THOM GUNN

FARRAR, STRAUS AND GIROUX

NEW YORK

THOM GUNN

A COOL QUEER LIFE

MICHAEL NOTT

Farrar, Straus and Giroux
120 Broadway, New York 10271

Printed in the United States of America
First edition, 2024

Background pattern on title-page spread by tmm / Shutterstock.

Library of Congress Cataloging-in-Publication Data
Names: Nott, Michael, author.
Title: Thom Gunn : a cool queer life / Michael Nott.
Description: First edition. | New York : Farrar, Straus and Giroux, 2024. |
    Includes bibliographical references and index.
Identifiers: LCCN 2023051870 | ISBN 9780374279202 (hardcover)
Subjects: LCSH: Gunn, Thom. | Poets, English—20th century—Biography. |
    Gay authors—Great Britain—Biography.
Classification: LCC PR6013.U65 Z75 2024 | DDC 821/.914 [B]—dc23/
    eng/20240206
LC record available at https://lccn.loc.gov/2023051870

To Mike Kitay

CONTENTS

THOM GUNN

PROLOGUE

At 9:55 a.m. on December 29, 1944, PC William Probert, responding to a radio message, cycled to a residential address in Hampstead, North London. "On arrival I saw Thomas William GUNN age 15 yrs and his brother Alexander GUNN age 12 yrs both schoolboys," he wrote in his subsequent statement. "Thomas GUNN said, 'It is my Mother she has gassed herself.'"[1]

Inspector Charles Hawkridge arrived twenty minutes later. "I went to 110 Frognal, N.W.3, and in the sitting room, ground floor, saw the body of deceased," he wrote:

> Mrs. Ann Charlotte Hyde, age 41, lying full length on her back about a yard from the fireplace. A travelling rug was near her head & a fire poker was fixed to a gas pipe at the side of the fireplace. When the flex was stretched out, this poker would reach deceased's head, which was resting on a cushion. Deceased was lying very slightly leaning towards her right side. The right arm was raised and flexed at the elbow. Everything in the room appeared to be in order, except that some furniture near the door had been pulled away from the wall. There had been a fire burning in the grate, but this appeared to have gone out some hours before. Deceased was wearing pyjamas & dressing gown.[2]

There were two notes. "Don't try to get in," read the first. "Get Mrs Stoney, my darlings."[3] The second was addressed to Ann Charlotte's first husband, Herbert Smith Gunn, then managing editor of the *Daily Express*, asking him to take care of the boys. "Everything as usual," she told him, "except pet them extra."[4] Ann Charlotte had separated from her second husband, Ronald Harry Picton Hyde, news editor of the *Evening Standard*, the previous morning.

Inspector Hawkridge interviewed the two boys separately, walking them each around the small walled garden at the front of the house. "I was informed by the eldest of the two boys that they had gone downstairs at about 9.50am 29/12/44, and having found a note outside the sitting room door, which would not open, furniture having been piled against it on the inside, they went for their charwoman, Mrs Stoney, who lives nearby," Hawkridge wrote.

> Having found that she was out shopping, the lads returned home and entered the sitting room through the French window at the back, which was closed but not locked. They found their mother in the position stated, but with the rug over her head & the gas poker under the rug. They turned off the gas & removed the rug & poker. Having removed the furniture, which had been placed inside the door, they phoned for the Police.[5]

The following day, the forensic pathologist Sir Bernard Spilsbury performed a postmortem examination in the mortuary of St. Pancras Hospital. The coroner's office concluded that the cause of death was "coma due to Carbon Monoxide (Coal gas) poisoning." On New Year's Day 1945, an inquest into the death was held at St. Pancras Coroner's Court. The coroner, William Bentley Purchase, recorded a verdict of "suicide while not of sound mind."[6]

Ann Charlotte's death was reported in that day's *Evening Despatch* and a few days later in the local Hampstead newspapers.[7] "Suicide follows separation," wrote the *Holborn and Finsbury Guardian*.[8] Ronald Hyde told the coroner's inquest that, having agreed to a temporary separation, Ann

Charlotte "telephoned me at the office and said she thought it was all a mistake—that she had made a mistake. I told her that we should stick to our agreement for a few days at least and left it at that." He continued: "She was a temperate woman and though she had said, in her recent anxiety, that she wished she were dead, she had never really threatened to do herself injury and I had no idea that she would take her life."[9]

Ronald did not return to the family home that night. "That was the last occasion that he heard from her," reported the *Holborn and Finsbury Guardian*, "and the next day he was informed that some children had found her dead."[10] Those two children, Ann Charlotte's sons, were the last people to see her alive, "at about 11.30pm when they went upstairs to bed," Thomas Day, of the coroner's office, wrote in his report. "She was then in the sitting room, reading. The elder son states that she was sad, otherwise normal."[11] The younger son told Inspector Hawkridge that "during the evening of 28/12/44, deceased had said that people ought to be allowed to commit suicide."[12]

1

BEGINNINGƒ

Before he was Thom, William Guinneach Gunn, born in Gravesend on August 29, 1929, was Tom.[1] "William" came from his paternal great-grandfather; "Guinneach," the Gaelic form of "Gunn," signifies "sharp, keen, fierce."[2] The summer of his birth was extraordinarily hot. A tomcat had sprayed inside the Gunns' house, "so that my mother," he wrote later, "always afterwards associated giving birth to me with the smell of cats."[3] He was never known as William. "I was Wm. Guinneach—but mother changed that," he wrote, "& maybe it's a bit characteristic that she did."[4]

Thom knew his mother—Ann Charlotte Thomson—as Charlotte. Almost twenty-six when Thom was born, Charlotte, too, had experimented with names: at times she went by Annie, Nan, Nancy, Nanette, Ann, and Charlotte, each a new identity or a play on an old one. Restless, she was the fourth of seven sisters, and seems to have found it hard to feel like an individual among "the Thomson girls." Charlotte was born in 1903: Barbara (1898), Margaret (1901), and Helen (1902) preceded her; Christina (1905), Mary (1907), and Catherine (1909) followed. They, too, played with names and nicknames: Barbara was Babs; Margaret, Peg; Mary, Mimi; Catherine, Kate—names that Thom would call his aunts well into adulthood. But Charlotte's name never stuck.

"Much of what I consciously am has been formed by my mother's family," Thom reflected, "or by what I know about it, or perhaps I should say by a mythology of it."[5]

The Thomsons were farmers from the northeast of Scotland. They were "a family of giants, 6ft. 3ins," recalled one friend, "well-read and cultured."[6] Thom called them "solid Keir Hardie socialists . . . pacifists, anti-Catholics, anti-royalists and Nonconformists."[7] Thom's grandfather, Alexander, moved with his widowed mother and six siblings from Echt, a crossroads village some twenty miles west of Aberdeen, to Kent's Medway Valley in 1887. Alexander's eldest brother, Charles, had seen "the fertile smiling land of Kent" for himself and was the driving force behind their passage south.[8] Charles ran Gig Hill Farm, in Larkfield, and each of the younger Thomson brothers subsequently took on their own farms. In 1897, Alexander leased Covey Hall Farm[9] in nearby Snodland. The following year, he married a local schoolteacher, Daisy Collings, whom he had met in the congregation of the West Malling Baptist Church.

So dominant were the Thomsons in his life that Thom "never saw much" of his paternal relatives and knew "little about them."[10] The Gunns were also of Scottish heritage. They had moved south earlier than the Thomsons and by the mid-nineteenth century had established a prosperous bakery in the heart of Gravesend.[11] Herbert, Thom's grandfather, chose not to continue the family business, however, and instead joined the mainstay of the Gravesend economy: shipbuilding. He rose from steam engine fitter to chief engineer of the *Gordon*, a War Office steamer stationed at the Royal Dockyard in Sheerness, and received two medals for service during the First World War.

Thom's father, Herbert Smith Gunn, known as Bert, was born in April 1903. He was the youngest of three children, and the family lived in a small row house in Sheerness. With their father often at sea, Bert looked up to his older brother, Malcolm, for guidance. In a photograph from his schooldays, Bert looks confident, almost cocky, and sports a slight sneer. Like his father, Bert wanted to make his own way in the world. Leaving Gravesend County School at sixteen, Bert followed Malcolm into a new career that, thanks to the popular press, offered intelligent young people from the provinces more adventure and excitement than ever before: journalism. Every young reporter had the same dream: to make it to Fleet Street.

Charlotte and Bert grew up some fifteen miles apart in Kent, but both saw their futures far away from home. By the 1880s, industry had transformed Snodland from an agricultural village into "Cementopolis," lined with yellow-gray row houses for workers at the quarries and paper factories.[12] Charlotte was "tired of the familiar" and "wanted her life to be grand and interesting. She felt constricted by this ugly overgrown village." She was bookish—the Thomsons "venerated education"—and reading had expanded her horizons beyond the Medway Valley. A nearby cousin lent her novels by Turgenev and Arnold Bennett; for a time, her favorite novel was *The Mill on the Floss*. In her late teens she conceived a passion for D. H. Lawrence, whose Brangwen sisters in *The Rainbow* and *Women in Love* she envied for their strength and feistiness. She even wrote a Lawrence-influenced novel, now lost, "in which the principal character," she told Thom, "was called Raven Jean and gave didactic speeches."[13]

When Bert started as a cub reporter at the *Kent Messenger*, he would have seen poems and articles written by "Nan Thomson." The weekly *Messenger* was the county newspaper of Kent, with offices in Gravesend and Maidstone. It usually printed one poem per paper, gentle pastoral verse in rhyming couplets by local authors. Charlotte's poems were more vigorous. Her first was a defense of the flapper:

> I sing of you, O English Flapper,
>> You so oft and cruelly abused,
>> And so slanderously accused,
> But when cold cynics loudly sneer,
> You scarcely deign even to hear,
> Shame to those liars and fools, O Flapper![14]

She had cut her dark hair short, started calling herself Nanette, and acquired what would become a lifelong interest in fashion, but for Charlotte the flapper denoted new levels of independence and rights for women in the aftermath of the First World War. Her poem was aimed at detractors in the national press: a writer for *The Manchester Guardian*, for example, thought "one of the unfortunate consequences of the war" was that "large numbers of women . . . had contracted a taste for a spurious kind of independence which led them to seek occupation outside the home."[15] An occupation outside the home was exactly what Charlotte wanted.

A fortnight after her flapper poem, she wrote a parodic article for the *Messenger* about the kinds of farmers a young woman might encounter at Fair Day. "A new type creeps in among the ranks of the farmer," she warned.

> The son of his farmer-father is there. But his ideas differ from those of his sire. (He has fought in the war, probably.) He has been to an agricultural college, perhaps. He has very up-to-date scientific theories (and practices, too, we hope). [. . .] "The old order changeth, yielding place to new," and farmers fulfil themselves in many ways, obedient to the law of evolution. Behold our New Farmer![16]

Having grown up on a farm, the last thing Charlotte wanted was to marry a farmer. She would watch as Barbara married a schoolteacher and Margaret a cement worker. Her teachers at Rochester Grammar wanted her to sit for a university scholarship, but Charlotte, impatient for life to begin, "was eager to escape into adulthood as soon as possible."[17]

With her bobbed hair and dark, serious eyes, Charlotte would have made quite an impression on Bert when their paths crossed at the *Messenger*. She was feisty, could quote D. H. Lawrence, and had a sharp tongue and temper. Bert likely saw her as a challenge. He himself cut a dapper and confident figure, tearing off on his motorcycle between assignments. A photograph depicts him, boyish and suited, astride a motorcycle: Charlotte annotated it "Tom Mix" after the iconic star of early westerns.[18] Bert was dashing and erudite. One future friend called him "that prince of good companions and [an] inveterate charmer."[19] Charlotte found him "attractive and ambitious . . . good-looking and light-hearted," according to Thom, and "worldly in a way which contrasted with her family's old-fashioned-ness." Immediately smitten, Bert wrote her "page after page of love letters, addressing her as Nanetta." Although Charlotte was "also courted by a local man of some wealth," Thom reported, "there was never any doubt in her mind that she should marry for love."[20]

By early 1925 they were engaged. Both would turn twenty-two that year. Their engagement became complicated when Bert accepted a three-year position as a junior reporter on *The Straits Times*, an English-language daily based in Singapore. The paper was nicknamed the "Thunderer of the East" for its strident criticism of the colonial administration.[21] Its editor, A. W. Still, had a "forceful personality" and led a five-man editorial team.[22] When Still addressed the Institute of Journalists in London in 1924, he encouraged young reporters "not to shirk opportunities for securing appointments abroad, because every year spent overseas added to their value, both as journalists and citizens. The creed of the new journalism was said to be 'give the people what they want.'"[23]

Bert sailed for Singapore in May 1925. The voyage took three weeks, with stops at Port Said and Penang. In a photograph taken onboard the SS *Patroclus*, Bert does not look entirely at ease. He wears a white linen suit and sports a topee, a curved white sun helmet reminiscent of the kind "you see British soldiers wearing on the march in India in television films of Rudyard Kipling's stories."[24] Arriving in the fierce, humid heat of Singapore, where the average temperature was eighty-six degrees Fahrenheit and it rained every other day, Bert was met by George Peet, a young English reporter who had made the same journey two years earlier. Peet thought Bert "a bit older" than him and found he had a "forceful character."[25]

Of his stint at *The Straits Times*, Bert later told the American magazine *Editor & Publisher* he "didn't like that very much."[26] Peet's relief at having a new colleague to share the reportorial load soured within a fortnight. "The newcomer reported precisely one soccer match, and then withdrew to his boarding house, refusing to do any more work," he recalled.

He told me he was engaged to a girl in England and had been assured in London that his salary would be enough to get married
in Singapore, but he had immediately discovered that he could
not hope to do that during his first three years. So, he declared,
the conditions of employment had been misrepresented, and he
was entitled to break his legal agreement with the *Straits Times.*[27]

Bert and Charlotte had likely planned to marry and settle in Singapore,
at least for the duration of Bert's contract.[28] Charlotte would have welcomed the adventure. Either Bert genuinely believed he had been misled
or realized within days of his arrival that he had made a mistake. The
"extraordinary position" continued for a week "until it was ended by the
management shipping him back Home." *The Straits Times* "denied that
there had been any misrepresentation," Peet recalled, "but the alternative
would have been to let him become a destitute European beachcomber
in Singapore, and a British firm could not afford to let that happen." By
early August, Bert was back in London. The "fiasco" lasted ten weeks:
three in Singapore, seven at sea.[29]

Six weeks later, on September 12, 1925, Bert and Charlotte married
at the Kensington Register Office. A photograph taken on the wedding
day shows a boyishly young Bert, beaming, with an arm around Charlotte, who offers a wry smile (plate 2). Charlotte stayed temporarily in
Kensington Palace Mansions, a block of short-term furnished apartments
overlooking Hyde Park, to qualify for residency in the borough. Thom was
told "their marriage was kept secret for a time" but had "no idea why."[30]

By the time William Guinneach Gunn was born, in August 1929, Bert
had made it to Fleet Street as a subeditor on the *Evening News*, then the
most popular evening paper in London. The young family took up residence in Gravesend, living in a detached late nineteenth-century house
on the outskirts of town, some twenty-five miles from London. Seventy-
eight Old Road East had a sprawling garden that backed onto an orchard. Beyond that, the chalky North Downs rolled to Snodland and

the River Medway. Thom's scrapbooks and Charlotte's albums are full of photographs taken in the garden of Old Road East. Both parents delight in their son: Bert, whom the infant Thom called "Wa Wa," helps pull a toy shopping trolley across the grass; Charlotte proudly shows off her wriggling son to the camera. Thom was a chubby baby. Within a year he had grown a mop of dark hair, like his mother's, and was tottering around the garden in striped shirts and leather sandals.

Having suffered an earlier miscarriage, Charlotte was somewhat anxious about her pregnancy.[31] When Thom was born, happiness mingled with relief. A strong bond developed between mother and son, born of Charlotte's protectiveness. In his early years, Thom was happy and boisterous, and enjoyed playing outside. Charlotte delighted in his energy. Her life by now was mostly domestic: on her marriage certificate she gave "no profession," which suggests her journalism career ended with marriage to Bert. "She stopped writing," Thom later wrote, "though for a few years she continued to do the occasional column."[32] She directed her vigor toward Thom and nourished his early intellectual and emotional life. Moreover, she seemed to delight in domesticity—a surprise, perhaps, given her longing for adventure and what her life might have looked like in Singapore.

Meanwhile, Bert commuted by train to Carmelite House, the *Evening News* office just off Fleet Street. As a subeditor on an evening paper, Bert started early and finished late: the final edition was put to bed around 6:00 p.m. Fleet Street culture was intoxicating for young, ambitious journalists like Bert, and he likely drank with colleagues most nights. The Harrow, on nearby Whitefriars Street, was the *Evening News* pub. Charlotte spent many long evenings alone with Thom. "Newspaper wives are much to be pitied," wrote Bert's future friend and boss Arthur Christiansen. "They are in many ways more lonely and frustrated than the wives of sailors. A sailor's wife at least knows when her husband's ship is in port, but a newspaperman's wife rarely has any idea where her husband is."[33]

Charlotte gave birth to her second son, Dougal Alexander, who would be known as Ander, in Gravesend in April 1932. Thom was not there: he had gone to Higham to stay with Aunt Barbara and Uncle Godfrey.[34] Thom's earliest memory came from that visit, when Barbara and Godfrey took him to a forge. "It was all very puzzling, the fire, the sparks," he wrote later, "& I think certain worry that maybe the horse was being hurt."[35] Thom, almost three, returned to Gravesend to find a baby brother. To mark Ander's birth, Charlotte began a new photograph album and wrote in the front: "Tom Gunn. Hys [sic] album and later pictures of Tom's Baby."[36] Thom continued to be his mother's favorite. "She put a lot of effort into Thom and rather ignored me," Ander remarked, reflecting on their childhood, "because she wanted Thom to be all sorts of things."[37]

Although Bert's parents lived only a short distance away on Old Road West, it was the Thomsons who most frequently visited Charlotte and helped with the children. If Bert felt overwhelmed by the Thomsons, Charlotte felt less than welcomed by the Gunns. Annotating one photograph of her parents-in-law, she wrote: "Mrs Gunn with her best Pussy face & H. G. senior looking So Pleased."[38] There was likely snobbery on both sides. Herbert Gunn might not have approved of his son marrying a farmer's daughter. On the other hand, the Thomsons' reverence for education lent them a certain intellectual superiority—"The tenant farmer's daughters acted like aristocrats," Thom mused—and they likely looked down on the merchant class. Charlotte realized early in their marriage that Bert only read newspapers and detective stories and that the Gunns were not literary. From Bert's parents' house she rescued from destruction an ornate family Bible in which the Gunns' births and deaths had been recorded since the early nineteenth century.[39] She was not religious—"Mother taught us that religion was a lot of foolishness," Thom summarized[40]—but appreciated the literary value of biblical stories.

With Bert in London most of the time, Charlotte welcomed some family company. Thom's "lively young aunts" Mary and Catherine, both in their early twenties, were frequent visitors.[41] Charlotte was closest to Christina, "the Beauty of the family, like the character in *David Copperfield.*" With her lover George Beldam, a former cricketer and pioneer of sports photography, Christina had been witness to the Gunns' marriage in Kensington. Beldam, from a wealthy engineering family, was almost forty years older than Christina. She began working as a nurse for Beldam's family in the mid-1920s and would return to Covey Hall with expensive new possessions—"crocodile-skin suitcases and the like"—that she could never have afforded.[42] A prolonged affair led to marriage and three children. The Beldams became regular visitors to Old Road East. Thom and Ander saw lots of their Beldam cousins, Josie and the twins, George and Goldie. "Auntie Nan," as the cousins called her, kept many photographs of the two families together at Rhodendale, the Beldam estate near Farnham, or their seaside estate, Kirklands, at Selsey Bill.[43] The children delighted in the company and surroundings; the adults less so. Bert Gunn was jealous of Beldam's "splendidly self-indulgent mode of living," Thom recalled, while Beldam was jealous of Gunn's "vigor and self-earned success."[44]

But Thom's favorite visitor to Old Road East was his grandfather. Alexander Thomson was well over six feet tall, but "quiet and gentle."[45] Like his brothers, Alexander sported a large, bristly mustache. To drink coffee, he used a mustache cup: its interior ledge—with a half-moon-shaped opening to allow the passage of liquid—enabled him to keep his mustache dry.[46] Alexander visited on Thom's third birthday: a photograph shows Thom wriggling on his grandfather's lap, as Alexander looks at the camera with wise, kind eyes. Another photograph depicts them standing side by side: Alexander is so tall he has to lean to reach Thom's outstretched hand (plate 3). Thom saw his grandfather's size in moral terms. "A good man—the good man in my memories, perhaps," he wrote later, "and if a little distant that added to the purity of his goodness."[47] Alexander was introspective: later, Thom thought him the model of "Thomson melancholia," a condition that also affected Charlotte.[48] Alexander's melancholia was likely due to the death of his wife, Daisy, from breast cancer in 1920. Charlotte was sixteen when her mother died. Thom met neither of his grandmothers: Bert's mother, Alice, died in November 1928.

Thom relished visiting the Thomsons in Snodland. "'We're going down to Covey to see the Girls,' Mother would say."[49] "Though I was born in Gravesend and have lived in cities most of my life, it seemed natural to think of Covey Hall as my source," he later wrote.

> Many of those brightly colored memories most people have from their childhood are for me of that house with nothing behind it but yard, farm buildings & orchard before you reached the fields; of Christmas parties and summer picnics on hills smelling almost rank with thyme; of long walks to pick blackberries and cowslips; of the orchard of variegated fruits and bushes & apples from Golden Knobs at the beginning of the summer and Blenheims at the end.[50]

Despite the grand name, Covey Hall was a two-story mid-nineteenth-century brick building, its exterior softened by climbing jasmine, yellow in winter, white in summer. Its heart was the parlor: Alexander lit the Kitchener range at four in the morning to keep the farmhouse warm all day; Thomsons from neighboring farms and villages congregated around the old oak table. It was "the hub of things," recalled Thom's cousin Margot, "a coming and going, a constant air of excitement, of expectation of something about to happen."[51]

The parlor led through a scullery to a kitchen garden full of raspberries, gooseberries, black and red currants; beyond, a small orchard with apple, pear, and plum trees. Stretching uphill toward Holborough Knob were fields of rich, fertile loam, given mostly to cereals: oats, barley, wheat, rye. Across Holborough Road, water meadows, used mostly for grazing, extended beyond the railway line to the Medway. When he was old enough, Thom played among the same old buildings as had his mother during her childhood: disused oasthouses, circular brick structures built in Elizabethan times, once used for drying hops. He enjoyed listening to stories about his mother's childhood. "Two of her first achievements were destructive," he later wrote:

> Among other relics, an ancient square of stale chocolate was preserved in the china cabinet of the Little Parlor: Queen Victoria

had personally presented it to a wounded soldier, some distant relative of the Thomsons. One day the child Nancy, feeling hungry, ate it. And another time, in the same room, wanting to clear space for some game she was playing, she moved the big belljarred stand of wax fruit into the sunlight, where she forgot it until the top half of it had melted over the rest. Thus she disposed of the Victorian age.[52]

Growing up, the seven Thomson girls had shared two upstairs rooms. To Charlotte, spending the night at Covey must have felt like going back in time. Alexander "lived much the same life," and Charlotte "now loved the house at Snodland as much as she had longed to leave it in her teens and early twenties."[53] Mary and Catherine ran the household, with help from Great-Aunt Alice, and sold milk from the back door. To Thom, life on the farm must have seemed terribly exciting compared to quiet days back in Gravesend. It was like peering into his mother's childhood: waking to the sound of milk churns being rolled across flagstones into the dairy; the harrumphing and stamping of horses in the yard; tramping up Ladds Hill and the Pilgrim's Way to pick blackberries and have picnics with his aunts. These Kentish hills and nearby marshes formed part of Thom's imaginative landscape. They opened his eyes to "an earlier time: an era of outlaws and pirates," which stayed with him for life.[54]

If Covey Hall was Thom's "source," it also proved the one constant of an itinerant childhood. While Thom was still a toddler, Bert had continued to climb the Fleet Street ladder. In 1931, Lord Beaverbrook poached him from the *Evening News* and made him a subeditor on the *Evening Standard*, thus beginning an association that would last two decades. Bert excelled in the role. He was "one of nature's chief sub-editors," recalled one colleague, "and at that level quite outstanding."[55] Bert also had the charm and ambition to excel in the social swirl of Fleet Street. Within two years he was made news editor of the *Standard*, a position that set his course firmly toward the executive level of Fleet Street editorship.

As news editor, Bert presided over the newsroom, assigning stories to reporters, determining the priority and importance of news, liaising with subeditors and photographers. It was a high-pressure job, coordinating the news output for six editions a day, six days a week, amid the "deeply infectious" air of "excitement and rumbustiousness": reporters rushing in and out, overhead pulleys transferring copy between desks, telephones ringing almost nonstop, and the clanking of presses beneath the *Standard*'s tumbledown offices on Shoe Lane.[56] The new role meant that commuting from Gravesend was no longer feasible. The Gunns bade farewell to their large house and garden. Thom, now almost four, would receive his first taste of London.

2

ITINERANCY

De Vere Gardens was a prestigious address. Charlotte knew it already: Kensington Palace Mansions, where she had boarded in the days before her marriage, was at the top of the street. At its foot was the Gunns' new town house, number 44. It was a desirable street for journalists, writers, and the political classes. Robert Browning and Henry James had lived there in the late nineteenth century. For the Gunns it was a significant step up in the world: Charlotte, a tenant farmer's daughter, was now the wife of a prominent journalist living among wealthy and respectable neighbors on an impressive London street.

Bert was proud of their new house, but George Beldam brought him down to earth. When Beldam "saw how small the house was he said contemptuously, 'There isn't room to swing a cat.'"[1] He had a point. The eight town houses at the southwestern end of De Vere Gardens are more like mews houses, incredibly narrow, and some three stories shorter than the rest of the houses on the street. Abutting De Vere Cottages, they have no backyards. To Thom, the house must have seemed claustrophobic after the openness and greenery of Gravesend. At least there was the escape to nearby Kensington Gardens, where he and Ander could play around the Albert Memorial. Thom was told to learn his new address in case he got lost. His cousin Margot recalled him saying "Tom Gunn 44 De Vere Gardens Kensington at great speed, all run together in one breath as if it had no meaning for him."[2] When, on one occasion, he did get lost, a policeman asked him to describe his mother. "A proud woman," he said, later thinking he must have learned the phrase from a fairy tale.[3]

The first book Thom owned was Robert Louis Stevenson's *A Child's Garden of Verses*.[4] Bert and Charlotte bought it for his fifth birthday. He devoured it. Almost sixty years later, he could still remember the two-line poem "Happy Thought": "The world is so full of a number of things / That I'm sure we should all be as happy as kings." "When I found those lines," he told a friend, "little goody-goody Thom ran to show it to his mother, who was cooking, saying something like 'Isn't that true, Mother?' She surprised me by telling me she thought it was complete nonsense. So I gradually got educated . . ."[5] On one occasion, watching his mother read a long novel, Thom "thought that reading must be a wonderful occupation."[6] He asked her what the book was about. "All the terrible things that people do to each other in wars, killing and maiming and sadness," she replied. The book was *Gone with the Wind*. "In spite of the fact that this *was* the formative encounter," he later reflected, "I have never even opened that book in adult life." He realized gradually that reading was "more private and involving" than the stories his mother read him at bedtime. It was "an important and adult activity" that he would one day get to do himself.[7] From her, Thom "absorbed the idea of books as a part of life, not merely a commentary on it."[8] "She was a good influence," he reflected. "She would have been very pleased that I became a writer."[9]

Thom's first experiences of bookshops were in Kensington, where Charlotte took him to buy Beatrix Potter's books. He thought "the rather colorless woman who sold us the books was also the author of them" and that her name was "Beatrick Spotter."[10] As a boy, Thom identified with a particular Potter character: Tom Kitten. Tom is a mischievous kitten who rebels against the "elegant uncomfortable clothes" his mother wants him to wear. In *The Tale of Samuel Whiskers*, Tom's adventuresomeness lands him in trouble:

> All at once he fell head over heels in the dark, down a hole, and landed on a heap of very dirty rags. When Tom Kitten picked

himself up and looked about him—he found himself in a place that he had never seen before, although he had lived all his life in the house. It was a very small stuffy fusty room, with boards, and rafters, and cobwebs, and lath and plaster. Opposite to him—as far away as he could sit—was an enormous rat.[11]

Tom Kitten's name and mischievousness appealed to Thom. The alter ego combines the feminine softness of the kitten with the masculinity of the name Thom Gunn: it must have felt like he himself was a character in a book. Thom was a bold and adventurous child—getting lost in Kensington Gardens, pushing against his own fears—and a risk-taking nature characterized his adulthood. Likewise, cats were important to him, as they were to his mother: almost every note and birthday card in his childhood scrapbooks features cats and kittens.

Bert sometimes brought home dummy newspapers for Thom to play with. They had *Daily Express* or *Evening Standard* mastheads: columns divided the pages but there were no words or pictures.[12] Thom remembered "spend[ing] an afternoon very busily scribbling until all the blank areas were filled in with wavy lines that looked to me like writing."[13] Charlotte encouraged Thom and lavished on him plenty of time and attention. Otherwise, she was not greatly happy in London. The "light sensual" days of her marriage were over.[14] She had two small children to look after while Bert, whose working and drinking had increased now that the family had moved to London, was out early and back late.

It became obvious to Bert and Charlotte that they were temperamentally unsuited. Thom, in a comparison likely suggested by his mother, thought it was "a little like the Wilcox-Schlegel marriage in *Howard's End* [*sic*]." Charlotte had a vivid, difficult interior life whereas Bert, rakish and charming, did not dwell on feelings and emotions. He was at home in the exciting, sensuous life of Fleet Street and began to have affairs. In Thom's account of his parents' marriage, likely furnished by his mother, Bert had dalliances with a neighbor, Mrs. Barnes, and "a certain Lady Mary," who gave Bert a large glossy photograph of herself. When Charlotte found the photograph, she passed it around a dinner party and "ridiculed it mercilessly—and her taunting was a thing to be feared," Thom wrote, "as everybody knew who ever suffered it."[15]

Bert's most serious affair was with Cecile Leslie. A Sorbonne-educated journalist, Leslie began her career on the *Evening Standard*. In 1935 she published a novel, *The Viennese Hat*, in which she included such a thinly veiled portrait of Bert, as well as "reflections of a personal character upon people in Fleet Street," that her publisher "decided to withdraw the book from further publication."[16] Bert was likely the model for Austin Taylor, the news editor of the fictional *Sun* newspaper, who hides his plain wife and attempts to seduce the novel's heroine, a young reporter named Sally Masters. Charlotte must have told Thom about the novel, but its portraits were not lost on contemporary reviewers. Writing in the *Daily Mirror*, Bookworm had "a nasty suspicion—has [Leslie] met all these odd people she talks about?"[17] Bert took little trouble to hide his infidelities. He "could never grasp the fact that a woman might have equal rights sexually," Thom mused. Charlotte soon "felt free to do what she wanted." A "habit of unfaithfulness" developed, wherein Bert and Charlotte lived separate sexual lives.[18]

One morning, Charlotte took Thom and Ander to Kensington Gardens. There they met Charlotte's friend Douglas, a young man in gray flannel trousers. "He was very agreeable," Thom thought, "and it seemed the most natural thing in the world to ask him back to lunch." The Gunns' maid had prepared a cold meal for the children; afterward they had their customary afternoon nap. Later, Thom came to think of his strong-willed and resilient mother as an early feminist. "She refused to use the word lady—to be called a woman was dignity enough for her," he wrote. "She stood up for herself, and she did what she thought was proper, and she was not going to take any nonsense from individual or society." Like her sisters, Charlotte did not accept "the convention that women were inferiors to be led by men, or had different rights."[19]

Despite their marital difficulties, and as was fashionable, the Gunns took a weekend cottage outside London. Pit Cottage, so called because it was built of chalk and bordered a large chalk pit, was "an incredibly wet and damp place."[20] It overlooked Snodland from the top of Holly

Hill, and its closeness to Covey Hall eased Charlotte's feelings of isolation. The cottage and its surroundings made a vivid impression on Thom.
He remembered his parents waking him late one night and carrying
him outside "to see hundreds of rabbits feeding on the grassy floor of
the pit."[21] Nearby, between the pit and the cemetery, was "The Witch's
Cottage." "What was that secret place, chimney & cellar, the enclosing
hedge grown up around them," he later wondered, "what secrets did it
really contain, did I/we want it to contain?" His imagination at the time
was "full of witches, moving in the undergrowth with sudden rustles."[22]
Years later, he told Ander about lying in bed at Pit Cottage, not daring to
stir, because "there was a witch in the garden and I would be in her power
if I so much as blinked."[23]

In 1935 the Gunns relocated to Shortlands, a southeastern suburb of
London on the Kentish border. Weekends at Pit Cottage may have given
Charlotte a desire to be closer to the Thomsons; likewise, with the boys
growing up, they may have wanted more space inside and out. A suburb,
perhaps, contained fewer temptations than Kensington. Regardless, their
year in Shortlands was not a happy one. Their house on St. Mary's Avenue was spacious and had a large garden, but the change of scene did
nothing to alleviate the Gunns' troubled marriage. A photograph taken
in Shortlands shows Thom, aged six, with his nose buried in a book.[24]

Another, bigger, problem soon arose. After three years as the *Standard*'s
news editor, Bert was promoted to northern editor of the *Daily Express*.
The significant promotion meant a significant relocation: Manchester.
Bert assured Charlotte it would be temporary: within two or three years
he would be promoted again, to managing or assistant editor of the
Express, if not the editorship itself, and they could return to London.
Bert "had his dreams," recalled one colleague, "and one of them was the
dream of the great Beaverbrook tycoon-editor."[25]

Charlotte balked. They had spent two years in Manchester as newly-
weds, Bert having taken a job at the *Manchester Evening News*, and she
had no desire to return north. The impasse caused their first separation:

Charlotte took the boys to Goudhurst, a village close to Maidstone and Snodland, where they lived in a cottage on the grounds of Oakley House, a walled estate that had once been a school for disabled children. Bert, meanwhile, moved temporarily to a flat on St. James's Street, near Green Park. "My impression during most of my childhood was that [my father] was usually wrong & my mother was right," Thom later reflected, "since there were many occasions when they disagreed." Bert, ultimately, was "attractive, ruthless, sentimental, unsubtle, humorous, irritable, cowardly."[26]

The separation lasted long enough for Charlotte to be listed in the telephone directory for 1936. With the boys in mind, the Gunns reconciled and moved north later that year. They settled in Cheadle, an affluent village south of Manchester. Thom called it "Lousy Land."[27] Their new house, a detached modernist pile on Daylesford Road, was close to prominent public schools. Now almost seven, Thom had barely been to school: he had briefly attended a primary in Kensington and had had a tutor while in Shortlands. The Ryleys School, in leafy Alderley Edge, prepared boys for "the Public Schools and Royal Navy."[28] Thom and Ander lived close enough to be day boys, not boarders. Thom thought it "very oppressive." Ryleys was dominated by the headmaster's wife, whom he and Ander found "something of an ogress."[29]

Busy editing a national daily, Bert seemed to be in the house only on weekends. "I think he started by trying to be a good father but hadn't much of a chance," Thom reflected.[30] Amid the itinerancy, this created a strange kind of continuity: Thom and Ander's home life centered almost entirely around Charlotte. At her encouragement, Thom read *Little Men* and pored over Arthur Mee's *The Children's Encyclopaedia*.[31] There he read all the Victorian poets and still recognized obscure names like Jean Ingelow and William Allingham when he came across them almost seventy years later. Charlotte read him Yeats's poems and Walter de la Mare's *Peacock Pie*. "I was continually given confidence by the admiration of my mother," he reflected.[32] He began to write poems and stories to please her. None of this juvenilia survives, but it set a precedent for Thom's childhood: he had found his chief audience and supporter.

What Thom remembered most about Cheadle, though, was his parents' social life. "Every weekend seemed like a party": as northern editor, Bert was expected to entertain, and the Gunns' house was always full of his *Express* colleagues and artier friends like the painters Owen and Sylvia Rowley. They all played with Thom and Ander and "told jokes that started 'Knock knock, who's there?' or ended 'as the girl said to the soldier.'"[33] One of the Gunns' closest friends was the journalist Vernon Noble, who joined the *Express* shortly before Bert became northern editor. They bonded quickly, and the Gunns were frequent guests of the Nobles in nearby Gatley, as were their colleagues Percy Elland, the chief subeditor, and Ronald Hyde, who later became news editor. Noble found Charlotte "vivacious" and recalled that, with Gunn, Elland, and Hyde, their "dinners together at various Manchester hotels were lively affairs."[34]

Ronald Harry Picton Hyde was the youngest son of the prominent Lancastrian political figure Sir Harry Hyde.[35] Sir Harry was a friend and associate of Max Aitken—later Lord Beaverbrook—and acted as his constituency agent in Ashton-under-Lyne during the December 1910 general election.[36] It was known around the *Express* offices that "the great Lord Beaverbrook himself" was Ronald Hyde's "sponsor," and although the *Express* was Hyde's first job, it did not take him long to become news editor.[37] By contrast, Bert had been a journalist for almost two decades.

Hyde was not typical for an era that mostly saw self-made reporters rise from local newspapers to the editorships of national dailies: men like Arthur Christiansen, Hugh Cudlipp, Percy Elland, and Bert Gunn. At Sedbergh School, Hyde had been head boy, president of the debating society, and president of the League of Nations Union, and had represented the school in cricket and rugby. He had gone on to study history at St. John's College, Cambridge, under the supervision of E. A. Benians.

The extended Gunn and Hyde families became close. They shared beach holidays to Southport and Llandudno and were frequent guests at each other's homes. Hyde's parents, Sir Harry and Lady Mary, lived in Sylvester House, a grand redbrick home in Ashton-under-Lyne, where the families would congregate. Hyde had two older brothers, Edgar and Gerald, and a sister, Lucy. She was "a plain rather plump person," recalled Ander, and the source of one of Thom's earliest poems. "We used to walk up this hill together and he'd sing, 'Here comes Lucy Hyde, wobbling from side to side.'"[38]

Almost a decade younger than Bert and Charlotte, Hyde cut a dashing, urbane figure: tall, handsome, "brimming brown eyes and long black lashes and the ridiculous George Robey eyebrows."[39] Thom thought Hyde "trie[d] hard to make friends," presumably because his university education and relationship with Beaverbrook set him apart in the newspaper culture.[40] But Hyde could not help but appear a cut above. "He spoke in a languid drawl," recalled his niece, "as one who was never in a hurry."[41] To Stuart Kuttner, later Hyde's deputy on the *Evening Standard*, he "was a rather grand, seemingly austere, Edwardian figure who could have stepped straight out of an early-twentieth-century English public school."[42]

Hyde ingratiated himself to colleagues in the way of all newspapermen, by showing he could hold his drink. "He would race one former editor of the *Standard* to the ceiling of the Two Brewers in Shoe Lane by shinning up the pub's wooden pillars," it was claimed of his early days as news editor of the *Evening Standard*.[43] Alcohol helped establish Hyde and Bert's friendship. Bert could also handle his drink. "Bertie's couple of quick gins did him a power of good, it was delightful to see him visibly thawing and becoming human," wrote one colleague of their midmorning routine. "I never saw him even slightly drunk in all the years I knew him. He could carry his liquor better than almost anyone I ever knew."[44] Charlotte also drank and smoked heavily. Noble recalled a meeting in London when "Ronnie Hyde and I entertained Charlotte Gunn at the Café Royal and we were asked to leave, because Charlotte drank too much, stood on a table and gave a political lecture (she was [on] the Left) to the other diners."[45]

Perhaps in rebellion against his Conservative father, Hyde also leaned left.[46] This appealed to Charlotte, herself a socialist. Later, during the Spanish Civil War, she hung red bunting from her house in Hampstead, took *The Daily Worker* as her morning newspaper, and volunteered to address envelopes and host fundraising events to help the Republican cause.[47] Around the same time, Charlotte made an appearance in the

"William Hickey" column of the *Daily Express*, then written by Tom Driberg. "Seen at a dance," Driberg wrote: "woman wearing spray of orchids pinned on by a hammer-&-sickle brooch."[48] Thom told this story to friends throughout his life. "Behind it was an impudent and witty proclamation that she wanted the best of both worlds," he mused, "but at the same time there was implicit a half-rueful self-criticism."[49] Bert, on the other hand, adapted his politics to his newspaper. "Since my father had no religious or political views," Thom reflected, "we were brought up to hers."[50]

It was not only Hyde's politics that attracted Charlotte. He was a suave, university-educated man ten years her junior, and she felt drawn to someone whose interior life seemed as rich and complicated as her own. Her feistiness and disregard for convention would have appealed to Hyde. She was strong-willed and attractive, in her mid-thirties, her dark eyes as piercing as when Bert had met her in the early 1920s. Moreover, she was the editor's wife, and rumors about the state of the Gunn marriage and their relative sexual independence may have circulated through the *Express* offices and piqued Hyde's interest.

Within a year of the Gunns' move to Cheadle, Charlotte and Hyde began an affair. It was easily more serious than any of Charlotte's or Bert's London infidelities. In summer 1937, Charlotte and Hyde holidayed together in Denmark. "Dear Tom," Charlotte wrote from Elsinore,

> I did enjoy the "Charlie" story. Tell father we all read his letters and larf. Do you know we have eiderdown in a sheet, like bag on top of us in bed, & no blankets. We have no bath in our bathroom, only a shower. I have to take care of my RED WAVES!!! xxxxxx CHARLOTTE xxxx[51]

In Thom's account, Charlotte and Hyde traveled with Charlotte's youngest sister, Catherine, under the somewhat improbable cover story that Catherine "was in love with" Hyde.[52] However, a photograph taken in front of Rudolph Tegner's *Heracles and the Hydra* statue, at the entrance to Elsinore harbor, shows Charlotte and Hyde with Christina, not Catherine.[53] Thom may have misremembered: given her marriage to George Beldam, Christina's being in love with Hyde would have been no less scandalous. Beyond Charlotte's postcard and the photograph, only Thom's account of the affair survives. According to him, Catherine was "so convincing in the part of '[Hyde's] girl-friend' because it was so unlikely for her to be deceitful."[54]

During her affair with Hyde, Thom's mother adopted Charlotte as her given name, leaving behind Nan, Ann, and Nanette for good. She also had a name for Hyde: Joe. It was likely an example of her caustic wit: Ronald Harry Picton Hyde became the ordinary Joe. He may have had a university education and a privileged upper-middle-class upbringing, but Charlotte was not easily cowed. He would be Joe to Thom and Ander, never Ronald.

Bert was only told about the affair, according to Thom, when Charlotte became pregnant. It must have been obvious that Bert was not the father. "An abortion was considered necessary," Thom wrote, somewhat baldly, in his version of events.[55] In 1937, this would have been difficult to obtain and almost certainly illegal. The 1861 Offences Against the Person Act made abortion illegal under all circumstances; the Infant Life (Preservation) Act (1929) allowed medically administered abortion "for the purpose only of preserving the life of the mother."[56] Many women had no choice but to resort to unsafe, backstreet abortions, done without anesthetic, sterilization, or adequate surgical instruments; or to abortifacients, advertised in newspapers to cure menstrual blockages, which were at best ineffectual and at worst poisonous. Because the Gunns were solidly middle-class, Charlotte's abortion was probably performed by a sympathetic doctor, perhaps discredited, during a clandestine visit to a secret address.[57] "If you had enough money," Thom wrote, "you could procure one safely and with apparent legality."[58] He was almost certainly wrong about the latter, but the Gunns' comfortable circumstances meant Charlotte likely had as safe an abortion as was possible.

"My father obviously paid for it," Ander recalled. "Did he know who the father was? People didn't tell you these things [as children]. They were secrets."[59] Thom and Ander boarded, miserably, at Ryleys while Charlotte recovered in a "nursing home." She did not tell them what had happened for several years. She thought "it was no evil thing in itself and that children should be able to handle the truth at the ages of twelve and fourteen," Thom summarized. "The consistency of her candor paid off. The children, as it turned out, handled it so well that they were not even interested."[60] Yet Ander wondered what lasting effect the abortion had on his mother. "I think she'd been damaged, probably, by rather crude surgery in those days," he reflected. "All these things have an effect on the children. And Thom was the one who was deeply affected."[61]

In January 1938, Thom wrote to thank his aunt Barbara for her Christmas gift of R. M. Ballantyne's *Martin Rattler, or A Boy's Adventures in the Forests of Brazil.* "We shall expect you quite a lot (at least once a month) when we are in London," he told her.[62] Bert's return to Fleet Street had come about sooner than anticipated: he was promoted to assistant editor of the *Daily Express* in London, where he would be right-hand man to Arthur Christiansen. For Bert, this was a step closer to the editorship itself. For Charlotte, it was a return to her family and an opportunity to leave Manchester behind once and for all. For Thom and Ander, it was farewell to Lousy Land: Charlotte photographed them, dressed in their Ryleys uniforms, waving goodbye to the house on Daylesford Road.

A press photograph from early 1938 depicts Bert's departure from Manchester: leaning out the window of a first-class train carriage, he is embraced by Charlotte, wearing her signature leopard-print fur coat (plate 5). Once Bert had found a new house in London, she and the boys would follow him. It was quite the send-off: colleagues and friends—including the slick-haired, laughing Ronald Hyde—thronged the platform, drinking and dancing. Charlotte's affair with Hyde, having survived the abortion, would also survive the Gunns' return to London. Hyde had also been promoted to assistant news editor of the *Evening Standard*, where he would occupy the same Shoe Lane offices that Bert had in the early 1930s.

3

HAMPSTEAD

"We lived on Frognal for 8 years," Thom once told a friend, "and that seems to be the place I always dream of as my home."[1] Back in London, the Gunns settled in Hampstead, then a "quiet and rather old-fashioned" district popular with artists and intellectuals.[2] Their house, 110 Frognal, sometimes called Grove Cottage, was built in the seventeenth century and was one of the oldest on the street (plate 6).[3] It had small front and rear gardens. Everything creaked. There was a fireplace in each room and dark-wood floors sloped toward a central chimney (Ander's clockwork train struggled against the incline). At the top of the house, Thom had his own room. Little larger than a closet, it had once likely belonged to a live-in maid. "It was just a bed and bookshelves and books," Ander recalled. "I don't remember him having any other hobbies except reading and writing. He really didn't seem to do anything else much."[4]

Frognal runs parallel to Hampstead High Street: at its top, Hampstead Heath and Whitestone Pond; at its foot, the senior branch of University College School. Thom started at its junior branch, Holly Hill, just past the top of Hampstead High Street, in 1938. He enjoyed posing for his school photograph: contact sheets show Thom, about nine years old, hair slicked to the side like his father, pulling faces and messing around. In others, he wears UCS's striped cap, burgundy and black, and looks at once serious and mischievous.[5] Thom's itinerant schooling meant he was behind for his age in some subjects, but, thanks to Charlotte, his reading level was already excellent. UCS proved a much more nourishing school than Ryleys for the gentle and bookish Thom. Its motto, *Paulatim sed firmiter*, "slowly but surely," aptly described its emphasis on intellectual curiosity and breadth of curriculum. Stephen Spender, who attended UCS in the 1920s, called it "the gentlest of schools." His biographer, John Sutherland, thought the "high intellectual tone and secular traditions" suited him.[6] The same could be said for Thom.

Holly Hill was a short walk from the Gunns' house, through narrow, cobbled lanes typical of Hampstead Village. On the first day of school, each child was given a Latin verb to remember. The headmaster, Dr. Lake, known as "Bunny," was a "small of stature, bespectacled, slightly rounded shoulders man with a shock of white hair."[7] Thom's housemistress was a part-Sicilian, part-German history teacher named Eugenie Polimeni, known as Polly. She taught at Holly Hill for some three decades and was considered lively and sympathetic. "In her imagination, which was enriched by her love of music and art," recalled one former student, "she saw what she was describing so vividly that her hearers were enabled to see it too."[8]

Thom thought Polly was "wonderful." He showed her some of his earliest poems, written when he was "about nine or something," and "she was very encouraging."[9] In July 1940, aged almost eleven, Thom published his first poem in *The Gower*, UCS's magazine. "A Thousand Cheers for Authors" evokes Thom's thirst for books and provides an insight into his reading habits. Its first two stanzas offer a concise history of literature and literary production, from campfire stories to the invention of the printing press. The poem's final two stanzas are its most metrically competent, and its repeated refrain demonstrates a flair for rhyme and meter beyond the skills of most ten-year-olds:

> In Mister Bumpus' bookshop—
> Oh, there is my delight!—
> Of books he has a monster crop;
> They are a lovely sight.
> I hope that authors never stop,

For reading gives the "wisdom-light."
A thousand cheers for authors!

I love to think of books of old
The great Greeks wrote so long ago.
Chaucer the first English stories told;
Sweet Shakespeare came and stout Defoe,
With Jonathan Swift and Bunyan bold,
Till Dumas—he's the best I know!
A thousand cheers for authors.[10]

Thom read widely and hungrily. By then, he knew *The Three Musketeers*, perhaps even *The Count of Monte Cristo*, and Charlotte encouraged him to read Jane Austen and E. M. Forster. Thom had read some Chaucer and Shakespeare—and Charlotte bought him *The Pilgrim's Progress*, despite her indifference to religion—but most of his early reading was prose fiction. He did not "get deeply into poetry" until he read André Maurois's *Ariel: A Shelley Romance* "at the age of about 13, but that kind of thing is probably unavoidable."[11]

By the time the Gunns returned to London, Thom had graduated from Beatrix Potter to E. Nesbit. He thought her writing generous and fair, and she quickly became his favorite childhood writer. Nesbit wrote about, rather than for, children: her books throw families of children into a mixture of realistic and magical adventures. *Five Children and It*, *The Would-Be-Goods*, and *The Railway Children* were among Thom's favorites; he liked that Nesbit wrote often about the landscapes of North Kent, with which he was familiar from childhood. Later, he called her "that sensible and imaginative woman" and admired how her children, though adventuresome, sought practical ways to cope in the grown-up world.[12]

In Hampstead, Thom borrowed *The Phoenix and the Carpet* from the local library. He enjoyed it so much, he worked his way through all Nesbit's other books. Dumas, Conan Doyle, H. Rider Haggard, A. E. W. Mason, and H. G. Wells all followed, but Nesbit was special. She was "one of the few authors I discovered without my mother's help": discovery was part of the thrill. In Nesbit, Thom liked "the idea of a big friendly family having adventures together." One of his most vivid childhood memories was "waking early & immediately starting the next chapter of *Five Children and It* before I got out of bed. I suppose she would have made me a Fabian, if my family had not already made me one."[13] Nesbit "gave me almost everything I needed," he wrote shortly before his death, "the feeling of a family as sociable, the commonsense style & good humour, the best political beliefs, & poetry as magic."[14] From her, he learned "'values' that moved into adult ones."[15]

As a reward for his writing "a very good horrible play," Charlotte gave Thom an autograph book to collect signatures.[16] As in Cheadle, the Hampstead house was full of Bert's newspaper colleagues. Vernon Noble, visiting from Manchester, called 110 Frognal "a gay gathering place for journalists, authors and artists, and we argued politics, philosophy and domestic affairs over drinks until dawn."[17] Sidney Strube, the *Express* cartoonist, drew a version of his bowler-hatted "Little Man," complete with clown nose and cigarette, in Thom's autograph book. Michael Foot, shortly to become editor of the *Standard*, wrote: "Before Paris, in Paris, behind Paris."[18] Ronald Hyde inscribed the Sedbergh motto, *dura virum nutrix*, "a stern nurse of men," to which Charlotte appended "Oh my! my!"[19] Thom was disappointed not to get Charles de Gaulle's signature. The exiled leader of the Free French lived at 99 Frognal; Thom and his friends spent two years, in vain, trying to solicit from him a "good morning."[20]

Thom was happy at Holly Hill. He wrote character sketches of every boy in his class and was "just as interested in writing about the boys I disliked or felt indifferent to as in writing about my friends."[21] In Hampstead, Thom began to develop a life away from his parents. "Growing up, I decided, is when there are some things you don't tell your mother," he later reflected.[22] School was one part of that independence; another was his best friend and neighbor, Ruth Pearce. They met when Ruth, the youngest of three sisters, dangled a toy steam engine over the high wall between their gardens.[23] From that moment on, they were inseparable.

Pretty and free-spirited, Ruth was two years older than Thom. They took the Pearces' Labrador, Beau, for long walks on Hampstead Heath. Thom recalled playing "an hours-long game of 'He' (Tag)" with other children in the surrounding streets, "the body getting strong through play . . . into the dark, delighted and sweaty."[24]

Their other favorite place, Church Row, had churchyards on either side and was strictly out of bounds. "We would have amazing games," Ruth recalled: "they were overgrown with wildflowers and roses in summer and we would stalk the visitors to graves and make up wonderful tragic stories about their lives." Indoor activities included dressing up and "reenact[ing] exciting moments from Dickens and the Russian classics." They borrowed Ruth's sisters and "little Ander" to be extras "while always keeping the dramatic parts for ourselves."[25] On one occasion, they ran naked around the Gunns' front garden and caused two old ladies who lived across the road in Frognal Mansions to complain to Ruth's mother. Ander recalled another occasion when Thom and Ruth "took all their clothes off and had a look at each other's bodies."[26] When Ruth signed Thom's autograph book, she drew a heart pierced with an arrow.

Ruth liked Thom's lack of inhibitions. She thought him "an unusual boy [. . .] kind and gentle" but with "a mature sense of humor—often with a cutting edge." He had "a fierceness of observation" and could "give an account of an event in minute detail." She was also impressed by Charlotte. "His mother gave us a tremendous amount of freedom," she reflected, of their license to play around Hampstead and, later, going on the Underground by themselves to first nights in the West End. "I think she trusted us a lot."[27] Moreover, Charlotte was chic: she kept her hair in a bob, her lips and nails a deep red, and wore hats with veils, tartan suits, and high heels. "What we didn't like was that she looked different from the other parents," Thom reflected. When Charlotte came to Speech Day at UCS, she let Thom and Ander choose her clothes: they invariably chose "her most anonymous outfit."[28]

Less than a year into their London return, the Gunns' marriage finally disintegrated. In November, Thom returned home from a Guy Fawkes party to find his father moving out. "[Charlotte] packed his bag with a bright smile," he remembered: "she got the maid to take down his suits ('Mr. Gunn is leaving us!'); and when [we] had gone to bed she positively ushered him out of the house." At first, Charlotte told the boys Bert had "gone to Scotland" on business.[29] Two months later, with Bert still away, Charlotte told them the truth: he had "run off" with Hilde Marchant, a star reporter on the *Daily Express*.

Marchant, "tiny, pert, pretty," according to one newsman, was "a Yorkshire girl of inexhaustible energy and a terrier-like disposition."[30] Bert was drawn to her immediately. At the *Express*, he became "her office impresario," recalled one colleague, "guiding her footsteps, ensuring that she was given top-class assignments and that her copy received first-class handling on the sub-editor's table."[31] Bert moved into a flat on Brunswick Square; Marchant left her husband, the *Chicago Tribune* war correspondent Sam Pope Brewer, to move in with him. Although Bert and Marchant never married, their relationship was not a secret on Fleet Street: *World's Press News* twice referred to her as "Mrs H. S. Gunn."[32]

Charlotte knew and liked Marchant. They shared political beliefs, and Charlotte admired Marchant's reports from Madrid about the Spanish Civil War. The boys also liked her, and she signed Thom's autograph book as "Hilde—STEP." "But for this I would have lived out my life talking on street corners to scorning men," Marchant wrote in Thom's book, quoting Bartolomeo Vanzetti, whose controversial execution for murder in 1927, with fellow Italian immigrant and anarchist Nicola Sacco, was an international cause célèbre. "My life is nothing. My death—it is all—but for this sweet agony, I would have forfeited my purpose."[33] Marchant "was able to talk to children without patronizing them," Thom recalled.[34] From one reporting trip to France, Marchant brought Thom back a box of condoms with "three cats making love to each other on the packet."[35] Ruth recalled that Ander "fixed [them] over all the taps" in the Frognal house and Charlotte had to convince the Gunns' charlady, Mrs. Stoney, not to give notice.[36]

Charlotte did not petition for divorce until October 1939, four months after the death of her father, Alexander, from a heart attack.[37] By the time of the petition, Ronald Hyde had moved into 110 Frognal; they had resumed their affair and intended to marry after Charlotte's divorce. Bert "gallantly" took the role of "guilty party."[38] However, Charlotte's affair with Hyde meant that she feared an investigation by the King's Proctor, "whose unpleasant duty it was to block occasional divorces because of collusion" where the misconduct of the petitioning spouse disqualified them from the right to divorce.[39] This perhaps explains why Hyde's sister, Lucy, also moved into the Frognal house. This gave the appearance that Charlotte was lodging with the Hydes, a situation that would not have survived even the gentlest of inquiries. "It seemed like a 'maison de trois'—there seemed to be a tolerant understanding between the three adults," Ruth recalled of Bert, Charlotte, and Hyde, "but to the neighbors it appeared shocking and something to gossip about."[40]

A fortnight after the divorce was granted in April 1940, Charlotte and Hyde married at Hampstead Town Hall.[41] Thom and Ander attended. Bert was one of the witnesses, Vernon Noble another. "One day when I visited London," Noble recalled,

> Charlotte and Ronnie Hyde met me at Euston Station, and Charlotte said: "We couldn't think of anything very interesting for you to do in London, Vernon, so Ronnie and I have decided to get married." They took me along to a register office and I witnessed their marriage, and the ex-husband Herbert Gunn was there and we all went back to their [house] in Hampstead for a party.[42]

After their separation, relations between Charlotte and Bert became more cordial. They remained close, not only for the boys but also because Bert and Hyde were good friends, as were Charlotte and Marchant. The terms of the divorce are unknown: Charlotte continued to live in the Frognal house even though Bert was still "the householder."[43]

Two months before the marriage, Hyde had become news editor of the *Standard*.[44] Newspaper work and separations meant Thom and Ander saw little of their father, and Hyde would prove just as absent a stepfather.

Their familial landscape, as children, was overwhelmingly female: Charlotte looked after them and, after Alexander Thomson's death, Covey Hall was run by their aunts. Charlotte must have felt a curious déjà vu when Hyde ascended to the same role Bert had held at the *Standard*. Once again, she was living in London, looking after two children, while her husband lived the exciting Fleet Street life she had once craved. Like Bert, Hyde was good company, and his charm helped him develop contacts throughout journalism and politics. As the Second World War progressed, the Savoy became the center of journalistic life. According to one American newsman, when Hyde was not running the news desk on Shoe Lane, he could "be seen in the hotel most evenings."[45]

For Charlotte and the boys, the war began during a holiday in France in summer 1939. They rented a house in Arcachon, a coastal resort near Bordeaux, with a French family named the Davids. During the trip, Thom got into difficulty in the sea and would have drowned were it not for the Davids' eldest daughter, Michelle, who swam to his rescue. With war imminent, Bert cabled Charlotte in early August and told her to return immediately to London. Charlotte ultimately took the boys to Covey Hall, where they listened to Neville Chamberlain's "lifeless voice" make the declaration of war.[46] Such was the initial chaos and uncertainty, it was not thought safe for Thom and Ander to return to London. To their horror, they were sent north to Ryleys, where they were to board until the situation in London became clearer.

Later, Thom based a juvenile novel on his three months back at Ryleys. Mrs. Woodhouse, the headmaster's wife, supervised the dormitory ritual of bedtime prayer. Thom acquiesced for two nights. On the third, he approached Mrs. Woodhouse and said: "'I don't want to do this. Could I just sit on my bed while they're doing this because I don't believe in God.' She looked at me in horror, but she had no choice but to punish me because of my beliefs."[47] Only the "humane influence" of an older boy, Porritt, prevented the other boys from punishing Thom for his rebelliousness. After lights out, Porritt told them stories from books he had read, "which were mainly by Dumas."[48] Thom enjoyed them so much he "read everything by Dumas" he could find in the school library.[49] Otherwise, separated from Charlotte and his friends, Thom spent his time writing "Wellsian stories about what would happen at the end of the world."[50] He was relieved when Charlotte collected them in December: the boys would stay in London until the Phoney War ended. Thom was overjoyed to be back at Holly Hill and to see Ruth. It was "like the end of a book by E. Nesbit," he wrote later: "they were back with their friends, back at the day-school that they liked, and there were games and adventures and parties."[51]

For the next six months, Thom and Ander lived with Charlotte and Hyde, their new stepfather, on Frognal. Ander thought him "a very laid-back sort of person, quite a sweet, loving sort of bloke."[52] The early days of the marriage were lighthearted and carefree, but a pattern of arguments and separations soon began. Hyde, a decade younger than Charlotte, was easygoing "and wanted a more even emotional life." According to Thom, Hyde "felt himself overwhelmed at times not only by her love but by her expectations of his love. He responded with a certain indolence; she pursued him with sarcasms; he got drunk."[53] Hyde, like many newsmen of that generation, was a functioning alcoholic. Come July 1950, he had to give up alcohol after a "depressive attack." Bert, then Hyde's boss at the *Standard*, told Beaverbrook, their proprietor, that "specialists have ruled that [Hyde] must be strictly teetotal for the rest of his life. He is 'alcohol intolerant,' which I suppose is another way of saying that drink poisons him."[54] For Charlotte, this was her daily reality in the early 1940s. Her second marriage was "not as happy as she had hoped it would be," Thom wrote, and recalled that she "once told [Bert], with a certain desperation, that she had to make this marriage work."[55]

For Thom and Ander, reunited with their mother, and with strawberry parties to enjoy through the long summer, the war seemed far away. Thom enjoyed mixing with his mother's new friends, artists and writers like Denis Mathews, Leonard Rosoman, and William Sansom. Rosoman painted Thom's portrait—he wears a blue shirt and lounges on a bed, reading—and Mathews, secretary of the Civil Defence Artists, later chose one of Thom's paintings for an exhibition of children's art at the Cooling Galleries. When they were not at the Holly Bush, a pub around the corner from Frognal, Charlotte held court in the house and encouraged Thom to mix with her friends. "I must have been an unbearably pretentious boy," he wrote later. "I can't see how they could stand me."[56]

The illusion was shattered in late summer when the Battle of Britain gave way to the eight-month Blitz. London was no longer safe. Charlotte took the boys to Surrey to live with Christina, then to a neighboring hotel when relations between the sisters broke down. "They didn't seem to know what to do with us," Ander reflected.[57] After four itinerant and uncertain months, Thom was sent to the progressive boarding school Bedales—and Ander to Dunhurst, its junior branch—in nearby Petersfield, Hampshire. If Thom feared it would be like Ryleys, he had a pleasant surprise. Bedales was founded in reaction to the strictures and tyrannies of Victorian boarding schools and was known for its informality, its encouragement of students' curiosity, and the innovative teaching methods that contributed to the welfare and happiness of its students. It "was a nice place (tho with a touch of earnestness)," he reflected, "and I started to grow up there."[58]

During his first term at Bedales, Thom wrote Charlotte "a novel." It was her suggestion: paper was in short supply, but Charlotte found him a large notebook with a shiny black cover. Each afternoon, Thom wrote a new chapter and illustrated it with pictures he had cut from her fashion magazines, mainly *Vogue*, during the Christmas holiday. "The Flirt," a comedy of manners, was the longest thing he had ever written: Olive agrees to marry Colonel Frobisher—"old enough to be [her] grandfather"[59]—much to the horror of her family and her lover, Charles. The colonel, the "flirt" of the title, is a great philanderer: Olive divorces him after finding him in bed with her sister. The story ends with a destitute Olive, in "thick, pink, sixpenny lipstick," prostituting herself outside a Lyon's Corner House. Charles whisks her away in a taxi, but she collapses before they reach his house. "Her head fell back, her eyes open— DEAD!" Thom clearly drew on his mother's own divorce for inspiration, although there is only a small allusion to Charlotte herself. One of the minor characters, "Ann," secretly marries "Harry," a "trapese-man" from the local circus. (Ann was Charlotte's birth name; Harry was one of Ronald Hyde's middle names.)[60]

Thom wrote more prose at Bedales. In "Rain," published in the school magazine the following year, a bomb explodes during a dinner party: the hostess runs outside and feels the rain "cool on my blood-spattered cheek."[61] Thom signed the story "Tommy Gunn," which attests to the influence of a new friend, the "epicene, outrageously funny" Michael Wishart. Wishart was "witty ahead of his years": his "outrageousness" appealed to Thom, as did his lack of concern for the opinions of strangers, something Thom had already learned from Charlotte. "We went around breaking conventions, parodying/mocking people, doing literary & artistic experiments," he wrote later.[62] Wishart was a year older than Thom and more daringly open than any boy he had ever met. "I guess we could discern in each other that we were queer already," Thom later remarked. "It was not conscious."[63] One "violent quarrel" seemed, in hindsight, "v[ery] like a lovers' quarrel."[64]

The attraction was mutual. "Thom had a quicker wit than all the other boys," Wishart wrote. "He was beautiful in a frail, dark way. Mindless fellows . . . mistook Thom's delicacy of form and thought for weakness, which developed his toughness."[65] Wishart taught him "to be naughty—being rude to teachers and shocking people."[66] Both boys had dysfunctional families and intense mothers. "Thom feared his father," Wishart reflected, "which was only one of our bonds."[67] Wishart's father, Ernest, was one half of the Marxist publishing house Lawrence & Wishart. In 1927 he married the sixteen-year-old Lorna Garman; Michael was born a year later.[68] "My mother, who was almost a child," he reflected, "treated me as a doll." Lorna was strikingly beautiful, with "vast ultramarine eyes": "dressed for dancing in clinging sequins [she] resemble[d] a sophisticated mermaid."[69]

Charlotte and Lorna met twice. "Mother [. . .] didn't like her, I wonder if a little jealous?" Thom wrote. "(I adored her.)" Wishart told

Thom about his mother's affair with the writer Laurie Lee. "'My mother's lover,' said MW airily & I was much impressed," Thom told Mary and Catherine years later. "I'm sure I then told him all about my mother's husbands."[70] At a Wishart party, Thom met Lee and Lucian Freud, another of Lorna's lovers, and found them "very dashing and attractive."[71] It "entered my mind," he later remarked, "that [Freud] might have been sleeping with Lorna."[72] Lorna's niece, Kitty—the daughter of Kathleen Garman and Jacob Epstein—later married Freud.

Thom's friendship with Wishart faded when he left Bedales. Wishart became a minor painter—he spent his career, as Philip Hoare remarked, "approaching but not quite achieving the first ranks of British art"—and lived a life that balanced "high-society propriety with Bohemian kudos."[73] "The Communist of his teens becomes a member of the Travellers Club," Thom mused. "What a characteristic course of life to take!"[74] Part of Thom's later aversion to Wishart was a response to his "egotistical" autobiography, *High Diver.*[75] More telling, even, is a remark about a boastful letter Wishart wrote to a mutual acquaintance. "As if experience can only be exciting for him when he can speak about it," Thom reflected.[76]

In four terms at Bedales, Thom learned to swim, paint, and act. He thrived in the artsy, coeducational environment and had "a series of girlfriends" in what he later compared to "the American institution of dating."[77] He loved Bedales's vast library and had a carrel next to "I" and "J." He noticed "all the books by Ibsen" and started reading him: "not the famous Ibsen," he later told a friend, but "a long strange romantic play about Julian the Apostate called Emperor of Galilean, I think. I must have been a strange child."[78]

Moreover, an "enlightened" teacher in English class taught from *The Poet's Tongue*, an anthology compiled by W. H. Auden and John Garrett.[79] Thom liked it so much he "read it beyond the assignments, out of class."[80] At UCS, Thom had only ever seen *The Dragon Book of Verse*, "which was all Lord Macaulay and the patriotic speeches from *Henry V.*"[81] The anthology showed Thom that "poetry could be anything at all: a counting-out game, a mnemonic for learning Latin verbs, a speech

by Shakespeare, or 'Frankie and Johnny,' a popular song, anything."[82]
He especially loved a line and a half from Donne's Elegy 16, printed as
though it was an entire poem:

> Nurse oh My Love is slain, I saw him go
> Oer the white alps alone.[83]

In their introduction, Auden and Garrett argued that poetry is "memorable speech" and that it appeared in their anthology not as "a cultural
tradition to be preserved and imitated" but as "a human activity, independent of period and unconfined in subject." This was the "first impression" they hoped to conjure in new readers.[84] Thom had already learned
from his mother that reading was part of life's "continuing activity."
Now, poetry seemed to open in front of him as both subject and activity.
Some thirty-five years later he called "memorable speech . . . still the only
workable definition [of poetry] I've come across."[85]

4

MOTHER

Coming down from acid in the early 1970s, living in San Francisco with his lover and a younger friend, Thom had "a flash of such certainty & suddenness that you don't know why you didn't see it all along." He realized he had tried "to reproduce the household of my mother and Ander and me. For when we came back from Bedales, there was no Joe," he wrote:

> he and mother had separated. I wasn't at all sorry, he had always struck me as rather tiresome, usurping my place in my mother's bed as it were, just when it seemed my father had been got rid of so successfully. (It never entered my head that these adults might have feelings of their own.)

Thom and Ander returned to Hampstead in summer 1942. "It was for the three years 1942–4 that I really entered upon myself," he reflected later. "I suppose I look back upon this as a golden period."[1]

In fact, Thom literally "usurp[ed]" Hyde's place in Charlotte's bed. "When Hyde left, she didn't have anyone in bed with her, so she brought Thom in," Ander recalled. "I thought, even in my child's way, that was a bit peculiar. It showed how close she was to Thom, how devoted." Thom stated that the arrangement was only to accommodate guests, but Ander disagreed. "There was no one else in the house," he recalled.

> They were quite open about it. It wasn't a secret. [. . .] I can't
> quite remember why it started. She was a very neurotic woman.
> She was obviously going around the twist, even then. If she'd
> thought about it, it wasn't good for Thom, this was not a sensible
> thing to do with your son when he was getting toward puberty.
> [. . .] She obsessed him. She possessed him.[2]

Writing about this custom, Thom claimed that, "being in fear of getting
an erection with her" once he reached puberty, he made "enough difficulties that she must have got the message."[3] He and Charlotte "were
lovers," he wrote.

> Of course. What, now, could be more obvious? I flirted with
> you constantly. I worshipped you. I was demanding. I hated my
> stepfather. (Poor man, he behaved toward me with care and re-
> spect, but I could not forgive him: he slept in the bed where I
> belonged.)[4]

Charlotte's devotion to Thom affected the relationship between
the brothers. They were "cast" into the roles of introvert and extrovert,
according to Thom, which "could be modified to those of kind elder
brother and mischievous younger brother." Thom was Charlotte's, Ander
Bert's, "though there was nothing explicit about such an arrangement."
Charlotte "loved Ander's independence and his vivid intransigence" in
contrast to Thom's "more passive spirit, his total acceptance of her."[5] At
home, Ander felt at a strong disadvantage. "I felt Thom got the best because he was highly intelligent and being worked on to be a genius," he
reflected. "That's why I had to hit him now and again, to put him in his
place." When Ander threatened to hit Thom with a coal scuttle, Charlotte called him a "fascist guttersnipe." In Ander, Charlotte induced "a
certain resentment, in the way she treated him against me. I think I was
an absolute nuisance. He was never a nuisance."[6]

That September, Thom, now thirteen, entered third form at UCS, a
year he later considered his "happiest time":

I had friends, no enemies, I was good at my work, I enjoyed
school and was happy at home. I wrote stories and poems which
I considered more than promising, but it was not an unhealthy
conceit, though it had no justification. I had contracted no violent friendships, and sex was still distant in the rosy sky. It was
known to me; but I was not entangled with it, and the boys who
were I looked upon with interest, pity, and contempt. It was a
healthy enjoyment I still anticipated.[7]

With a new friend, Peter Holgate, Thom played a "campy-historical
game" that involved staging Roman and Greek myths.[8] Moreover, he
watched convoys of "nice-looking" American GIs drive up and down
Frognal, newly arrived to support the European war effort. "The GIs
seemed sexier, on the whole, than the British soldiers because they were
better fed and their uniforms were of better material," he reflected. "They
looked like movie stars."[9] A late poem, "A GI in 1943," captures this
formative experience, describing "rough animal stubble above / the un-
disturbed beauty / of the farm boy's face." Thom's sexual interest was
aroused: when he wrote the poem, he had "learned nothing / fresh in
fifty-three years."[10]

By his early teens, Thom knew he was attracted to men.[11] The attraction was, in a sense, aspirational. When Thom reached puberty, his body
began to change. In 1943, he was still cherubic, a little short. Two years
later, a picture taken in the gardens of Hampton Court Palace shows
him tall, thin, and angular.[12] No great sportsman, at UCS he took up
rowing to develop muscles. Years later, he recalled a friend's remark that
seemed to capture his general sexual feeling from adolescence onward.
"In heterosexual love," his friend remarked, "you want to be <u>with</u> the
other person—& in homosexual love, you want to <u>be</u> the other person."[13]

As a child, Thom used to wear Charlotte's clothes. "I do remember my
mother saying, 'I don't want you wearing that dress out on the street,'"
he recalled. "I didn't know what she was talking about. It was not, in me,
consciously sexual."[14] His earliest fumblings with girls were "as clumsy as
if I'd been straight."[15] He recalled having a "hard on" in front of Ruth,

and a "vaguely romantic relation" with one of Ruth's friends. Under "non-sex" he listed several UCS boys and "an unknown girl."[16] "I had a non-existent sex life in my teens," he wrote later to a friend. "I don't count sex-games with boys at school and in any case I never got to do it with the boys I most wanted, just the ones who were available."[17] By his late teens, Thom felt "extraordinarily dishonest" with himself. "All my sexual fantasies were about men," he remarked, "but I assumed I was straight."[18]

Thom's sexual awakening occurred in an era of secrecy and shame for gay men. In the 1940s, homosexuality was illegal; men were prosecuted for committing homosexual acts in private.[19] Thom did not think his parents had homosexual friends; they likely did, but discretion was essential. "The only homosexuals I ever came across were these old men in raincoats jacking off in public urinals," he mused. "It's not a very attractive role model. There simply didn't seem to be any room for someone like me. I did not get the impression that attractive men were homosexuals."[20]

In a late interview, he remarked that, as a teenager, he would "love to have met some sporty young man who seduced me."[21] Something like that did occur. Drying himself in the changing rooms after a swim, Thom was approached by an older man, "perhaps in his mid-twenties," an "alumnus at the school I am going to." Thom was "perhaps . . . 11." They talked. "At one point while changing I get a hard-on, and since I don't know what to make of it, I decide I will just take no notice of it but go on talking to my new friend, who is being very flattering in his interest," he wrote. His new friend asked him to come swimming again that night, when the pool would be closed. "What an adventure, I think, not connecting his invitation with my erection. Much cross purposes, of course," he continued: "we do indeed climb the fence that night, but get in very little swimming. He grabs me in an uncomfortable hug from behind, but I doubt if he gets to come, since I break away too quickly. I feel silly. I imagine he thinks me a dreadful little flirt." In this recollection of the incident, written years later, Thom felt he was "so young I didn't understand all of this while it was happening."[22]

At UCS, Thom's new headmaster provided him with guidance.

C. S. Walton, nicknamed "Fruity" because of Walton's greengrocers, was "an impressive and exemplary figure."[23] He typically "brought out the shy and insecure," recalled one former student. "You felt he knew you, accepted you and appreciated your individuality."[24] According to UCS historian Nigel Watson, Walton was "a sexual innocent. One Old Gower recalled with disapproval instances where Walton kissed boys, but one assumes that if this was openly done, it was innocent in intention."[25] Thom's friend Peter Townsend, then head boy at UCS, thought Walton "had gay inclinations, but exercised a kind of self-discipline about that."[26] Thom claimed that Walton "covertly helped me through some early difficulties with my father."[27] What those "difficulties" were Thom did not elaborate, but it is possible that Walton intuited Thom was gay and had a difficult paternal relationship. "Like most homosexuals," Thom wrote of his childhood, "I disliked my father."[28]

Much had changed during Thom's childhood, but his love of reading, encouraged by Charlotte, remained constant. Back at UCS, he read outside class even more avidly than before. He read the Greek myths, then the major Greek tragedies, in Gilbert Murray's translations, all of which informed his own writing. One poem began:

> O peony you smell
> Like the heavenly nectar Hebe spilt
> On luxurious Olympus.[29]

But Thom's big discovery was Keats.[30] He fell for Keats "as you do for the first poet who really means something to you" and "liked him all, without discrimination." Moreover, Keats's connection to Hampstead enabled Thom to see his locale through a poet's eyes. Writing later about the "richness" of childhood, he felt he had wanted to capture "the sense of growing up with a sense of place. [. . .] It was on the one hand complacent and suburban, but on the other full of associations going deep and far back. Myths being given meaning."[31] In his early poems, he "encouraged [. . .] less the sharp-eyed exactness of Keats than an air of vague and nebulous beauty that concealed the actual world very nicely."[32]

Keats seemed to unlock all manner of possibilities. Thom began reading "everything," from Austen, the Brontës, and Hazlitt to Hardy, Herrick, and Marlowe. Dickens, too, was a revelation. Reading Dickens's descriptions of London in his early teens, Thom found "the romantic vision given body in bricks & flesh (& fog)."[33] In *Bleak House*, Thom recognized his own city, with its "pea-soup fogs" and "smoke so dense" that sometimes he could not see "more than a yard or two" down the road. Dickens also enlivened Fleet Street and Chancery Lane, areas of London Thom knew through his father and stepfather. Keats gave Thom a romantic vision of his locale, but to Dickens he owed a feeling for urban life that would shape his own writing. "Dickens also made me realize that I lived in a place where anything could happen," he wrote later. "The city is cruel and monstrous; my pulse quickens when I think about it."[34]

Thom's "golden period" dimmed in late 1943 when Charlotte and Hyde reconciled. Across London, Bert had moved to Chelsea, broken with Hilde Marchant, and planned to remarry. Olive Melville Brown had been one of C. B. Cochran's "Young Ladies," a troupe of singers and dancers, and had taken small roles in films like *Jubilee Window* (1935). Writing fashion reports for the *Daily Sketch*, she transitioned to journalism. Within two years she had become the *Daily Mail*'s star reporter and earned numerous front-page political and wartime scoops.[35] Like Charlotte, she was glamorous and strong-willed; Bert knew her by reputation long before they met in El Vino, Fleet Street's famous wine bar.

Bert and Olive married in January 1944 at the Chelsea Register Office. Ander recalled Charlotte "getting us ready and smartened up to go to the wedding, and she said: 'I don't know why he hasn't invited me!'"[36] Around the time of Bert's marriage, Thom began to notice "difficulties between father & mother."[37] Charlotte was used to having two husbands: when Hyde was absent, Bert likely provided Charlotte with emotional and financial support. That stopped when Bert remarried. Olive could tolerate Bert's children but not his ex-wife. The boys, however, could not tolerate Olive. "She was a terrible snob," Ander recalled. "God knows why he married her, terrible person. She was a phony."[38] Years later, when Thom's niece wanted to contact Olive, he warned her that Olive "eats boys and girls alive for breakfast every day."[39]

Charlotte envied Bert's glamorous new wife, some ten years her junior. When Olive became pregnant that spring, Charlotte's relationship with Bert quickly deteriorated. "She used to get very upset about him," Ander recalled, "but then she got upset about everything. When my father called her a hysterical woman, he was right. She wasn't very stable." At the same time, Charlotte found Hyde's absences increasingly difficult to deal with. "She went a bit crazy," Ander reflected. "I remember her in the latter days running around the house naked. She was in a state. I think that's when Hyde had left. I think she was probably impossible to live with. No wonder they couldn't stand her, poor thing. But Thom could, you see, because he was devoted to her."[40]

In December 1944, Thom published another poem in *The Gower*. He wrote "The Heights" after a trip to Scotland in August with his aunt Peg and cousin Jean, during which they climbed the Barmekin of Echt, the slopes of which had given the Thomsons' former farm its name: Hillside. Charlotte had visited Echt with her sisters in 1919. Thom may have recognized that he was following in his mother's footsteps, but it would be his only visit to Echt. "The Heights" uses a steady iambic tetrameter to echo the anticipation of his speaker, who imagines the wonders his party will see when they reach the top:

> We loved to walk the lower slopes,
> Smooth but interspersed with rocks.
> Of higher steeps we kept wild hopes
> And envied the adventurous fox.[41]

The "wild hopes" become progressively more elaborate, from "high-domed ruins" with "veiled kings" and "ghostly courts" to "inlets to undiscovered seas." Come the final lines, the reader knows what to expect:

We climbed the long-mysterious heights.
We climbed—but we found none of these.

Thom wrote the poem shortly after his fifteenth birthday. Its flatness of tone and replacement of the sublime with the mundane is teenage and speaks to something of the "Thomson melancholia" he saw in his grandfather and mother. While the poem is ostensibly set in Scotland, its tone matched his homelife on Frognal.

Shortly before Christmas, Charlotte and Hyde discussed a separation. Hyde recalled "domestic difficulties" and that "there had been talk of us parting—at her suggestion—for a while." Charlotte was in "a nervous state" around Christmas. On December 27, "it was agreed that [Hyde] should go away for a time." This would allow them to "think clearly and separately" about their future. Hyde left 110 Frognal at 8:30 a.m. on Thursday, December 28. Charlotte helped him pack his bag and "seemed very normal and reasonable."[42] Hyde went to the *Evening Standard* office on Shoe Lane and planned to spend the night at his apartment in Sloane Avenue Mansions.

After a telephone call to Hyde that afternoon, saying "she had made a mistake," Charlotte complained to her charlady, Mrs. Stoney, of "pain in her stomach." Until that day, Charlotte had seemed "in her ordinary health and bright," Mrs. Stoney recalled. When she saw Charlotte a few hours later, Charlotte was "a little better."[43] The evening proceeded ordinarily. At nine thirty, Thom and Ander listened to *Appointment with Fear*, their favorite program on the BBC Home Service. "It was a really frightening thing," Ander recalled. "That's what we used to listen to and drink our Bournvita."[44] That night, "The Man in Black" narrated "The Oath of Rolling Thunder," a western story written by the American mystery novelist John Dickson Carr.[45] While the boys listened to the radio, Charlotte read in front of the fire. They stayed up to listen to *The Making of a Poem*—that week, a discussion of Yeats's "Byzantium"—and went upstairs to bed around 11:00 p.m. Thom came back downstairs twenty minutes later, having forgotten his watch. He kissed his mother good night.

In the morning, Thom and Ander came downstairs around nine forty-five. They found Charlotte's "tender note against the parlour door" and went across the lane to find Mrs. Stoney.[46] "We thought, possibly, [Charlotte] had gone to see a lawyer," Ander recalled. "She was always going to see lawyers about my father."[47] Mrs. Stoney was out shopping. Ander noticed that the back gate was unlocked, as were the French doors into the parlor. This was strange, Thom thought, because "they had certainly been locked the evening before. Mother had done this, we supposed, to make it easier for us to get in." By now, the boys knew what they would find. "I guessed—though I hardly dared to even when I saw the note," Thom wrote a few days later. "I think Ander did too. But we did not dare mention our conjectures."[48] Recounting Charlotte's suicide fifty years later, Thom remained defensive about her actions and sought to absolve her from any blame. "My brother and I found her body," he remarked, "which was not her fault because she'd barred the doors."[49]

Beneath the bureau blocking the parlor door, Charlotte had stuffed newspaper to prevent gas seeping into the rest of the house. Opening the French doors, the "horrible smell" of coal gas hit them.[50] It "haunted" them "for the whole day afterwards." Charlotte, wearing her "beautiful long red dressing-gown," was lying on a sheepskin rug in front of the fire. A tartan blanket covered her face. In her hands, the gas-poker, used to ignite the fire. "Ander began to scream 'Mother's dead! She's killed herself,'" Thom wrote, "before I could even realise that she was."[51]

The boys ran back into the garden. Then they went back inside. Thom turned off the gas, Ander took the poker from her hands. They removed the blanket from her face. "How horrible it was!" Thom wrote. "Ander said afterwards to me that the eyes were open, but I <u>thought</u> they were closed; she was white almost, like the rest of her body that we could see. 'Cover it up. I don't want to see it. It's so horrible,' Ander cried. Her head was back, and the mouth was open—not expressing anything, horror, sadness, happiness,—just open." Charlotte's legs were apart, "one shoe half off, and her legs were white and hard and cold, and the hairs seemed out of place growing on them."[52] Thom kissed her legs.

After notifying the police, Thom contacted Hyde, Bert, and Thérèse

Megaw, a friend of Charlotte's who lived nearby. "His mother and I would always, during the war, have coffee across the road at about eleven o'clock in the morning," Thérèse recalled. "And that morning, Thom rang. He said, 'Thérèse, Mother won't have coffee with you this morning, she's committed suicide, and can I live with you?' Just all in one sentence."[53] He sent a telegram to Covey Hall saying "Mother has killed herself," among other things.[54] Much later, he reflected on "the incredible selfishness and thoughtlessness of the message" he had sent Mary and Catherine. "When I telephoned the telegrams office, and gave the message, there was a sort of whoop of excitement at the other end of the phone," he recalled.

> After about 5 minutes a grave kindly middle-aged woman telephoned from them: Are you quite sure that was the message you intended to be sent? etc.—"Oh yes" (I said irritably, or brightly, or tragically, or all three, I forget) "oh yes, they are very sensible people." I did not think for a moment that it was I who was not the sensible person.[55]

Bert "showed no sadness," Thom wrote. Hyde arrived an hour later and "drank a bottle of champagne we were keeping for the peace, & hid the bottle."[56] Thom blamed himself and Hyde for what had happened. "It was Joe perhaps who caused your death," he wrote a few days after Charlotte's suicide.

> He had left the house (for the second time since their marriage), on the early morning of the 27th; I had heard his voice, through my sleep, at her command. Oh mother, you could have called him back, but you knew we didn't like him! But we would rather you had 10,000 Joes in our house, rather than you had killed yourself.[57]

By the time Hyde left Frognal, he had been seeing somebody else for at least six months. Daphne Eddowes was "gay and attractive, with enormous china-blue eyes."[58] Hyde may have met her as early as 1941, when Daphne worked at the Savoy as an assistant to Hyde's good friend Jean Nicol, the press officer.[59] Daphne had divorced her first husband, the prominent divorce lawyer Michael Eddowes, and was living in Sloane Avenue Mansions, where Hyde also had a flat.[60] The Eddoweses had sent their small son, John, to Canada as a war evacuee in 1940. When John returned to England in August 1944, he found his mother "then with Ronnie."[61] Six months after Charlotte's death, in June 1945, Hyde married Daphne "quietly" at the Chelsea Register Office.[62]

In shock, Thom and Ander were taken to Covey Hall. There, Thom wrote about his mother's death in the first diary entry he ever made (plate 8). "Mother died at 4.0A.M, Friday, December 29th, 1944," he wrote. "She died quickly and peacefully, they said, but what agonies of mind must she have passed through during the night. I hate to think of her sadness. My poor, poor mother; I hope you slept most of the time, but however sad then, you are happy now. Never will you be sad again!"[63]

Thom kept this diary, containing his first attempt to write about his mother, for the rest of his life. He likely used it to write "The Gas-poker" in spring 1991.[64] The poem echoes the detachment of the diary in its cataloging of visual details. "This is partly the detachment of good writing," remarked Clive Wilmer, "though it is hard not to identify a wider habit of detachment that, even in the most extreme of circumstances, shuts off the expression of plain grief."[65] Part of the poem's detachment comes from Thom's decision to write it in the third person. He was "thinking in terms of a Hardy poem," he later remarked.[66] Its meter and disyllabic rhymes also recall Hardy. "Then it came easy," he remarked of the third person, "because it was no longer about myself. I don't like dramatizing myself."[67] In "The Gas-poker," he wrote that he and Ander

> went to and fro
> On the harsh winter lawn
> Repeating their lament,

A burden, to each other
In the December dawn,
Elder and younger brother,
Till they knew what it meant.[68]

He described the poker itself as a "sort of backwards flute," an allusion—
Wilmer argues, convincingly—to "the reed or pipe of pastoral song and
the myth of Pan and Syrinx," which Thom would have known from his
extensive reading of Greek myths as a teenager. "Where Pan . . . breathes
out through the pipe to make consolatory music," Wilmer writes, "the
dead woman has done the opposite, breathing in poison gas."[69] The poem
concludes:

The poker that she held up
Breathed from the holes aligned
Into her mouth till, filled up
By its music, she was mute.[70]

Shortly before he wrote "The Gas-poker," Thom wrote another poem
about his mother. "My Mother's Pride" begins with the lines, "She
dramatized herself / Without thought of the dangers."[71] This perception came from both his childhood and a conversation Thom had with
Thérèse in the 1970s. "She was very interesting about Mother," Thom
reported to Ander, "said she had a knack for the dramatic moment, and
also said that if she had waited a week she'd never have killed herself. I'd
never thought of that before."[72]

In his diary Thom had addressed his mother directly: "Never will
you be sad again!" He, too, vowed never to be sad again. As an adult he
became known for a booming laugh that, as one friend put it, "contained
the raucous completeness of life."[73] This was often the first thing people
mentioned about him: he laughed a lot, loudly, and was forever having
a good time. But not everybody was convinced. Tony Tanner, to whom
Thom was close in the 1960s, doubted whether Thom was as happy as he
tried to persuade people; that there was a deep sorrow he sought always

to disguise. "Tony made a point about the famous Gunn laugh," recalled Clive Wilmer:

> He said, "He laughs too loud, as if he's got something to prove."
> He was right about that. There was something about the laugh
> that was a bit too self-dramatizing; self-dramatizing in the sense
> of doing something you want other people to interpret in a cer-
> tain way, that isn't actually quite true to yourself.[74]

Thom may have admitted as much. "My Mother's Pride" concludes with the line, "I am made by her, and undone."[75]

All of that was to come. In the days following their mother's death, numb with grief, Thom and Ander had another immediate worry. "We are at Covey Hall now," Thom wrote, "though father wanted us to stay at his horrible house and with his horrible wife. He wants to live with us. Mother prophesied that he would if she should die."[76]

5

RECUPERATION

Thom called the years following his mother's death "more like a recuperation from an illness than anything else. I have an image of myself as dragging myself through them."[1] It was decided that Thom and Ander would not, for the moment, live in Chelsea with their father and stepmother. Olive gave birth to her first child with Bert in late January and did not want the custody of two grieving teenagers.

Instead, a temporary solution was found. The boys returned to Frognal to be looked after by their cousin Margot and her husband, John. Both had worked at Bletchley Park until John was transferred to London. Margot was twenty-two. John had never met Thom and Ander. Needing somewhere to live, they were "more or less commandeered by the aunts into moving into the house in Hampstead." The boys were "in a state of shock and grief," Margot reflected. "It was weird entering the house so soon after [Charlotte's] death. The fridge was still full of her food."[2] Thom, Margot felt, resented her presence. "You needn't think you can tell me what to do," he told her, "because you are only six years older than me and we played together as children."[3] He carried his cat "around inside his shirt all the time" and read by himself in his room. Ander, on the other hand, "was no problem at all."[4]

In a newsy letter to Mary, Thom reported that he and Ander had spent "a dull 2 hours" in Chelsea visiting Jamie, their new half brother. Thom complained that Olive's nurse had remarked "the English always have been honest" and wished he had "mentioned the Congress at Vienna and various other proofs of our hypocrisy!" Other matters surfaced—ration coupons, Bert's "meanness" with money, purchasing tickets for *Uncle Vanya*—and Thom told Mary that he and Ander were "very happy." He did, however, allow for one occasion on which he "woke up in the morning feeling quite prepared to follow Mother to the grave!"[5]

Thom's jauntiness masked his actual feelings. He was "numb for months," he wrote later, and the "numbness persisted in a minor way for a long time: it was as if for the first time I had lost my luck. (And, boy, hadn't I?)"[6] But in his letter to Mary, written six weeks after his mother's death, he was keen to demonstrate, in a curiously adult way, that everything was normal. Not everyone was convinced. Margot, obviously, could tell Thom was in an acute state of grief; to Ruth, who "loved [Charlotte] deeply" and thought of her as a second mother, Thom changed "dramatically" and "a kind of awkward embarrassment" developed between them. Their childhood intimacy evaporated. Thom "seemed to retreat," Ruth reflected, "and retire into a world of his own like some damaged creature hurt beyond help and condolence."[7]

There were some bright spots. When Victory in Europe Day was declared on May 8, Thom made "two lovely red flags [with] hammers and sickles on them" to hang on Frognal. He joined the "impressive" crowds outside Buckingham Palace and saw "their graceless majesties" George VI and Elizabeth wave from the balcony.[8] The boys spent the night beside an "enormous" bonfire on Parliament Hill, on which "was thrown a stuffed effigy of 'That man,' now said to be dead."[9] They "danced and sang around the fire till past one."[10]

Two months later, Thom took his School Certificate examinations. Understandably, given the circumstances, his results were not outstanding. He achieved "very good" in English Language, was awarded "credit" in English Literature, French, and Art, and passed British and European History, Latin, and Elementary Mathematics.[11] Thom wanted to stay on at UCS for two more years to sit the Higher School Certificate. University, however, was in some doubt. Bert told Thom "he might not be able to send me to a university because he wouldn't be able to afford it," Thom reported to Mary. "I think this is nonsense, but he seems weak on the subject, and liable to have his mind changed quite easily. If he needs any argument, I could tell him that Hilde [Marchant] once promised to pay for me, but I don't think it will come to that."[12]

But there was a more immediate problem. With the war over, Margot and John would leave imminently for postings in mainland Europe. Where Thom and Ander would live became an urgent matter. Bert quickly sold the Frognal house to the *Punch* editor E. V. Knox and a decision was made.[13] Ander would live with Bert, Olive, and Jamie in Chelsea while Thom would remain in Hampstead with the Megaws. It was what Thom wanted, but it was still a wrench to leave 110 Frognal, where he had lived almost half his life. It was the site both of his "golden period" and his mother's suicide, a place of love and grief. He kept a piece of it, his key to the front door, for the rest of his life.

The Megaws lived a five-minute walk from Frognal, in a smart town house on The Mount. Thérèse (Veder) Megaw was Dutch. After the breakup of her first marriage, Thérèse, aged twenty-six, had moved to London in late 1932. She stayed temporarily in Francis Bacon's Kensington flat, and married a young electrical engineer, Eric Megaw, in March 1933.[14] They had two sons, Vincent and Ted, both of whom were younger than Thom. Eric was conscientious and private, completely different to the newspapermen around whom Thom had grown up. He worked in his study "every evening often till two or three o'clock."[15] Thérèse was a bohemian figure with "a dark Jewish look."[16] She mixed with artists, writers, and actors, many of whom Charlotte had also known, from Denis Mathews and Leonard Rosoman to Nova Pilbeam and Eric Porter. Like Charlotte, Thérèse encouraged Thom's literary pursuits. "She was always wonderful to me," he told Ander in 2004, "considerate and sweet, and treated me better than her own sons, I thought."[17]

Thom lived in the Megaws' basement, a self-contained flat with a separate entrance. "I couldn't see any kind of happiness for myself except in hiding myself away in my room in Thérèse's basement and reading hugely and precociously, 18th & 19th century novels and Elizabethan plays," he wrote later.[18] For a while he carried around a small red book of George Meredith's poetry. "Love in the Valley," he thought, was "positively reckless in its sexiness," but he found Meredith's language a step down from Keats.[19] Reading provided an escape. Snodland, where Thom spent weekends and school holidays, was "almost unbearable."[20] He praised Mary and Catherine for their "generosity in taking over my awful adolescence after Mother's death,"[21] but "the irritation of adolescence" made visits difficult.[22] Thom likely found it upsetting to spend time where his mother had grown up, and where he had spent his own happy interludes during childhood. Now, he helped Mary and Catherine with their milk round, wheeling the pushcart and huge churn from village to village.[23]

Snodland, though, was preferable to Chelsea. Thom visited his father as infrequently as possible. In March 1945, Bert had become editor of the *Evening Standard*, his first Fleet Street editorship.[24] His Chelsea house was the scene of constant parties, "all these journalists and MPs," Ander recalled. "It was only a tiny house, but everyone was smoking and drinking and killing themselves." Ronald and Daphne Hyde were regular visitors. Thom had little time for them, or his father, but missed Ander. "The separation was a bit extreme," Ander reflected. "He used to come around occasionally, or I used to meet him. It was sad to be separated from your brother when these dreadful things happen to you."[25] They were "schizophrenic" years, Thom later remarked, contrasting his "upper middle class life in London" to his "lower middle class and countryish" life with his aunts.[26]

A year after his mother's death, Thom still "retired" and "hid." "The first winter had been misery," he remarked, "but by the second I had learned strategies."[27] One strategy, reading voraciously, provided escape, but he developed another based on the detachment of his letter to Mary. In an unfinished poem called "A Place Returned To," written in late 1966, he reflected on his teenage years in Snodland and included an unflattering self-portrait:

> His stoop, his forehead covered with dark hair,
> His pimpled face, his big hands with the book,
> [. . .]

> Over-emphatic, shrill,
> He was self-pitying, vulnerable, until
> He had to cultivate what he lacked most.

"But my past self, who lived here once, is dead," he continued. "I have learned the nonchalance of other men."[28] This was one of Thom's adolescent strategies, to protect his feelings and present a hard shell to the world.[29] It was as though he felt that the only way he could deal with his mother's death was to become a new person, to erase a childhood self he found "self-pitying" and "vulnerable."

Another strategy involved trying on new identities. In late 1945, Thom won the part of Orsino, Duke of Illyria, in UCS's Christmas adaptation of *Twelfth Night*. He had "fairly clear diction and a good feeling for his lines," wrote *The Gower*; "his presence was impressive, and one felt that his emotions were so genuine that they could not easily be brushed aside in a person whose birth and station gave him the luxury to be so arbitrary."[30] Escaping oneself was much easier if you could become someone else instead. For Thom, struggling not only with his mother's suicide but also his own sexuality, the Duke was an interesting role. He opens the play with a famous speech about desire and appetite—"If music be the food of love, play on"—falls in love with Olivia, then is drawn to Cesario, his new page. When Cesario is revealed to be Viola in disguise, the Duke's attraction does not waver. At UCS, all the roles were played by boys.

Discussing early struggles with his sexuality, Thom focused repeatedly on his perceived "dishonesty."[31] "It troubled me enormously in my teens," he remarked. "I felt I should assume that I was heterosexual, that this was—as they used to say—'a passing phase.' *I* didn't see any sign of it passing."[32] Literature provided a salve as well as an escape. Marlowe, for example, was "tremendously encouraging."[33] Years later, he described his ideal reader as "myself at the age of 18, feeling extremely unsure sexually, not really being quite honest with myself about being queer and needing reassurance."[34] To Ruth, homosexuality was "certainly not something [Thom] would have displayed openly," but she thought that it "surfaced" in the months following Charlotte's death. Thom "took up with a very camp lad and he didn't appear shy about him parading his sexuality."[35] It is uncertain whether Charlotte knew that Thom was gay. Later in life he remarked that she "would have taken it all right," but that Bert "would have been appalled and never spoken to me."[36]

Thom felt his "strategies" were "enforced by that unsureness of identity and that Werther-like depression that is (or was) regularly experienced by teenagers."[37] He typically sought to underplay the trauma of his youth. "15–18 are difficult years anyway," he remarked.[38] By spring 1946, his numbness and depression began to lift. His strategies had started to work. Acting in *Twelfth Night* was not simply a case of learning lines: Thom was forced to pay greater attention to his body—how and where he stood, gestures of head and hand, how he moved—while imaginatively embodying a different role. Some of Thom's earliest and most significant memories centered on what he called "a concentration of energies in me that built up and then suddenly burst free." The "energies" were "physical and of the emotions and . . . of the spirit too," and he came to refer to these experiences as "illuminations" or "revelations."[39]

Thom's first illumination had occurred in May 1942. Michael Wishart had obtained permission for himself and Thom to leave Bedales early one Saturday morning to travel to a party at Glebe House, the Wishart estate in Hampshire. "We woke, and since it was earlier than we normally woke, the dormitory—the twelve or so boys asleep in their beds—looked different from usual," Thom recalled. He and Wishart washed in cold water, dressed quietly, and with "barely suppressed excitement" set off outdoors and across the field toward the first bus. As they climbed over the stile and into the field, Thom's "feelings concentrated to euphoria—the unfamiliar hour, the excitement, my own energy, combining with the beauty of the grass (and hedge, and wild flowers, I think) in the warmth of the early morning sun." He remembered nothing of the party itself, but he never forgot that morning. "Every thing in the world seemed good, and also seemed concentrated in myself," he wrote: "my elation was too great to be contained in myself, in a sense, and it was as if the world was me, and I was the world."[40]

Four years later, Thom felt another surge of concentrated, bodily energy that seemed to be "a reaction to [the] depression" that had shaped his life since his mother's suicide. "I was on my way to school along Church Row—I remember other boys also going in the same direction, but I was alone at the moment so no especial friend can have been among them," he wrote.

> I became aware of the small tender green leaves appearing, after the hardness of the winter, on first one branch of a tree, then all over the tree, then on other trees. [. . .] Just that. It is difficult to explain, impossible to describe without sounding silly. I felt sudden, enormous happiness, in a big surge, focussed on the appearance of the minute leaves.

These "irrational powers and unforeseen energies," after a long, numb convalescence, were a release. "I apprehended possibilities again," he reflected. "I had a future again. [. . .] My elation continued for several days, and I hardly slept during the nights because I was not tired, I was all energy."[41]

University was one part of that future. First, Thom faced a period of national service.[42] In February 1947, Bert wrote to Robert Rattenbury, the senior tutor in charge of admissions at Trinity College, Cambridge, to "propose that [Thom] should serve his period with the Forces first" and go on "to the University in 1949."[43] Rattenbury warned that "the great pressure" on college accommodation following the conclusion of the Second World War meant that he could not "promise to admit [Thom] after his service," but assured Bert that Thom would make his "list of candidates" should he provide "good" qualifications and "satisfactory evidence of his character and ability."[44] Bert was "most anxious to avoid a situation where the boy . . . would thus be left in mid-air at a rather critical time in his life."[45]

C. S. Walton wrote to Rattenbury on Thom's behalf, observing that he had done "very well against quite exceptional background difficulty." Thom's parents, Walton wrote, candidly, if not entirely accurately, were divorced and married again and from time to time resumed their association, so that we never quite knew who was in loco parentis to the children, and the whole thing ended with the mother putting her head in the gas oven on Christmas Eve two years ago and being found dead by the two boys.

Walton felt Thom, then almost eighteen, was resilient and self-possessed beyond his years and "does not seem to have suffered as much as one would have expected." Thom was "unusually gentle and refined for a boy of his age," and had "an unusual degree of appreciation of literature and artistic matters in general." He was "still somewhat shy and diffident" but "a boy of very great promise."[46] Impressed and sympathetic, Rattenbury responded that Thom was "a boy whom we should be glad to have and to help."[47]

Matters were complicated that summer when Thom did not pass Latin for his Higher School Certificate.[48] He obtained a three-month deferment from the army to remain in London and sit School Certificate Latin that December. To his relief, Thom achieved a credit standard, which meant he did not have to sit Cambridge's Previous Examination as a de facto entrance examination.[49] Once he finished his Latin examination, Thom spent the winter of 1947–48 between Snodland and Chelsea. That was "one of the worst times," he reflected. "No school to go to, just waiting around to go into [the] army."[50] There was more disappointment: his deferred enlistment meant that going up to Trinity in autumn 1949 was now at best a remote possibility.

On April 1, Thom reported to the Wessex Brigade Training Centre in Bulford, Wiltshire. He entered the army tall and slim, at five foot eleven and 150 pounds. He gave cycling and rowing as his main physical activities and listed "reading" as his main "spare time" activity.[51] Thom completed "rather strenuous" basic training at Bulford and described army life as "very boring, stupid, useless, immoral."[52] In October, he was sent to the Royal Army Educational Corps to train as a sergeant instructor. This involved a three-month course at the Army School of Education, based in Buchanan Castle on the outskirts of Glasgow. The castle was impressive but "very badly organised," Thom complained:

> there are grotesque shortages—of electric light bulbs (only 5 among 30 of us), chairs (2), wash basins (2), lavatories (2), basin plugs (0), of door handles (every N.C.O. carries a spare door handle about with him as an essential part of his equipment).

The typical RAEC officer was "short and round and often with glasses," while the sergeant majors were "all aged guardsmen, <u>very</u> fierce, and at least 7 foot high." The castle had "a slightly more civilised atmosphere" than Bulford and "a library of reasonable dimensions," from which Thom was able to borrow D. H. Lawrence's *Kangaroo* and *Antony and Cleopatra* "in a very glorious edition."[53] The "enormous amount of reading"[54] Thom achieved in part mitigated the "boredom, drudgery, and endurance"[55] of military life.

Thom quickly determined that RAEC pedagogy was "bullshit."[56] "They talk too much about teaching," he told Ruth, "while only having the vaguest ideas of what it is really like 'in the field'! The heads of some of the instructors are way up above the clouds, and only a very few are any practical good."[57] Reflecting on this time in "Buchanan Castle, 1948," Thom felt that "the hierarchy based on fear" and "the taut perfection of the marching line" created a great stasis at odds with the great energy he felt as he turned nineteen and twenty. He wanted to be "released / Into my freedom, into the world at large" where he could "take charge."[58]

In the army, Thom's freedoms were intellectual and connected with two like-minded people. At Bulford he had met a short, energetic, opinionated boy named Derek Ingrey who wanted to be a novelist.[59] They exchanged writing samples. Thanks to his voracious reading, Thom also wanted to be a novelist and spent much of his spare time writing novels.[60] Ingrey was reading Henry Miller, Kenneth Patchen, and Céline; Thom, still on Hardy and Lawrence, was developing interests in Proust and Stendhal.[61] Ingrey called himself Ulysses: Ander thought that was his actual name. A memorable incident occurred when Thom and Ingrey visited Ander in Chelsea while Bert and Olive were away. "I gave them lots of drink and they were sick," Ander recalled. "My father knew someone had been at the gin. I told him Thom came round and brought his friend Ulysses. 'Oh!' my father said. 'Is he some sort of pansy man?' He didn't like Thom being gay. He found it intolerable."[62] Their friendship was short and intense. After the army, Thom saw little of Ingrey but later called him an "influence": he had helped to broaden Thom's awareness of novels beyond the Victorian era.[63]

Thom was mid-training when the Army School of Education relocated from Buchanan Castle to Bodmin. There, his main instructor was Archibald John Wavell, son of the former viceroy of India, Archibald Percival Wavell. Archie John, as he was known, was not a typical soldier. He loved poetry, and his real passion was Shakespeare, *Hamlet* especially, about which he exchanged long, animated letters with the author and explorer Freya Stark, a family friend.[64] Moreover, Archie John was "a gentle young man" and "an out-and-out intellectual," recalled the Canadian novelist David Walker. "Everyone liked Archie John and nobody understood him."[65]

Thom was drawn to Archie John's gentleness and wide-ranging intellectual interests; Archie John was likely thrilled to have as bookish and curious a national serviceman as Thom in his charge. They also shared political sympathies. Archie John was a socialist. "When I asked him why," remarked the Conservative MP and diarist Henry Channon, "he retorted that he wanted to be able to ask his batman to dine. I pointed out that he could do that now if he chose . . . but it didn't really require a social revolution."[66] When Thom left Bodmin to spend the remainder of his service at Arborfield, the depot of the Royal Electrical and Mechanical Engineers on the outskirts of Reading, he and Archie John shared "a most affecting farewell! I have still got one of his books," he told Mary and Catherine, "which he said I could send to him when I had finished it. Mark Myers showed him some poems by me (which I had lent Mark), and he said I had the Makings of a Poet and other flattering things, and asked for copies of them!"[67]

At Arborfield, Thom taught English and math to new recruits; in the evenings he monitored the library and television room. He taught so "badly," he claimed, that he "preferred" Saturday morning platoon drills.[68] He began reading James Joyce—presumably Ingrey's influence—and in summer 1949 discovered *The Brothers Karamazov*. He recalled reading it while on the train from Arborfield to London. "My excitement at getting away from the base for a little was folded into my excitement with the book," he later wrote. "We *all* have this kind of experience, in which our experience of the book is inextricably confused with the experience of reading it for the first time."[69]

It was a strange time for Thom. Against the stasis of army life, books excited him, he had "the romance of London" to explore on weekends off, and, as he turned twenty that August, he could finally see national service coming to an end. During the summer he experienced another "combination of really extraordinary energy and exhilaration,"[70] the third of what he later called his illuminations. It occurred during what he described as a "manic period."[71] He decided to use his overwhelming energy "to start, or write, a novel I had projected" and worked solidly on it "for about 5 nights, filling a number of notebooks, I think with very effusive writing, before the energy went away."[72] For Thom, at least in later life, this illumination seemed to connect "the body's vigor and the imagination's" in a new way.[73]

As autumn became winter, Thom felt a new "delight, anticipating getting out" of the army for good.[74] Moreover, the question of Cambridge was finally settled. In late November, he asked Robert Rattenbury "when it will be possible for you to tell me whether I have been accepted into Trinity College in Autumn 1950."[75] The answer came in early January: Rattenbury offered Thom a vacancy in English to start that October. Thom accepted, bringing three years of uncertainty to an end. "While I did National Service there was the possibility that I might not actually get [to Cambridge]," he later wrote: "it was in any case dreadfully distant, an escape from the drudgery of the army into the bright and tranquil life of the mind."[76]

6

CAMBRIDGE

Thom was released into the reserves in February 1950. With eight months until his Trinity matriculation, and keen for an adventure, he decided to spend as much time as possible in a country whose literature he had read voraciously while in the army: France.

By 1950 Paris had reestablished itself as a major intellectual and cultural center. It was the city of Robert Doisneau and Henri Cartier-Bresson; Camus, Sartre, and Beauvoir. Its rebirth would have come as a surprise to Thom, who had built his image of Paris—and France, more generally—from its nineteenth- and early twentieth-century literature. When he arrived in early March, his struggles with the French language—everybody spoke "at an awful rate"[1]—and his inclination toward solitude meant that he spent much of his time alone, though was "not particularly conscious" of feeling lonely.[2] He lived in the Villa Chez-Soi, a residential hotel in the Sixteenth Arrondissement, where he had his own room and his time was his own. Bert had arranged a sinecure in a translator's office, where Thom would work on publicity material for the Paris Metro. It was "poorly paid" but not onerous, and Thom had plenty of time to devote himself to his real purpose in coming to Paris. "I was a real mouse," he reflected. "I didn't know anybody, I didn't make any friends. I wrote and wrote."[3]

Paris was intoxicating. "I walked around it all the time," he recalled, "& for the first time in years did not feel a defeated melancholy."[4] He was full of writing plans and began to see the city through the eyes of a novelist. He made lists of people seen and things heard. Walking and cycling through the city, and speaking French daily, his confidence grew. "Very proud," he wrote, "because 3 people told me separately I was getting very Parisian in one day."[5]

Thom modeled himself on the heroes of his favorite French writer: Stendhal. He read *Le rouge et le noir* shortly before leaving UCS and reread it when he arrived in Paris. He identified with its naïve and energetic hero, Julien Sorel, with whom he shared a provincial background, a bookish nature, and a poor relationship with his father.[6] Later, he reflected that it was "a challenge" to be alone in unfamiliar cities, and that he had "a fantasy about myself as a kind of Stendhalian hero to whom heaven knows what may happen any moment."[7] Arriving in Paris, Thom read *La chartreuse de Parme* for the first time: it "knocked my socks off" and became a lifelong favorite.[8] Adopting a Stendhalian role was an important part of Thom's recuperation from his mother's suicide. "Looking back on myself at this time," he wrote of the period between Charlotte's death and going to Cambridge, "I see someone strangely withdrawn, deeply boring. [. . .] I was <u>present</u> at the activities of others, initiating nothing, passively taking stuff in like a sponge, and being completely unselective about what I took in."[9] Stendhal gave Thom "a sense of possibilities"—a literary equivalent, perhaps, of the all-consuming energy of his illuminations—and a feeling that "the recuperation [was] finally completed."[10]

If Thom tried to embody Stendhalian ideas, another French novelist had the greatest impact on his writing. Thom began Proust's *À la recherche du temps perdu* in the army and finished it in Paris.[11] It was the major influence on his main writing project while in Paris. *November* is a comedy of manners in which Quentin, the sixteen-year-old protagonist, has an affair with a much older woman. The novel refracts ideas first found in "The Flirt" through a sophisticated Proustian lens. "I wrote lots of it, but I lost interest when it wasn't even a third finished," he reflected. "I'd been reading Proust at the time and was totally corrupted by it, filling up a whole chapter describing one minute."[12] Proust was calamitous for Thom's nascent style—"the sentences got longer and longer," he joked, "and the insights subtler and subtler"[13]—but the experience of beginning "an immense novel and never finishing it" was an important step toward his becoming a poet.[14] "I realized I was more enthusiastic about poetry than the other forms," he remarked, "so that was what I wrote."[15]

Quentin embodied many of Thom's preoccupations. Worried that his adolescent passivity meant he was "without consistent character" and could be "different things to different people," Thom placed role-playing at the novel's center.[16] "How had Quentin the courage to continue acting a part that anyone must be able to see through?" the narrator asks.[17] For Thom, role-playing was an act of self-preservation rooted in anxieties about his sexuality. In *November*, he echoed the scene in Proust when Marcel sees Albertine for the first time, "the dark one with the fat cheeks who was wheeling a bicycle." Her "smiling, sidelong glance" makes Marcel wonder whether "she had seen me at the moment in which the dark ray emanating from her eyes had fallen on me?"[18] Thom's unnamed girl "seemed to dominate" her group of friends, "walking boyishly with her hands deep in her pockets." Quentin passes her in the street:

> I looked up and she gave me a strange look, which I took [to be?] merely mocking.—Her eyebrows rose, her eyes grew wide, her smile grew, it was confident and careless, seductive and melancholy, sad but inviting, at the same time a smile for me not for her friends, and it was, I suppose, this interest she seemed to feel in me that made me cherish the picture of that face and that expression.[19]

Thom either knew or suspected Proust was homosexual, but may not have known that a model for Albertine was Proust's secretary and driver Alfred Agostinelli.[20] "When you read all of Proust," he later remarked, "you live in a Proustian world for a moment. You know, that the bus conductor may be homosexual!"[21] Besides her "boyish" walk, there is little in Thom's "confident and careless girl" to suggest gender inversion; but, like Proust, he is unspecific about physical features, with nothing overtly masculine or feminine about arms, chest, hips, legs. Reflecting on his "imitative and dispiriting" early writing, Thom thought "there was some kind of material" he "wasn't able to face up to. I'm not certain what it was," he continued, "it wasn't simply that I couldn't yet acknowledge my homosexuality, though that was part of it. It was more that my imagination retreated too easily into the world before my mother's death, a world that in practice excluded most of the twentieth century."[22]

Abandoning *November*, Thom also abandoned stylistically and thematically similar short stories, such as "Blearing Park," "The Magnanimous Cuckold," and "The Wrong Sort of People." Part of his problem was overambition: plans for short stories quickly became plans for novels. Another intention was to write an introduction for a poetry collection called *Seasons and Poses*.[23] The most striking entry in the Paris notebook, however, is a list of suicide methods. Written in April 1950, the list does not appear to belong to a particular story, novel, or poem; neither is there any reason to suggest Thom was contemplating suicide, given that his Paris stay was energetic and restorative, albeit solitary, and he found himself "increasingly happy" there.[24] His list contained practical considerations. He ruled out an overdose of aspirin or angina medication as "too complicated." Jumping from the Eiffel Tower would be "dramatic," but the deep pit at Ladds Hill, near Covey Hall, was not thought "deep enough for instant death." Notre Dame was out because of its "horrid railings." Other methods included electricity ("no!"); gas ("but where?"); drowning ("how to stay under? I have almost drowned twice & it is a very horrible feeling"); starvation ("too long"); throat cutting ("no!"); cutting the posterior auricular artery ("instantaneous"); slitting wrists in a hot bath ("like the Romans. Very pleasant, but where obtain the bath?").[25]

Although Thom struggled to write poems—the best in the notebook is probably "The Hospital Ward," an extended metaphor for depression—Paris gave him a poetic gift. As with Stendhal and Proust, Thom's first encounter with Baudelaire occurred while in the army. "In Baudelaire I could read of evening approaching in Paris," he wrote, "when 'La prostitution s'allume dans les rues,' and though I had never been there, I knew I loved Paris—it too was the City."[26] Once in Paris, Thom challenged himself to read one Baudelaire poem a day.[27] *Les fleurs du mal* was Thom's introduction to urban poetry: his three favorites, "Le cygne," "Les petites vieilles," and "Les sept vieillards," are all from "Tableaux parisiens." He learned from Baudelaire that his walks around Paris could inform poems. Falling for Baudelaire and Stendhal at the same time fostered in Thom his "novelistic interest in people" and his lifelong interest in writing about desire. "It's not for nothing that I admire Stendhal and Baudelaire so much," he reflected, "because it's their preoccupation too."[28]

Before returning to England, Thom undertook a fortnight's tour of the Auvergne. He hitched and caught trains, but mostly he walked from Vichy through Clermont-Ferrand, Puy de Dôme, Puy de Sancy—following the volcanic mountains of the Chaîne des Puys—Pradelles, and Le Puy.[29] The experience was "almost like the day after acid," he wrote later, "clear, adequate, strange, beautiful."[30] The tour was part of an extraordinary summer of reading. Alongside Baudelaire, Proust, and Stendhal, Thom also read *King Lear* for the first time.[31] "My sense of [*La chartreuse*] was a great feeling of release, as if anything were possible, surely contradicted by <u>Lear</u>," he wrote later, "and yet of course the <u>language</u> of <u>Lear</u> demonstrates just the kind of possibility, and individual power to shape experience that its plot appears to deny."[32] Moreover, he found "an extraordinary sense of possibilities" in the idea that "one could contain romantic incident (dream, adventure, excitement of childhood game in adult life) in one's experience so long as it was sharp-edged, defined and . . . 'realized.'"[33] This was his inheritance from his mother: reading was not simply an activity in itself but a part of life, of one's lived experience.

University, Thom later remarked, "was an escape into my life. It was then that I started to spell my first name with 'h'. It seemed to me to be nothing more than a delightful affectation when I came to Cambridge, but I can now see that this was an attempt to become a new person; it was my announcement that I was going to be somebody new."[34]

The reality was more complicated. "I was christened William Guinneach Gunn," he explained to a Cambridge tutor, "but for some reason my parents immediately regretted this and I went through life as Thomson William Gunn."[35] That is the name on his UCS record card, typed in September 1942. This meant Charlotte knew him as Thomson while she was alive, and had perhaps even suggested the elongation from Tom to Thomson. When "The Heights" was published in *The Gower* in December 1944, he was "T. W. Gunn." On his application to Trinity College in February 1947, he wrote his name as Thomson William Gunn but signed himself "Tom Gunn." The following year he signed all his army paperwork "Thomson" except for the Official Secrets Act declaration, which he signed "Tom." In letters regarding his Cambridge admission, sent to Robert Rattenbury in late 1949 and early 1950, he signed "Tom Gunn (T. W. Gunn)."

Thom officially changed his name in September 1949.[36] "When I was twenty I thought it would prevent confusion if I became Thomson William Gunn legally," he later explained.[37] But in letters to friends and aunts, he would not be Thom until his return from Paris.[38] He worried, perhaps, that the "h" seemed like an affectation, although to the ear it would be no different. Why the change? Thom's new sense of "possibilities" made him determined to don his new name for good, especially when going up to Cambridge was a natural time for a new beginning. Its permanent adoption echoed Charlotte's changes of name throughout her life. "I wonder whether she was aware that she was marking a different personality in each case?" Thom wondered. "I don't think so. I wasn't aware of it in my own case, not until long after I'd made the change."[39] The definitive change from "Tom" to "Thom" looked backward and forward: Thom wanted to memorialize his mother and use her name on his own terms to become "somebody new."

In the army, Thom had written a poem addressed to Cambridge. "Shall I ever rest on your learned lawns?" he asked. "That was my impression of it, a lot of serene young men sitting around on the Backs reading serious books." Trinity did not disappoint. It boasted a wealth of poetic alumni, from Dryden, Herbert, and Marvell to Byron, FitzGerald,

Housman, and Tennyson. Thom walked through the sixteenth-century Great Gate, with its statue of Henry VIII, founder of Trinity, to enter the college. Its architecture had a "crisp beauty," Thom felt, especially Great Court ("for show") and Nevile's Court ("for perfection"). Meals were taken in the "big shadowy Hall," overlooked by full-length portraits of prominent alumni and college masters. Thom spent much of his time in the Wren Library, where he was impressed that the college librarian would show him fifteenth-century manuscripts of *Piers Plowman* at his request.[40] These buildings helped Thom to "love every inch of Cambridge with a total romantic love."[41]

Thom lived in Whewell's Court, on the other side of Trinity Street. It was "a fine example of heavy Victorian gothic," he thought, with two inter-connecting courts.[42] Unusually, he lived there for his entire time at Cambridge: his first year in L4, and last two in M7, both of which overlooked the junction of Sidney Street and Jesus Lane.[43] Thom shared L4 with his army friend Mark Myers, an ambitious and diligent law student, who "no doubt found me rather trying to room with."[44] Bedmakers brought shaving water each morning; winds rattled the window frames; thick, coarse blankets kept them warm against the fierce cold. Thom wanted his rooms to look the part. He hung two Sickert drawings in charcoal and red ink— *Paris Music Hall* (1907) and *The Handicap* (1913), which his mother had purchased from Sickert's retrospective at the Leicester Galleries in 1942— and reproductions of William Blake engravings from *The Book of Job*, as well as his aunt Helen's painting of Minor Canon Row, a street of town houses near Rochester Cathedral. "I must have plenty of room for books," he mused, "and a large flat table for writing."[45]

Entering Trinity, Thom was shy, gangly, awkward, pimply, and sexually confused. "I was a country mouse of no great development thrust right in the center of . . . tradition (in both the TSE and British Empire senses)," he wrote later, "of which the characteristics were both beauty and power."[46] His upbringing, solidly middle-class though it was, had not prepared him for the kinds of privilege and self-assurance he encountered at Cambridge. Attempting to assimilate, he bought a college blazer and tried to smoke a pipe. Although he was older than most new students—Thom was twenty-one when he matriculated—he felt "emotionally . . . very immature."[47] He counted only Mark Myers, his roommate, and Seth Caine, with whom he shared supervisions, as friends. He envied the "dashing undergraduates hurrying *somewhere*, gowns flapping in the wind, and it was evidently toward parties one wasn't asked to." Thom felt he had "the desire to be a social climber, but not the talent."[48] It took his entire first year, he claimed, before "my emotional age . . . caught up with my actual age."[49]

Thom's director of studies was Theodore Redpath, Trinity's first English don, and his supervisor was a young, Aberdeen-educated specialist in medieval and Renaissance literature named Helena Mennie Shire. Thom did not see much of Redpath, but Shire became a trusted friend and adviser. She and Thérèse Megaw were Thom's "two in-loco-parentis: they hated each other."[50] Shire's guidance and mentorship stretched beyond essays and into Thom's general reading and writing: building on the democratizing principles he had first discovered in *The Poet's Tongue*, Shire instilled in Thom a lifelong love of song, from anonymous Elizabethan street songs to Hardy's ballads to popular music like the Beatles. "[She] worked me hard and I liked her very much," Thom reflected.[51] Shire oversaw Thom's intellectual development for two years—Redpath took over in Thom's third year—and wrote extremely positive term reports about his progress. "Has worked and written with vivid interest and enormous enthusiasm," she wrote of his first term. "Width of view, incisive judgment, and lively intellectual curiosity. Already a good second, his work approaches A."[52]

Another Cambridge influence, unavoidably, was F. R. Leavis. Thom attended some of Leavis's lectures at Downing College but never had a tutorial with him. This meant Thom could absorb what he wanted from Leavis without the danger of becoming a disciple, or Leavisite, as his adherents were known. Thom later claimed that Leavis's value came from his view of literature "as part of life"[53]—something Thom had already learned from his mother—but his real, practical use came in what Thom could apply to his own writing. Leavis "was good for me in that he said things about the way a poem works, about the way movement can work with or against metre," Thom reflected.

One of the things I found especially memorable was for example the way he went through that speech in *Macbeth*: "If it were done when 'tis done then 'twere well / It were done quickly". He would point out the variations in speed with which Shakespeare is directing you to take your voice, corresponding to the emotional variations in Macbeth's attitude. This was the kind of thing that had never struck me before, though I had been moved by *Macbeth*.[54]

That year, Thom wrote "short Prufrockian poems about disillusioned middle-aged men walking through dead leaves." Knowing "they weren't good enough," he was unsurprised when undergraduate magazines rejected them.[55]

Thom's retreat into the nineteenth century—to avoid "this problem of a suicided mother"[56]—meant that he was unprepared, unable to write about his own emotions. Here, Leavis's example also helped. By concentrating on technical aspects of writing poems, Thom began to "deal directly" with his emotions, citing Leavis teaching him that "by reducing their diffusion, by concentrating them," his emotions could belong in poems.[57] Leavis railed against one such emotion, self-pity, thinking it, in Thom's assessment, "a limitation in moral fibre."[58] But Thom realized he could use Leavis's technical guidance to confront this much-deplored emotion. Using his example, Thom remarked, "one is able to hold in leash, or to a certain extent transform, one's own self-pity. One feels a tremendous amount of self-pity at our age."[59] Thom's undergraduate poems are by no means direct, but they do provide an early glimpse into the understatement that characterizes his later work.

Beyond lectures and supervisions, Thom concerned himself with poetry and politics. Sometimes, the two overlapped. At the Cambridge University Socialist Club he met John Mander, an "Etonian Marxist," whose poetry possessed "a vigor somewhat lacking" in his own.[60] At CUSC meetings they read aloud from left-wing poetry of the 1930s. That year, Mander cofounded *Oasis*, a poetry magazine that Thom helped sell in colleges and on the street.[61] Thom boasted to his father that he was treasurer of *Oasis* and that its first issue—which contained poems by Auden, Eliot, and Dylan Thomas—had sold 250 more copies than the average Cambridge literary magazine.[62]

When Tom Driberg, the gay Labour MP and newspaper columnist, addressed the Labour Club in February 1951, his speech likely contributed to Thom's decision to become a pacifist.[63] In July 1950, the United States had intervened in the Korean War, followed quickly by UN forces. Driberg was against British military involvement and wrote scathingly of "back-bench Tories who, true to their jungle philosophy, cannot help baying at the smell of blood in the air."[64] Thom had an interest in this, having been placed in the so-called Z-reserve after his national service. In January 1951, the government intended to recall up to 235,000 army reservists for refresher training.[65] Thom was not concerned about being sent to Korea—the chances were virtually nil—but objected to the possibility that reservists who refused the call-up could face a prison sentence. After watching the reissued *All Quiet on the Western Front*, "[which] shows in a most timely way the helplessness of all those who take part in war and the futility of killing," Thom left the cinema and saw an evening paper headline "that those who incite Z-men to object are to be imprisoned. A fitting contrast," he told his father. "And we say we're not totalitarian."[66]

Thom felt his "only proper course is to become a conscientious objector." He outlined his reasons in a long letter to Bert:

> I would like to emphasise, then, that (1) it is for moral reasons that I take this step (though of course I would disagree—who wouldn't?—politically with a war ~~with~~ against Russia), (2) I think it is usually only by individual action that one man can bring about any good, (3) I do not believe a bad means can ever bring about anything but a bad end, (4) this is not just an impetuous action on the spur of the moment—I shall not change my mind, and I have been thinking about it for a long time, (5) it is inconsistent with my already having done national service, but I feel no obligation to stand by something done at the age of 18, when I had not thought on the subject with any thoroughness.[67]

Bert sensed an opportunity. Having resigned the editorship of the *Evening Standard* in 1950, and left the Beaverbrook stable completely, he bought the ailing monthly magazine *Modern Housewife*, renamed it *You*, and installed Olive as editor.[68] Inviting Thom to write "a printable letter" for inclusion in the magazine, Bert planned a feature called "Son or Father—Who Is Right?" in which he would respond with his own letter.

"Son or Father" ran in April 1951, anonymously "in deference to the wishes of the father," as Bert wrote in its introduction. Setting the scene, Bert wrote that Thom "has always shown a tendency to the Left, though apart from an incursion into Communism when in his teens, he is not an extremist." Bert was "puzzled and dismayed" at Thom's decision to become a conscientious objector, calling it "an inexplicable line of conduct." He called Thom's choice "as personal as the decision of a man who resolves to end his life. And almost the same moral laws apply," he continued. "Individualism carried to its ultimate must surely result in a reversion to the moral code of the savage, the cat, the dog and the farmyard." Thom's letters to Bert were warmly distant; Bert's public reply, in *You*, strikes a similar tone. "You have my sympathy," Bert concluded:

> I want you to be happy and to lead a full life, with a contentment of spirit which must be the only motivating force for existence at all. You have decided to go a very difficult way to achieve it, and naturally I hope deeply that it will not bring too many complications and worries to you.[69]

Cloaked in anonymity, their stilted exchange in *You* is the closest thing to a dialogue between Thom and Bert that survives.

Toward the end of Thom's first year at Cambridge, he was asked to contribute a poem to an antiwar supplement of *Cambridge Today*. With pacifism on his mind, Thom had recently watched Lewis Milestone's gritty Second World War film *A Walk in the Sun*, which focuses on the psychology of a group of Allied soldiers as they attempt to capture a Nazi-held farmhouse in southern Italy. Milestone's film provided the occasion for Thom's "Poem," which he later renamed "The Soldier."[70] For the first time, Thom had a meaningful subject in which he had a personal stake. As a result, he wrote the poem "in a different way from any ever before—with a kind of sureness and concentration."[71] Its imagery recalls Wilfred Owen, although Thom thought it "predictably Audenesque in idiom."[72] He was especially pleased with his vigorous first and final stanzas:

> Yours is the brightness in orchards of bullets
> > Before day.
> Shake the wet bough and the drops will tumble
> > Quiet and gray.
> > > And lying in sterile mud,
> > > Hear them hiss in your blood.
> [. . .]
> You must know that the orchard exists for the maggots
> > You are the fruit;
> Your colours will soften when the coring bullets
> > Cut their own pain out:
> > > You'll make fine eating then,
> > > Flesh gone, and the worm in.[73]

Moreover, "Poem" got Thom noticed. Peter Green, editor of *The Cambridge Review*, wrote that, of the three poems in the supplement, "Only Thom Gunn / Shows really effectively how it can be done."[74] Thom felt "very encouraged" and, ripping up all the poems about middle-aged men and dead leaves, "decided to work hard at writing poetry all summer."[75] His "extraordinary sense of possibilities," first felt in Paris eighteen months earlier, was about to burst into life.

7

TONY

That summer, Thom returned to France to reprise the tour he had made the previous year. He walked and hitched south, sleeping beneath a blanket on the roadside. From Paris he passed through the Massif Central and the Auvergne: he wanted to go as far south as he could, and had designs on spending a week in Cassis, a harbor town with dramatic cliffs near Marseilles.

One day, walking along a straight dusty road through central France, Thom experienced "a revelation of physical and spiritual freedom that I still refer to in my thoughts as the Revelation. It was like the elimination of some enormous but undefined problem that had been across my way and prevented me from moving forward. But now I suddenly found I had the energy for almost anything."[1] A newfound self-assurance accompanied that energy, likely fostered by the success of "Poem." "Carrying my needs I carried all I was," he realized. "A gust on asphalt between origin / And destinations." With his newfound energy and vigor, he felt determined to live in "that 'between'" that, until now, he had "never thought of other than as way / To somewhere else."[2]

Back in England, he applied his energy to reading the entirety of Shakespeare: "doing that, as Helena Shire later remarked, adds a cubit to anybody's stature."[3] It was "probably what put the final stroke to my becoming a poet," he later reflected: "it was being plunged in a cauldron of language."[4] Reading Shakespeare and drafting new poems—"Mother

Love," "The Fable Is Different"—were the beginnings of "an apprentice-ship in poetry" during which Thom wrote an average of a poem a week for the next eighteen months.[5] Although he thought a lot of those poems "worthless, imitative junk," he took heart that "a new poem turned up just about every week."[6] Shakespeare and the Revelation meant that "the summer vacation was in fact as important as the whole of the preceding year."[7]

From the beginning, Thom's second year at Cambridge was busier than his first. "Poem" gave him status among Cambridge poets. He and John Mander started a reading group with Norman Buller and Harold Silver, which made Thom feel part of the literary community. The meet-ings had "practical" value in that "we tried to suppress our own vanities and be of help to each other."[8] But as Thom made new friends and as-cended the social ladder, these older friends fell by the wayside. Mander, he thought, was "manufacturing a synthetic tradition" in *Oasis*, and scorned one issue "devoted to horrid Harold S."[9] Thom still published in *Oasis*, but not everyone was impressed. Christopher Bayliss criticized his "insensitive ear" and judged that "Two Ghosts" "croaks from ambiguity to ambiguity."[10]

Another consequence of Thom's growing reputation was that he was asked to edit the Fortune Press anthology *Poetry from Cambridge 1951–52*. He threatened to turn down the invitation unless his new friend, the "affectionately witty" John Coleman, allowed him to "print 4 or 5 or 6" of Coleman's poems.[11] Coleman consented. One reviewer found Coleman and Thom "willing to let their technical requirements lead their phrasing astray once in a while [and] willing to revel in words."[12] Coleman was urbane and exciting. Thom "was once heard to say, 'Five minutes with John Coleman and all my problems are solved.'"[13] When Coleman was rusticated with his then girlfriend, a Girton law student named Margaret Baron, Thom attended their farewell party.[14] "We do so miss you both," Thom told him: "where is a cult without its objects of worship?"[15]

After the party, Thom polished off the remaining wine with an "argu-mentative, inquisitive, imaginative" young Scot named Karl Miller. His "abrasiveness was part of his charm," Thom felt, and he liked that Karl "seemed to have no preconceived ideas of what he might find at Cambridge and he wasn't going to accept anybody else's."[16] Karl's manner, wrote his and Thom's Cambridge contemporary Nick Tomalin, was "a peculiar blend of shyness and arrogance, perception and ingenuousness, tolerance and puritanism . . . Many times he will turn from reciting libellous verses about his acquaintances to water a sprig of heather he keeps on his mantelpiece to remind everyone of his intense Scottish patriotism."[17] Miller was in his first year at Downing but was already well-known as chair of *The Younger Generation* on the BBC Light Programme, where "under-twenties" discussed books and films.[18] A close friendship developed, based on shared literary passions and comparable backgrounds. Karl, who considered himself an orphan, had been raised by his maternal grandmother on the outskirts of Edinburgh.[19] Books, as they had for Thom, provided an escape from difficult teenage years. When Karl wrote Thom's profile for *Varsity*, the university newspaper, he felt "a very, very anxious honesty and a sadness are probably deepest in him."[20] Thom admired Karl's poems and included his work in *Poetry from Cambridge 1951–52*. Karl pinned Thom's new poems above his desk: his criticisms "matured my mind amazingly," Thom reflected, and he learned from— and assumed—Karl's "habit of questioning, questioning everything."[21]

The result was one of the most prolific writing years of Thom's life. During the 1951–52 academic year, he published eleven new poems. Some, like "Mother Love" and "The Fable Is Different," he later rejected as juvenilia, but others began to show a maturity of subject and style. Between February and May 1952 he published "A Mirror for Poets," "Helen's Rape," "To His Cynical Mistress," and "Lazarus Not Raised." All four drew on the classics for subject matter and/or the Metaphysicals for conceits. Donne became a significant influence. Thom had read Donne in his teens but "wasn't mature enough to know what to do with it."[22] Now, though, Donne gave him "the licence both to be obscure and to find material in the contradictions of one's own emotions."[23] This contributed both to the "meter & metaphysical ingenuity"[24] of his early poems but also to some of their flaws: obscurity, coldness,[25] and a claustrophobic inwardness. Concurrently, Helena Shire began to find Thom's academic interests "so exclusively and pointedly literary that it is apt to turn always inwards." She felt "a wider and more varied human concern" would see tutorial work move from second class to first.[26]

It is unsurprising that Thom's poems were inward-looking but not emotional. It is also unsurprising, given his inclination toward nineteenth-century novels as a mode of escape, that his poetic models were not contemporary. "There were no poets writing [in the early 1950s] who were enormously attractive," he reflected.[27] He found "energy" in "no contemporary English poets," by whom he meant people like George Barker and Dylan Thomas.[28] In American poetry—of which Thom was "extremely ignorant"[29]—he felt only Robert Lowell and Karl Shapiro came close to possessing it.[30]

Instead, Thom's closest "literary gods" were Auden and Yeats. Auden "made things seem easy" and was "tremendously helpful," he reflected, but there was a danger. Thom felt his early poems were "riddled with Audenesque mannerisms"[31] and thought that "imitating Donne and Auden at the same time" made him sound overly difficult and intellectual, "something like Empson."[32] Yeats, on the other hand, "wasn't yet one of the poets of authority" and was not on the Cambridge syllabus. His *Collected Poems* were published in 1950, "with the *Last Poems* added, and it was a revelation."[33] For Thom's generation, "Eliot was the king of the world" with "no possible rival": to discover Yeats, then, who promised "a lot more vigor, a bigger range," was "extraordinary."[34] Only later did the hazard of Yeats as an influence emerge, "in that one tends to pick up all the mannerisms but none of the intensity."[35] "Reading him liberated me into a lifelong oppression," Thom later remarked, "he was so important for me at that particular moment of discovery."[36]

Although Thom had grown less serious about acting after he left UCS, his broad reading in Renaissance poetry and drama developed his interests in theater and role-playing. At Cambridge he regularly attended opening nights at the Amateur Dramatic Club. In his first year he had seen *The Alchemist*, *Othello*, and *Coriolanus*. His second year began with *Edward II* and concluded with *Pygmalion*. That summer Thom took a small part in *The Taming of the Shrew*, his only acting credit at Cambridge, which Toby Robertson directed in the Fellows' Gardens of Trinity and King's.[37] It was "Cambridge at its sweetest," Thom felt: "Shakespeare, the moonlit summer night, the park-like private gardens of wealthy colleges, friends I hoped would be friends for life—different kinds of happiness rolled into one."[38]

Many of Thom's early poems feel like dramatic set pieces. His interest in drama and role-playing furthered "a rather crude theory" of "pose, based partly on the dramatics of John Donne, somewhat perhaps on Yeats's theory of masks, and most strongly on the behaviour of Stendhal's heroes."[39] Other sources included Shakespeare (the bastard in *King John*, Coriolanus) and later Sartre. While "literary in character," its heart was Thom's "Revelation on the road in France, with its intimations of unbounded energy." Taken together, Thom found that "viewing myself as an actor trying to play a part provided rich material for poetry." He was left "in an interesting place somewhere between the starting point— the bare undefined and undirected self, if he ever existed—and the chosen part." This place was "rich in tensions between the achieved and unachieved."[40]

Heroism was at the center of Thom's theory of pose. He acknowledged that "much of Shakespeare deals with the heroic of a certain kind" and that his early poems were an attempt to write "a modern equivalent to heroic poetry."[41] His ideas about heroism predated literary models such as Shakespeare and Stendhal; Charlotte taught Thom about heroes when he was about ten years old. "These are the heroes," she wrote in his autograph book:

Socrates, Jesus Christ, Lenin—Jeanne D'Arc, Leonardo da Vinci—Grandfather Thomson—Matteotti, Mazzini, Garibaldi, Karl Liebknecht, Rosa Luxembourg, Sacco & Vanzetti. ~~Thomas~~

Tom Mann.—François Villon, Shakespeare, St. Just. Mrs. Roosevelt. Madame Curie. Nansen. La Pasionaria. Carl von Ossietsky.[42]

From these predominantly socialist figures, Charlotte hoped Thom would learn values such as humility, gratitude, selflessness, honor, and integrity. Many, like Liebknecht and Luxemburg, Matteotti, and Sacco and Vanzetti, had been executed or assassinated for their beliefs; others, like Mazzini, were admired for their revolutionary fervor and support of women's rights. Thomas Mann, Shakespeare, and Villon embodied the peaks of literary achievement.

Thom did not recall "doing much about my theory in the actual living of life," but at Cambridge he found somebody who embodied many of these heroic values. Handsome, with a beautiful voice, Tony White was the finest student actor of his generation and destined to be a star. Before they met, Thom had seen him many times onstage, making "romantic-existentialist characters" of Aufidius, Gaveston, and Mark Antony. Toward the end of his second year, Thom met Tony at a party. They "joyfully discussed Stendhal for about two hours" and became "tied to each other by mutual enthusiasm." He was "a model as well as a friend," Thom reflected, and "helped me to shape my thoughts."[43] Ultimately, Tony "became a major hero of my poetry for some 15 years."[44]

With his abundance of energy, vigor, and panache, Tony "seemed to articulate in a bolder way than I ever could the kind of personal freedom that I had glimpsed on the road in France."[45] Writing Tony's profile for *Varsity*, Thom believed he "possesses the greatest possible amount of energy without being a monster. Sometimes one suspects that he is at least *trying* to act the monster," Thom continued:

> when one hears him recount with gusto some particularly savage and horrific story one can see that there is a positively Fascist streak in his admiration of successful violence. Just the same he is, secretly, rather a gentleman: he is considerate of other people's feelings.[46]

The doubleness of the last sentence could easily describe Thom himself. Tony seemed to embody contradictions in a way that Thom found exciting. He combined a tough exterior with a tender interior: exactly the kind of armor Thom had tried to cultivate in the years after his mother's death. "Like Coriolanus, his favourite hero, he refuses to be 'false to his nature,'" Thom wrote of Tony.

> And it is a supremely confident and active nature. One suspects that his real ideal is some swaggering unscrupulous Sabatini hero—and it is normally difficult to retain whole-heartedly such an innocent ideal at the age of 22. He is the sort of person who takes pride in doing what he feels like doing.[47]

Just as Karl saw a fundamental sadness in Thom, Thom saw vulnerability beneath Tony's energy and vigor. "As one of his friends observed, 'Tony gets beautifully depressed,'" Thom wrote, "something that is more surprising in him than in the rest of us."[48] Tony's depression and his "courtesy"—which Thom meant as "a giving of himself, in all his strength and sweetness, to others"—was "a direct result of the deep unease in him, a defiance of it."[49] Together they concocted a "home-made philosophy, the mélange of Rostand, Stendhal, Shakespeare, and Camus,"[50] and instigated an adherence to what they called "the Values," which Tony summarized in a card as "panache, logique, espagnolisme, l'imprévu, singularité and MAGNANIMITY."[51]

The effects of Tony's energy on Thom's poetry first emerged in a poem Thom wrote about an incident that occurred during the long summer vacation. To raise money for another European trip—this time to France and Italy—Thom spent six weeks at a farm camp near Cambridge. There he picked fruit and vegetables and found it "good to be in the open air all the time—a cure for introspection." From Priory Farm, Thom wrote Karl long gossipy letters. "As soon as I got here I found myself surrounded by girls, so as they flirted with me I flirted with them which is so easy," he wrote.

Round about the 3rd evening I became involved with a girl
called Ann—at first sight something very attractive about her.
A kiss became prolonged and the situation became inescapable.
I felt very vigorous during the first week or 2 and was prepared
to experiment without stop, and while we still had confidence in
each other and there was still exploration to be made everything
was well. [. . .] She never, I am convinced, suspected for a minute that I loved men, and I was very nice to her. She said at the
very beginning that as she was a Roman Catholic she would not
have intercourse with me: however it was obvious I cd persuade
her to in a few days.

Thom's sexuality was no secret to Karl, but his "experiment" was more
about conduct than desire. Tony had a reputation for affairs: Thom
wanted to copy him and play the heroic lover. "I was very interested until
my curiosity was satisfied," he told Karl,

[and] mere curiosity is soon satisfied, and I never for a minute
imagined I felt any passion. To my credit, I never pretended to
be more than casual. I carried off casualness with panache for a
while; but I began to get bored, & there is also a feeling of <u>fear</u>
of being committed to an attitude one does not sincerely feel so
I had to make the necessary break, and I now see I was more
unkind than I had meant to be. I knew that I cd have persuaded
her to do anything I wanted—but I would not have been adequate to deal with her afterwards.[52]

The word "panache" would have alerted Karl to the spirit in which Thom
had entered the liaison. "'Panache' was a word and a mode of the time
and place," Karl reflected, "and its prince was Tony White, saluted as a
local avatar, a fine ideal of tender toughness."[53] Jane Collet, who knew
Thom at Cambridge, married Karl, and had a son with Tony, recalled
"a famous occasion when Tony was supposed to have climbed up the
front of King's College in his socks and his *panache* and no more."[54]

But Thom did not yet have it in him to play the role: acting "more un-kind than I had meant to be" made him feel just as uneasy as the duplic-ity in pretending to feel sexual attraction. He learned from the encounter that "one must not enter on such things if one cannot be happy in them and make the girl happy. It is a pity to be perverted."[55]

The experience with Ann, and an abortive tryst with "a dear little girl from Leeds," also at Priory Farm, were the source of one of Thom's most accomplished early poems. "Carnal Knowledge" was his first poem about pose:

> Even in bed I pose; desire may grow
> More circumstantial and less circumspect
> Each night, but an acute girl would suspect
> That my self is not like my body, bare.
> I wonder if you know, or knowing, care?
> You know I know you know I know you know.[56]

The phrase "my self is not like my body" develops the idea of double-ness that Thom first explored in "To His Cynical Mistress" and "The Secret Sharer." The former, while establishing major Gunn conceits (love as conflict) and figures (manipulative Cupid), is a poem about saying one thing ("promising peace") and doing another ("calmly plot assassina-tion"); the latter introduces a doppelgänger or divided self, in which the speaker is both "here / Lying in bed" and "still here" on the street out-side.[57] Like "The Secret Sharer," there is little action or energy in "Carnal Knowledge." All the drama is psychological. The line "I am not what I seem, believe me" implies an interiority from which both addressee and reader are excluded. Feelings are kept at a safe distance: the poem is a kind of riddle—a form with which Thom was familiar from his interest in Elizabethan literature—but one that prevents any form of solution that is not wrought with ambiguity and paradox.[58] "I think I believed I was a cross between Hamlet and John Donne," Thom later remarked, "& the poem is like them, sexist, even misogynistic."[59]

Its sophisticated conceit and striking refrain make "Carnal Knowledge" one of Thom's most memorable early poems.[60] He later claimed he had no "explicit meaning other than simply being uncomfortable," but the subtext of the poem hints toward his disguised homosexuality.[61] "The thing known in the poem, of course, is that we don't love one another," he remarked. "However, something else that I was belatedly becoming aware of was that I was actually gay. [. . .] This might have been part of the poem; but it wasn't."[62] Thom felt a queer reading of "Carnal Knowledge" would be "a serious misreading, or at least a serious misplacement of emphasis."[63] Writing to a friend several months after he wrote "Carnal Knowledge," Thom explained that working within "the limitations of one's own sexual emotions" felt too narrow; that could come "later when I have tried out as many different ways as possible of expressing them." He did not mean "masks (in the sense of disguises) for homosexual passion": he wanted instead "to write of other things, so that I can work out relationships between them and myself—which I am still coleridgian enough to think is the best thing one can do in poetry."[64]

Plans to meet Karl in Paris fell through but, having left England, Thom managed to hitchhike to Lyon inside two days. The train to Florence took him twenty-one sleepless hours, during which he "was fed and amused by Italian companions."[65] He spent a week in Florence, another week "with dysentery" in Siena, before a final week in Lerici. He stayed in the Castello, then a youth hostel, with stunning views of the Gulf of La Spezia. There he wrote "Lerici," casting Shelley full of Leavisite self-pity, preferring death to life, and Byron more "worth the sea's pursuit." The poem's middle stanza, which at the time Thom called "the best and most Stendhalian thing" he had yet written,[66] offers an energetic ideal for how a hero should behave:

> Others make gestures with arms open wide,
> Compressing in the minute before death
> What great expense of muscle and of breath
> They would have made if they had never died.[67]

The poem drew energy from Thom's Italian adventure. "Italy had everything," he told Karl. "I stayed in high flats, ancient castles, old houses, I had dysentery and sex, I swam, I walked, I talked, I did everything."[68] His mention of sex is unusual. Given his discomfort at what had happened with Ann at Priory Farm, the experience in Italy was presumably homosexual. Little is known about Thom's first homosexual experiences, beyond the "sex-games with boys at school" and the incident with the older man at the swimming pool. By 1953 he "wasn't quite a virgin," he remarked later, but he had not had much experience, let alone a boyfriend.[69]

Returning to Cambridge, Thom learned he had achieved a first in part one of the English Tripos. For his final year, Trinity awarded him a senior scholarship. "I am equal to you now!" he ribbed Karl, a scholar at Downing.[70] Shire thought his concentration on literature "gives depth and intensity to his study and writing" and that, across the year, Thom had "achieved consolidation as a person."[71] Before Thom learned the news of his first, he had considered switching to the French Tripos for his final year, such was his interest in and passion for French literature. Rattenbury suggested Thom discuss the idea with R. R. Bolgar, a fellow of King's who lectured across classics, English, and modern languages. "His French is poor," Bolgar told Rattenbury. "He cannot at the moment make out accurately the meaning of even a simple text . . . but with reasonable industry and luck, he ought to be able to obtain a Third or even a Two-Two."[72] Rattenbury, and his first, persuaded Thom to stick with English.

There was more good news. Just as "Poem," twelve months earlier, had established Thom's Cambridge reputation, in September "The Secret Sharer" was broadcast on John Lehmann's influential BBC radio program *New Soundings*.[73] (Thom did not read the poem himself: he was still in Italy when the program was recorded.) Comprising new and established voices in poetry and fiction, *New Soundings* introduced Thom to a national audience. It was the first poem Thom "published" nationally, his work of the previous year having featured solely in Cambridge publications like *Oasis*, *Cambridge Today*, and *The Trinity Magazine*. Listening to the broadcast was a young American poet named Donald Hall, then at Oxford. "Gunn was *good*," Hall reflected. "He wrote in thunder . . . and poets of Oxford trembled in the storm."[74] Thom's appearance on the national stage confirmed him as "the Cambridge Poet," a position he was "happy to occupy." "My Forsterian fantasy had been brought up to date but also enriched by the fantasises of my friends," he reflected, with reference to other niches like "the Cambridge Politician, the Cambridge Editor, and the Cambridge Actor." These fantasies, "which we speedily fulfilled—had to do with success."[75]

Thom's status as the Cambridge Poet was bolstered in October when Karl wrote his profile in *Varsity*. "We all wrote each other's profiles," Thom reflected, "thus creating and perpetuating each other's celebrity."[76] Thom's second year had given him two major friends, academic success, and national acclaim for his poetry. Returning from Italy, he had high hopes for his final year. "I must have shaped myself & Cambridge into what they were," he later reflected. "Maybe [that] came from the 'revelation.' It was what I had wanted Cambridge to be, academically, with friends, becoming a poet, being pop-pop-popular & 'important.' It was the pimply youth come to power, a Julien Sorel dream and Cinderella story, all that I had ever wanted except sexual love, I got, and even that was to come."[77]

8

MIKE

That summer, Melvin Kitay, a blond-haired, blue-eyed Jewish boy, not long twenty-one, from Kearny, New Jersey, left America for the first time. Mickey, as friends called him, had been awarded a Woodrow Wilson Fellowship to read English at Cambridge; the first step, he thought, toward a career in teaching. Conditions aboard the *Arosa Klum* were cramped and lively. "On the ship I thought: Who is going to be my girlfriend?" He flirted with girls from the University of Iowa Scottish Highlanders, the largest female pipe band in the world. For the onboard talent show, Mickey made up new lyrics for "Carolina in the Morning" and performed it with one of the Iowan girls. He charmed everyone and everyone wanted to know his name. "Why didn't I just say Mickey when asked by the first person I met on the Arosa Klum?" he reflected. "No one had ever called me Mike, not even me. More adult than Mickey? Perhaps. The start of a new life in a new country? Perhaps . . ."[1] When he set foot in England, he was Mike Kitay.

Mike's parents came from what he called "the old country," the western fringe of the Russian Empire.[2] Abraham (Abe) Kitayewitz was born in Novogrudok, in modern-day Belarus, in February 1904; Dine (Dora) Kulew was born in Novita, in modern-day Poland, five months later. Both immigrated to New York when they were still children. The Kitayewitzes and Kulews lived on the Lower East Side, at the time the most crowded neighborhood, and the largest Jewish community, in the world. When they met, Abe worked in his father's dry goods store; Dora worked as a secretary and bookkeeper. Both were twenty-one when they married in December 1925. They soon moved across the Hudson to Kearny, where Abe ran the Marvel Dress Goods Store opposite the town hall. Julian was born in August 1927; Melvin followed in May 1931. Abe and Dora applied for citizenship in 1935 and changed their name from Kitayewitz to Kitay. By 1940 they had left the apartment above the store and moved to 17 Fuller Place, a detached house on the west side of town that overlooked the Passaic River.

Kearny was a multicultural crossroads, a small middle-class town with immigrant communities from Scotland, Ireland, Sweden, Italy, Portugal, and Japan. Newark, where Dora took Mike to department stores, was nearby. New York City, an hour away, "seemed like another country."[3] Through the store, the Kitays became an established part of the community. Abe had a reputation for giving good advice; Dora was friendly and outgoing, "up," where Abe could be moody. "Her favorite word, her ultimate compliment, was 'sensible,'" Mike reflected. Abe "loved Mark Twain and often quoted him," and had a practical intelligence that lent itself to carpentry, sewing, and mending things. Julian "resented my father because my father never said he loved him. I thought that was hogwash!" Mike recalled. "I couldn't imagine any father in Kearny at that time saying those words. They loved us, maybe too much. Nothing was more important to them."[4]

Abe wanted Mike to become a teacher and trained him in oratory. At Kearny High, aged fifteen, Mike won a National Sermon Contest with a sermon called "The Responsibility of the Jew Today."[5] But from a young age Mike's abiding passion was theater. His first performance onstage occurred at age seven during a family vacation in the Catskills, where he sang "Shortnin' Bread" at the Vegetarian Hotel.[6] In 1948, Mike enrolled at Rutgers, the state university of New Jersey, where he soon switched from a psychology to an English curriculum. Theater became his life. In his first year, he performed small, nonspeaking parts in Shaw's *Androcles and the Lion* and John Balderston's *Berkeley Square*. He audited a drama class at the New Jersey College for Women (NJC) and became a regular at the NJC's Little Theater. In his junior year he played Dickie Winslow in a production of Terence Rattigan's *The Winslow Boy*; in his senior year, he played the lead in the Prohibition-era melodrama *Broadway*.[7]

In *The Winslow Boy*, Mike was "the one gay, young, healthy, irresponsible personality in the show." His interpretation of Dickie "makes him more of a likable young chap and less of a weakling than the playwright intended." Dickie's sister, Catherine, was played by the "quietly effective" Polly Wilkes, a senior at NJC.[8] Polly had "a low vibrant voice, warm brown eyes, slender hands for accent and, underneath, an eager probing mind focused ahead to a realistic world beyond."[9] After performing together in *The Winslow Boy*, Mike and Polly started dating. "When I say, 'Did I love her?' I thought I did," Mike reflected. "Partly because of the sex. I'd never really had a girlfriend before. I was not very forward, so I really didn't date." Polly graduated that summer and moved to New York, where she worked in fashion. They continued seeing each other while Mike finished his senior year, although Mike's trips to New York became less frequent. "I didn't ask questions, but it occurred to me she was being kept or having an affair with some older gentleman," Mike reflected. "That was my suspicion."[10]

Although Mike slept with women—he lost his virginity to a camp counselor named Amy the summer of his freshman year—he felt sexually attracted to men. "They were attractive," he remarked of college boys at Rutgers. "They didn't have pimples. They were well coordinated. They played basketball, stuff like that."[11] He blamed Kearny for his youthful unease. "I never liked Kearny, mainly because I was Jewish—I didn't want to be different," he reflected, "and partly because I was homosexual. Not that I knew I was. I didn't know that, or acknowledge it, until I met Thom."[12] Mike "wasn't gay at Rutgers" but "had these questions." He developed a crush on a fellow student actor in his Shakespeare class. "He would make a point of sitting next to me and rubbing my leg. I wouldn't have any. That would mean I was a fruit," he reflected. "This wasn't conscious. I had a girlfriend, I wasn't gay. So I never followed up on it or in any way acknowledged it."[13] Similar to Thom's early impressions, to Mike homosexuals were those shady old men hanging around the urinals when he went to the cinema in New York City. At Rutgers, a neighbor in his residence hall was "very affected and effeminate" and Mike "laughed about him" with his roommate. "I wasn't being a hypocrite," Mike reflected, "because I didn't associate myself in any way with that person." Mike chose to ignore his questions. "You feel like you're the only person in the world," he reflected. "That's something Thom said to me, early on: he thought he was the only person in the world."[14]

Mike was midway through his degree when he was forced to register for the draft. He decided to join the Air Force Reserve Officers' Training Corps (AFROTC); as well as helping with his Rutgers tuition, it meant that, were he drafted, he would go to Korea as an officer. "My father freaked and said I'd got to do that and stay in school until I graduated," Mike recalled.[15] As a commissioned second lieutenant in the air force reserve, he would have to serve a two-year term once he finished his degree.

In his senior year, Mike was chosen as one of twenty Henry Rutgers Scholars, a prestigious scholarship for which he was relieved of half his course requirements so that he could pursue independent work in his chosen subject, English.[16] It was the crowning achievement of an already outstanding academic and extracurricular record: alongside his prominence in Rutgers's theater scene, Mike won prizes in oratory, was assistant editor of the *Freshman Handbook*, and was elected to the Philosophean Society, an honorary literature organization that hosted banquets for visiting writers.[17] Since switching curricula from psychology to English, Mike's academic work had improved to such an extent that he began to consider a career in teaching and scholarship.

As a result, he began to apply for graduate school. This would have the added benefit of deferring his service in the air force for at least a year. He applied to the Princeton-administered Woodrow Wilson Fellowship Program, with a view to pursuing doctoral studies and a college teaching career. On his application form, Mike wrote that he wanted to direct his energies "toward the literary present. Both as a creative writer and a potential teacher, the art of my time seems to me a more rewarding, more constantly interesting field of concentration than the art of times long past."[18] His referees—distinguished scholars such as J. Milton French, Donald McGinn, and Mason W. Gross—focused not only on his "modest, polite, sociable, and pleasant" character but also on his prodigious gifts as a writer and actor.[19] "Equipped as he is with intelligence, good health, and poetic genius," McGinn told the fellowship committee, "he should be able to make his mark in American letters."[20] Their praise focused largely on Mike's leading role in a one-act play he had also written: it was produced at the Little Theater as part of the end-of-year showcase for the directing class at NJC. McGinn thought Mike's play "distinguished by its poetic diction and its high idealism"; Gross felt Mike showed "great promise of a distinguished future in the field of playwriting."[21] "It was a verse play, I'm afraid: I'd seen Christopher Fry . . ." Mike reflected. "It was quite an occasion. Several of my professors attended. I think it was one of the reasons I got to be a Woodrow Wilson Fellow."[22]

Mike received the fellowship in April 1952.[23] He was chosen as one of thirty recipients, each of whom showed "marked promise for the teaching profession and possessing the highest qualities of intellect, personality and character."[24] Princeton administered the fellowship, but Mike was free to pursue his studies at an overseas graduate school of his choice. McGinn, a specialist in Shakespeare and Thomas Nashe, thought he should attend the University of Birmingham, in England, where Allardyce Nicoll had recently founded the Shakespeare Institute. "I appreciated his input," Mike reflected, "but I wanted to go to Cambridge."[25] Cambridge accepted him to study English, but Mike faced an anxious wait to discover whether there was room for him at one of its colleges. Jesus had "no room" for him.[26] It was the same story at Trinity: Robert Rattenbury wrote that they could take "only a certain number of men from abroad each year, and those places were all filled by the time we received [Mike's] application."[27]

But there was good news from Fitzwilliam House, which was "happy to accept him."[28] Having obtained his deferment from the air force in mid-May, Mike wrote to W. S. Thatcher, the censor[29] of Fitzwilliam, with his application. "Although the grant itself only provides expenses for one year, I plan to study for an additional year," he informed Thatcher, "either through a renewal of the fellowship or at my own expense, in order to become a candidate for a degree."[30] Mike would be admitted as an affiliated student—one taking a second undergraduate degree—and expected to complete his studies in two years instead of three. He knew that the Woodrow Wilson Fellowship was nonrenewable: by using it to pursue a two-year degree, he hoped, perhaps, to gain leverage over the air force when it came to the matter of a second deferment. If that attitude suggested a certain boldness of character, J. Milton French took pains in his letter of recommendation to Fitzwilliam to convince R. N. Walters, Mike's eventual first-year tutor, that Mike was "quite the opposite of the brassy American of the caricatures: modest, deferential, and eager to please. Despite his successful career in college he is far from being as sure of himself as he really has a right to be."[31]

On July 15, 1952, his place at Fitzwilliam secured, Mike sailed for England.

Cambridge was "like the movies."[32] Its cobbled streets, narrow passageways, and gowned students running every which way charmed Mike no end. His top-floor room on All Saints Passage overlooked the entrance to Whewell's Court. Mrs. Wooll, his landlady, lived with her daughter and son-in-law, and Mike had to pass through the sitting room to climb the stairs to his attic. There was no central heating or hot water. The outside toilet "was blue and white china and one hesitated to actually use it . . ."[33]

Away from home, knowing nobody, Mike was slow to settle academically. He joined the Fitzwilliam House Amateur Dramatic Society, as well as the university-wide Marlowe Society and Amateur Dramatic Club (ADC), and his theater activities consumed most of his time and energy. "His written work, though sound so far as it goes," wrote Walters in Mike's first term report, "usually gives the impression of having been done as an entr'acte at the A.D.C." Mike had a tendency, Walters reported, to arrive "quarter of an hour late for supervision" and would "profit by a good course in self-discipline."[34]

In lockstep with Cambridge's vibrant student theater scene was its periodical culture, and Mike felt his way into Cambridge through its newspapers and journals. Mike read Thom before he met him: in November alone Thom had "Carnal Knowledge" in *Granta* and "Round and Round" and "La Prisonnière" in *The Cambridge Review*. But it was Karl Miller's *Varsity* profile of Thom that caught Mike's eye. It included lines from a new poem called "The Beach Head":

> Shall I be John a Gaunt and with my band
> Of mad bloods pass in one spectacular dash,
> Fighting before and after, through your land,
> To issue out unharmed the farther side,
> With little object other than panache
> And showing what great odds may be defied?

Like many of Thom's undergraduate poems, "The Beach Head" blends the amorous and the martial. The speaker questions whether to "wait and calculate my chances," like Julien Sorel in *Le rouge et le noir*, before making a "pincer-move to end in an embrace, / And risk that your mild liking turn to loathing?"[35] Thom wanted the reader to think of the various embraces between Coriolanus and Aufidius—"Let me twine / Mine arms about that body"[36]—primarily because the addressee of the poem, Tony White, most admired Coriolanus.[37]

Reading the profile, Mike was "smitten" but did not know that the poem was addressed to Tony White.[38] Mike knew White, however, and not solely from the profile of White that Thom himself published in *Varsity* that November. In the ADC and the Marlowe Society, Mike was overlooked for major parts because of his American accent,[39] but he won a small role in that winter's ADC production of *Cyrano de Bergerac*. White played the lead. "Tony was a very attractive man, and I used to flirt with him when we were doing readings at the theater," Mike recalled. "I thought he was flirting back, or was at least aware of what I was doing."[40] Mike played the Meddler. He and Cyrano share an early scene in which Cyrano accuses the Meddler of staring at his nose:

CYRANO

Does it astonish you?

THE MEDDLER

Your grace

Misunderstands my–

CYRANO

Is it long and soft

And dangling, like a trunk?[41]

Cyrano opened at the ADC Theatre on Monday, December 1, and ran for six nights. Tony was lauded for his performance. "All but unrecognisable in his make-up," wrote one reviewer, "and with a new, controlled assurance of voice and movement, this was the best thing he has done."[42]

The following Sunday, Thom attended the cast party and saw many of his ADC friends, including Margaret Baron, Jane Collet, Peter Hall, and Sasha Moorsom. "We all knew Mike rather separately from Thom," Jane reflected.[43] "Thom's in with Karl," Margaret recalled, "and nobody quite *gets* Mike Kitay because they don't find him very intellectually stimulating."[44] At the party, Margaret introduced Thom and Mike, although little introduction was required. Mike had read Thom, and Thom had seen Mike act. To Thom, writing later, Mike was

a man already dreamt of
or seen in comic books or cowboy movies
or seen on the streets—the generous slick G.I.–
Crew-cut & clear eyed
firm in mind & limb:
American Boy

To Thom, Mike fit a certain American ideal: having dreamt of a man from "Henry James novels and comic books," Thom desired "the clear-cut simple-seeming goodness of the external looks & the complexity of what goes on inside."[45] Thom emphasized Mike's "rawly passionate" Jamesian quality, calling him "from the start, the example of the searching worrying improvising intelligence playing upon the emotions which in turn reflect back on the intelligence."[46] He intuited immediately that Mike was gay. Through Thom, Mike was able to answer some of the questions about his sexuality that had troubled him since Rutgers. For Thom, their first meeting was "fireworks."[47] For Mike, "apart from the ADC, my whole thing was Thom."[48]

Before meeting Mike, Thom had had a busy Michaelmas term. He was president of the English Club—Karl was secretary—and organized and introduced speakers. At its first meeting, Mike listened as Thom gave an "awkward but charming" introduction to Angus Wilson.[49] In late November, a "sober and punctual" Dylan Thomas addressed the English Club.[50] He and Thom were photographed together in Cambridge: Thom strides ahead while Thomas shuffles behind. To coincide with the reading, Thom reviewed Thomas's *Collected Poems* in *The Cambridge Review*. He found "a perceptible energy in his very mourning of the past" and called Thomas "one of our few imperfect poets from whom we can still expect signs of life."[51]

In the audience for Thomas's reading was E. J. Hughes, a second-year student at Pembroke College. Afterward, Hughes accompanied "Thomas and the society committee to the Eagle in Bene't Street so as to listen in on their conversation. Thomas and his acolytes spoke of filling Swansea Bay with beer."[52] As president of the English Club, Thom was likely among them. "E. J. Hughes of Pembroke was very retiring," he reflected later. "I am not sure if I even knew him to speak to while I was at Cambridge, though I did know what he looked like."[53] This was not quite true. In May 1953, Thom and Ted Hughes cosigned a letter to *Varsity*—with two other Cambridge poets, John Mander and F. S. Grubb—concerning "a New Venture" to take place at the Anchor pub: "poems will be displayed on the walls, and changed as often as new suitable poems are received. Writers are invited to send poems to E. J. Hughes, Pembroke as soon as possible."[54] Hughes remembered meeting Thom, briefly, around the time of this failed scheme.[55] Much later, after Hughes's death, Thom doubled down on his assertion. "Ted and I didn't know one another at Cambridge," he told Elaine Feinstein. "I'm not sure that I had even heard of him when I was there, the reason being that he didn't, I believe, publish any poetry until I had left: probably the first I read of him was in Karl Miller's anthology <u>Poetry from Cambridge</u>, which didn't impress me, and then <u>The Hawk in the Rain</u>, which dazzled me with its fearless energy."[56]

Within twelve months, Thomas was dead. When Thom heard the news, he went straight to Karl's room at Downing and, "not finding him there, left a solemn little note on his mantelpiece: 'This is a black day for English poetry', so that he should know I was feeling the proper grief."[57] Thom admired much of Thomas's early work—especially "The force that through the green fuse drives the flower"—but found that his own generation "couldn't <u>use</u> Dylan Thomas in the same way we could Auden."[58]

Thom was also working hard writing new poems. Lent term proved no less prolific than Michaelmas: Thom had "The Wound," "The Beach Head," "The Court Revolt," and "Wind in the Street" all published in early 1953. "Hardly a week seems to pass without the publication of some poems by Thom Gunn," remarked one reviewer that summer.[59] Thom also had "Carnal Knowledge," "A Mirror for Poets," and "Helen's Rape" in G. S. Fraser's *Springtime* anthology, which reached a national audience. Using the pseudonym "Apemantus," Thom reviewed *Springtime*. "We have seen better from Thom Gunn," he wrote dryly.[60] The anthology appalled him. He told a friend that "Fraser seems determined to make a modern movement: academic-cum-apocalyptic-cum-regional."[61]

After the *Cyrano* party, Thom "moon[ed] around" and, reading James's *Roderick Hudson*, "imagined either the hero or the narrator as being like Mike."[62] They did not see each other over the holidays: Thom invited Mike to join a New Year's trip to Paris with Tony, Karl, and several others, but Mike had already committed to a skiing trip with another American student. Thom made a cryptic reference to the rejection as "something sad-making" in a letter to Karl, saying it "partook of semi-hallucination & misunderstanding."[63] Mike was secretly relieved because Thom's friends "intimidated" him. He knew Tony and Margaret, but Karl, John Coleman, and John Holmstrom were all strangers. "I couldn't deal with that," he reflected. "I was a little overwhelmed because they were very close to Thom. And here I was, a total stranger and an American, so I didn't go."[64]

Stung by the rejection, Thom turned his amorous thoughts back to Tony and was "looking forward ecstatically" to seeing him again. "Somehow, without anticipating it, I have found myself thinking about him for days on end," he told Karl. "Perhaps there wd be a chance to sleep with him in Paris. Perhaps, but one mustn't set too much store on such a thing coming to pass."[65] It did not happen, but Thom had an "exhilarated stay" in Paris, lodging in a cheap hotel on the rue Jacob, eating "horsemeat steaks and black sausage on the Boulevard St.-Germain," and seeing "*Phèdre* at the Comédie Française, done in much the same style as in the seventeenth century."[66]

Part of his exhilaration came from the prospect of seeing Mike again. Thom hoped "it may be possible to remedy" their "misunderstanding" about Paris.[67] In early March he sent Mike a postcard of Degas's *Les Repasseuses* (*The Ironers*). "Come to lunch, and wine a repasseuse with me," he wrote.[68] "I got a card from Thom asking me to tea," Mike recalled. "Tea. That's what the English do."[69]

"We did in fact draw closer and closer until we were lovers," Thom reflected. "I was supremely—almost hysterically—happy, our life was all signs and tokens and allegories of our happiness."[70] They skipped college meals and ate together instead. Kohinoor, a cheap Indian restaurant, was a favorite, as was Lucy's Café, where they ate omelets and French fries. Evenings were spent in "such hot embraces in Whewell's Court."[71] "It was like Romeo and Juliet," Thom reflected:

> we were careful and we were dishonest when we needed to be
> because it was a question of preserving ourselves, but it was like
> any love affair. [. . .] I would falsify as little as possible, but I
> certainly omitted saying what I'd been doing sexually.[72]

They used codes: instead of "I love you" they said "fais" (I do). Thom came out to his friends in his early twenties—"long before I did in my writing," he reflected[73]—but otherwise it was an intense, passionate love nurtured mostly in secret. One consequence was that Thom "withdrew—if not myself then my interest—from most of my other activities."[74] This included his academic work. At the end of Michaelmas term, Redpath thought Thom was "just within First Class," but come the end of Lent term his work veered between "first-class, at other times low second class."[75] Their love quickly came to feel like absolute devotion. "There was an immature & hysterical & demanding aspect to my (our?) love," Thom later reflected. "I need you, devote yourself entirely to me. Maybe characteristic of most people in their first relationship. It took us a long time to learn."[76]

Jealousy was a major problem. Mike felt that Tony "wasn't an easy person" for him. "I was so struck by 'The Beach Head,'" he recalled, "because if Thom was addressing Tony, then where the fuck was I?"[77] Tony was the leading man, destined for stardom, whereas Mike's position in the Cambridge theater hierarchy did little for his own confidence. Conversely, Karl was jealous of Mike for taking Thom, his best friend, away from him. "Karl saw Mike as a stupid block, in between his relationship with Thom, and he couldn't understand why Thom would want Mike," Margaret reflected. "So that offends Karl's intellectual sensitivities, his critical faculties."[78] Thom and Karl had been inseparable, and their friendship intense. Mike's appearance, and the nature of his relationship with Thom, caused Thom and Karl to drift apart. "My father was not, I think, a homophobe," reflected Karl's son, Sam Miller, "but was sensitive to accusations that he might be."[79]

Such currents of jealousy contributed to Thom's own "pull away . . . from the 'Cambridge' I had helped create."[80] He apologized to Tony for having seen little of him during Easter term. "Which was mainly or completely my fault," he continued, "but not thro my lack of love for you—and I hope you haven't thought so. I'm glad you knew about the Mike K etc, for . . . it's some explanation for my having neglected you and Karl." Thom, "being in love," felt he had failed "to give all my time to loving and simultaneously remain the same person as before—that is seeing my friends as much." To Tony, he put his failure to reconcile these two commitments in typically heroic terms: "it was like holding on to a pendulum," he told him, "rather than being the perfect Existentialist who stands at the works of the clock & swings the pendulum." Tony, however, remained "exemplary."[81]

Nor was Thom himself immune to jealousy. Late in Lent term, to his bemusement and Mike's surprise, Polly Wilkes arrived in England for a monthlong visit. "I didn't invite her," Mike recalled. "She told me she was coming. I remember trying to explain to Thom. She had a right to do that considering we were boyfriend and girlfriend." They traveled together through Spain and North Africa. "Thom was jealous then," Mike reflected. "Having a girl come from America to see me and going on a trip to Spain together to fuck: I think that troubled him some."[82] Thom did not meet Polly; nor did Mike tell Polly about Thom. "I remember when you came back from Europe after the Polly thing," Thom told Mike years later, "and going to bed feeling terrible, and waking the next morning and crying for the first time in years and wishing I'd never been born, because I was convinced that I would lose you."[83]

With Mike and Polly traveling, Thom spent an uncomfortable Easter holiday in Allhallows, Kent, with Aunt Barbara and Uncle Godfrey. He wrote feverishly and sent a batch of new work to Karl, including the love poems "Tamer and Hawk" and "Without a Counterpart." Thom routinely used combat as a metaphor for love in his early poems, but until his relationship with Mike, he had no firsthand experience of such contests. In "Tamer and Hawk," his finest early love poem, Thom drew on seeling, the practice by which a medieval falconer trained a new bird by sewing its eyes closed. "I am no longer free: / You seeled me with your love," Thom wrote. "The habit of your words / Has hooded me." The poem's energy comes from the "demanding" nature of their love:

> I thought I was so tough,
> But gentled at your hands
> Cannot be quick enough

To fly for you and show
That when I go I go
At your commands.[84]

Thom had cultivated a tough, masculine self-image—modeled on Tony
White—to deal with his "fear of seeming not masculine, of <u>being</u> not
masculine." This, he later reflected, was "one of the most important consistent emotions of my life." He told Mike about it "at great length . . .
within the first months" of their relationship.[85] "In Cambridge there
were a couple of people you could tell were gay right away," Mike recalled, "and Thom didn't like those guys."[86]

The conflict between toughness and tenderness in "Tamer and
Hawk" belied Thom's more immediate fear: that his and Mike's love was
so intense that it would result in a kind of mutually assured destruction.
"Through having only eyes / For you I fear to lose," Thom wrote, "I lose
to keep, and choose / Tamer as prey." When Thom wrote the poem, he
had two major sources for this anxiety: first, that he would lose Mike to
Polly; second, their love "seemed so precarious" because Mike was due to
return to America that summer.[87] The "enforced separation" from Mike
made him "<u>cry</u> inwardly," and his spring poems reflected his anxieties.[88]
"Legal Reform" concerns two lovers "condemned to be condemned" to
love each other.[89] "Without a Counterpart" was "a self-projection into a
possible experience"[90] in which the speaker imagines waking "in fright"
to find his lover gone.[91]

In the spring, Mike wrote to the air force to seek a deferment. His
chances seemed unlikely: neither he nor Thom was confident. As a result,
Thom tried to make his own American plans. He applied for a Frank
Knox Memorial Fellowship at Harvard for the 1953–54 academic year
but was unsuccessful. He was "very sorry not to be going to America,"
he told a friend.[92] Come Mike's twenty-second birthday, in May, their
future was still uncertain. "I'm so permanently in love with you," Thom
wrote to him, "and I want there to be no Goodbye, no parting, and never
to share you, and love you and love you and love you."[93]

In early June, Mike received a letter from the air force, asking him to outline his academic position. Mike showed the letter to W. S. Thatcher, who replied on Mike's behalf. Explaining that Mike was "required to follow a two-year course in order to obtain his Honours Degree in English," Thatcher told the commanding general of the First Air Force that were Mike "called up now it means that he will have to abandon this course as it is a continuous one." Thatcher asked whether it would be possible "to defer Kitay's call-up until [he has] completed his studies and will have obtained a valuable qualification for teaching English?" Calling Mike "a valuable member of Fitzwilliam House," Thatcher concluded: "The break would be a serious thing, which I think would put him back for a very long time."[94]

It would prove to be an anxious wait. Thom and Mike had planned to spend summer touring Europe and left England in mid-June—around the same time Thatcher pleaded Mike's case to the air force—after Mike had performed a small role in the ADC's *Love's Labour's Lost*. They later described the tour as "like our honeymoon," but at the time, waiting for news, it perhaps seemed more like a long farewell.[95] After crossing the Channel, they traveled by train through Bruges, Ghent, Brussels, Cologne, Frankfurt, Heidelberg, Munich, Salzburg, and Innsbruck before sweeping across the Alps to Venice, Verona, Milan, and finally Rapallo, where they spent several weeks on the Italian Riviera. In a photograph taken outside Heidelberg Castle, Mike looks classically American: light slacks, polo shirt, hands in pockets. Thom, a sweater draped around his shoulders, looks casual, jeans cuffed, one hand in his pocket, the other gripping his belt: a pose that would become a signature (plate 10).

Opera punctuated their itinerary. They saw *Der Rosenkavalier* in Cologne, *The Marriage of Figaro* and Honegger's oratorio *Joan of Arc at the Stake* in Munich, and, best of all, Mario Del Monaco and Renata Tebaldi in *Otello* at La Scala. In Verona they saw Maria Callas star in G. W. Pabst's outdoor production of *Aida*, during which "a sacred bull . . . casually left droppings in the middle of the stage: laughter of 20,000 drowned [the] triumphal march."[96] It was an exhausting itinerary; Rapallo provided rest and relaxation. They stayed at the Albergo Pernigotti, a small hotel on the Corso Italia, and spent their days at the beach. While they were there, Mike received news from the air force. "I have finally learned that my appeal for another year's deferment from active duty in the American Air Force has been successful," he wrote Thatcher from Rapallo in mid-August. "This, I think, is largely due to the letter which you so kindly wrote for me last June. So it is with the utmost gratitude that I write to tell you that I shall be up next year."[97] Mike was thrilled. Thom recalled: "I did not know quite where I was for joy."[98]

Thom was twenty-three, Mike twenty-two. Fate had granted them another year together. "I think one reason why Thom and I stayed together in whatever way we did for so long was because we were our first," Mike reflected. "I was his first lover and he was mine. It was heavy duty because it's something that doesn't happen often."[99] Later, when Thom reflected on the loss of his mother and how his life changed for the better in the years 1951–53, in notes for a never completed poem called "Childhood & Youth," he was candid about Mike's role in his recovery. "I was saved by 3 freedoms," he wrote: "freedom of language, awareness of my freedom to do anything, & the freedom given me by meeting [Mike], freedom of love."[100] In the early 1990s, when he came to write "Rapallo," his poem about Mike and their European trip, his working title was "An Education in Love."[101]

9

POET

The year Thom fell in love, he also published his first poetry pamphlet and completed the manuscript of his first full collection: *Fighting Terms*. His success was due in part to a blossoming friendship with Donald Hall, then at Oxford, who edited the journal *New Poems* for Oscar Mellor's Fantasy Press. Having heard Thom's "Incident on a Journey" on *New Soundings*, Hall wrote to Thom, suggesting that he submit work to *New Poems* and that Mellor was interested in publishing Thom's work in his "Fantasy Poets" pamphlet series.[1] Thom was excited and sent Hall a list for a pamphlet. He wanted "Lerici," "Incident on a Journey," "The Beach Head"—his best poem, he thought—"The Right Possessor," "Wind in the Street," and "The Wound." Hall agreed but replaced "Lerici" with the inferior "A Village Edmund." Reviewing the pamphlet the following year, *The Times Literary Supplement* considered Thom to be "aiming at work on a larger moral scale than most of his contemporaries," the "ambitiousness" of which excused "the occasionally rough and coarse texture of his writing."[2]

Thom later acknowledged that "The Wound" was the best poem in the pamphlet. He called it "an attempt to deal with primitive and mysterious impulses, and about the failure of that attempt."[3] It is an extended metaphor of the divided self: "I was myself: subject to no man's breath: / My own commander was my enemy."[4] Drawing on his extensive knowledge of Shakespeare, he centered the poem on the homoerotic tension between Achilles and Patroclus in *Troilus and Cressida*,[5] although he "didn't acknowledge its sexual origins" at the time of writing.[6] Moreover, "The Wound" reads like a road map of Thom's early themes, concerns, and influences: it has a basis in mythology, has a soldier as its main character, privileges narrative over image, and places a high value on interiority. Perhaps most significantly, given his fear of "seeming not masculine," the subtext of "The Wound" is its correlation between action and masculinity. In *Troilus*, Patroclus warns Achilles that "a woman impudent and mannish grown / Is not more loathed than an effeminate man / In time of action."[7] At the end of the poem, when the speaker of "The Wound" resolves to act, his wound breaks open again.[8]

Thom was "terribly pleased" with the pamphlet and was flattered by Hall's "reports of Gunn-imitators in Oxford."[9] After Thom sat the second part of the English Tripos—for which he achieved an upper second, despite his submission of "original poems as supplementary to the papers," which Redpath hoped would secure him a first[10]—Hall invited him to Oxford and threw a party in his honor. "I think we expected him to be burly and tough, a poetic top sergeant," Hall reflected, "and instead we met a young man who was polite, witty, quiet, and fierce only in his literary intelligence."[11]

Thom stayed with Hall, and the visit cemented their bond. As with many of Thom's literary friendships, it would be sustained mostly via letter. That summer, Hall left Oxford for a creative writing fellowship at Stanford, where he would work closely with the American poet and critic Yvor Winters. Thom's plans were vague: the uncertainty around Mike's deferment created a kind of paralysis. Before his and Mike's European adventure, Thom learned that St. John's College had awarded him the Harper-Wood Studentship, a travel grant that would allow him to write poetry in an overseas destination of his choice. Its modest stipend, together with his state scholarship, provided him a frugal living for the year.[12] He decided to stay in Cambridge for Michaelmas term, then head to Rome, a new city to him, where he hoped to spend five or six months.

After his spring writing burst, Thom had "not written a line all summer."[13] He felt like "the proper Poetic vigour" had disappeared and that his recent work was "weaker and phonier, tho more polished—all my writing an artificial inducement, a recapitulation, by reference to past work."[14] Cramming for Tripos and traveling across Europe with Mike were not conducive to writing, however, and he knew that dry periods were inevitable. "I've been arranging a lot in my mind," he told Hall in September, "and hope that when I start again it will be a New Poetry."[15] At the start of Michaelmas term, Thom moved into the Central Hotel, "a mouse-infested box in the middle of Cambridge."[16] He spent his time reading "all the Eliz and Jac Drama besides Shakespeare,"[17] having told the Harper-Wood fund that "conceptions of Rome in 17th century drama" was his "possible thesis."[18] This did not spark "a New Poetry": instead, Thom returned to an older project, "The Furies," a long, mock-heroic narrative poem. He had felt "the Keatsian need to write 'something one can turn around in,'" but labored through draft after draft of turgid meter and heavy-handed irony before he eventually abandoned it.[19]

Through his appearances on *New Soundings*, Thom had fostered a warm correspondence with John Lehmann. An established editor and publisher, Lehmann had managed Leonard and Virginia Woolf's Hogarth Press and founded the periodical *New Writing*—later *Penguin New Writing*—which published an unusual assortment of literary criticism, poetry, writing in translation, and working-class writing in dialect.[20] Having "read and re-read" many issues of *Penguin New Writing* as a teenager, Thom felt they had "helped to form my taste and nourish my imagination."[21] Lehmann's publishing house, John Lehmann Ltd., collapsed in December 1952, and he set about relaunching *The London Magazine*, inviting Thom to contribute to its first issue. When Lehmann balked at excerpting "The Furies," Thom sent him "Earthborn" instead, and *The London Magazine* became a venue for what he called his "milky & drippy effusions," substandard poems and essays he did not collect.[22] "'I am become a name'—an OK name, which means I can now get bad poems accepted in important places," he told Tony, "so I must keep my integrity watchful."[23]

Grateful to Lehmann—he was "the first editor outside [Cambridge] to take anything I had written"[24]—Thom was nevertheless wary of him. Those who knew Lehmann, concluded his biographer Adrian Wright,

"tended to react [to him] with respect, but a feeling, too, of slight absur-
dity."[25] "Lehmann seems to have taken a big liking to me," Thom told
Hall after his first meeting with Lehmann in summer 1954. "I myself
consider him a fairly obnoxious bastard but probably a useful one."[26] His
problem with Lehmann, articulated later, seemed to be one of class and
sex. "[H]e was really a completely different generation from me sexually,
because all his ideas to do with sex were mixed up with ideas to do with
class," Thom remarked in an interview. "He was very much attracted by
working-class soldiers and things like that." Lehmann was born into a
wealthy family and educated at Eton and Cambridge. Thom was firmly
middle-class but had spent eighteen months "in the army with a lot of
poor boys" and was now "dealing with rich boys at Cambridge"; "the
whole thing [of class]," he claimed, "didn't mean anything to me, tremendously much, anyway."[27] Lehmann seemed to represent a world that
Thom instinctively resisted. He saw something pitiful in the duality of
Lehmann's situation: by day "London Smoothie"[28] and by night his consuming, often debilitating desire for young working-class men.[29]

The autumn was Thom's first "Bad Period" for writing,[30] likely because he was "in a giant confusion about everything, literary, academic,
pecuniary, social, amatory . . ."[31] He was excited to leave for Rome in
December but was anxious about Mike, to whom "it seemed like a 3
month desertion."[32] Thom delayed his departure to support Mike's busy
theater program through Michaelmas term. In October, Mike directed
the ADC's first play of the year, an adaptation of Henry James's short
novel *Washington Square* called *The Heiress*. It was a production "of great
integrity and conviction," wrote Stephen Haskell in *The Cambridge Review*, which "achiev[ed] a dramatic impact while preserving all Henry
James's irony, subtlety, and completeness."[33] The following month Mike
costarred in the Leslie Bricusse and Frederic Raphael musical *Lady at the
Wheel*, performing a "virtuoso meta-Charleston dance routine" that was
the talk of Cambridge.[34] Mike's "legs," wrote Stanley Price in *Varsity*,
"are only just joined to his body."[35]

In London, before Thom sailed, they saw Brando's *Julius Caesar* at the
cinema and Richard Burton's *Hamlet* at the Old Vic.[36] Between London

and Rome, Thom stopped in Paris, where he had secured introductions to several prominent literary expats, including the "amiably vague" George Plimpton, the founding editor of *The Paris Review*.[37] A "sort of dysentery" kept Thom in Paris longer than planned and he felt "bitter and dried out" from "French cigarettes" and "having read Dostoevsky all the past week."[38] Separation from Mike already caused him considerable anxiety. "Without Mike I'm incapacitated," he told Karl, "overcome with depression and inertia such as I didn't think I'd ever feel again once I'd turned eighteen." Solitude often made Thom feel uneasy and he sought distraction in sex, acting like a Stendhalian hero in a new city. "What is a male nymphomaniac called?" he asked Karl.[39]

Thom spent a few days in Rome before he met Mike in Venice for New Year's. "Snow came, deep, and the Venetians stared at it appalled, not knowing quite what to do with it."[40] It was so cold in their hotel, they stayed in bed, "deep beneath the covers," and ate cheap spaghetti Bolognese for breakfast. At the Scuola di San Rocco, snow on the skylights darkened the Tintorettos. On New Year's Eve, Mike pointed out "2 lesbians at a nearby table & we raised our glasses, toasting undying love."[41] After a few days together in Padua and Milan, Mike returned to Cambridge and Thom to Rome. Staying at the Pensione Imhof, he was five minutes from the Piazza di Spagna. "Rome is the best place I've ever been in," he told Karl.

> The right size, the right weather, the right proportions of good looking buildings to slums, the right complications. Also, the right attitude of the inhabitants. I mean as opposed to London or Cambridge or Paris. In London and half of Cambridge one tries like mad to conform; in Paris and the other half of Cambridge one tries like mad to nonconform. Here, nobody cares what you do, which is much healthier and less dull altogether.[42]

Thom tried to capture Rome's "nonchalance" in his notebook, but his sketches of city life failed to come off.[43] He published one—"A District in Rome"[44]—but found it "straightforward, perhaps to dullness."[45]

At the front of his Rome notebook, Thom quoted Yeats—"A style is found by sedentary toil / And by the imitation of great masters"[46]—and his attempted Rome poems struggled to avoid that master's "hypnotic" influence.[47] In fact, Thom's most promising poem from this period, "At the Back of the North Wind," was drafted before he left England. In his early work, Thom tried to "disguise" his "huge weakness"—meter—"by being very regular and rhymed": in "At the Back of the North Wind," however, he chose to "jump into the lion's mouth, and do away with most rhyme."[48] Its language is tough and clear: blank verse was a good vehicle for a poem of heightened sensory awareness that moved away from the pained interiority of *Fighting Terms*. Moreover, he drew the title from the nineteenth-century Scottish writer George MacDonald, a childhood favorite, and allowed himself to filter memories of Covey Hall Farm through the lens of MacDonald's romance novel.[49] Thom did not write well in Rome, but lessons learned from "At the Back of the North Wind" informed early drafts of "St Martin and the Beggar," "Jesus and His Mother," and "The Inherited Estate," written later in 1954.

Rome also saw Thom's first mature attempt to write about his mother's death. His source for "After a Dream" was the *Odyssey*, which he knew in Samuel Butler's prose translation.[50] In Book XI, trying to speak with Tiresias, Odysseus summons the dead but conjures his mother, Anticlea, whom he did not know to be dead. "Thrice I sprang towards her and tried to clasp her in my arms," he says, "but each time she flitted from my embrace as it were a dream or phantom." When asked why they cannot embrace, Anticlea replies that "all people are like this when they are dead. The sinews no longer hold the flesh and bones together; these perish in the fierceness of a consuming fire as soon as life has left the body, and the soul flits away as though it were a dream."[51] Thom drew on this scene and its language in "After a Dream":

> Much of the time I dreamt about my mother
> She seemed to be drugged and made a grunting sound:
> Are dead minds packed like fish in a narrow pond
> To wriggle feebly one against the other?

Perhaps my thoughts of her did really nudge her
And shake upon her the scarlet dressing gown
She died in, but her head only fell down
One side: it is not rest that I'd begrudge her,
She wanted it—I'd either have her dead,
Meteors raining on the shrunken pool
Where ceaseless tides were governed by her head,
Or else dreamed living—not a sweating post
But always taking notice, gay and cruel.

Where is that blood Odysseus gave the ghost?[52]

The ending collapses in the overcomplicated, unresolved syntax: Thom decided not to publish it.[53] But his mother was on his mind, not just in his recurring dreams. "Mother," he wrote while in Rome, "the arguments I've had with you / Since you were dead would fill another life / With a mother's rancour deep as that of wife / That killed you."[54]

Reflecting on the trip, Thom called it "a strange separate period which (in a way I'm unable to explain) was good for me." It gave him "a deepened and enriched sense of Europe" and also "a little more sense of the separate self before complete marriage."[55] Thom had matured since his last extended stay in Europe—Paris in 1950—and was less of a social dormouse. George Plimpton gave him a letter of introduction to the American publisher and patron of the arts Marguerite Caetani, married to an Italian prince and founder of the literary journal *Botteghe Oscure*.[56] Thom became one of her "hangers on" and she showed him "great kindness."[57] She invited him to her castle near Anzio, "beneath a mountain on which the Cyclopes are supposed to have lived. Last time I went to see her I met a funny tubby piggy man coming away," he told Karl, "& as soon as I saw her she said 'You've just missed Cyril Connolly.'"[58]

The "best person" Thom met in Rome was a German painter named Carl Timner. "He is, undoubtedly, one of the elect—he has the right pride and discrimination and sense of humour; and he does <u>do</u> things," he told Karl. "I mean, not only fucking, or painting for that matter, but he acts rather than talks about [them]."[59] Timner painted Thom's portrait: his downward gaze, lost in thought, is a more vulnerable portrayal than he would allow in later life.[60] Timner also introduced Thom to Caravaggio, many of whose works could be seen for free throughout Rome. In the Basilica di San Agostino they saw the *Madonna di Loreto* (1604–1606); in the Basilica of Santa Maria del Popolo, the *Crucifixion of St. Peter* (1600–1601) and the *Conversion of St. Paul* (1600–1601). There were also seven Caravaggios in the Galleria Borghese and three paintings on the theme of St. Matthew in the Contarelli Chapel. "My great find among painters is Caravaggio," Thom told Tony, "about whom I cd go on for pages."[61]

Caravaggio was a major part of Thom's "rich few months" in Rome.[62] Mike, however, was "stuck" in Cambridge. "We wrote, but Thom was busy," he reflected. "He may have missed me, but I didn't notice at the time."[63] The separation was their first real crisis and likely precipitated Thom's decision to leave Rome earlier than he intended.[64] "[Mike's] not being happy in Cambridge, I think, and perhaps I ought really to have stayed behind this term so as to be with him," Thom told Karl. "He's more wonderful the longer I know him—but a lover's ravings will bore you."[65] Jealousies continued to consume them. "Mike doesn't really like any friend of mine," Thom told Tony, "and every quarrel we've ever had has begun with friends or involved them in some way." Mike was jealous of Tony; Thom felt caught in the middle. "I don't know how I <u>should</u> have behaved, but I know I have behaved in the wrong way both to Mike and to you," he told Tony. "It's a case where existentialist principles fail to help: a Goetz would fling Mike off, but I've never had any intention or desire of doing that."[66]

Without previous experience of a relationship, Thom unsurprisingly saw his and Mike's difficulties in literary terms. Goetz, the warlord of Jean-Paul Sartre's *Le Diable et le bon Dieu*, attempts to renounce evil in favor of "good," noble deeds: Thom perhaps meant to imply that staying with Mike would not be noble or honorable. He was used to writing about heroic ideals, but his relationship with Mike made him question his literary preoccupations. "<u>How</u> does the hero treat a relationship?" he asked Tony.

> [Y]ou must admit that Goetz is incapable of contact with oth-
> ers except to dominate so much that there's no real give-&-take
> contact left, that Coriolanus though not stupid is no success,
> that Heathcliff's love would be—well, different, if he were not
> conveniently isolated by moors; and etc.[67]

At center, Thom was trying to articulate his difficulties in reconciling friendships with his relationship with Mike. The solitary, aloof hero was a much easier archetype to embody than the loving, beholden hero. Having spent the years since his mother's suicide arming himself against vulnerability, Thom was uniquely unprepared to respond with any emotional maturity to Mike, whose well-developed emotional intelligence, his Jamesian quality, made him Thom's antithesis. They were "so amazingly and disastrously different in just the wrong ways," Thom thought, and he reacted to their "awful and unnecessary quarrels" in "the worst way" while in Rome, "by a sort of indiscriminate & unpleasant recklessness."[68] His "sexual encounters" in Rome did little to effect a reconciliation.[69]

About to return to Cambridge, Thom asked Tony not to mention their correspondence "if we meet in front of Mike. That's weak of me," he continued, "but there's so little time left that I certainly have with him that there aren't enough hours for me to attempt once again to put my position before him and try to make it strong." Thom's position was that he wanted to follow Mike to America. "I can't bear to contemplate living without him & at the same time I don't see how (even after technical—sociological, passport, family (his)—difficulties are got over) we can live together," he told Tony. "If he was a girl it'd be so much easier! I'd marry him & it'd all be resolved." Though Thom found the whole situation "muddling and painful," he was sure of one thing: that Mike made him "more happy, & can still, than anybody else ever could."[70]

Mike's definite return to the United States meant that Thom had to find a way to follow him. He worried that his Frank Knox failure the previous year would invalidate a second attempt. Guy Lee was Thom's tutor at St. John's, where the Harper-Wood Studentship was administered.[71] Lee recommended he apply for an English-Speaking Union Scholarship, but felt competition for Commonwealth and Henry Fellowships would be "extremely keen."[72] It occurred to Thom that he might follow Donald Hall to Stanford on a creative writing fellowship. Thom had not told Hall he was gay, although that was the subtext of his expression of interest: he wanted to leave restrictive England for free America. "I feel it's an atmosphere better for writing, and in several ways better for living in," he told Hall. "Here people do get bogged down and impotent with their own complications."[73]

In Rome, Thom assembled an eight-poem portfolio and a statement about his writing interests. He focused on the importance of energy and railed against "the milkiness and the weakness and hesitation that attack human strength . . . and the vagueness and shiftiness that attack the adequate portrayal of it." In terms of style, he most admired "the compression of late Shakespeare, as in The Winter's Tale and Coriolanus, where everything contributes to the strong portrayal of strong emotion yet which leaves the reader enough doubt to be ignorant of the whole until he is finished."[74] Hall warned Thom that Yvor Winters, his director of studies, had a reputation for fierceness. "Thank you for all the advice about Wynters," Thom wrote him. "I was tactful in my wording—as tactful as I could be."[75]

Thom left Rome in mid-March, passed through Paris, spent several days in London, and returned to Cambridge, and the Central Hotel, for the start of Easter term in mid-April. In London, he received the letter that changed his life. "I appear to have got the fellowship," he told Hall. "I've only heard unofficially, but it seems definite enough."[76] The unofficial acceptance was his first experience of Yvor Winters. "They seemed to me definitely the best [poems] submitted," Winters told him: "I think there is little doubt of your literary gift." After praising passages of "Tamer and Hawk," "A Mirror for Poets," and "The Wound," Winters zeroed in on Thom's faults. "Your weakness, as I see it, is in your conception of what a poem is, in some measure," Winters continued, and beyond that of difficulty in choosing a theme solid enough for your purposes and in defining the total theme clearly enough so that each detail will really carry proper weight. Your novel in verse ["The Furies"] will never work, but I can't go into that here. [. . .] I won't object to your working on it, if you come, but I am sure I can talk you out of it.[77]

Thom would attend Winters's graduate-level poetry-writing seminar and his three lecture courses: The English Lyric; Chief American Poets, from 1630 to the Present; and The Theory and Practice of the Criticism of Poetry.[78] "It is in the three lecture courses that I can teach you most of what you need to know," Winters told him: "it is not the matter to be read which will be important, as what I shall endeavor to do with it."[79] Having spent "the whole of the last year in a state of poetic-looking but unproductive restlessness," Thom could not wait to get started.[80]

Fearing that too extensive a list of publications would count against him, Thom did not tell Stanford that his first book, *Fighting Terms*, was scheduled for imminent publication. Oscar Mellor had accepted Thom's manuscript the previous autumn. Seven poems were cut, including minor pieces like "Elizabeth Barrett Barrett" and "The Death of a Stranger." Of the remaining twenty-five, "Carnal Knowledge" began the book and "Incident on a Journey" ended it.[81] "To His Cynical Mistress" was the earliest poem included—Thom wrote it in late 1950—but there was no place for "Poem," the antiwar piece that had made his name at Cambridge. *Fighting Terms* was a "pretentious and memorable title"[82] and Thom dedicated the book to Mike, "as he has given me more help than anyone else."[83]

After several delays, *Fighting Terms* was finally published in late May 1954. *Varsity* called it "a national rather than a local event."[84] Reviews were enthusiastic: in *The Guardian*, Anne Ridler called Thom "a new poet of pith and promise"; G. S. Fraser in the *New Statesman* found "such independence [. . .] rare among young poets."[85] Most pleasing was the assessment of *The Times Literary Supplement*. "Mr. Gunn's blunt, open speech has great possibilities," the reviewer found, "especially in the short narratives where he deals with the kind of displaced person we usually find in a Hemingway novel."[86]

One such displaced character in *Fighting Terms* is the speaker of "Lofty in the Palais de Danse," a young soldier "gone to bad," who hangs around outside cinemas trying to pick up girls. "I thought of Lofty as a character who was supposed to be a stand-in for a part of me," Thom reflected, "in the same way as Yeats' Crazy Jane."[87] That "part" was the soldier in peacetime, "the national serviceman, the 'clumsy brute in uniform,' the soldier who never goes to war, whose role has no function, whose battledress is a joke."[88] Addressing a girl, Lofty remarks: "You are not random picked. I tell you you / Are much like one I knew before, that died." The girls "seem identical / To her original" but are discarded "as soon as slept with."[89] Elsewhere, in poems such as "Tamer and Hawk" and "Without a Counterpart," Thom wrote to "a genderless *you*" to disguise his sexuality. "I was never that dishonest that I translated a male into a female," he reflected. "I and those in the know would think it was a male, but the publishers and public would think it was a female."[90] Thom learned this technique from Auden: it worked, Thom reasoned, because "I didn't realise that [Auden] was queer when I first read him."[91]

One person "in the know" was Karl Miller, who reviewed *Fighting Terms* for *Granta*. He found "very few" poems that "rigorously develop a definitive attitude towards their theme" and detected "an occasional sentimentality" that he considered a weakness in poems like "For a Birthday." Thom had "grown more inward and personal," Karl thought, since "A Mirror for Poets," "one of his earliest and best poems." Karl concluded that Thom was "by far the most interesting undergraduate writer for some four or five years."[92] Thom kept a copy of Karl's review and intuited that, given the difference in tone to Karl's *Varsity* profile of him eighteen months earlier, Karl's boyish enthusiasm for him had dimmed to a professional regard.

Mike left England first, in mid-July, to begin his two-year posting at Lackland Air Force Base in San Antonio, Texas. Helena Shire had taken over from R. N. Walters as his tutor; with her guidance, Mike achieved a "Second Class, Second Division" in the English Tripos.[93] Thom helped, too: he wrote Mike a six-page crib sheet and advised him which background material to read for each exam question.[94] "Mr. Kitay did a vast amount of work during this term, enough probably to see him through," Shire wrote in her Easter term report. "He is a delightful personality who has not taken examination-taking seriously—but has undoubtedly profited from his time at Cambridge."[95] As W. S. Thatcher put it: "He has mixed very well and has been a great asset socially. He goes down having gained our very great respect and liking."[96]

With *Fighting Terms* published, Thom could concentrate on his preparations for Stanford. Staying in Allhallows, he was "living in a snow of leaflets, vouchers, visa, and—finally tickets"[97] and was "terribly excited at the thought of sailing so soon."[98] He was due to sail from Southampton, aboard the *Queen Elizabeth*, on August 26, and would spend his twenty-fifth birthday in the mid-Atlantic. Before he sailed, he wrote Mike a letter "to be given you if I die. I hope it'll never need to be given you, and we can open it and laugh at it together one day: and I hope that when we die, it'll be in each other's arms. But know this, my beloved; whenever I die, it'll be with thoughts of you—you who have taught me what it is like to live. I love you so passionately, so utterly, my darling, that I am sure my love will go on existing for ever, when I'm dead—long after that."[99]

10

STANFORD

Before sailing to New York, Thom discovered Hart Crane in *The Oxford Book of American Verse*. He called *The Bridge* "one of the influential poems of my life," and at an event to mark Crane's centenary in 1999 he read from "The Harbor Dawn":

> And you beside me, blessed now while sirens
> Sing to us, stealthily weave us into day—
> Serenely now, before day claims our eyes
> Your cool arms murmurously about me lay.[1]

In 1954, Thom did not know that the source for "The Harbor Dawn" was a letter Crane wrote to his mother.[2] At the Crane centenary, Thom read its last paragraph to introduce the poem. "There was a wonderful fog for about 18 hours last week," Crane wrote. "It was like wakening into a dreamland in the early dawn—one wondered where one was with only a milky light in the window and that vague music from a hidden world. Next morning while I dressed it was clear and glittering as usual. Like champagne, or a cold bath to look [at] it. Such a world!"[3] Thom's first impressions of New York were from Crane—"the darkling harbor, the pillowed bay," "dim snow," the howls of drunken stevedores—and he was moved to discover that Crane had shared so much of his sensory life with his mother.

. . .

Thom arrived in New York in the aftermath of a "runaway hurricane" that had flooded neighborhoods across Brooklyn and Manhattan.[4] Abe and Dora Kitay met him at the port—Mike was already in San Antonio—and drove him to Kearny. Thom had already met Dora in Cambridge; Mike had not come out to his parents and he and Thom acted out a friendship in front of his mother. "She and I kept our eyes from it as by an agreed consent," Thom reflected, "but how could she not have realised . . ."[5] Thom stayed in Kearny for three weeks; Mike was secretly pleased not to be there. "I couldn't deal with that subject," he recalled. "It was hard enough for me to imagine being gay, let alone with Thom there in my life."[6] Although Thom liked Mike's parents, he spent as little time as possible in Kearny. Mostly, he wandered around Manhattan in a state of "bewilderment and sickness."[7] En route to California, he was "still too excited by [New York City] to decide what I think of it," but found it "one of my big places, anyway: I'm fond of big dirty towns."[8]

A Fulbright grant paid for Thom's first-class train journey across America from New York to Oakland. From there he took the ferry to San Francisco, "a wonderful way of entering the city."[9] Thom arrived on a "hot, dry" day in mid-September and had a clear view of the skyline, from the recently constructed Bay Bridge to Coit Tower and the neo-Gothic Russ Building. He made the short train journey down the Peninsula to Palo Alto. Winters had arranged a room for him in an old wooden house on Lincoln Avenue "kept by a group of mad people."[10] It cost sixteen dollars a month and Thom could walk to campus in half an hour. Stanford itself "surpasses all my dreams," he told Hall,[11] partly because he found it a "refreshing change" from the stuffiness of Cambridge. He liked how "a positively rustic casualness and directness" had replaced "the big rush to be in the sophisticated social swim."[12]

Winters met Thom at the Southern Pacific railway depot and drove him through the California hills, "burned down to a gold from which the heat comes at you harder it seems than it does from the sky," to his house in Los Altos. Thom knew that Winters "had a certain reputation for ferocity, though I did not know what the reputation was based on."[13] It was not his appearance: Winters was in his mid-fifties, portly, wore glasses, and smoked a pipe. "Pleased or displeased, he was most of the time thoughtfully of the same expression," Thom reflected. His mind dulled from travel, Thom faced a poetry inquisition. Winters asked which poets he liked: Crane, Donne, Lowell, and Yeats elicited an uninterpretable grunt. Thom's thoughts about Edward Taylor and Elizabeth Daryush were met with the same grunt, "an ambiguous response, not always of appreciation." A difference of opinion about Daryush's "Still Life"—to Thom it was "lacking in substance," to Winters "a very funny poem"—made Thom think he "had failed a test or two most signally." He wondered how he "was going to get through a year" of Winters.[14]

When classes began, Thom's dread evaporated. Creative writing, as an academic discipline, did not exist in Britain.[15] In America, Iowa established its creative writing program in 1936: one of its first graduates, Wallace Stegner, founded the Stanford program a decade later. "I've always wished there was some equivalent for writers to the way Italian painters used to take pupils and apprentices," Thom told his aunts, "and here it is."[16] Classes were small and informal; the half dozen or so students crammed into Winters's small office on Tuesday and Friday afternoons. Winters faced them "in his morris chair, gently sucking his pipe."[17] They submitted poems to Winters earlier in the day: he read them aloud to the class, made comments, and invited discussion. Hall may have warned Thom about the severity of the Wintersian seminar. "If one of us committed a cliché," Hall wrote, "he would lean back in his chair, gaze toward the ceiling with a soulful expression, and intone with plush sonority, 'The pine tree, like a lonely sentinel, stood etched against the sky.'"[18]

Within weeks, Thom was praising Winters's "usefulness" and methods. "He had the knack—the genius perhaps—of divining your intentions," he reflected, "even if the poem was so obscurely or clumsily carried out that those intentions had become hidden."[19] Questions "were seldom left open."[20] He and Winters had "big arguments in class every day" and Thom found it "amazing . . . how much good I get from him."[21] Much of what Thom learned was practical and technical, just as it had been at Cambridge with F. R. Leavis. There were other similarities. They shared "the same stubbornness, rudeness, feeling of persecution once justified but no longer justified," Thom told Karl:

> His critical position is just about that of Dr Johnson if Dr J were alive today—rather too much common sense, and an acute dislike of anything "romantic," which term includes Lawrence, Yeats, & Eliot. So, as you see, he's a good deal more limited than Leavis.[22]

Leavis had disciples; Winters had "toadies."[23] Students in Winters's seminar often stayed on to do graduate work with him, finding in his set of beliefs "a refuge, a harmonious world where everything had already been decided in accordance with certain rules."[24] Later, Thom felt it "wonderful luck" that he had worked with Winters "at this particular stage of my life, rather than earlier when I would have been more impressionable or later when I would have been less ready to learn."[25]

Having written poorly for a year, Thom hoped Stanford would be "the place to train myself." His confidence was low: his short poems lacked energy; his long poem, "The Furies," lay abandoned. "The trouble is, hell, I don't really know whether I want to be a poet," he told Helena Shire. "I seem to have lost most of that inexplicable vigour I had when I was writing at Cambridge."[26] Fortunately for Thom, he was quick to absorb Winters's practical guidance: Winters's focus on correct meter and "intense verbal precision"[27] forced Thom to write with more rigor and discipline. These strictures helped rather than hindered him, as did the pressure to produce poems for Winters's biweekly seminars.

Thom did not lack ideas. At Tony White's encouragement, he had embraced existentialism as a valid model for heroism but struggled to write about it. In Rome he had started a poem called "St Martin and the Beggar"—in which St. Martin is "an early existentialist"[28]—and at Stanford developed it into its final, ballad form.[29] St. Martin held Christian principles but, in an act of existential self-definition, stated: "I cannot grow from them alone, / I must go out and fight."[30] Although Thom saw "a great deal of raw Sartre" in this and other early poems, Winters was also present in theme as well as style.[31] "Merlin in the Cave: He Speculates Without a Book" likely owes a debt to Winters, who told Thom to read E. A. Robinson's long poem *Merlin*; but Thom was drawn more to Winters's criticism of it. Robinson's Merlin, according to Winters, is "capable of more important work" than being a knight. "Merlin perceives that, given certain men of great force and limited understanding in certain initial situations," Winters writes, "certain disasters are virtually inescapable."[32] Thom saw the existentialist potential of this statement, and "Merlin in the Cave" examines the limits of existentialism.[33] Thom contrasted the "absolute prison" of philosophical reflection with the need for action. "I must act," Merlin states, "and make / The meaning in each movement that I take."[34] As was common in these early poems, Thom's dramatized speakers are not overtly different from the voice of the poet himself. "At least [Merlin] realises the important thing," Thom told Tony, "that by an effort of the will he may be saved."[35]

One of Thom's finest Stanford poems, "The Corridor," was Winters's favorite. It also showed his influence "more than any of the others."[36] Thom borrowed the central image—a voyeur watching people through a keyhole who sees his own reflection in a mirror—from Sartre's *L'Être et le néant*.[37] "It is Camus existentialism (*La Peste*) rather than Sartre," he told Tony. "The watcher is not an existentialist till the last stanza, but his situation is existentialist all through."[38] The watcher fears that by acting as a participant he "would be mastered, the inhabitant / Of someone else's world." However, when he sees the reflection of his own "[t]wo strange eyes in a fascinated face" watching himself through the keyhole, he realizes he is a participant and is confronted with a choice. "What could he do but leave the keyhole, rise," Thom writes, "And go, one hand held out, to meet a friend?"[39] An intelligent reading of Camus, Thom thought, would foreground Camus's "big emphasis on Reason for making one's choices."[40] Adapting his own "theory of pose" to existentialism, Thom realized that self-mastery was part of a larger, social complex. If Sartre and Winters were the main influences on his writing at this time, Camus provided a more humanistic outlook. "The Corridor" was Thom's attempt to marry Winters's reason with Camus's humanism. The marriage, though it would not last, prompted a shift in Thom's perspective that led to a valuable tension in his later work.

Winters also encouraged Thom to read as widely in twentieth-century American poetry as he did in the "plain style" of sixteenth-century poets like George Gascoigne, Barnabe Googe, and Fulke Greville. "He regarded that as an essential part of my education," Thom recalled. "And of course he was right."[41] Thom eventually became "immersed in, and excited by" poets whom he had previously only encountered in *The Oxford Book of American Verse*, but at first he was unconvinced. Of William Carlos Williams, he "<u>quite</u> liked about 4 poems out of 600."[42] With Wallace Stevens, he was "admiring but not in sympathy. In his best poems he seems to me to be saying, not 'something <u>is</u>', but 'something is <u>not</u>.'"[43]

While new idols rose slowly, others were quick to fall. In his lectures, Winters "set about the systematic demolishing" of Yeats, one of Thom's "literary gods," focusing on how Yeats presented "emotion lacking adequate source or motivation in the context."[44] That was one thing; another was a first meeting with W. H. Auden, who was passing through San Francisco on a lecture tour. Auden was "one of the few writers I've ever deeply wanted to meet," Thom told Shire, "but from curiosity & admiration not personal sympathy. After all, he's Part of One's Past, isn't he?"[45] He was disappointed. "I could hardly believe this was the Wild One of the Thirties," he told Hall, "who whatever his faults then at least had the virtue of a strident tone of denunciation. But now you'd never know: a flabby dilettante, gracious living, complacent and trite."[46] Thom wrote an unpublished poem about the evening, "A Visit from Mr Auden," in which "[t]he cocktail hour of death approaches fast."[47]

Thom called his year at Stanford "the most important single year of my writing life: Winters constantly encouraged me to extend myself, to take risks," he remarked. "At the same time I was learning (as I took them) the nature of those artistic risks and how closely they related to risks in my life."[48]

· · ·

Thom spent what little money he had in San Francisco. He divided his time "between writing and getting drunk in San Francisco, a town I'm crazy about."[49] It could "hold its own against some of the best European cities," he told Karl, and was "the queerest city I've ever been in."[50] Hall's friends Tony and Charlotte Herbold took Thom to his first gay bar, a North Beach hangout called the Black Cat.[51] It was "a great revelation," and he went back the following night by himself. "They were drinking and groping each other and they were having fun," he reflected. "I thought if I went back to the bar I could make it with them . . . But I wasn't very good at that kind of thing in those days."[52]

Thom embraced the promiscuous freedoms San Francisco provided. He wanted "some sort of relationship—either Body, or else Mind, if possible both—to fill in the year away from Mike."[53] He had a crush on "a beautiful black-Irish janitor" at Stanford but was "young & shy" and they shared only "long pointless boring conversations."[54] Already accustomed to leading a double life, Thom wrote at Stanford, went out in San Francisco, and was strict about their separation. "Most people were homophobic; whole departments of English were!" he later reflected:

> You couldn't be honest then. Sometimes young people say to me: "Why were you in the closet in those days?" I was in the closet because I would not only have lost my job, I'd have been kicked out of America and consequently would not have been able to live with my lover. That was a very practical reason for my behaviour, dishonest though it may have been.[55]

When Thom arrived in San Francisco, the queer bar culture that had emerged in the city through the 1940s and early 1950s was under threat. McCarthyism meant that "erotic communities whose activities did not fit the postwar American dream drew intense persecution."[56] Popular gay bars like the Paper Doll and the Black Cat relied on payoffs to beat cops and district captains for protection. Entrapment—undercover officers posed in bars, waiting to be solicited—provided the excuse to raid bars, remove liquor licenses, and eventually force closure. Gay bars were social hubs: the state actively sought to close them.[57]

Thom felt "there was no question of . . . being frank with Winters," who "would have been *appalled* at the idea that I was queer."[58] His relationship with Mike became an "engagement to the Texane"[59] and he told Hall he was seeing "a girlfriend (the Tamer & Hawk, etc subject)."[60] He maintained this in letters home. "Yes, thank you: the girls are just fine," he told his aunts.[61] To Ander he confirmed that "all the girls readily go to bed in California."[62]

He visited Mike at Christmas: it was their first time together since leaving Cambridge. Mike was finding their separation "very difficult" and struggled to make friends on base.[63] He taught an evening course in English literature at Trinity University and took a small part in a production of *My Three Angels* at the San Antonio Little Theater.[64] "I wasn't enjoying myself in any way," he reflected. "I wanted to be somewhere else." There was lingering jealousy about Thom "enjoying himself" and "meeting people" at Stanford.[65] To Thom it was a "terrific" reunion. "It was funny to find how that warm sort of relationship had really been forgotten by me except as a concept in the mind," he told Tony.

> I mean I had confidence in it & knew what it was, but it hadn't been "realised" in 6 months, & things can grow dangerously abstract even in 6 months. I find I tend to juggle with abstractions a bit too easily—juggle them into being something they may not be. So it was a good reminder to me (and him too, I think), and we were both happy.[66]

With Mike in service until summer 1956, Thom wanted to move to San Antonio at the conclusion of his Stanford fellowship. During his Christmas visit, Thom interviewed for an English instructorship at Trinity but would not find out for several months whether he was successful. Beyond a late, unsuccessful application to San Francisco State College, he did not apply for other positions. "Returning to England just then would sum up all my failure as a human being," he told Karl, "having made a tremendous effort to get what I have finally decided is the thing I want, and then coming back to where I started most decisively without it. And worse, much worse, than when I started."[67]

He wanted to stay with Mike, and felt as though he could write well at Stanford, but ambition was also part of Thom's desire to stay in America. He did not want to fall behind Cambridge friends: Karl had become a research fellow at Downing and would subsequently go to Harvard on a Commonwealth Fellowship. Tony had joined the Old Vic: in their 1954–55 season, he played secondary roles such as Aumerle in *Richard II*, Longaville in *Love's Labour's Lost*, and Mortimer in *Henry IV Part 1*.[68] Thom missed Tony the most. "I can't help feeling that you were the cause, direct or indirect, of my best poetry," he told him, "and by implication of my straightest thinking and strongest grasp on things." Even so, Thom was desperate to stay in America. "The job & extension of any visa are both still a bit up in the air," he continued, "& I may not get either."[69]

Back in California, Thom found his "restlessness has become dangerously less." With few friends at Stanford, his pursuits were mostly solitary. He could only afford to go to "wonderful" San Francisco once a fortnight. Instead, he "work[ed] off excess energy" at the gym and began learning Italian. Mostly he read—Valéry, Corbière, Baudelaire, "a few odd plays of Shakespeare"—and tried to write. "The restlessness before didn't exactly conduce to happiness of course, it never does," he told Tony,

> but without it, or rather with less of it (becos I'll never be completely without it) there's so much less drive towards any kind of fruitful action. Well (philosophically) one goes on, & I just hope one goes somewhere. Or, as the famous line in The Wild One: "You don't go to any special place, man, you just go." Indeed.[70]

That winter, *The Wild One* introduced Thom to motorcycle gang culture, the "myth" of which was "just starting up."[71] Marlon Brando embodied its virile masculinity. Dressed in black leather jacket, blue jeans, tilted cap, and heavy boots, Brando was an outlaw full of machismo, disaffection, and restlessness. That "famous line" in *The Wild One* became the epigraph for "On the Move," which Thom began in March and finished in May.[72]

Thom saw Brando as the modern embodiment of heroic values—the kind he discussed frequently with Tony—and, in the poem, "the Boys" become existential figures.[73] Thom equated "restlessness" with the search for value: "at best," he wrote in the poem's famous final lines, "Reaching no absolute, in which to rest, / One is always nearer by not keeping still."[74] Given his own worries about complacency, Thom wrote the poem as an exhortation to himself, to be more vigorous, energetic, independent. The motorcyclists are "self-defined, astride the created will" and embody the existentialist argument that each individual is responsible for him- or herself. Thom wanted the poem to capture some of the "physical energy of the body *and* the energy of the mind" he had felt during his "Revelation" on the road in France. To Thom, this energy seemed self-created, organic, which was why he "harnessed so much onto a Sartrean idea of the *will*" in his early poems, because "the will . . . seemed to be a way of channelling the energy."[75] This was a breakthrough moment in his poetry. Two years later, Thom called "On the Move" "the only time I have written adequately on one of the really important subjects: the poem is about movement as an experiment, and about 'the search for value' as a value in itself."[76]

In April, midway through "On the Move," Thom was offered the Trinity job. He looked forward to being with Mike, but not to teaching— "I shall probably be grey by 1956," he told Hall[77]—nor Texas, "a somewhat ghastly place, very huge, very arid, very boastful, very provincial."[78] Moreover, he worried that teaching would stifle him after some six months of fertile, explorative writing. This thought seemed to paralyze him: after finishing "On the Move," he wrote "nothing—not a damn thing except some revisions" in the month before he left Stanford. "Not doing anything makes me morose, ungrateful, arrogant, difficult to live with, etc.," he told Tony. "(Whereas working hard makes me morose, ungrateful, arrogant, and difficult to live with.)"[79]

In early June, Thom had a farewell dinner with Winters and his wife, the poet and novelist Janet Lewis.[80] Winters showed Thom his study, "a small one-room building across his backyard, with . . . cheap prints of the heads of favorite writers framed on the wall, Emily Dickinson and Herman Melville guarding his desk."[81] After a difficult start, Thom had "come to love Winters," he told Hall, "who has almost all the qualities one could want from a man—lack of cowardice, kindness, intelligence, and toughness."[82] He felt a great debt to Winters, but the strength of Winters's personality was such that it took Thom years to acknowledge it. "He was important to me in ways I'm not even sure I can completely identify or speak about," he reflected. "I think it would be fair enough to say that his definition of a poem is essentially my definition of a poem: 'a statement in words about a human experience'—which is rather large, but he meant 'with moral import.'"[83] Ultimately, Thom found Winters's ideas "rather narrow" and "overly rigid," and was glad not to have become a Winters toady.[84] But the picture was complicated: Thom admired Winters's early poems, his "very wild, very irrational" free verse, which he called Winters's "tangle with the forces of unreason."[85] The tension between early and late Winters informed Thom's relationship with the man he jokingly called a "father figure." Winters "tried to be a complete rationalist, though he was in fact a tremendous romantic," Thom recalled. "Nobody would be that much of a rationalist unless they were really romantic."[86]

On the long train journey to San Antonio, Thom drafted a laudatory poem, "To Yvor Winters, 1955." Drawing on Winters's late style and Greville's "At night, when colours all to black are cast," to which Winters had introduced him, the poem extols Winters's art of keeping "both Rule and Energy in view, / Much power in each, most in the balanced two."[87] It was a lesson Thom would keep in mind for the rest of his life. The literary toughness of his year in California was a fruitful contrast to his restless, romantic nightlife in San Francisco. It was, he reflected later, and perhaps with the benefit of hindsight, "a fucking beautiful year" in which he "wrote like a prince & cruised like a beggar."[88]

11

SAN ANTONIO

En route to San Antonio, Thom stopped in Los Angeles to meet Christopher Isherwood.[1] Thom was twenty-five, Isherwood fifty, "but I never for a moment felt that he was twice my age," Thom recalled. "We immediately started speaking together like long-time friends who hadn't met in years. He was tanned and youthful-looking, the famous bright eyes alert and observant; he perfectly adapted himself to his listener; his conversation was enthusiastic, lively, funny; and I said to myself, *this* is the way I want to age."[2]

Winters gave Thom a model for poetry, Isherwood a model for life. "I was especially impressed by the at the time uncommon ease, casualness, and openness with which he carried his homosexuality," he reflected.[3] Isherwood found Thom "intelligent, and warm." "He has pockmarks and a vertically lined face like a convict's," he wrote, "and his nose and chin are both too big—yet he's quite attractive, with his bright brown eyes." A shared ambivalence toward England was a natural bond. "He likes America, especially California," Isherwood wrote. "I warm to all Britishers who do that."[4] Thom later developed "an irrational terror" that he would "fall fatally ill" on a visit to England and die there. "I asked Isherwood once if he ever himself felt a similar fear. 'Oh yes!' he said, 'then my mother would have won!'"[5]

Thom also admired the "unremitting control" of Isherwood's prose.[6] In the opening paragraphs of "A Berlin Diary (Winter 1932–3)" he found "a proper model for poetry. So much is explicitly and concretely there, so much is suggested. It is fully prose, but it has all the concentration and scope of poetry."[7] In the 1960s, when Thom's subject matter gradually became more quotidian and humane, he found great value in Isherwood's style. It seemed to provide "no intermediary" between speaker and reader and enabled what Thom called "reticence" and Isherwood "evasiveness."[8]

Los Angeles provided other distractions. Hollywood was "just a bunch of ugly shacks"[9]—Isherwood, then a scriptwriter for MGM, took him around the set of *Diane* and introduced him to Roger Moore and Marisa Pavan—but Thom found "a genuine leather bar" called the Cinema on Santa Monica Boulevard. "I didn't really imagine that such a thing existed," he remarked, "[it] was just a fantasy." Inside, surrounded by butch men dressed head to toe in leather, Thom found it "very liberating."[10] Los Angeles, he reflected later, was "promiscuity given tangible form." He wanted to write about "the rich cool country C.I. has chosen to live in—its excitement." In one abandoned poem, set in the Cinema, he wrote: "I glimpsed romantic possibilities / in the eyes of over-cool strangers / who thought I might be a cop / so that night since I cdn't be vouched for / I never did get picked up."[11]

In Texas, on a high from the Cinema, Thom quickly acquired a secondhand Harley-Davidson, "engine re-bored and the whole thing repainted so it looks quite smart, at only $250."[12] Although the Harley was "positively sexually beautiful to look at," it threw Thom several times and he felt it was "going to fall to pieces under me."[13] He told Tony it was "something of a pose" but hoped "there is a chance of its becoming the real thing."[14] Thom rode his Harley to Trinity, telling Helena Shire that "only hoodlums ride" motorcycles in the United States and that "it is considered ODD for a teacher to ride one."[15] He later told an interviewer he kept the bike for "one month" and he had "figured by then that I was being rather phony with all this, so I retired it." He hung out with "people who owned bikes. But not with anyone so glamorous as outlaw bikers." Thom felt a "built-in sympathy" toward outlaws: the act of "defying" he found "interesting and attractive."[16]

Thom's arrival at Trinity was announced in the *San Antonio Light*, which called him "a modern English poet" but made no mention of his year at Stanford.[17] Teaching began immediately: Thom taught summer school courses to supplement his low instructor's salary. The English department was small, and Thom had a heavy teaching load. He taught freshman composition; a sophomore course that used Cleanth Brooks and Robert Penn Warren's *Understanding Poetry* as a textbook; and an advanced course in the English Renaissance. "The last is not too bad," he told Hall. "I plug Greville and [John Dowland's] Fine knacks for ladies, and [the students] are intelligent enough to be interested and innocent enough not to have too difficult prejudices."[18] He also taught an advanced course in creative writing, in which he adopted a stern, Wintersian approach to student poetry. One student, Doris Polunsky, published a poem called "Ode to Mr. Gunn; or, Trials and Tribulations of an Aspiring Poet" in the university newspaper:

> Our poor, defenceless poetry,
> Created with much care,
> Is criticized unmercifully
> By you in tilted chair.

> We hesitate to hand it in,
> Afraid of what you'll say;
> But, knowing that we must be brave,
> We hand it in and pray

> That you'll not find our phrases trite
> Or vague, or even worse,
> Reminding you of other poets'
> Well-known, published verse.

> But when you shake your head and say
> You'll read one through again,
> Then comment that it's "rather good,"
> Our labor's worth the pain.[19]

Thom liked his students, many of whom were not much younger than him. "The football players who were in my freshman English class were very amused by me," he recalled, "and I was very amused by them."[20] But he was impatient with the workload and routine and worried that he would have no time to put into practice what Winters had taught him. "I have no time to even <u>think</u> about writing poems," he told Tony in mid-August. "I fully expect to write nothing all year: and the thought of starting from bottom again at the end of the year fills me with despair."[21]

Living with Mike, however, was a comfort. They shared a wood-framed garage apartment near Woodlawn Lake. "We had each other, and I think that was what we wanted," Mike reflected. "But we didn't have much else."[22] Thom called them "sweetly domesticated" but was worried about their future. "I am equally afraid of sticking to him merely from habit, and of leaving him on some crazy impulse that I'd regret," he told Tony. "But this is everybody's trouble, I guess—homo or hetero."[23]

Much of their leisure time was spent at the movies. Thom thought *Rebel Without a Cause* contained "about the worst dialogue and story" he had ever seen "in a film with any pretensions. Still, I enjoyed it," he told Tony, "it's all about (good looking) young toughs in motorcycle boots."[24] He saw *Alexander the Great* twice—"the panachiest ever"[25]—and *Invasion of the Body Snatchers*, which appealed to his thematic interest in doubleness and duplicity. Through *The Blackboard Jungle*, "Rock Around the Clock" became an anthem for 1950s youth rebellion. The song was an enormous hit while Thom and Mike were in San Antonio; it spawned a musical starring Bill Haley and the Comets. "That was the big thing, because it was the first popular rock and roll film," Mike reflected. "Thom and I loved it, just as we loved Elvis."[26]

Elvis was the soundtrack to 1956. His self-titled album was released in January, followed by four consecutive hit singles: "Heartbreak Hotel," "I Want You, I Need You, I Love You," "Don't Be Cruel," and "Hound Dog." For Thom, Elvis became a heroic figure, embodying the toughness of bikers and soldiers; his pose and showmanship were actorly and recalled the energy and strength of Shakespearean heroes. Elvis "turns revolt into a style," Thom wrote later:

Whether he poses or is real, no cat
Bothers to say: the pose held is a stance,
Which, generation of the very chance
It wars on, may be posture for combat.[27]

In the poem, Elvis is "[o]ur idiosyncrasy and our likeness." The music "pitches through some bar" from a jukebox and the speaker imagines the "gangling finery," "crawling sideburns," and wielded guitar. Elvis was an erotic figure, as erotic as Brando and Dean, and Thom's version of him, the "idiosyncrasy," is that of uniformed soldier. The "bar" of the poem is likely a leather one; the "gangling finery" of the patrons' leather jackets and Levi's: in Thom's 1950s poems, "combat" is almost always seduction.

In San Antonio's gay and lesbian nightlife, drag "grew dramatically in the 1950s" to become the predominant scene.[28] There were no leather bars. Several downtown bars had a mixed clientele. Mike recalled "a sort of arty, gayish bar where a black woman played the piano and sang."[29] Thom was used to the relative openness of San Francisco, whereas Mike had lived with the fear of being a gay man in the military for more than a year. "You had to be very careful. Even in the bars you were taking a risk," he reflected. He found those mixed bars "very closeted, very uptight." With his boyish good looks and blond hair, Mike attracted people easily. "I had an admirer who would call at 2 or 3 o'clock in the morning," he recalled, "and I would hear heavy breathing . . . Flattering in a way." Mike knew another gay man in the military who "would always say, in a camp voice, 'Yes Lieutenant Kitay . . .' He would make a point of saying my rank."[30] Thom already hated San Antonio, "a horrible town with a sluggish river,"[31] and its limited gay life and repressive atmosphere compounded his dislike. Having a lover in the military was "hard," he reflected. "I was duplicitous. I lied where I needed to."[32]

One of the few poems Thom wrote in San Antonio was "The Allegory of the Wolf Boy." It added to his tradition of doubles, divided selves, and secret lives. A boy transforms into a wolf: the allegory itself is left open, but the boy "plays us in a sad duplicity." His "sad" is Shakespearean, meaning steadfast and grave, thus the boy's "duplicity" is unchanging, inescapable. His physical transformation allows him to "loose desires hoarded against his will." Thom insisted that homosexual readings of early poems like "Wolf Boy" and "Carnal Knowledge" were at best limited,[33] but acknowledged that "Wolf Boy" "is" about being a homosexual.[34] "It is about queerness—or rather a certain type of queerness," he told Tony at the time of writing, "but I think it is acceptable, because the allegory applies equally to any person who lives one life and fails to connect it to the life he really wants."[35]

"Wolf Boy" was also an important step in terms of technique. Three years later, when Thom planned a poem called "On Witches," he drew a parallel with "Wolf Boy." "Like a man who knows himself homosexual & becomes a ponce," he wrote, "the fact that she is not society's ideal makes her espouse an exaggerated anti-ideal which without her doing this wd not exist. [. . .] Keep the likeness to sex in mind; do not state, but make clear as in Wolf Boy."[36] Stylistically, Thom compromised between wanting to write about his life (including his sexuality) and disguising it. "Do not state, but make clear" is his stylistic equivalent to the genderless "you" he borrowed from Auden (and perhaps Crane). There was power in this approach. Thom found he "express[ed] better thro images than thro direct statement."[37]

Thom also continued to publish in England—*The Spectator* published "The Separation" and "The Silver Age" during his first weeks in America; he contributed regularly to *The London Magazine*; "On the Move" appeared in *Encounter*—but he felt removed from the London literary scene. "I know little of how my book goes in England, except that the Spectator is always claiming me as one of its tiresome group of new metaphysicals," he complained to Hall. "Just because one's coherent, it doesn't mean one is metaphysical."[38] The metaphysical question was part of a wider argument—a largely "journalistic contrivance"[39]—that poets like Thom, Donald Davie, Elizabeth Jennings, and Philip Larkin were part of a group called "The Movement." Work by these poets shared similarities of style (plain), diction (colloquial), tone (witty, ironic), situation (commonplace), attitude (commonsense), approach (realistic), with a preference for clarity; symbol, metaphor, and imagery were used with restraint.[40] Movement poetry, moreover, seemed to coalesce around a rejection of Modernist innovation and a revival of interest in traditional forms.

Like other supposed members, Thom denied all knowledge of, and participation in, the Movement. He had to articulate his views when Robert Conquest wrote asking him to contribute to an anthology of Movement poetry called *New Lines*. Thom's appearances in prominent publications like *New World Writing*—"a fashionable collection of shit," he told Karl, "but it has a fantastic circulation"[41]—and the rapturous critical reception afforded *Fighting Terms* meant he was one of Britain's most exciting young poets: his accordance with some, if not all, Movement attitudes, styles, and themes meant he would be key to any Movement anthology. "What it really comes down to is that I don't think the Movement is a movement in the same sense that, say, the Imagists, the Thirties, the Apocalyptics, were movements," he told Conquest. "The different writers you name . . . share a healthy destructive attitude but very little else."[42] Seeking John Lehmann's advice, Thom said he "wouldn't mind at all being printed by Macmillan's" and that he would "rejoice in the company" of Jennings and Larkin. "Old Gunn is in a Dilemma, you see," he wrote Lehmann, "between principle and desire for self-display."[43]

Self-display won. Thom offered Conquest his choice from *Fighting Terms*, but the seven poems chosen—including "On the Move" and "Autumn Chapter in a Novel"—were all more recent. When *New Lines* was published in June 1956, Thom was relieved that Conquest's introduction echoed his own thoughts about shared intentions: Conquest remarked that the connection between poets was "little more than a negative determination to avoid bad principles."[44] Thom warmed to Kingsley Amis and Davie's work and thought Larkin "the best of the lot." Moreover, he was glad his "misgivings of eighteen months ago didn't make me refuse to be in it."[45]

During his back and forth with Conquest, Thom argued, unsuccessfully, that Donald Hall's poems deserved a place in *New Lines*.[46] This was his attempt to return a favor: he called Hall "a hell of a good friend"[47] for his help with the Fantasy pamphlet, for introducing him to Oscar Mellor and the publication of *Fighting Terms*, and for alerting him to the Stanford fellowship. Hall thought Thom "not the Best Young Poet, but something considerably better: a poet who will be read for years if you die next week; I mean hundreds of years."[48] Thom valued Hall's poetry but thought his collection *Exiles and Marriages* was too long. He felt a book "should be as cut-down and tight as a single poem."[49] He worried that Hall's quality dipped as he became more prolific. Winters put it succinctly in a letter to Thom: "I suspect that he is more interested in being a popular poet than a good one."[50]

Thom had published "Lofty" in *The Paris Review* in 1953, but other early attempts to publish in the United States had failed. During his year at Stanford, he had received rejections from *The Virginia Quarterly Review*, *The Hudson Review*, and *The New Yorker*, all of which made him question what he had achieved since *Fighting Terms*. In April 1955, when he sent a batch of nine poems to *Poetry*, one of the most prestigious literary journals in America, Thom expected another rejection.[51] To his surprise, *Poetry* accepted all nine poems and later awarded him the Levinson Prize. "I am preening myself," he told Tony, "because the previous recipients include Stevens, Hart Crane, Edwin Arlington Robinson, D. Thomas."[52]

When Henry Rago, then acting editor of *Poetry*, wrote to accept Thom's poems, he expressed reservations about the opening of "Lines for a Book":

> I think of all the toughs through history
> And thank heaven they lived, continually.
> I praise the overdogs from Alexander
> To those who would not play with Stephen Spender.[53]

Rago thought the lines about Spender were libelous and asked Thom to cut them.[54] "By all means cut those two lines," Thom replied. "I think it is a bit of a pity they should go, but if you think the reference to Spender is libellous it would be best that they should."[55] When he restored them in *The Sense of Movement*, he was widely criticized for what Kenneth Allott called "an emphasis on will, deliberate choice, toughness, 'Rule and Energy' that seems almost to turn sensitivity into a dirty word." The poem itself was "a fair enough joke at the expense of what is regarded as the aesthete's effeminacy, but it is something more, with a dark T. E. Hulme-ish flavour of action worship as the badge of an élite."[56] Thom later called it "foolish and fascistic in the extreme," but insisted he was not attacking Spender's homosexuality. "I wouldn't have done [that]," he reflected. "I was attacking a kind of namby-pambiness which I don't associate with homosexuality any more than with heterosexuality." It was more a question of "assert[ing] myself as being apart from an older generation."[57]

Thom's breakthrough appearance in *Poetry* convinced him that he could write well in America. In San Antonio, his daily life was busy with teaching but otherwise uneventful. Only correspondence seemed to bring any excitement: there he kept in touch with poetry and, through friends and family, what felt like the outside world. In late 1955, he began to plot a path back to Stanford. He agreed to review Wallace Stevens's *Collected Poems* for *The London Magazine*. Having not warmed to Stevens while at Stanford, Thom felt curiously enthusiastic about the assignment. He approached it as "an attempt to give a reader new to Stevens somewhere to start from," he told Lehmann. "I think this is necessary—I needed some help of this sort myself when I first started reading him."[58] Such systematic reading opened Thom's eyes to Stevens's power. He saw in Stevens's best poems "a statement not of a solution nor of the simple predicament but of his *awareness* of this predicament without solution." Thom himself specialized in predicaments without solutions—"The Secret Sharer," "The Allegory of the Wolf Boy"—and where he does offer one, in poems like "On the Move," it is by "not keeping still": the search for value in a valueless world was itself a serious and worthwhile pursuit. Thom recognized something similar in Stevens—

he thought *Harmonium* was "committed to a subject—the search for value"[59]—and finding a new poetic ally renewed his own strength and commitment to that value.[60]

Thom's sudden enthusiasm for Stevens gave him an idea. He wrote to Yvor Winters proposing a return to Stanford: he would write a doctoral thesis on Stevens under Winters's supervision. This would free him from the "hell" of San Antonio, create an intellectual atmosphere more conducive to writing poems, and develop options for him and Mike to stay together. His decision, he told Winters, was "not only because it would be good for me, but because it will be necessary if I want to teach in America, which is what I think I want to do."[61] This was "a big reversal from my previous attitude," Thom told Tony. "But teaching is about the only job I could do which would give me the leisure for writing . . . and the university atmosphere in America—at least at Stanford—is not so sterile as that in Cambridge."[62] Thom felt he needed America, California specifically, to write. "I feel I'd never stop writing if I lived on the West coast," he told Hall, while "in England I'd gutter at thirty and extinguish at 40."[63]

After Harcourt, Brace & Co. expressed interest in seeing his recent work, Thom began to think more seriously about assembling a new collection. He heard from Hall that Pegasus Publications, an imprint of *The Harvard Advocate* that had published Hall's *To the Loud Wind*, was interested in publishing a booklet of his poems. The thought excited him, but no sooner had he collected around twenty poems—some from *Fighting Terms*, some new—under the title "The Sense of Movement," than Hall wrote again with bad news: Pegasus had folded.[64] Frustrated, Thom sent twenty-three new poems to Oscar Mellor at Fantasy—who had an option on his second collection—as *The Sense of Movement*.

This was reluctantly done. Thom thought Mellor had "mildly swindled" him over *Fighting Terms*: he did not receive any royalties from the book, and their agreement included a 50 percent fee for poems published in journals.[65] Mellor did not acknowledge receipt, and after three months of silence Thom sent him an angry letter. "But you really are very annoying—I have written to you quite a few times in the last 18 months," he wrote, "asking about copies of *Fighting Terms*, reviews, accounts, and now this, and only had one answer—and that was a year ago."[66] Mellor replied, saying Fantasy was in danger of collapsing. Thom, "ashamed" at having written so irritably, told Mellor to keep the "little money" *Fighting Terms* had made "as a present from me. If it helps to lighten any of your difficulties, I shall be glad."[67] In return, Mellor released Thom from his obligation.[68]

After another rejection, this time from Macmillan, Thom must have thought *The Sense of Movement* was cursed.[69] When Macmillan returned the manuscript, Thom, "acting like a Bronte sister," sent it to Faber and Faber by the next post and enclosed a check for five shillings for its return, should they refuse it.[70] Charles Monteith, a commissioning editor at Faber, wrote to Thom within six weeks promising to publish *The Sense of Movement* in 1957. "Mr Eliot has asked me to send you his own personal congratulations on the poems," Monteith wrote, "and to say how much he has enjoyed reading them."[71] "I must be slipping," Thom told Tony, but secretly he was delighted.[72]

More good news followed. Stanford awarded Thom a fellowship and a half-time teaching position. Moreover, Mike would also be going to Stanford: he was awarded a fellowship to pursue graduate work in the speech and drama department. "So the happy Kameradschaft will not be broken up," Thom told Lehmann.[73] He sounded flippant, but that spring a crisis had developed that threatened their future: the air force investigated Mike for alleged homosexual activity. "They told me I had been charged with having homosexual activity with this young man who had been in the army. He was in my class at Trinity," Mike recalled. "I could tell he was interested in me, but I wasn't interested in him in any way." To his "amazement," Mike was allowed to telephone Thom and instructed him to get rid of anything incriminating at their apartment. Thom disposed of some letters from an actor friend of Mike's at Rutgers who addressed Mike as "darling."[74]

At the start of the investigation, Mike was interviewed for two hours a day. Then it was Thom's turn. "I said a magnificently cunning and duplicitous thing," he recalled. "I said, 'I'm absolutely certain that Mike could not be homosexual, because I've lived with him so long if anyone knew about this I would.' It was a complicated deceit within deceit." It was "an arduous time," Thom reflected, and the air force "really wanted to get Mike" and "did try everything they could" including "getting some poor privates that were frightened out of their minds, that came up with the most extraordinary lies about him. Like they'd been to our apartment and had sex with us and there was pornography all over the walls."[75] Mike risked a court-martial, Thom possible deportation. "Thom was paranoid," Mike recalled, "because of how he got into the country, and the passport, and being kicked out. It was a very trying time."[76]

Mike had a "genius for organisation," Thom reflected, "organising witnesses, anticipating questions."[77] He was asked about the inscription "Baby, read this and return" on a letter he had forwarded to Thom at Stanford. Mike said "Baby" referred to his English girlfriend. Thom wrote immediately to their Cambridge friend Sasha Moorsom, via Tony, asking if she would act as Mike's alibi. "If they approach her, she would say . . . she read [the letter], but remembers nothing about it except that she returned it to Mike" and that "Neither Mike nor I are homosexuals."[78] Sasha was not called upon, but Thom thanked her anyway:

> Mike (and I too) sends his eternal gratitude for your help in L'affaire Kitay. It is still on, and the complications would fill a book. However, you have not been brought up, and the next stage (we hope, anyway) is the judgement itself—however that will turn.[79]

The investigation dragged on for weeks. "It was like waiting for the trapdoor to open, or the guillotine to come down on me," Mike reflected.[80] He spoke to "a sympathetic colonel" who promised to "bring it to a conclusion" before his imminent discharge. Thom felt confident enough to tell Tony that "it seems probably everything will go well, from lack of evidence," but they faced a nervous wait.[81]

12

LEATHER

Mike's discharge date passed, without any action having been taken against him. He and Thom set out on their planned summer tour: after visiting New Orleans, they would head up the East Coast to New Jersey, where Mike would see his parents, and New York, where Thom would renew his visa. It was "an enjoyable and eventful trip": Mike crashed his Oldsmobile in Opelousas and was arrested for dangerous driving. Thom had to bribe an "amiably corrupt" sheriff to avoid one hundred dollars' bail. In New Orleans, waiting for the car to be mended, they were arrested again, this time for loitering on Bourbon Street, and would have spent the night in prison if Thom "hadn't luckily happened to have had the unused bail from the previous day to use as bail for this."[1] Winters had warned him about the South. "Beware of rattlesnakes, copperheads, cottonmouths, alligators, Mississippi dogfish, bad liquor, and characters out of Faulkner," he told Thom. "Beware also tellers of tall tales. Do not allow your speech to be corrupted, no matter what strange predicament you may encounter."[2]

In New York, Thom stayed at the William Sloane House YMCA, a fourteen-hundred-room residential hotel on West Thirty-fourth Street. He fell for the city "in a big way," so much so that "San Francisco seems a let down after New York."[3] He made "various interesting inconclusive experiments with the more extreme evidences of perversion,"[4] and explored the city's leather bars—notably the Lodge, on Third Avenue between East Fifty-third and Fifty-fourth Streets. He bought his first black leather jacket. "I'm not sure what it meant to me," he reflected. "I thought I was the only pervert in the world."[5] The visit likely inspired "The Beaters," a poem about sadomasochism:

> And what appear the dandy's affectation
> —The swastika-draped bed, or links that press
> In twined and gleaming weight beneath a shirt—
> Are emblems to recall identity.[6]

Although Thom later rejected "The Beaters" as "an early and bombastic poem" in which he was "childishly trying to shock," at the time it was a serious attempt to examine his own thoughts and feelings about sado-masochism.[7] It was "an examination of sadism as a personal perversion," he told Conquest, "i.e. the romantic Nazism, the set of fetishes."[8] This New York sparked "mixed feelings" about "homosexuality, leather, s&m. [. . .] DH L[awrence] believes in the sexual self as a consistent part of the whole self. But I can't."[9]

In Kearny, Mike's mother, Dora, was taken ill—"psychosomatically," Thom thought[10]—and Mike had to stay behind: he cut the autumn quarter and did not enroll at Stanford until January 1957. "When I came home and said I was going to Stanford, my parents freaked," Mike re-called. "My father said why didn't I go to Yale? A good question. But Thom was in Stanford, and I wanted to be gay with Thom. So I wanted distance."[11] Thom spent his first months back at Stanford in his old room on Lincoln Avenue. He attended Winters's poetry seminar: he was one of "the three best people in the group," Winters thought, alongside Ellen Kay and Alan Stephens.[12] To his surprise, Thom found he was much better at teaching than graduate work. "I am beginning to feel that my days as a student should have been over long ago," he told his great-aunt Alice. "Working for a doctorate is only an excuse for staying in America, anyway."[13] With the autumn quarter barely underway, Thom began to have "long self-questionings" about "what I'm doing here and why I'm doing it." He told Tony he would fulfill his teaching obligations, but that "next summer will be the occasion for a big Choice: continuing to teach or becoming a postman."[14]

Between teaching and study—a workload that rivaled San Antonio—Thom surprised himself that autumn by "writing furiously, many hours a day—in a way I haven't done for about 18 months." He experimented with new forms, from syllabics ("Vox Humana") and canzone ("The Beaters") to terza rima ("The Annihilation of Nothing"), although beside Stevens's "The Snow Man" Thom felt "like dead wood."[15] By Christmas, however, he asked Monteith whether it was not too late to expand *The Sense of Movement*.[16] Monteith consented, and Thom took considerable care incorporating new poems and rearranging them, grouping them by theme or idea, with one group developing or expanding on another. The center of *The Sense of Movement* comprises four poems: "Market at Turk," "In Praise of Cities," "The Allegory of the Wolf Boy," and "The Beaters." First, the hustler "gestates action" on the street corner; second, the Baudelairean city contains all lives and possibilities; third, the "sad duplicity" of living a secret life; fourth, the thrill of meeting like-minded people, "careful still to break their loneliness / Only for one who, perfect counterpart, / Welcomes the tools of their perversity, / Whip, cords, and strap."[17] Using existential vocabulary like "will," "choice," and "action," these poems constitute a disguised coming-of-age story, drawn from Thom's experiences in New York and San Francisco.[18] "Being in the closet," he later remarked, "I saw being homosexual as a deliberate choice. [. . .] It's got nothing to do with choice or the will, but I was being defiant about it."[19]

When Mike arrived at Christmas, he and Thom moved to a small apartment on Alma Street "with all the modern conveniences except a cat."[20] They shared a lawn with neighboring apartments and, with no bedroom, pulled down a Murphy bed from the living room wall. Behind their apartment was El Palo Alto Park, with its hilly trail along San Francisquito Creek. Early on at Stanford, Mike directed the first act of John

Whiting's *Marching Song*. As the curtain rises, the characters are watching the end of a movie: the audience sees it, too, so Mike needed a minute or so of silent film. "Luckily, I had an agreeable cast of one: Thom. He asked me what he should do," Mike recalled. "I was distracted, trying to figure out how to use the borrowed camera. 'I don't know. Whatever you feel like. Go crazy.' Who knew he'd take direction so well? He ran down the ravine behind Alma Street, where we lived, pretending he was being chased, tearing off his shirt and waving it over his head and laughing that laugh." Thom was apt to "clown around" at home, doing "his Vincent Price limp; his Instant Face Lift; make one of *many* rude sounds," or using his "awesome energy" to do his "kind of tap dance with a big finish."[21] "[Mike] and I gradually civilise each other," Thom told Tony, "but sometimes I get the feeling we're neither of us fit for the company of others just yet. Very unstable young men."[22]

Despite early success with *Marching Song*, Mike did not find the Stanford program a good fit for his directorial ambitions. The speech and drama department focused on acting, and graduate seminars on playwriting and the theory of stage art and techniques[23] gave Mike little opportunity to hone his directorial skills. In consultation with his director of studies, Mike decided to leave Stanford in the summer and try to find work in Los Angeles. Wanting to help, Thom introduced him to Isherwood, who invited them to a party with Aldous and Laura Huxley, and Janet Gaynor and her husband, the celebrated costume designer Adrian.[24]

With Mike in Southern California, Thom spent the summer in England to renew his visa. He had spent three years away and he returned, according to Ander, with "a very fine American accent."[25] His first week in London was "really nightmarish"—everything felt familiar and constricting—and to escape he slept a lot and saw American movies every afternoon. He desperately wanted to see Tony—"the great man of my life (friend only) next to Mike"[26]—but Tony was in Ireland for much of the summer and missed all but a few days of Thom's visit. Thom had "secretly" expected his return would be "rather marvellous . . . returning in triumph to the ways of my youth," he told Hall, but was confounded by a "complicated dislike of England" with which he seemed to "associate the unsatisfactory side of myself."[27] Visiting Mary and Catherine in Snodland, he looked out the train window "with the eyes of ten years ago, the self I thought I had ceased to be is back, naked, ignorant, stupid as a dinosaur / primitive man to whom all things can hurt."[28] Self-reflection was "neurotic-making," as was the disconnect between his self-image and how friends and family treated him.[29] "Too many people [were] expecting me to be something they had decided I was at 17 or 21 or 24," he told Tony. "And I couldn't be bothered to try to show them I wasn't that any longer."[30]

Thom arrived in England shortly after *The Sense of Movement* was published. In a short piece for the *Poetry Book Society Bulletin*, he wrote that the book was about "a specifically contemporary" kind of "malaise," the attempt "to understand one's deliberate aimlessness, having the courage of one's lack of convictions, reaching a purpose only by making the right rejections."[31] This was "_the_ big subject," he told Hall, and was "at its nakedest in America" with "the wild one, the J. Dean cult, Elvis."[32] An existential spirit underpinned these modern images, and is captured in the book's epigraph: "Je le suis, je veux l'être" ("I am that, I choose to be that").[33] Moreover, in his poems Thom wanted to "convey an experience [and] try to understand it," an approach modeled on Baudelaire, who "combined the two as a single process as well as any writer I know."[34] Combined with Winters's influence on both style and form, Thom found *The Sense of Movement* "much more sophisticated" but "much less independent" than *Fighting Terms*, and thought it "a second work of apprenticeship."[35]

Reviews were broadly positive. Conquest thought Thom had "something of Yeats's power and technique" and argued he was already "a major poet."[36] Frank Kermode called the book "*serious* and *important*" and Thom "an enormously gifted young man."[37] He was praised for energy and vigor but criticized for butchness and violence: one reviewer complained that the choice of "James Dean-like heroes, of Motor-cycles, of

Elvis Presley as a vehicle for metaphysical speculation does not help."[38] Most criticism manifested itself in puzzlement: serious engagement and judgment were postponed until Thom's next book. His "newness of vision has still to be tested by time," hedged one;[39] "the next book may make the poet's own direction clearer," stalled another.[40] Graham Hough thought Thom lacked "an assured poetic personality" but was "in process of making one."[41] Such tentative assessments persisted throughout Thom's life. A restlessness of style and theme, a desire to experiment, and a growing insistence on contemporary (American) culture as a viable, necessary source for poetry meant that Thom's changes of direction were taken not as signs of an exercising intelligence but as departures from the rich potential and excitement of *Fighting Terms*.[42] With the book published, Thom had an "awful final feeling that a phase is over" and that he had to find "a new set of subjects or at least a new way of looking at them, that I can't risk self-repetition."[43] England did not help his mood: he could not wait to return to Stanford.

Mike returned from Los Angeles without work but quickly found employment in Palo Alto. A former Stanford classmate, Peter Kump, formed the Comedia Repertory Company and hired Mike as a director. From humble beginnings, Comedia became one of the most important small companies on the Peninsula. Through 1957 and 1958, Mike directed *The Chalk Garden*, *The Mousetrap*, *An Italian Straw Hat*, *No Exit*, and *Separate Tables*. "Comedia is making serious drama, performed with near-professional competence," wrote *The Stanford Daily*.[44] Thom thought it "a good job" with "a large and important amateur group," and Mike developed a reputation as a highly intelligent and sensitive director. "He's being most successful, anyway," Thom told Lehmann, "and we're hoping it may lead—eventually, somehow—to a job in New York."[45]

Between productions, Thom and Mike began to spend promiscuous weekends in San Francisco. "We'd married at such a young age and we were our first partners, in a way," Mike reflected. "We'd never experienced other people, so it had its attractions for me." Heading back to

Palo Alto, they would stop for hamburgers at Mel's Drive-In and swap stories. "Thom was always much luckier than I was," Mike mused. "Thom would go and no matter what he'd come home with somebody."[46] But the novelty quickly wore off; nor was Mike comfortable "with the whole motorcycle image thing."[47] "I didn't particularly like it when Thom would suddenly meet someone in leather and [the attraction] was immediate," he reflected, "just because they were dressed in those clothes."[48]

Before the city's first leather bar opened—the Why Not? on Ellis—in 1960, San Francisco leathermen patronized the Spur and the Hideaway, both in the Tenderloin. The Spur "was rather awful but it was all we had," Thom reflected. He much preferred Jack's on the Waterfront—"a leather bar by the standards of the time"—which was a good Sunday afternoon haunt for "poppers, which was very advanced drug use for those days. That was all we knew."[49] Leather was part of an outlaw sexuality, and Thom cultivated its tough, masculine image. Photographs taken in New York in 1956 show him standing wide-legged in a leather jacket, Levi's, and a Harley cap (plate 12). Though his face was craggy and pockmarked, he was also tall and skinny—butch in costume only. "Thom was enamored of the subversive aura of the clubs and the whole idea of breaking sexual taboos, even if he himself wasn't necessarily breaking them," recalled one fuckbuddy. "Thom's principal (and perhaps only) physical fetish was, as far as I could tell, leather itself. Wearing it, touching it, using it."[50]

That autumn, Thom wrote another leather poem after reading a news article about three motorcyclists who had died in high-speed races in Angels Camp, California. One "was a member of Hell's Angels and had the group's name tattooed on his right shoulder," reported the *San Francisco Chronicle*. "On his other shoulder were tattooed the words, 'Born to Lose.'"[51] Thom included this expression in "Black Jackets," in which the boy wears "loss" "to assert, with fierce devotion, / Complicity and nothing more."[52] At first, "loss" appears to undercut the otherwise concrete imagery of "Black Jackets"—creaking leather and "cycle boots"—but for Thom, "loss" was something he had lived with for more than a decade. Like his adoption of the Sartrean will in *The Sense of Movement*, which allowed him to treat queerness as a defiant choice, the idea that loss could be mastered or controlled gave him reassurance. There were two major losses: his mother, and the queer self he hid behind leather jacket or wolf-skin. This restless exploration of an idea characterizes Thom's first three books: ideas like loss, choice, risk, energy, and the will are explored in depth and at length, and do not mean the same thing at the end of *My Sad Captains*, published in 1961, as they did at the start of *Fighting Terms*.

In the late 1950s, Thom felt life impinge more and more on his art. "One of <u>my</u> problems is how to get the important sexual business into poetry," he told Lehmann. "I mean one can't write of motorcycles and hoodlums etc <u>all</u> the time, and there are other problems in dealing with the actual mechanics of sex. It isn't that I don't dare, but that I don't have the technique yet, I think." Ideally, he wanted to combine the "rational-statement poem" of Stevens, Robinson, and Hardy with the "near-sexual energy" of Crane or Dylan Thomas.[53] This would "<u>include</u> more than the Stanford style permits." Moreover, he wanted to write about "cities; perversion; the exhilaration after sex; delinquency" but felt he risked repetition if he did not replace "motorcycles and hoodlums" as his symbols for sex. Thom planned a "Book of the City" in which the city represented "choice" and "the moment of unrest" and felt that, while he still took Baudelaire as his "guide," "Tate, Auden, Crane, Pound can help, if one is careful with them."[54]

Crane helped the most. Thom began reading his letters and saw "rather frightening" resemblances between them. "I don't mean just queerness," he told Tony. "Queerness is not a disease, but the way society looks on it is liable to cause reactions in one that are, at least, destructive. The lack of rest can become an inability to stay in one place, to keep up one pursuit, to think about one subject." Those latter two reactions, Thom thought, "caused Crane to practically stop writing after the age of 30 . . . which, I take it, was the main reason he killed himself."[55] Thom copied extracts of Crane's letters into his notebook, notably his description of the city as "a place of 'brokenness,' of drama."[56]

Thom drew on this "brokenness" in the concluding lines of "A Map of the City": "Endless potentiality, / The crowded, broken, and un-finished! / I would not have the risk diminished." The key lines of the poem, though, are: "I watch a malady's advance, / I recognize my love of chance."[57] "The 'malady' is perversion of course—in heterosexual parlance," he told Tony, "but in the terms of the poem it is 'love of chance.'"[58] By "perversion," Thom meant leather, sadomasochism, and promiscuity, not simple homosexuality. He felt he wrote about "two themes, always: the extreme—the despair—the man who refuses to admit the malady, & dies fighting it. The man who makes terms with the malady." Thom credited Crane with "helping me towards the 3rd style," shown in "A Map of the City," by which he means technique as well as subject: "meaning must be more of an implicitness between words."[59] Emphasizing this, Thom could be suggestive but indirect, trying to "make terms" with the malady and reclaim some of his lost selfhood. "The malady of queerness," he reflected, "is only part of the malady of living more clearly concentrated, focussed, as it were."[60]

Thom's continued indirectness was the result of his decision—in fact never realized[61]—to become an American citizen, "quite as much to dissociate myself from England as to associate myself with America."[62] He later called his writing "a certain stage in my coping with the world," but at this stage, were he to have written about his life directly, he would have risked deportation.[63] This raised a moral issue for Thom, who valued straightforwardness and honesty. "I can't come out into the open till I get my citizenship," he told Hall, "and it's 4½ years till I can apply for that."[64] He laughed off his frustration at being unable to write openly. Once he became an American citizen "and thus unextraditable," he told Hall, "there will be my life work, published by the Obelisk Press but deserving better—an anatomy of homosexuality."[65]

Before he could apply for citizenship, Thom had to find a way to stay in America. By November 1957 he had decided to leave Stanford. "I can't stand working for a doctorate down here in such poverty," he told Lehmann. "I earn less than the dole, believe it or not—2 dollars less a month!"[66] Moreover, he was thoroughly bored by Palo Alto. "My longing to live in a city again gets greater and greater all the time," he told Tony.

"I go up [to San Francisco] on a spree every now and again . . . but knowing I'm there only for the day makes me set too much store by it, I try to cram in too much, I exaggerate the pace."[67]

A chance gift brought him a new opportunity. Earlier in the year, Thom had given a reading at the University of California, Berkeley, at the invitation of the poet and professor Thomas Parkinson. He stayed overnight with Parkinson: thanking him for his hospitality, Thom promised to send him a copy of *The Sense of Movement*. Parkinson thought the book brilliant and lent it to his Berkeley colleague the poet Josephine Miles. She admired it "immensely" and asked Thom whether he would be interested in teaching at Berkeley.[68] "This is strictly off the cuff and my own idea," she told him, "just to see what you'd feel about it."[69]

Thom responded to Miles's offer "with enthusiasm" and felt he had two options: "teaching full time on a good salary at Berkeley" or "a job, any job, in San Francisco."[70] He talked himself into going to Berkeley because it was "a good university," the salary was "princely," and "best of all [it] is only a few miles across the bay from San Francisco."[71] Thom was offered a one-year contract as an acting instructor with a salary of almost five thousand dollars. "I cannot refuse so much money," he told Hall, "though full-time teaching will be bad for my writing (it was before)."[72] Anxious to avoid a repeat of his burnout in San Antonio, Thom determined to leave Berkeley when his yearlong contract ended: he hoped to have saved enough money to support himself for six months, during which he would write solidly.

Come summer, and having finished up at Stanford, Thom could not "work on a <u>line</u> without getting restless" and resolved to stop writing until he felt "something really jogging my elbow." He spent June in New York, another "revelatory" visit, seeing plays and patronizing Third Avenue leather bars. "I learn more about people and myself in NY than anywhere else," he told Tony. The visit intensified Thom's self-questioning about whether he saw his working life—outside poetry—tied to universities. While in New York he was "offered a job in a tough-<u>queer</u> bar" and would have taken it if he "hadn't already signed this damn contract" with Berkeley.[73] He had "3/4 decided to give up universities," he told Lehmann, and "drag Mike along" to New York where Mike could achieve "enormous success" as a director. Thom was "no longer interested in educating people—if I ever was—and the process of doing it takes up too much mental energy."[74]

Thom and Mike had lived together for three years. At first, he found that "living with Mike is equivalent in most ways to actually being married," he told Tony in summer 1956. "We are really pretty happy together, and we both intend it to be for good. But doing this—living with someone, or marrying—is the most crippling choice." Thom found that living alone gave him "absolute freedom, an enormous independence, the power to change oneself constantly," whereas a "chief value" of living together was "the power to completely know, almost to be, someone else." He wanted them to be "completely individual and still have the other thing as well."[75]

Now, they faced a choice. Staying in Palo Alto would mean a draining commute for Thom, whereas moving to Berkeley would mean the same for Mike, who worked around the clock for Comedia. "We're mostly happy, really, though the devil in various forms gets into us at times," Thom told Lehmann. "I hope the devils will never get strong enough to split us. In certain circumstances I would conceivably be capable of bringing that about—not from lack of love but from self-love."[76] Uncertainty about jobs and living arrangements was a source of continual tension. Mike decided to stay in Palo Alto and Thom moved to Oakland, a "shabby transit town" far enough away to "avoid the highly-charged self-conscious atmosphere of Berkeley itself."[77] Reflecting on this decision later, Thom thought there was "an air of decay about our love."[78]

Greater proximity to San Francisco meant Thom would find promiscuous sprees easier to come by. "I said to Thom once, 'You'd do anything for a trick,'" Mike recalled. "And I wasn't wrong." He later dated their effective sexual separation to Thom's last year at Stanford. "We slept in the same bed—we always slept in the same bed for many, many, many years," he reflected. "But we weren't sexual with each other."[79] For Thom, the city meant sex: he hoped a new poetry would follow.

13

BERKELEY

Thom's "enormously dirty" apartment in Oakland was just what he wanted. His building was half "old, genteel leddies," half "old, tattooed laborers" and stood almost at the foot of Telegraph Avenue, then the main thoroughfare through Oakland and into Berkeley. "Motorcycles hurtle past my window all day," he told Ander, "and I do little besides watch them."[1] Thom could walk up Telegraph to campus in about an hour. Its northernmost blocks, from Sather Gate to Dwight Way, contained the Berkeley life Thom hoped to avoid: "coffee shops full of boys in grotesquely thick sweaters and girls in black stockings, all dropping names like Kierkegaard." He much preferred Oakland's "shabbiness and impermanence."[2]

The Department of English had quarters in Dwinelle Hall, a sprawling, multilevel labyrinth of classrooms and offices. Henry Nash Smith, whom Thom affectionately called Henry Smash, was department chairman and, while "very bright and intelligent," seemed "completely mystified by all that goes on."[3] Vice chairman Ian Watt, Thom's "self-appointed protector,"[4] taught him to "ALWAYS keep your office door open" during student meetings.[5] Thom already knew Josephine Miles and Thomas Parkinson; he gravitated toward the affable Mark Schorer, a scholar of Blake and Lawrence; the medievalist Charles Muscatine; James D. Hart, who was born in San Francisco and specialized in the literature of the American West; and Ralph Rader, a year younger than Thom and another recent hire, whose interests ranged from Gray and Tennyson to the theory of the novel. It was a stimulating intellectual environment, and the department welcomed numerous visiting professors and scholars. Thom was most amused when Stephen Spender arrived as a visiting professor in the spring semester.[6] Spender "acted very nervously, as if I'd offered to knock him down," Thom told Tony. "I flattered myself that this was because of my reputation as a Tough, and because of my Restoration-like lampoons on him but noticed afterwards that this was his manner with everybody,"[7] though Spender must have read "Lines for a Book," to which Thom had restored the offending lines when *The Sense of Movement* was published in 1957.

In both fall and spring semesters, Thom taught freshman Reading and Composition, and the sophomore survey English Literature from Chaucer to T. S. Eliot. In fall he also taught an upper-division, invitation-only seminar in verse composition. This was a typically heavy load for an acting instructor, but Thom approached it in a valedictory spirit, believing it would be his final year of full-time teaching. While "stultifying," Thom thought teaching likely provided "far more leisure . . . than in most jobs."[8] His resolve to leave was quickly tested when he learned, "unofficially, that if all goes well I could stay on at Berkeley indefinitely" and gain tenure. "But I am only 29!" he told Tony. "What I mean is, do I want to stay here, in the same job, in the same area, all my life?" He felt "being in a new place, and new circumstances" was necessary for his writing, and that a life at Berkeley would reduce his poetic output "to three pieces of Horatian verse a year—or, since I have a conscience, perhaps to nothing." Writing was so "precarious," he thought, "that I feel whatever I do will be the wrong thing."[9]

Thom and Tony were in similar positions. Tony's promising acting career had stalled. He had grown so tired of the phoniness of the theater world that he refused to perform on the Old Vic's 1956 American tour and subsequently quit the company. He took on various jobs in order to support himself as a writer, including a stint as a lamplighter in London's East End.[10] Some of Tony's Cambridge friends saw him as "a Romantic hero in the making . . . doing what no one else dared," whereas Thom saw the anxiety beneath the pose.[11] One letter from Thom enormously cheered Tony, who was "going through one of those lapses of vitality when you are convinced you have made an utter balls-up of your life and there is no retreat."[12] Thom tried hard to change Tony's mind about acting, but his two-year campaign by correspondence left Tony unmoved. "An actor is by definition an interpreter," he told Thom, "and nothing is ever his own creation. [. . .] You are not using the material; you are the material."[13] In early 1959, Tony decided to spend six months lobster fishing in Ireland, earning some money and using his free time to write. But in a more fundamental sense, he was lost.[14] "I wish I could see some way of reconciling the worlds of idea and action," he told Thom, "which I suppose I've always been trying, and failing, to do. The hopes seem remoter than ever."[15]

Tony remained "a major hero" of Thom's poetry. After stints as a lamplighter and a lobster fisherman, he was variously a translator, bricklayer, and delivery driver.[16] Tony "dropped out, coolly and deliberately," Thom later wrote, "from the life of applause."[17] As Tony changed, Thom's conception of heroism changed. His heroic figures grew more nuanced and humane, no longer drawn from classical mythology, or even contemporary counterculture, but from ordinary, vulnerable people on the street. This change began with "In Santa Maria del Popolo," which Thom drafted in early 1958 and which is based on his time in Rome four years earlier. The speaker enters the Cerasi Chapel and sees Caravaggio's large oil painting of St. Paul's *Conversion on the Way to Damascus* (1601). In the painting, Saul lies on the ground, eyes closed, arms raised upward. "O wily painter," Thom asks, "what is it you mean / In that wide gesture of the lifting arms?" The poem concludes when the speaker turns away from the painting,

> To the dim interior of the church instead,
> In which there kneel already several people,
> Mostly old women: each head closeted
> In tiny fists holds comfort as it can.
> Their poor arms are too tired for more than this

—For the large gesture of solitary man,
Resisting, by embracing, nothingness.[18]

Before this moment, tired old women would not have appeared in a Gunn poem. The painterly depiction of "the large gesture of solitary man" seems to lose its meaning, set against the weary defiance of "tiny fists" that the speaker witnesses for himself in the dark church. The sympathetic conclusion signals Thom's change in attitude toward the heroic: the Shakespearean-Corneillean pose was out.

At the same time as "In Santa Maria," Thom drafted a poem addressed to Tony. Using the working title "Loot,"[19] he tried to articulate their theory of poetry as a "reaching out in the unexplained areas of the mind" to find "loot" that was "of value as an understanding or as a talisman, or more likely a combination of the two, of both rational power and irrational."[20] For Thom, Tony was model, teacher, co-conspirator. "But remember you started my education," he wrote in notes for the poem, "taught me the Virtues: Magnanimity, an Energy, generous & disinterested and discipline[d]."[21] In the poem, Tony is not presented as a typically heroic figure: he hunts a pig, "mind[s] an Irish pond," and spends evenings reading. Thom's point was that "one hoards the record of constant practice" so that it is "always at hand the / Loot of conduct."[22]

The poem was a failure—Thom wrestled with it for two years before he abandoned it for good—but the process was useful. From it, he realized that one's conduct, *how* one acts, was more important than action itself. He found it "the only positive left in a world without God (human relationships are subsidiary to it—or rather, rightly, it forms the relationship itself)." He decided his next book would be "an examination of Conduct."[23] In his review of *The Sense of Movement*, A. Alvarez saw Thom "writing about choice," whereas he found that the "tenseness" of *Fighting Terms* came from "a man actually in doubt."[24] This hung around in Thom's mind for six months. He asked himself what comes after "doubt" and "choice" and discovered that "conduct" was "the direction in which I ought to go."[25]

Thom doubted he would "ever be able to do anything adequate" about conduct, but soon found a model for his idea.[26] Tony sent him a copy of *The Shirt of Nessus*, Constantine FitzGibbon's account of the botched attempt to assassinate Hitler in 1944. Claus von Stauffenberg, who brought the briefcase bomb into the conference room at Hitler's "Wolf's Lair" military headquarters, was executed for his role in the plot. Von Stauffenberg became Thom's "hero,"[27] and he thought him "the perfect subject . . . for a modern tragedy—the great noble figure (no Willy Loman), magnanimous, the courage, the plot, even perhaps hubris— having favored the unknown of Nazism in the first place as being preferable to the known evils of Communism & the W. Republic."[28] In his poem "Claus von Stauffenberg," Thom felt he had "come near" to what he wanted to achieve: "a poem statue-like without being frigid (like a Cornelian hero). Something composed and powerful."[29]

Moreover, Stauffenberg came close to reconciling what Thom and Tony called "the worlds of idea and action." "I have no comfort for you," Thom told Tony: "it is bad to compromise, it is bad to fail, it is bad not to attempt their reconciliation. At least one mustn't give up. The most one can hope for is a few short periods when they appear to be reconciled, and also for a bit of knowledge about them as one goes along."[30] One of those "short periods" appears in Thom's poem, when Stauffenberg "fails, honour personified, / In a cold time where honour cannot grow."[31] By early 1958, Thom was moving away from the "splendid egotism" of Sartrean heroes and coming instead to "value much more somebody who gets involved with people and gets rid of his egotism"[32]—people like Claus von Stauffenberg, people like Tony White.

So far, Thom's American reputation rested on two suites of poems published in *Poetry*. The first won him the Levinson Prize in 1955; the second, in October 1958, coincided with his first American book, a revised edition of *Fighting Terms* published by Jerome Rothenberg's Hawk's Well Press. Thom had wanted to revise the book ever since it was published in England four years earlier—"Too much of what I meant to be energy

and complexity is just posture"[33]—but, in making the poems more metrically perfect, he removed much of their jauntiness and edge. Alvarez
still called it "the most impressive first book of poems since Robert Lowell's,"[34] but when Faber published its own edition in 1962, Thom mostly
restored the text of the Fantasy edition.

In April 1959, the University of Chicago Press published *The Sense
of Movement* and brought Thom to a broader American audience than
had the small-press edition of *Fighting Terms*. He was thrilled to have a
major American publisher but was less thrilled with the book's critical
reception. In *Poetry*, John Thompson called him "intelligent, ingenious,
and formally capable within the limits that would be expected, say, in
Advanced Verse Writing."[35] A year later, in the *Sewanee Review*, James
Dickey remarked he had "seldom read a duller book than *The Sense of
Movement*" and had "nightmares thinking of the energy and the good
intentions that went into it."[36] Thom tried to shrug them off, but the
reviews stung at a time when he was not writing well. After finishing
"Claus von Stauffenberg" in summer 1958, Thom wrote sporadically for
the next two years, revising poems like "A Map of the City" and "The
Book of the Dead" and finishing "The Monster" and two poems called
"Modes of Pleasure." Through 1959 Thom felt he had "perfectly good
ideas for poems" but not the energy to work on them.[37] "I may be better
than anybody else in England but Larkin and Ted Hughes, but that isn't
particularly good," he told Tony. "I want to be better than Rimbaud &
Baudelaire & Donne and unfortunately do not look likely to be. Too
mousy, alas."[38]

Like their British counterparts, American reviewers struggled to
know what to make of him. "Do you know that reviewers have accused
me of being 'influenced' by Auden, Graves, Empson, Winters, Stevens,
'the American metaphysicals of the Forties' (whoever they are), the Beat
Generation, Edwin Muir, and several others I forget," he told Hall. "I
wonder how many of these names cancel each other out."[39] Comparisons
with the Beat Generation amused him most. "I'm not <u>really</u> beat anymore than Ginsberg is," he told Hall, "but at least I don't claim to be it. I

just take beatness as a subject, sometimes, just as anyone does."[40] He disliked the Beats' inflated reputations and what he considered to be technical shortcomings. Free verse, he thought, was "a valid and difficult form" and "in an odd way very restrictive as to tone—but it is <u>not</u> incantatory prose." "Howl" he felt "(apart from being nonsense) is a mere catalogue, as bad as Whitman (who is always bad, anyway)."[41] "They are not worth taking seriously for a moment," he told Conquest. "I mean, their like has occurred so often before that they are old-fashioned."[42]

Despite his lukewarm American reception, Thom's star was on the rise in England. In 1959 *The Sense of Movement* won the Somerset Maugham Award, a prize given to young writers to fund foreign travel. "Eliot adds his own warmest personal congratulations," telegrammed Monteith.[43] Press coverage of the award made Thom shudder at his English reputation. One article claimed he lived in Mexico, that his relaxations were "motorcycles and weight-lifting," and that he was "building up a legend of himself as the Marlon Brando of English letters."[44] "I am assumed to be a character in one of my poems," he told Karl, now literary editor of *The Spectator*. "I suppose I asked for it, partly, but never thought it would reach the degree it reached in the Mail and Express."[45] But the award came at a good time. Without his verse composition class in the spring, he had "quite a bit of leisure" and was "50–50" about staying on at Berkeley. Winning the award convinced him to stay: with enough money and "excuse to dive off to Mexico or Germany" for a semester, he could be secure and restless at the same time.[46]

Thom spent some of his newfound leisure time in San Francisco. On Thursday nights he went to the "Boot Party" at Castaways, a leather-friendly bar at the top of Market. He invariably wore leather jackets, Levi's, motorcycle boots. "I wear my German belt, by the way, constantly," he told Tony. "It is admired, envied, and despised—but more admired and envied than despised."[47] He "paint[ed] the town my own colour" and "got in good with the local down-and-outs."[48] These adventures provided material for two minor poems: "All-Night Burlesque" and "An Inhabitant." The first, he feared, was an example of how he was "constantly caricaturing himself";[49] the second was so outwardly queer it "will have to await my Opus Postumus for publication."[50] "An Inhabitant" covertly foregrounds cruising, a gay hustler, and is "all accurate in details."[51] "Market at Turk," which deals with similar thematics, is descriptive, whereas the speaker in "An Inhabitant" takes part in the interaction:

> Watching you try to size me up, I pause
> To tease the teaser, but admire meanwhile
> The candour in your assessal of the market
> From the snowy pillars by the Bank: the style
> With which you loaf there planning to break laws.
> [. . .]
> You tilt back with a silent gap-toothed laugh,
> Deciding that I'm equal to you; then,
> That problem over, turn away, resuming
> The appraisal of more profitable men;
> And throwing back a nod and wink pad off.[52]

The hustler is not like the butch, military figure of "Market at Turk" but "bourgeois and good-humoured." The poem turns on the word "equal": the hustler may decide the speaker is another hustler, hence his decision to seek "more profitable men." In a different reading, the poem may resume the code of sadomasochism Thom explored in "The Beaters": "equal" implies that hustler and speaker both perform the same role—likely top, or dominant—and that the hustler seeks a bottom, or submissive. The title alludes to Thom's comment about "Wolf Boy," in that the hustler appears to inhabit, and be enjoying, the kind of life he really wants.

Thom knew these negotiations from San Francisco leather bars. He wrote more successfully about cruising and promiscuity in the two "Modes of Pleasure" poems. They form a diptych about the dangers and rewards of promiscuity, and he later referenced the first, "I jump with terror seeing him," in an argument with Mike about their differing attitudes. "It can be as you say: and result in 'bankruptcy'—and you don't give me credit for having realized this myself," he wrote: "if . . . you had read a poem called Modes of Pleasure a little more carefully you'd see I realized <u>all</u> the <u>bad</u> possibilities of promiscuity when I wrote it in Spring 1959." Thom felt "cleaner after promiscuous sex [than] I do without it," and thought promiscuity "<u>can</u> be positive: i.e. it is adventurous, active, exciting, and energetic."[53] The second poem, "New face, strange face, for my unrest," explores those positive aspects, where "sharing an anticipation / Amounts to a collaboration." This is the "chance" Thom anticipated in "A Map of the City" and the "commotion of bar or bed" alluded to in "Market at Turk."[54] Thom's implicit practice in the late 1950s was to carve out a social space for queer men in the city: this approach, if not disguised then at least coded, allowed him to write poems that were as honest as possible without jeopardizing his residency in the United States.

When Thom moved to Oakland, he and Mike shared "a weekend relationship." Thom thought this "½-assed, to put it mildly,"[55] but he also relished the "enormous freedom" of living alone.[56] Within months, however, Mike quit Comedia and left for New York, "either for a couple of months, for a year or two, or for ever," Thom told Tony, hoping to prove himself as a good director. "If he can't stick it, he'll come back here; if things go well with him, I'll join him there." Their plans, "as hazy as ever,"[57] changed once again when members of Comedia staged a mutiny against its "stupid producer," Peter Kump, "who was inefficient, had managed to lose $7,000, and was a cynical-sentimental piece of shit."[58] The rebels resigned and invited Mike to return from New York to form a new group. With financial backing from Mike's friend Sheilah Dorcy, they formed Phoenix and put together a musical revue called *Six Appeal*. Directed, initially, by Glenn Jordan, a recent graduate of Yale Drama School, *Six Appeal* garnered rave reviews throughout the Bay Area.[59] Mike wrote parts of the show and was one of its six performers. He put New York on hold and threw himself into Phoenix. "We felt good that we were striking out on our own," he reflected.[60]

With Mike back in Palo Alto working on *Six Appeal*, Thom had a stop-start writing year. He began it "writing with mad and concentrated fury"[61] but wrote nothing from March onward until "the goddess Fluency" returned in December.[62] He found it "ironical" that he had received the Somerset Maugham Award and a prize from the British Arts Council "in my most unproductive year since I was 20."[63] It did not help that he had become regular poetry critic for *The Yale Review*. This was not unfamiliar work: he had reviewed for *The Spectator* and *The London Magazine* throughout 1957 and 1958 but had done so as a "way to make money" to supplement his low earnings at Stanford. Writing reviews "wrecks one's prose style, perhaps one's judgment," he told Hall, "but means you don't have to work too hard."[64] Now at Berkeley and no longer as desperate for money, Thom discovered that reviewing drained both his time and energies. For *The Yale Review* he had to write two long pieces a year, which in practice meant reading most of the poetry collections published in Britain and America. "What I've always wanted, to be the Tynan of poetry," he wrote to Lehmann.[65] He stuck with it until 1963, when, "tired of sitting in judgment on people," he gave up reviewing. "I don't like the false position of omniscience that one gets from cutting down other poor bastards," he told Tony.[66] He resented "making comparatively fast judgments" and realized instead he "had to live with a book for some time before I could really find out its value for me."[67]

That summer, Thom returned to a valued book: Camus's *La Peste*. After a solo visit to New York, "mak[ing] the usual dozen new friends I always make there," he came back to California to spend time with Mike in the Palo Alto hills.[68] While Mike worked on *Six Appeal*, Thom read voluminously. "I became more interested in Camus, who seems to take some of the same ideas [as Sartre], but to use them much more humanely," he reflected, "and to carry them to much more interesting ends."[69] Rereading *La Peste*, Thom was more attracted than ever to its small acts of heroism, the selflessness of Dr. Rieux, and its shared values of love, generosity, and happiness. As a plague sweeps the city of Oran, its citizens try to find ways to resist, to continue to be human. "I feel more fellowship with the defeated than with saints. Heroism and sanctity don't really appeal to me," remarks Dr. Rieux. "What interests me is—being a man."[70] The book reinforced Thom's realization that heroism did not have to be a bombastic Shakespearean ideal of dominance and military valor: it could be ordinary, quiet, unassuming, and, ultimately, shared. "It struck me even more than before as the great book of the century," he told Tony. "I can't think of a single other work of prose—nor a Collected Poems by anyone, for that matter—which is as important, as well done, says so much. I mean since Stendhal."[71]

Camus's influence on Thom was evident as early as 1955, when Thom wrote "The Corridor," but it was not until the late 1950s that he became perhaps Thom's most dominant philosophical model. His humane attitude informed Thom's idea of conduct: the connection comes from a comment Camus made about honor. "I have always felt myself at one with the obstinate, with those in particular who have never been able to despair of a certain conception of honour," Camus told *The Observer* in 1957:

> I have experienced many of the frenzied feelings of our time, and I still do, but I have never been able to bring myself to despise the word honour, as so many people have done. Doubtless that is because I have been, and am, conscious of my human weakness and of my unjust actions, because I have always known instinctively that honour is (like pity) that unreasonable virtue which takes over when justice and reason become powerless.[72]

Thom told Tony of his feeling that Camus "makes clear several things that have been fuzzy in my mind."[73] Namely, Thom saw that honor and conduct were more outward-looking and social than doubt and choice, the central ideas of his first two books. In the same piece, Camus continued: "Personally I have never desired to be cut off. Modern man is subject to a kind of solitude which is certainly the cruellest burden his age has laid upon him. I feel the weight of this burden, believe me."[74] Thom had grappled with solitude in his life—his loneliness after his mother's death *and* the feeling, shared with Mike, that being gay and closeted makes you feel like the only person in the world—and many of his early poems feature solitary heroes who are banished from, adrift in, or set against their societies. Camus's focus on humanity and community, both in his *Observer* interview and in *La Peste*, encouraged Thom to develop these ideas in his own work and reimagine some of his earlier concerns, like magnanimity, which he and Tony called "The Values."

Thom thought deeply about Camus for the rest of the year[75] and finally "returned . . . to the practising writers" shortly after Christmas. "At my darkest hours too," he told Lehmann. "I got drunk and drunk again until New Year. Then, exhausted, limping home, I found I had ideas again, and not only ideas but ideas in <u>words</u>." He always felt his writing was "crap" when he was "this close to it," but he kept up his momentum into February.[76]

By this time, Mike had left again for New York "to see what can be done for a young director."[77] Thom wrote to the actress Irene Worth, whom he knew through Tony, asking if she could help by letting Mike attend a rehearsal of her upcoming Broadway production of *Toys in the Attic*. Describing Mike as "a much better [director] than I am a poet," he told Worth that one of Mike's "difficulties in NY is that he hasn't been able to watch professional directors at work."[78] If Mike could find work, Thom planned to leave Berkeley and join him that summer. They would travel together to Europe on Thom's Maugham money—"I'm sure Mr M would approve," he told Hall[79]—before settling for good in New York. Thom hoped the European trip would be reconciliatory: he had realized that, since he moved to Oakland, they had spent more time apart than together. "No," he told Lehmann, "in answer to the inevitable suspicion—this does not mean we have broken up. (I don't see any likelihood of our ever breaking up.)"[80]

14

INNOCENCE

Although by 1960 Thom had lived in America for more than five years, near annual relocations meant he had made few friends. At Stanford there were the graduate students Thomas Arp and Ted Tayler;[1] in Los Angeles there was Isherwood, although Isherwood's partner, Don Bachardy, was "furious" because Thom "didn't take any notice of him."[2] In New York there were the poet Ralph Pomeroy and the minor playwright Con Smith. At Berkeley he warmed to his officemate, the novelist Jackson Burgess, and was "terribly happy" that the poet Louis Simpson was on the faculty.[3] In his freshman Reading and Composition course, Thom developed a friendship with Belle Randall, an aspiring poet and actress whom he found his most able and engaging student.[4] She had a crush on him. "It would be years before I fully grasped that the friendship he offered wasn't something second best," Randall reflected, "but deeper and more lasting than the love affair I imagined could ever have been—a romance in its own right."[5]

Moreover, Thom's self-worth and his writing were intimately connected. During blocks, at times he felt he neglected his old friends. "I've hardly written to a soul, even my brother, for months," he told Hall. "I think in a curious way it had to do with writing almost zero poems last year—shame, withdrawal, feeling of wasting one's life if one doesn't write, I don't know which."[6] Of such friends, Tony was uppermost in his mind. "I often find myself telling people about you, how admirable a person you are," Thom told him. "You had more to do with making me the kind of person I am than anybody else I've known—something you probably realize as well as I do."[7]

At Berkeley, Thom became close to another Englishman named Tony. Tony Tanner was twenty-three when he arrived in Berkeley on a two-year Harkness Fellowship. He worked closely with Henry Nash Smith and Frederick Anderson, the librarian of the Mark Twain papers, on Twain and the American Transcendentalists.[8] "We immediately took to one another hugely," Thom recalled. "After that we went everywhere together, like Two Musketeers."[9] Tanner was witty and perceptive. He liked Frank Sinatra, spent his evenings in little jazz clubs in San Francisco, and was "endlessly fascinated by every aspect of American life," according to his friend and roommate William Plowden, "from small to large: the novels of Saul Bellow, the music, the hot roast chickens sold in supermarkets." He was "passionate, deeply sincere,"[10] and had an appetite for life that Thom found enormously appealing. "Apart from him," Thom told Tony White, "I have virtually nothing to do with the people at the university."[11]

In February, John Berryman joined Berkeley's Speech Department as a visiting professor. Carolyn Kizer offered to introduce him to Thom. "I brought along Tanner, partly for protection I think," Thom told John Haffenden, Berryman's biographer. "I didn't know what I was in for with Berryman, and I've never been good at meeting other poets. [. . .] [Kizer] assumed that Tanner was my boy-friend, I gather; I think Berryman was too sensible to do so."[12] At Berkeley, Berryman mostly felt isolated and depressed.[13] Thom and Tanner, however, made him feel "very up" and invited him to a double bill of *The Wild One* and Fellini's *I Vitelloni* that night. At Robbie's, a cheap restaurant on Telegraph, Berryman was late, "already drunk when he arrived, and he didn't eat but just went on drinking." At the movies, he "laughed extremely loud at odd moments" and "fell into a loudly snoring sleep."[14] Berryman found Thom "a good guy" and called the "wild & ebullient" Tanner "the only real friend" he made at Berkeley.[15]

Six weeks before he joined Mike in New York, Thom moved another man into his Oakland apartment. Clint Cline was a navy veteran from

Michigan, short and ruddy, with "a kind of generosity of spirit that I've almost never come across before," Thom told Tanner, "an insistence that I should enjoy everything as much as he enjoys it, and having himself an unequalled capacity for enjoyment." Confused, Thom thought he was "in love with two people" and was "classically unable to see a way of resolving the classic situation."[16] Clint was the first of Thom's major friendships that began with sex; Thom felt that sex helped to form "a solid foundation for a long & loving friendship."[17] He later remarked that friendship "must be the greatest value in my life. [. . .] Unlike Proust, I think that love and friendship are part of the same spectrum. Proust says that they are absolutely incompatible. I find that they are absolutely intertwined."[18] At this stage, however, Thom could not see how to integrate these friendships into his life with Mike, who preferred the "limitation" of "being married."[19] When Clint temporarily roomed with Thom, "Mike didn't like [it] at all."[20]

When Thom arrived in New York, Mike was tired and stressed. He was not in the city but in Liberty, a small town upstate, where he performed in stock dramas and musicals for the Stanley Woolf Players, a repertory troupe that toured the Catskills resort hotels. Thom stayed with him in one of the actors' residences: after a week he complained he had "no sex, no friends, no good bars, not enough money, not enough books to read, not enough talent to write poems." Needing the money, he worked at three long reviews, two for *Yale* one for *Poetry*. He saw Mike for less than an hour a day and felt "less close to him than when we were writing to each other with 3000 miles between us." Mike's lack of success made him "vague and irrational and irresolute," Thom felt, and believed it was a "delusion that there's a Chance waiting for him somewhere in Manhattan. (There isn't.)"[21]

Moreover, Thom doubted whether he could convince Mike to join him in Berlin, where he planned to travel using the money from the Somerset Maugham Award. Mike "wants our relationship exactly as it was eight years ago," Thom told Tanner, "and he treats any change as a deterioration. Well, he knows I love him, and I know it too, so he'll just have to get used to it, I suppose. A somewhat brutal remark, but what happens when Tristan and Isolde (or Roland & Oliver, for that matter) marry? The old intensity of passion becomes something out of place, and should give way to something equally good but different."[22] He tried writing a poem about their problems. Mike is "all I have for a center / to keep me aware of what is / tangible," reads one draft.[23] Losing him would be "a despair I know otherwise only in dreams,"[24] a reference to his frequent dreams about finding his mother's body. Unused to writing so openly and confessionally, Thom abandoned the poem.

Instead, he wrote "Das Liebesleben," a poem that drew on his reference to *Tristan und Isolde* to compare the quieter aspects of love to grand Wagnerian passion:

> this, we know, was Love: high-toned
> sexual play bound for death or
>
> disaster. Off stage, no doubt,
> matters are a bit different.[25]

Thom's restlessness in Liberty seemed to fire a new creativity. Having not written any poems since February, he told White in late August that he had written "more this year than any year since I got to this country" and had "almost genug [enough] for a new book."[26] Moreover, his new work excited him. "Big departures," he told Conquest. "The New Gunn continues."[27] "Das Liebesleben" was one of several poems he wrote in a seven-syllable line and a casual tone, privileging an everyday perspective over the operatic theme. He had tried syllabics as early as 1955, in "Market at Turk," but thought that poem sometimes seemed to have "just the right irregularity, and sometimes it seems hopelessly regular."[28]

Other syllabic poems had followed—like "Vox Humana" and "Waking in a Newly Built House"—but Thom was slow to feel he had made a breakthrough. "Waking" responded to the challenge Thom had set himself in "Vox Humana," to articulate "an unkempt smudge, a blur / an indefinite haze,"[29] and drew directly on William Carlos Williams. "There I found a way, with Williams' help, of incorporating the more casual aspects of life," he reflected, "the nonheroic things in life that are of course a part of daily experience and infinitely valuable."[30] "Waking" was "a turning point," but it took until late 1959 for subject and form to coalesce.[31] Part of that process was Thom's reversion to the seven-syllable line—"Waking" used lines of nine syllables—which he found "full of very exciting possibilities."[32] Syllabics suited "the casual perception," whereas he felt metrical verse made him commit to "rather taut emotion, a rather clenched kind of emotion."[33]

Thom had worked through some of these ideas back in Oakland. "My Sad Captains"—an allusion to *Antony and Cleopatra*[34]—makes a definitive break with Shakespearean heroism. It is one of several poems in his next collection to use celestial imagery, drawn from Greek and Roman mythologies in which the hero becomes as immortal as a star. Thom's heroes "withdraw to an orbit / and turn with disinterested / hard energy, like the stars"[35] and he acknowledges that, through heroic acts, they have "separated themselves a bit from the rest of humanity."[36] This is demonstrably "Old Gunn": having absorbed lessons from Camus, his conception of the heroic had come to encompass more quotidian, humane acts of heroism in the manner of Dr. Rieux. To demonstrate his change of direction, Thom used star imagery in "'Blackie, the Electric Rembrandt,'" which he wrote that summer in Liberty:

> . . . Now that it is finished, he
> hands a few bills to Blackie
>
> and leaves with a bandage on
> his arm, under which gleam ten
>
> stars, hanging in a blue thick
> cluster. Now he is starlike.[37]

Thom liked "the idea that an ordinary kid like that could be star-like," and was "poking fun at him. He thinks he's making himself heroic by getting a tattoo."[38] The poem was rueful self-criticism on the one hand, on the other the exploration of "a whole new terrain."[39] A third poem from this period—"Considering the Snail"—examines the life force of a snail, an attempt to capture the "intensity of attention" he admired in good poems.[40] Embracing uncertainty—"What is a snail's fury?" he asks—Thom transformed the "doubt" that Alvarez had identified in *Fighting Terms* into a positive trait, a restless curiosity in, and respect for, experiences and perceptions other than his own.

As Thom prepared to leave Liberty, Mike decided not to accompany him to Europe. In a draft poem, "Yet Another Parting," Thom described their "pitch of deprivation" and his desire to "embod[y]" their love "in the casual errand and housework / and jokes."[41] He was exploring everyday occurrences and humane conduct in his more casual poems, but that tone seemed ill-fitting for a poem about him and Mike. In another draft, "A House Without Doors," he explored the aftermath of his saying "harsh words . . . a trifle priggishly" to Mike: "How indirect we have got! Two houses without doors. / This is the body I said I wd never hurt / & Oh God! the face I know so well / . . . It is more: it is all I mean by love."[42] Thom allowed himself to embrace vulnerability in his syllabic poems, but it was not something he would yet allow himself to embrace in his relationship with Mike.

Thom spent two weeks in England before he sailed for Germany. Charles Monteith took him and Ted Hughes for lunch at the Travellers' Club, a venerable private members' club on Pall Mall.[43] Thom promised to see Hughes again in January, when he returned from Germany.[44] En route to Berlin, he spent a week in Hamburg, a city he found every bit as "licentious" as its reputation.[45] He was amused to find, on Herbertstrasse, "a whole street of middle-aged Huren, who sit at little windows on display."[46] Splitting his time between St. Pauli, the red-light district, and the gay bars clustered around Grossneumarkt, he stayed at the Klopstock-Pensionat, a boardinghouse once used as a training school by the Abwehr. His favorite bars were Stadt-Casino, La Bohème, Flamingo, and David-Klause, but he made no mention of Kaiserkeller, a music club at the busier end of Grosse Freiheit, where the Beatles began a residency that same week.

When Thom took the train to Berlin, there was still free passage between East and West.[47] "You do not feel the nearness of Communists, in fact you have to keep reminding yourself of East Berlin," he told Tanner. "West Berliners go into East Berlin as little as possible . . . and obviously they try to keep the whole problem out of mind as far as possible."[48] Thom had not known what to expect: "the Berlin of Mr Norris and Sally Bowles with a lot of rubble, maybe," he told Lehmann, but found it "hard to imagine Isherwood's Berlin as having ever been here."[49] That said, rereading *Goodbye to Berlin*, Thom found "detail after detail . . . as a marvellously accurate description of the feeling here now," he told Tanner. "There is the same kind of recklessness, nonchalant hedonism, unscrupulousness—but totally without the feeling of immanent catastrophe in the early 30s."[50]

Thom stayed in Berlin for two months and moved between three hotels near Nollendorfplatz.[51] Isherwood had lived on Nollendorfstrasse in the early 1930s, and while the neighborhood looked considerably different when Thom arrived, it remained Berlin's queer center.[52] Thom visited its many bars, including Robby-Bar on Fuggerstrasse, Zweilicht on Motzstrasse, and the legendary Kleist Casino on Kleiststrasse.[53] He was mostly disappointed, telling Lehmann that Berlin queer bars were "very epicene, very girly. I think it must be only in America you get bars exclusively for the butch (as opposed to money-butch)."[54] One exception was Inkognito, a bar in Charlottenburg where Thom likely met a motorcyclist named Klaus Stötzner, who lived nearby. Thom kept a photograph of Stötzner, dressed in full leather, and thought he exhibited "energy that is not brutality."[55]

Berliners spoke "only a few words" of English; Thom's German improved dramatically and he soon made friends "from All Walks of Life." That he lived in the United States was a source of fascination. "My identity bracelet charms everybody out of their senses," he told Tanner. "I have been on the backs of more motorcycles & drunk more cognac (prost, gulp, prost, gulp, etc) than ever before in my life."[56] Elli's Bier

Bar in Kreuzberg appealed to Thom's rugged tastes and attracted hustlers, writers, and artists from East Berlin and farther afield. On one occasion, Thom spotted "two young Americans nattily dressed alike in brimmed hats and expensive raincoats." They were James Merrill, with whom Thom had given a reading the previous year, and his "attractive" partner David Jackson.[57] Merrill thought Thom "lean & hungry" and "dressed classically in black leather, boots, keys, etc."[58] The next day, Thom swapped leather for Levi's and Merrill and Jackson took him to the zoo.

Berlin became one of Thom's favorite cities. He was "disgruntled and bewildered" for a fortnight, then found himself "in the place, and knowing it, and loving it the more I know it." It helped that he was flush with Maugham money. The weakness of the deutsche mark meant Thom had more money than he knew how to spend. He sent some to Mike and Clint, "both of whom need it. (And I don't even feel generous, as I would if it were dollars)."[59] He felt his comparative wealth most acutely in East Berlin, where "the ruins are still very much ruins," he told Tanner; "many of them are being dynamited, either because they are irreparable or because they are Imperialist or Fascist in association." Wandering around Prenzlauer Berg and Friedrichshain, Thom saw "everybody in working clothes (tho blue jeans are frowned upon), hearty exhorting posters, and everywhere more cops than you've ever seen before—though they all look about 16 years old."[60] In East Berlin, one new friend had worked for Claus von Stauffenberg during the war but refused to talk about it. He "was in the Hitlerjugend," Thom told White, "and is scared to talk about the past at all in case this gets known by the wrong sort of person."[61]

Thom bought several small notebooks in Berlin and wrote a statement of intent: "The next poems must be personal, flat, almost casual. The form of syllabics is all that will give them tightness—a form all but invisible to the reader, but for me the difference between order & disorder."[62] Two "flat, almost casual" Berlin poems—"Kurfürstendamm" and "Berlin in Ruins"—were moderately successful, but Thom continued to struggle with "personal" poems. He abandoned "A House Without Doors," about Mike, and "Loot," about Tony White, which he thought "a dead loss" after two years of work.[63] Thom felt that "Loot" explored a version of White that no longer existed. "He has looked outward, at the tangible world, without wanting to make it refer to himself, but with a sense that it existed in its own right and that something could be learnt from it," Thom told Tanner, in what was as much a statement of his own new poetic intentions as it was a description of White.[64]

Thom drew on his experiences in Berlin to write "Innocence." "It's about the sort of thing we've often discussed," he told White, later dedicating the poem to him.[65] "Innocence" is about history, not street life, and Thom wrote it in his old style, not his new, but he did not mind: it was a new take on an old subject. "In it I'm trying to deal with a problem I've never before fully faced in a poem," he told Tanner, "the problem of the consequences of energy (which I admire) without moral sanction."[66] In the poem, a soldier of "the Corps"—implicitly the SS[67]—stands guard while a "Russian partisan" is burned alive and "feel[s] disgusted only by the smell." Such was the soldier's training in "the Corps," he developed "a compact innocence, child-like and clear, / No doubt could penetrate, no act could harm."[68] "I am trying to show how like he is to most people, or rather how easy it would be for most people to (in the right circumstances) be in the SS," he told Tanner. "By attributing innocence to this man I am not exonerating him or the SS, but I <u>am</u> attacking innocence."[69] The poem's quiet opening echoes the hardening of the soldier's emotions; Thom uses cold, direct language to describe how the Russian's "ribs wear gently through the darkening skin." Challenging old ideas in "Innocence," Thom learned the value of understatement—a technique that would shape his subsequent poems.

"Innocence" became his central statement about conduct. Treating Nazism with contempt, Thom departed from the borderline fascistic emphasis on heroism in his earlier poems, his admiration for which he found difficult to explain. His use of the term "Nazism" was cavalier: he seemed to treat it as an abstract philosophical concept rather than a recent political, cultural, quotidian reality. "The Nazis are a great subject for a whole set of poems," he told White in 1958. "Sometimes it seems to me that Nazism, and its spread, are related to the sort of contagious attraction of various sadists I have known. I mean for their practices, not their physical attraction."[70] Thom mentioned a "swastika-draped bed" in "The Beaters"—to which "Innocence" is a sequel, "a beating party that went too far," as Richard Murphy put it[71]—but his main concern was to explore Nazi ideas as an extreme extension of his own obsessions. Earlier that year he watched the "tremendously impressive" *Triumph of the Will* by Leni Riefenstahl and thought "the audiences all come out at least ½-Nazis."[72] He wondered if Nazis had "the intellectual daring of completely surrealist or nihilist motives, of a complete negation of humane values? Not this, either," he continued:

> And if they are not (1) either compulsively or fashionably sadistic, (2) mere greedy fools, or (3) existentialists more daring than have ever existed before, then what are they? One's forced back on the possibility of the image of people who are sentimentally patriotic, and just happen to have greater technical resources and less scruples than their like ever before.[73]

Working on "Innocence" for two months in Berlin drew Thom away from Nazism as a "more daring" form of existentialism and toward the more humane values of his later poems. He dropped the philosophical entanglements, but some of the fetishism remained. In Berlin he tried "to get a Nazi belt" for a Californian friend but struggled to find one.[74] Wearing black leather in California was a countercultural statement; wearing it in Germany risked the taint of Nazism.

Thom returned to England via Denmark and the Netherlands. In Amsterdam he stayed at Hotel Argos, a converted cigar shop popular with leathermen from across Europe, and palled around with its proprietors, Sako Jan Tiemersma and Anton Johan ("Ton") Kennedy.[75] In Copenhagen, a Dane named Bent Kilaa told him about the London leather scene: this word-of-mouth knowledge exchange was essential in an era before *Damron* and other gay guides.

Thom made notes about the Ace Café, on the North Circular; the Busy Bee, on the outskirts of Watford; the Spartan Club, in Victoria; and the Coleherne Arms, "way along Old Brompton Road," but his London stay was too brief to involve any visits.[76] Instead, he had lunch on Chalcot Square with Ted Hughes and Sylvia Plath, whom he found "most compatible."[77]

Charles Monteith took him and Hughes for another lunch at the Travellers' Club. Thom had lived out of a suitcase since leaving Oakland six months earlier and turned up wearing a leather jacket and a pair of leather chaps bought in Berlin. "The dress of your guest at luncheon yesterday caused a good many members to complain to me," R. P. McDouall, secretary of the club, told Monteith, and he was obliged to report the incident to the committee.[78] Monteith assured McDouall that he had "no idea at all that [Gunn] would arrive so bizarrely attired" and tried to account for Thom's "informality . . . either by the general informality of Californians—to which perhaps he has become accustomed—or by the exigencies of travel"; Monteith had "decided—obviously wrongly—to brazen it out."[79]

On a borrowed typewriter, Thom compiled the manuscript of what would become *My Sad Captains* and sent it to Monteith before he returned to California. Already thinking about his next book, he wanted his "starting points" to be "of ordinary life, in all their resistance, their warm detail, their inertia or fluctuation. They are not principles, but rather modes discovered empirically, modes that work. (It is from them that principles are formed.) Casual, unassertive, and there." He saw William Carlos Williams and D. H. Lawrence as potential models and vowed to "drop discussion of the Will. It has become a bore, & I doubt if there is anything new to say about it."[80] He had already started this project in the "jubilant, new, primavera, bouncing, syllabic" second half of *My Sad Captains*.[81]

Waiting for Thom in Oakland was a letter from Monteith accepting the book. This enhanced the upbeat mood Thom had brought back with him across the Atlantic. London was "something of a surprise," he told Isherwood. "People seemed much more relaxed and happy than I'd ever found them before."[82] Berlin and London had made up Thom's mind to live once again in a big city. That spring, a chance arose: Thom found "a big and cheap apartment" in North Beach and jumped at the opportunity to move to San Francisco. "I'm very happy about moving there," he told White, "though it'll mean about ¾ hour journey each way to work."[83] Thom moved to 975 Filbert Street the first weekend of March 1961. Only Mike was missing.

15

SAN FRANCISCO

Thom moved to San Francisco, in part, to be "in the middle of all my friends and all the bars."[1] He spent Sunday afternoons at Jack's on the Waterfront. "It's very full," he told Mike, "everybody's tanned, & everybody is relaxed & not worrying whether they make out or not." Moreover, Jack's gave him a new sense of belonging. "I like the masculine-queer atmosphere," he continued, "it is one of the few I feel at home in."[2]

Mike felt the opposite. He was still in New York, poor and depressed, and did not appreciate Thom's accounts of his sprees in Berlin and San Francisco. They had not seen each other since Thom left Liberty the previous summer: a "series of awful quarrels"[3] meant Thom was terrified Mike would leave him. "My sweet, handsome, noble man, forgive me for all I am and have been. And trust me. Because I love you and need you," Thom wrote to him, "and I am paralysed with fears that I will lose you some way. You are the only precious thing there is."[4] Early in the year they exchanged two or three letters a week and Thom tried everything to effect a reconciliation. "If I agree I am what you say in the letter (i.e. . . . like 99% queers, sex on the brain, loving novelty, voyeur, experimentalist, etc) and I do, then I have two choices," Thom told him:

(1) to stay as I am and reject you (since you say there is and can't be any compromise)

or (2) try to be completely faithful & hope we don't explode.

Well, in that case, I guess your decision is simply to accept my decision. I decide the second, my darling, because I love you, and I will try. I do not know whether I can succeed, at this stage, in something so unqualified, but I will try, since it is the only way I can keep you.[5]

Thom knew he could not keep this promise, but his entreaties aided a "big making-up" and convinced Mike to return to California. Just as Mike was packing his bags, however, he "got hepatitis, which sometimes lays people up for about 4 months. Last time he phoned he was so weak that he could hardly speak."[6] With Mike unable to leave New York, Thom felt hopeless. He did not want to pressure Mike to return before he was ready; nor could Thom drop everything at Berkeley and fly east to take care of him.

Bedridden, Mike required complete rest. Alcohol was verboten. A friend nursed him—an "attractive" antiques dealer named Donald Magner—with whom he subsequently had "a bit of a thing."[7] Thom, meanwhile, took their postponed reconciliation as carte blanche to sleep around. "I haven't slept with anybody worth talking about," he told Mike in mid-March.[8] He was more intrigued by Mike's affair with Magner: he hoped it would alter Mike's views about promiscuity and bring them closer together. "Oddly enough, for someone I've never seen, I have a most complex relationship with Don, wrong as I may be," he told Mike. "I mean I have an obsessed feeling of him as an alter ego—more good-looking than I, and more dumb—with many of the same problems and attitudes at bottom. I suppose tho, it's mainly that I am always interested in someone who's in love with you."[9]

Since Thom's move to Oakland in 1958, he and Mike had spent so little time together that sex was no longer part of their relationship. "Our trouble sexually—Well, I should say my trouble, is that sex became for us in the last 2 or 3 years something increasingly associated with sadness," Thom reflected. "You would weep almost every time we had sex. I once said this to you and you merely said 'Well, I'm like that.' No wonder I got inhibitions and Stendhalian fiascos with you." Thom hoped that Mike's fling with Magner would loosen him up. "I do not want sex with you

3 times a day as I did 8 years ago," Thom told Mike, "but then nor do you."[10] Mike remembered things differently. "When we met it was like sparks flying," he reflected. "I think in a way it stayed that way for him more than it did for me."[11] Thom wanted it both ways and wanted Mike to want the same: sex with each other, sex with other people, and their loving relationship as the solid foundation. "I've known for almost 8 years the one thing about which my life could revolve," Thom told Mike, "yet here I am, in the same absurd and awful pain as always at having achieved it."[12]

Quarreling through letters turned sex, love, and promiscuity into abstractions. "You say 'To love is to submit . . . To love is to cease being one's own man . . . To love is to be less than yourself in order, finally, to be more than yourself,'" Thom wrote Mike. "You also say love is to conquer. God knows love isn't such an abstract thing that it is always the same, and with the same effects." Thom's own tendency toward abstraction and his desire to intellectualize created an impasse. Perhaps with "Das Liebesleben" in mind, Thom thought that the "love of operatic heroes and heroines" could exist; it was a glorified death wish "in which the validity of any other kind of action is denied" and that "should always end in the tomb."[13]

Thom had "sometimes wanted the death-wish love" but had "more consciously wanted" the love that "conquer[ed] without submission." In that kind of love, he told Mike, "since we were both men, there should be no submission; and, yes, in spite of the New Testament tone of paradox, in which you were all of yourself and more of yourself. How else, I thought, could it be worth it?" He tried to convince Mike that "love is a kind of unevenness" between the two forms. "There is a terrible danger— and I mean to me, just as much as to you—in unconsciously modelling one's love on het. love," he told Mike:

> But one can't, our love has to make its own, homosexual terms,
> which CANNOT be the same as between a girl and a man. Babe—
> I'm not clinging to unattachedness, to uncommittedness—but I
> am, or want to be, a man just as much as you are. I wanted us to
> be individuals, "our own men," and each other's men.[14]

For Thom, this was the heart of the matter. Being a man meant constancy and adventure: they did not negate each other but created instead an intricate emotional complex of sexual freedom within a committed, loving relationship.

It was a difficult balance to maintain. Arguments with Mike could spur Thom's cruising. "When I have been angry at you and gone and picked someone up, it was not to spite you—because I'd never want to do that, I think," he told Mike, "but to feel that someone (even a casual trick) thinks I'm worth something."[15] Thom knew he could be "a selfish fucking bastard"[16] and was loath to admit to himself his own "enormous" "unscrupulousness," "self-pity," and "an extent of liking popularity."[17] "I don't know why you love me, babe," he wrote. "I am a waste and an approximation—I am not a fake, I think, but that's all the good I can see in me. I sometimes wish for the simplicity of an animal. Animals have it made."[18] He encouraged Mike to pursue relationships with other men, but Mike resisted: he wanted a monogamous relationship, and feared that taking a major lover would jeopardize his life with Thom. "The time of the letters was the closest I came to [saying] I can't go on like this," Mike reflected. "We are too different. I didn't like living, and having my pleasures, and going out trying to meet [other men]."[19] Thom did, and he tried to balance that with gaining Mike's approval, "one of the things I crave most in the world. You have given me, by it, a kind of strength in moving that I never dreamed I could have & never would have had without you."[20]

Through the spring, as Mike slowly recovered from hepatitis, Thom sank into depression. "After these last few months I'm not what I used to be," he told Mike. "I mean your letters, the phone calls, the accusations and counter-accusations, almost breaking up, your trying to kill yourself. I even think I LOOK older. I feel, if you'll forgive the phrase, as though something died in me, some kind of energy or something."[21] Thom cried regularly and felt "moments of incredible bitterness" toward Mike, but wanted them to persevere. "I love you, my darling, very very much, more than I can ever explain to you, but there comes a depth of misery (a degree of incompatibility, maybe) which eats away at the love," he wrote.

I am sure, as I said, a few days ago, that we can get back a trusting, un-fighting, unanalytical love, but we must work for it, and—as you said—nothing is altered, none of our problems, neither of our theories about what love should be, what people should be, by your having had hepatitis.[22]

Mike agreed to return to California in mid-June. Thom thought he should come as soon as possible: New York debilitated Mike's mental health to such a degree that Thom thought he was having "a sort of breakdown." He wanted Mike "for the time being [to] wash your hands of NY, and do it at once, baby."[23]

There was another factor behind Mike's decision to return to California. His friend Sheilah Dorcy had purchased the Pagliacci Playhouse in Redwood City, renamed it the Tunn, and wanted Mike to be resident director. Dorcy had produced *Six Appeal*, was "hugely impressed" with Mike's ability as a director, and had the money to set him up as head of a local group.[24] Thom had to convince him: if he could not find success in New York, Thom argued, "wouldn't it have been a good and satisfying thing to do with your life if you could end it in control of a small group you knew to be excellent?" Mike's other option was to teach, but Thom warned him off. "I teach as a way of keeping myself so that I can have the leisure to write poetry," he wrote. "Teaching & the practise of an art is OK. Teaching alone is ridiculous." He felt that "what one does with one's energies should be an act of love for life." Mike scribbled a note at the bottom of Thom's letter. "Sometimes it is finally better & less painful to try to do without what one loves," he wrote: "i.e. Us—I love you & have gone thru hell for you—I don't believe that you love me—so why suffer?"[25]

Throughout their quarrels, Thom had emphasized his need for queer friends. "I have always needed people around me," he told Mike. "And, as I said, a few days ago, straight people who know nothing of me sexually are not the answer."[26] He wanted "butch queer goodlooking friends" whom Mike would also like. "Having finally realized I'm nothing special, but a run-of-the-mill queer," he reflected, "I want to be (I want us to be) in the company of other run-of-the-mill queers."[27] In his first few months living in San Francisco, Thom made three important queer friends.

In Jack's he met a young British medical student. "There is a queer, colossally big London Jew called Wolf . . . who says my poetry changed his life," he told Mike: "it caused him to get a bike and wear leather, and he tears around like a whirlwind—and [he] came out here to be a doctor, here because I live here. And he really means it, too."[28] Wolf's real name was Oliver Sacks. His friend the theater director Jonathan Miller had given him a copy of *The Sense of Movement* and said, "You must meet Thom; he's your sort of person."[29] Flattered, Thom broke one of his central rules. "Yes, I did make it with Wolf & it was indefensible, since I find him extremely unatt," he told Mike. "But for the first time in my life I did what I consider so wrong, i.e. slept with someone because he was so devoted, which I find immoral, really, the one form of sexual immorality." Sacks was overwhelming and Thom felt "a rather owing responsibility, since he wants me far too much (though it's not love, by my definition, it's obsession)."[30]

That summer, Sacks planned to ride his motorcycle across the country. "I am not sure what Thom saw in me at this point," Sacks reflected, "but I found in him great personal warmth and geniality mixed with fierce intellectual integrity. Thom, even then, was lapidary and incisive; I was centrifugal and effusive. He was incapable of indirection or deceit, but his directness was always accompanied, I thought, by a sort of tenderness."[31] Knowing that Sacks also wanted to be a writer, Thom encouraged him to keep a diary of his adventures and send him installments.[32] Thom thought Sacks's writing lacked sympathy and wanted him "to put himself inside the skin of others": "the Great Diary," as Thom called it, would give Sacks the perfect opportunity.[33] "He was much more transparently self-dramatizing in those days," Thom reflected. "It was never unpleasant posturing at all, he was always nice, but in his youthful enthusiasm he was always trying on poses."[34] Thom perhaps saw a little of himself in Sacks: "trying on poses" had been precisely what he had been doing in *Fighting Terms* and *The Sense of Movement*.

Around the same time, in Crossroads, a leather bar on the Embarcadero, Thom attracted a tall, wiry man named Chuck Arnett, a dancer with the National Ballet of Canada. Arnett was on tour, performing *Bye Bye Birdie* at the Curran Theater, and staying late at Jack's and Crossroads. "They were groovy people," he remarked of the leather crowd, "they all had office jobs in brokerage firms and at night it was a whole other world."[35] He subsequently moved to San Francisco and became a major figure in the leather community.[36] Part of his attraction, thought Thom, was his strength. "I am attracted to people who take charge, who decide what the party's going to be, who give the parties—not by Hitler-like leaders but by people who organize things," Thom reflected. "I think that's very sexy and very attractive. I admire people who are stronger than me, in fact, and although I may appear like a strong person, I appear to myself as a weak person so I'm always attracted by the strong." Arnett was "always in the middle of a group" and Thom felt drawn to his energy and generosity. "We were all followers of Chuck," he reflected, "even Don Doody, strong as he is and obstreperous as he is."[37]

That spring, Thom cruised a law graduate named Donald Doody at Gordon's, a supper club for the "fuzzy sweater set" at Sansome and Broadway, a mile from Thom's Filbert apartment.[38] Two years Thom's junior, Don was cerebral and opinionated; short, stocky, and high-strung. After a tough Irish-Catholic upbringing in Chicago, Don joined the US Air Force, learned Russian, and held a low-level intelligence position in Germany in the mid-1950s. The attraction was immediate. "I thought he was a good-looking fellow," Don recalled. "He had very bad skin at the time. He had acne, but other than that . . . I remember mostly that he smiled and laughed a lot."[39]

At Gordon's they were both "doing our bar persona." The next morning, while Thom made coffee, Don scoured the typewritten pages strewn across Thom's desk. "I'd never heard of him," Don recalled. "I read some and he was watching me. After a while he began using me as his proofreader. [. . .] We didn't really discuss the larger issues of poetry. I was the detail man." Don was passing through San Francisco from New Orleans: he had graduated from Tulane Law School and was about to start a graduate degree in English. He defended his dissertation—"Shakespeare and Opera"—at Tulane in summer 1962 and shortly thereafter moved to San Francisco, where Thom had recommended him for the PhD program at Berkeley. To make ends meet, Don started tending bar at the Tool Box, San Francisco's newest leather bar. He "liked it a lot" and would "come back from classes in Middle English to start tending at this pseudo biker bar."[40]

At Harrison and Fourth, the Tool Box was a block from Folsom, then an unfashionable neighborhood far from the historically gay centers of Polk Street and the waterfront. When Jack's and Why Not? were shut down, the Tool Box became the center of San Francisco's leather scene. Rudolf Nureyev called it "that funny little bar under the freeway"; Arnett thought it "looked like a set for a Eugene O'Neill play."[41] South of Market was a warehouse and manufacturing district close to downtown. Its main thoroughfares, Folsom and Harrison, spawned myriad alleys and side streets that attracted "artists looking for affordable studio space, musicians in search of practice venues where they would not bother neighbors, squatters who took up residence in abandoned factories, and gay leathermen."[42] The Tool Box opened in 1962, Febe's and Ramrod followed in 1966, and Folsom became known as the "Miracle Mile" and the "Valley of Kings," stretching from Fourth in the northeast to Twelfth in the southwest. Arnett's enormous leathermen mural at the Tool Box became internationally known when it was featured in the "Homosexuality in America" spread in *Life* magazine in 1964.[43]

Mike returned to San Francisco in July. Thom thought six months of unhappiness had "toughened me up a lot emotionally,"[44] but, six weeks later, he called their domestic situation "pretty unhealthy."[45] He felt he had to choose between "a comfortable domesticity, in which I am bored to the point of not writing a line" and an "endurance in a vacuum, given a local meaningfulness . . . by affairs and poems," but he felt "too much of a goddamn coward" to plump for the latter. Nor was it a "clean choice" because of the impact on Mike. "He has come to depend on me, on my being there, in a way that terrifies me," he told Tony Tanner. "I don't feel up to such a need, and at the same time I feel guilty in that it's my fault that it's there, and I encouraged its growth in the first place."[46] With the atmosphere on Filbert Street tense and anxious, Mike spent most of his time "working his ass off" preparing *Son of Six Appeal*, which opened at the Tunn in January 1962 and received "very fine notices."[47] Its skits, wrote the *San Francisco Examiner*'s reviewer, were "sparkling, topical, attractive and razor-sharp."[48]

In September 1961, *My Sad Captains* was published simultaneously in Britain (by Faber) and the United States (by the University of Chicago Press). Thom called it "a rather dull book," full of repetitions, and thought he should "wait ten years" before publishing another collection.[49] At best it was "experimental," at worst "a complete withering of talent."[50] In America, it was not widely reviewed. John Simon called it "a disappointment" and thought Thom "gets worse as he becomes more sucked into America."[51] M. L. Rosenthal, conversely, found "a quick eye, a moral and psychological keenness, and a visionary power."[52]

British critics were generally impressed, although Thom's use of syllabics was greeted with uncertainty. Anthony Thwaite felt they "dribble on, line by line,"[53] whereas Bernard Bergonzi thought they showed "great technical accomplishment" and that the book "makes it clear that Mr Gunn is one of the leading poets of his generation."[54] Frank Kermode praised his "remarkable advance towards transparency, towards a new austerity."[55] In *The Observer*, A. Alvarez praised *My Sad Captains* as "another step forward, this time into a new clarity of theme and style" while maintaining that *Fighting Terms* was Thom's best book.[56] Thom had courted Alvarez: as poetry editor of *The Observer*, he was an influential figure with the power to make or break reputations. Thom published in *The Observer* beginning in the late 1950s and, a fortnight after Alvarez's review, published four new poems: "From an Asian Tent," "The Goddess," "Knowledge," and "Kurfürstendamm." Introducing them, Alvarez called Thom "the poet of the 'shook-up,' Marlon Brando ethos [who] dresses accordingly, in the best 'Wild One' style—black leather jacket, jeans, cowboy boots."[57] Later that year, when Thom received page proofs of Alvarez's major anthology *The New Poetry*, he realized "with great depression" what Alvarez liked about his work: "topicality."[58] Thom grew warier of Alvarez and later agreed with Donald Davie's assessment that "violence and psychic disturbance" were Alvarez's "touchstones for contemporary poetry" and that he had sold Thom "on the same ticket."[59]

Of the poems Thom published in *The Observer* in September 1961, "From an Asian Tent" was "rather a brutal" attempt "to deal with my father in a poem."[60] Thom imagines Alexander the Great, away in east Asia, receiving news of his father's death. "Father, I scarcely could believe you dead," it begins, and concludes:

> Remembering that you never reached the East,
> I have made it mine to the obscurest temple;
> Yet each year look more like the man I least
> Choose to resemble, bully, drunk, and beast.
> Are you a warning, Father, or an example?[61]

Thom later claimed the "autobiographical" element of the poem was "a secret source of feeling that might really be half-imagined, some Oedipal jealousy" and felt "freed by the myth from any attempt to be fair or honest about my father."[62] At the time, he found it "bad enough . . . to know that I'll look repellent as <u>my father</u> before I'm 45."[63] Moreover, it is a poem about failure: Alexander had set out to conquer what his father had failed to conquer; Thom sought to be what his father had not, but felt hamstrung. He thought Bert was weak and saw parallels in how they conducted themselves in relationships; he was "terribly much a failure" to Mike and wanted "to be someone of complete strength. [. . .] I suppose, in Freudian and very relevant terms, I am tormented by not being what my father ought to have been."[64]

In September 1960, before he visited in Berlin, Thom had seen Bert in London and they had quarreled for the "first time in 10 years."[65] Bert was a reduced figure. He was no longer a frontline Fleet Street editor. His tempestuous editorship of the *Daily Sketch* had ended in late 1959 with an editorial reshuffle at Associated Newspapers, and he had taken on editorship of the *Sunday Dispatch*. "Apparently his drinking at work has become serious enough for quite a lot of people to know about it," Thom told his aunts. "He's a sad man now."[66] In summer 1961, the *Dispatch* was merged with the *Sunday Express*, and Bert "had the mortification of seeing the [*Dispatch*] die under his feet."[67] Bert, Ander told Thom, was now "on the great industrial scrapheap."[68]

Bert and Olive planned to sail around the world, starting with an Atlantic cruise. When they arrived in New York, Bert cabled Thom that he had caught a virus and a doctor advised him to return to London. Thom felt "heartlessly, somewhat relieved" that they would not make it to San Francisco.[69] Bert's condition was more serious: in London, he was diagnosed with terminal lung cancer and deteriorated rapidly through the winter. "Father was lying propped up on a pillow looking very thin and weak living on liquid foods," Ander wrote in January. "I must say it is rather sad to see a formerly active man on his back in such a short time. He threatens to send you a cable for what reason I know not but presumably he expects you to come rushing across the Atlantic just before he dies."[70] Bert's condition was common knowledge on Fleet Street. He was too ill to write, so Olive replied to the many compassionate letters he received from friends and former colleagues. "He was deeply touched to hear from you," she told one, "for it is letters such as yours that make him feel he is not forgotten."[71]

In March, Thom was on a reading tour when he heard his father had died. Olive telegrammed San Francisco; Mike forwarded the message to Thom in New York, where he was due to read that night at the Poetry Center at the 92nd Street YMHA. "Got the telegram and fais molt," Thom replied.[72] He sent Olive a condolence letter but did not return to England for the funeral.[73] He kept several obituaries, including *The New York Times*' critical assessment of Bert's legacy,[74] but was otherwise "very matter of fact" about his death.[75] "My father died recently," he told Robert Conquest, "and I was rather shocked that I couldn't feel anything at all. I'd half expected I might feel something in spite of the fact that I'd never had much to do with him and he was, finally, a ruthless and self-pitying man."[76]

16

HEPATITI/

Thom came to see 1961 and 1962 as two of the worst years of his life. He struggled to remember them, "either because there isn't much to remember, or because I don't want to remember it."[1] His self-esteem was low: he was mildly depressed, drank too much, wasn't writing, and felt his relationship with Mike could collapse at any moment.

In the spring of 1962, Mike "fell in love" with a handsome law graduate named Thomas Gee. "And it was love on his part too, but he was very slow to recognize that," Mike reflected. This was Thom's greatest fear: while he had encouraged Mike to be promiscuous, he knew that Mike's monogamous nature meant that falling in love with somebody else was a real possibility.[2] "They didn't particularly like one another," Mike recalled, and he felt "uneasy, guilty" about bringing Gee to Filbert Street.[3] "I am not blaming you more than myself for Tom," Thom told Mike the following year, "but the fact that he was your husband meant that I wasn't your husband."[4]

Thom explored questions of monogamy and queer relationships in his notebooks, but his difficulty writing personal poems contributed to his ongoing block. In "The Justification," quickly abandoned, he used an image of embrace to describe his dream of a successful open relationship:

> What I envisioned: 2 planets
> revolving on themselves, equal

& self sufficient
yet locked in the invisible
firm embrace of gravity.
[. . .]
From a distance they look one
but—tho eternally reconciled–
they are two.[5]

In another abandoned poem from the same notebook, Thom felt he and
Mike had become so entrenched—"only the / distant see the mountains
whole"—that a positive resolution, a compromise, seemed remote. Their
relationship limped on, he thought, "between friendship & fury."[6] Although Thom felt "a generalized pleasure at living in SF,"[7] he called his
life "not worth living" and 1962 "the worst year of my life. You must
be able to understand this," he told Mike, "it must surely have been the
worst of yours. The emptiest."[8]

Everything in those two years made Thom "too depressed to do anything but drink."[9] His drinking was "getting ridiculous" in early 1961
and he realized how "people can depend on drink—it's not that it gets rid
of your unhappiness but it seems to make you a person more able to face
it."[10] Through 1962, Thom spent more time than usual in the Tool Box,
where Don Doody was tending bar. "He was very romantically interested
in me," Don reflected. "He would come alone and he would drink a lot."
Thom was often "so sloshed" that he could not find a cab: Don "got into
the habit of driving him home." Don often rebuffed him, but felt they
had "a romantic friendship for several years." Don knew about Mike but
sensed he had "his own separate life." Thom was "always into new things
and new people," Don reflected. "But he found certain values in some
people that he appreciated and kept those people tied to him for a long
time."[11]

In fall 1962, the success of Son of Six Appeal prompted a revival of
the original Six Appeal. It was staged at On Broadway, an avant-garde
cabaret theater a few blocks from Filbert Street. Sheilah Dorcy and Tom
Gee coproduced it. Afterward, Mike traveled to New York once more

to look for work. Alone in San Francisco, unsure whether Mike would return, Thom began to make his own plans for 1963. "I am taking off the spring semester," he told Hall, "and will be taking off Eastwards about halfway through February, and will probably spend most of the time in Europe."[12] He was enthusiastic about London and "travel[ing] randomly around Europe for a month" before returning to California,[13] and had previously raised the idea of "returning to Europe for good."[14]

Thom's plans collapsed in December when he was taken to Mount Zion Hospital with hepatitis, not helped, most likely, by his excessive drinking over the last two or three years. "I am on cortisone, after 2 weeks of jaundice & getting worse," he told Sacks, "& maybe show a bit of improvement. What a laugh, anyway! I am full of optimism."[15] He was kept in the hospital for a month and knew his recovery would be long and slow: he lacked energy, struggled to concentrate, and required good nutrition and plenty of bed rest. "I sleep most of the time," he told Hall. "Useless to ask a man with hepatitis for a poem. [. . .] Useless to ask him for anything much except self-pity, actually."[16] He knew that hepatitis was a virus, but felt it was also "a logical combination of [the last two years]," he told Mike, "the liver (the center of the body) turning against the rest of the body in revulsion at a life it doesn't want to lead."[17]

When he was discharged in January, rather than return alone to Filbert Street, Thom stayed with Don and his roommate Bryan Condon in their Victorian apartment on Fell.[18] He slept on the couch and lived off hamburgers and orange juice. He planned to stay for a month but was there until the middle of May, in part because he had a "strange, largely superstitious feeling about Filbert Street," that he would "fall into a kind of hepatitis depression . . . and that my perception about myself will become self-pity and so unworkable."[19] Don was good company: he had amassed a large collection of opera LPs and could talk engagingly about Dostoevsky, Tolstoy, Camus, and Thomas Mann, all of whom Thom read and reread extensively during his convalescence. He also saw plenty of Tony Tanner, who was visiting UC Berkeley on an American Council of Learned Societies fellowship to work on his first book, *The Reign of Wonder*. Thom "resigned" himself to a "temporary dependence": Don became "a kind of father figure, doing everything" for him.[20] Mike was familiar with this idea. "You need Tristan, and I need the Father-Figure," Thom had told him. "I am not being sarcastic about you any more than I am about me, just using shorthand. And I am not Tristan. And you are not the Ideal Father."[21]

Thom came to see his hepatitis-enforced break from a self-destructive spiral of drinking and cruising as a blessing in disguise. "It has been interesting, in a way, standing back from things for a while," he told White a month into his convalescence. "I think I see myself a bit more clearly."[22] He noticed a "curious coolness" in his attitudes and perceptions. "It is something to do with the pleasure of regaining strength (which I am, steadily) combined with the residue of that distance that illness gives you to your life," he told Mike. "I could finally, for the first time in several years, make a large perception about what I am rather than what I want to be. (I have often been perceptive about what I want to be, cf. most of my poetry. It is not difficult like the other, though.)"[23]

Standing back from himself, Thom felt able to write to Mike with greater emotional honesty. Mike had credited Thom, in Thom's phrase, with "lack of feeling because I often don't show feeling." Thom replied that he "admire[d] the understatement of feeling more than anything."[24] His distrust of overt feelings meant that, quarreling with Mike via letter, he could sound extremely rational, cold, condescending, and impatient. Feelings and emotions were more Mike's domain. "A difference between us: for you, love must be passion at all costs—the trouble is that there are a few passions that work strictly against love, for example the passion to humiliate," Thom told him on one occasion: "for me, love must avoid hurting at all costs—the trouble is that this is a negative and in my case I've hardly been successful."[25]

Determined never to live through "a repetition of what we've had together in the last years"—"we'd have had more if we were separate"—

Thom tried to convince Mike to return to San Francisco and draw a line under their quarrels.[26] He still felt Mike's insistence on monogamy was a "fiercely clung-to abstraction," but tried to broker a compromise based on the acceptance of differences. "I love you and I would like us always to live together, but I cannot promise you anything besides love and shelter," he told Mike. "On the other hand, I expect no promises from you—there will be a succession of Toms, and though I may like some more than others, I assume none of them will bring you much happiness. I will always be here, and I will always love you. I hope you know that. And I hope you come back here."[27]

It would be "a new start" and a "modest one," Thom hoped. "Modest in that we live together because of our need for each other, and recognize that, and want to make each other stronger, not trying to deliberately weaken each other."[28] Thom saw Mike's relationship with Tom Gee as "an abortive attempt—at a 2nd marriage" in which Mike was trying to "get a reaction" from him. "It was partly (entirely!) my awareness that made me think to hell with you both," Thom wrote, "I'll feel nothing & show nothing."[29] In acknowledging that "there will be a succession of Toms," Thom realized he needed to incorporate Mike's desires into their shared life: he could be promiscuous, but Mike would need a marriage. He found it "difficult to tell," as things stood, whether they were still together. "You go on loving somebody however badly you treat each other," he told Lehmann, "and after you've stopped wanting sex with each other."[30]

Thom was also more honest about what he wanted. "I didn't— I couldn't—write a line during the era of the great quarrels and the era of Tom Gee, the whole time you were here," he told Mike. He did not blame Mike, but "it contributed to my unhappiness," he continued, "which in turn made it more difficult for me to write again. Writing was once easy for me: it is when you start, I guess, but now it is very lengthy and difficult, so if I do not arrange my life according to it I simply do not have a chance."[31]

Convalescing on Fell Street gave him plenty of time to think. He began a new notebook and vowed to finish poems like "Breakfast,"

"The Doctor's Own Body," "No Speech from the Scaffold," and "Driving to Florida," for which he had made notes throughout 1962. These were ambitious poems: he spent a lot of time and energy on them, especially "Tending Bar," about Don, and "The Doctor's Own Body," but was ultimately dissatisfied. "Tending Bar" was too "abstractified" where he had attempted a more concrete examination of "strength."[32] His interest in doctors came from his recuperation: doctors and bartenders "typified" a kind of man who "learns, gradually, to control his experience," whose strength "is never absolute or invariable."[33] Thom tried to turn his recovery of strength into poems and drew on his sickbed reading for supplementary material. He copied sentences from *The Magic Mountain*—"disease was a perverse, dissolute form of life"[34]—into his notebook and tried to apply his new subject matter to the humane values he had sought to embody in *My Sad Captains*. "To diagnose the ailing / Must be my sympathy," remarks the speaker of "The Doctor's Own Body," echoing Camus's Dr. Rieux. Heroic aims—"Who can reform a sea?"—were out.[35]

Other poems were too personal for Thom to complete. One fragment called "The Queer" relates to what he called "the problem of the personal poem." "I'm not sure that I want to write 'confessional' poems of the recent Lowell type," he reflected, "or if I do, I want them to be happy poems, because most experience is finally happy—or it is warm and indiscriminate."[36] For Thom, sexual desire was a good, happy thing—despite the masks and disguises he felt necessary in his poems—although he acknowledged that "queers too / use love as a weapon." "To hold a woman in your arms is to hold softness / but to hold a man is to hold a hardness / equal to my own," he wrote. "The thickness of men's necks, the way thr pants are drawn tight across thr asses—I understand that the same things may not attract you."[37] His defiant tone would not emerge publicly for another decade, but his notes were an indication that he saw his life, his queer marriage to Mike, as one future strand of his work; he began keeping a diary, documenting his life, their life together. He called it "The Record" and, as he became stronger, steadily made notes about meeting people, going to bars and movies, general gossip, reflections on his writing and relationships, often no more than a line or two a day. "I want all the people in the world to be in every poem I write," he reflected, "the heroes and the ordinary people."[38]

When Thom returned to Filbert Street in mid-May, he was almost fully recovered. "I have really had a very good 6 months," he told his aunts. "I have got a lot done, and been very happy. Also I have put on 12lbs, which is good, since I was always too skinny. Next month I can drink a beer occasionally."[39] Mike returned days afterward with a "very good attitude," but their reunion was short-lived because Thom had agreed to accompany Don on a road trip across Mexico.[40] Driving south, they dropped Tanner in Los Angeles to visit his American girlfriend, Marcia Albright, and spent a few days at Laguna Beach before heading east through Yuma and Tucson. They crossed into Mexico at Nogales and visited Guaymas and Mazatlán, drove inland to Guadalajara and Morelia, and arrived in Mexico City some twelve days after leaving San Francisco. They slept in the car as far as Guadalajara and suffered periodic bouts of "dysentery." Thom thought Mexico was "the loveliest country" he had seen, and enjoyed the "incredibly varied" landscapes of "desert, tropical vegetation, bush mountains."[41] In Mexico City he found bullfights "mediocre" and "distasteful."[42] One evening they were "misled by guide to highclass whorehouse," and the next "misled by queens to highclass roadhouse."[43] From Mexico City they drove to Acapulco, then to Tampico, their final Mexican stop, where they spent nights among the bars and whorehouses of the waterfront district.[44]

Thom had promised to accompany Don north to Chicago, where he planned to enter the construction business with his youngest brother. En route, they stopped in New Orleans and stayed with Don's "warm and generous" friends Bob Barron and Mike Chittim.[45] Barron was a physician and a connoisseur of Chinese pottery, Chittim an attorney for an insurance company: "elegant gays," Thom later called them.[46] He slept with Chittim (his first sex of the year) and got drunk (his first time in eight months) with more of Don's friends at La Casa de los Marinos.

Don introduced him to Clay Shaw, a businessman he had met while at Tulane through their mutual interest in playwriting.[47] Shaw was "urbane, accomplished, cultured," and widely respected in New Orleans's civil and social life; when Thom met him, he was managing director of the International Trade Mart and actively involved in the restoration of the historic French Quarter. Don was drawn to him for the same reasons as he was Barron and Chittim: Shaw was tall, distinguished, fluent in four languages, widely read, and frequented the ballet, opera, and symphony.[48]

New Orleans was the high point of the trip, Chicago the low. "Don's relations with his parents are too complicated for an outsider to be able to deal with either them or him," Thom told Mike. "His father is almost exactly my father, down to manner & speeches."[49] Tanner visited for an afternoon, witnessed the toxicity, and left almost immediately. Both he and Thom were convinced that Don's return to Chicago would be "a tragic mistake," but Don was stubborn and stuck to his decision.[50] First, though, Don had to go to San Francisco to settle his affairs. Thom had seen little of America beyond California and New York, so Don swept him and another friend, Thom O'Malley, through Oklahoma, Texas, New Mexico, Colorado, Utah, and Nevada en route to California. "Flat, gentle, expressionless, beautiful country," Thom wrote of the stretch from Dallas to Amarillo, "full of beautiful men with blond hair & uncomplicated faces."[51] They arrived in San Francisco on Thom's thirty-fourth birthday. "I wish I could keep travelling for ever," he told Tanner. "I wouldn't write anything, but I'd have a great time."[52]

In the fall of 1963, Thom's life changed again as he prepared to start teaching for the first time in eight months. He decided to curtail his reviewing commitment to *The Yale Review* and give only one poetry reading every two years. "Both these occupations take up more of my energy than I'm interested in giving them," he told Lehmann, "and also bring into play emotions in myself that I dislike." It was also a step toward arranging his life around writing poems, something he hoped would help renew his relationship with Mike and continue the fertile creative period he had enjoyed while recovering from hepatitis. He also determined to "write some serious prose" about "the poets I like best."[53] This, he hoped, would also help his composition. When Thom had seen Yvor Winters in spring 1961, Winters "told me all my recent poems (including 'Innocence') were journalistic and melodramatic and I ought to give up poetry for a few years and concentrate on criticism."[54] He had no desire to go that far, but he thought deeply about Winters's advice about how writing "carefully considered essays . . . would improve your thought, your scholarship, your perception, and your poetry."[55] With this in mind, he had started to plan an essay about William Carlos Williams, but did not commit to writing it until 1965.[56] It would prove one of his most important essays, not only for his analysis of Williams but also for the effect that his deep reading of Williams had on his own poetry. Without Winters's advice, Thom might never have written it.

That semester, Thom taught freshman composition, his usual verse-writing class, and a new course on recent British and American poetry. That was during the day; at night, he nursed Mike, who had come down with hepatitis again. "I am being a nurse at the same time as starting work again at the university," he told White. "Lucky I have been in hospital, or I wouldn't know how to wash somebody in bed."[57] For Thom, the irony was that "for the first time in 3 years" he and Mike had "a definable relationship."[58] Illness, and uncertainty about his future, meant Mike was "close to a nervous breakdown."[59] He depended on Thom, a situation Thom found "terrif[ying] and inhibit[ing]" and which filled him "with cold impulses of self-preservation."[60] The winter was "crisis after fucking crisis," he reflected. "I do not know why I love life still. Insensitivity? Blind stupidity?"[61] When he could leave Mike resting, Thom was "dazzled by fleshly splendors" at the Tool Box.[62] Sexually the year was "deeply unsatisfactory" and, with Mike convalescing, Thom felt "hampered by [the] set-up" because he could not bring tricks back to the apartment.[63] "I will not be able to think calmly about this time of my life for another 10 years. [. . .] I am a tenant in my apartment, and a tenant to

M's tyrannous misery, which he cannot help," Thom wrote. "I must be strong, I must contain myself, & not complain. It is my choice to live with him, after all."[64]

Difficult domestic circumstances spurred Thom to live by the values—openness, sympathy—he espoused in his work. Between teaching and nursing, he managed to finish "The Vigil of Corpus Christi," which examines how a man, "like a sentinel / at limits" is reawakened to physical and psychological "fulness" when a dog licks his ankles. In a departure from more typically Gunn-like hardness of "stiff blanket" and "unrelated edges," the man "grinned // with an unsoldierly joy" and felt a new appreciation of "soft sweet power."[65] Moreover, it is a bodily "fulness" Thom experienced firsthand during his own recovery from hepatitis. In "Vigil," Thom no longer privileged the complex, inward philosophizing that characterizes his early work and began to write of the value of the body alongside the mind. "What revives me (i.e. brings back my sense of life) is that sense of being one's body," he wrote later, "no more, no less, filling it exactly, beautifully, adequately."[66]

Thom was working through major changes in subject, style, and outlook, and found writing more difficult than ever. Acute self-questioning made "The Doctor's Own Body" and "The Vigil of Corpus Christi" transitional poems, unsatisfactory in a technical sense but important staging posts on Thom's route toward a more open, relaxed, humane poetry. Around the same time he wrote "Vigil," Thom labored over "The Girl of Live Marble." He sent an early draft to Tanner and White, who discussed it over dinner. White "saw it as among other things a poem about 'seeking,'" Tanner reported, "ie . . . that most love, so called, is in fact a narcissistic 'seeking', and the seeker in fact only wants to find his own reflection."[67] This was Thom's intention. He felt his main subjects were awakening and recognition: "Awakening as pure experience; awakening as proof of identity; awakening as prelude to identity," he wrote, with poems like "On the Move," "The Vigil of Corpus Christi," and "Waking in a Newly Built House" in mind. He felt "recognition (i.e. of other human beings)" was a subject he had "made tries at & haven't really succeeded in."[68]

"The Girl of Live Marble" combines awakening and recognition and was an important step for Thom. Between its first publication, in *The Observer*, and its collection in *Touch*, Thom revised the ending to show "as the watcher / Moves close, it is himself he sees."[69] Thom thought his poems about "recognition" would "constitute the first real step forward in thought." He wanted from his new work "the new vision fastened in the material world by the style." It was a vision of "strength, variety, validity of life, implying the ethically good. The good must be in commerce with other people, in that delight at their freedom which also makes one's freedom more precise."[70]

As his poetry became more populated, Thom's life felt more solitary than usual. With Mike unwell, Tanner in England, and Don in Chicago, he felt "a constant poignancy this fall—of loss everywhere."[71] He was "Mr Limbo," he told Tanner. "I don't go out much to drink, I work hard, I spend hours writing, I go to bed surprisingly early." Only writing kept him from "self-reproach."[72] Hepatitis had derailed his European plans for 1963, but Thom arranged another sabbatical from Berkeley in order to visit England in 1964. Tanner told him there was "a new nation gestating,"[73] and he "look[ed] forward enormously" to "living in London" for a while.[74] Thom wanted to know how he felt "about living there for more than just a summer,"[75] as he seemed to think about "moving to England" for good "every year."[76]

In March 1964, Thom was awarded a grant from the National Institute of Arts and Letters that would enable him to stay in England for a year. He was delighted: he had twelve months to write, free of teaching, and could "pay M's bills, bring him to Europe for summer."[77] Happy and full of anticipation "to travel & see all my friends this year," Thom seemed to enjoy day-to-day life again in a way that had been impossible for several years.[78] Coming home from a party at the Tool Box, "the best in years," he had "the feeling of adequacy in myself, in the experience. The ability to be. The ability to be happy."[79] Mike was also "happy & bewildered at thoughts of going to Europe,"[80] and looked forward to leaving behind his latest day job as a bank teller. At night, he directed a musical revue, *Pocketful of Wry*, at the Old Spaghetti Factory, a beatnik cabaret-restaurant in North Beach where he and Thom had struck up a friendship with Fred Kuh, its colorful proprietor.[81] In June—when *Pocketful of Wry* had finished its short run—they sublet the Filbert apartment to the poet Donald Justice and made separate cross-country journeys to New York: Thom via Chicago to see Don, and Mike via Kearny to visit his parents.[82]

In New York, they reconvened in the city most nights to go to the theater. Thom stayed once again at William Sloane House and spent his days cruising Greenwich Village. He worked his way down Christopher Street from the Stonewall Inn to Keller's, a "super-butch" leather bar on the West Side Highway.[83] In the Village he met Doric Wilson, a "handsome & sexy 25-yr old red-haird dramatist" with whom he spent "about 4 hrs in bed."[84] Wilson was resident playwright at Caffe Cino, a Village coffeehouse and Off-Off-Broadway avant-garde theater.[85] After Thom and Mike saw *Three Sisters* at the Actors Studio Theater, they ran into Wilson and took him to Keller's. Thom thought Mike "sour & rude: it cd have been the best evening in NY," he fumed, "and it was the worst."[86] Mike was likely jealous that Thom's latest trick was building a career for himself in New York theater, something Mike had been trying and failing to do for the past six years. The day before Thom left for England, he and Mike had "a terrible quarrel [about] 'roles and relationships.'"[87] Thom feared that their reconciliation, still delicate, was about to collapse. Before going to the airport, he "walked unhappy all day" and saw Mike in the evening. Mike was "very cold—he may not come to Europe, everything may be finished."[88]

17

RETURN

Thom's excitement at being back in London was mixed with "depression at the almost inevitable split with M," who was "probably rightly" leaving him. "Yet that situation is given unreality from being in London again—a London exotic & without the strain of Father's presence."[1] The Beatles were the soundtrack to a more optimistic, vibrant, aspirational city than the one Thom had left a decade earlier; his year in London "mov[ed] to the tunes of the Beatles," beginning with *A Hard Day's Night*, "and was punctuated by the rebellious joy of their singles."[2]

Mike decided to visit London after all, a prelude to a driving holiday across Europe with Tom Gee. "Everything totally meaningless," Thom wrote. "I cannot alter what happens to me. I can only try to control my attitude to it."[3] At one point he "absolutely broke down,"[4] feeling two fevers: "the Mike-fever of despair and the (allied?) cruising fever."[5] Mike visited for four days and returned to London for a month after his European trip. Thom's life changed "from writing poetry and having sex to writing criticism and going to shows."[6] He and Mike saw everything, from *The Jew of Malta* and *The Birthday Party* to *Les Enfants du Paradis* and *Entertaining Mr. Sloane*. But Thom felt Mike was "very cold to me, consistently,"[7] and his feeling that they could reconcile—prompted by Mike's "absolutely wonderful"[8] first visit—evaporated. Mike was set on living with Tom Gee when they returned to San Francisco. "[Gee] was not somebody who committed," Mike recalled, "and I wanted him to commit. I love you and I'm yours forever. And finally he did, on that trip."[9]

Thom felt "empty and sad" when Mike flew home. "I miss you very much, sweetheart, and worry about you," he wrote. "Forgive me for such a short letter. I am not quite sure how to write, or what to write."[10] Resigned to Mike's decision, Thom was nevertheless shocked that, after their protracted series of quarrels and reconciliations, they had finally separated. He was "deeply depressed" and his "own deep selfishness" hit him "like a revelation."[11] Mike wrote him from San Francisco, "heartbreaking in [his] kind but firm distantness."[12]

When Thom arrived in London, he stayed in Tony White's flat in Notting Hill.[13] He liked the neighborhood's "rich jostling flow" and "promiscuous mix" of people[14]—Poles, Italians, Irish, Jamaicans—and found himself "a large room on the second floor of a handsome Victorian house" on Talbot Road, three streets from White. From his window he could see a young boy in a house across the street, "gazing at what went on below him on Talbot Road. He sticks in my mind as an emblem of the potential and excitement and sense of wonder I found all about me in the London of that year."[15] He saw White almost every day. They worked in their separate flats each morning—Thom writing poems, Tony translating French novels[16]—and emerged on their balconies at midday to "signal to each other (through binoculars) if we wanted to go for a beer and lunch together."[17] On Monday nights they would discuss a book over dinner, cooking for each other on alternate weeks, and continue their discussion at the Britannia, a favorite pub on nearby Clarendon Road. They worked through Aristotle, Camus's *La Chute*, *The Count of Monte Cristo*, Valéry's "Ébauche d'un serpent," *Billy Budd*, and works by Keith Douglas, Robert Lowell, and Shakespeare.

Later, they discussed Thom's own poems-in-progress. In London he finished a project that he had started during his recovery from hepatitis. Under the draft title "For the Survivor," he worked on the sequence that became "Misanthropos": a series of seventeen linked poems about a man who believes himself the sole survivor of a global war.[18] The project originated in "wide-ranging discussions" between Doody and Tanner, Thom reflected, "some of them across the bed of my recuperation."[19] Writing to Mike about his "longish poem" in spring 1963, Thom felt "scared, since it is at the stage from which it cd become the best thing I ever wrote or the worst."[20] His central character, a "courier after identity," faces a similar problem. He has "the entire world to choose from" but the choice paralyzes him and leads to "the onset of hatred, until / the final man walks the final hill // without thought or feeling, as before."[21] Thom hoped that poetry could "once again become a major genre," and "Misanthropos" was his attempt to create something similar to what he found in "Mann, Proust, Conrad, Camus, Lawrence . . . a complete attitude to experience worked out in detail, qualified, supported, given an imaginative realization." He thought that "the examination of such attitudes" helped him "in an indirect but very important way, to live my life."[22]

Thom described "Misanthropos" as "a combination of science-fiction and pastoral,"[23] but its most pervasive influence is Thomas Mann. Its first poem, "The Last Man," develops an idea Thom found in *The Magic Mountain*: that physical recuperation could act as a metaphor for moral and spiritual recovery. Thom copied into his notebook a passage from the novel in which Mann asks whether life was "perhaps only an infection, a sickening of matter? Was that which one might call the original procreation of matter only a disease, a growth produced by morbid stimulation of the immaterial?"[24] Thom drew directly on this passage in "All that snow pains my eyes," the tenth poem of "Misanthropos," in which a disease, never named, is "life's parody."[25] Mann's suggestion that "the first step toward evil, toward desire and death" occurred at "the primeval stage of matter, the transition from the insubstantial to the substance"[26] provided Thom with his subject in "Misanthropos": his "last man," through concurrent physical, mental, and spiritual recovery, could become the "first man." In an early note, Thom wanted the poem to be about "the psychology leading to the act of sympathy (thro perceptions of the meaningless, guilt, the presence of others). You start as the last man & end as the first man."[27] The "presence of others" was Thom's primary concern. He wanted "to write a kind of poetry that hasn't been much written this century. Hardy writes of relationships, and WCW of all the living world, so some have done it." In "Misanthropos," this meant exploring what happens "when my survivor meets all the other survivors. I want to be thro with the Lonely Man. How he helps them, how they help him."[28]

This figure, "the Lonely Man," was Thom's latest poetic alter ego. He called 1963 "an interesting & unexpected year" in which he learned a surprise lesson. "I tend to create alibis everywhere, with everyone, and for everything," he felt, whereas Don was "lacking alibis," was upfront and honest with everyone, and made of his life something "genuinely strong and achieved."[29] He began a poem called "The Alibi," in which he realized how he manipulated situations with Mike:

> Now my mind catches up & glances back
> & wreckages of trust litter the track.[30]

Thom dropped the poem but mounted a similar examination of alibis and shifting identities in "Misanthropos." "I was presence without full / being," the speaker remarks. Wearing dark glasses, "Nobody in the street could / see if my eyes were open."[31] Until "Misanthropos," hiding in plain sight was the modus operandi of Thom's doubles and doppelgängers. Now, he wanted a greater self-honesty to underpin poems about relationships, community, and sympathy. "Misanthropos" concludes on a didactic note: Thom encourages the reader to "Turn out toward others, meeting their look at full, / Until you have completely stared / On all there is to see."[32] As he reflected later, "the process of understanding" meant "more than the business of merely comprehending the text. [. . .] Understanding means taking [poems] to heart, means—ultimately— *acting* on them."[33]

It seemed fitting that Thom began his most ambitious poem in America and finished it in England. It bridged his geographical imagination. "The hill to which the last man has retreated," he explained, "shares characteristics with both Ladd's Hill in North Kent and Lands End in San Francisco."[34] He spent the autumn and winter revising "Misanthropos," asking Tanner and White for guidance. The poem helped clarify two years' worth of thinking and gave Thom greater confidence in his change of direction. He felt he was "searching for . . . a way of defining a type of energy that *doesn't* infringe on other people's energy—that possibly may even help other people."[35] The British stage actors Alan Dobie and Julian Glover read the poem on the BBC Third Network in March 1965, and it was published in *Encounter* that summer.[36] When "Misanthropos" was included in *Touch* two years later, Thom was surprised and disappointed to find his writing was "still very English, in spite of my long stay in America & my attempts at experiments."[37]

The success of his joint *Selected Poems* with Ted Hughes, which Faber published in 1962, meant Thom was one of Britain's most read and recognized young poets. "If people who don't read poetry know about me it's because of the leather jacket and the years in America," he reflected. "I have no illusions about the true value of my image. It's a pose, but when somebody wears a suit he is posing as much as I am."[38] When Thom returned to London, he found himself in demand. His "lunches and dinners" with John Lehmann and others were "awful enough,"[39] as was the party Monteith threw for him at the Faber offices on Russell Square.[40] There, a fortnight later, he met T. S. Eliot for the first and only time.[41] Eliot was still a director at Faber but, in ill health, visited the office "two afternoons a week."[42] Thom found him "an immensely big man" who "would start long sentences and get lost in the middle of them."[43] When Eliot died four months later, Thom wrote a condolence letter to Monteith.[44]

Thom also saw plenty of Tony Tanner. In Cambridge he attended the conferral of Tanner's doctorate at King's College, along with Tony White. In London, Tanner often joined Thom for convivial weekends spent drinking and talking. Soho was their stomping ground, from the Romano Santi (Italian) and Madame Maurer's (German) on Greek Street, to the Golden Lion on Dean Street, and farther afield to the Salisbury in Covent Garden and the Duke of York in Fitzrovia. Marcia Albright, Tanner's American girlfriend, often accompanied them. She had joined Tanner in Cambridge earlier in the year and worked in London as an editorial assistant at *Encounter*. "My boss was Stephen Spender," she recalled, "if you could call Stephen Spender a boss . . . He was the literary editor." Marcia preferred London to Cambridge. "It was very misogynistic," she recalled. "It was just taken for granted as part of the culture, that there were things that men talked about among themselves."[45]

Marcia was youthful and vivacious, a combination that Thom sometimes saw as flighty and incessant. His feelings could manifest themselves in ways similar to some of the misogynistic treatment Marcia had experienced in Cambridge. When Tanner and Marcia saw Thom, often in the company of Tony White, at times it could feel like a Cambridge dinner party. "I always felt I was excluded from the 'serious' conversations about literature and poetry," she reflected. "It was lovely having [Thom] around. I got to know him a bit better, but I was not privy to the literary conversations that they had. I was considered a girl . . ."[46] That was Thom's attitude. "Marcia is a good girl," he told Tony White. "I hope things turn out all right with those two."[47] After a few months spent in Tanner's and Marcia's company, Thom wondered whether "on the whole they slightly get on each other's nerves."[48] But Marcia grew on him as the months passed. "It is quite surprising how I steadily like her more & more," he observed in a letter to Mike.[49] By the time Thom left London, he was "completely at ease with her now, & she with me."[50] Marcia, however, "never felt like there was this real intimacy that he would allow. I always felt he was very, very guarded in terms of allowing his inner self to emerge."[51]

Regardless of the true depth of their personal relationship, Marcia championed Thom's work and helped to convince Spender to take "Misanthropos" for *Encounter*. "I read it and thought it was an amazing poem. Stephen would come back for five minutes every three months and look through the [submissions] pile," she recalled, "and he'd put 'Misanthropos' at the bottom because it was so long. Finally I just said to him: 'How would you feel if you were the editor who turned down *The Waste Land*?' It was easy to make Stephen feel guilty. He had a lot to feel guilty about. So he read it, finally, and thought it was extraordinary."[52]

In November, at Tanner's invitation, Thom traveled to Cambridge and gave a reading at King's. He read at his "very best," he reflected, and enjoyed meeting Tanner's students, "who had Beatle haircuts and were far brighter and better-informed than I ever remember our frivolous generation."[53] One of Tanner's students was Clive Wilmer, who had first come across Thom's work in Alvarez's 1962 anthology *The New Poetry*. "Thom was terribly famous in those days," Clive reflected. They got into "a real conversation" after the reading, "in a way that you don't often at parties. I felt I'd gotten quite close to him, talking about poetry. He had a knack for making other people feel important." Clive subsequently visited Thom in London and showed him some of his own poems, including "The Burial Mound." Thom suggested he cut the second stanza. "I made some protest that that fouled up the rhyme scheme," Clive recalled, "so one of the rhymes would be incomplete. [. . .] He thought about it for a bit and said, 'I think those rhymes are more for you than for the reader, and the poem can do without them.' I went off home and thought about it, and he was right."[54]

Writing well and seeing friends in London made Thom think seriously about a permanent return to England. He was committed to teach another year at Berkeley, but felt like "giving up teaching for a few years."[55] When he learned from Mark Schorer, chairman of the English Department, that he would be eligible for tenure in 1966, Thom "wonder[ed] if I'll still be there."[56] But it was London, not teaching, that gave Thom pause. "Partly London (& England) are so much better than they used to be—they have grown into what I wanted them to be," he told Hall, "and partly my need to be an exile has vanished. It is wonderful being able to explore with recognition."[57] Moreover, Thom was beginning to think of a future without Mike. "One never knows, of course," he continued, "there are so many new phases that get entered just when you think everything is over, and he is certainly someone worth holding on to, though I must say it's I who have behaved badly to him always, not him to me."[58]

By "explor[ing] with recognition," Thom meant living in London as a gay man for the first time. With White he frequented neighborhood pubs like the Britannia, but he ventured farther when cruising. His favorite haunt, the Coleherne, attracted a butch leather crowd and hosted "a dynamic West Indian Band" on Sunday mornings.[59] Its packed saloon bar was "smoky with that extraordinary, slightly predatory, suspicious atmosphere that hung around most gay venues of the times," recalled one of Thom's friends, the actor Gil Sutherland. At closing time, everyone moved outside "in what became a bit of a 'meat market.'" Thom often made the short walk to the Place, off the New Kings Road, which "operated 'officially' as a coffee bar" to circumvent licensing laws. A rickety wooden staircase led to a two-room basement. "It was quite outrageous and the anonymous sexual activity that went on in the almost pitch darkness was astonishing," Sutherland recalled. The Place was "immensely popular in those hedonistic days" and Thom went as often as he could.[60]

Thom saw "promiscuous sex as an attempt to gain power over the world."[61] It was not always joyous. Some nights at the Coleherne were "desperatesville"; other times he felt "oddly inhibited."[62] After a night with "Graham of East Ham," he experienced "a great feeling of simultaneous loss & preservation of detachment."[63] He was not "a depressed person," he told Mike, but felt his "depressed periods . . . have a kind of clinging persistence, and hold on faithfully."[64] The relationship between his two fevers—cruising and despair about Mike—intrigued him, but writing about them was, for the moment, beyond him. His recovery from hepatitis had been an important period of self-reflection, but he struggled to reconcile the sympathetic, outward-looking, peopled poetry of "Misanthropos" with his desire to write more openly about personal subjects. In his early poems, he was "attempting to realize the Man of Energy," he reflected. "Now I am attempting to find an adequate embodiment of the man who helps, really an extension of the other. [. . .] The helping must be unheroic but with a chance of effectiveness." He wondered whether this could be "an attempt to do in poetry what I have failed to do with Mike?"[65]

With "Misanthropos" finished, Thom tried to reexamine his attitude toward personal poems. Clive lent him copies of Sylvia Plath poems that were later collected in *Ariel*. Thom did not value Plath. "The trouble is with the emotion, itself, really," he told Clive: "it is largely one of hysteria, and it is amazing that her hysteria has produced poetry as good as this."[66] At the same time, he read Robert Lowell's *For the Union Dead* and thought "The Flaw" "one of the most beautiful poems he has written."[67]

When Lowell's *Life Studies* was published in 1959, Thom privately found it "much less important, more light-weight, than his earlier work."[68] In print, he applauded its "virtue," by which he meant its account of "a human experience that is so recognizable" in a style "honest and clear, with little attempt at any rhetoric but the simplest." He also criticized the "flatness" of its "rather loose prosy style."[69] Stylistically, Thom preferred *For the Union Dead* because it seemed the height of Lowell's "idiosyncratic way" of combining "the greater toughness of poetry written in meter" and "the tenderer measures of the present in free verse" in a single line.[70] He also preferred its subject matter: personal but less overtly confessional than *Life Studies*. By 1966 he counted Lowell among his poetic "heroes."[71]

Moreover, Lowell's poems reminded him of Thomas Hardy, whom he thought a model for poetry about relationships. He wanted to "learn from" both but was "careful not to get too close to either." He wondered whether "a form of disciplined exploration" could facilitate the writing of personal poems. "For [Hardy] it was the prose autobiographies of his wife, for [Lowell] too it was a prose autobiography he wrote," Thom reflected. He resolved to write "a prose autob. essay, <u>not</u> to be published. Of total honesty."[72] A transitional step seemed necessary: writing personal poems was "difficult," Thom found, because his "own outline [was] so blurred" and his "own desires so unclear." He saw in himself:

> (1) a desire for a consistent and unbrutal strength, which I know I come nowhere near achieving (2) feelings of guilt about M (3) a liking for being alone, but a liking for others, even random others (4) a readiness to enjoy my experience (5) various complicated different kinds of cowardice (6) the ability to become depressed or happy at the touch of a hair. These do not constitute much by way of character.[73]

While writing these notes, Thom cruised daily and felt alternately "terrible" and "manic-ly chipper."[74] In the middle of a manic period, he received a letter from John Lehmann about "Misanthropos." "Lehmann makes an interesting comment," he told Mike. "'What I wish is that you didn't pull your poetry-making self so far away from your life-enjoying self.' [. . .] I think he is on to a fault of mine but hasn't phrased it very accurately."[75] The comment struck a nerve because Thom was attempting such a reconciliation in his notebook. He acknowledged to Lehmann that he struggled "to get down on paper the whole of what I find valuable or true about what I experience." He found "a great delight in the trivial and casual—things one may see on the street—that are somehow lovely because they are part of the whole absurd and pointless and wonderful expression of energy ('life-energy,' that is)."[76] Thom's "great delight" echoed his plan for a new series of poems that were "autobiographical, to some extent," and included "the mystique (my mystique) of the City" and a "sequel to Misanth in sense of people together, their withness with each other, mine with them."[77]

Alongside Hardy and Lowell, Thom drew on a third poet: William Carlos Williams. In the spring, he began two projects about Williams. The first was a major essay about Williams's poetry to mark the publication of several Williams volumes in England.[78] Thom praised Williams's authenticity and originality, how his poems "embodied a desire that the unknown and unexpressed should not be treated in terms of the already known and expressed. [. . .] He was in love with the bare fact of the external world, its thinginess; and the love mastered him for a lifetime."[79] Thom felt that Williams's "stylistic qualities" were "governed . . . by a tenderness and generosity of feeling which makes them fully humane. For it is a humane action to attempt the rendering of a thing, person, or experience in the exact terms of its existence."[80] It had taken Thom a decade to come around to Williams, and he used the essay to articulate some of his own new ideas about poetry. He thought it his "best piece of prose"[81] and was delighted when James Laughlin, Williams's friend and publisher at New Directions, wrote "saying he wished 'Bill' had been alive to read my [essay]."[82]

For the second project, Thom collaborated with Ander, by then a respected photographer, on a book of poems and photographs. In *Positives*, Thom wrote short poems in response to Ander's black-and-white photographs: the book traces a life arc through scenes of infancy, adolescence, youth, work, relationships, and old age.[83] Thom had "always wanted to work with pictures" and he felt Ander's photographs "made a good starting point for my imagination."[84] He wanted to capture "the sense of crowded, detailed London" and explore his major themes—awakening and recognition—in "photograph poems."[85] "Thr are endless possibilities in it," he felt: "the idea of the beautiful being of—not only one's own life but—another's life, and the types of connection possible."[86] Thom used the project to develop "a free verse based on the seven syllable line; physical perception emphasized."[87] Syllabics allowed him to write about "smaller subjects" in a "more relaxed and casual" tone than was possible in metrical verse.[88] Thematically, Thom saw *Positives* as "a continuation of Misanthropos i.e. life in the world, signs of an undertaking, the nature of being committed to the humane & poignancy of the concrete."[89] They were not personal poems, but they demonstrated his newfound "commitment to oneself-as-part-of-others."[90]

On April 1, Thom booked his return ticket to the States. "[Ten] weeks from Tues," he wrote, "when I could do with 50, starting to write so much."[91] A typical day involved work on a new edition of Fulke Greville for Faber, lunch with White, an afternoon drafting *Positives* or working on his Williams essay, and an evening at the Coleherne or cruising Hampstead Heath. He submitted *Positives* to Faber in June, calling it "The Gunn Brothers' Guide to Humans."[92] Thom was pleased with "Misanthropos," *Positives*, and another long free verse poem called "Confessions of the Life Artist," but his prolific year had not shaped a new collection. "As for my next book of poems, I really don't know," he told Monteith. "I told you I thought I'd be able to send it to you this summer, but I'm afraid it'll be more like the end of the year." He knew "Misanthropos" would make up half the book; shorter lyric poems the other half, "but [I] won't be sure of them for some time."[93]

Thom's cruising fever abated, but his feelings of "guilt & despair" about Mike intensified as his return to San Francisco drew closer. "I have after 13 years thrown away the precious jewel I had," he wrote, "the one thing of value in my whole life."[94] His own emotional doubleness confused him: on alternate days he felt "the indifference . . . to what Mike is feeling" then "the craving for him, compounded of love & guilt, the selfish need for him. The one feeling without warmth, the other without dignity."[95] He tried to enjoy his last weeks in London, most of which he spent with White and the recently engaged Tanner and Albright.[96] White organized a farewell party on a canal boat, which slid through the "watery network of London" from Little Venice to Greenford and back.[97] Thom liked "gliding through the open secret"[98] and came to see the canals as an apt metaphor for the tension between openness and secrecy, his main obstacle to writing personal poems.

In later years, Thom overstated the singular joy of his year on Talbot Road. It had been "a year of great happiness," he felt, in which he reveled in an "openness and high-spiritedness and relaxation of mood" he "did not remember from the London of earlier years."[99] That was true, as was the pleasure he took from seeing friends like Tony White and Tony Tanner, as well as Ander and his Kentish aunts. He wrote well and was more productive than he had hoped to be. Moreover, it was a "year of reconciliation / to whatever it was I had come from."[100] It was the first time he had felt comfortable in London, and its pull made him contemplate a return. The shadow of Mike, however, and the breakdown of their relationship undercut his otherwise happy year and lent it a sense of unreality. Preparing to leave, his thoughts turned to a San Francisco with and without Mike. "Well, I certainly have my moments of depression, but there's no point in burdening you with them," he wrote to him, shortly before leaving London. "I often think that the only time in my life when I have been solidly and confidently happy was 1953–4. I guess that will remain so. You are very precious to me, my darling, and always will be the one person in the world I could ever love. And I love you."[101]

18

TOGETHER

Returning to San Francisco in mid-June, Thom had nowhere to live. In March, Donald Justice had left the Filbert apartment unexpectedly, and with Mike temporarily in New York working as a writer for *That Was the Week That Was*, a quick fix was required. Tom Gee moved their furniture into the basement and sublet the apartment to students for the rest of Justice's tenancy. When Mike returned to San Francisco in May, he moved in with Tom Gee, who lived two blocks away on the same street. With students still at his apartment, Thom had no choice but to do the same.

Mike was mostly absent: his musical revue, *Funny Side Up*, opened at the Sir Francis Drake Hotel the week Thom returned.[1] Thom avoided Gee, keeping to the Old Spaghetti Factory and a new Folsom bar called Detour. When he returned to 975 Filbert a week later, he expected Mike to come with him. Instead, Mike stayed with Gee. "I was somewhat pissed off at Mike over this at first, but one can hardly blame him," Thom told Tony White, "and actually we see quite a lot of each other and get on better than in several years, so maybe it is a good idea."[2] Privately, he was "in a daze, unthinking, not sad or happy" but was pleased to see Mike "happy & healthy."[3] Thom found it "much easier to talk to him frankly about himself, myself, and us," he told Tony Tanner, "in a way that he always (rightly) complained I didn't for the last two years."[4] Mike considered returning to 975 Filbert in August, but Thom felt they were "getting on so well with each other"[5] living apart that he did not want to risk renewing their quarrels. He had "moments of violent jealousy" about Mike and Tom Gee but mostly kept them to himself.[6]

Thom was "sleeping with the sexiest people ever."[7] He still thought San Francisco "one of the most attractive cities in the world," but London had made him sense that his future was elsewhere. "Nothing has really occurred to make me want to stay here longer than a year," he told White.[8] He tolerated living alone for the sake of his relationship with Mike and sought to explore his feelings in new poems that capitalized on the advances he had made in free verse. "Object of journal poems," he stated. "I want it to be a means of grasping the concrete—the casual perception which is rich in implication of the general, but thro which the general is not necessarily explicitly stated. Also attempt in this form (as in metrical form) to make the personal palatable." With this last aim in mind, Thom's first journal poem addressed his feelings of hopelessness and despair at how his and Mike's love was "getting lost":

> Living without you, where
> we used to live, I find
> the whole flat has gone sour.
> Living alone, trying
> to manage, I
> start filling the bare place
> with habits, but your absence
> is like a continual draught.
> Yet how they linger, the
> smells of a vacant flat!
> Every night, I sleep covered
> with more blankets than
> I ever needed before.[9]

Thom abandoned the poem, but, to his relief, the apartment was not "vacant" for long. By early October, Mike was "growing rather tired of Tom Gee" and wanted to return to 975 Filbert. "It's something I've always been a little ashamed about," Mike reflected, "because I just moved back, and I never said anything to [Tom]. We used to have good times together, but when push came to shove I just didn't want to be with him. I just couldn't see my life without Thom Gunn." Mike's return concluded more than five years of near-constant quarrels. "When I went in," he recalled, "Thom said, 'Let's have no more of that nonsense.'"[10] Their resolution to live together laid the foundations for what they knew, despite their differences, would be a shared life.

Thom returned to Berkeley that fall to teach a "dreadfully ambitious" course on the history of English lyric poetry from Chaucer to Hardy, as well as his usual verse-composition class and a course on recent British and American poetry.[11] Reading and planning, on top of committee meetings and graduate examinations, now that he was eligible for tenure, meant he was working "off my feet."[12] "He made us write a two-page paper every week—he was very strict about the two-page limit—and he always expected from us more sophistication than the other professors did," recalled his student Joan Acocella. "He gave us idiosyncratic material—more difficult, less lovable than the usual—and then he gave us his reasons for liking it, which were bound up with his moral personality: his reserve, his distance."[13] In his English poetry course, Thom leaned on Leavis's *Revaluation* and Winters's work on the Elizabethans. "Gascoigne is a fine poet," Thom told Tanner, thinking Winters "dead right," "and Ben Jonson (whom I read thoroughly for the first time) is one of the most exciting poets in English."[14] Thom could be distant and reserved in the classroom, but also mischievous. "Knowing full well I was probably the only teacher at Berkeley who had a tattoo," he later remarked, "I would wait till about the third week of term before rolling up my sleeves and watching the reaction of the students. They were shocked."[15] Lyle Tuttle, later Janis Joplin's tattooist, had inked the large black panther on Thom's right forearm in early 1962.[16]

One of Thom's new colleagues was his old Stanford friend Tony Herbold. "At that time, I now realize, he was a kind of epitome to me of romantic America," Thom reflected, "being a kind of married James

Dean (and this was a little before James Dean too.) And now he is very settled, with a mustache and 5 kids—though still a very nice man. Circles sure are starting to close, Algy old man."[17] Herbold's reappearance, full-time teaching, and an exhaustion so pervasive he could not write spooked Thom into thinking tenure would be a disaster. Shortly before Christmas, he approached James D. Hart, the new department chair, to discuss his future. "I told Hart that I was leaving in the summer," Thom told Tanner. "'Weally, Thom, I'm stunned,' he riposted." Thom agreed to take another sabbatical year, without pay, and make a final decision in summer 1967. "I don't see myself changing my mind," Thom continued. "San Francisco meanwhile has never seemed so exciting, but maybe this is partly because I know I shall be leaving it."[18]

In early 1966, an awareness that he would not teach again "at least for some years" seemed to free up Thom to write. He finished "Snowfall," a poem begun hesitatingly in London, and "No Speech from the Scaffold," which he had begun metrically in 1958, tried in syllabics in 1961, and, to his surprise, "[now] emerges in free verse!"[19] Another, "Back to Life," was an attempt "to get a form that combines the virtues of the iambic line (which deals with the past) and the virtues of the free verse line (which deals with the present)."[20] Thom's "wild experiments"[21] were poems with lines of variable length: the variation, he hoped, would work against the rhyme and meter to create a casual tone suitable for everyday subject matter.[22] He was most pleased with "Pierce Street," in which he used line breaks as caesurae to split pentameters into lines of two and three feet.[23] "Pierce Street" was originally a five-poem sequence before Thom cut it to a single poem about the apartment Chuck Arnett shared with several friends.[24] Thom regularly hung out with Chuck and friends at Pierce Street and was photographed in front of Chuck's "twice life-size" leathermen mural, "soldiers of the imagination."[25] He used the figures to examine his new interest in the body. "I am bodied in my skin," he wrote. Compared to the "silent garrison," "[t]hose who are transitory can move and speak." That transience, Thom suggests, is a more precious thing than static permanence.[26]

· · ·

Reading for his American poetry and English lyric courses, Thom found that his new writing interests in sympathy and humaneness opened new perspectives on old poems. "What bugs me so especially about Yeats and Eliot is their inhumanity," he told Tanner, "i.e. lack of humaneness, their contempt for ordinary nice rather silly harmless people."[27] Tanner cautioned that "humaneness . . . on its own could never produce major poetry."[28] Thom recognized the dangers: he thought the ending of "Blackie" was sentimental because "I tend to get sentimental about pretty boys"[29] and that *Positives* was "sentimental at best, but maybe there is a kind of sentimentality that constitutes a valid minor branch of art—valid so long as it doesn't pretend to majority."[30] He came to see sentimentality as his "chief danger," such was his "placing of a high value on such things as wonder, acceptance, etc."[31]

He found his heroes were "increasingly Pound, Williams, and Lowell" above Yeats and Eliot.[32] He came to Pound through Donald Davie's *Poet as Sculptor*, which Thom thought "a book of criticism that not only helps one's reading but could help one's writing."[33] He called "most of the second canto and the whole of the 47th . . . as good as anything in the last 50 years,"[34] a reassessment of his 1963 position in which he called the *Cantos* "the biggest con-job of the century."[35] From Davie, however, Thom learned that there was "ultimately something of an impersonality about Pound," whereas "Yeats' poetry is almost strictly poetry of personality." Thom considered this "by and large very obnoxious. And when personality becomes such an important part of the <u>content</u> of a man's poetry, I am unable not to judge it."[36] He valued Elizabethan songs like Campion's "Now winter nights enlarge" and sought to emulate its "certain anonymity of tone."[37] Avoiding the pitfalls of personality was a major part of Thom's continuing struggle to write personal poems. "I'm not aiming for central personality," he later remarked. "I want to write with the same kind of anonymity that you get in the Elizabethans and I want to move around between forms in the same way somebody like Ben Jonson did. At the same time I want to write in my own century."[38]

Thom's enthusiasm for Pound coincided with his discovery of Gary Snyder, whom he found one of the most exciting young poets in America.

He thought Snyder a "careful craftsman" who was influenced "in the best way and by the best of Pound (e.g. E.P.'s Cantos 2 & 4!)"[39] When Fulcrum published Snyder's *A Range of Poems* in Britain, Thom reviewed it for *Agenda* and examined how Snyder used Pound and Williams to write a poetry "of fact, not of metaphor or symbol; statement does all the work."[40] Snyder's "personal perceptions" were "made from the middle of work or of love" and were "those of a modest and honest man entrusting himself to his experience."[41] Two years later, reviewing *The Back Country* and *Six Sections from Mountains and Rivers Without End* for *The Listener*, Thom called Snyder's poetry "'personal,' in that it is almost all written in the first person," without being confessional. Its modesty, Thom argued, "comes from the fact that he is interested not in the unique experience but in the shared or sharable experience, the successive awakenings to wonder, to awareness and to sympathy."[42] Snyder's "attentiveness" was "a form of moral discipline."[43] Thom saw some of his own aspirations embodied in Snyder: a first-person poetry of moral responsibility that "patiently records the world, as an act of love."[44]

During his early-year "writing streak," Thom also experimented in free verse.[45] He sought the spontaneity of "unarranged exploration, perceptions crowding in, used, deserted for other perceptions."[46] As Clive Wilmer has noted, Thom's approach to writing free verse can be traced to Yvor Winters's scansion of Williams's poem "By the road to the contagious hospital" (known as "Spring and All"), in which there is "an even number of major stresses to the line, with lines ending as often as possible in mid-phrase."[47] Thom wrote "Touch," one of his finest free verse poems, in this rhythm. It privileges tactile sensation and describes someone climbing into bed beside a lover. Extreme enjambments—"I feel a is it / my own warmth surfacing or / the ferment of your whole / body"[48]—evoke the crowding in, and desertion of, perceptions that Thom saw as vital to the spontaneity of free verse. His source for the bed scene was Robert Creeley's poem "The World," in which Creeley follows "the mind, wandering, but at the same time trying to focus in on its own wandering and to map a small part of its course accurately and honestly."[49] In "Touch," the lovers create a place of warmth that is self-perpetuating, that "seeps /

from our touch in / continuous creation." This place is theirs alone, their "dark enclosing / cocoon," and their connection to the "dark / wide realm where we / walk with everyone."[50] The movement recalls "The World," in which, Thom wrote, Creeley contrasts "the real world with its commonplace light" with "the grey light of the love-making and the ghost."[51] Thom was pleased to have worked so many of his recent touchstones—modesty, sympathy, honesty, shared experiences—into one poem and felt that he had made, at last, an important and necessary advance.

Thom had hoped to finish his next book before Christmas 1965 but did not send it to Monteith until September 1966. It had taken him twice as long to write as any of his previous three collections and contained poems written as long ago as his Berlin stay in 1960. With "Misanthropos" alongside Thom's recent work in syllabics and free verse, the book was a bold experiment. He attributed its experimental nature to his "real indifference to being a career poet"[52] and decided to call it *Touch* after his best poem in free verse. The same day Thom sent the manuscript to Monteith, he also sent Winters some of his recent poems. "Your dissipated adventure in syllabics (or something) has weakened the whole texture of your perceptions," Winters replied. "Your rhythms, when I can find them, are uninteresting; the diction is genteel but unimportant. [. . .] You simply approach polite journalism."[53] When Thom replied, two months later, he conceded that Winters was "probably right" about the poems and reassured him that he had given up free verse "since I don't seem to be doing very well with it, and am going back to meter."[54]

In early June, grading exams on the Filbert roof, Thom felt "sad, puzzled, confused, v. much off sex."[55] A "moment of sadness"[56] colored his final day on campus: leaving Berkeley felt like the first of many impending departures. "I did so much writing last year, and grew a cubit," he told Hall, "which is why I must stop teaching a year or two, so as to fill out to justify that cubit."[57] He planned to spend autumn in San Francisco, "then take a roundabout route back to Europe" and arrive in England for Christmas.[58] "Why I am leaving Mike I really don't know—maybe I won't," he told Hall. "Decisions are easier to make when you're absent from someone than when you're around the actual warm vulnerable human being. So maybe I'll stay on here, for all I know."[59] When he learned he had received a grant from the Rockefeller Foundation, Thom adapted his plan: he would visit London in early 1967 with a view to a permanent return.[60] "I don't think about long-range plans very much," he told White, "and am acting like a low-grade slug, living from hour to hour."[61]

Shortly before the term ended, Thom had seen a friend take LSD. "Resolution," he wrote afterward, "to take LSD first thing of vacation."[62] His only previous experience with a hallucinogen was in 1958, when Paul Bowles, passing through the Bay Area, gave him a mescaline capsule. "I went through all of the effects," Thom told White at the time,

> uplift, giggles, supernatural confidence plus the uplifted feeling, mighty perceptions, calm and adoration at the "rightness" of everything ("rightness" is the only word), then colors—rockets exploding in green, much green, much blue, then shapes—ugh—fat and with turbans on (must come from De Quincy, though I've never read him), then cramps in my legs, and the most appalling sense of isolation imaginable—the only person in the world—like being the first man on another planet. I'd take one again if I had the chance, though: it was fascinating.[63]

Thom was first "offered" LSD in autumn 1965 but thought "maybe mescalin will do me (that one time with it) for a few years."[64] By summer 1966, however, he felt ready. Don took him to Jere Fransway's place in Brisbane, on the outskirts of San Francisco. Originally from Wisconsin, Jere had served in Korea and set up in the Bay Area as an electrician before dropping out to deal drugs. Six feet tall with a ruddy complexion, he was exactly the kind of take-charge figure Thom admired. Jere "presided," recalled one friend, "[often] wearing nothing but a smelly, old burnoose."[65] On this occasion, Chuck provided the LSD and they all dropped together. "Beautiful, none of the pretentious bullshit about it is true," Thom wrote of his first trip, "it is merely a gt awareness, sensitivity to what there is. Flowers, trees, the view thro binoculars, fruits, people. Pancakes, beer & pot also. Hot, hot afternoon, seemed to last a day. Very good, must repeat."[66]

A week later, Thom split some acid with Chuck at the Grant Avenue Street Fair and found himself high, stripped to the waist, dancing in the Capri.[67] Thom called himself "about the last of my friends . . . to take it" and planned to introduce Mike to it later that summer.[68] "My 'connection' (slang) tells me this shipment is twice as strong as the kind I had before," he told Tanner, "and marvelously 'hallucinogenic' (scientific term)."[69] He and Mike dropped at Aquatic Park, a cove on the city's northern shore, and were "hallucinating solid for about 3 hours."[70] Thom, in a "panic," felt they should go home. "I change my trip from bad to good by concentrating on M," he wrote.

> The woodwork in the room disintegrates "the world meeting me, me meeting the world." Curtains billowing w/out a wind. The light & dark of a god's wingbeat, pulsing. The brightness, almost too beautiful & terrible to bear.—We were still having slight hallucinations nine hours after taking capsules (12.30–9.30), and the actual center (vortex) of the trip was dementia.[71]

Thom did not drop again for a month, when he shared a tab with Don, who was taking LSD two or three times a week. However, the experience with Mike spooked Thom. "I've begun to change my ideas about LSD," he told Tanner in October. "The apostles of it . . . say Trust your body. But unfortunately I think my body must be rather untrustworthy. Much incipient paranoias, etc."[72] Although he found it "interesting to hallucinate," Thom's "strange paranoias" meant he would not take LSD again until spring 1968.[73] "I'd always assumed in my lazy and rather imperceptive buoyancy on the fairly warm upper waters of my life that the lower waters had an average or below average population of monsters," he reflected.[74] In fact, a bad trip could bring one of his recurrent nightmares to life. These were death dreams, either about his mother or, as was the case that autumn, "Bryan's suicide, deaths of M. & Don, my survival."[75] In his nightmares, Thom always survived.

Without courses to prepare and teach, Thom lacked structure and struggled to write. He visited New York, his first trip outside San Francisco for more than a year, thinking "if I really fucked off for 3 weeks away from home I'd be able to discipline myself when I came back."[76] As usual he stayed at William Sloane House and saw old tricks like Doric Wilson and James Dimitrius.[77] He saw Peter Tangen's first one-man show at the Bertha Schaefer Gallery and spent a day with Oliver Sacks, "who has really grown up a lot, & was very likable."[78] Thom cruised the Empire Theatre on West Forty-second, which showed old war movies and was popular with the leather crowd.[79] While he was away, Don Bachardy passed through San Francisco and took Mike for lunch. Mike "looks older but is on the whole unchanged," he told Isherwood, "except he seems less sulky, less rigidly success-minded, and decidedly less stuck on Thom."[80] Their relationship was beginning to change. When Thom returned, he realized he "missed Mike this time—far more than I did the whole of that year in England."[81]

Thom's trick did not work. Back in San Francisco he began to find himself in "a state of largely unmotivated but deepening depression."[82] He tried working on his Greville edition, now almost a year overdue, and hoped prose would be "good for getting me started on poetry."[83] Instead, he felt like "a kind of grotesque Oblomov," he told White, "totally incapable of decisions, and not really caring that much about anything."[84] He took to spending whole days on the coastal trail at Lands End, a favorite spot on which he had part-modeled the "final hill" in "Misanthropos." He liked its craggy, windswept shoreline, where he could walk and think. He started to realize that teaching "inhibited" him in "certain ways I can't clearly define," and looked forward to a period without its "responsibilities."[85] He also felt full of misgivings about *Touch*. "I rather wish, now, that I'd never sent it," he told White, "since it will be more uneven than any of my other books, and I'm beginning to suspect about half of it is not worth publishing." More charitably, he realized that the circumstances of its writing—some six years of great personal confusion and upheaval—contributed to its experimental nature, and that it was "a way of clearing things out, starting clean."[86]

Although he did not write for the rest of the year, Thom took Winters's criticisms to heart and decided on a "revival of meter <u>and of metrical qualities</u>." He also resolved to "step down" from his obsession "with self-definition, with tracing the stages of the flux of self." With *Touch* finished, Thom summarized his "thought" to date and laid the groundwork for his next book. "In abstract terms," he wrote,

> the progress of my thought (my thought selectively parasitic on that of others) is from Yeatsian Fascism, though Sartrean attempts at self-definition, toward (a) WCW attempts to possess the external world of things and (b) Camusian attempts to make myself equal, as a helper, to the world of people. Through all of this, there has been no supernatural world except as a metaphor.

He thought "in (b) there is still some future left for me" but worried it was "a future without clear shape except schematically": he felt "Misanthropos" began promisingly but ended as overtly didactic and symbolic.[87] Thom hoped London would provide new subjects. In February, Mike drove him to the Berkeley campus to pack up his office and collect his books. The department was "intent on getting me back,"[88] but Thom was not to be dissuaded. He sent his resignation letter to James D. Hart and was told that Hart remarked, "Why, Thom Gunn gave up tenure just as if he was getting off a streetcar!"[89] "Very good things are happening to me," Thom explained to Thomas Parkinson, "which I hope will show up eventually in my writing, and I really think it will be better for me to take off from teaching for a few years."[90] With his poetry, and his future, in mind, Thom flew to London.

19

ACID

Thom's first stop was Cambridge, where he spent a week finishing his Greville book in the University Library. Staying with the Tanners, he talked a lot with Tony about Tony White. "He had reached some sort of extreme edge," Tanner had written, before Thom arrived, "as though the hidden logic of his previous years had finally emerged and handed him the bill—no job, no prospects, no money, no place to live, no inkling of what he would even like to do—except retire deep into a physical life in Ireland."[1] Thom had heard from Ander that White was "jobless and homeless" and had resolved to move to Cleggan, on the Galway coast, where he had worked on a lobster farm, off and on, since the late 1950s.[2] But for the moment White was in London and Thom took full advantage. Their new haunts included Henekey's, "one of the centres of the Flower Power generation," on Westbourne Grove, and the Prince of Wales in Holland Park, whose multiple entrances on different streets "made it very popular with the local villains who could make a quick getaway whichever side the law entered."[3]

When Thom relocated from Cambridge to Kent, where he stayed with Mary and Catherine in Snodland, he took White on a day trip. "We drink 6 beers in the Ship & Lobster on the waterfront & walk 8 miles along sea wall," he wrote, "me drunk the entire time, cutting inland at Cliffe, climbing a fine tree, & then bussing back to Gravesend."[4] It "really was one of the nicest afternoons in my life," he told White, "and also one of the funniest."[5] Moreover, the walk provided Thom with the occasion for "Flooded Meadows," most of which he wrote in England. The poem begins, "In sunlight now," the first trace of Thom's growing interest in light and perception as metaphors for self-definition:

> Yet definition is suspended, for,
> In pools across the level listlessness,
> Light answers only light before the breeze,
> Cancelling the rutted, weedy, slow brown floor
> For the unity of unabsorbed excess.[6]

"Flooded Meadows" is a sonnet. Thom had become "rather tired of people saying the sonnet is dead,"[7] and it is a typically Gunnian joke to write about "the unity of unabsorbed excess" in such a tightly controlled form.[8] Moreover, Thom thought the light was "solipsistic in a sense, and cancels all the accretions of experience, simplifying it into maybe one marvellous LSD trance where the real world has been glamorized as pure abstract light."[9] Although he had stopped taking LSD, it was still on his mind: while "Flooded Meadows" is not ostensibly a poem about acid, Thom tried to incorporate the positive aspects of his experiences with hallucinogens into his work, using light and perception as metaphors.

Spending a week in Snodland, he wrote in the mornings while Mary and Catherine, now in their late fifties, did the local milk round. In the afternoons he joined his aunts on long walks up Holly Hill and along the Pilgrims' Way that recalled his childhood. Disoriented from traveling, and with "a neurotic deprivation of M[ike]," he heard "Penny Lane" on the radio and thought about San Francisco.[10] Back in January, walking along Ocean Beach with some friends, Thom had been "suddenly astonished by the appearance of a bunch of surfers." The image stuck and he began writing "From the Wave" in the old parlor at Covey Hall.[11] He saw "From the Wave" as "answering an earlier poem like 'On the Move,'" in which he replaced the hardness of the motorcyclists and their movement for movement's sake with something more versatile, together, and purposeful.[12] The surfers are "half wave, half men" and move with rather than against nature; they search for the "right waves" on which "Balance is triumph . . . / Triumph possession."[13] "From the Wave" is a more joyful and tender poem than "On the Move," and Thom wanted its tone to shape his future writing. "My poetry is rather unpopulated right now," he told Mike at the time, "I mean not enough people in it."[14]

In London, Thom returned to Notting Hill. He found a "small, dim, but adequate room" in Hedgegate Court, just off Talbot Road. White was nearby in Powis Court. Thom still felt "displaced,"[15] and back at the Coleherne he had a "profoundly depressing" night where he was "turned down by 5 I liked. I suppose I am getting old."[16] More promisingly, he renewed his friendship with Mick Belsten, a member of the Gay Liberation Front, and his lover, Peter Flannery. Belsten was "lovely, humane, witty, sensible"[17] and Peter "one of the most amusing people I've ever met."[18] Days spent together in East End pubs renewed Thom's spirits and energies and, a few weeks later, he realized "disastrously" that he had "become happy in London, wh/ I did not intend."[19] Although London was still as thrillingly attractive as it had been in 1965, two things had changed his mind about making a permanent return. First, he realized he could not live without Mike; second, as he later summarized, in mid-1965 San Francisco "was only a little behind London in the optimism department," but, as he had learned through LSD, it "was prepared to go much further."[20]

Thom's mind was still in San Francisco. News reached him that Don Doody had been subpoenaed as part of New Orleans District Attorney Jim Garrison's investigation into the Kennedy assassination. A friend sent Thom a newspaper clipping that described "mystery witness" Don as "a balding red-bearded man of about 35."[21] Doody's connection with Clay Shaw brought him to Garrison's attention: Garrison believed Shaw had conspired with the CIA to assassinate Kennedy.[22] Thom found it unlikely that Don, "the friend of a friend of a possible conspirator," was "in real trouble" but found the situation "a little frightening."[23] During his two-hour interview in Garrison's office, Don was asked about his trip to Mexico in 1963. He named Thom as his traveling companion and said he introduced Thom to Clay Shaw. "I think we had lunch or something," Don said, "but I wouldn't guarantee it."[24] When Don summarized the interview for Shaw's lawyer, he remarked that Garrison and his staff "gave him the impression they were certain Clay Shaw was a CIA agent. They also gave Doody the impression they felt he was also a CIA agent."[25]

Worried that Thom would get caught up in Don's difficulties, Mike wrote him a note emphasizing how much he stood to lose. "Not because of job and position in community," Mike wrote, "but you are an alien. [. . .] Bryan says that Garrison has a 'thing' about deviates. Which I can understand. I do too."[26] Thom ignored Mike's advice and sent Don a blank check to help with his and Shaw's legal expenses. "Listen, stupid," Mike wrote Thom when he found out,

> how stupid can you get? Sending Don Doody a blank check!!?! I mean REALLY! What an ill-timed beau geste. Like it's a witch hunt, dopey! like my investigation in the air force, and YOU SHOULD COOL IT! I mean it was fine to send him the money but you could have / should have done it thru Bryan or Mike Chittim or Jerry or even me. All of Garrison's "suspects" have one thing in common—and one thing only. A thing not unknown to yourself. [. . .] Anyway, do please be a bit more careful.[27]

However, Don was not interviewed again, Thom was never contacted about the investigation, and the blank check was never used. When Shaw was brought to trial in 1969, a jury acquitted him in less than an hour. Several years later, after he had given a reading at Southern Methodist University in Dallas, Thom told Tanner that "Dallas itself (which I hadn't seen since the time when Don and I planned Kennedy's assassination) is falling to pieces."[28]

By early May, Thom had "written, or almost finished" six new poems while in England: "Flooded Meadows," "From the Wave," "Sunlight," "North Kent," "The Moon's Dark," and "Walks Round Silvertown."[29] He found

"Sunlight" especially difficult to judge, thinking it was at once "something of a departure," "probably the most <u>formal</u> poem (in tone, anyway) I've ever written," and "terribly close to poems I wrote a long time ago."[30] Like "From the Wave," "Sunlight" was a transplant: conceived in San Francisco, written in England. Back in January, Thom had attended the first Human Be-In in Golden Gate Park. Allen Ginsberg, Gary Snyder, "and a crowd of twenty thousand people chanted to the setting sun," he recalled; "Sunlight" was "my own address to the sun." Thom's diction and tone are elevated, but the poem can be incanted: this felt like new territory. He had "written a lot about the defining impulse" in man but, in "Sunlight," he felt he was "examining the idea of acceptance."[31]

Usually, Thom struggled to write between finishing and publishing a book. With *Touch* due for publication in the autumn, he was surprised at how many new poems he had already written, even if they did amplify his concern that *Touch* "doesn't really add up to very much."[32] In comparison, Ted Hughes's new collection, *Wodwo*, made him "almost melt with envy."[33] While Thom was pleased to have made physical touch "an allegory for the touch of sympathy that should be the aim of human intercourse,"[34] he felt that *Touch*, as a book, was a "mess" because he had failed "to connect the poetry of everyday life and the heroic poetry (which is greatly to oversimplify the two kinds)."[35] Not everyone agreed with him. Clive Wilmer wrote an insightful piece in *Granta* about Thom's work to date, including *Touch*.[36] Isherwood was "tremendously moved and impressed and sort of <u>haunted</u>" by *Touch* and called it work "which <u>really</u> <u>deserves</u> the title La Condition Humaine."[37] But the reviews stung, especially Ian Hamilton's summation in *The Observer* that *Touch* "is not the fresh start one had been hoping for." He found "Misanthropos" full of "a leaden allegorical deliberateness" and material "Gunn has already worked to death." "The final man could as well be a lonely sentinel, a callous lover, Elvis Presley," Hamilton concluded, "and the flurry of good companionship with which the poem ends fools no one, least of all Thom Gunn."[38] Hamilton "has a way of hitting nails on the head (and driving them right out of sight)," Thom told Tanner. "I expect he's right about me."[39]

Nonetheless, *Touch* was a Poetry Book Society recommendation and, while in London, Thom wrote a short piece about the collection for the PBS *Bulletin*. It concludes with a statement of intent that matched his optimism around "From the Wave" and "Sunlight":

> There remains open the possibility that one can deliberately and consciously attempt to create in oneself a field which will be spontaneously fertile for the tests of sympathy[.] . . . I do not mean that one can simply love everybody because one wants to, but that one can try to avoid all the situations in which love is impossible.

This, he felt, "could be a proper exploration for several lifetimes of books."[40] Excited by his recent productivity, Thom felt he would continue to write well when he returned to San Francisco. *Touch* "is a boring book," he told Tanner, "but the next book will be my best."[41]

Thom returned to San Francisco just in time for the Summer of Love. Haight-Ashbury was now the countercultural epicenter. Timothy Leary encouraged everyone to "turn on, tune in, drop out"; countercultural newspapers like the *San Francisco Oracle* and the *Berkeley Barb* were passed around. Owsley Stanley, already a major underground figure for his involvement with the Grateful Dead and Ken Kesey, had White Lightning LSD freely distributed by a community anarchist group called the Diggers, and everyone dropped acid as Jefferson Airplane and the Dead played Golden Gate Park. Hippies flocked to the nearby Monterey Pop Festival, then came up and stayed on in the city. Others heard what was happening and hitchhiked west. Colorful clothes, flowers, and psychedelic drugs flooded the Haight. A feeling of great communal togetherness presided: openness and tolerance were championed over more traditional middle-class values. The slogan "Make Love Not War" embodied both the advocacy of free love and the growing opposition to the American presence in Vietnam.

Thom was initially wary of hippie culture. He stuck to his usual

North Beach hangouts and Folsom bars and went only occasionally to the Haight. "It all seems very unrelaxed there now," he wrote in July, "as compared to Jan & Feb this year."[42] He spent most of the summer in "high jinx" and "drinking orgies" with the visiting Tanners.[43] Don was away at the Montreal Expo and Mike had taken a job in New York, for Channel 13, as story editor for a series of plays by emerging writers. Before leaving San Francisco, Mike was "beautifully up," but as the days passed Thom felt "a bit nervous & down by it all" and a "stranger after only 10 days w/ him."[44] When the Tanners left in mid-August, he "felt despondent out of all proportion."[45] Without close friends nearby, without Mike at Filbert, Thom—who needed good company to balance the solitude required for writing—felt anxious and uncentered.

In late July, he mailed his Greville book to Faber—"At last!!!"[46]— and walked to Lands End, "very sunny, rivers of flowers," bursting with giant hollyhocks and wild mustard. There he saw "a naked family bathing in the cove." Their little boy "[r]uns up to me: / Hi there hi there, he shrills, yet will not stop."[47] Thom could not stop talking about the innocence of the scene and realized he wanted "to write a poem about the naked family," having "found an embodiment" for his preoccupations with "trust, openness, acceptance, innocence."[48] The parents "had to learn their nakedness"—what he called an "educated innocence . . . that knows the world"[49]—whereas the boy, in his nakedness, experiences "his body which is him." The day after seeing the family, Thom, whose work became more tactile and bodily after *Touch*, found himself writing "ptry that much excites me"[50] and worked steadily on "Three" for the rest of the summer.

In New York, Mike was regretting the Channel 13 job. "He has always wanted this kind of thing—cocktail parties and Show Business— until he actually got the offer," Thom told White. "Then he said: 'I've decided I don't really want that kind of thing after all. I like being lazy in the sun in San Francisco and wearing old clothes and being unambitious.'" It seemed "unlikely" he would stay in New York—Thom, relieved, had promised to follow him if it worked out—and "it looks like he'll be returning here for good."[51] Mike was spending weekends in Kearny with his parents. "Faintly depressed," he began smoking marijuana to help him sleep, at Thom's suggestion and supply.[52] His father, Abe, was showing early signs of Alzheimer's, and Mike "persuaded himself" he was showing similar symptoms like "absence of mind, desire to retreat from everything, etc. It's a self-delusion," Thom told Tanner, "but it's a further strong appearance of that huge melancholia he is subject to so much of the time." Thom often felt guilty that he was "able to dismiss the problems of those close to me with a quite sinister ease," although he felt "that at 14 I was made to feel too much for my age and have become rather unequipped for deep emotions as a result."[53]

At Stanford, Donald Davie had agreed to replace Yvor Winters as head of the creative writing program. Winters retired in 1966 and, the following year, Thom received a copy of his latest critical book, *Forms of Discovery*. "It confirms my best hopes and worst fears," Thom told Tanner, including a "dogmatic, arrogant, defiant" tone and "a deplorable last chapter in which he discusses most of his students."[54] Thom's work, according to Winters, "exists on the narrow line between great writing and skillful journalism."[55] Thom wrote him, lightly criticizing the tone ("a bit defensive") and the final chapters ("too personal") while calling individual readings of poems "the best I have read in any criticism, even in yours."[56] Winters had written the final chapter in a hurry: he was suffering with late-stage throat cancer; his health deteriorated through 1967, and he died in early January 1968. When Thom heard the news, he wrote to Janet Lewis, Winters's widow, that Winters "will go on influencing the minds of those of us who worked under him, for the rest of our lives." He found it difficult "to speak about the love we felt for him, a love the extent of which he was too modest to realize."[57] Thom mourned Winters more than he had his own father. "He meant quite a lot to me," he told White, "even though I've seen him only once a year for the last nine years. And a very loveable man, in his dogged and awkward and sometimes outrageous way."[58]

A few days after Winters's death, Thom gave a reading at Stanford.[59] It was the prelude to a month of readings on the Southern California poetry circuit. "I hate the thought," Thom remarked, "but shall need the money."[60] In Los Angeles he stayed with John Zeigel, an English instructor at Caltech and a friend of Isherwood's, whom he knew from Folsom Street. Thom was pleasantly surprised: the circuit was a blast and Zeigel "a prince of generosity." His "splendid hedonistic" days began with Bloody Marys and ended at bars like Falcon's Lair, Tool Shed, and Tradesman. After five weeks of readings, Thom's nerves had disappeared and he was reading "better than ever before."[61] A "monotonous and limited" voice worked in his favor: "I can afford to dramatize my work as much as I want and still will not seem overdramatic."[62] He read at Caltech, UCLA, LA State, Cal State Poly Tech, Occidental and Claremont Colleges, and UC campuses at Irvine, Riverside, Santa Barbara, and Santa Cruz. Afterward, he made short reading visits to New York, Boston, Vancouver, Denver, and San Jose. After two more readings in Los Angeles in June, he planned to "call it quits" having earned enough money to live for the rest of the year.[63] Moreover, he had not written a poem since December. "Not that my non writing is caused by my whirl of performance," he told White. "I am also in one of those in between periods, when ideas etc are taking their time to settle."[64]

In May, Thom accompanied Don, Chuck, and Jere Fransway to the Northern California Folk-Rock Festival in San Jose. The Doors played, as did other Gunn favorites including Jefferson Airplane, the Grateful Dead, and Country Joe and the Fish. Thom took a Desoxyn (methamphetamine), and Chuck gave him psilocybin (magic mushrooms). "A man & woman turned up at the fairgrounds and, Kesey fashion, gave away 4000 capsules," Thom told Tanner. They were "hogs"—a hallucinogen, PCP, later called angel dust—and the "Hogman" distributed them "to promising looking people, one of them Jere," he continued. "I had an afternoon that was—well—memorable. A steady euphoria for hour after hour . . . I would stand in the sun with one or two of [my friends] & have a prolonged wordless euphoric understanding with them. We would start sentences and there would be no need to finish them, the sympathy was so great." It was such a good, comfortable, joyous experience that Thom felt "ready to take acid again. You remember I had scared myself out of it," he told Tanner, "now I feel good & confident that I can handle it as at the start."[65]

Several of Thom's friends were serious dealers, and he had easy access to marijuana, psilocybin, and LSD. The center of his drug life was Clara Street, an alley between Fourth and Sixth, parallel to Folsom and Harrison. Chuck Arnett had left Pierce Street and moved to 32 Clara (now demolished), where he "maintained a 'salon' upstairs, while Jere Fransway did the same downstairs," recalled Thom's friend Mike Caffee; "they ran a 24-hour party-pad and sold pot, LSD, and whatever drugs were currently popular."[66] Thom found it "like home industries, the whole week there were guys in the kitchen putting the white powder into capsules (and licking their fingers and getting loaded), the phone went continually, people kept dropping by to pick up their 'lots.'" The customers were typical hippies, "hair down below their shoulders, colossal earrings etc."[67] Arnett and Fransway's supplier was Gary White, a former marine, who had a connection to "Mr. LSD," Owsley Stanley. According to Thom, when Stanley's lab in Orinda was raided in December 1967,[68] White had "the last lot of Owsley caps before O was arrested. They are buffered & capped [at 32 Clara], & thousands change hands every day there."[69] Gary was cheerful and generous but private: he kept apart from the Arnett and Fransway communes. When there were acid parties, Gary brought "carefully diluted bottles of pure LSD that we would dose onto sugar cubes or bits of blotter paper using eye-droppers."[70] His manufacturing and distribution outfit was so profitable that he bought and restored a large house at 400 Clayton and amassed a collection of art and antiquities that one friend called "probably one of the very fine and most eclectic collections in the country."[71]

Mike returned to San Francisco in July. He turned on with marijuana most days and felt he was loosening up. Thom bought him a pair of leather bell bottoms. "At one time I would have been like, 'You must be out of your mind, dear,'" Mike reflected. "It was much more of a distance to travel for me than it was for Thom because he'd always been a wild thing." In the Capri one afternoon Mike took a pill from the bartender and Thom "was impressed I would take [it] without knowing what it was."[72] Come autumn, Thom thought it "nicer (almost than ever before) living with Mike."[73] "Quarrels such as we used to have are almost unimaginable," he told Tanner. "Look, we have come through."[74] Mike felt that "in hippie days we entered a new chapter. It was a very, very good time for us."[75]

Thom's drug life had restarted, but poems were slow to follow. In mid-September, "feeling Creative for the first time this year," he began a new notebook.[76] "New notebook, new determinations, new assessments of intentions," he wrote on the first page. "What I most want to (continue to) do: pass the romantic impulse through the classical scrutiny. The scrutiny is both the experience and the poem's form. It is destructive (or should be) of all that is not hard and genuine in the impulse." Moreover, Thom asked himself: "Possibility of a personal poem? [. . .] The subject, if it is the proper one, is a liberation of thought by developing it."[77]

With that in mind, Thom used one recent poem to cultivate another. Earlier in the year he had finished "The Garden of the Gods," a poem about "all mythological gardens, and even the mythological garden one inhabits on acid trips."[78] For Thom, that garden was a place of birth and death. "I trace it downward from my mind," the speaker concludes, "Through breast and calf I feel it vined, / And rooted in the death-rich earth."[79] While in Los Angeles in February, he "drafted a poem" after attending a reading by Lawrence Ferlinghetti at Caltech.[80] This poem was "Rites of Passage": he did not finish it until he began his new notebook in September.[81] The speaker metamorphoses from boy into a horned, hoofed, rough-skinned animal[82] and prepares to gore his father. "I stamp upon the earth / A message to my mother," he says. "And then I lower my horns."[83] In his "supplanting" of his father, Thom suggests that "it looks strongly as though he is going to castrate his father." In an interview, Thom mentioned an equivalent from Greek mythology—Zeus castrating Kronos—but was keen to avoid any specific references in the poem itself. "Myth is being used not as decoration but as indicating certain forces within us," he reflected, "that we are not able to come to grips with very rationally and that are rather strong, dark forces."[84]

In writing a poem about a father and son—and one that directly addresses the father and alludes to the mother—Thom achieved something he had been attempting "for about twenty years."[85] In "Rites," there are two mythological gardens, one belonging to the father, one to the mother.

"I make my way / Adventuring through your garden," the speaker tells his father. "In the back of my mind was a bit from that French folk song . . . Dans les jardins de mon père," Thom later remarked. "This is a phrase I've always liked, 'in the gardens of my father.'"[86] Of the mother's garden, Thom said: "I am there referring back lightly . . . to the idea of his mother being the earth itself, as in the original myth . . . It's simply the idea of maybe the mother is dead or maybe the mother as being elsewhere."[87]

The garden in "Rites" is not, strictly speaking, an acid garden as in "The Garden of the Gods," nor is the poem directly an acid poem; instead, it is one in which "acid in some sense altered some of my perceptions."[88] Thom wanted to use "plain language" but "give a kind of oddity to it": his language is formal, his tone abrupt, his sentences short. "We don't know at any point whether this is actually happening or whether this is his fantasy, whether it's a kind of hallucination," he remarked.[89] It is a plainly personal poem in which Thom used mythology and his acid experiences to liberate and develop feelings that had remained trapped since his first attempts to write about his parents. Mythology was still a kind of conduit—one he had tried before in "From an Asian Tent"—but acid gave Thom the courage to attempt a new kind of poem. "You looked back and you saw a lifetime of shit and hiding and dishonesty," he later reflected, "and you suddenly saw no point in it any longer. Particularly if you were taking acid every day."[90]

The day after starting his new notebook, Thom read some of his poems at Robert Duncan's poetry workshop, a weekly meeting run by a homophile organization called the Society for Individual Rights.[91] Thom invited Duncan to Filbert Street a few days later. "He is on the whole likeable but is fond of doing most of the talking," Thom reflected. "Typically, I avoid disagreeing with him since I search for strong points of contact before I am prepared for theoretical argument with him."[92] He found it strange that Duncan had "taken me up lately" when they had known each other "slightly" for a decade.[93] A friendship slowly developed. Spending time with Duncan was "an extraordinary experience," Thom later said. "I would go away with my head teeming with ideas and images and I'd write them down in my notebook and feel like writing poetry."[94]

No sooner had Thom lost one mentor in Yvor Winters when he gained another in Duncan. It was a remarkable contrast. "I am the only person in the world ever to have dedicated poems to both Winters and Duncan," he later remarked. "They hated each other. They didn't meet but they hated each other. When they referred to each other it was with contempt."[95] Winters was "deliberately a poet of closure" and taught Thom to distill his images and ideas into finely constructed poems; through Duncan, a poet of openness, Thom became "more interested in . . . writing as a process and being open to things happening while you're writing."[96] He did not want to emulate Duncan's process; rather, as he had with Winters's ideas, he wanted to absorb what he found useful and discard the rest. "If one believes in the validity of the different poetries," he reflected, "then one can in some way marry or digest whatever is in them."[97] By opening up his writing process, Thom wondered whether he could achieve something more personal within the constraints of rhyme and meter, his most comfortable form. "What Duncan has stressed is the importance of the *act* of writing," Thom reflected. "It is to reach into the unknown, an adventuring into places you cannot have predicted, where you may find yourself using limbs and organs you didn't know you possessed." He felt that the importance of such "adventuring . . . had been minimized in favour of the end result, 'the poem on the page'. Duncan sees the adventure as ongoing, unfinished and unfinishable, and the poem on the page as marking only one stage in it."[98] Thom's language recalls "A Map of the City," in which, drawing on Crane, he describes the city as "Endless potentiality, / The crowded, broken, and unfinished!"

With Duncan in mind, Thom considered writing directly about his experiences. In late October, at the Renaissance Pleasure Fair in San Rafael, Thom had his first acid trip in two years. "There we all drop acid (350 & a little speed)," he wrote. "Possibilities of all good & bad trips apparent. Many lovely things happen. The boy on horseback, the speed family of dancers. I dispel cramps successfully. Dale falls from a tree. A walk w/ Jerry at closing time—the great vision I have: 'Le Son du cor, le soir,

au fond des bois.' The buckskinned foresters, somewhat elongated, at evening, blowing horns & merging into the similar colors of wood & earth.
[. . .] A fine day, & I have confidence in myself w/ acid again."⁹⁹ Thom
found a distinct parallel between acid trips and an open writing process:
both were "an adventuring into places you cannot have predicted." Two
days later, Thom began "The Fair in the Woods" and felt it was "a new
departure." All the details were "literally true," he told Tony White, "but
I don't care if it is read as a 'vision' and if a reader were to treat them all
as dream detail." It was "a kind of poem I've wanted to write for several
years."¹⁰⁰ By contrast, writing to Tanner about "The Fair in the Woods"
made Thom "question the solidity of the acid poem." He wanted to write
it, "valid or not," and thought about it as belonging to the "Blake–St John
category" of poetry "in that it tries to present an unshared experience."¹⁰¹

The Renaissance Pleasure Fair confirmed to Thom that if acid were
to become a major experience in his life, he had to write about it. Moreover, it would allow him to write personal poems by focusing on experience rather than confession. But his immediate problem was *how* to write
about it. Thom had not written any free verse since "Touch," in mid-1966,
and that, somehow, seemed too loose a form in which to write about essentially unstructured experiences.¹⁰² In the "unpremeditated movement
of free verse," acid poems risked "unravel[ing] like fog before wind."
Rhyme and meter were his strengths: these seemed "the proper form for
the LSD-related poems," Thom reflected. "The acid trip is unstructured, it
opens you up to countless possibilities, you hanker after the infinite. The
only way I could give myself any control over the presentation of these
experiences, and so could be true to them, was by trying to render the
infinite through the finite, the unstructured through the structured."¹⁰³
Thom wrote "The Fair in the Woods" in iambic pentameter; its quintains
rhyme *ababa*. This regularity makes the line-break caesura after "Landscapes of acid" more dramatic—it is a literal drop, as one drops acid—and
it convinced Thom to trust himself: writing about acid would require the
rigor of Winters and the adventure of Duncan.

20

THE *S*TUD

Thom thought the Stud was a "terrible" leather bar.[1] That was in 1966, when it opened at 1535 Folsom. By the spring of 1968 it had become "a strange French cooking western bar," recalled Don Doody, who tended bar there, and "it was really, really empty."[2] Don persuaded the owners to let Chuck Arnett paint murals and decorate it. "Don was going to be John Lennon and Chuck rather astonishingly was going to be Paul," Thom laughed, "the beautiful one who was responsible for the art as opposed to the ideas."[3]

Chuck's psychedelic black light mural depicted a Tool Box–style leatherman dropping acid and transforming into a hippie drag queen. Don wanted to make the Stud the hottest bar in town for music, dancing, and LSD. "Dancing in those days . . . meant swinging your arms around and jumping around," Don recalled. "They had a policy not to give dancing permits to gay bars, only to straight bars. I said [to the local beat cop], 'They're not dancing. They're just feeling good.'" The Stud was one of the first bars, if not the first, to play taped music—including the Grateful Dead, Jefferson Airplane, and other local bands—rather than a jukebox. "All of a sudden the place was really jammed with lines outside," he recalled, "because it was the only place in town where you could hear that music."[4] By September, Don had "succeeded magnificently" with the Stud. "There are now more murals, there is dancing and affability," Thom told Tanner, "and it is probably the most packed bar in town."[5] It was "a bar like no other in the world," he later reflected, "a gay druggie bar, not particularly a leather bar."[6]

Chuck and the Clara Street family moved into the apartment above the Stud, which ensured a steady supply of drugs into the bar. A hit of anything cost no more than a dollar. Don ensured his bartenders had easy access to methamphetamine. "It was easy to get lots of pharmaceutical speed in those days, like 'Christmas trees' and . . . 'Black Beauties,'" Thom recalled. "Bartenders took it to be good and alert whatever trips they'd been on the previous night." Everything was shared, "like 'a new drug, hey, try this pill. You'll love it.'" Everyone wore large wooden beads and, on one occasion, a guy "showed a larger bead, just the size of a capsule, to a friend of his," Thom recalled, "and the other guy just took it and thought he was offering him a capsule and swallowed it!"[7]

The Stud became the center of "a spiritual quest to save the world with Love," reflected Mike Caffee. "LSD has done this for us and we expected the world to follow. Thom was an integral part of this."[8] It also brought Thom and Mike Kitay closer together. "I was a dancer," Mike reflected. "I loved getting high and getting stoned on acid and hearing live music and dancing."[9] This affected Mike's relationship with Don, whom he had found abrasive and aloof; Don had thought Mike uptight. "Don has started telling me he likes Mike," Thom told Tanner. "He likes him because he is in general more relaxed, is liked by various of Don's friends, turns on, and enjoys the Stud . . . [I]f they continue getting on together it could certainly make an old lady's life easier."[10]

For eighteen months, the Stud became the center of Thom's San Francisco. The highlight of the year was the party Don held at the Stud on December 17 to celebrate the Roman Saturnalia.[11] Don invited 150 friends and patrons to the Saturnalia, which he modeled on the Acid Tests held by Ken Kesey and his Merry Pranksters.[12] Its theme was "Psychedelic Freak Out." Arnett decorated the bar "to look like a kind of Venusian Fingal's Cave, with flexible stalactites," Thom told Tanner. "And everybody, including Mike and me, said it was the best party they'd ever been to. One thing that helped was that everyone was offered acid, and so about 70 of us were on a reasonably heavy trip."[13] Thom and Mike, still "tripping our tits off," tried to leave around two in the morning. "The buildings on Folsom were leaning together like the buildings in *The Cabinet of Dr. Caligari*," Thom remembered. "Mike and I got in our car and before he put his key in he said, 'YOU MADE IT MOVE!'"[14]

They stayed: Chuck hosted an after-party upstairs, at which Mike had "long sex" with a dealer named Alan Anderson.[15] "He was around the Stud a little bit," Mike recalled. "He was like a minor villain—that's too strong a word."[16] Thom and Mike were both attracted to him. Thom thought him "very bright & lovely . . . & has spent 1½ years in prison (6 months of which in solitary) and is really very Alyosha like."[17] This gave Thom the idea for "Street Song," his Elizabethan-influenced peddler song about a drug dealer on Haight Street.[18] Thom and Mike liked Alan so much that, just before Christmas, Thom asked him to move in with them. "I mean it," Thom wrote, "but Mike feels doubtful."[19] In the event, a crisis developed around New Year's when, at Thom's invitation, John Zeigel arrived to stay at Filbert and drop acid on Folsom. "After we go to Stud, & to E. Bishop's very groovy party," Thom wrote, "Alan & [John] make out in back room, & it turns out M is in love with Alan. This I had not even guessed at."[20] Mike left the apartment early the next morning after he and Thom had their "first quarrel for a very long time."[21] Thom asked them to leave, but Alan and John slept together in the back room the next night. Mike left again, calling Thom a shit. "AA of course will not be living here," Thom wrote. "Probably it is best M has discovered AA cannot be owned, now rather than when he was living with us. What an awful complicated & unnecessary business!"[22]

Thom blamed himself for what had happened. "It was all my fault," he told Tanner. "Mike has come an awful long way in 6 months, and I was trying to push him too far at that point I think."[23] Thom admired Chuck Arnett and Jere Fransway's families and thought he and Mike could add to their own family if Mike could find the right monogamous partner. Not everybody was convinced that Thom had Mike's interests at heart. "Tom Gee tells M I am fucking M up," he wrote. "Then at Stud . . . [another friend], shit-faced tells me DD & M that I am fucking up M's life."[24] Before Mike flew east in late January to visit his parents, he and Thom had "a good talk" that "clear[ed] up many difficulties."[25] Thom had hoped to see Alan—whose "friendship (not sex)" he wanted "more than I have wanted anything in many years"[26]—while Mike was away, but he discovered Alan was visiting Zeigel in Los Angeles. "This is a blow I am not ready for. Hardly slept and on Sunday morning ended up in tears! [. . .] Stupid teenage sentiments."[27] With Mike and Alan both away, Thom felt able to clear his head. "It is good, every now and again, to live alone for a short spell," he told Tanner.[28] After the Alan situation, Thom became less prone to possessive infatuations. When Alan called, a fortnight later, Thom felt "over the hang up & can just love him in the good unpossessive way now." Mike called later the same day: "It's no trouble loving him."[29]

Thom may have been feeling sentimental. He was "already a bit distraught," having agreed to teach the winter quarter at California State College at Hayward.[30] Between January and March—"the most depressing three months" he had had "in a long time"[31]—he caught the bus there twice a week, "a real drag—1½ to 2 hrs . . . each way," and found that "the students are not quite up to Berkeley standards."[32] Moreover, Thom found the heightened tensions on campus unsettling. "Since the Chicago convention I have come round to believing that 'the revolution' will take place," he told Tanner.[33] In California, students were "being beaten up very bloodily and usually without provocation, by cops, at San Francisco State College and at Berkeley, and the right wing is presumably getting stronger and stronger," Thom told White.[34]

Politically, Thom kept a low profile, but that February he took part in a benefit reading to support the SFSC strike organized by the Black Student Union. At Glide Memorial Church, he read with, among others, Robert Duncan, Lawrence Ferlinghetti, Elizabeth Bishop, and Michael McClure. He also met Freewheelin Frank, the secretary of the San Francisco Hell's Angels, who passed him a joint. "I passed it on to Elizabeth Bishop," Thom told Tanner. "She puffed it manfully."[35] That spring, Thom also participated in a mass reading for the Society for Individual Rights.

He had a minor affiliation with the SIR, having attended Duncan's SIR poetry workshop the previous year. He had also appeared in their magazine, *Vector*, in 1967 as an independent sponsor for Proposition P—the immediate withdrawal from Vietnam—in local elections. "I thought I would be in the list of famous writers, along with Isherwood and people," he told Tanner, "but actually I was in the list of local homosexuals . . . I was rather pleased by that!"[36]

Having come to trust himself with LSD, and because teaching at Hayward was not onerous, Thom continued dropping acid on weekends. A blue barrel[37] at the Stud gave him a "harsh and ragged" trip, but he had now learned "to deal with the difficulties." He emerged from that trip "with what struck me as a mighty apothegm: 'the experience is learning to live with the experience.'"[38] More confident, he decided to "drop a 'paper,' acid on litmus," his heaviest acid yet. "My first impulse was that I wasn't up to it," he told Tanner. "But I thought about it 2 days, and felt it was a challenge." He said the "two hours at the center of the six or so I was on it were about the most interesting of my life." His hallucinations were "so strong that it was completely part of reality" and "nothing had a permanent identity, least of all myself." Don had also dropped "and became a lot of different people to me, at one stage my father." They went up to the roof of the Stud together and Thom "had a conversation with God . . . the source of the universe. I can tell you," he told Tanner,

> I put some pretty challenging propositions to God, and he gave
> me no answer. Of course I didn't see him, because it was not a
> human-shaped god I was speaking with. But I could see any-
> body who was relevant—as I say, including my father—except
> for Mike, interestingly enough. And there was a time when I felt
> quite a need for Mike to be there.

Don "didn't <u>comfort</u> me when I asked panicky questions . . . but answered them honestly with difficult answers, which made me work out the problem on its own terms rather than dismiss it. E.g. at one time I said 'Well, if I don't have identity and I don't have love, what is there?'

And he said 'honor.' Though I didn't understand what he meant till some hours later, when he said that by honoring oneself one can honor other people."[39] The "'loss of ego' bit was difficult," but he began the following day with "a cleaned-out brain . . . full of peace & self-control."[40] He decided to drop acid "once a week or, if I can take it, twice a week" once he had finished at Hayward. "I want to see what will happen," he told Tanner. "I won't turn into an angel and I won't go mad, but it does burn the chromosomes very nicely and doing so cleans a nice hole in the brain which can be filled by what one chooses to put there."[41]

Thom had written steadily through the winter, drafting "Street Song" and finishing "For Signs," "Words," and "Justin." In the spring, he turned his "loss of ego" trip into "At the Centre," his first acid poem since "The Fair in the Woods." Its first five stanzas begin with unfinished or interrupted questions—"What place is this," "What is this steady pouring that"—concluding with "What am," in which the missing "I" represents the loss of ego.[42] Thom surrenders to the "all-river"—what he called "a complete flowing" in a letter to Tanner[43]—his metaphor for the perceiving mind. "Experience is a pouring of images," he noted. "The things imaged are not always importantly distinct from each other, they are at all times part of an unstopping process of merging, blending, reforming, like currents in a fast river."[44] Images pour "in cascade over me and under" in such profusion it is difficult to distinguish between them. The last two stanzas, Thom felt, were about "the source overlapping its creation" and that, while humans "abstract things from the flux," it is important to "acknowledge the flux" as much as possible. At the center of the trip, the mind "is not concerned with identity, least of all human identity," he concluded, hence "What am" rather than "What am I."[45] In the poem, the trip focused on the beer sign on top of Hamm's Brewery—the glass filled as its lights came on—which Thom felt was "a most extraordinary image of the whole created world, filing up with good things then draining out again."[46]

In April, Thom joined the Stud family on a bus ride across the Golden Gate Bridge to Kirby Cove, a private beach near Fort Cronkhite. He dropped a "strawberry barrel" as they came down "the long road to the cove, overlooking the sand." As was usual by then, his trip was "a bit hard in the first stage (fantasy of rebirth)" but became "the most beautiful yet."[47] It was "a kind of barely controlled euphoria," he told Tanner, "a feeling of discovery & a feeling of adequacy and delight in the things discovered."[48] The Kirby Cove trip inspired two poems: "Grasses" and "Being Born." The first is a scene of rest and concentration, in which Thom compared the natural world and the LSD vision by adapting the pouring, river imagery he used in "At the Centre." More significantly, "Being Born" was Thom's attempt to examine the difficulties he faced at the beginning of trips. He saw in his drug experiences "<u>glimpses</u>, but only glimpses, of other ways of knowing, and of forces beyond you," he told Tanner:

> I have had a curious fancy more than once on acid that just
> at the edge of my vision there are a few giant pillars or maybe
> figures. I do not want to see those figures very clearly, because if
> I do they may turn into the doctor and the mid-wife delivering
> me into a new life, to which this life is only a preface.[49]

These pillars became the "vague pillars, not quite visible," of "Being Born," which, upon closer examination, were revealed as "Midwife and doctor faintly apprehended." "Must I rewrite my childhood?" he asked, fearing what "mergings of authority and pain, / Invading breath, must I live through again?"[50] Birth imagery often featured in Thom's acid poems from 1968 onward. "For Signs" featured his "birth-hour"; the speaker finds "the garden's place of birth" in "The Garden of the Gods" and feels it "vined, / And rooted in the death-rich earth"; "Rites of Passage" concludes with a "stamp upon the earth / A message to my mother"; and "Tom-Dobbin" features a platypus mother and a male pup "hatched into separation."[51] In September 1968, almost six years into keeping his diary, Thom wrote, "Mother wd have been 65 today," the first time he had marked her birthday.[52]

. . .

Of the three poems Thom finished in late 1968, "For Signs" is the most significant. He was not averse to astrology, which exploded in popularity in the 1960s as part of the hippie aesthetic; the poem is set when the moon was in Scorpio, "that sign / It stood in at my birth-hour," and which Thom was told meant "sexual perversion."[53] The poem is in three parts: waking, dreaming, and waking again.[54] The speaker—whom Thom calls "Dream mentor"—dreams a "cool fantasy of violence." The second part of the poem begins:

> And sleep like moonlight drifts and clings to shape.
> My mind, which learns its freedom every day,
> Sinks into vacancy but cannot rest.
> While moonlight floods the pillow where it lay,
> It walks among the past, weeping, obsessed,
> Trying to master it and learn escape.[55]

Thom was used to bad dreams. Earlier that year he had "a very strange dream where I found my mother dead. I thought, callously, 'Oh no, not <u>again</u>. I think I'll let somebody else find her body this time.' Which I did! Also in this dream I got on very well with my father."[56] In an early draft of "For Signs," the "cool fantasy of violence" is an explicit description of finding his mother's body:

> The dreams begin. Real things are recombined.
> On different carpets, detail rearranged,
> A corpse is found, in scarlet, as at first.
> The body, open-eyed, . . . is unchanged,
> Only the finding variously rehearsed
> Within the rooms/vaults/chambers that honeycomb the mind.[57]

Thom cut the personal details, but "For Signs" was an important part of his "push outward," he told Tanner, "a Romantic push—towards dream, hallucination, etc."[58] The poem was prompted by, and reflects on, his acid experiences, and balances his "Romantic push" with an acknowledgment that his past is inescapable: "Cycle that I in part am governed by / And cannot understand where it is dark."[59] It capped "a great burst of writing" that made Thom feel "more confident about what I've been doing than any time in about 10 years!"[60]

Writing about his mother in "For Signs" was no coincidence. Thom had family, and ideas about family, on his mind. "Family" was Thom's word for communes and collectives, gay and/or hippie; groups with Don, Chuck, or Jere at their center were families. He loved that acid trips were communal occasions, either at the Stud or on Kesey-style bus rides with Don, Chuck, and their extended families. After a "very euphoric" trip in Golden Gate Park, Thom received a telephone call from a young artist named Bill Schuessler.[61] They had met during the Summer of Love when Bill, then twenty, had left Sheboygan, Wisconsin, with his best friend, Michael Belot, to travel to San Francisco. "We wanted to wear flowers in our hair, as McKenzie says," Bill recalled. "Walking down Haight Street barefooted and acting like we're so natural and people would open their windows and shove out balloons that they were blowing up all night. And it was wonderful. It was like just any kind of thing was going on." Days were spent in Haight-Ashbury and Golden Gate Park, but at night Bill snuck into leather bars on Folsom Street. "I saw [Thom] at the end of the bar in a sort of leather corner," Bill recalled of the Tool Box, "and I flashed on him and cruised him. He cruised me back and we ended up on Filbert Street."[62] Thom referred to Bill in his diary as a "21yr old from Milwaukee . . . groovy & gorgeous."[63] He showed him around the city, taking him to Lands End and the de Young Museum. Bill wanted to stay in San Francisco, but Thom gave him "the wonderful advice" to return home and complete his degree at the University of Wisconsin–Milwaukee. "He said that, even if you don't use it, you'll always be happy that you did it," Bill reflected, "because you'll know that you finished it. So I did, and he was right."[64]

Two years later, in spring 1969, Bill was ready to return. Thom brought him to Filbert Street for dinner: "Very good vibrations between

Bill S & me," he wrote.[65] Mike felt the same. "The evening I met [Bill] there were very good vibrations," he recalled. "That's kind of what got us together." Mike guessed how Thom and Bill knew each other. "Neither of them ever explained it to me, nor did I ask," he reflected. "I'm pretty sure they'd met in a bar and did whatever they did." For Mike, an affair with a younger man—Bill was fifteen years his junior—was a new experience. "It was parental. Not consciously, but because of the age difference," he reflected. "That was at the height of drugs and the Stud. Bill doesn't have much to say. He never did. That was fine with me." They liked dropping together and going to the big open-air concerts in Golden Gate Park. Thom sometimes went with them but mainly left them to themselves. "[Thom] was thinking of my happiness with Bill," Mike reflected. "They had been close at one time. I've never known Thom to be so sweet, and fatherly, as he was with Bill."[66] Within two months, Thom asked Bill to move in with them. "Michael and I were having a mad affair," Bill recalled, "and [Thom] invited me rather than Mickey, which I found very nice in the sense that I didn't feel like I was stepping on his toes when I did move in."[67] "When I say Thom was generous," Mike reflected, "he was the one who invited Bill to live at Filbert Street, which I wouldn't have done on my own."[68] Thom was "very glad" that Bill decided to move in with them. "Everybody is very happy!" he told Tony White. "It really makes me feel, for almost the first time, that one can successfully manipulate one's life if one tries hard enough."[69]

Although his writing year ended in September, Thom was pleased with his recent poems. "I have gone through a change in the last 10 years, but it has been pretty gradual," he told White. "Away from closed-ness and Sartrean self-definitions, toward open-ness and an attempt to accept other possibilities than the strictly rational." Dreams and hallucinations were the latest stage of that journey. "The trouble is," he continued, "in the taking the direction I am taking, I may be going toward mush, and marsh, and general vague squishiness."[70] In taking "pure romantic experience-for-its-own-sake" and attempting "to give it meaning by rendering it through the human inventions of metrical and stanzaic form," Thom saw his "difference from most of the good people around" as his interest in "<u>why</u> [the experience] seems important," not merely "capturing the thing-in-itself or the experience-in-itself" and "producing it on its own terms." He saw "experience as a good" and approached it "without pre-assuming what its meaning will be."[71] Thom needed this kind of rigorous intellectual exercise to ensure his poems about wonder and togetherness did not fall into "general vague squishiness." Within eighteen months, LSD had become the focal point of Thom's life and work. It gave him "more of an accepting attitude toward the world."[72] In poetry, this meant writing about sympathy and acceptance; in practice, it was a fulfillment of the ideal: Mike had a monogamous lover and they were bringing him into their Filbert Street family.

Thom spent the first fortnight of October 1969 in New York before embarking on the Michigan poetry circuit, a series of fifteen readings in eighteen days that began in Ohio. Unlike on the California circuit, Thom had little company and spent some "memorable mornings, on my own, in hotel rooms, of real neurosis." It felt like his "period of most concentrated strain" since "the first few weeks of basic training in the army."[73] In Ann Arbor he stayed with Donald Hall, now a professor at the University of Michigan, who was "having much melodramatic trouble w/ a melodramatic girlfriend."[74] The first night, "DH v drunk, & propositions me!!!!!!!"[75] Several days later, when Hall was "sober & there," Thom mentioned "Tues night to reassure him,"[76] and later wrote, hoping Hall was "a bit happier now. You really did seem pretty distraught . . . The girl, however good in other ways, sounds like she has a gift for melodramatics."[77]

The circuit introduced Thom to "several new Americas" outside California. "An intensely political person will say to me every now and again: Why do you choose to live in America when you can live in England?" he told Tanner.

Well, quite apart from personal reasons, I'd say that whereas there are several Englands (Philip Larkin's England, Agatha Christie's England, the Beatles' England, Tony Tanner's England and a few others) there are <u>hundreds</u> of Americas, and I haven't got to the end of them yet.[78]

Thom felt he was at his best "in writing, anyway—when I am trying to reconcile opposites," he reflected. "E.g. Apollonian—Dionysian, impulse & self-discipline, etc. [. . .] & one of the most important of these living-between-opposites is being an Englishman in San Francisco."[79] In notes for a poem called "Looking for America," Thom thought that "to find America you have to find a new self." There was "no fixed self, a continual emerging, a process."[80] LSD certainly helped Thom's process. He did not think of himself as American, "but I'm not (<u>really</u>) English either," he told Tanner after the Michigan circuit:

> The one thing I share with Sylvia Plath is that we are both Mid-atlantic poets. And I'm a Midatlantic <u>person</u> too. At least I believe so. Even if I were to go back and live in England for the rest of my life (God Forbid) I'd stay Midatlantic—or, let's say, half-San Franciscan half-English . . . I find London exotic and I find San Francisco exotic.[81]

Back in San Francisco, Thom capped an excellent year with the Stud's second Saturnalia party, "A Day in the Park." It was "a kind of Beerbohm Tree Forest of Arden," he told Tanner, "pools, glades, three real birds, stage turf on the ground."[82] He dropped violet-colored acid ("with speed, I'm certain") and was "really out of it for a couple of hours."[83]

Although he had not dropped acid once or twice a week as planned, between the two Saturnalia parties Thom had tripped sixteen times. Personally and poetically, 1969 had been one of his best years. "Mike's happy, Bill's happy," he told Tanner.[84] In notes for a poem called "The Lovers (M & Bill partly, M & me partly)," he wrote: "thr love is of the

other's uniqueness, thus of humanity."[85] On the subject of "making it &
not wanting to make it," he felt "M has genuinely got so much farther
than I have."[86] But Thom was happy, too. He felt LSD "helped my writing in many ways where my writing needed help."[87] Having turned forty
in August, he was glad that he had not started taking LSD until early
middle age. "It opens up possibilities," he reflected. "At twenty, one is
all too aware of the nature of possibility; when one's thirty-five, one has
become a little enclosed in one's mind."[88] Come 1970, Thom had four-
fifths of a new book that promised to be almost entirely about acid. He
was pleased his poems had stylistic and thematic consistency; something
he felt lacking in *Touch*. Although it was not finished, Thom felt his next
book would be a great leap forward. "The poems all seem to 'cohere'
at least," he told the Tanners. "The reviews will be really interesting. I
mean, it's almost as if I am <u>inviting</u> them to discuss acid and homosexuality rather than the quality of the poems."[89]

21

MOLY

Thom began 1970 as the Bain-Swiggett Lecturer at Princeton, a visiting professorship for poets, and taught there twice a week from January through May. He thought it was "clearly a sinecure"[1] and, with no desire to live in Princeton, arranged to stay at the Albert Hotel in Greenwich Village. The Albert had been home to numerous musicians in the 1960s, from Tim Buckley and the Byrds to Muddy Waters and the Mamas and the Papas. Thom found it "full of groovy people" but "incredibly dirty, even by my unfastidious standards." He stayed "from sheer lethargy" and because he liked "to be in the middle of Greenwich Village."[2] His room was broken into twice and his marijuana, typewriter, and white fringed jacket all stolen.[3] He moved his remaining valuables to Princeton, where he already kept his passport and acid, and arranged to sublet the art critic Lucy Lippard's "supersplendid loft" on Prince Street from mid-March to the end of his stay.[4]

Thom experienced his usual "melancholy of disorientation"[5] and had "vivid obsessions . . . that Mike would die while I was away and I'd never see him again."[6] Loneliness and the freezing cold kept him mostly indoors, but sometimes he cruised Central Park in the snow with "sex in the head."[7] "For the first (and I hope only) time in my life I seem to be using sex as something interesting to engage in because I can't think of anything better," he told the Tanners. "I mean, one can read only so many hours a day."[8] He carried "a San Francisco in the head"[9] and tried to write, but thought he was producing "very thin stuff."[10] Tanner had criticized "Grasses" as "another sitting and watching poem," which did not make Thom feel confident about his other recent poems.[11] He began revising "Phaedra in the Farm House," written in San Francisco in the autumn, which drew on memories of Covey Hall Farm. "I'm a bit cross with myself for having written it," he told Hall. "I never intended to do that kind of updated mythologizing any more."[12] In the Greek myth, Phaedra, wife of the hero Theseus, falls in love with his son, Hippolytus. The story ends with Hippolytus's death at the hands of his vengeful father; Phaedra commits suicide in remorse. "I think of her as Racine's Phaedra, for her emotions—hysterical and vulnerable," he told Tanner. "Except she is in a farm-house like my grandfather's in Kent."[13] The Covey Hall setting, and Phaedra's eventual suicide, conjure Thom's mother, "hysterical and vulnerable" in the last days of her life. He wrote the poem in Phaedra's voice[14] as she looks at Hippolytus "in from the stable," smelling of "soap, ghost of sweat, / Tractor oil, and the yards." The voice is Phaedra's but the memories are Thom's, like the sound of "slow-rolling churns" on flagstone, the "parlour's polished smell," and the "rabbitting" of summer evenings at Pit Cottage.[15]

Thinking about his mother, Thom wrote a series of five poems called "Tom-Dobbin," which touches on doubles and metamorphosis as well as the relationship between motherhood and queerness. "Tom-Dobbin" is a centaur, human from the waist up (Tom), horse from the waist down (Dobbin).[16] "Tom is me of course," Thom later remarked, recalling his boyhood name.[17] Man and horse compete, share, and, in the second poem, briefly combine:

> Hot in the mind, Tom watches Dobbin fuck,
> Watches, and smiles with pleasure, oh what luck.
> [. . .]
> In coming Tom and Dobbin join to one—
> Only a moment, just as it is done[.][18]

In his notes, Thom's centaur was "homosexual" and the poem was "a rejoicing in being queer."[19] The joy came in recognition—"from distinction to unity"[20]—that is, recognizing your own queerness and discovering you are not alone. "Knowledge of my uniqueness joins me to fellowship w/ everything," Thom wrote, reflecting his concern with humane, sympathetic values.[21] In a similar scene of joining and separation in the fourth poem, Thom describes a platypus mother feeding her "young one":

> The brown fur oozes milk for the young one. He,
> Hatched into separation, beaks his fill.
> If you could see through darkness you could see
> One breaking outline that includes the two.[22]

This scene anticipates Thom's realization, later in the 1970s, that it was "obvious" he and his mother "were lovers." "If it is true to say that living with you made me queer," he addressed her, "it is equally true to say that living with you made me a poet."[23] He did not push this idea in "Tom-Dobbin," but his placement of the motherhood scene after the centaur "plunges into orgy" implies a connection. The final poem of "Tom-Dobbin"—originally a much longer stand-alone poem called "We Are Centaurs / Being Queer / Making Love"—concludes: "we enter / The haze together—which is me, which him? / Selves floating in the one flesh we are of."[24] Thom's allusion to Genesis—"Therefore shall a man leave his father and his mother, and shall cleave unto his wife: and they shall be one flesh"[25]—solidified the ethics and philosophy of queer life that he had been building for almost two decades. "Tom-Dobbin" allowed Thom to reconcile the contradiction between the familial and the erotic, and acted as a coming-out poem that few recognized as such. Moreover, it speaks directly to the life Thom had first experienced in San Francisco—in particular at the Stud—and had wanted to build with Mike for the last decade: inclusive, supportive, sympathetic, familial.

Thom wrote "Tom-Dobbin" to feel close to his family. In New York he spent most of his time alone, and at Princeton his past seemed to confront him at every turn. The campus reminded him of Cambridge—

cold evenings, dripping trees, Gothic buildings—and the English faculty conducted itself "with a tweediness I imagine you'd have to go far to find in <u>England</u> nowadays."[26] Thom was one of several visiting English and Irish writers that semester, from Elizabeth Bowen and Lawrence Durrell to Frank Kermode and Nathaniel Tarn.[27] He found the faculty "formal, gracious, and damned distant" and received few social invitations.[28] "Not that I want to go to their houses particularly," he told the Tanners, "but I wonder why they don't ask me."[29] He liked A. Walton Litz, whom he recognized from Oxford in 1953, and Lawrence Lipking, but the only person to invite him for dinner was the young instructor and poet John Peck, who had the office next door to Thom in the basement of McCosh Hall. "The shabby and stuffy reception given him by the department was predictable in some ways," Peck recalled, "but painful to witness."[30] Thom thought Princeton students were like the faculty, "prep-school boys—not grown up at all," he told Donald Davie. "It's going to help a lot when they bring in many more girls into the university (right now there is only a to-ken 70!)."[31] In late spring, Thom concluded his semester at Princeton with a public lecture on Thomas Hardy and a public reading.[32]

In mid-March, after he left the Albert Hotel and moved to Lippard's loft in SoHo, Thom wrote to the Tanners: "I feel a bit like those charac-ters in Les Enfants Terribles camping (bivouacking) in the ball room."[33] Smells from the bakery downstairs filled the loft in the morning. As with Talbot Road, Thom caught SoHo "at the moment of change . . . just as it stopped being an Italian neighborhood: the first art gallery appeared round the corner while I lived there." Moving to the loft soothed his disorientation; he enjoyed "working only two days a week [and] running loose in the West Village every night."[34] Thom still frequented the leather bar Keller's but also enjoyed new bars: his favorites included the Zoo, on West Thirteenth Street, and the Den, a members-only leather bar at West Twelfth Street and Greenwich Avenue.[35] There he saw his "favour-ite" graffiti: "'We are the people our parents warned us against' . . . It's a sentence that burgeons in the mind as the months pass."[36]

After a month in SoHo, Thom was "finally starting to enjoy New York."[37] He also sensed that "the mood was changing everywhere."[38] He felt "proud" of Princeton for the first time when more than four thousand students, faculty, and staff voted to strike in response to President Nixon's invasion of Cambodia.[39] There were "numerous bombings": Thom witnessed "a rather famous town-house go up in smoke,"[40] an allusion to the Greenwich Village explosion of March 1970, when bombs being prepared by leftist militant group the Weather Underground exploded in the basement of a town house on West Eleventh Street.[41] "The feeling of the country was changing," he reflected, "and one didn't know into what."[42]

In New York, amid those uncertainties, Thom wrote "some curious, rather grotesque poetry."[43] Alongside "Tom-Dobbin," he wrote what became the title poem of his next book: *Moly*. Originally called "The Witch (Circe)," the poem draws on the scene in the *Odyssey* where Circe turns Odysseus's men into pigs. Moly is the name of the magical herb that Hermes, "the down just showing on his face," gives Odysseus to protect him from Circe's magic.[44] One of Odysseus's sailors awakens from Circe's spell, not knowing what he has become:

Nightmare of beasthood, snorting, how to wake.
I woke. What beasthood skin she made me take?[45]

Thom was thrilled with the poem: it encapsulated all his interests and concerns since he started taking acid again in 1968. "I see Moly as the antidote to the piggishness in man," he told the Tanners; "(some might see it as the Thorazine to be used for an acid freak-out, but let it be, that ambiguity)."[46] That "piggishness" was a settling of attitudes in middle age: acid, he thought, "shakes these complacencies by offering new perceptions of yourself and of the world."[47] Writing "Moly," Thom realized that "all the poems in the book are about changes in people." He joked that "The Metamorphoses" would make a good title, "but a Roman chap [already] used that one." Instead, he settled on *Moly* but worried it was "rather too much like a Ted Hughes title."[48] Thom sent *Moly* to Faber in late May. He saw it as a progression from "the primitive & the innocent" through "anxieties assoc. w/ consciousness" and "certain (pre-acid) attempts to reach beyond consciousness" in the first half, to "tripping and the consequent openness & the comparative success in reaching thro & beyond consciousness" in the second.[49]

As usual, after finishing a book, Thom felt "faintly depressed nowadays, with no reason."[50] He had written well, taught well, and largely enjoyed living in New York, but it had been a subdued six months and he was happy to leave. "I strongly get the feeling that I will never leave San Francisco for such a long time again," he told Belle Randall. "I miss San Francisco, and Mike, and friends, a lot."[51]

But Thom's travels were not yet over: he flew to England for the summer and split his time between London and Kent. He had agreed to take part in the Poetry International Festival and for his sanity had determined "to avoid reading all weeklies and Sunday papers . . . except the Listener. Even the TLS rouses me only to amazement at England's provinciality."[52] At the opening press conference for the festival, Thom had "6 cameras on me at once!!!" and had his photograph in the *Evening Standard*, the *Financial Times*, and *The Guardian*.[53] He participated in an "absurdly boring" reading at the Queen Elizabeth Hall, "at the heart of the establishment," and spent the next day drinking in Frick's with Tony White before a second group reading at the same venue. "During the first part I chat w/ Allen Tate, a very good gentle man," Thom reflected. "I speak briefly to WHA. I read I think even better than yesterday."[54] Auden was the star attraction, and Thom read with him, Carolyn Kizer, Dennis Brutus, and Sándor Weöres in the George Street Assembly Rooms in Edinburgh. The following year, when Thom read at Colgate, a liberal arts college in upstate New York, he was told by Richard Murphy, his host, "that Auden has a great distaste for me (something I'd been suspecting for some years)."[55]

Thom was amused to see how the British press reported his appearance at the festival. "Here was a poet whose image to many readers must be that of an abrasive character writing about Presley and motorbikes," wrote Robert Tait in *The Scotsman*. "Well, not only was that a long time ago, but by listening to the man, one can detect the subtler feints of thought and feeling there all the time."[56] Thom sometimes played up to his tough-guy reputation, but in London he projected a subtly different image. In a photograph taken at the festival, sitting next to Kizer and Stephen Spender, he wears a fringed leather jacket and a tie-dye singlet. In another photograph, he removed the jacket and, in the words of festival organizer Charles Osborne, "flash[ed] his tattoos at the press."[57] Thom was comfortable in front of the cameras and liked the attention, but his general hostility to fame and public life was well known. "Gunn now lives permanently in San Francisco," reported the *Evening Standard*, "where, he says, he is lucky enough to have just the right amount of fame—enough to be helpful, not enough to be inconvenient."[58] He was pleased that when the festival was over he could return "from celebrity to the anonymous life, thank god."[59]

The anonymous life meant staying with Mick Belsten and Peter Flannery in Barnes and drinking in Becky's Dive Bar with Tony White. Becky's, a below-street pub in Southwark with beer cellars "thought to be the cells of the old Marshalsea debtors' prison,"[60] was a squalid place. There Thom saw the "Nameless Wildness" graffiti that he later used in his diary to describe memorable trysts.[61] Visits to Kent punctuated his time in London. He saw Mary and Catherine in Snodland and Barbara and Godfrey in Sittingbourne. Not knowing when he would next return, he thought it might be his "last sight of B & G."[62] He also helped Ander, his wife, Margaret, and their children pack up their London house—the subject of "Last Days at Teddington"—before they moved to Cornwall. He adored his niece and nephew, Charlotte (eight) and William (nine), and they adored him. "The excitement of him being there," Charlotte recalled. "He brought this energy. He looked so exotic. I'd never seen anyone in leather trousers before."[63] It was an enjoyable stay, but Thom "wasn't entirely contented in England this time," he told White, "though it beats me to explain why not: staying on Talbot Rd., many lovely times with you, the Anders euphoric at their move, even the aunts were really at their best."[64] Thom could never shake his "extreme" reactions to England. "I suppose in a sense it is revisiting past selves," he told Tanner, "and measuring myself against them."[65]

When Thom returned to San Francisco in August, after a seven-month absence, he felt the same "strange" atmosphere that had affected him in New York. "There was a certain strain in attempting to preserve the euphoria of the sixties," he reflected; "one's anxieties seemed obstructive."[66] His unease had begun in the aftermath of the Altamont Free Concert the previous December, during which four people had died amid extreme violence. Thom and friends were "about half-way back" and "saw no trouble" but thought the Rolling Stones were "crazy" to have hired the Hell's Angels to guard the stage.[67] If the Summer of Love was a new beginning, the Altamont chaos—*Rolling Stone* called it "a fundamental lack of concern for humanity"—felt like an ending.[68]

Although he was "full of happiness at being back," Thom spent several weeks "in a bit of a slump" and did little "except sit in sun & feel confused."[69] He felt "full of vague but <u>very</u> grandiose literary projects"— and even started a "jocular pornographic novel" called *San Francisco Romances*—but did not want to start writing poems again until he had the proofs of *Moly*, "to find out where I'm at."[70] Even so, he wrote three songs—"Hitching into Frisco," "Baby Song," and "Sparrow"—and made revisions to "Wrestling" and "Diagrams," early versions of which he had drafted in New York. The homeless man in "Sparrow"—"in a leaky doorway in leaky shoes"—became a common figure in Thom's poetry as he began to write more directly about San Francisco street life. "Baby Song" continued the maternal imagery of "Moly" and "Tom-Dobbin" and, in a baby's voice, describes life inside its mother's womb. "Things were different inside Mother," it says, although Thom decided to cut his original last line: "Now I am suddenly on my own."[71]

Around Christmas, two events occurred that heightened Thom's perception of the new, strange mood in San Francisco. Earlier in the year, Don Doody had left the Stud, moved his family to Campus, "an ailing gay bar" two blocks away, and hoped to transform it into "somewhere very nice, like the early Stud."[72] At their New Year's party, six people had their tires slashed outside the bar: Don learned "such things had been happening outside the bar for years" and resigned, "figuring—very honorably—that you can't turn people out into a night full of paranoia about knives."[73]

Simultaneously, Thom's use of LSD began to decline. Gary White had manufactured "a large quantity of pure acid" and Thom "bought 100 [doses], to sell half."[74] Thom dropped some of White's "v strong" blue acid on Christmas Day and "hallucinated, quite uncomfortably, for well over two hours." On this trip, he "discovered" how he had "succeeded in reconstructing" his "idealiz[ed]" childhood household of "my mother and Ander and me" with "Mike as my mother, Bill as my younger brother." He hoped Mike and Bill were not just "symbolic embodiments of needs" and was disturbed "that the submerged part of myself is still that far lost in the primeval jungles and swamps."[75] Thom's "need created a place that must always be filled" with opposites: "Father / Apollo-Dionysus / tricks" against "Mother / the Goddess-Muse / Mike."[76] This LSD trip revealed the central contradiction of his life, the two needs he had fought to reconcile. He later ascribed his retreat from LSD to "a couple of rather bad trips that taught me no end of unpalatable facts about myself, to my great edification,"[77] but at the time he felt acid "seemed to annihilate the ego & reawaken one into an ego-less self as innocent as the newborn, one carried the whole of one's previous self, one carried one's full burdens, weakness, cowardices, obsessions." With this in mind, Thom felt that his next book "cd be about burdens—how they are carried with you but—accepted, translated, made use of."[78]

A new drug quickly replaced LSD and would make a significant impact on Thom's poetry. MDA, nicknamed "the love drug," was "a mild psychedelic, and a very wild aphrodisiac."[79] Lighter than LSD, MDA never gave Thom a bad trip. Its effects were more bodily: Thom felt "total immersion in sex for 6 hours,"[80] but its comedown caused feelings of depression and fatigue that could last for several days. Returning to the water metaphor of "At the Centre," Thom explored how bodies merge in drug-enhanced orgasm in "The Plunge."[81] If Thom's LSD poems dwelled more on consciousness and perception, "The Plunge" is more physical—

> the brute thrust of
> entering this all-
> alien like a bitter
> sheath
>   each
> nerve each
> atom of skin
> tightens against it[82]

—and bodily desire became a much greater force in his poetry, replacing intellectual ideas like will, conduct, and chance. "The Plunge" began Thom's broader interest in "the totally non-verbal experience" conducted through the body and prompted a return to a style of free verse comparable to "Touch."[83] He wanted his "non-verbal" poems to "plung[e] deep into the center till I can be high, fucking like a cat, fucking *for* fucking, at the mercy of (and at the same time) dominating the experience."[84] Such a plunge was "essential for keeping the senses pure," and was not hedonistic but "an act of sympathy."[85]

Faber published *Moly* in March 1971, and Thom was surprised when the Poetry Book Society made it their "Choice" for the quarter. "I suppose Ted and I really are The Establishment now," he told Tanner. "Dear me. Well, we can still be a surprising Establishment."[86] Thom thought *Moly* was an invitation to discuss homosexuality and LSD: most reviews dealt with the latter and elided, either willfully or naïvely, the former. Alan Brownjohn found the book "often exciting" but not "the kind of breakthrough—or break-out?—that one might have hoped for at this stage in Thom Gunn's career."[87] Michael Fried complained that the poems "do not *smell*."[88] Ian Hamilton criticized the "obediently trotting metric" and "murderous line-breaks," and found Thom "essentially an intellectualiser."[89] Donald Davie, appalled at *Moly*'s reception, thought British reviewers found Thom's "aggravating coolness" offensive.[90] Clive Wilmer argued that Thom's "ability to draw visions of wonder into the language of discourse" and his "self-discipline [which] has long resisted the orthodoxies of inarticulacy and hysteria" set him above his contemporaries.[91] Thom thanked Clive for his review, noting he was "the only person who realised that the rhythm of the book was working between the moon at the start and the sun at the end. It is very good when somebody gets something like that."[92]

In early 1971, Thom taught a poetry seminar at Stanford, "a very nice easy job" in which he saw a lot of Donald Davie, then head of the creative writing program, and the two poetry fellows: Rod Taylor and his friend and former student Belle Randall.[93] In the spring, Tony Tanner arrived to teach a course on the American novel at Berkeley. Thom met him at the airport and found him unrecognizable. "He is very worried," he wrote, "anxious about everything & worrying to us, that we can't do much about it."[94] The previous year, Tanner had suffered a minor nervous breakdown, which he ascribed to "nervous exhaustion from overwork," and took time off to recover.[95] Now, Tanner's anxiety focused on his recently published second book, a study of postwar American fiction called *City of Words*. Tanner had pushed himself to finish it and was disheartened by its poor reception in England. Seeing his friend in such a state shook Thom, especially because Tanner had seemed in good health and spirits when Thom was in England the previous summer. "I spend a depressing morning trying to cheer him up," Thom reflected, "but he finds fresh worries to give body to his anxiety."[96] He hoped that Marcia's arrival, in April, would revivify Tanner, as might the presence of Tony White, who stopped in San Francisco for a fortnight while traveling across America. "Some good things come in small doses," Thom told White after the trip, "but next time let's have a larger dose of you."[97]

Tanner's anxieties worsened as the quarter progressed, and in mid-May his therapist told him to stop work immediately and return to Cambridge. The night before he and Marcia left, they joined Thom, Mike, and Don Doody to celebrate Mike's fortieth birthday at a Berkeley restaurant. It was a tense evening. "Don didn't have a good word to say about [Marcia]," Mike recalled.[98] "I'd always had this very strange feeling about

Don," Marcia reflected. "Not that he really was evil, I could just never quite understand what his motives were, what power he had over Thom or why Thom had this worshipful feeling toward him."[99] After dinner, Thom and Mike walked with Marcia while Don and Tony had a lingering talk. "When we were driving Don back to San Francisco, Don told us he'd said 'everything' to Tanner," Thom told Tony White, "about how Marcia is Big Nurse all set to turn Tanner into a basket case . . . It doesn't leave Tanner anything to do except worry more: he loves Marcia and is not going to leave her, and so he thinks of us as all being in a kind of silent conspiracy against her." Tanner called Thom the next morning and they had "a very painful conversation" in which Thom attempted to "distinguish between Don's opinion of Marsh and my own." Thom thought that she and Tanner did not make a good psychological match, but could do little to assuage Tanner's feelings. "He got quite angry with me," Thom told White, "but for some reason it seemed really impossible for me to lie about the whole business." Thom worried his friendship with Tanner would not survive the fallout. "It's true we probably won't see each other for a couple of years, but it's going to be difficult by letter and difficult when we do see each other," he continued. "It's all really a great pity: I'll write him friendly letters, but I get a feeling he may not answer them."[100] Thom wrote Tanner a few days later. "I am often wrong about everything, as you know," he told him. "But I hope you know I love you."[101]

The cooling of his friendship with Tanner was personal, but it contributed to Thom's larger feeling that the general atmosphere in San Francisco was beginning to darken. He had "friend after friend busted for dope" and others were "freaking out on bad acid." Nixon was "losing his temper at the top," Thom felt, and, with an election eighteen months away, it seemed as though Nixon would win a second term. "What are we left with?" Thom reflected. He thought 1965–69 were "years of great experiments in music, drugs, the consciousness, society" and felt people had made "beautiful anarchic gains" in terms of "knowledge of possibilities, knowledge of change."[102] Midway through 1971, he held little hope for the next decade.

22

AUTOBIOGRAPHY

When Thom received a Guggenheim Fellowship in April 1971, he knew exactly how he would use the money.[1] "I'd make the down payment on a house, for my growing family," he told Ander. "Houses are quite cheap still in quite pleasant areas which are predominantly Black, Mexican, or Hippie. I have a black heart, a Mexican tongue, and I dig drugs and long hair, so I have nothing against such districts, myself."[2] The Haight was one such district. The neighborhood had become "violent and disturbing"; drugs like heroin and new "superpsychedelics" like STP and PCP, initially developed in military laboratories, fueled the "growing craziness" of Haight-Ashbury.[3] In May, Thom and Mike viewed a house on Cole Street, some seven blocks up the hill from Haight. Four days later they bought it, using thirty-three hundred dollars of Thom's Guggenheim grant as a down payment.

Mike thought the Haight was "very iffy," but Thom did not agree.[4] He called it "very cool" and thought "North Beach is going through rather bad changes and the Haight is going through some pretty good ones." They would miss North Beach, and "the Bay right beside us," but Thom looked forward to having "the whole of Golden Gate Park just around the corner."[5] For Mike, the house was "love at first sight."[6] It was a duplex: 1214 upstairs, 1216 in the middle, with a garage at street level. Each apartment had a separate entrance on Cole Street with a steep interior staircase. An exterior staircase connected them at the rear. Thom,

Mike, and Bill took 1216, which had "big bright rooms, a studio for Bill, and a small back yard with sun on it all day."[7] Mike and Bill had the back room, an extension, which opened into the yard; Thom took the front room, overlooking Cole; and Bill used the middle room as his art studio. They knocked down the wall between kitchen and dining room to create a large communal living space that Mike decorated with his collection of tin advertising signs. He had begun to amass the collection—from flea markets, antiques fairs, defunct bars, and house clearances—since returning to San Francisco in 1968. Rows of vintage soft drink bottles— American brands like Kist, Dodger, Royal Crown, Hires, Nesbitt's— lined the room and the staircase up to the apartment.[8] Thom took great pleasure in tending the garden and within a year had planted "radishes, onions, scallions, chives, parsley, lemon bergamot, mint, hollyhocks, nasturtiums, lupins, alyssum, sweet william, stock, phlox, pinks, sweet peas, snapdragons, tomatoes, basil, pansies, polyanthus."[9]

Thom, Mike, and Bill spent August renovating the house. It was "a somewhat troubled time" full of "strange dreams," Thom thought.[10] He ascribed his "frequent downers" to the instability of moving after a decade in one place, "longer than I've ever lived in one house in my life."[11] They moved into 1216 on September 1. A fortnight later, Don Doody—"the spiritual director of our lives"[12]—moved in upstairs with Stud friends Al Hilliard and Paul Feola. "We are become in our modest way a kind of commune," Thom told Tony White; "we are in & out of each other's places all day, and very pleased with ourselves and the place. I have never seen DD so domesticated, he spends his days scraping paint off his kitchen walls, hardly goes out at night, and speaks about 'the nesting instinct.'"[13] Having spent the 1960s close to Clara Street and the Stud, Thom was delighted to have his own family in his own house. "It is really, I realize, the way of living I've wanted for the last 6 years or so," he told Tanner. "I guess I am something of a bully, in my quiet way: first I manipulate things so that Bill comes to live with us, and then I manipulate things so that Don does too—and it happens with just the two others I'd hoped for (Al & Paul)."[14]

From Cole Street, Thom could stride up to Seventeenth and down the hill into the Castro. Walking the length of Haight took him almost to South of Market, where the "Folsom St circuit" extended from the Stud at 1535, through Febe's at 1501, to the Ramrod at 1225.[15] A new bar at 1347, the In Between, was so called because it was in between Febe's and the Ramrod. Boot Camp, two blocks over at 1010 Bryant, was a new favorite. He kept up with new bars and theme nights in Mr. Marcus's gossip column in a new gay newspaper, the *Bay Area Reporter*.[16] In the Haight, Thom's neighborhood gay bar, Bradley's Corner, was already an institution. Shortly after moving to Cole, in Buena Vista Park he cruised a "really chunky young beauty" named James: they bought some speed, returned to James's place, "shoot up 3 times (a first for me) & have sex for 12 hrs . . . Really beautiful."[17] Thom wrote about this experience of intravenous drug use in "Faustus Triumphant":

> The dazzled blood
> submits, carries the
> flame through me to every
> organ till blood itself
> is flamy
> > flame animates me
> with delight in time's things
> so intense that I am
> almost lost to time[18]

Like "The Plunge," "Faustus" is a free verse poem that evokes a nonverbal experience through an insistent focus on bodily sensation. It also began a new interest in "get[ting] inside of people in slightly unusual & so interesting situations." Thom connected it to his subsequent poem "The Idea of Trust" in which "'pretty' Jim," a thief who briefly lived upstairs on Cole Street, defined trust as "an intimate conspiracy." The "act of writing" about it, Thom remarked, "made me more sympathetic to him than I'd guessed—getting into his head had surprising results."[19]

Moving house effectively ended Thom's writing year. He had expected to edit a monthly poetry page for *The Organ*, a countercultural newspaper based in San Francisco, but contributed only one page before it folded that summer.[20] In December he gave two readings in New York State, at Rochester and Colgate, that paid for a fortnight in the city. His new favorite haunt, the "best L bar ever," was Eagle's Nest, also known as the Eagle, on West Twenty-first.[21] There, he cruised two guys he recognized from his hotel, "Electric Cowboy" and Frank. "Cd have made it w/ them, don't know why I didn't," he reflected. "Am aware of renewed danger of succumbing to 'the mythology.' Necessity of holding out, however attractive it may seem."[22] Thom had grown more suspicious of symbols and simulacra. Hypermasculine leathermen on motorcycles were symbols of power and strength, but they were also a type, a sexual fantasy. He felt there was a danger, a loss of selfhood, in becoming one's fantasy. Instead, he came to value leather bars as part of ordinary, everyday life—for friendship, conviviality, drugs, cruising—thus blending desire and fantasy with reality. When he returned home from the east in mid-December, he looked again at notes made the previous year for a poem called "Acid Cowboy / New York Billy," in which the protagonist loses his sense of self by becoming the symbol of his desire. "He sups on what he has become," Thom wrote, "then for a moment / does not even savor himself, he's / so completely his fantasy."[23]

Thom returned home from the East Coast in mid-December and found an "odd situation upstairs—too many people."[24] Back in October, Jere Fransway's commune, a craft store and artist workshop called the Handmakers, was raided. Police called it a "drug supermarket": in a "fortified cellar storage room" they found "sixty pounds of marijuana, 20,000 tablets of LSD," plus peyote, mescaline, cocaine, and barbiturates.[25] Lonnie Leard, Thom's friend and a clerk at the store, was one of five arrested. There was a warrant out for Fransway's arrest: a few days later, Thom found him sleeping on Don's floor upstairs. Al Hilliard moved out; Paul Feola had already left, having quarreled with Don. While Thom was in New York, a fire at the Handmakers, "a gingerbready . . . frame post-earthquake structure," razed it to the ground.[26] Now doubly unable to return to the Handmakers, Fransway moved his "really vast entourage—usually 15–25 people" into Don's apartment, including his dog, a Chesapeake Bay retriever named Jeffrey.[27] This made Don "freaky-irritable."[28] Returning from New York, Thom walked into the middle of the upheaval, but Don reassured him that Jere and entourage would not be upstairs "for much longer."[29] Fransway's eventual departure, shortly after Christmas, precipitated a near-friendship-ending quarrel between him and Don. "We have a democracy," Thom explained to Tanner. "Don Doody has an autocracy."[30]

Thom felt confident that order would be restored in the New Year: Don planned to share with James Dondson, "a person so generous, open, and tactful that it is difficult to find any flaw in him."[31] Thom became used to other people upstairs and to the more mundane aspects of commune-dwelling, especially since he was responsible for the house. Doody could come across as cantankerous and quarrelsome; Thom found him "an incredibly generous person, but the good he does is so much by stealth that you have to nose around to find the number of people he is feeding, visiting in prison, giving things to, and in general sheltering."[32] Thom enjoyed having the house both ways—a hippie commune upstairs and the stability of him, Mike, and Bill downstairs—but for the first six months the drama upstairs added to his strange feelings about the move. "I take as a motto for this period of my life," he wrote, "'Been having a hard time / Living the good life.'"[33]

Thom described 1972 as a "pretty good year. If some trying things have happened," he told Tanner, "my spirits seem able to cope with them OK, and the good things have far outnumbered the bad ones anyway."[34] Most of the "trying things" were drug busts. Thom had "known 10 people at least" from whom he could buy drugs, but by the year's end it was "hard sometimes to find one."[35] In August, one friend, Harold Cartlidge, known as Dale, was sentenced to six years for "smuggling into Denmark enough LSD for 72,000 doses," then the heaviest sentence a Danish court had imposed in a narcotics case.[36] Closer to home, Thom, Mike, and Bill all grew marijuana, as did Don upstairs. One May morning, Thom was walking up Cole Street from the grocery store when he saw "five young men in suits, with short hair, who had parked on a sidestreet. I thought, if I were asked to describe what I thought a narc looked like I'd describe them," he told Tanner. "Wouldn't it be funny if they <u>were</u> narcs and they were going to our house? I then saw four of them flatten themselves against our wall (so nobody from the upstairs window could see them), while one rang Don's bell—and then they all went in." Thom rushed inside and "removed all Mike's enormous marijuana plants from the back windows" and hid them in a closet.[37] Upstairs, Don was busted for possession of marijuana and five thousand speed pills: Don claimed his older brother, a doctor, had given him the pills when amphetamines were still readily prescribed to aid weight loss. Don escaped prison but received three years' probation and a one-thousand-dollar fine.

The night before the raid, Thom had brought home a young leatherman from Folsom. Larry Hoyt was a conscientious objector during the Vietnam War and worked in the Sonoma State Hospital teaching children with learning and behavioral difficulties. Thom saw him "a lot" during the summer. Larry was "alarmingly young—21, certainly young enough to be my son," he told Tanner. "Very attractive and very bright." They were not monogamous—"unimaginable, dahling"—but "we are seeing a lot of each other, which is a bit unusual for me," he continued. "I'm trying to do things for him I would have liked someone to do for me when I was his age."[38] Thom claimed to need "the Father-Figure" but often acted like one to younger men like Bill and Larry. "At 21 / he cd be my son / or my own past self," he wrote in notes for a poem called "The Visionary Son." Glossing those lines, he reflected: "These boys who come to my bed each night & think I am their father & I, meanwhile, trying to think them mine." Describing his "visionary son," a kind of doppelgänger, Thom wanted him to be "an improvement over me" but "not a 'success,'" with "imagination & good sense" and a "great laugh too but quieter." For the same poem, Thom listed his own qualities: "lucky, abstracted, talkative, without death wish (or addiction wish), orgiastic, a great enjoyer."[39]

A month into their friendship, Larry took Thom to his parents' summerhouse in Forestville, on the Russian River, and showed him the Sonoma State Hospital. The visit, and Larry's stories about teaching the

boys, informed Thom's poem "As Expected."[40] From the hospital, Thom
and Larry spent a long weekend at the Geysers, a camping spot some hundred miles north of San Francisco. Many of the city's motorcycle clubs
made runs to the Geysers, and its natural steam and mud baths made it
a popular draw for hippies. Its "ancient bath houses" reminded Thom of
"the baths at the start of Fellini's Satyricon." Thom had first experienced
the Geysers the previous summer, "a total nudity trip" of young and old,
male and female, longhairs and hippies, all of whom "lived naked most
of the time they were there." There was "quite a bit of both heterosexual and homosexual orgy," which "seemed very natural—just like the
world ought to be." Thom slept on hillsides and swam in the cool stream.
"Maybe this is what Clive would call hippie sentimentality," he told Tanner, "but the beautiful naïve impulses that started up about 6 years ago
are much too powerful to be obliterated by the shit that has been piled
upon them, and that they have sometimes directly caused themselves."[41]
Thom thought that "hedonistic and communal love" could be "extended
to the working life of the towns," but the Geysers paradise was short-lived.
Thom went three times—in August 1971, with Larry in June 1972, and
with his friend Roy Siniard, the writer Jack Fritscher, and Fritscher's partner, David Sparrow, the following month—before the Geysers shut down
in 1973. "The Geysers were no scrubbed German Spa," Fritscher recalled.
"No health department would have approved."[42]

After his 1971 trip, Thom sketched a few lines for a short poem called
"At the Geysers." He did not return to it until summer 1972, after his
two subsequent visits, and began writing a four-part sequence called
"The Geysers."[43] His early work on the sequence coincided with work
preparing an edition of Ben Jonson for Penguin.[44] Rereading Jonson,
Thom found points of comparison between them. He thought Jonson
"strangely neglected," he wrote in his introduction to the Jonson edition, in part because much of his work "can be damned as 'occasional'"
and written off as "trivial or insincere." Thom argued that "all poetry
is occasional: whether the occasion is an external event like a birthday
or a declaration of war, whether it is an occasion of the imagination, or
whether it is in some sort of combination of the two." The occasion was

the "starting point to which the poet must in some sense stay true," he continued. "The truer he is to it, the closer he sticks to what for him is its authenticity, the more he will be able to draw from it in the adventures that it produces, adventures that consist of the experience of writing."[45] Thom took the epigraph for "The Geysers"—"Thou hast thy walkes for health, as well as sport"—from Jonson's "To Penshurst" because "the place embodies moral virtues for me in the same way P. did for BJ."[46]

Moreover, in the final poem of the sequence, "The Bath House," Thom wrote openly for the first time about an erotic gay scene in which he himself had participated. The Jonsonian couplets of the first three poems fragment: seemingly random line breaks and caesurae disguise the rhyme and meter. The poem concludes:

> I am part of all
> > hands take
> > > hands tear and twine
>
> I yielded
> > oh, the yield
> > > what have I slept?
> my blood is yours   the hands that take accept
> > > . . . . . .
> torn from the self
> > in which I breathed and trod
> I am
> > I am raw meat
> > > I am a god[47]

Images of disintegration and community compete: "I am part of all" is repeated, first with reference to "bobbing in the womb, all round me Mother."[48] In the final lines, the speaker—no longer a watcher, as in poems like "From the Wave" and "Grasses"—is "torn from the self" and discovers himself to be "raw meat . . . a god." It is a moment of bodily, sensual rebirth—comparable to the psychological rebirths of *Moly*—into a world of greater openness, acceptance, and freedom. The poem was the answer to a question Thom posed to himself about why he remained "in a place by myself" after every good communal experience. "Why can't I stay here, <u>with</u> the world, <u>with</u> others," he asked.[49] The elation of "The Geysers"—the experience itself and its writing, the combined occasion—demonstrated that he could.

The autobiographical nature of "The Geysers" compelled Thom to return to a much-considered project: a prose autobiography, "the attempt to define yourself completely, accurately, without rhetoric." He felt "somewhat disturbed" that he wanted to write one, but had "come back to the idea again & again in the last 6 yrs or so." He began a new notebook in autumn 1972 and outlined his early life. "I am interested, indeed, in my experiences & in my poetry more than I am in <u>me</u>," he wrote; "(is that possible?)." He worked hard, writing outlines and drafting early chapters, and came to see his most important task as "reproduction of the 'atmosphere,' i.e. the sniff of the air."[50] That phrase became "the sniff of the real" in Thom's poem "Autobiography," written concurrently, in which, aged seventeen, "life seemed all / loss, and what was more / I'd lost whatever it was / before I'd even had it."[51]

Progress on the prose autobiography was slow, but the project had a major effect on the themes and ideas of Thom's poems. He thought the "subject" for his next book would be "the conditions of acceptance," a kind of process in which "you have to wait for the time, work toward it, as it involves a special kind of understanding that has its own time for maturing i.e. Breaking Ground, & the time it took to write it."[52] Thom began "Breaking Ground" that October when he heard that Uncle Godfrey had died: he thought about Aunt Barbara, whose "voice / intonations I've known / all my life," and whose death he would find difficult to "accept."[53] He comforted himself with the idea that, when Barbara died, her "sweet character" would be "distributed" among others and she would be "renewed again / and again throughout / one great garden which / is always here."[54] Acceptance, like writing, is a process. Writing poems about family, and prose about himself, helped Thom accept himself, from his fear of death to adolescent shame about his sexuality. Thom had this in mind when he discussed "burdens" in a subsequent interview. "You carry the burden of everything you know on your back: it's a very interesting burden, I don't regret it, I like it," he told John Haffenden. "What I want to get across is that one can learn from the ecstasy just as well as one can learn from the mistakes and unhappiness. They modify each other."[55]

"Breaking Ground" is about origins and sources. Thom's interest in these themes prompted the mother imagery of *Moly* and the birth imagery of "The Geysers." He wrote "Bringing to Light," a companion poem to "Breaking Ground," in 1973. Initially called "Origins," he took for its premise "the idea of origins, the multiple going back to the single."[56] Experiences were layered: Thom drew a diagram in his notebook, with "present events" on the surface and, below it, "remembered/unremembered events," "psychological events," and "dream/unconscious/mythological events" like layers of bedrock beneath the earth's surface.[57] "Bringing to Light" is autobiographical insofar as Thom reflected on his own memories and experiences in the poem. For example, he mentions a "forgotten" picnic in Kent when he was six years old, for which he has "a page of snapshots" in his album. "It still takes place," he wrote, "but in / a cellar I cannot locate."[58] The idea of layers merged with rooms and spaces because Thom wrote the poem at a time when part of Covey Hall Farm had been sold to developers. "Orchard, granary, barns, stables, all farm buildings are coming down," he reflected.[59] "I'll miss not seeing the yard again," he told Mary and Catherine.[60] For Thom, who had dwelled on Covey Hall, his prehistory, in his prose autobiographical writings, the farm would come to exist only in memories and photographs, slipping through the layers to what he called "foundations under the foundations." Moreover, the farm was a connection to his mother's origins. In "Bringing to Light," he depicts a "common root" that tied everybody together as a mother–son relationship:

> joining each other in their origins
> separate words return to their roots
> lover and mother melt into

one figure that covers its face
nameless and inescapable

need arrayed like a cause[61]

In dreams, and after his difficult acid trip about childhood and family, Thom worried that "it is only my need, these others are not really Mike, Mother" but become "the same person: person-who-fills-my-need."[62] He acknowledged that Mother was his "inescapable" origin and that Mike had filled his need for a stable, familial relationship.

Thom felt fertile and productive through the autumn. Only Nixon's landslide reelection ("that barrel of slime") took the shine off what he still felt, by December, had been "a really good year in most ways."[63] His writing momentum slowed in the new year when he agreed to teach the winter quarter at Berkeley. He thought it would be his "last teaching job for a while," but as the quarter progressed two things changed his mind.[64] The students, he found, were livelier and more intelligent than he remembered, and he enjoyed seeing old colleagues like Jackson Burgess and Thomas Parkinson. Moreover, when the dollar was devalued in February, Thom discovered he did not have enough money to visit England in the summer. Food prices had also increased: the household could only afford meat once a week. Thom did not want to increase the rent at Cole Street. Instead, he persuaded the English Department to let him teach the winter quarter on a permanent part-time basis. "Won't know till toward the end of the year," he told Barbara. "I think they are well-disposed toward me (in spite of the fact that I left them) but of course they may not have enough money to take me on. Gov. Reagan has kept them very short of money, since he hates education!"[65]

Drugs were still cheap, however, and Thom's drug life became more experimental. Acid was weak, grass strong, but he was more interested in PCP, MDA, and speed. "Thom was always taking speed," Mike reflected. "If Thom was on speed, it would depend on the drink. If he took them together . . ."[66] Early in the year, Mike told Thom "nicely" that he had "become nervous, a chatterbox, and inattentive & restless to everyone."[67] With Don (and sometimes Jere) upstairs, drugs were always nearby. Thom took speed to go to the bars, give readings, write essays, and do household chores. He picked up methamphetamine users— "speedfreaks"—on Folsom and, for a time, would refuse to play with other tricks unless they were also on speed. "He was not willing to continue to play with me unless I joined him in taking a speed pill," recalled one trick from the mid-1970s. "Although I found Thom to be sexy, the requirement to do speed was a turnoff for me. We never had sex again."[68]

As the winter quarter concluded at Berkeley, it had been two years since Thom published *Moly* in Britain. But the collection had still not appeared in America. The University of Chicago Press had rejected *Moly* in 1970 on the grounds that the "success" of *Touch* had been "modest" and they were "not . . . anxious to endorse" another Gunn book.[69] W. W. Norton & Co. and Oxford University Press's New York branch had also rejected it.[70] Robert Giroux, of Farrar, Straus and Giroux, made an offer for *Moly* in late 1970. A contract was produced, but UCP wanted "an entirely unreasonable" sixty-five hundred dollars for Gunn's American rights: this impasse would preclude the future publication of a collected edition of Gunn's poems by Farrar, Straus. Thom was so exasperated that he told Peter du Sautoy, the chairman of Faber, that he wanted to see *Moly* published in America "even if it comes out from some minor publisher in the end. In spite of the lousy reviews it mostly got in England, I still feel it is my best book."[71] An agreement was reached: Faber agreed to pay around two thousand dollars for the return of the rights, and UCP remaindered its stock of *My Sad Captains*, *Positives*, and *Touch*. Farrar, Straus brought out *Moly* in a joint edition with *My Sad Captains*. Thom was "very happy at the prospect" of his "two best books" appearing "between two covers."[72] *Moly and My Sad Captains* was published in April 1973. American reviewers echoed their British counterparts. "Some idiot woman thinks I am trying to be like Roethke!" he told Tanner. "Well, I can see why she thinks I've failed."[73] But Thom was delighted with Robert Duncan, who responded to *Moly* with his own suite, *Poems from the Margins of Thom Gunn's "Moly"* (1972).[74] Thom was pleased that Duncan "<u>chose</u> to interpret [*Moly*] as gay poems"—something every critic ignored—"and I'm grateful indeed considering the richness of his poems that resulted."[75]

Thom wrote a lot through 1973 but felt his poems "lack[ed] that concentrated sense of direction of the Moly poems."[76] He knew "a single 'feeling'" had characterized each of his books so far—with the exception of *Touch*—but struggled to recapture the "risky and rich" feeling, "a very full excitement" he had grasped in "The Plunge" while writing about acceptance and burdens. He felt "excitement seems to be always involved with my real poetry."[77] He thought that sympathy could connect excitement with acceptance and turned to Oliver Sacks's recently published *Awakenings*, in which sympathy was "literally the organizer of [Sacks's] style" and allowed the book "to be so inclusive, so receptive, and so varied."[78] Reading *Awakenings* confirmed to Thom that, to write most convincingly about sympathy, he had to write about other people. He began a new poem called "The Street / Ars Poetica," an early version of what became "The Release." Its subject was "the validity of the imagination—my sense of imagination—how it must be literal not symbolic."[79] It is a simple premise: Thom watches a "beautiful, eager" man, "maybe speeding a little," sit on some steps in the sunshine. "He eases to and fro in his consciousness," Thom wrote, "he moves in and out of my poem."[80]

The purpose, and paradox, of the poem was "to keep him other but alive." Thom did not want to "attribute motive" to the man: that way, "he'll simply be me."[81] Keeping him other, separate, was an act of sympathy and respect. Thom took this experience as an occasion to write a poem about poetry and about his own efforts to be more sympathetic to others and truer to himself. As he said of "excitement," he wanted "to get the reader to feel the Feeling when he reads the poem."[82] There are many kinds of release in Thom's work—sexual, emotional, psychological, pharmaceutical—and, on a literal level, "The Release" releases the man, "clean of me," back into the world.[83] Like "The Geysers," it signaled a greater openness to include autobiography in his poems. To emphasize that new openness, in summer 1975 he published "The Release" in *Gay News*, his first London appearance as a gay poet.[84] After years grappling with identity and autobiography, Thom felt ready to be himself.

23

RELATIONSHIPS

In 1974, Thom learned his San Francisco family was not infallible. Mike and Bill separated. "It has been 5 years of very great happiness for me," Thom wrote, "and I've been lucky to have it at all."[1] In notes for a poem, he wrote: "Perhaps it's a punishment for pride. I was so proud / of our beautiful family. Five years / the three of us stayed together / while other families fell apart."[2] Although Mike and Bill patched things up and Bill returned to Cole Street within a month, it was a warning.

Moreover, Thom was in physical pain. He spent a week in bed "with fucked up back," the result of a pinched nerve, and began a course of neck traction using what he called a "portable gallows."[3] Speed provided temporary relief, and Thom spent two exciting weeks in New York before he arrived in England for the late spring and early summer. What proved "psychologically, an exceptionally difficult time,"[4] began with "jetlag and despair" on arrival.[5] Tony White was away; Thom stayed in his empty flat. Lunching in Hampstead with Thérèse Megaw and Ruth Pearce (now Townsend), who told him about "lots of deaths," did little for his mood.[6] When White returned, he took Thom to a party in Kensington thrown by the poet Derek Mahon. Thom acted "rather disgracefully" toward the poet and children's author Kit Wright. "He said 'I like your poetry,' & I think I said 'I like your body,'" Thom wrote. "I also said 'Are you interested in leather?' and he blanched." That evening: "Tony's big surprise, 22 years late."[7] Thom later told August Kleinzahler that Tony had performed oral sex on him. "Not only did Thom not refuse Tony's attentions," Kleinzahler recalled, "he told me it was the happiest moment of his life."[8]

Two days later, Tony introduced Thom to an old flame, the actress Rachel Roberts, whom Tony knew from the Old Vic in the 1950s. Roberts had especially asked to meet Thom but "ignore[d] me for 2 hours" before she disappeared to her flat to get ready to join them at a Dr. Feelgood gig at the Hope and Anchor in Islington. Thom and Tony waited for her in a pub, and Thom later wrote about this incident in "Talbot Road":

> When once in a pub I lost my temper,
> I shouldered my way back from the urinal
> and snapped, 'I was too angry to piss.'
> The next day he exclaimed with delight,
> 'Do you know that was the first time
> you have ever been angry with me?'
> As some people wait for a sign of love,
> he had waited how many years
> for a sign of anger,
> for a sign of other than love.[9]

They left without her, saw Dr. Feelgood, and ended the night at a Brinsley Schwarz gig at Dingwalls in Camden. "Very Rolling Stone's idea of London, nice & exciting," Thom reflected. When they returned to Tony's flat, there was a "rep[eat] of [the] surprise."[10] In June, Thom and Tony spent five days in Paris, paid for by Thom's big reading at the Mermaid Theatre.[11] "T likes to wander the same way I do," Thom reflected as they explored the arrondissements and visited Tony's friends and family. A favorite place was Julien, "a fabulous restaurant, cheap, beautiful, & jovial" on the rue du Faubourg Saint-Denis, where they ate almost every day: heart with carrots; kidneys and mushrooms; tripe. The trip was "magnificent" and Thom enjoyed having Tony to himself for a few days.[12] "I won't thank you again for all your kindness & generosity," he told him. "It was endless, and made my three months."[13]

Paris was the high point of Thom's visit. England was mostly distressing. He spent a fortnight with Aunt Barbara, who gave him a "3hr blow by blow of [Godfrey's] death & funeral."[14] Thom felt "suicidal" and had "a vision of life & being pushed around, powerless, & nothing else."[15] He dreamed "of never coming to England again."[16] His "rather unpleasant nostalgia"[17] wandering around Hampstead later informed "Hampstead: the Horse Chestnut Trees," in which "Forms remain, not the life / of detail or hue / then the forms are lost and / only a few dates stay with you."[18] He found a new wall around the front garden of 110 Frognal; a familiar chestnut tree from across the street had been felled; at 108 Frognal, the decrepit wooden fence was falling down. Down the hill, Thom was swept along by "rosy UCS boys coming home from school—longhaired & with knapsacks." The same day, Thom received an "unhappy letter" from Mike: he and Bill were having problems again.[19]

It was an itinerant visit: Thom barely spent a week in any one place. He made a brief trip to "cold & damp" Cambridge, where he read at the English Club and visited the Tanners in their large corner house on Alpha Road. Thom had not seen Tony for three years—since Tony's abrupt departure from Berkeley—but was pleased to find him "in control of himself & his situation."[20] He also enjoyed seeing Clive Wilmer, "unrecogn. in glasses & beard," and meeting a "handsome young poet" named Robert Wells.[21]

En route to Cornwall to see Ander, Thom stayed overnight with Ted and Carol Hughes at Court Green. "Long talk w/ Ted," he wrote, "partly on what compels people to write. The compulsion, Ted says, is not necessarily a poetic one—e.g. Dante, Owen (an anti war manifesto), Sylvia (i.e. 'her poems were telling me how things really had been' (setting him right). (e.g. 'the hare bowl abortion'))"[22] Ander met Thom off the train in Penzance and drove him to St. Just, the closest town to Land's End. Charlotte and Willie were "more charming than I can say," Thom thought.[23] They visited St. Ives and explored the hills and coves of Cape Cornwall. Thom was most curious to see Ander. After his visit to England in 1970, Thom had started a poem called "A photograph of my brother":

I often think how
grown up I am, the
exotic experiences I've had
but looking now at your picture
I can see that the more I deviate
from the family the more
I am of it[24]

This was the presiding feeling Thom had of England in 1974: he could live five thousand miles away on the western edge of the world, but he would always look like a Gunn. There would always be a part of him in Snodland, shackling him to a past he no longer wanted. At best he would look like Ander; at worst, their father. In the late 1970s, when Thom slicked back his hair and went clean-shaven, "I found I had been hiding my father's face / Beneath it all these years."[25] In England he became neurotic and unsettled. "My great nightmare is I'll never see you again," he wrote Mike, "which is silly of course but I can't help it."[26]

Returning to San Francisco, Thom spent another fortnight in New York. He stayed with Allan Noseworthy III, a "big 23 yr old beauty" whom he had met in New York on his way to England.[27] Noseworthy was a doorman at Ty's, a Christopher Street leather bar, and lived in a loft on Bleecker Street with a Newfoundland named Yoko and two "dyke parakeets" named Hank and Lotsa.[28] He was "flighty, highly strung, at times silly, but so good in every important sense." Thom was "not in love with him," he told Tony White, "but I love him a lot."[29] After a night at Keller's and the Ramrod, they returned to Allan's loft, took Placidyl, "& [Allan] asks me 'Are you in love with me?' & falls asleep before I have time to answer." The next day, Allan gave Thom his father's gold wedding ring.[30]

Allan took Thom to his first gay pride parade. They joined the crowds marching from Greenwich Village up Sixth Avenue to Central Park. Thom wore full leather and dropped acid. "The whole thing was rather

good for me," he told White. "I'm not sure whether it made much difference to the people watching the parade: there were a few smiley straight
people who obviously appreciated it—but most of the faces were unsmi-
ley, puzzled and rather contemptuous."[31] He joined the parade "more
because it seemed to me cowardice if I didn't than from real enthusiasm"
but appreciated its "good explicit political purposes" following the defeat
of the Gay Rights Bill in New York City.[32] He contemplated writing a
poem about the parade:

> What does it feel like to be a queer?
> I'll tell you. Cutting a swathe
> thro the middle of Manhattan, the traffic
> being held up on 42nd street,
> jubilant & boisterous
> with forty thousand others
> handsome, homely, exotic, pedestrian
> to feel the kinship,
> having deserted the family
> —the more I deviate from the family the more I am of it—[33]

England and the United States had become the choice between one family and another, between past and present—what Thom later called his
"continuities"[34]—and the increasing openness of the 1970s encouraged
him to come out in his poetry. "I was delighted by it," Thom later remarked of the 1974 parade. "Or, as they nowadays say, 'empowered!'" He
claimed that, after the parade, he "admitted [queerness] in" to his poems
for the first time, "whereas formerly I had covered it over or disguised
it or excluded it. I was now *able* to include it."[35] This comment perhaps
pertains only to a straight readership. Queer readers likely would have
recognized the queer code of lines like "their hum / Bulges to thunder
held by calf and thigh"—from "On the Move"—and entire poems such
as "Market at Turk" and "The Beaters" from their first publication in the
1950s.[36]

Before the parade, Thom had already made an understated coming out: he had lent "The Feel of Hands" and "'Blackie, the Electric Rembrandt'" to Ian Young's "gay anthology" *The Male Muse* (1973). "I don't think much of the idea of such an anthology," he told Tanner, "but it seemed to me it would be cowardly to refuse permission to be in it."[37] In a subsequent interview, Thom implicitly criticized *The Male Muse* when he argued that "[Robert] Graves is right, that the muse has to be female. The Goddess is a mother, not a wife or a lover. The feminine principle is the source and I think it dominates in male artists whether homo- or heterosexual."[38] This is the subject of Thom's earlier poem "The Goddess," in which he addresses Proserpina: "it is we, / vulnerable, quivering, / who stay you to abundance."[39]

Back in San Francisco, Thom began a new notebook. On the first page he quoted Gertrude Stein: "She always says she dislikes the abnormal, it is so obvious. She says the normal is so much more simply complicated and interesting."[40] In England, Thom had made a list of subjects for poems, among which he listed "the (sudden) unavoidable realization of how self-destructive I am . . . when I have always—always—assumed I was the opposite."[41] Dropping acid at an Eric Clapton gig, he felt "very introspective" and saw himself "as in many ways worse (not more fucked up, but worse morally) than anyone I know. Besetting sins: cowardice & selfishness."[42] These "sins," as Thom saw them, were perhaps two aspects of his response to his mother's death. If he had been selfish in assembling the Cole Street family according to his needs—in an attempt to re-create his ideal childhood household—his cowardice was perhaps in his refusal to confront feelings and emotions, choosing instead to shield himself behind an armor made of jollity and deflection. In that sense, Thom was his father's son. Always upbeat, his bonhomie could echo Bert's social ease, charm, and affability, themselves a defense against emotional difficulties and unpleasant situations.[43]

England had unsettled him. He sensed his "sins" were connected to the "confusion of values" he felt in post-acid San Francisco. "How do I work out the relation of my in general hippie values, I mean I do believe in love & trust etc, & then the other thing?" he asked himself:

> I say that s&m is a form of love. I think it is, but I don't think that goes quite deep enough. It is compulsive behavior perhaps, but how does it relate to my conscious values? The behavior is symbolic of exactly the opposite values. So, is that behavior—(1) merely excretion (i.e. getting rid of stuff that can't be digested); (2) a rebellion against conscious values; (3) self dramatics, romantic escape from the real; (4) a need. . . . Father? or wot?[44]

That summer, Thom began planning "English poems." One abandoned poem focused on his father's love of control; another, "Poem in Kent," returned to an old idea: "the Self-Who-Stayed; (& go into all that)."[45] Of his proposed "English poems," he wrote only "The Cherry Tree"—the titular tree grew in his Aunt Barbara's garden—and "Hampstead: the Horse Chestnut Trees." Of all the trees in Thom's work, those in the latter poem are some of his least comforting: they "have no sentiments / their hearts are wood / and preserve nothing."[46] There is an "uneasiness" behind the poem: Thom questioned "whether it's possible to remember the past with any accuracy," a concern that became more prominent the more he experimented with autobiographical subjects in his poetry and prose.[47]

Thom's fragile selfhood was behind these ideas. "Poem in Kent" imagines him "whining from village to / village, persistent gnat" on a motorcycle, "the self who never found a village." In the margin of one draft he wrote, "I seek a way to lose the self, using the self to lose it"—the same double-bind he had explored since the early 1950s.[48] Another poem in progress was "The Reflections"—which later became "Behind the Mirror"—in which Thom explored the difference between one self and another:

> Once in a dark restaurant I caught the eyes of another,
> they stared back at mine with unflagging interest.

Another! no it was my own eyes from a recessed
   mirror.

I and the reflected self seemed identical twins,
   alike yet separate, two flowers from the same plant.[49]

The second part of the poem tells the story of Narcissus—Thom had
Caravaggio's painting in mind[50]—and suggests that Narcissus could only
become "of it"—that is, be with his reflection "where both water and
earth" combine—by drowning himself, by suicide.[51] He "would come to
rest on a soft dark wave of soil / to root there and stand again"—a conclusion that echoes the "place of birth" and "death-rich earth" of "The
Garden of the Gods." In one plan for the poem, Thom wondered whether
it "cd have the structure of a love affair: 1) difference 2) attraction 3) love
4) difficulties 5) suicide (but w/ a different meaning here)."[52] That meaning, perhaps, was Thom's acknowledgment that while he would never
recover from his mother's death, he needed to leave behind England and
"the Self-Who-Stayed" before he could wholly immerse himself in his
life in the United States.

That August, Thom turned forty-five. "I'm reading almost nothing. I'm
doing too much speed, I want to get the sinisterness of JS's Castle out of
the way," he wrote. "Yet in a way the last 2 months have been among the
best of my life."[53] The "sinisterness" began the previous autumn, when
Thom wrote several poems about "freaks."[54] He called the first poem
"Jack Straw's Castle" and the series "Night Work," a title derived both
from Freud's "dream-work" and Thom's own recurrent nightmares.[55]
When he moved to Cole Street in 1971, Thom experienced "a series of
anxiety dreams" that persisted for the rest of the year. "I had moved into
the wrong house. I had moved in with the wrong people. Once to my
horror I found I was sharing an apartment with Nixon," he said with a
laugh. "Very often I would keep discovering new rooms in the house that

I'd known nothing about."[56] Thom used the metaphor of rooms to explore his own unconscious: he called it "being loose in one's own castle," the nightmares of a bad acid trip.[57] "The drug dreams of *Moly*," he later reflected, "have all gone sour in *Jack Straw*."[58]

Thom wrote the first, seven-poem version of "Jack Straw's Castle" between autumn 1973 and spring 1974 and published it later that year.[59] But when he returned to San Francisco following his unsettling stay in England that summer, he told the Tanners: "I think I must rewrite Jack Straw's Castle."[60] He wanted to include the "confusion of values" he felt and his perceived "self-destructiveness," which he saw as "oneself stoking the fires that burn the self in a central courtyard."[61] The revised "Jack Straw's Castle" became "a poem about sickness" in which "the central sickness [is] the central self-destructiveness." He felt that "the I/he in the center shouldn't be merely suffering [but] acting out something that he doesn't realize is self-destructive."[62] Confusion and uncertainty conclude the poem: echoing *Richard III*, Jack speaks about himself in the third person: "With dreams like this, Jack's ready for the world."[63]

The final poem provides the most significant change to the revised sequence. "I'm in bed with a man," Thom explained: "it would not have ended that way twenty years before. I'd have found some other way of dealing with it."[64] The idea came from a fragment, "Midsummer Night," that Thom wrote about sleeping beside Allan Noseworthy in New York:

> but we went to bed
> between two windows
> & lay ass to ass
> out on Placidyl
> with not even a sheet over us
> & felt the air as cool
> as the green water
> of a swimming pool, I'd wake
> & feel you, close enough & cool.[65]

Thom admired Allan—"he was a pure example of a gay man during that time," recalled one friend, "very sexual, very druggie"[66]—and his openness may have helped convince Thom to rewrite the poem and come out publicly. Having contributed to *The Male Muse* and marched in the gay pride parade to avoid "cowardice," Thom concluded the title poem of his new collection with two men sharing a bed and would come out to a national audience on his own terms.[67] This was important to him. His image of two men sharing a bed is obvious yet understated, a likely response to those who had missed a more subtle coming out in earlier poems like "Tom-Dobbin." Given Thom's interest in doubles, doppelgängers, past selves, and hallucinations, "the man I gave my key" in "Jack Straw's Castle" seems to hover between real and imagined, an alter ego or a sexual partner. When Pat Strachan, Thom's editor at Farrar, Straus and Giroux, wrote a publicity statement for *Jack Straw's Castle* that dwelled mostly on Thom coming out, Thom replied with his own statement. "I like what you say about Jack Straw, but I think I prefer what I say," he told her, "in that homosexuality only comes at the end of the poem and is not really what the poem is about."[68]

Thom finished the new, eleven-part "Jack Straw's Castle" in October. "I have had a wonderful six months, unlike the rest of the world," he told Tony White in mid-December. "I'm not completely sure why, either. I've had a peculiar sense of having got it together at bottom, as if my understandings of my own contradictions were getting a little greater." It was his "best time since 1968," which he called "ACID YEAR."[69] Privately, he felt he had "not been abnormally silly"—by which he meant allowing drinking, drugging, and tricking to become self-destructive cycles—and that "writing something that meant something to me" in "Jack Straw's Castle" was his "reaction from England."[70]

Thom felt so up that he was able to handle the slow disintegration of Mike and Bill's relationship. Their year concluded with a PCP-fueled car crash in which "Bill went mildly into the windshield" and Mike went through it, appearing afterward like "a picture of Jesus in the crown of thorns done by a particularly literal and sadistic Meister of painting in medieval Germany."[71] The PCP came from their new upstairs neighbors, Lonnie Leard and Michael Grove. Thom's year ended in New York, where he stayed with Allan Noseworthy and they "laid a solid foundation for a long and loving friendship." Thom thought Allan "an extraordinary person—living on impulse, but all his impulses are good, & his vibes about people are <u>always</u> right."[72]

In January 1975, Thom began the permanent part-time position at Berkeley that he would keep for almost twenty-five years. "No promotion, but who cares," he told Barbara, "there will be no administrative work either. The head of the English Department said, 'Would you believe it? This kind of job (permanent part-time) is so unusual it took the university nine months to get it arranged.' I said, 'That's nothing, it took <u>me</u> nine years of scheming.'"[73] Thom taught the winter quarter only. His two courses were not new: he had taught Modes of Writing and Verse (advanced composition) during his first stint at Berkeley. The position gave him a steady if small income—"about half that of a local bus driver or street sweeper," he wrote in 1978[74]—and six months free to write poetry.

Although Thom came to think of Modes of Writing as his "albatross,"[75] he was initially enthusiastic about "push[ing]" beginners into discovering whether they had talent for poetry, fiction, or drama. "At that stage of one's life one simply needs to be pushed," he reflected, "to get out a lot of work and get through one's mistakes, to see how one can grow. It's an exciting and arduous course." He preferred Modes of Writing to Verse because it was more "exciting, getting someone from nowhere to somewhere else. But they've got to find out for themselves whether or not they really are writers. You've got to feel the pressure of a certain kind of subject matter within your own life. It might be your everyday experience or your imagination, though more likely it's a combination of the two. But to be a writer you've got to feel that pressure working on your language and your rhythms, and you've got to work this out yourself." Conversely, Verse could "get too pleasant." "Let's say they do have some talent—it should be more difficult for them," he reflected. "It's very easy to have fifteen or twenty young people sitting around you . . . and have them pick up a poem and say, '[. . .] Rob writes about eagles so well. Let's have another eagle poem, Rob!' [. . .] Maybe they should tell Rob to try something different, extend himself a little."[76]

When the quarter began, Thom was "full of optimism" but was distressed to learn that he had eighty-five students for Modes of Writing, far more than was practical for such a class.[77] Six weeks in he had "gone through the customary development from anxious ineptitude and hatred of all those dumb students to a kind of sunny glibness and a slightly patronising friendliness for all those people I think I've helped so much."[78] As the quarter concluded, he thought "some really good writers started to emerge."[79] Even more pleasing, he still found the time to write: he used Whitman and Stein as models for "Yoko," a poem about Allan's dog, and used a similarly long, flexible free verse line to revise two cruising poems—"The Release" and "Fever"—on which he had been stuck for more than a year. Thom had come to realize that he required a balance between the university-imposed discipline of teaching and the self-discipline he needed to write.

In May, with his teaching quarter finished, Thom gave a reading at Stanford. Mike drove him down the peninsula: they planned to spend the evening with Tony Tanner, then a visiting fellow of Stanford's Center for Advanced Study in the Behavioral Sciences.[80] Before the reading, Thom had decided to come out. "I stumble a little, being nervous," he reflected, "becos I decided I will say I am gay in the explanatory remarks about JS's Castle. I do OK but not really well."[81] Many in the audience—Tanner, the Davies, Janet Lewis, Robert Conquest—already knew Thom was gay, but because he took care to compartmentalize his life, Thom remained closeted to a broader literary audience. "He wasn't passing for straight, he was passing for not gay, because the world was different," Mike reflected.[82] Thom chose Stanford for three reasons: it was where his American adventure had started; he was guaranteed a friendly audience; and Stanford was separate enough, atmospherically, from San Francisco that it satisfied Thom's desire for compartmentalization: he did not, after all, want to be recognized on Folsom Street as a famous poet. For Jack Collins, a former student of Tanner's who came to know Thom and Mike well, Thom came out at a time of greater openness for gay people. "We were all realizing that we don't have to be ashamed or afraid, being gay. We just have to see how many of us there are. We just have to look around us at all the other gay people. I think that was the context for Thom. I think he didn't like being in the closet. It wasn't him."[83]

In the spring, Mike and Bill separated for good. They "resolved their worst difficulties," Thom told Tony White, and "decide[d] to go on living together but to have a bit more independence in their sexual lives. Thank god for such sensible and unhistrionic people, who can place the importance of continuing a relationship over the more dramatic and picturesque alternatives."[84] Mike kept the back room. By this time, Thom had moved into the middle room and was "really digging it," so Bill moved to the front room, overlooking Cole. "When I told Bill it was over, it was very, very hard for me to do that," Mike reflected:

> What was unusual about Thom and I, I think, is that we were able to segue from the physical into nonphysical, and still we would share the bed, we would share stories; we would share, you know, like lovers. And that's how we thought of each other. So I wasn't sure what that would be like to have Bill, too. And even when Bill and I were together, Thom was very paternal with Bill.[85]

Thom was "a person to listen to," Bill reflected, "because he knew what was generally right in a fatherly way."[86] Mike felt Thom was "more protective" of Bill after the separation.[87] When Bill, "alarmingly yellow," came down with hepatitis weeks later, Thom nursed him back to health.[88]

In early June, while nursing Bill, Thom settled into a routine. Mornings were spent preparing the manuscript of *Jack Straw's Castle*; afternoons were spent reading for a (never-completed) selection of John Donne.[89] He planned to submit Donne in July and *Jack Straw's Castle* in October, but told Monteith that "things have got strangely reversed":

he had barely started on Donne, while "the book of poems has filled out its particular shape."[90] Thom was anxious that Faber might reject it. "I hadn't thought of it before," he told a friend, "but maybe some of the language is a bit 'strong' for them. Can it be so, in 1975?"[91] His fears were unfounded: Faber accepted *Jack Straw's Castle* without comment. "Let's hope this one gets <u>reviewed</u>, at least," he told Ander. "Well, the important thing is getting it published, so at least it's there for people to read if they hear about it. It's a wild book, I hope."[92]

Submitting the book, Thom felt the onset of "depression." "I suddenly realised that <u>that</u> was the cause of it," he told Tony White. "I suppose it gave me the sense of disposing of five years of my life, and what next? A silly way to feel, and one I rather disapprove of, but one doesn't feel the way one does for very good reasons."[93] Thom had learned that, after submitting a book, he was slow to restart writing poems.[94] He turned to prose instead. "I'm reading all of Robert Duncan (and that's a lot) because I have to write an article on 'Homosexuality in RD' (and that's a lot)," he told his new friend Douglas Chambers, a gay Canadian professor of English he had met at a literary festival in Toronto.[95] Duncan had come out publicly in 1944, to little precedent and much hostility, in his article "The Homosexual in Society."[96] Exploring the "artistic freedom" that Duncan had "bravely" won, Thom drew on Duncan's 1972 preface to *Caesar's Gate*. "Today I see Love and that Household in which I live, as I saw it in its beginning twenty years ago," Duncan wrote, "as a homestead I and my companion there would create, even pathetically, within Man's nature, 'shelterd by our imaginary humble lives from the eternal storm of our rage.'"[97] Thom recognized that the household was "the place of growth and harmony" but "also contains a fury."[98] This struck a chord: the household seemed to embody his own confusions, between hippie values and S&M, between domesticity and promiscuity, between limits and risk. Uniting them, however, was a quality he found in Duncan's poetry. "A man loving a man beholds somebody *like himself*," Thom reflected, before quoting Duncan's lines: "Nature barely provides for it. / Men fuck men by audacity."[99] From Duncan, Thom had already learned about writing as process; reading through his poetry, systematically, he also drew strength from Duncan's emphasis on audacity: that a queer life, however it was lived, was a statement of boldness and courage. Moreover, it was thanks to Duncan that "modern American poetry, in all its inclusiveness, can deal with overtly homosexual material so much as a matter of course—not as something perverse or eccentric or morbid, but as evidence of the many available ways in which people live their lives, of the many available ways in which people love or fail to love."[100]

It had been another "very happy" year.[101] Writing to Ander shortly before Christmas, Thom reflected on how he no longer worried about not writing. "Dry periods seem to be necessary to me, like a kind of pregnancy for the fertile periods," he remarked, having not written a poem since April. "But then writing also seems to be a necessary part of the way I live, when I write I start to really understand things and connect different things. If something matters enough it always gets into my poetry sooner or later. [. . .] (Maybe one day I'll manage to write a poem about Mother, a subject that has always defeated me.)"[102] He was thinking about his mother because he had recently reread Duncan's poem "My Mother Would Be a Falconress," which "dramatize[s] the whole series of conflicts involving possessiveness and love on the one hand and freedom and identity on the other."[103] In the poem, the falcon is sent out to kill birds, but must return to his mother without having eaten them, so that she can reward him with the meat.[104] Thom probably saw himself in the "obedient little falcon" whose life is "patterned" by his mother's "contradictory demands."[105] ("Who could equal you, dazzling contradictory woman?" Thom later asked.[106]) The poem had come to Duncan in a dream, which would have resonated with Thom given his recurring dreams about his own mother.[107] Moreover, it seemed to confirm for Thom that an "ideal Mother [is] the muse and the principle of generation."[108] Like the little falcon in Duncan's poem, Thom knew that his connection to his mother, even after her death, would not be severed. "I would be a falcon and go free," says the falcon, years later, after his mother is dead. "I tread her wrist and wear the hood, / talking to myself, and would draw blood."[109]

. . .

In the new year, Thom's connection to his mother, and his response to her death, was evident in his behavior. When he wrote to Douglas Chambers in early January 1976, he had cowardice, one of his "besetting sins," on his mind. "Many of my friends and acquaintances seem to be going through crises, so I attempt to help, either by talk or letter," Thom told him. "I don't have crises. Not because I am so emotionally balanced, but because I am so cowardly about emotions that I make sure I am never put in a position where a crisis can happen to me."[110]

24

LOSS

In September 1975, Tony White left London for good. He stored his books in a friend's attic and moved permanently to the cottage he had built for himself on the Galway coast. "I am now officially an Irish resident or resident of Ireland, which pleases me a lot," he told Thom. "I really love this country, in spite of its flaws, even for its flaws and like being associated with it. The unpredictability of it. You feel that anything can happen, even if it generally doesn't."[1] White seemed "brimming over with delight," Thom told Tanner. "I have never read a happier letter from him."[2] Tony lived on fishing and did odd jobs for the villagers; milk, potatoes, and onions were free. "He is apparently much liked by everybody in the village and says he is really happy for the first time in his life," Thom wrote to Barbara. "Nice to know that one of my friends is happy besides me. Sometimes I'm afraid it must be just because I'm insensitive."[3] Thom stuck a photograph of White, surrounded by friends in a pub, above his writing desk (plate 33). "It's the best picture I've ever seen of him," Thom told Ander, "getting his big bear warmth and his twinkly eyed beautifulness just right."[4]

Thom traveled to campus three days a week for the winter quarter. He was busy and tired but had "a good start to the term, much better than last year."[5] Sifting through student manuscripts for his poetry class, Thom remembered it was almost Tony White's birthday. "I suddenly realized you are about to reach my age, so this is the first birthday card I've ever sent you," he wrote. "I think of you snug in your cottage listening to the haystack & roof-leveling wind from the Atlantic. Will write you a letter soon, in answer to your double letter."[6] In fact, Tony was in London: he had agreed to help a psychiatrist, Dr. Lambert, "put together a book on his specialist study, 'Impotence'!"[7] Tony had spent Christmas with John Holmstrom in his north London flat. While there, playing football for Battersea Park, Tony broke his leg: "Some young cowboy scythed me down as if I was an offending thistle."[8] Tony's leg was put in a heavy, uncomfortable cast and Holmstrom's flat became his sickroom. In January 1976 he moved to the Lamberts' house in Twickenham. "There is a small and affectionate dog called Parsnip," he told Holmstrom, "who pops in now and then to see if I've got all I need."[9]

By the time Thom wrote his birthday card, Tony was dead. "Yesterday he had a heart attack & was rushed to hospital, but died soon after admittance," Holmstrom wrote Thom on January 10. Thom did not receive the letter until the nineteenth. "It seems it was a blood clot that caused it, possibly from the immobilised leg," Holmstrom continued. "We mustn't be sad for him. His death will have taken him completely by surprise. [. . .] I don't think anyone was ever more generally loved than Tony. He can't be replaced. It's us I'm sorry for."[10] Thom was devastated. "His last letters to me were the happiest I had ever had from him," he told Ander and Margaret. "I cannot believe I shall never go round the pubs with him again. He did mean an awful lot to me—as he did to a lot of other people. He made a better thing of his life than almost anyone else I know."[11] Teaching kept Thom busy through the difficult days and weeks that followed. "'Losing oneself in one's work'—I guess even that's a cliché," he told Tanner. "I doubt if there's anything new to be said. But perhaps that's ultimately a comfort, in a strange kind of way, that you join everybody's situation at certain times in your life."[12]

Thom found some comfort in the shared grief for Tony. Although he declined Karl Miller's request to write something about Tony for *The New Review*—"Tony would have hated it"—Thom felt that, among the "private remembering," receiving letters about Tony helped him come to terms with his death. "I must say I haven't felt a loss like that since my mother died," he told Tanner. "It is probably worse for you over there, because you were at least in the habit of seeing him every now and again—that old duke of the dark corners; but in any case the world does seem enormously diminished, and I still can't altogether believe it."[13] Holmstrom and Sasha Moorsom were inconsolable; Richard Murphy, who lived close to White in Cleggan, could no longer face the village and moved to Dublin.[14] "The awful realisation is how much one <u>depended</u> on him," Holmstrom reflected, "the one thing he never wanted!"[15] "The way he accepted the worst about you was the most extraordinary thing," Sasha wrote. "It's as if he even liked you better when you showed your frailties."[16] Bill, away in New Orleans, wrote to Thom and Mike: "his love for you all and his trustful acceptance of me made him most beautiful to me. [. . .] Our family is one smaller."[17] Thom kept all the letters. They "make an amazing memorial, summing him up better than his own letters," he told Tanner.

> Your own letter; Ander and Margaret's letter—much less articulate, but carrying something of the same; a card from Bryan, beautifully saying "what a pity, just as everybody was letting him down off the pedestal they'd put him on" (I assume that "everybody" to be me); Holmstrom's letter; and Don Doody calling from New York, somewhat drunk late one night. He did teach us all an awful lot: it somehow shows in all the above, though in no decipherable configuration—but there is something there that might be a key to him. Better leave it undeciphered, though![18]

Ander and Margaret told him about Tony's funeral. "We went to Becky's Bar and had Ruddles bitter, faggots & mash," they wrote, "a menu which would have had Tony's full approval."[19] That pleased Thom: he felt the best way to celebrate Tony's life was "to act as usual and have a good laughy drunken evening."[20] In what proved his final letter to Tony, Thom had thanked him for two decades' worth of help with his poems. "I wonder what I would have done without your good sense and penetration to get me out of obscurities and sillinesses," he reflected. "I don't know whether I've ever thanked you adequately for your help. Well, believe me, old thing, it has meant everything to me. And of course you have always been 'inspirational' as well."[21]

Thom had known Tony and Mike for almost the same amount of time. He met Tony some six months before he met Mike, and Tony's death caused him to reflect on their similarities. "The two people I know who grew into wisdom have been Mike and Tony—and such a flexible and practical wisdom," he told Tanner. "Maybe wiseness would be a better word. And maybe it means something that they both dropped out from the world of applause, the world of actors and directors, to be able to become unique."[22] Mike had "dropped out" because he wanted to "take acid and drugs and live the life," but felt, consciously or otherwise, that he wanted to help others—not that he would use the word "wisdom." "That's how I wanted to distinguish myself," he reflected. "Since I wasn't an achiever anymore, that's what I wanted in life."[23] Mike wanted to help Thom after Tony's death. "We talked about it a little bit, because it was such a shock," Mike recalled, "but it was very held in, which is Thom's way. He didn't want to bring me down, he didn't want to rain on my parade." At times of grief or stress, this could create distance between them. Mike, too, was grieving: his father, Abraham, died in late February and he had to fly east immediately to attend the funeral.[24] However, Thom's way of dealing with grief set the tone for the household. "In the early days, when I learned that Thom couldn't deal with—didn't want to deal with—my depression or anything heavy," Mike reflected, "I made that adjustment, that if I didn't respect that we were going to be in trouble. I was always angry, pissed, that I couldn't share that. I share, I'm a sharer. Thom was not a sharer and remained not a sharer."[25]

Thom struggled to come to terms with Tony's death because they did not regularly see each other. "I still keep thinking of things I want to tell him and then having to remember he is dead," he told Tanner. "I suppose his death will hit me afresh when I next go to England, which I certainly hope is not too soon."[26] He was reminded of Hardy's poem

"The Walk," in which a husband, after his wife's death, goes for his usual walk. "What difference, then?" he asks. "Only that underlying sense / Of the look of a room on returning thence." "Maybe my 'room', in this situation, is England," he told Holmstrom. "I need some confirmation of Tony's death from it which I haven't yet had."[27] Writing was the only way he could try to come to terms with Tony's death. That spring, Thom wrote an essay called "Cambridge in the Fifties" for a collection of Cambridge memoirs.[28] Thom's grief lends the essay a strange poignancy: he mentions Tony's death, aged forty-five, but it is not obvious that his death was so recent. The essay concludes with a paragraph about how many of Thom's Cambridge contemporaries had flourished as magazine editors, historians, reviewers, novelists, theater directors. "Only Tony White, among my close friends, became an exception," Thom wrote. "He dropped out, coolly and deliberately, from the life of applause, having come to see how the need for it complicates one's existence quite unnecessarily." He was grateful to Cambridge for many things, chief among them his friendship with White, "someone who could eventually teach me that the real business was elsewhere completely."[29]

Writing to Holmstrom in the summer, Thom was "enjoying every enjoyable thing, as it occurs, but once it has stopped occurring I return to the same hungover unease. I don't know why I had assumed this sadness would be less deep after six months, or would resolve itself: loss is loss, and time often only helps to show how deep and wide it is."[30]

When he finished "Cambridge in the Fifties," Thom began another autobiographical essay. He wrote "My Life Up to Now" as an introduction for a bibliography of his work that George Bixby, a rare book dealer, and Jack Hagstrom, a physician, had compiled.[31] In the essay, Thom felt he was "letting it all hang out," and was distressed to learn that Bixby and Hagstrom wanted to offer the book to Faber rather than a specialist publisher of bibliographies. "It is not that I'm being cowardly," Thom wrote Hagstrom,

but if the book comes out from Faber it will get reviewed, get
sought out by people who have no interest in my poetry, and
cause a focussing on my life and motives that I have no wish to
invite. [. . .] So if you do want the book to come out from F&F
I'll rewrite it in a more reticent way.[32]

Faber did not publish the bibliography, but Charles Monteith liked
Thom's essay and felt he should develop it into a full autobiography.
"Something in me refuses to do it," Thom told Monteith, having toyed
with the idea for a decade. "It would certainly be nice to capture certain
things before they get forgotten forever. On the other hand, I think I'll
wait about ten years, and then think about it again. I still feel very much
in the middle of things."[33] Thom knew that his biographical unease—"I
rejoice in Eliot's lovely remark that art is an escape from personality"—
"troubled some readers."[34] Others took him too much at face value. Donald Davie's poem "To Thom Gunn in Los Altos, California" begins:

> Conquistador! Live dangerously, my Byron,
> In this metropolis
> Of Finistere. Drop off
> The edge repeatedly, and come
> Back to tell us![35]

"Maybe you trust a little too much that I really am as I am in my poems,"
Thom teased him.[36] He repeated this to Davie in person but thought
Davie "just considered I was being modest," he told Tanner. "I suppose
one adopts an attitude implying strength and charm as a way of coping with the world, but I never thought anybody believed that that was
where I began and ended. It's a strange feeling when one feels like crying
out, 'But I have conflicts and weakness too, don't you see?'"[37] However,
Thom was happy to project an image of "a cheerful and rather superficial
person most of the time."[38] Mike's old friend Glenn Jordan thought this
"a perfect description of the self he presented to most of us."[39] Thom's

general behavior was "lively, animated, high-spirited, vivacious," Jordan reflected, "and he had an adolescent sense of humor, often ribald, sometimes seemingly simple minded. It was hard to reconcile the Thom that one knew with the man who wrote the poetry."[40]

Come summer, Thom had not written a poem since December. "If you tend to hyperactivity, I tend to lethargy," he told Tanner. "Writing seems very difficult, and all I've really done this year has been bits and pieces of prose."[41] Holmstrom told him to persevere. White's death "is bound to inhibit your poetry for a time," he told Thom, "but that too will pull itself together."[42] He wrote nothing during that "odd stagnant summer" and spent his birthday evening talking with Mike and Bill about Tony.[43] A week later he received "a good letter from Holmstrom"—now lost—and decided "to stop whining to myself about TW."[44] He told Ander he wanted "to concentrate on being the kind of person [Tony] would be proud of. Come to think of it, I think—completely seriously—I've been trying to live up to him, trying to be 'worthy' of his friendship since I first knew him at Cambridge. Shouldn't think I'm alone either."[45]

Instead of writing, Thom spent the summer on Folsom Street. The Castro had become the center of local gay politics, while Folsom had cemented itself as the city's sexual center. Thom's favorite bathhouse was the Folsom Street Barracks, which opened above the Red Star Saloon in 1972. It quickly became "one of the most famous, one of the most lurid" bathhouses in the city.[46] Thom wanted to write about it, but felt it would be "easy to fall into Baudelairean novelo-drama, but that is untrue to the experience," he reflected: "[bathhouses] are places of joy & excitement, not of despair, or rather they are places to which we bring what we want them to be."[47] Another favorite was the Slot, at 979 Folsom, "for those who kept their fingernails clipped short and carried a can of Crisco."[48]

Thom's social hub and extended family was the Ambush, on Harrison between Ninth and Tenth. It opened in 1973 and "[broke] the old idea that a beer and wine bar can't make it in SF."[49] Regulars called it "the Bush": you parted the heavy black leather drape across the door and entered a room with cool gray walls, meat-rack seating around the edges, and "dozens of old chandelier crystals" suspended from the ceiling that made rainbows cascade across the bar as light poured in through the large front window.[50] The Ambush became a hub for South of Market artists and writers, "born out of the bowels of gay liberation," according to Mark I. Chester, the radical S&M photographer who lived and worked on Folsom, "carrying on a spirit that flowed from the Tool Box, the Folsom Prison, and the Red Star Saloon."[51] Chuck Arnett designed its flag and logo; the bar hosted a monthly art exhibition as well as beer busts and slave auctions; upstairs, a deli kept everyone fed. "The Ambush was a special little niche of the South of Market Sexual Outlaw subculture," recalled tattoo artist and Ambush deli-counter man Robert Roberts. "The regulars seldom went to any of the other bars. There was simply no need to go anywhere else."[52] Its men were "slightly greasy, sleazy, unshaven, unkempt, and oozing with sex." What kept it all together was "a sense of belonging and family," Chester reflected, "a sense of community and a shared vision, desire and experience. It was a bar owned by men in the community for other men in the community. We weren't just customers, we were friends."[53]

Chester was one of many radical gay artists to exhibit at the Ambush. Others included Rex, Tom of Finland, and Thom's friends Chuck Arnett and Tom Hinde. Poet friends like Ron Johnson and Jack Sharpless were also patrons. From the Ambush the following year, Thom "br[ought] home great NY Robert (fotog. SB etc) for nite. He has lots of coke for us."[54] It was perhaps surprising that Thom had not met Robert Mapplethorpe sooner, given their shared patronage of an S&M leather club in New York called the Mineshaft, the definitive sex club of the late 1970s and early 1980s. Located in an old Meatpacking District slaughterhouse, the Mineshaft opened in October 1976. Thom made his first visit a month later and called it "the worst (i.e. best) orgy house in the whole world."[55] Edmund White was also a regular. "Inside was the big bar area with its low lights and pool tables," he recalled.

Behind a partition was the "action" part of the club on two floors. There was an entire wall of glory holes with people kneeling in front of crotch-high holes and servicing disembodied erections. A fist-fucking sling was suspended on heavy chains from the ceiling, and a small crowd of men stood around looking at the nearly gynecological examinations. A whole rabbit warren of small rooms was downstairs and in one was a bathtub where men would take turns being pissed on.[56]

The dress code was strictly enforced: no colognes, perfumes, suits, ties, dress pants, rugby shirts, designer sweaters, tuxedos, disco drag, or dresses. Approved attire included cycle leather and western gear, Levi's, jocks, uniforms, T-shirts, plaid shirts, patches, and sweat. Mapplethorpe wanted to do a book with Thom, "hard core & kinky," but Thom hesitated.[57] Later, Mapplethorpe took Thom's photograph.[58] "Thom loved that picture," Mike recalled, and it was later used on the cover of the Farrar, Straus and Giroux edition of his *Collected Poems*.[59]

Jack Straw's Castle was published in autumn 1976, dedicated "to the memory of Tony White." It was a Poetry Book Society Choice in England and garnered better reviews—albeit with some reservations—than Thom had expected. "I see from the TLS that I write, not good poems, but simulacra of good poems," he told Wilmer.[60] Peter Porter praised Thom's "achievement in finding a voice"—Thom rolled his eyes at that one[61]— and "had not expected to hear Gunn speak so directly, and yet with such a sense of vulnerability and trepidation." Porter found the "sensuality" of the poems "more explicitly homosexual than previously, but it doesn't exclude heterosexual concern."[62] One reviewer found the title poem "highly personal, almost to the point of embarrassment to the reader."[63] "I don't care much what they think," Thom told Ander, and was pleased to learn, in early 1977, that Faber was already reprinting the book.[64] "It seems that what pleases people," he told Monteith, "is to include plenty of English place-names and to avoid explicit drug references!"[65]

The book was published at the same time in the United States. For Thom's reading at Paperback Traffic, a Castro bookstore, he had Chuck Arnett and Bill Tellman design a poster: a reclining leatherman grabs his crotch and surveys a distant, many-turreted castle (plate 25).[66] He also gave interviews to two gay publications: *The Sentinel*, a local newspaper, and *The Advocate*, a national magazine.[67] "Maybe I will capture the gay audience!" he joked.[68] "Much of Gunn's verse, when its subject is not explicitly homosexual," wrote W. I. Scobie, reviewing *Jack Straw's Castle* in *The Advocate*, "is imbued with a gay sensibility and is almost totally free of the *machismo* that made for some disagreeable moments in earlier books."[69] Douglas Chambers reviewed the collection for *Body Politic*, a gay Canadian magazine. "The title poem of this collection is a labyrinth into the modern mind," Chambers reflected, "but it is so effective because its images of loss and isolation come with the sharpened vision of the gay experience. [. . .] Jack Straw, the man of straw, the man of no account—all of us sooner or later on some dark night."[70] Thom felt Chambers was "completely right, i.e. accurate, about my intentions" and had "perceive[d] the emphasis made" in a way few reviewers had.[71]

Thom's correspondence with Tony Tanner had helped both men grieve for Tony White. Although they saw each other less often than in the 1960s, their friendship had slowly started to recover from Doody's disastrous intervention in 1971.[72] When Thom did not hear from Tanner for several months over the spring and early summer, he worried he had said something to irritate his old friend. When a letter finally arrived in July, Thom was "relieved" and replied immediately: Tanner had accepted a permanent American professorship, at Johns Hopkins, and was preparing to leave Cambridge.[73] Charles Newman, Tanner's old friend from Northwestern, directed the Writing Seminars at Hopkins.[74] "One huge bond was that they were both marathon drinkers," Marcia reflected. "They would stay up for hours drinking and talking each other under the table." Newman had "moved heaven and earth" to get Tanner to Hopkins and had convinced them to pay his shipping costs—including thousands of books—buy him a car, and rent him a "sumptuous" apartment close to campus.[75]

Tanner had separated from Marcia and was now seeing an Italian academic named Nadia Fusini. Thom felt that he had chosen Johns Hopkins over UC Santa Barbara with Marcia in mind: following their split, Marcia had moved to San Francisco. Thom, "for purely selfish reasons," was sorry that Tanner had not chosen Santa Barbara—"we'd have seen more of you"—but tried to lessen his "anxieties" about Marcia. "Without any loss of the old sweetness," he reassured Tanner, "she seems to have become rather coolly capable in her expressed attitude to herself."[76] After Tanner and Marcia separated, Thom softened toward her. She was an occasional guest on Cole Street and remained a friend of the family. "I've never known her so good," Thom reflected after she came to dinner that summer, "not silly or apologetic, just nice & even sensible."[77] He was more concerned about Tanner. From Tanner's "semi-breakdown" of 1974 to the "exuberance" of his visit to San Francisco in summer 1975, Thom feared "such an extreme contrast" anticipated "another period of emotional troubles."[78]

Beginning in Atlanta in early November, Thom gave a series of readings on the East Coast. He worked north through Baltimore, Hartford, and Boston, spent a fortnight in New York, and returned to San Francisco in early December. In mid-October, Tanner had written him "a neurotic letter saying don't come to Baltimore, but in eve [he] fones saying do."[79] He then received another "worrying" call from Tanner and, preparing to leave San Francisco, felt "slightly hysterical."[80] At Emory, his first reading, he felt "more or less in self control."[81] Two days later, in Baltimore, he spent the afternoon and evening with Tanner, "trying to reassure him, he being in terrible shape, unable to live in present, only in an imaginary Cambridge & England."[82] Thom gave a "goodish" reading and saw Tanner the next morning before he flew to Hartford. "My selfish thought of TT," Thom wrote: "thank god I'm not where he's at."[83] Shortly after Thom left, Jack Collins visited Tanner. "He was stuck in his apartment building," Collins recalled. "He was really in despair. He talked a lot about suicide. He was drinking heavily. [. . .] If Tony was threatening suicide, it would be a sore subject for Thom."[84] Writing to Ander a month later, Thom thought Tanner was "in a state of acute anxiety" and "having his fourth emotional breakdown in six years." Thom found it "very difficult and painful, all the more because he is one of the friends I love most, but I'm not a professional psychiatrist and don't know how to deal with such cases except with sympathy and common sense. And common sense is just what a person in such a condition is most inaccessible to."[85]

At Thom's invitation, Tanner spent a month at Cole Street over Christmas and New Year. "He is <u>far</u> better," Thom thought, "though very nervous & even apologized to an empty can he kicked."[86] One evening they had dinner with Jack Collins and his partner, Marty. "Further work is put in on TT's case," Thom wrote, "with which I am getting thoroughly bored."[87] Mike was "very fond" of Tanner and tried to keep things light.[88] "Tony Tanner was a good example of a smart friend Thom had, but he didn't like Tony's problems," Mike reflected. "Thom had no patience for that, just like he had no patience toward himself. He didn't have any for other people, too."[89] After a week or so, Thom left Tony to his own devices and spent "frenetic" evenings getting stoned at the Ambush.[90] When Tony returned to Baltimore in mid-January, Thom felt it was "good having him here" and hoped he would fare better at Hopkins having spent a happier month among friends.[91]

Three weeks later, Thom heard that Tanner had returned to England on compassionate leave: his father was seriously ill. "When I would no longer accept Tony's despairing phone calls, and Tony was disintegrating in Baltimore," Marcia recalled, "Charlie [Newman] began phoning me regularly for advice. [. . .] I told Charlie that if they let Tony return to Cambridge he'd never come back. Charlie refused to believe that Tony could be so feckless. But that was what happened."[92] In late February, Thom heard from Tanner. "I had resigned from Hopkins and they cancelled my courses—no doubt some will see it as rank flight," Tony wrote.

> Maybe it was—anyway after a few days of being sick-room help and errand boy I finally collapsed. [. . .] I am right down to the extent that the doctor won't countenance my going back. It wen got my legs this time and I can't walk properly—so much for my euphoric idea of emigrating all on my own.

Tony spent several weeks in a rehabilitation clinic, wheelchair-bound: for the rest of his life, he struggled to walk without the aid of two sticks.

His guilt at leaving Hopkins was compounded when somebody told him "that I had alienated many of my friends—which I can understand because depressives are colossal bores" and that he had "ascrib[ed] malevolence and negative feelings to old friends." He apologized for the negativity of his stay at Cole Street. "That I never meant and I was only aware what princes you all were while I was being, as it were, the beast," he told Thom.[93] No apology was necessary, Thom reassured him. Tony returned to the house on Alpha Road and was able to resume his old position at King's. "They took him right back," Collins recalled. "Tony really needed that matrix. King's kind of mothered him."[94]

For Thom, 1976 was defined by Tony White and Tony Tanner. His grief for White was still raw, and his friendship with Tanner, one of the deepest and dearest of his life, struggled to recover from the difficulties of that winter. "I wrote him a lot of letters and got no answer," he told his aunt Barbara a year later, "but finally I said that no news means bad news as far as I am concerned and he did write."[95] Thom found it difficult to process what, for him, was akin to a double bereavement. "I must say," he told Barbara, "I feel rather as if I have lost two of my best friends this year, not one."[96]

25

BLOCK

"1976 was a lousy year," Thom told Mary and Catherine, "but I can already feel 1977 will be good."[1] He taught well and maintained a "euphoric" nightlife on Folsom—THC and speed were the drugs of the day—without downturns in focus and energy in the classroom.[2] "I taught better than I have in years," he told Barbara, "and of course when I teach a lot I learn a lot from my students as well."[3]

In February, Douglas Chambers and Allan Noseworthy visited in consecutive weeks. Douglas would become a regular visitor on Cole Street: he taught at Trinity College, University of Toronto, and usually visited Thom during spring break. Douglas was witty and kind: Thom had warmed to him immediately, and he admired Douglas's wide-ranging interests, from Milton and John Clare to horticultural history and modern drama. Douglas was also a gardener and gave Thom advice about what to plant in the small yard at Cole Street. In the mornings they talked about literature; in the afternoons they dropped acid and went to the Ambush.[4] Thom was also able to talk to Douglas about gay relationships. Although Douglas lived and worked in Canada, where he had boyfriends, he spent part of the year living in London with his long-term lover Brian Norbury, a civil servant. Douglas was intrigued about Thom and Mike's setup. "I have no rule against a sustained sexual relationship," Thom told him. "It just seems that sex seems largely promiscuous since living with Mike I get all the love I need."[5]

Where Douglas was constant and dependable, Allan was flighty and irresolute. He had split from his boyfriend, a sometime Mapplethorpe model named Larry Lavorgna, and came to San Francisco to recuperate. He "gets on terribly well w/ M[ike] & B[ill] & is good for me," Thom reflected.[6] In New York, Allan's life was a mess: he was broke, had an empty apartment—he had sold all his furniture when he moved in with Lavorgna—and wrote Thom letters by candlelight because the electricity had been cut off. "I don't know how to extricate myself from the whole mess," he told Thom.[7] One option was to cut his losses and move to California. "If and when I do come, can I sleep on your couch until I find an apartment. Yoko too?" he wrote Thom. "I hope you don't mind me calling when I'm all down and depressed but I always feel like talking to you makes me feel better."[8]

When the winter quarter concluded, Thom embarked on a fortnight's tour of the Midwest. He took a weeklong stint as poet in residence—a title he "hated"—at Lake Forest, a liberal arts college north of Chicago, "to pay Mike back for the new pipes I had to have installed in the house last year."[9] Thom did not take to the well-heeled Illinois suburbs, nor his residence at the Deer Park Inn, an English-inspired boutique hotel. "I was crossing the hotel lobby one evening, looking quite like myself but not contemptibly so," he told Douglas, "when an eighty-year old Lady Britomart remarked in an Edith Evans voice to her companion: There goes one of the great unwashed hordes." He was grateful for the gas station across the street, which "with a rather too characteristic Gunnesque sentimentality" he treated as his "hold on reality."[10] Breakfast cost $7 and was "terrible," he told Mike. "Thank god for valiums, that's what I say."[11]

At Lake Forest, Thom gave a public lecture called "An Apprenticeship." He drew on his recent autobiographical writing and dwelled on Christopher Isherwood as a model for both his work and his way of life. "People sometimes ask me if I think [of] myself as an English or an American poet," Thom told the Lake Forest audience. "I suppose that one of the attractions of Isherwood for me has been that he was an Englishman who has become a kind of writer neither completely English nor completely American, hovering somewhere in a mid-Atlantic where such distinctions no longer apply."[12] Thinking about Isherwood's coolness—his "devot[ion] to getting it right," as Thom put it elsewhere[13]—likely informed a poem Thom wrote about his Lake Forest residency. Originally called "Poet in Residence," "Expression" derides his students' "very poetic poetry" about "breakdown, mental institution, / and suicide attempt, of which the experience / does not always seem first-hand."[14] The girls, he told Douglas, "were still (still) imitating Sylvia Plath."[15] In the second half of the poem, Thom visits the Art Museum and sees an "'early Italian altarpiece'" of a mother and child, "Solidly there . . . two pairs of matching eyes / void of expression." It is a wry, knowing conclusion: to find an impersonal analogue—"The sight quenches, like water / after too much birthday cake"[16]—for a subject he had experienced firsthand, and which had so far "defeated" him in his own poetry.[17]

When he returned to San Francisco in May, Thom was impatient to start writing. He began a new notebook—"a new morning?????"—but struggled to overcome his block.[18] He wrote two minor poems—"3 AM" and "Walker"—and made tentative first drafts of "The Cat and the Wind" and "Expression," but was not happy with them. "I have written very little I can even stand in the last two years," he told Charles Monteith in June. "It has been as if I was 17 again, and completely uncertain of where I am going."[19] He had written almost nothing since finishing *Jack Straw's Castle*, and 1976 was completely barren. "Whether that had to do with Tony W's death, or getting old, or a combination of the two, I have no idea," he told Barbara.[20] He wondered whether committing to a prose autobiography was "the inevitable next step. Inevitable for my imagination, such as that is."[21] He drafted the first page of "Accounts (Histories?)" while in the Midwest and wrote of its first chapter that "it may be the basis of my myths, but treat it (Mother's family) as objective history, in their terms, not mine (which are less interesting)."[22] Thom wrote four chapters through 1977 and 1978: he stalled having reached Bedales and "The Flirt" in 1941, and gave up prose autobiography for good.[23]

Throughout 1977, Thom wondered whether he was finished as a

poet. "I keep thinking I haven't written any poetry since the beginning of last year, but that isn't really accurate, it's just that I haven't written any good poetry," he told Ander in November. "Well, it doesn't matter too much: I'd like to feel I had another book on the way, but I can't really be bothered with what the newspapers think."[24] Through the summer he wondered: "If I am an ex poet, & thus not a poet any longer, I wonder what I am?"[25] Thom was beginning to tease out the implications of a poetics he had established in 1962. "A good poem is simultaneously a tentative and risky cruising," he had written, "a complete possession and orgasm, and a huge leather orgy. (Whether its subject is related to sex or not.)"[26] Throughout the summer, Thom cruised feverishly: new tricks alternated with a lonesome long walk home. "I am being a sybarite," he wrote. "Summer-anxieties alternate with brief euphorics."[27] Thom's motives in sex and writing were the same, but the acts were also mutually inclusive. His life was finely compartmentalized, but Thom tended to feel and write at his best when his compartments—writing, teaching, family, promiscuity—were balanced. His summer cruising was likely an attempt to kick-start his poetry, underlaid with the fear that, nearing fifty, he would soon be "dredging" the bar like the "Fallen Rake" in "Modes of Pleasure."[28] "Poetry was never the major thing in my life anyway," he told Holmstrom in December. "I regret not writing it now because it did constitute a stage in the attempt to understand whatever I was going through, or had gone through; but if it's gone, well then it's gone, and I should be happy I was allowed to write such an enormous quantity of it."[29]

Thom tried to convince himself that "'achievement' is mainly a lot of bullshit" and that he would "far sooner be Tony White, with very little achievement in the ordinary sense but a full man—the fullest!—than Ted Hughes, with a splendid poetic achievement but not somebody I even want to know very well."[30] Thom thought Hughes "by far the best person writing nowadays" but remained wary of "the bombast, the romanticism."[31] That summer, Thom introduced Hughes's reading at San Francisco's Museum of Modern Art. Remarkably, it was the first time

Thom had heard Hughes read in person. "My eager curiosity was not completely satisfied," he told Holmstrom:

> It was partly the <u>selection</u> of poems: it was as if Ted completely subscribed to his newspaper reputation of the poet of animal violence. He wasn't violent in the actual reading, though some crazy in the audience went violent and started screaming to his ex-wife that she had slept with Sylvia Plath (she was far too young), it was just that each poem was a typical Hughes anthology poem. I could make a far better case for him, I know, than he did for himself.[32]

Plath had thought Thom was Hughes's "poet-twin": Thom perhaps agreed. For a time he judged his own collections against Hughes's—he wished *Moly*, with its "Hughesian title," was more like Hughes's poems[33]—and while he cooled on Hughes after *Crow*, Thom retained a sense that, of the rising stars of 1962's joint *Selected*, only one had achieved his potential. The story was somewhat similar with Larkin—the other component of the "triple-headed creature" Edward Lucie-Smith had dubbed "the Larkin–Hughes–Gunn"[34]—whose work Thom found best "when he is untypical . . . when he shows unexpected sympathies or when he writes a marvellously Symbolist ending to the poem High Windows." When Thom learned that *High Windows* had sold more than twenty thousand copies in Britain alone, he questioned "what that says about Britain. Most of those readers don't like L for the beauty of his form (though that is what I mainly like about him)—so what do they find attractive about his most prominent attitudes—his closed mind, his sour & begrudging tone, his assumption that provinciality is a virtue?"[35] Ultimately, Thom thought Larkin "a terrible influence on British poetry because if you admire somebody like that so much it means you're not going to be aiming very high."[36] To Thom, especially during a block, it seemed as though contemporaries like Hughes and Larkin had little trouble writing. "I always tell myself it must be better to have difficulty in writing, as I usually do, than to be facile," he told Monteith, "but I must say there are times when I wouldn't mind having a bit of slick facility!"[37]

Excessive cruising and writer's block were not Thom's only problems that year. He felt that Bill had struggled to move on from his split with Mike and that living in the same apartment created more problems than it solved. Thom was "very concerned" about Bill in "his mixture of intense aggressiveness & vulnerability. Also his attempt to put on a new personality like a jacket."[38] When Mike briefly dated another man, it proved a "tense time" for the household.[39] Bill's "bitterness" made Thom question whether the family could survive when Mike, given his nature, inevitably found a new long-term partner.[40]

Thom's fears were tested that summer. At the Stud, then in its classic 1970s dance bar iteration, Mike met a tall, handsome Ohioan named Bob Bair. Bob was twenty-six—two decades Mike's junior—and had never had a serious relationship. They started hanging out at the Stud and going to big open-air concerts. "The Grateful Dead and just about anybody," Bob recalled. "And we took lots of drugs, a lot of acid. Snorted coke. Smoked grass. It was fun for me, coming from Mansfield, Ohio . . ." Bob had lived in the Bay Area for a couple of years, working construction before becoming a stable hand at Grizzly Peak Stables and, later, a zoo-keeper at the Oakland Zoo. "I had been cut off from my family when I told my father I was gay," he reflected. "I didn't really speak to him, and rarely to my mother. There was a period when I didn't really see them. Maybe one of the reasons this house has meant so much to me is because it became my family, which is what happens with gay people. They have to create families wherever they can find them."[41]

As his relationship with Mike became serious, Bob spent more time at Cole Street. "I didn't know who Thom was. I didn't know that Mike had had a relationship with Thom already, and that he had had a relationship with Billy already," Bob recalled. It took him almost a year—shortly before he moved in with Mike in 1978—to learn the family history. "Mike would mention things like he had known Thom for a long, long time and they were very close, but I didn't realize that Mike was never going to leave Thom, that they had made a pact in some way," Bob said. "When I discovered that, it was hard for me because I realized that Mike was in a relationship with someone else. I didn't know how to handle that. It's sharing. You can imagine being in love with someone, but sharing them with people who they've already had relationships with? I was young enough to think that maybe that's the way gay people do it."[42] Bill was a more immediate concern. Bob thought Bill saw him "as kind of an enemy at first."[43] Thom witnessed Bill's "crisis" in the summer when Bob spent two nights with Mike on Cole Street.[44] A week later, Bill decided to spend the rest of the summer with friends in Big Sur. Thom had mixed feelings: he was happy for Mike but "rather sad to see [Bill] go," and worried that the family would not be able to stay together.[45]

With Bill in Big Sur and Mike and Bob spending more time together, Thom was mostly alone and relied on bars and visits for company. Jere Fransway, "at his most genial & lovely," had returned temporarily upstairs.[46] Thom looked forward to a visit from Allen Day, a Bostonian leatherman who worked as a commercial illustrator and pornographic artist.[47] Meanwhile, Allan Noseworthy had decided to move to California: he drove himself and Yoko across America and arrived on Cole Street in early September. "Lovely full house," Thom wrote, with Day and Noseworthy visiting at the same time, "like Christmas when little."[48] With little space, Noseworthy and Yoko had to bunk with Thom. "The other day we all three woke up to find that I was crushed against the wall, with no blankets, on one side, and Allan was almost fallen out of bed on the other side," he told Barbara, "and Yoko was stretched out very comfortably between us."[49] Mike and Bill liked Allan and "regretted we don't have another bedroom so they could live here permanently."[50]

In the autumn, Thom spent his traditional fortnight in New York. He stayed with Don Doody, Thom O'Malley, and their friend Martin Rosen—"the three wise men of Gotham"[51]—on East Twenty-second. In Boots and Saddle, a Christopher Street gay bar, he met "all timer" Norm Rathweg, an architecture graduate student. Norm was twenty-seven, stood six foot four, had scruffy blond hair, and wore leather. With his lover, Louis Keith Nelson, he had built the Chelsea Gym, an icon of gay Chelsea, and knew Edmund White from the Sheridan Square Gym. "I'd see Norm marching down the street with four other young men all in their thirties, wearing jeans and leather jackets, their hair cropped short, their voices loud," White recalled. "They weren't bullies or pigs. They read books. They listened to classical music. They fell in love. Their politics were progressive. They talked about ideas. But Norm could command a team of straight workingmen on a building site and hide his emotions under a gruff exterior. He was the New Gay Man." On subsequent visits to New York, Thom stayed with Norm and Louis at their Colonnade Row apartment, on Lafayette Street, and mixed with their group of "big, hearty sensitive men." Thom was "one of the stars of the group," remembered White, "tall, bearded, lean, a serious leather guy and a decade older than all of us (though he looked our age). He was fascinated by Norm and maybe just a bit in love, even if his 'type' was younger and frailer."[52]

Back in San Francisco, Thom made some New Year's resolutions for 1978. "Resolutions: (1) drink less, (2) be nicer to people, (3) try to find what makes me keep checking out (e.g. Dec 31, Nov 28 etc), (4) get off ground w/ aut[obiography], (5) get ptry going again, & (6) find some way of dealing with Bill."[53] Taking MDA and amyl nitrite at the same time had caused Thom to "lose consciousness" twice.[54] More immediately, however, Thom began to suffer from debilitating sinus trouble and had to take a powerful antihistamine: this meant he could not "drink and drug" for almost the entire winter quarter.[55] He taught "the best 141 ever, and prob[ably] the worst 143B," he reflected, the latter being one of the strangest groups he had ever taught: "stringent Wintersians, [. . .] pure eccentricity, sophomoric girls, a Robt Service admirer, a Swinburnian; very strange lot indeed."[56] By spring his dizzy spells and sinus headaches had worn off, but he continued to feel "dogged by this strange disproportionate depressed feeling of not being well underneath."[57]

After finishing the winter quarter at Berkeley, Thom returned to teaching almost immediately. He had agreed to teach the spring quarter at UC Davis because he needed the money to fund an autumn visit to England.[58] A scenic bus ride took Thom to the "nice bland blond campus" on the outskirts of Sacramento.[59] He taught each Monday, stayed overnight in a dormitory, taught again on Tuesday, and caught the bus back to San Francisco. The job itself was "easy & pleasant" and Thom liked the students. "There is a curious innocence about the whole place which could become very boring," he told Belle Randall, "but is delightful for a change."[60] The change also proved unexpectedly good for Thom's writing. It became clear that one of his students, John Caire, was "a very good poet."[61] Caire helped him "by example," Thom remarked: "his work is so simple, so clear, and so good, I think I figured 'Well if he can do it at 20, why can't I at 48?' So I'm writing something."[62] He began quickly, spending "a very satisfactory day" at Davis working on poetry and memoir, and kept up the momentum.[63] "I wrote nothing but awful stuff for two years and five months," he told Clive Wilmer, "but recently like magic it all came back to me, and I've been writing all the time I can for the last seven weeks or so. Makes me very happy, I must say."[64]

Thom blamed his writing block on three interrelated reasons: aging, Tony White's death, and his usual struggle to write again after finishing a book. But there were other theories. In May, "M tells me DD thinks I am writing so little because of speed."[65] Mike would not have repeated the remark unless he thought Don had a point: when Thom was struggling to write, he took more drugs and hit Folsom Street harder than usual. With Caire's example and Don to prove wrong, Thom began writing with an urgency he had not possessed for several years. "I hate to call it inspiration, that is such a philistine word," he told Monteith. "An urgency, a pressure that pushes you through a poem so that you are at your best while you are writing it, alert to all possibilities that present themselves <u>during</u> the writing, something like that."[66]

Some ideas took a long time to gestate. Thom had wanted to write a poem about Bill since the split with Mike. In "Selves," Thom pictured Bill painting a literal and figurative self-portrait, "laboured at these two years / since you broke with your lover," symbolic of his "new self." Completing the painting "freed" Bill: Thom missed Bill's old "vulnerable and tender" self, but rebuked himself for wanting Bill to conform to a particular role:

> I suppose
> it was an imaginary son
> that I held onto during this time
> of mess and misunderstanding.
> But sons grow up,
> imaginary ones as well,
> and perpetual children are tedious.

Bill had grown up and was "learning / to carry the other, / the constant weight, the weight / it is necessary to carry," an echo of the "burdens"— good and bad—that Thom thought necessary for self-reflection.[67] Moreover, the poem contains a hint of future happiness. Freed from his self-portrait, Bill could focus on "other subjects," one of whom, Jim Lay, "a nude / loll[ing] on some cushions," would become his new lover.[68]

Other ideas were happenstance. Running errands on Castro Street, Thom ran into Gunner, "the hottest man in town," whom he often saw playing pinball at the Ambush.[69] Thom had tricked with Gunner, a sometime centerfold model and actor, years earlier: Gunner thought their "mutual 'play' session [was] non-traditional and erotic as hell. A nice change of pace from the standard BDSM fare that I encountered in the leather community."[70] Thom wrote "Bally *Power Play*" about Gunner, "the cool source of all that hurry / and desperate activity, in control," that recalls the toughness and absorption of "Market at Turk." Gunner is a tender tough: between games "he tells me about broken promises / with a comic-rueful smile / at his need for reassurance, / which is as great as anybody's."[71]

Come August, Thom had written solidly for three months. He was most proud of "Sweet Things," a street-life poem about running into an old trick and knowing "delay makes pleasure great."[72] "Bally *Power Play*" and "Sweet Things" are partner poems, written concurrently and featuring a typical Gunn figure. As he noted in one draft of "Sweet Things," "No wonder the figure of authority is sexually appealing; he takes charge."[73] The poem was one of several that caused Belle Randall to write Thom about the differences between his life and his work. "In poetry you present yourself as promiscuous ('the man I gave my key'), but it is hard for me to make that image jive with the man I know," Randall wrote. "The way I see you: you are too affectionate a man not to care about the whole person and wellbeing of anyone you came across, even a stranger on the city bus, and therefore you would not use people as objects in the way promiscuity requires."[74] "I don't think promiscuity necessarily involves using people," Thom replied. "Short relationships can be just as full of reciprocity as long ones. (Fun's fun, said the Duchess.)"[75]

Thom was flippant with Belle, but while writing "Bally *Power Play*" and "Sweet Things" he was thinking more about "'the gay sensibility,' a phrase rather popular around the newspapers these days." He consistently rubbished the idea and used the phrase interchangeably with "homosexual lifestyle." "That we have a specialized sensibility, somehow frivolous, and unsuited to the rough and tumble of real existence, is just what straight people have been saying about us all my life, and just what I have been trying to reject," he wrote in his notebook:

> So I have never been affected by people like Ronald Firbank or Norman Douglas, whom I've always found rather tiresomely silly. I am far more influenced by The [Manhattan] Review of Unnatural Acts (STH), with its wit and style; or by the drawings of Rex (Icons, etc), with their eerie contradictions. His men are sheathed in a strange ordinariness—gaze at each other, themselves, or nothing, and pausing with a kind of veiled attentiveness, abstracted yet obsessed.[76]

Figures in Thom's poems could be hypermasculine, but he incorporated a Rex-like "ordinariness" that humanized them: the unexpected vulnerability of "Bally *Power Play*" and the handshake of "Sweet Things," "a dry finger playfully bending inward / and touching my palm in secret."[77] Speaking a decade later, Thom still felt the idea of a "gay sensibility" was just as ludicrous. "I don't want to disown a gay audience, but I don't want to limit myself to that, because one can get very limited," he told Alan Sinfield. "One thing I'm trying to do, implicitly, is to show that being gay is as normal as anything else; so when I write about my life as a gay man, or with a gay emphasis, I am implicitly saying that I don't have to put on a special voice to speak about such matters."[78]

In September, Thom arrived in England. John Holmstrom put him up for two nights and together they saw the Marvell exhibition at the British Museum and the Rubens ceiling at the Royal Banqueting Hall. Thom felt "turned on by all English boys" and had "strange unexpected feelings about London, better than any since 1965—its uncarefulness—I like its not being a major city."[79] But London's punk scene was not enough to distract Thom from "identif[ying]" the city with Tony White, nor did it make his jet lag any less acute.[80] Waking one morning at five o'clock, Thom spent the next four hours "thinking about one's failing creative powers, one's lost attractiveness, Mickey's death, the approach of one's own death, human nastiness, life's meaninglessness, etc."[81]

The itinerant nature of the visit did not help Thom to relax. He visited Mary and Catherine in Snodland, then Barbara in Sittingbourne. Much of Covey Hall Farm had now been redeveloped, and the vast backyard was reduced to a small patio beneath ivy-covered walls. Mary and Catherine, both around seventy, had retired from their milk round and now picked fruit at neighboring farms. With Barbara, Thom "got happy" digging her garden and making himself useful. He felt "sad to see Bar maybe for the last time, she tightening her mouth to keep from crying."[82] In Cambridge, Thom spent two nights at Tony Tanner's house on Alpha Road. Tanner was in "good enough shape," Thom thought, and benefited from having a new housemate, the "very good-humord & bright" Chris Prendergast, a professor of French whose marriage, like Tanner's, had recently broken up.[83] "Tony was back on the booze and I was a seriously unhappy guy," Prendergast reflected, "so we spent most of a year drinking, and listening to Carly Simon, Joni Mitchell, and Linda Ronstadt, though, as not for the first time, with Tony it got out of control and

towards the end he was on a vodka for breakfast jag."[84] Thom also saw
Clive Wilmer; Thom had agreed that Clive should introduce and edit a
collection of his reviews and essays—the book that became *The Occasions of Poetry*. He enjoyed seeing Tony and Clive but found Cambridge
"faintly depressing. I don't know why," he told Barbara, "because I loved
it the whole time I was an undergraduate."[85]

From Cambridge, Thom traveled to Leeds to see Ander, who was now
working for Yorkshire Television. His children, William and Charlotte,
lived with him; Margaret had stayed in Cornwall. "My brother's marriage is not in the healthiest shape," Thom told Holmstrom. "But my
niece and nephew are. Particularly my nephew, who is heading toward
the position of most gorgeous member of the family. He is now 17, and
a nice bright boy to boot."[86] Will "seems all potential, to himself seems
lost," Thom thought, and developed his perception into "Slow Waker,"
perhaps seeing something of his own adolescent self in his nephew. "He
wants to withdraw into / a small space, like / the cupboard under the
stairs," Thom wrote, "and get in nobody's way."[87] Ander drove them all to
Cornwall to visit Margaret. That night in the pub, Thom was "a besieged
celebrity" and slipped away to watch television with Will and Charlotte.[88]

Thom had purposefully left a week in London until last. He stayed in
his old room at Thérèse's house and, after a few days, felt "a certain high"
from being in the city.[89] He was bracing himself: on his final weekend
in London, he returned to Notting Hill for the first time since Tony
White's death. He bought gifts for Mike and Bill from Portobello Market and walked along Talbot Road, "expecting grief but feeling nothing
much."[90] He had expected "floods of tears," he told Holmstrom, but instead "felt very bored."[91]

Back in San Francisco, Thom reflected on the understated grief of
his London stay and made notes about a conversation he had had with
Thérèse about his mother:

> An old friend said two things
> a few weeks ago to me.
> First, that if you had waited a week

you'd never have done it.
What a waste, what a waste.
I had never known that.
Secondly, she referred
to your flair for dramatic timing
& I, who loved you so,
and who think I hate
those who dramatize themselves.
I keep thinking I have you complete
but I don't—you are
unpredictable even after your death.[92]

The notes formed part of an abandoned sequence called "Letters to the Dead," in which Thom addressed his mother, father, and Tony White. "You played invulnerable, particularly before me (at Cambridge)," Thom wrote, addressing Tony, "because you knew (whether consciously or not) you were my subject matter."[93] Thom had visited London expecting to grieve for Tony, but left with a new perspective on his mother. His dreams that autumn were more vivid and nightmarish than usual:

I have dreamt of you
a hundred times. You are back:
Hello my darlings, you say
as you embrace us. I was away.
I was not dead all that time,
I was away. And every time
I have thought, 'How could you,
how could you do this to us?'
[. . .] in dreams, Mother,
I invent a fiction
in which I seek to give color
to my reproach
  that you deserted us, that
    you deserted me.[94]

Charlotte's suicide and Tony's death were comparable: both were sudden and unexpected and both left Thom feeling abandoned. With this new perspective on his mother, Thom questioned what he knew about her. "I grew up to be a writer, just what would have made you most proud," he wrote, addressing her. "I also grew up to be what you wd have called a bugger. Wd you ever have understood? Perhaps in the end, but we wd have had some awful years at the end of my teens. I wd have been defensive & you wd have been tyrannical: you wd have made me go to a psychiatrist etc, you wd have stuck at nothing to separate me & Mike. Or do I do you an injustice? Wd you have been able to love me enough to realize that the man-&-woman love you so valued cd find an equiv between men?"[95] Writing about his mother and Tony was Thom's attempt to regain agency in the relationships. "I am not ready for you to slip / into history, / the pain less sharp," he addressed Tony, in words that could have been written about his mother, "the loss at one with all loss."[96]

26

MARRIAGEſ

In summer 1978, Mike raised the idea of Bob Bair moving into Cole Street. "Thom said the same thing, really, as he had with Bill," Mike recalled: "if that's what you want, it's going to be fine with him. And it wasn't fine. There was a certain friction at the beginning between Thom and Bob, but it didn't last very long."[1] Thom was in a difficult position: he liked Bob and wanted Mike to be happy, but he also wanted to support Bill and emphasize that Bob was not replacing him in the family. "Thom was so nice to me, and so open and sweet," Bob reflected, "that I couldn't dislike him, even though I felt a little jealous at times."[2] The new arrangement needed some time to settle. When Thom returned from England, Mike was cold toward him: after a few weeks they "finally had it out (quite nicely, but honestly)" and Mike "finally said he loved me, for the first time since my return."[3] Mike operated at a higher emotional pitch than Thom. Consciously or unconsciously, Thom was not always well attuned to Mike's depressions and anxieties, and their occasional flare-ups could seem sudden and unexpected. Thom toyed with a poem about Mike, a companion piece to "Selves," but wrote only notes and fragments. "You are not easy / to come across unawares," reads one, "But I can do it, / because I have yrs of practice."[4]

Marriages were much on Thom's mind through winter and spring. One of the final pieces he wrote for *Occasions* was a review of James Merrill's *Divine Comedies* (1976) and *Mirabell: Books of Number* (1978).[5]

Thom was largely indifferent to Merrill but found his recent collections "the most extraordinary stuff."[6] He found "extraordinary" the twenty-year project Merrill had undertaken with his partner, David Jackson, to communicate with spirits on a Ouija board. Specifically, Thom admired Merrill's "portrayal of the domestic situation" in which the action occurs. "It is also, not incidentally, the most convincing description I know of a gay marriage," Thom wrote:

> Much of what makes any marriage successful is the ability to take the importance of one's partner for granted, to *depend* on the other's love without being in a state of continuous erotic or passional tension. Merrill's indication of these abilities is the firmer for being indirect. The men's life together is presented to us in detail which is almost casual: we see them choosing wallpaper, keeping house, travelling, entertaining, and above all sitting at the ouija board.[7]

Thom knew this firsthand: at home, he and Mike did everything together. They chose fixtures and fittings for the new bathroom; repainted the kitchen and dining room; shared cooking and shopping duties. "They were always lovely to each other when I saw them together," recalled one friend. "Often when Thom and I would come back from lunch, Mike would be at the house. We'd all have a little chat and there was a definite old-married-couple feeling to their interaction."[8] Writing the Merrill review helped Thom cultivate another project. "I begin to see the Marriage Group more clearly," he wrote. "I have had it in mind I don't know how long. A year—as long? more than a year?"[9] He wanted the "Group" to start with "wooing and go through all sorts of marriage (including gay) and separation and end up with Philemon and Baucis," he told Belle Randall. "I have much of a novelist's interests in me, but none of the novelist's staying power."[10]

Moreover, the family was going through a period of transition. Bob had moved in with Mike, and Bill's new lover, Jim Lay, a neurosurgical technician at the nearby University of California San Francisco Medical

Center, was often at the house. More people meant more relationships and more complications. "A lovely eve w/ Bill, we smoke roaches from a tin he has collected, & talk & talk," Thom wrote that spring. "Never have evenings like this w/ Mike anymore."[11] For a time Thom found Bob's "constant presence" irksome and thought Mike "shd know w/out being told."[12] In an abandoned poem called "Matrimonial," Thom mused that "all marriage problems are the same," the result of "a commitment / that was not a contract / but is treated like a contract."[13] Thom and Mike had overcome those problems, but Mike experienced them anew with his separation from Bill and marriage to Bob. Early in that marriage, Thom thought Bob, when drinking, was "<u>always</u> antagonistic" toward him and ascribed it to "jealous[y]."[14] After a night when Bob's "ranting & weeping" kept the house awake, Thom talked to him "for hours—he eventually makes sense—his jealousy of me, the household."[15] Bob's assimilation into the family was not easy: it took him and Thom several years to become close. They worked to overcome their mutual suspicion through frank conversations and a shared love of Mike.

"Extremely complex relationships, need I say, are built up," Thom wrote in his Merrill review.[16] That summer marked twenty-five years since Thom had left England and followed Mike to America. Reflecting on their Cambridge courtship, he drafted a poem called "The Married Men":

> Away from you my need
> flares/wakes into its (full life) wakes to its old energy.
> I call it "yearning."
> Walking between hedgerows in Kent
> I slash at the nettles
> with a switch I picked up
> as savagely as if
> it were 26 years ago. I need
> to touch you as hard
> as I did then.
> I need to confirm yr reality,
> my own, and the life

I have led since I met you.
Without you it is like
having hardly lived.

The poem pivots to San Francisco, where Thom holds Mike "each time we pass / your firm slim body / on the way to the kitchen" and "quickly take you for granted," echoing the depiction of marriage in his Merrill review. Thom wondered whether everything remained "understood / in our arrangements / that 'we' is still most important." The draft concludes:

All my needs are not yours,
nor yours mine.
We have a house
into which others come.
We sleep in separate rooms.
You sleep in one room with one man
I in another w/ a lot / I with a series of symbols.
We arrange, we arrange.[17]

That was their essential arrangement: Mike was a serial monogamist, whereas Thom needed a stable loving relationship—Mike, his mother—as well as novelty and promiscuity—tricks, "symbols," father-like authority figures. Leather bars were the backdrop of Thom's life: he went most days, for the conviviality as much as the sex. "I never thot my life's gt love wd be like this," he wrote, "(such freedom w/ such trust)."[18] It was a hard-fought victory: Thom and Mike, for all their different needs and wants, knew they would never leave each other.

"The Married Men" is a plainspoken, anxious poem: Thom did not intend to publish it in that form but knew a "marriage group" was worthless without an exploration of his own marriage. In one draft of "The Married Men"—called "The Need / The Yearning"—Thom reflected, "I love a lot of people a bit / but only you completely." In notes for a conclusion, he wrote: "At times I sit in one room / knowing you are / only a room away / & I 'yearn' for you."[19] This conclusion inspired another poem, "June," about daily life with Mike, in which Thom used a botanical analogy to offer "a definition of love—that the summation is so hard because of the texture of a love of almost 30 years, it is also the texture of the basis for a life—the house I return to after my brief flights/adventures."[20] In the garden, "[s]eparate in the same weather," buds from the Oriental poppies

> rise from different plants together
> To shed their bud-sheaths on the bed,
>
> And stretch their crumpled petals free,
> That nurse the box of hardening seed,
> In the same hour, as if to agree
> On what could not have been agreed.[21]

It is a quietly beautiful and triumphant poem: the "crumpled petals" protect the incipient seeds. Thom intended this unspoken togetherness to reflect daily life—he called one draft "The Silences"—and his and Mike's comfortable distance. At first, he wanted its final rhyme to be "need"—"i.e. They quietly accommodate the same needs" or "And share the same (quiet life) & needs"—but felt that "need" carried too much personal weight, settling instead for the more intimate and companionable "agreed."

In 1982, Thom published a different poem called "The Married Men." Like "June," "The Married Men" is metrical; unlike "June," it is doggerel, perhaps intentionally. The poem explores a family dynamic comparable with Bob's assimilation into Cole Street:

> There is a boy who hangs on your speech
> And watches you jealously
> Would like to have you out of my reach
> Although he bears with me.
>
> I will do everything I must
> To help, as you would do.

And if I try to get his trust
It is for his sake too.

Just for a moment, a moment he goes.
You give me a candid stare.
You keep our faith. And I suppose
There's plenty of you to share.[22]

The poem is a partial family portrait. Missing from it are Bill and Jim, who now shared the front room. Thom had lived in the middle room since summer 1974, when noise from overnight roadwork on Cole Street forced him inland; "really digging it," he made the move permanent.[23] A small window looked onto the yard. There was just enough room for a futon and a bureau. He kept his black boots in a row outside the door; his leather jackets, checked shirts, and blue jeans hung in a narrow wardrobe. In the upstairs apartment, with Don living in New York but continuing to pay rent, Lonnie Leard and Michael Grove had lived in relative harmony for several years. That summer, Leard moved in with his new boyfriend, a PCP dealer named Paul Olson, a few blocks away on Schrader. Grove was left alone upstairs and his "zombie-like drug states" meant Thom wanted to find him a dependable roommate as quickly as possible.[24] "Much as I like him, I'd as soon kick him out," Thom mused, "it makes him a physical risk to the house (he cd burn it down)."[25] Leard recommended a friend to replace himself. "We hope to have a nice, firm-minded woman here as [Grove's] roommate to look after the place," Thom told his aunt Barbara. "I have never met her but her name is Joy, which surely promises well."[26]

Work on the "Marriage Group" filled Thom's summer. He was "pleased to be so busy" and felt that his new poems seemed "to be different from anything I wrote before." He felt "a constant sense of risk: when I look forward, every poem I write might be the last I ever write. Which gives an extra happiness to the writing of each poem."[27] Working concurrently on a new *Selected Poems* sharpened his focus. "I think it is a solid book," he told Jack Hagstrom, "showing me as good as I can be, short of the new things I shall be trying out in this next book which is taking such a long time to write."[28] Having written poorly, if at all, for two and a half years, Thom felt an almost euphoric enjoyment in writing and felt emboldened to take risks. Although his next book "might be a long time off," it had started to take shape in Thom's mind and he could "see so much detail that needs putting in."[29]

Much of that detail related to San Francisco. In late 1978, the gay community experienced an unprecedented trauma: Harvey Milk, the self-styled Mayor of Castro Street—who, ten months earlier, had become the first openly gay man to be elected to public office in California when he was sworn in as a city supervisor—was shot and killed alongside city mayor George Moscone by "clean-cut cry-baby" Dan White, his former colleague.[30] "I am as shocked as I was at JFK's assassination," Thom wrote, "& feel more grief."[31] As the news spread, thousands began to converge on Castro Street: that night, Thom joined more than forty thousand mourners on a candlelit march through the city to Civic Center, where Joan Baez sang and acting mayor Dianne Feinstein addressed the crowd. Thom drafted a poem about the march, never completed, in which he called Milk's life a search for "social beauty, / learning more clearly as he searched / to cope, to organize, to bring health / to the great wide-flung organism / of a city. A civic health." Milk saw "the beauty of variety . . . like a wood / where the trees are planted / so that when they grow up together / they allow each other room." Milk's murder "cut off" that "vision of the growing wood," but Thom was "rather proud of San Francisco" in its response to the shootings.[32] "I always seem to be marching to City Hall for some reason or other," he told Ander.[33]

Thom had lived in San Francisco for almost two decades and had seen the city undergo rapid change. The late 1970s, notwithstanding Milk's assassination, was the heyday of gay San Francisco. There were exponentially more gay bars and bathhouses in summer 1979 than when Thom arrived on Filbert Street in 1961. Not only were the old neighborhoods like Polk, Folsom, and the Castro still mainstays of gay life, but also new neighborhoods had sprung up around clusters of new bars. By the late

1970s, the Haight had undergone significant regeneration: urban blight, hard drugs, prostitution, and street violence were in decline. Property was cheap, new people moved in, and the neighborhood fostered a gay community to rival Folsom and the Castro. Bradley's Corner remained a popular hangout: other bars followed, like I Beam, DeLuxe, and Question Mark (later Trax), all along Haight Street. "I am reckless & SF is good to me," Thom reflected. "Sex, Joan Baez, drugs, writing poetry—there is time for everything."[34] His new favorite bar was Gus's Pub. Covered in an outrageous collage of hippie wallpaper, Gus's served beer and wine and had a large, "very druggy" backyard where "every possible different kind of person" would go to smoke marijuana and drop acid on the weekends.[35] To Thom, the city was a place of community and conviviality; a place of shared experience, whether that was drinking at the bars, watching movies at the Red Victorian, or catching the bus across town. "I don't like people getting movies in their own homes, and I don't like people driving around in cars," he reflected. "I think people should take public transportation and be with other people in movie theaters. Merely sitting near another person on a bus or in a movie theater is good for the sense of community."[36]

New bars and new friends made Thom reflect on how his own history was interwoven with the city. The germ of an idea came from a remark Don Doody had made the previous autumn: "Doody's idea of poetry about the complications of friendship."[37] He thought about "Poems to/ about friends: DD, TT, AN3"—the latter Thom's shorthand for Allan Noseworthy—although the friend who seemed most apt for a treatment of complications was Jere Fransway, "a Falstaff: first part jolly side, second part treacherous—what connects is his wanting to bring people in with him."[38] Since the Handmakers' bust and fire in 1971, Thom had seen Jere infrequently. He would sometimes sleep upstairs on Cole while on the run; upstate, he often fell foul of the law. In 1972 he was charged, with five others, with "possession of dangerous drugs, possession for sale of dangerous drugs, and possession of marijuana."[39] One mutual friend recalled that Jere "became notorious for surreptitiously dosing victims with marijuana laced with PCP, a paralyzing downer, then sexually exploiting them."[40]

The idea gestated for almost a year before Thom felt ready to write.

He set himself an ambitious target of twenty poems—from Chuck and Jere through Mike and Tony White through Ruth and Thérèse to Don Doody, Allan Noseworthy, and Tony Tanner. "I have tried so often to get [Mike and Tony White] but in truth don't know where to begin," he reflected. To get to Bill, in "Selves," he had "had to work through about 40 lines I later cut."[41] He wanted each poem to demonstrate "the movement constantly toward greater opening of the self" and saw the project in relation to the marriage group.[42] His draft title for the sequence was "Love Without Wings," an allusion to Byron's refrain—"Friendship is Love without his wings!"—in "L'Amitié Est L'Amour sans Ailes." Thom called friendship his "greatest value" and thought that love and friendship "are part of the same spectrum."[43]

In the event, the project proved too ambitious: the final sequence, "Transients and Residents," comprises four poems: "Falstaff," about Jere; "Crystal," about Chuck; "Crosswords," about Don; and "Interruption," about Thom himself wanting to make his "snapshots" of his friends "accurate." Sitting at his desk, Thom does not write. His lamp "describes a circle round me with its light /—Singling me out; the room falls back unseen. / So, my own island." Staring at the window, his "reflection glows"—an image he had used in "Behind the Mirror" to examine the differences between self and other.[44] In this instance, Thom was interested in the way friendships changed him. He wrote poems about Jere, Chuck, and Don because they were all figures from his past: he did not see Chuck and Jere frequently; he saw Don, itinerant and evasive, perhaps once or twice a year. He found that "the less I know the person from inside, the easier to write." Chuck and Jere came easy: they were more like symbols to Thom—of power and taking charge—than close personal friends, especially now that a decade had passed since he saw them most days on Clara Street or at the Stud. Don, meanwhile, was "so definable [in] his characteristics, but how hard to grasp."[45]

Thom also chose to write about his 1960s friends because their shared world no longer existed. "Crystal" and "Falstaff" "are about distance, tho w/ DD the distance is not from me[,] it is from an earlier part of his life."[46] Chuck had reinvented himself as a speed dealer on Folsom: Thom found him "almost heroic," as "magnificently self-enwrapped" as a foxglove, and "feel[ing] complete" only in the "crowded night."[47] Jere was generous but domineering—he would cook "each evening for some twenty heads" yet had a "bullying love," a "ruthlessness" that "showed itself more nakedly as need"—but had disappeared and was rumored to have cancer.[48] Thom was drawn to these men and they were an important part of his LSD period in the late 1960s, but now, at a distance of ten years, he felt able to express reservations about them. There is a hint of self-reflection, too: Chuck was a kind of role model to Thom, a leader, but he now questioned Chuck's reliance on "the chemical" and saw that, like the foxglove, he would flower in "damp solitude / Before its energy fades."[49] Jere, a calculating bully beneath the jolly exterior, perhaps reminded Thom of his own (self-perceived) "[b]esetting sins": selfishness and cowardice.[50]

Don Doody was a subtly different proposition. That summer, "to the great pleasure of all," Don made an extended visit to San Francisco and stayed on Cole Street.[51] He and Thom had "many a good chat" but, to Thom, Don had retreated from the world.[52] "Your cup of instant coffee by the bed / Cold as the sixties," Thom wrote in "Crosswords":

> You have seen reason to remove your ground
> Far from the great circle where you toiled,
> Where they still call their wares and mill around
> Body to body, unpausing and unspoiled.
> You smell of last week. You do not move much.[53]

More so than with Chuck and Jere, Thom's friendship with Don was also a mentorship. In early 1963, while Thom recovered from hepatitis, Don's insights into Camus and Mann had helped Thom develop the idea for "Misanthropos." At Don's "school," as Thom put it in "Crosswords," "it's through contradictions that I learn."[54] Don had taught Thom to live without alibis, introduced him to LSD, and encouraged him to question everything.[55] Once ringleader of the Stud, Don now "watches TV most of time in back room—does crosswords, makes lists."[56] This was in stark contrast to the restlessness Thom had admired in Don; when Don decided to leave the Stud, then the most popular bar in San Francisco, Thom mused: "he cannot ever live with success too long."[57] Don's contradictions were part of that restlessness. In "Crosswords," Thom portrayed him as "Obsessive and detached, ardent and cool," keeping himself in his own "companionable / Chilled orbit by the simultaneous / Repulsion and attraction to it all."[58] Don, meanwhile, saw Thom as his "anchor."[59]

Although Don spent most of his visit in bed, Thom was still grateful for his company. Mike and Bob had rented a cabin for the summer on the Russian River; Bill and Jim hid themselves away to smoke PCP. Thom "really suffer[ed] from lack of company (family)" but knew it was important for Mike and Bob to spend time on their own, away from Cole Street.[60] "Tho it is fun to be alone for short periods," Thom told Douglas, "it gets lonely after a while. I do NOT like being pushed back on my own resources, since I don't have many of them."[61] By the middle of August, with Don also away, Thom felt "like a mother whose numerous children are at the seaside."[62] Nor was Thom having much success at the bars. "My sex life is nonplussed by my head," he reflected, "which is going thro a mild hysterical reaction to being 50."[63]

That autumn, Catherine came to San Francisco, Thom's only aunt to visit him in the United States. Thom "hate[d] being a host," especially for longer than a week. "C's small talk is endless," he complained, "well meant but gets on my nerves."[64] Catherine seemed content to look after herself; Thom sometimes played the tour guide, showing her around Ghirardelli Square, North Beach, and Sausalito. Mike helped to keep things jovial: he took Thom and Catherine on day trips to Port Costa, a small village on the East Bay, and across the Golden Gate to Mount Tamalpais and Muir Woods. Catherine "had a wonderful time," Thom wrote at the end of her fortnight's visit, "& liked all my friends." The night she left, Thom decided to share his birthday cocaine with the house:

Then grass, then Billy brt out peep [PCP]. Shortly aft, Bill sat crying.—Shortly after, I heard him running upstairs, short hysterical steps. I caught him as he was going into Joy's room, waking her up, looking for something. I brt him down & M asked him what he was looking for. He said "The shotgun." (We believe Joy's boyfriend, a Michael, has a gun up there.) At that point, Mike & I had 3 people freaking out on our hands, Bill, Jim on peep, Bob on alcohol.[65]

It was a "dreadful" night: they were "all v tender toward each other" the following day.[66] Bill, "after his brush w/ suicide is bright and affectionate" and decided to start painting again.[67] With Bill and Jim at the front, Thom in the middle, and Mike and Bob at the back, all in the same apartment, Mike suggested that Bill and Jim move upstairs to give everybody more space. Thom agreed in principle—Joy was about to move out and he was not keen on any of Michael Grove's candidates to replace her—but put off the decision until he returned from England. He had agreed to give a poetry tour of England and Wales, reading to secondary school audiences, before a big joint reading with Ted Hughes in London. "It's got slightly out of hand," he told Holmstrom, "in that I'll be doing far more readings than I intended, and they extend from Cardiff to Sunderland, but my fare got paid for so the 'Poetry Secretariat' (which sounds like something out of 1984) is using me to the maximum."[68] Feeling "uniquely unprepared" for the trip, he started smoking again.[69]

The schedule, not confirmed until Thom arrived in England in November, made little geographical sense. He was back and forth to London for the next fortnight. First were Cardiff, Pontypool, and Bristol; then Maidstone and Chislehurst; back to London, down to Hove, and back to London for two readings in one day. Next, the Wirral, West Kirby, and Bury, with a night in Manchester; then Sunderland, Durham, and Stoke for a reading at the University of Keele. Swindon and Cambridge were last, before a final return to London and readings at the Poetry Society in Earl's Court and with Hughes at Riverside Studios. Thom managed to squeeze in family and friends between readings. After a day of farewells in London, and having given seventeen readings in fourteen days, Thom was back on a plane to the United States. "It all went excellently," he told

Barbara. "The schools readings were among the best: anywhere from 150–300, volunteers from the top forms of the many schools in a district."[70]

Thom enjoyed visiting new places—almost every town and city was new to him—but his abiding memory of the tour was "that gaze of hero-worship" from the children at the school readings.[71] Seeing how Ted Hughes was "positively beleaguered by celebrity" confirmed what Thom had always known. "I couldn't live in England now and be a poet," he told Douglas. "I am a good deal too famous there to be comfortable [. . .] and it was simply ludicrous being introduced to audiences as if I were Yeats, for Christ's sake; and it was fun being a star for a while. But if it had gone on much longer I'd have started to believe it—my greatness, that is—or at least in the possibility of it, and that would make writing (never that easy, after all) that much more difficult." Despite his misgivings—"I was speeding on my own vanity," he concluded[72]—it was one of Thom's happier England visits. The hectic schedule helped prevent lethargy and depression, nor were there long visits to his aunts where the pace of life slowed almost to a standstill. Nevertheless, he was pleased to return to San Francisco, where he could slip back into a comfortable anonymity.

Exhausted from travel and suffering from a violent cold, Thom felt awful. Noticing "a weakness" in his right eye, he wondered if he had had "a small stroke." The right side of his mouth also seemed to be "malfunctioning."[73] Thom "wept with fear" before a doctor's appointment, only to discover he had Bell's palsy.[74] "I was scared shitless," he told Douglas, "partly because it could have been a tumor of the brain, and partly because if it was Bell's Palsy then it can sometimes take as much as a year to get your face straight again."[75] After five days, Thom's face began to return to normal; after ten days he was "about 95% symmetrical."[76] His episode of Bell's palsy concluded a difficult year. There were "too many dramatic crises for my liking," he told Douglas, and wished for "a Bland New Year."[77] Unable to drink while receiving cortisone injections, Thom stopped going to the bars. When teaching began in January, he felt "excessively up & vigorous & energetic . . . partly because of lucky escape from Bell's Palsy, partly becos I've been sleeping full nights."[78] Feeling vigorous, he wanted to write, but teaching meant he had to wait and "accumulate lots of plans for poems."[79] He had one particular poem in mind. "I've been thinking," he told Ander in February, "maybe I am at last ready to write something about old Tony."[80]

Although 1979 concluded with more domestic problems—"Bill still smoking peep & Bob still getting drunk," Thom wrote, "which makes me feel my life here isn't that terrific"[81]—a positive step was taken early in the new year. Bill and Jim decided to move upstairs: to Thom, that meant "we'll be a regular commune of the 1980s!"[82] Thom told Michael Grove to vacate by May: with Bill's sometime PCP supplier gone, Thom thought they could help him quit. "It was a very powerful drug," Bob recalled. "It takes you out of this world and puts you in another world. Thom was smart about that. He had done it a couple of times but didn't like what it did to people." Jim also used PCP, but it was not initially clear that he was as addicted as Bill. "They were both really hooked on it," Bob reflected. "Jim was just hallucinating and seeing stuff and hearing things. He wasn't living in the real world anymore."[83]

Lonnie Leard's boyfriend, Paul Olson, was also a PCP dealer. In March, Thom, Mike, Bob, Bill, Jim, and Bill's friends Michael and Thierry, visiting from Paris, went to a "magnificent turkey & ham" dinner at Lonnie and Paul's house on Schrader. Thom was tired: alone, he returned early to Cole Street and promptly fell asleep. A phone call woke him at six o'clock the following morning: "It is Billy saying 'we are all in jail.' Shortly after I left, the cops raided the place, breaking in & behaving like pigs, keeping them handcuffed hours, drinking the wine, beating on them."[84] Police found "a ledger book containing . . . a list of narcotics transactions."[85] "We were all peeped," Mike recalled:

> It was like a movie. They took us in a small paddy wagon, some of us on one side and some of us on the other, and they booked us. I don't think they found any drugs—they didn't need to, we were stoned out of our minds. Somebody advised us to go to the queens' tank because we didn't want to have to deal with straight people who didn't like gay people.

Michael and Thierry were frightened: the police thought there was a possible "French connection" to Olson's operation. Outwardly, Mike kept
his cool. "I made one of the jokes I'm known for," he reflected. "I said,
'Why on earth is it so terrible? Well, I don't know, a coat of paint, some
new curtains . . .' I handled it well."[86] Thom spent the day on the phone
to Tom Gee, trying to organize "a good lawyer" and release on bail. It
was evening before Gee phoned to say they were getting out. "Suddenly
I cry & cry, for about 10 minutes," Thom wrote. "I felt like a woman all
of whose men have gone out to battle." No charges were brought: Thom
took "the Cole Street Six" out to dinner to celebrate.[87]

When term ended, Thom felt ready to write. Now that the family
occupied both apartments, he took a new workroom upstairs. His desk
overlooked the gardens of Cole and Alma (plate 31) and he could watch
their cats laze on the roof of Mike and Bob's room. There he began the
collage that would spread across two walls, floor to ceiling, and contained
personal photographs, postcards, newspaper clippings, posters, leather
ephemera, and his own drawings, often arranged in playful juxtaposi-
tions.[88] "Thom was very talented at drawing cartoons," Mike reflected,
"and they were sometimes dirty—Mickey Mouse with a huge erection,
stuff like that."[89] Thom asked friends and family to send him specific
postcard images: he collected English gardens, the backs of heads, tattooed bodies, and classic "Greetings From" postcards.[90] He stuck photographs of important friends, family, and mentors—Mike, Tony White,
his mother, Ander, Isherwood—directly above his desk. "It is going to be
wonderful to have my own work room with <u>only one door</u> (my present
work room is a little distracting as it has two doors and people are always
passing through it from one place to another)," he told Barbara. "Still,
you know me, I do more than half my reading and writing sitting in the
garden anyway!"[91] The new arrangement was just what he wanted: they
gained an apartment and extended the family. "Mike, Thom, Bill, Bob,
& Jim," he told Jack Hagstrom: "we all have very undistinctive names."[92]

27

AGING

"Subject to confirmation that you are still British Citizen as I am sure you are," Charles Monteith telegrammed Thom in December 1979, "you are winner WH Smith Literary Award of £1,000. Torrential congratulations."[1] Thom won the award for *Selected Poems 1950–1975*, which had been well received. Writing in *The New Republic*, Donald Davie cited Colin Falck's assertion that Gunn had produced "'the lines of most near-to-Shakespearian power in twentieth-century English or American verse.' It is an astonishing claim to make for anyone," Davie reflected, "and a higher claim than is usually made for Gunn; and yet I think it is just."[2]

Teaching prevented Thom from attending the London ceremony. Instead, he had Charles Monteith read a "cutely worded message"[3] about an obsolete proverb he had found in *Little Dorrit*:

> The proverb is: A cat in gloves catches no mice. [. . .] I mentioned my proverb to a San Francisco poet, and he capped it with one of his own: And mice in high heels have a terrible time getting away from cats. [. . .] I want to assure you moreover that the sudden access of riches will not go to my head: my paws will remain ungloved, I shall try to go on catching the mice of poetry, and as for mice in high heels, I never had any particular interest in catching them anyway.[4]

Thom caught plenty of mice once teaching had finished. "Being <u>prevented</u> from writing for 10–12 weeks, because I am too busy," he reflected, "seems to concentrate the faculties."[5] After reading Walter Jackson Bate's biography of Keats, Thom "thought it wd be great to write a sonnet on Keats. I mean who wd think of doing such a thing in 1980. And did it."[6] The result, "Keats at Highgate," is one of his most technically accomplished poems, written mostly in a day. Others followed. Thom wrote most of "Crosswords," his poem about Doody, in April; the same month, after Robert Mapplethorpe took Thom's photograph "in full leather in my room," he began writing "Song of a Camera."[7] After an encounter with "the sexiest cabdriver in the world," Thom began "Night Taxi," a poem he called "the ultimate promiscuity."[8] England, too, provided inspiration, and Thom worked on "The Girls Next Door," about Ruth and her sisters, and "Slow Waker," about his nephew, Will.

Thom was writing "with the gusto of a teenager"[9] and felt assured enough to tell Monteith that he would deliver his next book the following summer. "And if you know how superstitious I am about this sort of thing," he told Douglas, "you will be STRUCK by my confidence."[10] Thom's confidence was hard-won: his blocked period in the mid-to-late 1970s, while difficult, had been instructive. "I learned nothing from the experience," he told Ted Hughes, "except that I have become very dependent on the process of writing poetry and that it will probably always return to me; but I learned nothing, I mean, about how to deal with the dry spells, or about what brings them and what ends them." All he knew was that he seemed so receptive to ideas that he had trouble keeping up with them. Poems like "Crosswords" and "Keats at Highgate" he finished quickly, but others bubbled away in his notebook for weeks and months. Having entertained the possibility, during his block, that "maybe there was no more poetry to come from me," Thom was excited, and relieved, that it had all come back just as easily as it had disappeared.[11]

In July, he accompanied Robert Duncan to New Mexico for the D. H. Lawrence Festival. He expected "a lot of bullshit" and had "enough sense to avoid most of the worst" including "a trip to the 'Shrine' where girls in white dresses strewed white rose-petals on said shrine at sunset, and also the DH Lawrence Festival Gala Ball, where people were supposed to appear as a character from one of the books."[12] He also avoided a recital of Lawrence's work, collected as "Eagles in New Mexico," read by actors including Julie Harris, Ian McKellen, and Elizabeth Taylor. Thom contributed to the festival's opening poetry reading, where he read with A. Alvarez, Duncan, Allen Ginsberg, N. Scott Momaday, and Stephen Spender, and contributed to a panel about Lawrence's influence on poetry and criticism.[13] "Stephen Spender was very good, and A. Alvarez patronising in a kind of neglectful fashion," he told Monteith. "20 years ago I never dreamt I would be praising Spender and contemptuous of AA!"[14]

At the festival, Thom met Ginsberg and William Burroughs for the first time. Ginsberg "hugely impressed" him. "I'd always imagined he might be a bit hysterical, like some of his poetry," Thom told Douglas, "but he is <u>sensible</u>, and <u>kind</u>, and takes charge and looks after people in a way I admire."[15] Besieged by questions at a cocktail party, "I say to AG, 'I hate this kind of thing, don't you?' He says, 'I look on it as a Buddhist exercise.'"[16] Thom stayed in the same house as Burroughs and his entourage. "Whether he liked me or disliked me I have no idea," Thom told Ander. "He looks like Buster Keaton, the great stone face."[17] They went around together, "to the conference, to gay bars, on one occasion to Los Alamos, through the most spectacular landscape I'd ever seen, to see what remained of the exclusive but rather spartan boarding school that had been there when WB went there in 1929, at 15."[18] This provided the occasion for Thom's poem "A Drive to Los Alamos."

As he had the previous year, Thom spent much of the summer alone. Mike and Bob had decided to buy their own cabin on the Russian River. "I only had a certain amount of money," Mike reflected. "It was cheap because it was a dump." Bob, a carpenter by trade, saw it as a challenge, and he and Mike began spending time there through the year, from long weekends to months at a time. "Thom didn't like that we had the cabin," Mike recalled. "He didn't like it when we were away all summer."[19] Thom's concern, as ever, was loneliness, not that Mike and Bob would outgrow the family. "I think [the cabin] allowed Mike and me to have our own life separately," Bob remarked. "We felt that Thom also needed his own life, separately, too. He tried to do that, but some of the characters he tried to do it with . . ."[20] Occasionally Thom visited Mike and Bob, but rarely for longer than a few days: he missed the excitement of the city and beat a hasty retreat to San Francisco. That August, with Bill and Jim in Big Sur, Thom "d[id] not look forward to being alone" in an entirely empty house.[21] He sought company at the bars but spent his fifty-first birthday alone. "I no longer attract anyone," he wrote a few days later. "Why should I, at 51?"[22]

That summer, Thom had more success writing about bars than cruising them. He finally finished "The Menace," a poem he had "always wanted to write about leather bars, s m games, etc."[23] The poem is not about the Mineshaft but "is recognizably about the meat district, and some of it does take place in a kind of generic leather bar (I had in mind the Den, 1970), from which the poem's hero goes back with somebody to that somebody's small room where he wakes at the end of the night."[24] "Central" to Thom's "intentions" in the poem is a quotation from Gregory Bateson's *Steps to an Ecology of Mind*—"The playful nip denotes the bite, but it does not denote what would be denoted by the bite"— which Thom quotes and analyzes within the poem.[25] He wrote "The Menace" in part "to release leather bars from the rather crude assumptions made about them by straight people, newspapers, and gays who have either never been in one or have only gone to one to find in it what they expect." He wanted to "emphasise the importance of improvisation and play" at the expense of "the dreary mythology of s and m, involving as it does all the rigidities of role and routine which I find repulsive."[26] In notes for an essay about cruising, written around the same time as "The Menace," Thom called it "an activity . . . fertile in the side products of the active but undirected mind (like poetry)" and concluded that "I am an authority on cruising in the same way I am an authority on breathing."[27] Improvisation—Thom's new take on his youthful idea of risk— fired his imagination. He drew energy from leather bars and cruising but was equally keen to emphasize that his work was not one-dimensionally queer. In another unfinished, unpublished essay, "Poets and Gay Poets," Thom argued that in "On the Move" he "was sexually excited by the subject matter, but the sexual excitement is not my <u>subject</u>, I want the excitement to come over but if anybody misses the sexual overtones they are missing nothing important in the poem." He was writing in response to "a recent phenomenon: discovery & naming of Gay Poetry," a "category" that he thought "releases but in the same moment it imprisons." Thom's impatience with the phenomenon is evident in the essay's concluding sentence. "It may be difficult to accept in 1980," he reflected, "but there are larger concerns for a human being than the important one of sexuality."[28]

With "The Menace" written, Thom felt his next book was finished barring the "insanely ambitious" sequence "Transients and Residents."[29] He tried, but failed, to add to its four poems—"Falstaff," "Crystal," "Crosswords," and "Interruption"—but surprised himself by returning to notes he had made about Tony White the previous year. He worked solidly on the poem, "Talbot Road," and finished it in early October. "I think it (the pome) is the best thing I've done in some time," he told Douglas. "Hope I'm right."[30] Its five sections recount the circumstances of Thom's year in London in the mid-1960s; the poem is both an elegy for White and Thom's reckoning with his own past. He examined the "damp smoulder of discontent" behind White's "mighty giving of self, / at the centre of the jollity." For Thom, in retrospect, it was "the year of reconciliation" in which "I forgave myself for having had a youth."[31] The poem follows "Transients and Residents" in *The Passages of Joy* but is not part of it. "Talbot Road" does not criticize an old friend the way "Crystal," "Falstaff," and "Crosswords" all do, but, like that sequence, "Talbot Road" turns from the account of a friend to an account of the self. Thom is more forgiving of himself in "Talbot Road" than in "Interruption," in which he finds himself "Colourless, unjoined, like a damaged moon."[32] But Thom had always hitched his cart to Tony: as Tony changed, Thom tried to change, too, and live by his friend's example. That was still true, even though Tony was dead. "The mind / is an impermanent place, isn't it," he asks, "but it looks to permanence."[33]

Making his annual autumn visit to New York, Thom stayed with

Allan Noseworthy—whose stint in San Francisco had not worked out—at the latter's new apartment on Elizabeth Street. It was near where Thom had lived on Prince Street in 1970, and he enjoyed wandering around the old neighborhood. He made the rounds of the Mineshaft, the Spike, the St. Marks Baths, and a new leather bar called Jay's on Hudson and Fourteenth.[34] Norm Rathweg invited him for dinner at the novelist Coleman Dowell's Fifth Avenue apartment; Thom and Norm spent the rest of the night with Ed White and the writer Stephen Koch at the Bar, "the nicest neighborhood gay bar ever," on Second Avenue and East Fourth Street.[35] Thom also met the composer Ned Rorem, who had set his poem "Back to Life" to music. Rorem thought Thom's "foreignness comes not from being English but from being Californian. Attractive, ill at ease, he's one of America's (England's?) three true poets."[36] Thom called the trip one of his "best times" in New York, but his pleasure was short-lived: the day after he left town, a mass shooting at the Ramrod, a popular leather bar in the West Village, left two people dead and six injured.[37]

Looking to England, Thom was unimpressed with a series of articles in *PN Review* that seemed to confirm an antigay bias. Michael Schmidt, the head of Carcanet Press, founded *PN Review* in 1973; by 1980 it had become Britain's preeminent poetry journal. Thom had been close to it from the beginning, through his friendship with Donald Davie—who coedited the journal with C. H. Sisson, under Schmidt's general editorship—as well as his admiration for regular contributors like Robert Wells and Clive Wilmer. Wells, who worked for Carcanet at the time, had asked Thom to submit poems to *PN Review* in 1977 but was concerned Thom thought the journal "too closed and rigid."[38] Thom did not disagree, finding its central tenet "a conservatism of outlook and of politics."[39] This appeared to be confirmed in spring 1980, when Sisson wrote an editorial about the "wilful distortion of language for political ends," focusing on the word "gay." "What is particularly *gay* about homosexuals?" Sisson asked:

How idiotic to attach to that adjective a meaning so irrelevant that the word has been more than half-killed and we are left without a substitute! A more general threat is posed by those who think it a shame on women that ordinary usage allows a masculine gender where no distinction of sex is intended. Everywhere indignant people get up and declare that one must say "his or her" whenever one is not speaking exclusively of one sex or the other.[40]

Thom dismissed this as "trite."[41] Eight months later, however, he "exploded" when he read an article in which Dudley Young attempted, in Thom's summary, "to render the word faggot respectable for straights to use."[42] Thom found it "so outrageous I am surprised it was not accompanied by an editorial disclaimer."[43] Having promised to send new poems to the *PN Review* for several years—his only contribution, so far, had been poems previously published in America[44]—Thom decided "fuck it, if they are going to be anti-gay, they don't get this gay's contributions."[45]

Ordinarily, Thom avoided conflict at all costs and wrote to Schmidt, without relish, explaining that he could not submit work to *PN Review* while it printed homophobic articles and editorials. Schmidt's response surprised him: he asked for Thom's permission to reprint "June" and "The Victim," which Thom had originally published in the American magazine *Inquiry*. "So I have been spending the morning trying to explain to him how a queer like me can't very well contribute to a consistently queerbashing mag like his," Thom told a friend. "I would have thought it was obvious."[46] Thom did not want to fall out with a journal that had been "extremely generous" to him, but did want to make known his objection to its "antigay stance that has nothing whatever to do with poetry."[47] Schmidt found Thom's refusal to contribute work "upsetting and—frankly—incomprehensible" and claimed "there is no anti-gay stance (there quite simply could not be)."[48] Thom was surprised to learn that Schmidt himself was gay, although it did explain some of the hurt Schmidt felt at their quarrel. By the time Thom replied to Schmidt's long letter, he was bored by the argument. "It is true that I have no right to assert that <u>PN Review</u> has an anti-gay policy, since I could not possibly know that," he told Schmidt. "Nevertheless, it is the <u>only</u> magazine I have ever come across that has contained both an article attacking the use of the word gay (for whatever reason) and another freely using the word faggot. At the very least I wish to convince you that a very unbalanced <u>effect</u> has been brought about." Thom felt that if Schmidt was now "concerned about the balance and fairness of the <u>PN Review</u> on the subject of homosexuality," then he had, in a sense, "succeeded."[49] He gave Schmidt permission to reprint "June" and "The Victim." This was lucky for Schmidt, because the poems were "already in PNR 22 which went to press yesterday. Your letter reached me this morning!"[50]

Thom was "bored by school," and the quarter was enlivened only by the quarrel with Schmidt and the arrival of a new colleague.[51] Robert Pinsky had been Winters's student at Stanford in the mid-1960s—on the same fellowship Thom had had a decade earlier—and had arrived from Wellesley College to teach creative writing at Berkeley. He had given a "v. good reading" there the previous year, after which Thom had introduced himself.[52] Thom thought Pinsky's *The Situation of Poetry* "one of the better books of criticism" he had read but was less sure about Pinsky's actual poetry.[53] "<u>He</u> would never believe with Bunting that a poet's best friend is his wastepaper basket," he told Davie.[54] But Pinsky and Thom hit it off and Thom was "very glad" that Pinsky was "to be head of creative writing."[55] Tall, charming, and savvy, Pinsky made a good colleague as well as friend: Thom tried to avoid academic politics wherever possible, but he was not about to alienate a useful ally in the department.

When teaching finished, Thom typed the manuscript of his new book: *The Passages of Joy.* The title came from a Samuel Johnson couplet— "Time hovers o'er, impatient to destroy, / And shuts up all the Passages of Joy"—and Thom liked it "since it seems to refer to the ear-hole and the cock-hole and the nose-hole as well as to all the other possible meanings of the word passages."[56] He had "the usual misgivings" and wondered

1. Charlotte Thomson, circa 1923

2. Charlotte and Herbert Gunn,
circa 1925

3. Thom Gunn and Alexander Thomson,
circa 1932

4. Herbert Gunn outside 4 Daylesford Road, Cheadle, 1938

5. Herbert and Charlotte Gunn with Ronald Hyde (third from left), 1938

6. Grove Cottage, 110 Frognal, Hampstead, where Thom lived between 1938 and 1945

7. Thom as Horatio in a University College School production of *Hamlet*, late 1946

Mother died
at 4.0 A.M, Friday,
DECEMBER 29TH
1944 —
She committed suicide
by holding a gas-pipe
to her head, and covering
it all with a tartan rug
we had. She was lying
on the sheepskin rug,
dressed in her beautiful
long, red dressing-gown
and pillows were under
her head. Her legs were
apart, one shoe half off
and her legs were
white and hard and cold,
and the hair seemed

out of place growing on
them.
We had awoken at 9.45,
and had dressed leisurely
but were puzzled by a
tender note against
the parlour door, saying
"Don't try to get in.
Ask Mrs Stoney to help you
darlings."
Then we realised that
both the parlour and
kitchen door were locked.
So we did go over to
Mrs Stoney, who lives
next door. But only
her son was in, she
having gone out shopping.
Then Ander tried the back
gate, which was unlocked
and went in through the
back door into the parlour
but I guesses—though I hardly dared
to even when I saw the note. I think

8. Thom's diary entry written in the days following his
mother's death, January 1945

9. Thom in the British Army, circa 1948

10. Mike Kitay and Thom outside Heidelberg Castle, summer 1953

11. Mike Kitay in the yard of 143 Alma Street, Palo Alto, circa 1957

12. Thom in Greenwich Village, New York City, summer 1956

13. Oliver Sacks, circa 1960   14. Yvor Winters, circa 1950s

15. Thom on the campus of the
University of California, Berkeley,
circa 1960

The ~~S.P.C.G.~~ / On the Move
'Man, you've got to go', ~~got~~

The blue jay scuffling in the bushes follows
Purpose of instinct
The gust of ~~birds~~ that spurts ~~across~~ across the field
Has an intention & some resting place.
~~But~~ One seeks the graceful instinct , and moves with uncertain violence.
~~(to the~~

We Scare the birds, whose value is in a nest, an egg;
~~Here~~ But man was made to frighten ~~him~~
    Scare himself to the future
    Mastered by ~~some~~ what he controls
    Not perfectly.
    Scare himself

Orderly as the flight of birds
Nearer until you see the goggles

Dots in the ~~distance~~ here the come, the Boys,
    the
Tough as they may, leather jackets ~~covered~~ Covered in dust
~~S~~ Hearing themselves in most noise.
    upon themselves,
They spin, intent, ~~past~~ in a second. They move because they move.

Meaningless to the passerby
Danger to themselves & to the old on foot.
They seem to go nowhere, just to go

Values come from an improvisation.
You have them, they are gone

It is a sort of self examination, a part solution
(this is the self examination) ~~For But~~ one is not damned becos, part animal
    One lacks direct instinct —
One is ~~not damned where we have woven of a valueless world~~
    ~~movement in a void~~ ~~towards toward~~ ~~& having left, always~~
    towards another
    one more
    By refusing to be pathetic
    Daring oneself
Driving ~~carrying~~ one's danger

    You hurl yourself into some future
    Complex as a city
    The least you'll get is freedom from other's slowing pity / & the most
    Self justification of the exertion for its own sake.

16. Manuscript draft of "On the Move," 1955

17. Marcia and Tony Tanner,
circa 1960

18. Don Doody and Thom,
San Francisco, circa 1963

19. Tony White and Thom, Cambridge,
circa 1965

20. Thom and Tony Tanner,
King's College, Cambridge, 1967

21. Thom, Bill Schuessler, and Mike Kitay
at Stinson Beach, summer 1967

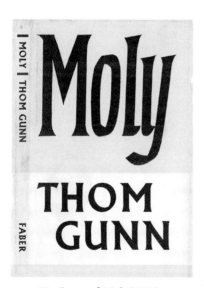

22. Cover of *Moly* (1971)

23. The Stud, 1535 Folsom Street,
San Francisco, 1970

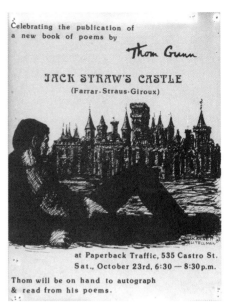

24. Mike Kitay and Bill Schuessler, circa 1969

25. Advertisement for
Jack Straw's Castle, 1976

26. Robert Duncan, circa 1970s

27. Entrance to the Mineshaft,
835 Washington Street, New York City, circa 1979

28. Thom's diary, June–July 1978

29. Thom in the yard at 1214–1216 Cole
Street, San Francisco, circa 1980

30. Ander Gunn, undated

31. The view from Thom's workroom, upstairs at the rear of 1214–1216 Cole Street, circa 1970s

32. Mike Kitay and Bob Bair, undated

33. Tony White (second from right), circa 1970s. Thom liked Tony's "big bear warmth" and stuck this photograph above his desk.

34. Norm Rathweg, circa 1980s

35. Charlie Hinkle, circa 1980s

36. Allan Noseworthy,
late 1982 or early 1983

LAMENT

Your dying was a difficult enterprise.
First, petty things took up your energies,
The small but clustering duties of the sick,
As irritant as the cough's dry rhetoric.

And hours of waiting for pills, shots, x-ray
Or test (while reading novels twice a day)
Already with a kind of clumsy stealth
Distanced you from the habits of your health.

[Filling your time with these officious, bland]
[routines and duties of an altered life]

In hope still, courteous, but tired and thin,
You tried to stay the man that you had been,
Treating each symptom as a mere mishap
Without import. But then the spinal tap : (or person?)
It brought a hard headache, and when night came
I heard you wake up from the same bad dream
Every half hour with the same short cry
Of mild outrage, before immediately
Slipping into the nightmare once again
Empty of content but the drip of pain.
No respite followed : though the nightmare ceased
Your cough grew thick and rich, its strength increased.
Till after four more nights we brought you from
To the Emergency Room. That frown, that frown
I'd never seen you show such rage before

Four nights,
that frown, that
frown!
Your face had never
shown such rage before

37. Early draft of "Lament," about Allan Noseworthy, August 1984

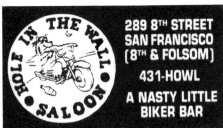

38. Mike Kitay and Wendy Lesser at
Thom's memorial at the
Doe Library, University of California,
Berkeley, August 2005

39. Advertisement for the
Hole in the Wall Saloon,
289 Eighth Street,
San Francisco, circa 1995

40. Thom outside 1214–1216 Cole Street, circa 1980s

how the collection would be received.[57] "I think its sexual content, as they say, will make it very embarrassing to reviewers," he told Douglas. "I suspect English reviewers will be unbelievably catty about it, as they well know how to be, and that American reviewers will simply not touch it. And yet I mean even the comic stuff seriously and want it to be taken seriously, as I think people shd always be interested by insights into another human being's experience. Maybe I'm wrong and they will be all delightfully fair and sympathetic."[58] But Thom had little time to dwell on its future reception. Knowing that he usually dried up after submitting a book, he had arranged the rest of 1981 to keep himself busy. For spring he lined up a three-week stint as a visiting poet at Amherst College; then, through autumn, he would be Elliston Poet-in-Residence at the University of Cincinnati. Preparing to leave for Massachusetts, Thom was rocked to learn that Mike and Bob were "apparently having great (unspecified) troubles, as each have told me separately. [. . .] Must the house be dismantled again? I have come to love Bob."[59]

Before arriving at Amherst, Thom gave readings at Dartmouth College and "the Eton of America," Phillips Exeter Academy. At the latter, "the content of some of Thom's poems and his unabashedly gay attire (leather jacket, skintight jeans, pointy-toed boots and earring) ruffled the feathers of many of the teachers."[60] At Amherst, Thom was "'Robert Frost Library Fellow in Poetry' (good lord)"[61] and tasked with giving a public lecture called "Yvor Winters, His Poetry and Opinions."[62] Otherwise, his schedule was light: he gave classes on Marvell's mower poems and held office hours for the students. Few came to see him, but one young local, Daniel Hall, took him to the Drake, a local dive bar, "and he enjoyed it so much we went back again the following night."[63] Thom spent most of his time alone, although he enjoyed hiking around Quabbin Reservoir with Joseph Langland, a poet who taught at the nearby University of Massachusetts. "He is nice, child-like in a good sense," Thom thought, "[and] showed me his favorite places, & where he has little bks of poetry or bottles of retsina hidden."[64] Allan Noseworthy visited for a weekend and introduced Thom to his college friends—two couples, John and Suzanne, and Tod and Margaret—who spent weekends in Massachusetts.

But the rest of his stay was "rather lonely and boring."[65] Rather than spend nights alone in his "pigsty" apartment, Thom often went to the movies and called them his "best friends here."[66] He saw *The Return of the Secaucus Seven* and wrote home: "you'd all like it, it's about us and all our friends if we were str**ght."[67]

After a month away, Thom returned to San Francisco in May. He spent a "lazy" summer, mostly alone at the house or among friends on Folsom.[68] In late July, he began an affair with a twenty-seven-year-old drifter named Joe Dunn. They met at the Brig, split some MDA, and spent the night on Cole Street. Joe was "everything one could want in bed," Thom told Douglas, "but out of bed was one of the more dumb, pretentious, and egotistical people I have ever had to do with."[69] Thom had not had a major infatuation since Allan in 1974. Joe's flightiness was attractive and dangerous and he made "AN3 look as stable as the Rock of Gibraltar."[70] Thom was a stickler for arrangements, timekeeping, and courtesy, but always forgave Joe for letting him down. "I am in love with Joe," Thom wrote on his fifty-second birthday, "for better or worse."[71] A few days later, Thom seemed to come to his senses after finding Joe passed out in a South of Market sex club. "I think I understand him much better now—a beautiful man, but so unstable, so fucked up," he reflected. "Maybe I shd open a home for wayward boys instead, then at least I'd get govt backing."[72] The affair petered out in part because Thom was due to fly east in late September to begin his Cincinnati residency. He put Joe up on Cole Street for a week before moving him to a South of Market rooming house. "Regret & relief in equal measures," he wrote. "I get so fond of people."[73]

In Cincinnati, Thom had a dormitory apartment on campus that overlooked "two highways—one of them just beyond a rather strikingly bare parking lot."[74] Don Bogen, a professor at Cincinnati—who had been Thom's teaching assistant at Berkeley in the mid-1970s—helped him with supplies and errands, but Thom was "mostly alone."[75] Downtown was "not much of a place to stroll—or be" and the locals were "friendly but unattractive."[76] The Cincinnati Art Gallery in Eden Park lasted him "several Saturdays," but the gay bars, Badlands Territory and

Under Construction, were woeful.[77] "The time certainly has changed when I <u>liked</u> being alone in a strange place, considering it a challenge," he told Clive Wilmer, "and I suspect having a fantasy about myself as a kind of Stendhalian hero to whom heaven knows what may happen any moment."[78] He attributed it to age: he seemed to have lost some appetite for risk and adventure, and some nights "end[ed] up feeling the most unattractive person in the bar."[79] He kept "very usefully occupied" on campus during the day, but found evenings "a terrible drag," split between reading *Middlemarch* and haunting the periodicals room of the university library.[80] When Mike phoned after a fortnight, it was "easily the best thing that has happened since I arrived."[81]

Thom's only real fun came during a visit to New York, where he "compressed into 5 days what I hadn't been able to do in 5 weeks." He spent nights at the Bar, Hellfire, and the Mineshaft; enjoyed *Taxi Zum Klo*, "a movie which is the story of all our lives";[82] and adored the "gorgeous punks" of the Lower East Side.[83] Listening to Allan Noseworthy discuss affairs and romances reminded Thom of Joe Dunn. Reporting the conversation to Mike, Thom wrote: "[Allan said,] 'Affairs are when you have lots of nice sex with somebody, and you have fun together and make each other feel good, but romances—' And I interrupted 'Are when you make each other feel bad?' 'Yes, that's right,' he said grinning. What a silly old sweetheart he is."[84]

As Elliston Poet-in-Residence, Thom gave a public reading, a lecture about his long poem "Misanthropos," and a lecture about Basil Bunting, whose poetry he had recently discovered. He called the Bunting lecture "an introduction" because professors in the Cincinnati English department would ask him: "'but <u>who</u> is Basil Bunting?' [. . .] pronouncing Basil in the American way, which indeed makes him sound very unfamiliar."[85] Preparing the lecture was slow and difficult work, and Bunting "more and more of a challenging subject the more I get into him."[86] Thom was keen to make a compelling case for Bunting, whom he considered "the best poet writing in English alive."[87] He shared Davie's view that "whatever BB's weaknesses of execution and theory, his actual practice is such as to make him the only poet in England who points a way forward, the grasp on what is important about his life being equaled by a grasp on language and the way it can be made to work rhythmically."[88] That way forward was most evident in Bunting's long poem *Briggflatts* (1966), which Thom found "perhaps the richest and most alive twenty pages of poetry written in the language this century." Bunting's attraction for Thom was a densely woven combination of qualities, from the "oppositions and contradictions" of Bunting's imagination—he was both poet and soldier; he knew "the North of England as only one born to a place can know it, but he also knows it only as one returning to it after long absence can know it"—to the "rich power of implication" in Bunting's "juxtapository method."[89] Such a method—as Bunting had learned from, and discussed with, Pound—was central to the idea of poetry as "condensation."[90] Thom agreed that "in condensed language thought and feeling are so concentrated that precisely *there* is that intensity of effect that the most admired poetry consists of."[91] Moreover, Bunting called *Briggflatts* "an autobiography, but not a record of fact," a description that resonated with Thom's own long-running conflict with personal poems.[92] Noting that "the personal is central to *Briggflatts*," Thom thought Bunting's statement meant "he has transposed and compressed, as all artists do, so as to make his instances more typical and at the same time more specific."[93] This was also a statement of Thom's method, in that he thought the personal was a much broader subject than simple autobiography allows. He placed *Briggflatts* "in the same class" as Robert Duncan's "A Poem Beginning with a Line by Pindar," not only for its "marriage of Modernist and Romantic possibilities" but also for its "personal enterprise . . . being both 'an autobiography' and a quest."[94] Bunting's method was not so much a model for Thom—as Duncan's was in terms of adventure, exploration, and process—but a jolt of recognition: "condensation" had been Thom's mode all his writing life. Moreover, he had long sought to write an intensely personal poetry that was, as Bunting put it, "not a record of fact," and had come to appreciate that the personal had to be an "enterprise" that combines inward look and outward quest. This is what Thom was getting at in "Interruption," where he writes:

Starting outside,
You save yourself some time while working in:
Thus by the seen the unseen is implied.
I like loud music, bars, and boisterous men.
You may from this conclude I like the things
That help me if not lose then leave behind,
What else, the self.[95]

Thom gave his Bunting lecture in mid-November and left town two weeks later. "He hated Cincinnati," Mike recalled. "First of all, he didn't like being away from home for that long. When Thom would come home, he was full of vinegar, telling you whatever he wanted to tell you. He loved to share funny experiences."[96] Those had been thin on the ground in Cincinnati, so Thom set about finding "loud music, bars, and boisterous men" in San Francisco. Almost immediately he hosted a four-way that became "a good long session on acid."[97] It was, he reflected, "wonderful to be home."[98]

28

FOREBODING

In July 1981, San Francisco suffered its worst fire since the 1906 earthquake. It started on the site of the old Barracks bathhouse and ripped through the mostly wooden warehouses and apartment blocks on Hallam and Brush, a cul-de-sac behind Folsom. Twenty-five buildings were damaged, eighteen destroyed, and more than a hundred people displaced. The *Bay Area Reporter* was critical of how the wider media reported the fire. "In his local news segment on Channel 4 [David] Fowler was devastating in his preoccupation with what he described as a 'Gay Ghetto,'" wrote Allen White. San Francisco fire chief Andrew Casper stated that "people may be chained to beds," and Fowler doubled down "with such phrases as 'slave headquarters,' 'sado-masochistic rituals' and references to the 'Gay bath house.'"[1]

Three days after the fire, Tony Tavarossi—the legendary local leatherman who had managed the Why Not?—died of a mysterious illness at San Francisco General. As the news spread, an impromptu "wake with free cocktails" was held in the Eagle and "at least 25 100-proof Schnapps wafted heavenward where . . . Tony was cruising a groovy angel."[2] Tavarossi was forty-seven. A fortnight before Tavarossi's death, the *Bay Area Reporter* had run its first article on Pneumocystis carinii pneumonia—what it called "Gay Men's Pneumonia"—and encouraged gay men experiencing "progressive shortness of breath" to visit their doctor.[3] It emerged that this strangely aggressive form of pneumonia had been the cause of

Tavarossi's death. Cases were also being reported in New York, as were cases of Kaposi's sarcoma, a rare cancer in which tumors appear on the skin as purple lesions. It was uncertain exactly what caused this cancer to affect otherwise healthy young men, but its spread in the gay community led to its being dubbed "gay cancer" and "gay plague." "The best evidence against contagion," remarked a doctor in *The New York Times*, "is that no cases have been reported to date outside the homosexual community or in women."[4] Between June 1, 1981, and September 5, 1982, the Centers for Disease Control and Prevention (CDC) recorded 593 cases of what was first called "Kaposi's sarcoma and opportunistic infections in previously healthy persons." Of those 593, "death occurred in 243 cases (41%)."[5]

Into the new year, Thom's most pressing concern was the household. Mike and Bob were breaking up; Thom hated being caught up in the tension. "I also feel very sorry for both of them," he told Douglas. "What a miserable business Romantic Love can be. Sometimes it seems to me one of the most monstrous and self-deceiving of human inventions. & I'm no cynic."[6] At Berkeley, Thom found his "'nerves' all shot."[7] It took Mike and Bob until April to "officially" separate: Mike left for a fortnight in Kearny and Bob moved into the front room. Thom felt "very comfortable" with Bob in Mike's absence.[8] They needed each other's support because, upstairs, Bill and Jim were in "one of their peep periods."[9] One night, Thom heard Jim cry out upstairs. "I run up," Thom wrote, "& he is giving the kiss of life to Bill, who has stopped breathing." By the time an ambulance arrived, Bill had revived. Thom was "very angry" and told Bill "he must take responsibility for his actions and not be a baby."[10] "The rule for our house seems to be: When things stop jumping on one floor, they start on the other," he wrote Mike. "Maybe I'll go back to Cincinnati. I'm afraid this is just not a good year for any of us."[11] Thom could only process what had happened once Mike was back from Kearny. "After everybody has gone to bed I cry uncontrollably, but without sadness for anything," he wrote, "simply to get rid of all the tears that had collected inside of me. Delayed shock, perhaps."[12]

At the bars, a "notable rejection" made Thom "wonder what I will find as substitute for sex?"[13] "Why is my impulse to write poetry so closely connected—so much a part of—my sexual impulse?" he wondered, and considered it his "limitation." "I feel it necessary sometimes to steer my energy into nonsexual subjects almost by an act of will, since I don't believe all the important parts of life are sexual," he reflected. "And when I succeed in doing so, I'm quite often successful. Yet it does, even then, derive from an energy that is sexual energy—it's the same kind of concentrated excitement that lights up everything in a limited area."[14] By May, he had not written "any real poetry worth calling such" for about a year but hoped that, with *The Passages of Joy* coming out in the summer, he would make a tentative start on some new poems. In the meantime, he was "sensible and practical" and kept himself active writing criticism "by an act of will."[15] He wrote about Bunting, Eliot, and Pound for the *PN Review* and about Bunting for *The Threepenny Review*.[16]

In spring, Thom gave a version of his Bunting introduction at 544 Natoma, the first openly gay arts and performance space in San Francisco.[17] In the audience was August Kleinzahler, a young poet who had been Bunting's student a decade earlier.[18] Kleinzahler was in his early thirties and had just moved to San Francisco: he lived on Frederick, a few blocks down the hill from Thom. To Kleinzahler, it seemed "somewhat implausible" that this "rather traditional English poet" was going to talk about Bunting at a venue "usually given over to colossally boring readings and talks by LANGUAGE poets and theorists in the deconstruction mode." But he went and was "unusually impressed."[19] Kleinzahler sent Thom a copy of his debut collection, *A Calendar of Airs*, and Thom invited him for a beer on Cole Street. Kleinzahler realized he had met Thom before: his gay older brother had introduced them over the pool table at the International Stud in New York in 1970. "One time my brother introduced me to a 'famous English poet,' a tall, handsome-looking galoot in a T-shirt and leather vest, with lurid tattoos on his arms," he recalled. "He didn't look like any sort of poet to me, more like a predatory sex addict. Had someone told me then that he would become one of my dearest friends I would have laughed in disbelief."[20] Thom's friendship with Kleinzahler became one of the most satisfying of his life. They attended readings together and went on martini-fueled cinema trips; August brought beer to Cole and told stories about Bunting; Thom helped August find a British publisher. "Thom was interested in my poetry, and I was evolving then," he reflected. "I'd send stuff I was working on to him, and he'd write back, usually a postcard. That went on for years."[21] Although Thom was concerned that August's scope was "ultimately too confined," he still called him "the ideal heir of WCW [and] better than anybody on this continent of his age (30 or so) that I have read."[22]

In July, Allan visited Cole Street. His new job, membership director of the Saint, a gay nightclub in New York—"like a maitre d's job for 3,000 queers every weekend"—meant he was in the best financial shape of his life and could afford to send money home to his family in Ohio. Allan also volunteered at Gay Men's Health Crisis, a community-led group that provided support to gay men who had contracted Kaposi's sarcoma and pneumocystis. When he arrived in San Francisco, one of his friends was seriously ill with Kaposi's. Michael Maletta, with whom Allan had worked at the Creative Power Foundation, was in San Francisco General. "I tried calling him but had to hang up," Allan told Thom. "I just didn't know what to say. So, I wrote him a little note."[23] Maletta was diagnosed in late 1981; he was thirty-nine when he died in August 1982. Allan attended the memorial service in the Castro. Maletta was praised in the *Bay Area Reporter* for his contribution to the gay community through the big parties he organized at the Creative Power Foundation. "He made things happen that never would have happened otherwise," remarked a friend. "He changed people's lives."[24] Not everyone agreed. "You can't disco and popper your way to Gay Liberation," replied gay rights advocate Arthur Evans. "The lifestyle we have created for ourselves is as lethal to us as the Moral Majority."[25] Maletta's death occurred at a time when knowledge of the disease was still scant. In June, the CDC made the first connection between possible sexual transmission and the outbreaks of Kaposi's sarcoma, Pneumocystis carinii pneumonia, and other opportunistic infections among gay men.[26] The disease was informally called GRID—Gay-Related Immune Deficiency; the term "AIDS"—Acquired Immune Deficiency Syndrome—was not used until September.[27]

As he had predicted, Thom began writing tentatively again in the summer. He worked on "a Haight St poem" called "Skateboard," about a tow-headed boarder he used to see on the street. Its muscular free verse recalls "Bally *Power Play*," as does its central figure, "emblem extraordinary / of the ordinary."[28] In August he finished the five-part "Bow Down"—originally called "City Poem (San Francisco)"—but had "no confidence in it."[29] "Most of the poem is about something I have worked to death," he told Belle Randall, "the notion of the interchangeableness of personality or even identity, especially in dream."[30] Feeling "discouraged," he resolved to "go back to meter—the meter of To Penshurst & To Sir Robert Wroth." He wanted a "synthesis of styles" but was unsure how to combine them. "I move from free verse to meter, from meter to free verse," he reflected, "hoping that by doing so I will infect the one with the virtues of the other."[31] He began a poem called "Thinking of M at RR," which, over the next year, he would revise into a poem about recovery called "To a Friend in Time of Trouble." Its couplets marked Thom's return to meter, and the poem as a whole combines his interests in mind and body: hard physical work creates inner tranquility. Thom pictured Mike alone at the cabin, dealing with the "grief and rage" of his on-again-off-again relationship with Bob. Mike was always willing to help and counsel others: he "learns, and learns" in order to share his knowledge.[32] "I thought it would be nice if I was that person," Mike reflected, "but I don't think of myself that way."[33] But that was how Thom saw him: he learned from Mike's ability to learn from experience. His long block after *Jack Straw's Castle* taught Thom that writing "had become through the years a stage in the process of my dealing with what happened to me—not the first stage and not the last one either, but an important one, for me, in considering it and following through its verbal implications." Every important matter became, "sooner or later, sometimes much later, subject to the worrying out that attends composition."[34]

Thom's lack of confidence likely stemmed from the reviews of *The Passages of Joy*. "Apart from Davie & Ricks, transatlantic travellers, it is a massacre," he thought. "Ranging from snide to vicious. Ian Hamilton crowns a career based on malice. Still, it's what I might have expected, however disappointing."[35] Hamilton scorned the "good deal of 'coming out'" in *Passages*: "coming out of men's rooms, gay bars, one-night stands. Much of this, however, is done with the dizzy relish of one who has for years believed that he would never get to write about such things." The book was "wet and bogus."[36] This marked the nadir of Thom's English reputation. Gavin Ewart called him "a very talented writer who has not found very much to write about—though he has tried." His condescension was born of a received idea: that Thom was doomed as soon as he "moved to the States, and began to write American."[37] In the United States, *Passages* was well but not widely reviewed. "These poems are smart, sincere, humane," wrote Mark Caldwell in *The Village Voice*, "but tamer than Gunn's own experiences suggest they ought to be."[38] The *San Francisco Chronicle*—in, remarkably, their first full review of one of Thom's books—praised his "deep empathy and understanding of others and their problems."[39] Mary Kinzie praised *Passages* in *The American Poetry Review* and called "Talbot Road" "the clear triumph" of the book.[40] In *The Threepenny Review*, Don Bogen called *Passages* "a vigorous and important book."[41] The reviewer for *The Advocate*, America's major gay magazine, thought Thom was "at the peak of his poetic powers."[42]

Thom's exception of Donald Davie was complicated. Davie reviewed *The Passages of Joy* and *The Occasions of Poetry*, Thom's prose collection that was published at the same time, in what Thom called the only review "that addresses itself responsibly to questions of style and subject matter."[43] Davie called *Passages* "as fine a collection as [Gunn] has ever published" but felt it "lacks the resonances that some of us have come to expect and delight in."[44] The implication of Davie's review, although he does not directly say it, is that Thom's poetry had declined since he had come out. Davie told Thom that "between the lines" of the review he should read that "Gay Liberation has been bad for you because it necessarily foreshortens your historical perspectives to post-Enlightenment times, in ethics and consequently in politics, in aesthetics, even in metaphysics." He thought it "not just priggish prejudice" that made him "prefer those earlier poems of yours where your sexual proclivities were left ambiguous and undefined (as after all were Marlowe's)." But a "priggish prejudice" colored Davie's tone in their correspondence. "Who am I to be required to explain myself as to homosexuality in poetry," he asked Thom: "the testimony of the centuries is on my (heterosexual) side, and if the onus of justification lies anywhere, it lies with you and your fellow-Gays, not with me."[45] Davie had joked, in an earlier letter, that Thom must think him "a scourge of the 'gays.'"[46] Thom disagreed but questioned Davie's doubt, apparently expressed in a letter to Marjorie Perloff, that "a homosexual (except, you rather sweetly said, for me) could write good poetry. I've thought about this statement for several years, and I still don't know how you could deny the title of poet to say Marlowe or Whitman."[47] A decade later, when Clive Wilmer asked Thom about Davie's review, Thom was phlegmatic. "I'm terrifically grateful for that essay and for everything Donald has written about me," he remarked. "Nevertheless, his particular point [in the review] is that coming into the open about homosexuality— not *being* homosexual, but *speaking* about it openly—has been a diminishing force in my poetry. I don't see that at all."[48] Theirs was an unusual and unexpected friendship. "He has about the best critical mind around at least for poetry being written, and I am proud to be the object of its, er, scrutiny," Thom told Douglas. "He may be basically homophobic, but he tries not to be, and he is certainly <u>fair</u>."[49] Thom did not forget Davie's review. He told Wilmer that, while writing his next book, *The Man with Night Sweats*, "something that was in my mind the whole time . . . was how can I show [Davie] that he's wrong?"[50]

Thom felt full of "good fruitful thoughts" but struggled to write.[51] He was either too lonely or too busy. Mike and Bob, reconciled again, were at the cabin; then, through the autumn, Thom hosted his niece, Charlotte. At twenty, she struck him as feckless and sheltered; Thom gave her his room and moved upstairs to his workroom. "She is a darling, and everybody likes her," he reflected, "and she seems to like everybody."[52] At first he thought her a "perfect guest" but, "not happy as a host," his patience quickly frayed.[53] "Even though he was incredibly social and generous of spirit, he did have his limitations," Charlotte reflected. "He should have said to me, Charlotte, you've been here long enough. You're cramping my style. Can you just . . . move on now? But he didn't. Perhaps like my father, he didn't like confrontation like that. It's funny because they're both very outspoken and say what they think, but perhaps they find confrontation uncomfortable."[54] Bob thought Thom's behavior was "shocking." "We didn't understand why he was so cruel to her," he reflected. "He didn't like the idea of someone being around who wasn't hip, who didn't get his scene."[55] Mike thought Thom was "nasty" to Charlotte because "he was embarrassed a little bit, because she was so provincial."[56] For Charlotte, Thom was "a typical Thomson—outspoken, never letting anything lie, picking up things and talking about them, challenging them." One evening, they watched Jonathan Miller's *King Lear* on television. "I remember laughing at something," Charlotte recalled. "He looked at me and went, 'Hmm. I've never heard anyone laugh at *that* part of *King Lear* before.' I immediately felt very small, and that I shouldn't have laughed when I wanted to laugh." Thom "would leap down your throat if you put a toe out of place. Mike would just shrug his shoulders sometimes at Thom's behavior. Mike and Bob were always the sweet ones. They could see it all happen."[57]

Charlotte stayed for five weeks. "Thom showed me around a little bit," she recalled, "and then he just left me to it when he realized I wasn't just staying a week." Thom carried on with his daily life, with Charlotte sometimes tagging along: it was not quite an example of his sometimes childish desire to shock, but Thom did not want to conceal anything from her. On one occasion, Thom took her to a joint reading with Michael McClure at Cody's bookstore in Berkeley. Driving back across the Bay Bridge in McClure's car, Thom "got a twenty-dollar bill out and they both snorted cocaine. I know my uncle Thom did it because he wanted to be naughty," Charlotte reflected, "because he had this virginal, heterosexual, nondrinking, non-drug-taking niece come to see him. He knew I was in awe of him, which he was uncomfortable with, and by the end of the stay I wasn't quite so in awe of him." On another occasion, Charlotte was reading *Tess of the d'Urbervilles* "in this kind of cubbyhole next to the kitchen. Thom came out [of his room], naked, with a bloke or two, and he was laughing away . . . He saw me there and I must've looked a bit shocked. He saw that I was reading *Tess* and made some remark about Thomas Hardy. He opened the fridge, took out some beers, and went back to his room."[58] When Charlotte returned to England, Thom wrote that it had been a "great pleasure having you here, and getting to know you a little bit—the little bit that I do know you."[59] He told Barbara that Charlotte "kept me more at arm's length than she did some of my friends" and thought she had been "in awe of the 'famous poet.' A pity," he thought, "since for me one of the advantages of living in SF is that here no one has heard of me, and I certainly don't put on airs."[60]

With few exceptions, Mike thought Thom "wasn't good with women."[61] His world, since moving to California, was almost exclusively masculine: masculinity attracted and interested him; femininity did not.[62] At Berkeley, Thom taught women and had female colleagues, but the main women in his Californian life initially came from Mike's involvement in the theater scene. In the late 1950s and early 1960s, Mike's patron, Sheilah Dorcy, often visited and monopolized Mike's attention. Thom, jealous, tried to provoke her. "When Thom first knew her, he would say, 'Come here Sheilah, I have something to tell you.' She'd go over and in her ear he'd go, 'Fuck fuck fuck fuck fuck,' gradually getting louder," Mike recalled. "She wanted me to herself. One time, things were tense because she didn't want Thom around, so she shoved him into his room and closed the door."[63] That jealousy was early enough in their relationship that Thom likely still had Polly Wilkes in mind—worried he had lost Mike only months after they had first gotten together.

On other occasions, Thom could exercise a flippant misogyny. "I'm sorry I told [Forrest Gander's] sister that 'oh, women don't matter,'" he wrote to August Kleinzahler, "but it was the Kingsley Amis in me, and the shock my remark registered was amply worth the untruth. (Of course women matter: they cook us cakes, don't they?)"[64] He could also betray a touch of misogyny when discussing female poets. In the 1950s, for example, he called Marianne Moore a "typical woman writer" but later included her in his laudatory essay "Three Hard Women." In that essay, he deliberately avoided using the term "poetess" because "it is not without its associations, and they are precisely those that Moore and Loy were trying to escape from."[65] He valued the work of Elizabeth Bishop, Janet Lewis, and Ruth Pitter and often taught female poets who he felt were undervalued and deserving of a wider reputation, like Mina Loy and Lorine Niedecker, and, later, emerging poets like Daisy Fried.

Although he saw Belle Randall infrequently, they maintained a warm correspondence and Thom was highly supportive of her poetry and fiction. His main female friend in the Bay Area was Wendy Lesser. Theirs had begun as a professional relationship: in 1980, Thom joined Lesser's new magazine, *The Threepenny Review*, as a commissioning poetry editor, "imposing the condition that he really be allowed to do work for it." Thom resigned after twelve issues, telling Lesser, "in essence, that now that we had definitely made it he felt able, in good conscience, to resign his official position."[66] Thom continued to work for *Threepenny* in an unofficial capacity—as well as contributing poems and reviews regularly—and his friendship with Lesser blossomed. "He was comfortable with her, in her world, and he liked her," recalled the poet Robert Glück. "I would see them at events together and they were on each other's arm."[67] In letters "he would often address me as if he were talking to Pip out of *Great Expectations* or something," Wendy reflected, "but not as though I belonged to that despised female category or anything like that."[68] Ultimately, Thom was a homosexual man who was attracted to masculine men. Taking him in his time and place: most of his colleagues at Berkeley were men, most of his students were men (although two of his best—Belle and Deborah Treisman[69]—were women), most of his friends were men, and all his lovers were men. Very few women had any part in his life once he left England.

Thom's general indifference toward women was one response to his mother's suicide. Women like Thérèse Megaw and his aunts Barbara, Mary, and Catherine were caregivers whom Thom needed during his adolescence—Helena Shire performed a comparable role at Cambridge— but they were also part of the England he had chosen to leave. His mother's suicide set Thom's attitudes toward women for the rest of his life: they were flighty, self-dramatizing, not to be trusted. His flippant behavior—

"they cook us cakes, don't they?"—was part of the armor with which he had equipped himself after his mother's death. Margaret Baron (now Owen)—Thom and Mike's friend at Cambridge—felt that Thom's "great warmth" for his friends masked the intimacy he was unable to give. "In Thom's eyes there was always that tragedy of his mother's suicide," she reflected. "That child of fifteen had nothing."[70] One woman, his lost mother, had played an outsized role in his early life. Caught between wanting to forgive and wanting to blame, Thom never got over losing her.

Through 1982–83, Berkeley converted from quarters to semesters. Thom decided to teach the spring semester full time and give a literature class on top of his two creative writing classes. He spent December "working my ass off" planning the literature class, a survey of twentieth-century poetry from Eliot, Pound, and Stevens to Bishop, Bunting, and Duncan.[71] The change in system meant Thom would teach fifteen weeks instead of ten; this drained his energies and gave him less time to write. With the domestic situation on Cole Street remaining tense, and with a constant stream of guests through the winter and spring, Thom spent more time than usual in his Berkeley office. "For once I am trying to disregard emotional home dramas," he wrote. "I just can't deal with them."[72] Absenting himself, however, led to internal struggles. "Impelled into so many actions through fear, during them haunted by fear," he reflected, "I am today suddenly astonished to think that anybody could be considered weaker than me."[73] He thought about "my mother, Tony. The most poignant loss is of the sense of loss itself."[74] Thom felt he was slowing down as a poet—gaps between collections became progressively longer—and his worries about writing ran in tandem with his fears about aging and how he would cope without sex. "'Wanting to be a poet' this is probably the most heroic thing to 'be.' Better than a novelist, more romantic somehow. It sums up freedom of activity, the imaginative life, on all levels," he wrote. "A poet is only a poet while he is writing poetry . . . and that, perhaps, is why the name and role of poet continue to elusively attract me: here is my row of books on the shelf, but that is dead achievement, that is by another self—he possessed a mysterious power of imagination and understanding: I would like to be him. I would like to be a poet."[75]

Alongside Thom's anxieties was the worsening threat of AIDS. In January, Ward 86, the world's first dedicated outpatient AIDS clinic, opened at San Francisco General. Until now, Thom had not engaged deeply with the ongoing health crisis but received regular updates from Allan in New York. "Another friend died of Aids yesterday," Allan wrote in mid-February. "It's been on N.B.C. news every night this week."[76] In May, Thom wrote in his diary: "I make certain notes about sex, becos of prevalence of Kaposi's Sarcoma. Hygiene, Restraint, Selectivity, Rationality. After all, I do like living."[77] In later years, Mike often joked that "Gunn control" was an oxymoron. "Thom always wondered how all these people he knew got it and he didn't," Mike reflected. "God knows he was sexually active."[78] Thom still believed in promiscuity as a way of life—he called it "an entrance into all humanity"[79]—but realized that there was a greater need for caution. "I try not to go to the Caldron (in fact I go only about twice a month), because of AIDS," he told Douglas. "I keep thinking I shd make out with less people, but God keeps throwing such wonderful-looking men in my path. Maybe I shd cynically get a lover for the sake of hygiene . . ."[80] The Caldron, a sex club on Natoma, opened in 1980 and was extraordinarily popular; Thom called it "Mine Shaft West (i.e. with smiles)."[81] He eventually let his membership lapse. "I haven't been there in some time & I guess I'd better not go again," he told Douglas a month later. "What a pity that such a generous place shd come to an end, but it's necessary for all the sex-places to, I guess. I'm trying just to have sex with a few regulars & making it as safe as possible. (Prodding each other with broomsticks held in welding-gloves.) No more 'exchange of body fluids,' alas."[82]

Thom thought "AIDS presaging a new era" was a good subject for a poem: "look back on last 20 years as a golden age of permissiveness betw penicillin & AIDS."[83] Trying to write it, though, "words go dead on me," Thom remarked, and ascribed his difficulties to "post-publication blues."[84] A review of Robert Creeley's *Collected Poems* was one of only two things Thom published in 1983—the other was "Bow Down"—but writing essays gave Thom "the feeling of being still a writer, and also the chance to exercise my small intelligence."[85] An essay about Winters was less successful: Thom gave it up midway through a fourth draft "and threw the whole thing across the room in exasperation." His tentative return to writing the previous summer had proven a false start. "I wonder if my life is worth anything at all, which is silly because I think I make several people happy (as they do me)," he told Ander, "thus I am delighted when anything, even a review can prove to me that I can still put two words together in a way that is meaningful."[86] Writing two years to the day since submitting the manuscript of *Passages*, Thom thought about how he could break his writing jinx. One option was to mimic Robert Duncan, who, after publishing *Bending the Bow* in 1968, entered a self-imposed publishing exile and vowed not to publish another full collection for fifteen years. "Fifteen years: 1997? Hmm, seems rather a long time," Thom reflected, "I'd be almost 70." He compromised with himself and planned not to publish his next book "at least till I'm halfway into the book after the one I haven't even started yet."[87]

Thom liked to adopt a sunny disposition, but constant worries—both at home and abroad—affected his mood more than he cared to admit. In May he learned that Ander and Margaret were to separate; in the summer, he learned Tony Tanner had suffered "the worst breakdown of all."[88] Thom felt sad for Ander—he wrote, saying "you are loved and admired more than you suspect"[89]—but was even sadder for Tony. "You see people disappearing down a whirling funnel," he told Douglas, "and there's nothing you can do to help them."[90]

In San Francisco, Clint Cline, one of Thom's oldest friends, had suffered a heart attack and needed surgery. Since living together, briefly, in 1960, Thom had seen Clint regularly. Theirs was a light, convivial friendship, sustained over drinks in Badlands, Clint's local bar, but Thom was always there to support Clint when he needed help. At Clint's request, Thom attended his "holy union" to his lover, Bill Coleman, who was dying of terminal cancer, an experience that Thom "found . . . v difficult."[91] Similarly, Thom helped Clint deal with his "emotional trouble" when it began to emerge that "he was a battered child."[92] "Thom was very loyal to friends, particularly if they were needy in some way," Mike reflected. "It's quite possible Clint needed money. Thom would never mention anything like that, that he had given somebody money."[93]

Clint had "a 50% chance" of surviving the "open heart surgery (again) & a bypass," Thom wrote. "He is relaxed, sweet, generous as always."[94] Clint survived the operation but suffered kidney problems, contracted an infection, and became "deeply depressed."[95] The infection spread to Clint's right arm and caused the amputation of a finger. "I'm afraid he will lose the arm," Thom told Barbara. "He is only a year or two older than I am but he has started to look as if he is 90." Thom "really hate[d] visiting hospitals . . . but when I remember how much visits meant to me when I had hepatitis in 1963 I know it's worth it, so I grit my teeth and get on the bus!"[96] Thom offered to put Clint up on Cole Street while he recovered, "as he'll need a bit of nursing."[97] Clint left the hospital in September and returned home. Thom visited him twice a week for the rest of the year and helped him with things he could no longer do, like cutting his fingernails.

Thom began to see death all around him. The *Bay Area Reporter* published a front-page article about fears that visitors to the gay pride parade in June would spread AIDS and that bathhouse owners should do more to educate their customers about the virus.[98] The San Francisco Board of Supervisors unanimously approved $2.1 million for AIDS projects, on top of the $2 million budgeted for AIDS by the city's Department of Public Health.[99] For all that support, Thom knew he would make plenty more hospital visits in the coming years. When it looked as though Clint might not survive, Thom reread "the 2nd of Donne's Anniversaries again," the long poem "Of the Progress of the Soul," which Donne wrote to commemorate the death of Elizabeth Drury.[100] Thom had first read the poem at Cambridge, three decades ago, and knew it well. Now, in summer 1983, he felt death approach:

> Thinke then, My soule, that death is but a Groome,
> Which brings a Taper to the outward roome,
> Whence thou spiest first a little glimmering light,
> And after brings it nearer to thy sight;
> For such approches doth Heaven make in death.[101]

29

ALLAN

"This is the most fantastic July weather ever," Thom wrote. "But I am drained of language."[1] Unable to write, Thom gardened and went to the movies instead. Old friends kept showing up, like Larry Hoyt one Sunday afternoon at the Eagle. "We ran around together for quite a while when he was 21!" Thom told Douglas Chambers. "Now he is over 30, very handsome, & was in full leather. Luckily he is a gerontophile so he spotted my double chin, my hundred of grey hairs, my craggy face etc. & we had a riotous evening together at home."[2]

Thom also made some new friends. At the Castro Street Fair he ran into "a handsome tall boy with bike boots outside Lp & a T shirt saying 'Mean & Weak.'" They went back to Cole Street, took speed, and had "wonderful sex together, from 6pm to about 3am . . . His name is Randy Glaser . . . as bright as he is handsome & sexy. I could really fall for him. I wonder if I will." Randy was a curly-haired, green-eyed pastry chef; at twenty-seven he was exactly half Thom's age.[3] Almost immediately, Thom started to write about him: "I am 54 / but then I think of Jonson / his 7 & 40 years / making fun of his own looks," he wrote, recalling Ben Jonson's "My Picture Left in Scotland," in which Jonson mused that no amount of sweet talk could persuade his young love to "embrace / My mountain belly and my rocky face."[4] Thom knew about infatuation and wondered if it was "all a mirror / merely a form of my self-regarding?" But he also "recognise[d] selfless love in myself / & will wait for it &

strive for it."[5] Randy became Thom's regular lover. "He has it all," Thom told Douglas. "He is also fun to be with, intelligent, and barely literate. I'm just keeping up with him sexually. Aren't gerontophiles wonderful? (I was 54 yesterday.) He looks great in leather & has a big cock."[6] He found it "difficult to believe that [Randy] is as infatuated w/ me as I am with him, but I think he is."[7]

Infatuation, combined with worries about AIDS, made Thom consider monogamy. This was unusual for him, but he was "crazy about [Randy]."[8] However, as the weeks passed, he felt strange that love had not followed infatuation. "Oddly enough, I'm not in love," he told Douglas, "I'm not sure why."[9] Less strange, however, was that, since meeting Randy, Thom had felt "the old Creative Juices . . . stirring again."[10] He quickly wrote "Well Dennis O'Grady" and "Outside the Diner," which with "Skateboard" formed "a sort of dwarfish triptych of the streets." They were a start, but Thom wanted "to produce a few chubby poems, positively belching from their repleteness with the morsels of experience."[11] That meant returning to meter. "I'm working diffidently at a few rhymes," he told Douglas. "I think I have to get back to meter for a while—to hell with what's fashionable, free verse is too limiting."[12] A rare visit to see Mike and Bob at the Russian River saw Thom "getting lost" in Yeats and returning to notes made the previous year: by December, he had finished "To a Friend in Time of Trouble."[13]

In New York, Thom stayed with Allan for a fortnight. They had known each other for almost a decade, during which Allan had become more emotionally sure of himself, a little less vulnerable, but remained the "pure of heart" softie Thom loved.[14] "A[llan] no longer equates love with hysteria," Thom wrote after Allan split with his porn-star boyfriend, Richard Locke, "which is terrific."[15] In memory of Michael Maletta, Allan had cofounded the AIDS Resource Center in New York; by the autumn, the ARC had begun to offer housing to destitute AIDS patients. Allan himself was "rather sick" and "[slept] a lot," leaving Thom to catch up with old friends like Robert Mapplethorpe, Ralph Pomeroy, and Ted Tayler.[16]

Back in San Francisco, Thom's affair with Randy began to fade. "Though we have a sensational time in bed," he told Douglas, "I am afraid I'm really terribly bored with everything about him that cannot be used sexually."[17] Thom probably thought Randy was tiring of him. "Back home we have rather fast sex," Thom wrote on one occasion, "& he does not stay the night, although he has said he will earlier."[18] Although he valued flightiness and risk, Thom liked to know where he stood: anticipation and delay were just as thrilling as the sex itself, and he did not like to be let down or have somebody change his mind. Thom wrote about Randy and his "great / Halo of aureate-/ brown curls" and "hard-filled lean / Body" in "Bone," a poem he later called "a piece of elegant self-delusion."[19] They still saw each other through December, but Thom's infatuation with Randy was already over. Perhaps on account of Randy's physique, Thom joined a nearby gym. Bob joined, too. "We work very hard down there and look like gods," Thom told Charlotte. "That's not really true: we look much the same, but we _feel_ like gods. Everybody else in the house is rather sarcastic (jealous?) about us."[20] Thom did not like to see himself or his friends age. When Isherwood and Bachardy visited, Thom found it "surprisingly boring, lots of small talk and not much else. Ish himself is lots more doddery, on his feet and in his memory. He was really quite vague."[21]

That Christmas, Thom invited Paul Joseph—Bill's friend and sometime dealer—for dinner at Cole Street. Joseph had AIDS: he had had "a series of illness[es] that always looked like flu all year," Thom told Douglas, "so he really only has a year of life left." Joseph was the first friend of the house to have AIDS; it made Thom "think of Tom Nashe's poems about the plague."[22] He had in mind "Autumn hath all the summer's fruitful treasure," from Nashe's play _Summer's Last Will and Testament_:

> London doth mourn, Lambeth is quite forlorn;
> Trades cry 'Woe worth' that ever they were born.
> The want of term is town and city's harm;
> Close chambers we do want to keep us warm.
> Long banished must we live from our friends;
> This low-built house will bring us to our ends.
> From winter, plague, and pestilence, good Lord deliver us![23]

Thom copied "This low-built house will bring us to our ends" into his notebook and listed the nine people he knew who had, or had died of, AIDS.[24] Another Nashe couplet from the same poem—"Cold doth increase, the sickness will not cease, / And here we lie, God knows, with little ease"—echoes Thom's interest in confined and troublesome spaces. The "Little Ease" of "Jack Straw's Castle," a cell where one cannot stand, sit, or lie, now looked like a grave.[25]

Christmas proved a disaster. "We sat down to the meal & [Paul] started coughing & rubbing great globs of spit into the cloth," Thom told Douglas. "He then started (he thought surreptitiously) licking bits of food & placing them on people's plates. Since he has AIDS, this wasn't nice. So I asked him to leave & when he refused I & Bob & Jim & Bill carried him out (he resisting), put him in Jim's car, drove him home, wrestled him into his building's doorway, & left him there."[26] Thom had a better Boxing Day. "I go to Trax, see what I take to be a hustler—rather long hair, blond, stocky, & the kind of face that slays me—playing pool & video machines," Thom wrote. "I go to DeLuxe, return, he comes over, & says 'You're hot.' I bring him back for a GOOD night of coke & leather & love. He is 26, went to Wesleyan, has travelled a lot, works in a warehouse & likes Moly the best of my books."[27] Charlie Hinkle was also a poet. Thom ran errands the next morning and left him asleep in bed. "He had to leave before I returned," Thom wrote. "Boy am I lucky."[28]

Thom saw Charlie almost every day for the next fortnight. They made a date for New Year's Eve but Thom felt "slightly uneasy" that Randy was still on the scene. "It's good to be off with the old love, Mr. Gunn," he admonished himself, "before you are on with the new."[29] A "good, nice, honest, explanatory" hour with Randy made his feelings clear.[30] Thom and Charlie hit the bars, from Rawhide and Line-Up to Manollo's and Stables, and were among the thousands-strong crowd that amassed in the Castro to protest Dan White's release from prison.[31] Charlie came for family dinner on Cole Street. "Of course everyone likes him," Thom wrote. "We go to Stables, a very sleazy empty bar nowadays, & have a hugely good time. We eat after at Orphan Andy's, come home, have sex, hug all night."[32]

The new romance contributed to what Thom called a period of "exceptionally good health."[33] He felt euphoric and vigorous, but beneath his excitement about Charlie was another feeling. Thom could not shake the fear that Charlie—who, like Randy, was half Thom's age—would quickly grow bored and leave him. He did not think he could "satisfy him sexually. Not completely, that is."[34] Thom felt teenage pleasure and anxiety. After a movie, they slept "with the sound of a thin rain. Wonderful to wake with him, his blond hair all over pillow, & have sex with him."[35] He loved the "deeply shared intimacy" of waking together, and sleeping "always in contact, lightly, an arm about a waist, bodies touch at the hips, or at the farthest with our feet resting against each other."[36] He knew it was too good to last. When Charlie returned from a family visit to Washington, DC, Thom could not get hold of him and wondered if he had been "jilted."[37] Thom was wrong but knew he should manage his expectations. "I am crazy about him but I guess shd settle for friendship," he reflected. "He is 26, his energy takes him in every direction, he has everything to give to the whole world, & my instincts with him are greedy & possessive as in a French novel."[38]

When Thom did not see Charlie for another fortnight, he felt "awful" and "walked & moped. I guess Charlie has lost interest in me."[39] Thom had "seldom been hurt by my jealousy," he claimed, "but always by a feeling of neglect. With Charlie, I find myself recognizing the torments of imagined neglect by first TW & then MK. Is that then what it's really about? Or, is that what I want? No, I do not think so. But the feeling of not-being-important in some way balances out the feeling-of-being-important. And I suppose I do need that: the feeling of being important."[40] Thom began writing "The Differences," a poem about Charlie. It focused on their most intimate moment—sleeping together, their bodies touching—and inevitable fade. They had been "touching at the hips, / As if we were two trees, bough grazing bough, / The twigs being the toes or fingertips."[41] He drew a deliberate comparison with "To a Friend in Time of Trouble." In that poem, Mike enacts "a giving of the self," whereas Thom, in "The Differences," "tried to lose my self in you" but "turned into the boy with iron teeth." The next time they met, Charlie told Thom he wanted to pursue graduate work in Portuguese literature and planned to spend the next year living in Brazil.[42]

Two quickfire romances had excited Thom's imagination and he hoped to "write one poem a month this year!"[43] Despite the new fifteen-week semester—"In the eleventh week an alarm started going in the heads of me and all my students: <u>term should be over</u>, it shrieked"[44]—he had managed to finish "To a Friend in Time of Trouble," "An Invitation," "Bone," and "The Differences" since December. He looked forward to "a summer of poetry writing (I hope), reading, exercise, & Latin grammar."[45] He also had sick friends in mind. Robert Duncan was recuperating from "massive kidney failure" and receiving "dialysis three times a week."[46] Another friend, Roy Siniard, had developed a form of motor neuron disease and planned to leave San Francisco. Thom went to his farewell party at the Ambush. "He is 46, has 1–5 more years to live," Thom wrote. "He is happy: I can do anything, he says."[47] In the *Bay Area Reporter* he read obituaries for two friends—Gemini Mike and John Ponyman—the latter "the 6th I have known die of AIDS, and the best."[48] On Folsom, Thom went less frequently to bathhouses and sex clubs. Through spring 1984, there were rumors of their imminent closure. "A proposal to close bathhouses," he reflected. "I think they shd."[49] When the order came in October, the closures had a dramatic effect on the South of Market area. For the first time since the 1960s, new bars and clubs did not replace the old ones.[50] Thom wondered whether the neighborhood would survive and made notes for a poem: "A farewell to South-of-Market."[51]

In early 1984, Allan Noseworthy reconciled with Richard Locke and moved with him to Palm Springs. Allan was thinking about Thom, though: an article in the *Los Angeles Times* about "a woman recovering from attempted suicide" made him think about how Thom had helped him through several dark times. "That's when I smiled," Allan told him, "and thought of you and how much I love you and did I even thank you enough for being there? Here I am, thanks to people like you."[52] When Locke gave a show at the Caldron in early April, "Putting Safe Sex

Principles into Action," Allan was too sick with salmonella infection to accompany him.[53]

Thom gave his last class of the semester on Friday, May 4. Saturday was "a happy day" spent at the gym, grading papers in the garden, and flirting with a street boy on Haight. That evening, his life changed. "AN3 phones & tells me he has Kaposi's sarcoma," Thom wrote, "i.e. AIDS."[54] With treatment available only in New York and San Francisco, Thom insisted that he stay indefinitely at Cole Street. Allan arrived three days later. He was thin, "has lost 20lbs," Thom wrote. "He is composed."[55] Thom gave Allan his bedroom and moved upstairs to the workroom. He felt he could still "organise myself inside & out, so as to write ptry all summer."[56] For the first week, Allan was in and out of San Francisco General. "He shows no self-pity, he makes jokes, he is absolutely wonderful," Thom wrote: "never did anybody dramatize himself less."[57] Allan was a model patient. Thom told Douglas, "I would like to act like him if I find myself with the condition. (As, after all, I well may.)"[58] Although Allan had lost a noticeable amount of weight, Thom either did not realize the imminent danger or tried to convince himself otherwise: "I am 54, have 5–20 years to live, probably no more, very likely will die within that span," he reflected. "A[llan] is 35, has 1–5 years to live, almost certainly will die within that span. In either case time of death is not now—instead it is undetermined tho within limits."[59]

On June 1, Allan ran a "high fever" and Thom took him to the hospital. Allan was released that afternoon but continued to deteriorate. "AN3 has pneumocystis—gets worse and worse," Thom wrote three days later.[60] "We took him to the emergency room at the hospital about midnight," Thom told Barbara: "poor man, you get so depressed and irritable when there is not enough oxygen in your blood (as if being ill wasn't depressing enough), and two days later he was in a breathing machine, with a tube going down to his lung."[61] For Mike, Allan was the first time he had seen AIDS up close. "I cried," Mike reflected. "You could tell the minute you went into the hospital room that he wasn't going to survive."[62] Thom visited Allan in the hospital every day: knowing Allan would not return to Cole Street, Thom moved back downstairs from his workroom. "I find

I can concentrate on little else," he wrote. "I read [Francis] Parkman & spend a great amount of time dealing with phone calls: dr, Richard [Locke], Pete N, mother, Lou, some of them twice a day."[63] "There's usually lots of tears on the phone," he told Barbara. "Well, you can imagine."[64] Allan's father and younger brother arrived on June 12, his mother a few days later. "Apparently he was reconciled to his father, with tears and embraces, after several years of estrangement," Thom told Douglas, "and his nurse, a Philippine woman who had become quite knowledgable in working with AIDS patients, asked Allan if this was his 'special friend'!"[65] Allan "was v touched by his father's coming," and his mother was in time to see him "coherent and quite relaxed."[66]

For a few days, Allan was able to breathe unassisted. He used a notebook to communicate. When Thom and Mike visited, Allan wrote "lots of sentences to us on his pad ('conversation')—and Mike was wonderful giving him news & making him smile."[67] But he "looked startlingly worse," Thom wrote, "cheeks sunk like a skull."[68] "It's almost impossible he will make it now," he told Barbara in mid-June:

> So it has been a sad month for us, and it's getting sadder. There is theoretically a small chance that he will survive, and it will be wonderful if he does, but if he does die in about 10 days time then it seems hard that his life has been prolonged for such a length of time when at this stage it is nothing but continuous pain.[69]

Four days later, Thom visited with Bob: they found Allan "much worse, in fact dying. His lung collapsed, he had convulsions twice, he is back on machine, never to come off. Opened his eyes when we came in, & watched from under the blanket," Thom wrote. "Having difficulty with each breath, his body heaving up each time."[70] "It was like seeing somebody being crushed by a gigantic stone," he told Ander.[71] The next day, Allan was "quite lucid" but Thom knew he "must be in horrible pain" and wondered, "Why do they have to keep him alive?"[72] He visited with Mike the following day. "We knew he was pretty near the end," Thom wrote. "He held both our hands and went to sleep." Allan's mother called Thom early the next morning and told him to visit as soon as possible. "I came over for morning, he was just about focussing on trivia," Thom wrote. "Nurse gave him a big shot of morphine, I suspected it was the end, I left at end of morning & Mrs N phoned me he was dead when I came home. He must have died between 12 & 1. I shall miss him horribly—nobody was like him. I knew him just over 10 years. I didn't know I had tears left, but cried a lot."[73] Thom worked in the yard all afternoon and took some of Allan's things to his family. "The doctors and nurses could not have been better," he told Mary and Catherine. "So he was 2½ weeks in hospital before he died."[74]

Sitting in the yard, the day after Allan's death, Thom felt "as if I have been a rocket going through a tunnel at supersonic speeds for the last month & now I am suddenly—too suddenly—come to a dead stop in my back yard, surrounded by a stagnant heat."[75] He was "surprise[d]," the following week, to find himself "in tears at least once a day still."[76] Only a month on, he felt he had "been through a year of sadness" since Allan died.[77] An old, persistent fear reemerged. "I don't know what I'd do without Mike," he wrote. "M reminded me, last week, how AN3 had called us his 'role models' on his first visit here."[78] The shock, and a health scare—while Allan was in the hospital, Thom worried that a mark on his chest could be Kaposi's sarcoma, a false alarm[79]—spurred Thom into action. He visited the San Francisco Recorder's Office to take the "first step toward changing ownership of house to joint ownership (with M)."[80] The virus's incubation period was still unknown: an additional spur may have been the "not particularly safe threeway" Thom had had with Charlie in mid-May.[81]

By mid-July, Thom was "trying to write a poem about A's illness."[82] He kept regular writing hours and felt it "good to work, tho on a bad subject."[83] Reading Parkman's *The Jesuits in North America* lent Thom his opening line: "Your dying was a difficult enterprise." The "far Canada of a hospital room" extended the metaphor, and Thom used Parkman to "trace the fortunes of 'the body' (flesh)."[84] "At some stage, realising that the seventeenth-century reference implied was a bit much in a poem which in various ways might already have been a little close to Jonson's and Donne's elegies on the dead and dying," he told Clive, "I tried to take out the Canadian reference—but it was stuck there, subsequent images depended on it."[85] Comprising fifty-six rhyming couplets, "Lament" is Thom's longest single poem. It is an unsparing account of Allan's final days that concludes with Thom "think[ing] about yr trust in the body (which I share) & how it lets you down."[86] Thom witnessed that process, hour by hour. "[I]t was yours and gave you what it could," Thom wrote of Allan's body,

> Till near the end it let you down for good,
> Its blood hospitable to those guests who
> Took over by betraying it into
> The greatest of its inconsistencies
> This difficult, tedious, painful enterprise.[87]

For years after Allan's death, Thom dreamed about him. "How like you to be kind, / Seeking to reassure," he wrote in "The Reassurance," his poem about Allan returning to him in a dream. "And, yes, how like my mind / To make itself secure."[88] In early drafts, called "Of the Dead," Thom broadened his focus to include his persistent, lifelong dreams about his mother's death:

> Of the dead who return in dreams
> one comes back, reenacts her (death / suicide)
> breathing the gas in her red dressing gown
> for ever and ever she dies again
> while I reproach her, for the bitter drama
> she had to act out.[89]

Thom contrasted his reproachful feelings toward his mother with the reassurance Allan sought to offer. Therein lay another comparison: for all Allan's flightiness, hysteria, and emotional crises, as he approached death, "never did anybody dramatize himself less." Thom abandoned "Of

the Dead" because it seemed too confessional. "I don't like dramatizing myself," he later remarked. "I don't want to be Sylvia Plath."[90] Beneath his appearance, Thom preferred the stoical Jonsonian reticence
of "Lament" to self-dramatization and displays of emotion. In writing
about Allan's death—as he would some years later when he wrote "The
Gas-poker" about his mother—Thom sought a quiet dignity in his depic-
tions of pain, suffering, and one's reactions to them.

In September, Thom was pleased to welcome Ander to San Francisco
for a three-week visit. Thom had long wanted Ander to visit and wrote
a poem—"An Invitation"[91]—encouraging him to come. Ander's visit
snapped Thom out of the emotional jet lag he had suffered since Allan's
death. "Ander & me, knowing so much together, being able to take so
much for granted, as if sometimes we were 2 aspects of oneself," Thom
reflected, "antagonism contained, balanced in the love."[92] It took a week
for the brothers to get used to each other, a fact Thom attributed to the
fact "we have not spent 3 weeks (or 3 days, probably) perpetually in each
other's company since well before the age of 20."[93] Thom found it strange
how "remnants of childhood combativeness" arose in him "without any
warning at all."[94] The rest of Ander's visit went well—Thom remembered
how he delivered Aunt Catherine's verdict on *The Passages of Joy*, loudly,
in a genteel restaurant: "Well, Thom has really ripped his flies open this
time!"[95]—and Thom enjoyed showing him around San Francisco, from
Coit Tower to Golden Gate Park. "I love him a lot," Thom wrote after
the visit, "& find myself <u>missing</u> him the next day."[96]

In November, Thom gave a reading in New York at the 92nd Street Y.
He felt "peculiarly restless and uncertain—really about NY without Allan" and considered canceling. "One moment I want to go, the next I
don't."[97] He drew parallels between the effect on him of Allan's death and
that of Tony White. "Now, as when TW died I lost the London I had
acquired through him," he mused, "so now AN3 has died I have lost the
NY I have acquired through him."[98] The trip went ahead: Thom stayed

with Norm and Louis on Colonnade Row and read "Lament" for the first time at the Y. He filled a week seeing old friends and visiting old locales but grew "progressively sadder & sadder at the loss of Allan."[99] He met some of Allan's friends to help go through his belongings, most of which were still in the apartment he had sublet when he moved to Palm Springs. "All his things were still there," Thom told Mary and Catherine. "I did notice that he had kept every letter, it looked like, that had ever been written to him, so I located an enormous bundle by myself and dropped them in a dustbin outside. As a friend said who had to clear out Sylvia Plath's flat after her suicide: 'The dead leave everything behind.' Don't they just."[100] Thom flew back to San Francisco and "luxuriate[d]" in his return "as if I had been away 3 months instead of 8 days."[101] He wondered when he would next visit New York. "Not next year, certainly," he wrote. "Perhaps this is goodbye to its stimulating abrasiveness I have loved so long!"[102]

Allan's death changed Thom's perception of AIDS. "San Francisco is not the happiest of places now," he told his aunts. "I know a lot of people who have died of AIDS. As everybody says, it is like the Plague—you don't know who is going to get it next but it's going to get a lot more people before it is finished. They now think the germ has an incubation period of up to five years. And it is always—eventually—fatal."[103] That "five years" of incubation haunted Thom. "One man a day dying of AIDS here," he reflected. "I realise I must face the fact that the probability is I may find I have it one of these days. I wanted to have an old age of considered metrical poetry written at leisure: now I must think otherwise. I must try to concentrate, consolidate while I can, my old age might consist of 1985 only, or less, or not much more."[104] He saw in AIDS "the impending loss of our fire (newly won) pugnacity and openness," the gains of the 1970s.[105] "It is by audacity," he wrote, "by trying to go beyond 'what is natural' that the human enterprise has continued."[106] Thom felt "the odds are surely high that I contracted it in the years before I started to be careful, and I must think of myself as possibly having only 2 years left." He wanted to write "ten poems a year" for his remaining years, "most of them in meter, since in the metrical poems I seem to get deeper into my feelings & thoughts about things and make a solider construction out of them."[107]

One solace came in the form of Charlie Hinkle, who had not yet departed for Brazil. "I had one of the best times ever w/ Charlie," Thom wrote after they spent Thanksgiving together at Cole Street. "To think our connection almost vanished early in the summer & now we are really close again. He said 'I never knew what you wanted from me.' (I told M afterwards, & he said 'You are often rather overwhelming to him.') But now I feel we are firm & loving friends—& that is great, because I love being in his company, & at last we are comfortable together."[108] On New Year's Eve, Thom went to Folsom with Charlie but they lost each other. Thom ended up in the Brig, from which he brought home a tall, handsome leatherman named Dennis Hrlic. "With my poor coke & his excellent mda we have a wonderful night," Thom wrote, "'unsafe' sex (which makes me feel guilty later)."[109] Feeling "stupefied & ripped," Thom was not himself for several days.[110] Having resolved, a fortnight earlier, to stay safe and devote himself to poetry, his risky behavior confused him. If the "odds were high" he already had AIDS, he felt guilty at having potentially exposed Hrlic. Thom knew he had destructive tendencies but struggled to avoid them. He was right to be worried, but for a different reason. "I see from [the *Bay Area Reporter*] that Dennis Hrlic died in July," he was to write in August 1988. "I must assume that he if no one else exposed me to the plague."[111]

30

ILLUMINATIONS

In September 1984, Thom attended Robert Duncan's much-anticipated reading from *Ground Work: Before the War*, his first major collection in fifteen years. Thom was "surprised" that Duncan read so many "Moly poems (his, I mean)" and when "he announced 'in that period, I had a crush on Thom Gunn,' and all this time I thot it was my mind!!"[1] Thom felt honored. "I feed on you like some nasty critter I learned about in school, inside the crab's shell," he told Duncan afterward: "no maybe more like a sparrow on a crocodile, since that doesn't kill what it feeds on. And I was proud to be mentioned by old Pa Crocodile too."[2]

In his self-imposed hiatus, Duncan had wanted to move on from the "overcomposed" poems of *Bending the Bow* and "write poetry again not haunted by a book."[3] This inspired Thom. "I would settle on an arbitrary date—1992—for the publication of my next book," he told Tanner. "By that time, in all probability, I will have completed at least one and a half books, so possibly with half of an unpublished book still in my drawer I won't feel that drained sense that I have nothing left to give anyone in 1992. I will have something left—half a book!"[4] Thom established 1988 as the "cut off date for contents," thinking he would be "nicely into the next book" by then, thus defeating the "tyranny" of the jinx.[5] His flurry of metrical poems in early 1984 had set him up well, but Allan's death and the emotional energy expended on writing "Lament" effectively dried him up for the rest of the year, and he felt "troubled" that he could not finish poems he had drafted.[6] But he did finish one more poem that year. After Duncan's reading, he wrote "an extra Moly poem"[7]—"Odysseus on Hermes," which he called an "Appendix to RD's Moly Suite."[8] "I took his drug," says Odysseus, "and all came out right in the story."[9]

Thom knew that his writing plans were subject to AIDS: he feared that he had already been exposed to, and was incubating, the virus. As intended, he treated 1985 as a year of consolidation. He planned poems about childhood and adolescence, particularly the four incidents he called his "Illuminations," and felt he could perhaps succeed in verse where he had failed in his prose autobiography. In February, he made extensive notes about the "Illuminations." "They were like a concentration of energies in me that built up and then suddenly burst free," he reflected: "what kind of energies I cannot even say, since they were so strong that they were physical and of the emotions and yes I think of the spirit too, though I wouldn't want to explain too closely what I mean by that." The four incidents were: the morning walk to the bus stop with Michael Wishart in 1942; feeling revivified while walking to school some eighteen months after his mother's death; an early attempt to write a novel while in the army; and a "revelation" of freedom while hitchhiking across France in summer 1951.[10]

Feeling "harried from left to right" during the semester, Thom had neither the time nor the energy to draft the "Illuminations" poems.[11] But other ideas emerged. One night in the Watering Hole, a hotel and bar built on the site of the old Folsom Street Barracks, Thom ran into "2 ganz hairy guys" and wrote "an extempore" about what had happened.[12] He called it "In Time of Plague":

> This bar, this place is full of death,
> but it is drawn
> so oddly from the sexual
> that I am confused
> confused to be attracted
> by, in effect, my own annihilation.
> Who are these two, these fiercely attractive men
> who want me to stick their needle in my arm?[13]

Thom had written about limits and risk in his early poems, but now, at the center of an epidemic, he found people "testing themselves against risk, / as a human must," as he wrote in the final version of "In Time of Plague," which tested his own resolve: his desire for sex—the men "thirst heroically together / for euphoria"—against his instinct for self-preservation. The interior monologue unfolds in real time: Brad and John "get restless" with his "indecisiveness" and move off through the bar, "carrying in their faces and throughout their bodies / the news of life and death."[14]

The same day Thom wrote "In Time of Plague," he also wrote a long letter to Tony Tanner. He had not heard from Tanner for several years[15] but had received a "wonderfully encouraging" report from Jack Collins, who claimed Tanner was "eager to deal with everything, to read and to teach and to walk."[16] Tanner had quit drinking and he was in his best mental shape for fifteen years. "Tony used to tell this story that he woke up one morning and told himself he didn't have to live a life like this," Clive Wilmer recalled of Tanner's revival. "He could choose to live a happy life; he could choose to just be happy. He changed his behavior, and just put up with the disadvantages of his condition and got on with life. He wrote a lot, made new friends, and it lasted for about ten years."[17] Thom expected to see Tanner for the first time in six years: he had agreed to visit England and participate in the Cambridge Poetry Festival. Tanner had moved from Alpha Road to rooms in King's College; Thom hoped to stay with him "if you find yourself able to bear with my elderly jocularity."[18]

The festival was scheduled for the summer, but in mid-January Thom began to feel uncertain about leaving the States. He worried that the "new Reagan anti gay imm policy might just mean I cdn't get back in country" and decided to cancel.[19] "The sexual bigotry that is usually not far beneath the surface of any immigration official at airports and 'points of entry' has indeed surfaced," he told his aunts, "and immigration is giving a hard time to foreign homosexuals entering the country. Worse than hard time, I should say—turning them back. So I would run the risk of not being able to get back here, my own home."[20] It was a real fear, but also an excuse. "I don't want to [go] anyway," he wrote in his diary.[21] He did not want to give any "big celebrity readings" and was "working (successfully it seems) at stopping being famous."[22] Thom likely had Ted Hughes in mind, whom he thought "an idiot" for having accepted the position of British Poet Laureate following John Betjeman's death.[23]

Without England on the horizon, Thom could relax. Back trouble meant he was unable to go to the gym, breaking a thrice-a-week habit he had maintained since joining with Bob two years earlier, but he could still manage the garden, which looked "wonderful, pinks, foxgloves, oriental poppies, etc."[24] He wrote two minor poems called "Fennel" and "Nasturtium" but worried there was "too much poetry about flowers" and felt he "must get back to people as subject matter."[25] His back trouble made him more sensitive to aging. "I am looking rather sagging in general," he told Tanner, "and am fast approaching that look of the armored reptile behind which the old man's eyes dart furtively, seeking refuge."[26] Mike, on the other hand, "is 53 and white haired with a white mustache, and also the body of a 25-year-old."[27]

The family had not lost a close friend to AIDS since Allan, but other deaths contributed to a subdued atmosphere. Of their cats, only Lucy survived: Rhoda, sixteen, had died the previous summer, and Pearl, the same age, went missing, returned a day later, "weak and drowsy," and died during the night.[28] Thom buried them both in the garden. Bob's dog, Spitfire, had "massive cancers" and died that spring. "I don't know when I have been more fond of an animal," Thom reflected.[29] "He had only about 2 days discomfort," he told Ander, "wagging till the end lest we should feel unhappy."[30]

In poetry, it was also "a Spring for deaths," Thom told Douglas, "the two best poets in English die within a few [weeks] of each other—J. V. Cunningham and then Basil Bunting."[31] Thom knew neither—he had met Cunningham once, Bunting never[32]—but admired both, remarkably different as they were, much as he admired both Winters and Duncan. Sadder for Thom, though, was the death of his old patron Josephine Miles, who had recruited him to teach at Berkeley. Her health had been deteriorating for several years; her failing eyesight led Thom to visit her, weekly, and read aloud from poetry and novels. He visited her for the last time in April and she died a month later. "She sat in her chair and tried to speak sentences, but she couldn't get out more than a few words, and <u>she didn't like it</u>," Thom told Douglas of her final months. "It is merciful that she did die. One could only verbally caress her, poor thing."[33] Thom wrote her obituary for the *California Monthly* and spoke at her memorial service.[34]

With his thoughts "so crowded with death," Thom contemplated his own mortality. "I am glad, on the whole, that the last part of my life doesn't look as if it will turn out too easy: out of difficulties only can I resist the sloth which is the reverse of life," he reflected. "This is the only way I can triumph—from grazing failure . . . until at last I fall right onto it & through it into annihilation."[35] Thom learned his old friend Gary White was "in hospital, viz. with AIDS."[36] Charlie Hinkle "says his immune system is in bad shape," Thom wrote, "but he doesn't have AIDS." Thom thought Charlie looked "rather thin & grave. He is tired & his T-cell count is down. However, this can be recovered from, with care & luck."[37] Thom also paid regular visits to the ailing Robert Duncan and took him for short walks around the neighborhood. That summer, Thom heard that another of his models was in poor health. When he mentioned to Armistead Maupin that Isherwood was "really showing his age nowadays," Maupin "told me . . . that Isherwood himself said (of himself) 'The entire East Wing is dark.' How terrific to be able to kid about one's own failing powers. People really do set me admirable examples."[38]

Thom could joke about his own health—"the only part of me where the lights are still blazing are the kitchen and the Servants' Quarters," he told John Lehmann[39]—but he was sensitive about aging. "Nothing gets better," he warned Clive: "you can drink less, erections occur more seldom, you get tired more easily, the poetry gets sparser, and a general silliness sets in."[40] Writing blocks heightened his sensitivity to aging: his recent poems "disgust[ed] me by the poverty of their invention and performance" and his current notebook felt like "a symbol . . . of my aridity, inactivity, inanity."[41] He felt "internally vigorous but outwardly sick," he told Douglas, reassuring him that it was "<u>not</u> 'AIDS-related'" but back pain and an "intermittent toothache."[42] At the Folsom Street Fair, however, Thom "caught sight of faces, familiar from about 10–15 years ago . . . faces of men in their seventies, though neither of them could have been much more than 40."[43] Beset by "an overwhelming melancholy," Thom went home early.[44] After the Hrlic encounter at New Year's, Thom's instinct for self-preservation kicked in. "Every now and again I have sex—<u>always</u> 'safe', I may say—but not as often as I could," he told Douglas. "Lots of people here are still nuts, & the bathhouses that are still open have reverted to what they were. People find it very difficult to stop doing what they like best, which I completely understand—but you'd think they'd try to modify it when it will lead almost certainly to a painful and drawn-out death. Promiscuous sex is no longer political, just suicide."[45] He wondered "at what point does the search for euphoria become self-destructiveness?"[46]—a question partly answered in "In Time of Plague"—and contemplated writing another poem about "an orgy in 1982 . . . a fine picture of trust, sharing, frankness, openness— what was being shared, in that euphoria was a sense that we are all one— hugging, containing that fleshed knowledge—also hugging to them a killing virus."[47]

Although Thom practiced safe sex, his appetite for risk was undiminished and he sought danger elsewhere. He regularly tricked with two men he called the "speed brothers" or "the nefarious Peep Brothers," Eric and Rick, the subjects of his later poem "Nights with the Speed Bros."[48] They had first met at the Brig in 1983 and hooked up every few months for night-long party and play sessions. "Crystal again," Thom wrote on one occasion. "This had better be my last crystal marathon (12 hrs) or I'll kill myself."[49] "Rick is immensely blond and immensely silent," Thom wrote of their fifth session that October, whereas Eric "is older—also handsome, a streaky blond, he likes to be in charge, he calls the sexual plays as it were." Having partied for fifteen hours, Thom wanted to leave their Castro apartment and go home: Eric accused him of "leaving not from tiredness but from sexual guilt." Keen "not to get into a speed argument," Thom kissed them both goodbye and left: he realized, "after such an ending, it is unlikely I can ever go back."[50] Crystal marathons helped Thom "get out of myself . . . in spite of the risk to my health—(speed with a high blood pressure condition!)"[51]

Losing Eric and Rick created another drawback: sleeping with regular, trusted partners reduced the likelihood that Thom would be exposed to the virus. "I have been extremely careful, sexually, for almost three years now," he told John Holmstrom. "Being careful has certainly been made easier by the complete loss of any physical attractiveness I might ever have had, but I do tend to fall in love as foolishly as ever, and there is the occasional gerontophile who apparently doesn't care at all about the visual."[52] Thom was being disingenuous—when Clive Wilmer saw him the following year he thought Thom looked "extraordinarily young for his age, very fit and lean"[53]—but had another, fortuitous, reason to feel more confident about dodging AIDS. "I count myself lucky because I have never much liked anal sex," he told Holmstrom, "and that certainly seems to be the most common method of transmission. I have always been terribly oral, sucking and being sucked like some shellfish in the tides."[54] Sometimes San Francisco seemed to challenge him directly. He saw the graffiti "I LOVE YOU, DESIRE" scrawled on a bus stop. "Maybe it meant / Desiree?" Thom wrote, "but I do too, desire / itself."[55]

Thom was careful, but he could not shake the fear that he was already infected. When he began writing again in November, his anxiety prompted one of his new poems: "The Man with Night Sweats." Working made him "happy, in an odd kind of way," he told Ander. "I actually got a kind of satisfaction from writing that long poem about Allan's death: I thought of myself as fashioning a kind of monument for him, and using all my skill at its most elaborate—even showing off with it—so as to make that monument worthy of him."[56] If writing about Allan was a personal monument, "The Man with Night Sweats" looked outward. "Everybody here seems to know (from newspapers etc) that nightsweats (with weight loss) is one of the first symptoms of AIDS," Thom told Clive.[57] He saw the poem as a monologue "spoken by a dying man" about "the realization that this is a symptom of fatality. How can you live with such a realization? You don't, you die with it."[58] Showing the poem to friends like Clive, Holmstrom, and the poet Jim Powell, Thom found that they all felt the line "I cannot but be sorry" inadequate. Powell thought it "all too distanced," but Thom had "intend[ed] the distanced effect" and "was aiming for a kind of diffident under-statement."[59] He structured the poem around images of embrace—recalling the "hugging" image he had used to describe the never-written "orgy in 1982" poem—and presented the body as a shield uniquely unequipped to deal with a virus. "Hugging my body to me / As if to shield it from / The pains that will go through me," Thom wrote: "As if hands were enough / To hold an avalanche off."[60] The "hands" are Thom's but, more broadly, they represent the great effort of the gay community to help and support AIDS victims. He was keen to stress that not all behavior was as reckless as "In Time of Plague" and that lovers, friends, and acquaintances rallied round to support one another, just as Cole Street had helped take care of Allan. Thom thought that "sex, friendship, and love are all to an extent mutually inclusive, overlapping considerably w/ each other," and was heartened to see how, in a dark time, despite fear and anxiety, those overlaps existed everywhere in the homes, bars, and streets of San Francisco.[61]

Finishing "The Man with Night Sweats" gave Thom the spur to write the "Illuminations" poems he had planned at the beginning of the year. In "The Liberty Granted"—its working title, "A Place of First Permission," he borrowed from Duncan—Thom wrote about the first flush of childhood liberty he had experienced at Bedales in 1942. He asked himself "how has the promise of joy been fulfilled?" and concluded it had been "self-fulfilling," a promise of "joy thro complete participation in love, sex, and poetry."[62] Shortly thereafter, Thom began "South," another "Illuminations" poem, in which he explored similar ideas of energy, liberty, and release he had experienced while hitchhiking through France in 1951. "I came to realise / That I was not encumbered otherwise / By furniture or promises," he wrote, "because / Carrying my needs I carried all I was."[63] The years between his mother's suicide and meeting Mike were like a slow recovery from a debilitating illness; in hindsight it looked to Thom as though his revelation of freedom on that long dusty road in France, as he wrote in one draft, "wd bring me to a readiness for him / whom I had not yet met / by whom the boundaries of my life / were to be changed for good."[64] Thom had a complex idea of "needs," and "South" was his attempt to articulate not only his newfound selfhood but also the connection between his mother and Mike. Written during the early, devastating stages of the AIDS crisis, it also sounds a note of rueful self-criticism. In the poem, the moment passes; the young Thom continued his walk "and it was not the same." Expecting the euphoria to last was a mistake, he seems to say, as was the expectation of complete self-reliance: thirty-five years later, Thom realized that he needed other people and that those connections could be, were always, fragile.

In his "mensus mirabilis for writing," Thom finished seven new poems and drafted several more. "Would every month could be like that," he mused.[65] But it was not altogether a happy month. Gary White died of AIDS in mid-November; Don, who had been looking after Gary, arrived that night on Cole Street "drunk & very tearful."[66] Thom found Don "terrific" in that, "when real need occurs, he will just turn over his life to help a friend."[67] Then, a week before Christmas, news came that Isherwood's prostate cancer was terminal. Thom wrote a short elegy—"To Isherwood Dying"—and learned, a few days later, that Isherwood was dead. Thom was saddened but not surprised: he had known for some time that Isherwood's health had been failing. He later learned from Don Bachardy that Isherwood had had cancer since 1981 "but kept forgetting, gt memory failing in those last years."[68]

Teaching his new course on the English lyric poem, alongside his creative writing classes, Thom had "little time to write" during the semester.[69] He was "mulling over" a poem about "All Hallows marshes" that would become "A Sketch of the Great Dejection."[70] Set between his mother's suicide in December 1944 and his "illumination" while walking to school in spring 1946, the poem identifies the "place of poverty, / of inner and outer famine" as a cross between the Allhallows marshes—close to where Aunt Barbara and Uncle Godfrey lived—and the marshes of *Great Expectations*.[71] Resting "upon a disintegrating gravestone," the speaker asks himself: "How can I continue?" Thom felt conflicted about his desire to consolidate: he struggled to see his attempt to write poems about foundational moments of his youth as anything other than selfish at a time when life—when *poetry*—seemed to demand of him monuments to friends like

Allan and other victims of the AIDS epidemic. Although "A Sketch" is not an AIDS poem, one interviewer called it the "gravitational centre" of *The Man with Night Sweats*.[72] The teenage Thom resolved to keep going, rather than "sink into the mud":

> My body insisted on restlessness
>   having been promised love
> as my mind insisted on words
>   having been promised the imagination.[73]

Promises of "love" and "the imagination" were the architecture of "South," too, where Thom felt "language & body wd potently combine" to prepare him for his eventual meeting with Mike.[74] If Thom had learned anything, it was to persist. "I fared on and, though the landscape did not change," he wrote in the concluding lines of "A Sketch," "it came to seem after a while like a place of recuperation."[75]

Thom sent "The Liberty Granted" and "A Sketch" to *Threepenny*, explaining to Wendy Lesser that they were "two parts to the same poem, the second a sequel to the first, so they would ideally be printed together."[76] He subsequently withdrew "The Liberty Granted": he claimed he "shouldn't let it be printed as it stands" and thought he would "either rewrite it or throw it away."[77] He had similar misgivings about "South," which he called "100% boring" and vowed "never [to] print it in book or pamphlet."[78] Neither poem was his best work, but Thom's distaste for them was rooted more in the circumstances of their writing. "I bore my-self even, in the return—no the prolongation—of adolescent longings," he wrote shortly after finishing "South":

> I am surrounded by shipwrecks, friends dead & dying of AIDS or the evils of old age, poets I admire and novelists, acquaintances, dead and dying also, & yet in this storm I fret, like an adolescent, like a spoiled young aristocrat, about my incompletions, about the things I can't have that I feel I need for my completion.

He felt guilty about what seemed his miraculous, ongoing escape from AIDS. "Everything's great with my body, it says: I am surrounded by a storm of death but everything's <u>fine</u> here," he wrote. "It's not good sense, it's pure 14 year old's animal vigor saving the day again." But Thom knew his vigor could not last. "I will write good poems again, I will make love again—those lithe poems and lithe men that seem to make me feel most whole," he reflected, "but they will become fewer and fewer."[79] With "South" finished, Thom abandoned the "illuminations" for good: he would have to seek a different kind of consolation.

Some of Thom's "adolescent longings" emerged when Charlie Hinkle left San Francisco to spend a long-awaited five months in Brazil. This was a prelude: Charlie planned to move to New Orleans and begin graduate work at Tulane. "A sadness. He says he may be in SF over Xmas," Thom wrote, "but given the state of his health, thinness, constant tiredness, I wonder if I'll ever see him again."[80] He worried Charlie was "in that bad year of tiredness, susceptibility to every germ, night sweats, that comes before AIDS itself."[81] Charlie left without saying goodbye; Thom spent his departure day "w/ sentimentality as I passed Charlie's apt in the bus. I am so juvenile."[82] Thom reflected on their "kind of affair" in a letter to Tanner. "Something was never right about it, we were never close in the right way," he mused. "Well, we are still very fond of each other— I don't let people go, as you know."[83]

AIDS cases in San Francisco had remained a constant 60–65 per month in late 1985, but in February 1986 the number leaped to 102. "We all hope this was a freak and not a new tendency," Thom told a friend. "Sometimes I think there are not going to be many of us surviving this generation—if indeed we are lucky enough to survive."[84] Thom worried about Charlie, but in May he received a late-night call from Norm Rathweg in New York: he had developed an AIDS-related condition. Thom invited him to visit over the summer, thinking "it may be his last chance to do so."[85] "The approach of death to the young and healthy gives rise in me to the tritest sentiments," he told John Holmstrom after Norm's call, "but it is so very sad. I keep having the image in my mind of a body being crushed by a mountain, the crushing gradual, complete, and absolutely irreversible."[86]

Norm did not make his summer visit. "Kaposi's turned up" in August, Thom wrote, and he was too sick to travel.[87] When Thom saw him in September—passing through New York to judge the General Electric Award for Young Writers—Norm was much improved. "His attitude is wonderfully healthy," Thom told his aunts; "he keeps his strength up by eating 3 hot meals a day, and enjoys what is left of his life to the utmost."[88] Thom welcomed other visitors that summer: Ander came to stay with his new partner, Bett, whom Thom found "intelligent, good-looking, sensible, fun to be with" and a "good" influence on Ander.[89] Clive Wilmer also visited. "I don't think I ever knew before he was <u>that</u> good company to be in," Thom reflected.[90] Sensing that he could spark a friendship, he introduced Clive to August Kleinzahler. "I think he thought in his schoolmasterly way that it would be 'good for us'—i.e. mind-broadening," Clive reflected. "It *was* good. The two of us hit it off."[91] August visited Clive in Cambridge the following year. "Their obvious closeness was a bit daunting to me at the time," August reflected. "Englishmen, I had to be on my best behavior!"[92]

Having finished "A Sketch" and labored through countless drafts of "South," Thom was "all poised to write my head off," he told Douglas, "but somehow none of the planned poems is working out."[93] By the end of June he had "done nothing at all" and was preparing to make visits of his own, to read in Seattle and Arizona.[94] Shortly before leaving for Seattle, the house was thrown into disarray. "Jim so sick so often I can tell we are all worried about what may be behind it," Thom wrote.[95] Bill and Jim had kept to themselves for much of the year—Thom thought they were "slightly peeped all the time"[96]—and the extent of Jim's sickness was not revealed until Thom had returned from Arizona in mid-September. Thom spent the evening "full of my worry over Jim, who does have AIDS, & even greater worry about the effect on Billy. I don't know, the house is in for a very difficult time."[97]

31

THE MISSING

Jim had contracted AIDS "by a grotesque chance, years ago," Bill told Thom, when he was "stuck accidentally by a needle that had been used to inject an AIDS patient being operated on."[1] Bill devoted himself to Jim's care, but Jim "was always an obstinate man who didn't like anybody to even suggest what he should do."[2] Thom had not always seen eye to eye with Jim but had welcomed him into the family because Bill loved him. He made notes for a poem about Bill and Jim's relationship, never written, called "Love, an Ordeal."[3] "Your love for that man in his life & during his dying. I observed it 10(?) years, from close quarters, living in the same house," he wrote in October, "and went thro stages of irritation, disgust, pity, & finally awe at a love given so completely. [. . .] Yr love I thought at first too self-effacing. I felt betrayed. We all did."[4]

Bill and Jim had known that Jim had had AIDS since Thanksgiving 1985. Thom found the secrecy "not altogether unreasonable" and felt that, were he to contract AIDS, he "certainly won't give speeches from a float in the Gay Parade [. . .]!"[5] The family was not told until "it became obvious," Thom told Ander. "Jim has started to look so old. And the last few days his physical & mental situation have been alarming. We are very afraid his mind is going."[6] Thom thought it "the saddest thing to see Bill helping him: I keep thinking of Enter King Lear, led by a Boy."[7] Thom was deeply affected: watching Jim wither away was like witnessing Allan's demise all over again. "I don't think I could bear to see Mike, for example, gradually waste away before my eyes," he told Ander.[8] On one occasion, Thom watched Bill help Jim down the stairs and made notes for the poem that became "Terminal":

> The eight years difference in age seems now
> Disparity so wide between the two
> That when I see the man who armoured stood
> Resistant to all help however good
> Now helped through day itself, eased into chairs,
> [. . .]
> I think of Oedipus, old, led by a boy.[9]

Jim was very weak, but Bill hoped he still had "a couple of years"; Thom thought Jim had "a long time yet. Unless he gets struck down."[10] Bill was "heroic" and "determined to come up to every occasion"—he planned to take Jim to the Russian River and to Paris—but Jim "want[ed] 2 things at once—to die & to live, but making it Bill's responsibility to keep him alive."[11] Thom was also "very concerned about Bill, who is being resourceful and brave and practical and loving," he told Ander, "but whom I know well enough to know that it is already (going to even more) affect his emotions to the point of desperation."[12] He had "seldom felt the precariousness of the world so much, a selfish feeling no doubt, since what I want is simply the security of my family."[13]

Seeing Charlie Hinkle did little to restore Thom's equilibrium. Charlie, now twenty-nine, had returned from Brazil and started graduate work at Tulane. He visited San Francisco from New Orleans to see a friend, Alan Rockway, who had recently been diagnosed with AIDS. "We have dinner at Disk & spend all eve talking," Thom wrote. "Good to see him, he is still thin, hates N Orleans, but we had a good time!"[14] Charlie had told Thom that his health was "OK, especially when I think I should have dropped dead long ago," but added the proviso that he still had "a lot of trouble concentrating." Were he to die, Charlie wanted Thom "to promise me you'll wear your biggest boots and all your leather to my funeral." He had started writing short lyric poems and sent them to Thom for comment. Thom's favorite was "Rain," which begins: "I want death to come during a downpour." Charlie was grateful for Thom's help. "You certainly diagnosed my antipathy to personal pronouns," he told Thom. "I get to a stage in the writing process where I 'de-Charlie' the poem. It's something I do almost automatically."[15] Thom would have approved. He felt Charlie, with so much potential, "left the self in balance" while he decided which of his "multiplying talents" to develop.[16]

In early December, Thom received a phone call from Larry Hoyt's lover, whom he had never met: Larry had "a respiratory complaint" and was "in Franklin Hospital, his kidneys almost gone, dying."[17] Thom visited him the following day. "Poor Larry! He was out on morphine, breathing through one of those same tubes as Allan had; his skin yellowish-grey . . . I spoke in his ear to say goodbye & stayed an hour or less: I <u>shall</u> miss him."[18] Larry died that afternoon, aged thirty-five. Thom could not shake "the arrested angle he held his head on the pillow, as if caught in astonishment, to take the tube."[19] Thom later wrote about Larry's death in "Still Life," concluding with the image of "[t]he tube his mouth enclosed / In an astonished O."[20] Thom was stunned: Larry's death was completely unexpected. He had seen little of Larry in recent years and was "surprised at how stricken" he felt.[21] Larry had been "such fun, & so good, & even so useful to the world—a generous & robust man."[22] Thom attended his memorial service at the San Francisco Columbarium. "One guy had the courage and (I thought) taste to wear full leather (I told him so too). (I was chicken)," Thom told a friend. "I suppose the fact of such ceremonies helps to allay grief, but really the grief is unallayable."[23]

On Cole Street, Jim's affairs were a mess. Thom offered to pay for his funeral; Mike sold Jim's car to cover some of the medical expenses.[24] A week before Christmas, Jim "start[ed] phoning home, dr, airlines, having decided to spend Xmas in Tennessee," Thom wrote, "a delusion, since he cd never travel, prob cdn't get to foot of stairs."[25] Jim was confined to bed and looked "like a survivor from a concentration camp. It's grim," Thom told Clive Wilmer, "and will probably get a good deal grimmer before the end."[26] Jim was in and out of consciousness; Bill nursed him around the clock and "seems to almost never go to bed these days," Thom reflected. "Jim is lucid again, says to Bill 'I hope I wasn't mean to you.'"[27]

Thom looked after Jim on Christmas Eve. "I am so shocked by his weakness I have to go off and cry," he wrote, returning to "moisten his brow with little sponges."[28] Jim weighed little more than forty pounds, "all bone," and could barely swallow liquids.[29] On Christmas Day, Thom, Mike, and Bob ate downstairs; Bill stayed upstairs with Jim. He came downstairs in the early evening "& said 'I think Jim is not alive,' so we went up, & he had died, his eyes fixed, crossed as if staring at the end of his nose, his mouth gaping, poor baby." Thom brought Bill back downstairs and "he sat on the sofa holding my hand for an hour or so."[30] "It was a horrible illness and a painful death," he told Belle Randall the following year, "but I am beginning to realise that death (not just from AIDS) is almost always painful and difficult, and that the image that us sheltered children have always had of dying sweetly in one's sleep is one most seldom realised in experience."[31]

The next day, Thom took Bill for lunch in the Hyatt Regency's revolving restaurant "because he said he'd like to do 'something grand.'" Thom thought it "a very healthy thing for him to say."[32] There was "relief" in the house, after three traumatic months, "Bill most of course from his constant anxiety, but all of us, that poor Jimmy's pain is ended at last."[33] Bill "talk[ed] lucidly and at length" about Jim, which Thom also thought "healthy," but he feared that Bill, struggling to accept Jim's death, would start taking PCP again. "It was that much worse having to go through it stage by stage in your home, I find, than it is in hospital," Thom told Douglas. "Now Bill is recuperating, and clearly the recuperation is not going to be fast. We do what we can, which isn't much."[34] A few days later, Mike had to stop Bill from "running up the street in his slippers thro rain (peeped), to meet Jim's astral projection."[35] For Thom, it was already a sensitive time of year. "Forty-two years as an adult," he wrote to mark his mother's death.[36] On New Year's Day 1987, Thom went with Bill to collect Jim's ashes: later in the year, Mike and Bill scattered them along the coast at Big Sur. "May you lastly reach the shore, / Joining tide without

intent," Thom wrote in "Words for Some Ash," "Only worried any more /
By the currents' argument."[37]

Despite the trauma of the Christmas period, Thom began the new year
vigorously. He had "a last sexual fling" before teaching started and a
"marvellous" first day of classes.[38] At one of his regular lunches with
Robert Duncan and Robert Glück, Thom mentioned to Duncan that
"I am so ebullient these weeks I believe I must be rebounding from a
bigger depression from Nov–Dec than I was aware of at the time." Duncan replied, "Yes, we think that for a depression to be real we have to
illustrate it."[39] Thom found that "a prolonged depression is almost always
succeeded by a prolonged euphoria, as if the emotions are compensat-
ing!" He was "terrifically busy" but was "loving it all, the teaching, all
my students' problems etc. I even wrote some poetry," he told Ander,
"which I seldom do during term."[40] He called his new group of poems—
"Words for Some Ash," "Still Life," "Terminal," and "The Man with
Night Sweats"—"Terminal Studies."[41]

Thom's euphoria was at odds with the rest of the family. Their sixteen-
year-old cat, Lucy, was ailing and needed "an expensive operation she
was probably too old for anyway." Taking her to the vet, Thom "[felt]
like Lady Macbeth."[42] Bill, "deeply sad," decided to visit Bob Barron and
Mike Chittim in New Orleans, hoping that several weeks away from
Cole Street would help his grief.[43] Downstairs, Mike and Bob had separated "to the extent that Bob has moved into the front room, and is now
a roommate rather than a lover," Thom told Douglas. "Someone once
told Mike that he was a Serial Monogamist, which I find a vastly comic
label for him, but I do wonder who the next will be, and will we have to
make room for him too?" Thom was "sympathetic to both sides" and neither Mike nor Bob seemed "too crushed by the situation." Having lived
through their numerous separations and reconciliations, Thom himself
felt no desire "to remarry: my emotions are quite fully enough occupied
with all this kind of thing!!!"[44]

In March, a phone call from Charlie put an abrupt end to Thom's ebullience. "He was in hospital, with pneumocystis," Thom told Ander. "But now it is curable, tho painfully, by chemotherapy, so he hoped to be out in a few weeks—though of course he will still have AIDS."[45] Charlie was relieved to be treated as an outpatient: hospital stays "sapped" his "stamina" and he was "quickly" losing his eyesight. "I'm afraid I don't have any nice things to say," he wrote Thom in mid-April from New Orleans. "I think that the worst thing actually, apart from feeling crummy all the time, is that I have to listen to everybody's stupid opinions and advice."[46] Thom knew, but did not admit to himself, that Charlie would be blind, and likely dead, within twelve months. Each week he recognized "at least one name" among the obituaries printed in the *Bay Area Reporter*. "Strangely enough," he told Ander, "I have stopped worrying about myself: I don't fear about having gotten it from Charlie, because we both knew to have 'safe sex' by that time in history. And if I do have it incubating in me from before then, why then I do, but there is no point in worrying about something before there is any need."[47]

Within a month of Charlie's call, Thom learned that two more good friends of the Cole Street family were seriously ill. Allen Day phoned to say he "has 'the big one'—is recovering from abscesses on the brain & pneumocystis."[48] Thom visited Allen and his partner, Louis Bryan, a few days after Allen's call: he looked "terribly thin & wd seem to have brain damage."[49] "Overnight Allen went from a man who did his income tax by hand to a man who couldn't add 200 and 200," Louis recalled. "His sense of numbers was just totally blitzed. Our phone bill was full of his attempts to call people, but having got one or more digits wrong, he ended up with someone else."[50] A few days later, Thom discovered that Lonnie Leard, who had lived upstairs at Cole Street for many years, "was in hospital with pneumocystis."[51] Thom and Mike visited him immediately and went several more times through the spring. Lonnie "was lovely, v tired but loving," Thom wrote, "we held hands for about ¼ hr & I did most of the talking."[52] "We have been visiting hospitals," Thom told Ander, "and worrying about our friends a lot."[53]

Norm Rathweg had hoped to visit Cole Street that summer—to make up for his aborted visit the previous year—but in April Thom heard from Norm's partner, Louis Keith Nelson, that "poor old Norm will not be up to coming here after all."[54] At first, teaching became "a refuge from troubles," but, come May, Thom was "pleased that term will soon be over. 'My nerves are shot.' Everything is just being too much for me: I think all my friends, 4 close friends, with AIDS is what is doing it to me."[55] With Bill visiting Michael Belot in Paris and Bob away seeing family in Ohio, Thom felt fortunate to have Mike's company and support. "M & I meet in the evenings," he reflected, "2 old people 'without dislike or suspicion.'"[56] They made several trips to Santa Rosa to see Lonnie in the hospital, and Thom called on Allen every few days. He claimed he was "not working well, either on poetry or prose"[57] but began to think of his sick friends in terms of his early poems. "I hungered once for the heroic: a social rhetoric examples from Shakespeare, Rostand, Sartre (Goetz) of stoical bravery, magnanimity," he wrote. "Now, my friends dying young / I see such virtues daily." Thom saw their "gallantry, cheerfulness, considerateness toward the rest of us, as if we were suffering."[58]

In May, Charlie returned to San Francisco to apply for Medi-Cal "to avoid having to pay the $10,000/yr for the AZT," an experimental drug that he hoped would repair his failing eyesight.[59] Charlie had "black patches . . . holes in his eyesight," and was so thin that Thom doubted he would recognize him in the street.[60] Charlie lived in Noe Valley: Thom began taking the J Church streetcar to Church and Twenty-ninth to visit him. Most often, he took Charlie for lunch at Speckmann's, a German restaurant, "whr I do not make a secret about trying to stuff him & get him to put on weight." Thom thought Charlie was "much more cheerful. But says he will be blind in 3 months. His left eye has already gone. I leave, look at the young moon, the beauty of physical things, and think of what he will be losing."[61] By mid-June, Charlie had "lost weight more than ever" and looked like a "shadow."[62] Thom took him for big lunches as often as he could, but "a recurrent inflammation & swelling of an artery in his brain" left Charlie "disoriented, unable to think or talk."[63] A year later, Thom wrote "The J Car" about his lunches with Charlie at Speckmann's, where they sat "like children good but fearful / Who think if they behave everything might / Still against likelihood come out all right." Thom could hardly look at Charlie, still "an apprentice to his trade," without guilt, "leav[ing] him to the feverish sleep ahead, / Myself to ride through darkened yards instead / Back to my health." The end of the poem touches on Charlie's unfulfilled promise—"Unready, disappointed, unachieved"—and Thom's sadness, not for his own unreciprocated love for Charlie but because Charlie himself "would not . . . help create / A love he might in full reciprocate."[64] Mike saw Thom worry about Allen, Lonnie, and Norm, but sensed that Charlie was an altogether different proposition. "He was, as I say, my one rival," Mike reflected. "I think Thom loved him."[65] Thom did love him and readied himself, as best he could, for what he knew would come.

On August 8, Thom received a call from New York: Norm had died of pneumonia that morning. "Never to see that huge handsome man again," Thom reflected, "or hear his lovely drawl . . ."[66] Four days later, "Norm's death really gets to me," Thom wrote. "Charlie to hospital (briefly, he says), sounds tearful; Lonnie released."[67] On August 17, Lonnie returned to the hospital, "frighteningly thin—suddenly he looks 80."[68] Early the next morning, Lonnie died. Hours later, Louis called: Allen Day had "died this morning after 20 hrs in a coma (pneumocystis)."[69] Thom barely slept that night. He had lost three friends in ten days. "It has been a difficult August," he told Ander. "And we shall be losing Charlie very soon, he is in hospital, shockingly thin, and gone blind, poor baby. It seems sadder to die at 30, as he is, than at my age. I have done so many things that I wanted to, and have had such a full life, and he's still only at the start of it. [. . .] Well, it's all sad, and there's nothing to do about it."[70]

On August 24, Thom received news about Charlie. "Alan Rockway's mother says 'I think the poor kid's had it,'" Thom wrote after a phone call; "he has been in bed several days with fevers."[71] Thom tried to see Charlie the following day but was told he was "too uncomfortable to be visited now."[72] That night, Thom drafted "a very plainstyle poem" called "On the Death of Friends," a lament, which he later revised as "The Missing."

"Now as I watch the progress of the plague," it begins, "The friends surrounding me fall sick, grow thin, / And drop away."[73] The virus, passing between them, "might have no end, / Image of an unlimited embrace," and the speaker seems helpless and passive, frozen "Between potential and a finished work" in "raw marble," an allusion to Michelangelo's *Prigioni*, unfinished statues of slaves or prisoners.[74] Thom felt helpless and passive visiting Charlie two days later. "He was drowsy," Thom wrote. "I am blind he said, my retina is detaching. He can still see a tiny corner. Held my hand, went to sleep."[75] That night, Thom drafted "Her Pet," in which he described the tomb of Valentine Balbiani and its side relief.[76] On her tomb, Balbiani is at ease: she reclines but remains alert, propped up on an elbow reading, while her pet dog gazes up at her. The side relief depicts her skeletal appearance in death, where "everything is loosed." Thom's frequent hospital visits are the subtext, not the subject, of the poem; he saw in the main tomb a poise that sought "to pretend / And, hope dismissed, she sought out pain at length / And laboured with it to bring on its end."[77] "The Missing" and "Her Pet" explore Thom's own anxieties about his role as a poet in the middle of the AIDS epidemic: how to craft monuments of, and memorials to, his dead and dying friends.

In early September, Charlie was moved to the Ellipse Care Center, a hospice in Redwood City. Thom tried to phone him "but was told he was in too much pain."[78] On the afternoon of September 9, "dear difficult beautiful Charlie died, in pain & longing for death, as Alan Rockway told me on the phone."[79] Charlie's death hit Thom "very hard indeed." He blamed "the accumulating impact of Norm's death only 4 weeks before, then Lonnie's, then AD's. But Charlie was so full of an exquisite promise—it was not merely his looks, merely his intelligence, merely his loyalty & feistiness, his wonderful combination of opposites—there was so much still to come. Poor darling brave wonderful little fucker." Thom attended his memorial service; afterward he felt "exhausted."[80] He thought he was "holding up surprisingly well," he later told Belle Randall, but Charlie's death "really did me in."[81]

Thom had lost four close friends within five weeks. Norm was thirty-six; he and Thom had been friends for a decade. Lonnie had just turned fifty; he and Thom had been friends for twenty years. Allen Day was also thirty-six, Thom's friend of twelve years. Charlie was thirty. His friendship with Thom—some three and a half years—was short and intense. "When near your death a friend / Asked you what he could do," Thom wrote of Charlie in "Memory Unsettled," "'Remember me,' you said. / We will remember you."[82]

One of Charlie's friends, the novelist and journalist William McPherson, had stayed for a couple of days after Charlie's death: Thom found him "very good company, esp now."[83] After McPherson flew home to Washington, Thom was alone on Cole Street: Bob and Bill were away, Mike was at the cabin. Thom could not deal with the empty house and caught a Greyhound bus to the Russian River. "When I went to the cabin, I was in a bad way," he wrote in his diary. "I kept crying— anywhere, any time—in a way that had me concerned about <u>myself</u>. For the first time with any death, I didn't care if I died myself. & I was consumed with guilt that I cd have done more."[84] Mike knew the depth of Thom's feelings for Charlie. "This was not playing," Mike reflected. "God knows I was not one to complain about Thom being in love. But it was so unexpected and so different . . . I was used to Thom dealing with people not in an emotional way, not in a caring way, just fun and sex and drugs. Charlie was different, but we never talked about it."[85] Spending time with Mike was "very good" for Thom. They did ordinary things: shopped at Western Hill Nurseries, ate out in Guerneville, drank at Rainbow Cattle Company. Thom helped Mike with cabin chores, read Emily Dickinson, and began a poem about Charlie. "At least I stop crying," he wrote.[86] Earlier in the summer, Mike had written Thom from the cabin. "Lonnie's death—why his more than anyone else's I don't know—has me thinking about dying," Mike wrote. "I love you babe. I hope you know I always remember that. Because I do. I hope I'm not a disappointment to you."[87] Mike's note deeply affected Thom. "I was just thinking yesterday," Thom wrote, "how knowing him 35 years has been an education in love."[88] In the days after Charlie's death, Mike saved Thom from himself. He thought Charlie's death "brought me as close as I have ever come to a breakdown," he told Clive. "Anyway, Mike made sure I got my grasp back on the real world and I don't want to exaggerate."[89]

Back in San Francisco, "much delayed by all the troubles," Thom began to prepare his lectures for the winter semester.[90] He had "3 new death poems": "The Missing," "Her Pet," and a long elegy for Charlie called "The Schools."[91] Charlie's ashes were scattered among the cacti at the San Francisco Arboretum. Thom visited regularly for the rest of the year and "liked being there."[92] Charlie reminded him of Tony White. "Ch wd not let anyone keep an emotional hold on him for long, but he kept hold of you," Thom reflected. "He was elusive, but he was also loyal. (In these ways like TW.) How grateful then I was for his loyalty, for the love firmly behind all the disappearances, the absences." Charlie was also as difficult to write about as Tony. "I turn you into someone else—like Lycidas, [Robert] Gregory, [Sir Robert] Wroth—a myth, however distinguished," he mused. Even Charlie's "presence . . . turns to a myth, recedes, when I write about it."[93] Dissatisfied with "The Schools," Thom cut all but its final two stanzas and kept them as a stand-alone poem: "To a Dead Graduate Student." By October, Thom had "written about 20 poems in the last 12 months—3 times what I usually write in a year. Most have to do with death."[94] With "Memory Unsettled" and "Death's Door" finished, and significant revisions made to "Courtesies of the Interregnum," Thom found he had enough elegies to fill an entire section of his next book. "I suppose this has really been the worst half year of my life," he told Ander. "Maybe next year will be even worse, though I don't see how it could be, since none of my close friends with AIDS is left!"[95]

In November, Thom heard again from Alan Rockway's mother. She asked Thom to collect a stained-glass panel Charlie had made. "So I did, & visited A, who seems on the point of death," Thom wrote.[96] "His mother for some reason thought he might like to see me," he told Ander. "It was an unwise, though well-intentioned thought. He was always rather jealous of me with Charlie, and I suppose the poor guy couldn't control his feelings at such a point. He was beyond speaking, but when I took his hand he first turned his eyes away and then closed them—with distaste."[97] Rockway died the following day. Thom later wrote about this incident. His poem "In the Post Office" is "about possessiveness": Rockway is "[Charlie's] dying friend, who was in love with Charlie, as many of us were."[98] In the poem, Rockway's "bitterness and anger" are the result of Thom's roles "of victor" for Charlie's affections, "of heir" to the stained-glass panel, "And of survivor, as I am indeed, / Recording."[99] Thom began the poem in late 1990: he kept Charlie's panel behind a filing cabinet and did not look at it again until the poem was finished in summer 1991. It "surprised" Thom and he wrote "Postscript: the Panel," quoting the panel's inscription: "'The needs of ghosts embarrass the living. A ghost must eat and shit, must pack his body someplace. Neither buyer nor bundle, a ghost has no tally, no readjusting value, no soul counted at a bank.'"[100]

Writing "In the Post Office," Thom had "become the representative of all the dead / people I have loved" and felt a keen responsibility to write about them.[101] "They are no good to me, of no value to me, but I cannot shake them and do not want to," he wrote. "Their story, being part of mine, refuses to reach an end. They present me with new problems, surprise me, contradict me, my dear, my everpresent dead."[102] One of those deaths had haunted him for decades. "Of course the dead outnumber us," he wrote in "Death's Door" in late 1987, "—How their recruiting armies grow! / My mother archaic now as Minos, / She who died forty years ago."[103]

In mid-December, Thom made a list of thirty-seven friends he had lost, or would soon lose, to AIDS.[104] Bill was "living largely in Jim's old room, keeping much to himself,"[105] but Thom felt he had "come through wonderfully in the last 12 months, and has shown his great sanity and good sense and lack of self-pity."[106] Rather than host Christmas dinner at Cole Street, the family went out to a restaurant to escape the "dreadfulness" of Jim's death the previous year. After the meal, everybody went their separate ways. Mike and Bob, reconciled, left for the cabin; Bill shut himself away upstairs. Thom went to Folsom Street, came home, defrosted some carrot soup, ate a brownie, "and thought how glad I am I have a family & am not alone like this all the time."[107]

When Thom published *The Man with Night Sweats* in 1992, he wrote in an explanatory note that the elegies of its fourth part "refer to friends who died before their time." He named them in an appendix, "For the record—for *my* record if for no one else's, because they were not famous people."[108] Many of those on his mid-December 1987 list were not famous, either: some were, some were well-known figures on Folsom Street, and some are the subjects of those elegies. Thom's list of thirty-seven names is recorded here, with accompanying life date information, where available.

AN3 [Allan Bertram Noseworthy III, May 30, 1950–June 21, 1984]
Larry Hoyt [Larry Timothy Hoyt, April 4, 1951–December 5, 1986]
Jim Lay [James Harold Lay, May 26, 1939–December 26, 1986]

Lonnie Leard [July 25, 1937–August 18, 1987]
Norm Rathweg [Norman Joseph Rathweg, September 22, 1950–August 8, 1987]
Allen Day [Allen James Day, July 28, 1941–August 18, 1987]
Charlie [Charles Kilburn Hinkle, May 7, 1957–September 9, 1987]

Scotty shirtmaker [Robert Leroy Scott, August 10, 1938–March 27, 1987]
John Ponyman [John Kuhner Ponyman, January 27, 1942–February 4, 1984]

Gary White [Gary James White, December 31, 1933–November 12, 1985]

Paul Joseph [Paul Pedman Joseph, May 23, 1949–June 8, 1986]

David Williams [David Lee Williams, October 12, 1934–
   October 31, 1987]

Chuck Arnett [Charles William Arnett, February 15, 1928–
   March 2, 1988]

Jack Sharpless [John Richard Sharpless, August 12, 1950–May 4,
   1988]

Paul Marras [Marrah?][109]

Jon Anthony [John Anthony Crachiola, September 13, 1953–
   June 5, 1988]

Mapplethorpe [Robert Michael Mapplethorpe, November 4,
   1946–March 9, 1989]

Timo Butters [Timothy Adams Butters, July 15, 1954–
   November 12, 1987]

Gemini Mike [Michael James Shiell, June 13, 1944–April 18,
   1984]

Tony Tavarossi [Elloyd Joseph Tavarossi, December 17, 1933–
   July 14, 1981]

Michael Maletta [December 30, 1942–August 4, 1982]

Paul Olson [Paul Aaron Olson, October 27, 1940–November 22,
   1984]

Dinos Patrides [Constantinos Apostolos Patrides, April 20,
   1930–September 23, 1986]

Ken bartender of Trax [Ken Smith, d. March 17, 2003]

Christian H. [Christian "Chuck" Haren, February 1,
   1935–February 27, 1996]

Billy of Nada's Flowers

José, one of Ch's roomies

Clayton St. Al [Albert John Talley Jr., August 24, 1946–May 23,
   1989]

Spenser the candlemaker

Allen Rockway [Alan Michael Rockway, November 18,
    1942–November 10, 1987]

Dan Sharp [Daniel Edward Sharp, August 27, 1940–March 26,
    1986]
Bill Son [William Monroe Son, January 31, 1937–April 14, 1988]
Pete McCann [Pietro Narciso Maccan, June 29, 1933–January 24,
    1986]

Bob Davis [Robert Bowne Davis, April 30, 1946–April 9, 1987]
Claude Duvall [Claude Mareen Duvall, August 30,
    1941–December 18, 1988]

not to mention two neighbors: Claud opposite & the red haired
    man w/ the jeep on this block

32

CONSOLATION

In December, Thom learned that his old friend Chuck Arnett was "close to the end."[1] Chuck had been a major figure on Folsom Street for two decades, painting murals and holding exhibitions at the Tool Box, the Stud, the Red Star Saloon, No Name, and the Ambush. His AIDS diagnosis and heavy use of methamphetamines meant, as Don Doody wrote in Chuck's obituary, "his work in recent years has been less public."[2] Chuck died on March 2, 1988. Although their friendship had peaked in the late 1960s, Thom still thought of Chuck as an exemplar of strength and power. "If he hadn't had AIDS, he'd still be around," Thom remarked in 1996, "probably exploring new drugs that we don't even know about. He was extraordinarily strong."[3]

More poignant for Thom was the slow decline of Robert Duncan. "Robert is amazingly cheerful, and has gone on this way for several years now, but it is no life," Thom told Jack Hagstrom in late 1987. "For him, more than any other writer I have known, he defined his life as being a practising poet, and now he can't concentrate enough to either read or write and what he leads is a posthumous existence."[4] Early in the new year, Thom returned home to find a message on his answering machine: Duncan had died of a heart attack. "Poor RD," Thom wrote, "a posthumous poet for 4 years."[5] Within the month, Thom had written a short piece about Duncan for the *European Gay Review*. "He wrote magnificent gay poetry, I think as good as 'Hero and Leander' and 'The Sleepers,'" Thom reflected. "He considered the mutual love of men as proper and beautiful as any other branch of Love, and wrote about it in all its variety . . . He did not believe, I think, in the gay sensibility: he believed in anything but specialisation, and aspired to as inclusive a sensibility as any poet this century."[6]

Thom planned "to write more fully about Duncan," but, through the first half of 1988, teaching absorbed his time and energy.[7] As a "visiting lecturer," Thom was not on the faculty: a union contract meant he received no additional remuneration for teaching "approximately double what anybody else is teaching at Berkeley."[8] On top of his creative classes—Modes of Writing and Verse—Thom also taught a literature class: a survey of British and American poetry from 1900 to the present. Late in the semester, he had August Kleinzahler read to his literature students. "It was like introducing a friend to one's family," he reflected, "but I didn't know which was friend & which was family." Unable to pay Kleinzahler using department funds, Thom "paid him 100 bucks of my own & pretended it was from school fund."[9] Kleinzahler was not easily hoodwinked. "If I discover that 'other fund' was the 'Thommy-san Fund' I will stick hundred dollar bills in both your nostrils as you sleep," he warned, "& pour cocaine down them & watch your head snap around like a kite in a stiff wind."[10]

Despite his complaints, Thom secretly welcomed his heavier-than-usual teaching load. Absorption in classes, essays, and grades helped him deal with his grief. When spring break arrived in late March, he wrote a poem that had been on his mind since January. One morning, taking the bus to Berkeley, Thom had seen through the window a friend walking along the street with his four-year-old adopted son. Thom had first met Steven Fritsch Rudser—"ganz, a 29 year old 'Daddy'"[11]—on Folsom in 1985 and brought him home for the night. "He was very genteel," Rudser reflected:

> People talk about his poetry being a formal expression of dirty
> things, of drugs and sex and all that kind of stuff. That's true:
> even though he was into leather sex and bondage and whatever,
> he was really personable, and he was one of those people who, in
> my interactions with him, I always felt better after I talked with
> him for a couple minutes. He was very sweet. He'd always say

nice things, "Sexy Steve," that sort of thing. That was a special thing for me to receive. I don't think that was a special thing for him to give.[12]

"A Blank," originally called "The Last Poem," focuses on Rudser holding his son's hand, which Thom saw as an image of hope and optimism, "the year of griefs being through." It would be "the final poem in the next book, rebirth, upbeat sentiment, a new generation, etc.," he told Jack Hagstrom, "after all those poems about death. I planned it as the final poem even before I wrote it."[13] Thom knew that Rudser had planned "to educate, permit, guide, feed, keep warm, / And love a child to be adopted" and was now delighted to see this "four-year-old blond child tugging his hand."[14] Thom sent Rudser a copy of the poem, asking his permission to publish it.[15] Rudser replied by sending an "immense" bunch of flowers.[16]

When term finished, Thom kept writing. He drafted "'All Do Not All Things Well,'" about two mechanics who lived nearby and ran an improvised garage outside their apartment building.[17] "People who can forget the self for love of something else—math, poetry, & think of auto-freaks," Thom reflected: "by doing that, rest the self, so that it grows untampered with, and becomes more worth the giving."[18] Thom admired, and wrote about, this giving of the self to something else: the "auto-freaks" had their cars; Rudser, in "A Blank," gave himself completely to the care of his adopted son. Thom also saw Charlie Hinkle in that light: he had taught himself Portuguese "for the love of it, & taught himself so well that 6 universities wr prepared to give him money to do graduate work."[19]

Thom devoted himself to Charlie's memory that summer: he wrote "The J Car" and worked on a project he had discussed with William McPherson shortly after Charlie's death. Together they would "bring out a booklet of Ch's 10 best poems," some of which Thom now found "incredibly moving."[20] They selected the poems and had the booklet, *Poems*, printed that summer by Eon Press. "It looks good," Thom thought, "he would have liked it."[21] He advertised it to "friends of the late Charlie Hinkle" in the *Bay Area Reporter* and sent forty-five copies each to McPherson and Charlie's brother, Wade.[22] "His death still tears me up when I think of it," Thom wrote, "more than that of most of the others—because he was so unfulfilled, so unfinished."[23] He knew that editing *Poems* was not only a memorial to Charlie. "Of course, the irony is that I think I am doing this for Charlie, and I am really doing it for myself," he told Jack Hagstrom. "Charlie couldn't be more indifferent to this kind of thing where he is now. And perhaps I'm trying to make myself more comfortable that I didn't do more for him when he was alive."[24]

Writing "The J Car" that summer, Thom knew he had finished his next collection, the as yet unnamed *The Man with Night Sweats*, "even if I do have more poems about the death of my friends." The book would end with the optimism and hopefulness of "A Blank," and Thom wanted his future poems to "start from my idea of aliveness, not of getting on with life, merely, but of the intensity of lives in past and in present." He saw it as a continuation of the project he had started in poems like "The Geysers," the promise "sketched out at the end of the sixties and embodied in the seventies" through gay liberation. He felt an urgent need to record "the way we have tried to 'make it up as we go along'"—quoting from Duncan's "Sonnet 2"—and how the "tragedy of loss" was "inevitable, though who wd have dreamt so dramatically—is so great because of the essential optimism of the centerpiece."[25] Reviewing Duncan's final collection, *Ground Work II: In the Dark* (1987), that summer, Thom quoted with approval Robert Creeley's description of Duncan as his "hero of possibility."[26]

But writing about "aliveness" was easier said than done in San Francisco in 1988. "I don't have to visit friends in hospital this year, as I no longer have any close friends with the plague," he told Clive. "I hope I shall never have to live through a time like that again, but I probably shall."[27] He still recognized people in the *Bay Area Reporter* obituaries, some "I once had crushes on, or tricked with years ago—I am sad," he told Jack Hagstrom, "but since I haven't seen them in years I have already assumed their deaths."[28] Thom downplayed it, but he struggled to shake that sadness. One evening, watching *Taps*, a movie about military students who attempt to take over their school to prevent its closure, Thom abruptly turned off the television and heard "a city sound, a distant motorcycle, and get an image of it for some reason going through the deserted streets of the Financial district." The image "chilled" him, and he wondered if it had "something to do with the silly heroism of the movie & the wasted death." The motorcyclist, such an important figure in his early poems, was now "the man doomed to loneliness—as, really, holding in him all the people dead of the plague, and dying of it, and destined to die of it." With Mike and Bob at the cabin, Thom was alone again. "I do indeed believe in the humane values—friendship, kindness, loyalty, responsibility—but finally, though they are all there is, I do so envy the religious, the people like Eliot who can however doubtfully <u>know</u> there is something beyond all this," he reflected:

> I "know" there is nothing beyond all this—I lack that assurance of a spiritual dimension & I could never even begin to acquire it, but it's a difficult business being simply a humanist. The only value I have that goes beyond all this is embodied in Mike, but he also embodies most of the humane values I believe in, and I cannot believe in a love that goes beyond the grave. The warmth I know comes from his love and from community, but the members of a community of friends in any case die one by one . . .
>
> I think constantly of the dead—not only of those who meant most to me, like Tony and Allan, but of those I would scarcely miss if I knew they were still living far away somewhere—the terrible sadness that so much was involved to make them what they were—they learned, they changed, they went from generic baby to unique adult, & then suddenly they died, and they could help nobody any longer by their example, their work & their friendship. Sad thoughts at night from an empty unspiritual aging man.[29]

Thom did not like the word "spiritual"—"it seems to make a claim to a category of wish-fulfilment"[30]—but his relationship with Mike was perhaps the exception. "The closest to spiritual I can come is in my love of Mike, which is quite extraordinary," he wrote in the early 1980s, "as the family love superseded the sexual love, so something like a spiritual love superseded that. It is intense and enormous, but I think only myself & perhaps he can understand that."[31]

Thom also drew warmth from the wider gay community, most notably in street fairs. "You know how I love street fairs," he told Jack Hagstrom in 1995. "They are my model for what everyday life should be like."[32] In August, Thom attended one of his favorites, the Dore Alley Fair—also known as Up Your Alley—which was smaller and more intimate in feel than the internationally known Folsom Street Fair. Dressed in full leather, he chatted and flirted with thousands of other leathermen. "Spoke with many people," he wrote. "As for the crowd—I know it's impossible to sleep with <u>everybody</u>, but I sure wish it wasn't."[33] The following day, he made "notes for a poss poem about street fairs" and within a week he had written his "strange new poem."[34] It was "a poem I'd been wanting to write for years," he told Douglas, "either about this street fair or another, and finally I combined a description of the event with a tribute to Duncan's Opening of the Field I'd just been rereading."[35]

"At the Barriers" uses "a deliberately Whitmanian line for all its references to Jacobean masques," Thom reflected, "i.e. it's in a completely different style from what I've been doing this last fourteen months or so."[36] He had written most of his AIDS elegies in couplets or rhyming quatrains; "At the Barriers" was reminiscent of the long free verse line he had first used in "Yoko." The poem begins:

> The fog burns off and the crowd mingles promiscuously,
> they gaze at each other with a lazy desire
> —the whole city block, its trade suspended for today,
> is warmed by the sun and by this prolonged friendly lust
> that envelops us like an atmosphere, a perfume of the place.[37]

It is a manifesto for "aliveness," the euphoria and possibilities of the gay community that Thom saw as an optimistic coda to his elegies. He dedicated "At the Barriers" to Robert Duncan and published it in the *San Francisco Sentinel* in October, two months after the Dore Alley Fair.[38] Its last stanza evokes Duncan's emphases on possibility and community:

that there was a place for anyone who sought a home in which difference is celebrated. "Each of us a sum of specifics," Thom wrote,

> each an Arcadian
> drawing attention to our difference, our queerness, our shared
>   characteristics,
> as if this were an Italian-American street fair, or Hispanic, or Irish,
> but we include the several races and nations, we include the
>   temperaments,
> the professions, the trades and arts, some of us alcoholic bums,
> our diverse loves subsumed within the general amity,
> and "returning to roots of first feeling"
> we play, at the barriers, the Masque of Difference and Likeness.[39]

Later that year, Thom wrote "Duncan" "about Duncan's ideas of closure, not just an elegy."[40] With its expansive line, "At the Barriers" honors Duncan's ideas of openness; in "Duncan," Thom used rhyme and meter to explore closure, and in turn used closure to explore the idea and limits of openness. "It's as though I'm taking street noises and turning them into a string quartet," he explained. "One finds out more about the rough and unformed and also about the elegance as well. I was aware of doing this in the Duncan poem and that, in a sense, is part of my subject matter in the Duncan poem. I'm writing about open poetry."[41] "Duncan" concludes with an image of closure, which Thom meant to suggest the open-endedness of Duncan's work. Nearing death, Duncan was

> soon to be enclosed
> Like the sparrow's flight above the feasting friends,
> Briefly revealed where its breast caught their light,
> Beneath the long roof, between open ends,
> Themselves the margins of unchanging night.[42]

Thom may even have seen a little of himself in Duncan, especially "[t]he habit of his restlessness," and shared a similar fear: unlike Duncan, Thom did not "dread" closure, but he did fear that he would someday become "a posthumous poet."[43] A year later, Thom wrote a long essay about Duncan called "Adventurous Song" in which he contended that "Duncan, like Bunting, married Modernist with Romantic influences."[44] For Duncan, "poetry was adventure," and Thom found "a clear connection between adventure and spontaneity" in his work.[45] He could not help writing to friends about his Duncan obsession. "Did I ever tell you Duncan's definition of the Romantic movement," he asked Douglas: "'the intellectual adventure of not knowing.' [. . .] Duncan was a stunning thinker."[46]

Although 1988 was a year full of good writing and free from hospital visits, Thom retained one major source of anxiety: Bill. He had "seldom been off" PCP since Jim's death, Thom told Ander, and "has not given himself a chance for what you might call emotional healing."[47] Instead of confronting him, Thom tried writing Bill a letter. "I do know you well after all these years, and my dear I do know what a huge potential you still have in every way," he wrote, "but this drug is not only inhibiting that potential, it is destroying it, turning you into somebody you would never have wanted to be and would still not want to be if you ever let yourself think about it."[48] They had a "<u>fairly</u> good talk," Thom thought, "at least in that everything was dealt with, but it was unsatisfactory in that I cdn't get him to decide on any course of action."[49] He changed tack and wrote a poem about Bill's addiction. "A System" compares PCP to a lover who "takes a bully's pleasure of him, yet / Represents freedom like a first affair." Bill is "the lost son," stuck inside "his closed system, maze / Of solitary cell."[50]

Early in the new year, there came another blow. Thom came down with a fierce flu that spread through the house. Bill caught it "very violently": Thom persuaded him to see a doctor, who in turn told Thom to take Bill to the emergency room immediately.[51] "If we had insisted, we'd have taken him two days before & he wouldn't have been in such danger," Thom told Ander. "As it was, I had to force him to go & in fact took him there in a taxi!"[52] Bill's flu turned into pneumonia. "It may be pneumocystis," Thom wrote in his diary. "I find it very difficult to deal with this idea."[53] He kept Bill company at the hospital. "Looks as if he will get better—tho he was <u>very</u> seriously sick—today actually eating, talking, aware," Thom wrote two days later. "I thot we'd lost him. I can't say how relieved I feel."[54] Thom, "<u>somewhat</u> reassured," flew to Yale, where he was to judge that year's Bollingen Prize.[55]

When he returned two days later, Bill was still in the hospital. "He pretty certainly has ARC," Thom wrote. "Mickey & I are devastated."[56] An AIDS-related complex meant that Bill was highly likely to suffer from opportunistic infections. "This will turn into AIDS as his immunity goes down year by year," Thom explained to Ander, "but I don't think that will happen for five years or so, and he might well outlast both Mike and me."[57] Bill came home in late January, "underweight and depressed," but a subsequent visit to the doctor provided some relatively good news.[58] Bill's T-cells were in "good shape [and] it is only 5% likely he'll get full blown AIDS for 2 years."[59] Thom felt relieved, but his "terrible anxiety" absorbed so much of his energy that "teaching 2 courses seems to fill my life just as completely as 3 courses did last year."[60] Bill's diagnosis reinforced Thom's sense of the precariousness of the family he and Mike had built. "I am not—none of us are really able to deal with the thought of his death," Thom told Ander. "He has been part of my family for exactly 20 years!!"[61] Charlie's death had brought Thom close to a breakdown; Bill's death was unthinkable. "I have been thinking about the importance of the household—Mike, Bill, Bob," he wrote. "Living with me longer than a blood family would, they are positively part of me, & I of them. The thought of losing Billy is unspeakable. A void opens before me of which I cannot even guess the dimensions."[62]

Thom was also concerned about Mike. He found Mike's "physical and mental problems . . . so interwoven" that he struggled to distinguish between them.[63] When Mike returned from a visit to Kearny, he struggled "to concentrate on what he reads" and worried this was "the first stage of his father's [Alzheimer's] which was hereditary." If Mike were to develop it, he wanted Thom "to give him an OD of sleeping pills. Of course I said yes," Thom wrote. "The question remains: how to get them, and what is an overdose, how make sure I don't fuck up?"[64] On top of Mike's health anxieties, there was the situation with Bob. Although they were now housemates rather than lovers, Mike seemed "to want, all at the same time—(A) a non-sexual friendship with Bob, (B) a full marriage again with Bob, (C) the absence of Bob."[65] Thom knew better than to interfere. "I had no hand in moving him in," he reflected, "[and] I shall have no hand in moving him out."[66] In July, a possibility was raised: Bob "may leave family for a trial year."[67] Thom blamed the breakdown of the family on "the terrible follies of romantic love—its selfishness, exclusive jealousies, possessiveness, its neglect of anything but itself," all things he had hoped could be "muted by the growth of a family." Thom thought "there is room for everyone," and Bob's imminent departure hurt Thom more than he let on.[68] Through the fall, Bob made arrangements to leave. "Thom always said you've got to come back," Bob reflected. "We want you back here because you're part of the family here."[69] He left in November. "The front room looks very empty without him," Thom wrote in his diary. "Mike in eve, explodes in grief & rage, against him, me, everything. I hope he can get some rest in his emotions, finally."[70] Thom was "very sorry indeed" that Bob left but, as he explained to Douglas, it was "necessary" because he and Mike were "getting along so badly. I suppose my idea of a family had to come to an end sooner or later," he wrote, "but it's a great pity."[71]

Between finishing "Duncan" in late 1988 and his sixtieth birthday in August 1989, Thom wrote only two poems, both minor: "The Beautician," from an old idea, and "The Antagonism," for a festschrift for his old Cambridge tutor, Helena Shire. He had typed the manuscript of *The Man with Night Sweats* in summer 1988 but did not plan to publish it until 1992. Instead, he sent copies to friends for safekeeping. "I am haunted by the thought that I might be devoured by a dragon, that the house might spontaneously combust, and that the remaining inhabitants of San Francisco might suffer from the Witch Hysteria of Salem etc in the 17th century," he told Douglas. "My manuscript would inevitably be lost, and what would the world do then?"[72] With only two new poems since "Duncan," Thom began to doubt his "boast about having cheated the infertility jinx."[73] Instead, he wrote prose: an essay about Janet Lewis's poetry for Wilmer's journal *Numbers*, and reviews of Jim Powell's debut collection, *It Was Fever That Made the World*, and Donald Hall's *The One Day*.[74] He worked hard on a short essay about Whitman for *The Times Literary Supplement* and harder still on a long-planned essay about Isherwood for *Threepenny*.[75] "It is important to stress [the importance of sexual desire] about Whitman because there was 100 years of pretence that he wasn't talking about what he was talking about," Thom told a friend; "it is less important to make the point with Isherwood since he himself forced the emphasis so admirably for the last twenty years or so of his life."[76] Writing prose kept him active and alert. "My mind is void of ideas for poetry: but I'm comfortable with that," he reflected in mid-summer. "I'm being patient."[77]

In August, to mark Thom's sixtieth birthday, Clive organized a special supplement in the *PN Review* and Douglas compiled a festschrift called *A Few Friends*.[78] The supplement "dazzled" him. "I only hope it doesn't go to my head and I start imagining I am a living classic," he told Clive. "Literally, I can't thank you enough: whether I deserve it or not, the whole collection of kind people make it seem as though the subject of it all should be read, and even have his books bought!"[79] In fact, Thom felt embarrassed to receive such fulsome praise when he had written so few poems in the last twelve months. He also felt confused that he was "not feeling that terrible sterility of the wordless world" that he usually felt during periods of block. "I am not feeling anything very much that wd go into poetry—I feel simply as if the batteries are getting recharged (as they probably are). So maybe my 'game' is working: a book & 5 subsequent poems are like money in the bank: my imagination need not think itself bankrupt." Thom knew he would "always <u>sooner</u> be writing poetry" but kept himself "busy by writing reviews & articles."[80]

In December, Thom received sad news from England: Barbara, aged ninety-one, had died of a lung infection. "Not a very difficult death," he reflected. "One of the people I have most loved in my life, but I did not cry. The preparation for her death by her muted senility & last few years in a home take the worst edge off it."[81] Thom had not seen her since 1979 but had written her letters through the 1980s: Mary and Catherine read them aloud to her. "Till she was about seventy she was such a splendid woman, not an ounce of selfishness in her," Thom told Ander. "I think of her remembering how she had bicycled all the way from Higham in to Strood to see Mother when she (Mother) was first married. Quite a few miles, that. 'What energy I must have had then,' she said—but she still had terrific energy when she was telling me about it. I love to think of the young Barbara pink-faced and pedalling and long-haired on her bicycle."[82] Barbara's death concluded a bleak decade. Thom made a list of "what happened to me in the eighties":

1. AIDS invented itself
2. Jim died
3. Billy got AIDS (ARC)
4. Allan died
5. I met Charlie, & he died of AIDS
6. others died of it, in 1987, Allen Day, Norm, & Lonnie, as well as Charlie, all died in one month
7. I didn't go to England; & I stopped holidaying in NY after Allan & Norm's deaths
8. Mike & Bob split up; Mike is sad all the time; Bob moved out, effectively ending the idea of the family
9. In England, Barbara dies at 91; and Ander remarries (and that's good).
10. I wrote a lot of good poetry, which is the only other good thing that happened, of importance.

For New Year's, Mike took Thom to the movies. They saw *The Fabulous Baker Boys*, came home and opened a bottle of wine, and "talked (not about Bob) but about ourselves & families etc."[83] Their love transcended such lists. "Mike is quite a considerable source of happiness to me, and I am pretty lucky that we have been able to live together most of the last forty years," he told Tony Tanner. "Every now and again we spend a wonderful time together, as for example New Year's Eve, and I know I must have somehow done the right things all along after all, and the rest is just bad luck and good luck over which I didn't have much power."[84]

33

NEEDS

For the new semester, Thom continued his two-course teaching load: verse composition and Modern Poetry, his survey of twentieth-century British and American verse. In the summer he had been granted "security of employment." "Not that I was in danger of losing my job," he explained to Ander, "but this means additional pay, dental and optical insurance, and even a bit of retirement, though since I have only just started paying into the retirement fund it surely won't amount to much in 2000 A.D."[1] His new status was, in effect, a promotion from lecturer to senior lecturer. The pension plan and increased salary were welcome, but Thom was more pleased with the continuation of his ideal arrangement: teaching only the spring semester left him free to write for the rest of the year.

Thom was a conscientious and exacting teacher. He updated his notes and varied his course content each year, came up with new quizzes and assessment questions, and generally encouraged his students to explore their own reading and writing interests.[2] When he had learned, in 1987, that he would no longer have to teach his "albatross"—Modes of Writing—he was "so happy about this I kept waking up at night & thinking about it."[3] In its place, he was offered Introduction to Poetry. "I responded to the chance of getting at so many students in the lower division (and teaching them how to write about poetry) with a certain enthusiasm," he told Douglas. "The thought of it all rather excites me."[4] Although this

Introduction proved a one-off, Thom then alternated between two other literature courses: Modern Poetry, and Lyric Verse, a course whose scope encompassed anonymous fifteenth-century ballads through Kipling and Hardy. "It's really what I most want to teach, though, literature," he had told Douglas, after teaching Modern Poetry for the first time in 1984. "It's lovely forcing oneself into close reading about which one has to be explicit in a class."[5] He also derived enjoyment from his determination "to demonstrate what is to be liked about every poet I am teaching. [The students] can always find out for themselves what is to be disliked."[6]

His verse composition class was composed mainly of juniors and seniors. "I think it's entirely possible to teach undergraduates [to write poetry], provided they start with some talent in the first place," he told August Kleinzahler. "I figure it's like freshman English: they hand you in something, and you give them some idea of how it could be better written. That way you're helping them in the long run with their writing and their reading and with relating their perceptions of their lives to their language. It's called education."[7] Although graduates sometimes joined his verse class, Thom "strongly doubt[ed] that I have anything to teach [them]."[8] Sometimes he felt that they had learned to be abstruse; referring to one Berkeley professor, Thom felt his own teaching "will be made more difficult by the students who have learned from him how to be obscure!"[9] Otherwise, graduate students already had their own fascinations and prejudices. "By then they have gotten too sophisticated for anyone like ME to help them," he told Kleinzahler. "They're off on their own pretentious trips, they are imitating Ashbery or someone like that, they have read obscure French critics."[10]

Thom's teaching focused on practical analysis that could help students both understand poetry and write it themselves. The screenwriter Michael Colleary attended Thom's Modes of Writing class in 1982. "He didn't speak abstractly or thematically about any piece of work," Colleary reflected, "but about how the author specifically achieved the effect he or she sought."[11] Thom valued a certain straightforwardness and made his lectures and classes accessible to the students. The poet Anne Winters, one of Thom's teaching assistants, admired "his understated but thorough professionalism." She thought his "style of teaching was straightforward, responsible to an unusual degree and reticent—no panache. If one approached him he was approachable, and listened. He was easy to work for."[12] Thom's reaction to the "many splendid looking young men" in his classes was "to try to charm them off their feet, and their girlfriends too," he told John Holmstrom. "They all know I am queer, I imagine, and find me a sweet old man who every now and again engages their fine young interest with some slightly unexpected aperçu about poetry."[13] Because he rarely discussed his own poems—except at readings—his students did not always realize who he was. "Nor even, at school, would he talk of being a poet," recalled David Gewanter, a former student of Thom's, "so that a student, near the end of an Introduction to Poetry course, once asked, 'Mr. Gunn, there's a poet in the *Norton Anthology* called "Thom Gunn": is that you?'"[14]

Sometimes, Thom also had to adopt a more pastoral role. On one occasion, entering "the supposedly-locked faculty men's room," he found "a tall handsome boy humping another similar in the middle of the room."[15] He told them to use a condom. On another occasion, after a midterm, one of Thom's students approached him and said "he hadn't done well because he hadn't been able to study . . . because he took the HIV test and is waiting for the result. I felt so bad for him I went back to my office and cried."[16] The student later told Thom he had tested negative.[17]

Although Thom doubted he had anything to offer graduate student poets, he was not averse to supervising graduate dissertations. Joshua Weiner had arrived in Berkeley in 1986 and worked with Thom on an MA degree. Subsequently, Thom was Weiner's dissertation director for his doctoral work on Mina Loy.[18] Thom admired Loy—he had written about her in his "Three Hard Women" essay and later taught her in his Modern Poetry course—and introduced Weiner to her work. "Thom got excited when I suggested the dissertation topic," Weiner recalled, "and was the most involved, most engaged of the people I worked with at Berkeley." Weiner ultimately proved to be Thom's only graduate student, likely because, as Weiner put it, "Thom held the rank of lecturer and doctoral students anticipating the job market shied away from anyone who did not have rank of Professor."[19] Their relationship began as that of teacher-student, but they soon became friends. That semester, Richard Murphy gave a poetry reading at Berkeley. "I have never been to a reading at which the audience was so against the reader," Thom reflected; "he was both ridiculous . . . and vain and complacent, and of course the poetry was dreadful."[20] At one point, Murphy stopped mid-poem and asked Weiner, who was sitting next to Thom, "to leave the room for laughing, something I've never known to happen in a poetry reading before," Thom told Ander: "asking someone to leave, I mean, not the laughing."[21] "Wish I'd gone out with [him]," he wrote afterward.[22]

A few days later, Thom met Murphy for coffee. "He did tell me 2 interesting pieces of gossip. 1 woman came to him in London who said TW gave her the best 7 years of her life. She said look at my daughter in the garden—that is TW's daughter. [. . .] Similarly, RM is convinced Karl & Jane Miller's 2nd son Sam is really Tony's. Same looks, same behavior, etc."[23] Thom was not convinced. "It's certainly nice to think of there being another Tony," he told his aunts, "but I suspect it's wishful thinking."[24] In fact, Murphy was right: Sam Miller was Tony's son, but Thom never knew this for certain.[25]

In March, Thom sent the manuscript of *The Man with Night Sweats* to his new editors—Craig Raine at Faber and Jonathan Galassi at Farrar, Straus and Giroux—with a view to its publication in 1992. Raine thought it "the finest thing" Thom had ever written, with "strong emotion . . . and perfect artistic control."[26] Raine had not always valued Thom's work. Reviewing *Jack Straw's Castle* in 1977, Raine dwelled on "The Left-Handed Irishman," a minor poem originally in *Positives* and reprinted in Thom's *Selected Poems 1950–1975*. "It aspires only to frigid competence," Raine remarked. "Is Gunn, we wonder, writing the poem in pencil on his knee, using his other hand to stop him yawning?"[27] Thom may have recalled Raine's review when he learned that Faber had refused proposals from Clive Wilmer and Neil Powell to write critical books about his poetry. Raine "says F&F didn't sell enough copies of me to make it worth their while," Thom reflected, alluding to a letter Raine had sent Wilmer in 1988.[28] "In order to sell a critical study—as opposed to the poems themselves—Thom's reputation and (horrible concept) visibility would have to be higher than it is at the moment," Raine had told Wilmer. "He is, of course, highly respected but doesn't have a large enough popular following in this country—largely, I suspect, because he lives in the States."[29]

Unimpressed, Thom wrote "a long mediated letter" to Raine, detailing his "numerous complaints about the mercenariness & inefficiency of F&F."[30] He complained about the lack of ads for his books in his sixtieth-birthday supplement in *PN Review*; the justification for refusing the critical studies; all but two of his collections being out of print in Britain; and his uncertainty about which of Raine, Charles Monteith, and Christopher Reid should be his principal point of contact.[31] Raine addressed each point: Faber was not reluctant to purchase advertising space; their short-lived critical series, with the exception of Neil Corcoran's introduction to Seamus Heaney, "lost money quite badly"; Thom's sales were "steady but slow" and Raine committed to "gradually re-issuing [Thom's] collections in paperback"; and, with Monteith retired and Reid working in a different department, Raine himself was the man "you should deal with."[32] Easily placated, Thom found Raine's answer "very reassuring" and was pleased Raine had taken his grievances "seriously [and] in such a friendly manner!"[33]

Thom remained sore about the critical book. With no other publisher willing to cover permissions costs, Thom thought "no such book will ever be written—in my lifetime, anyway."[34] He was not "so conceited as to <u>need</u> a book about me," but he did want to see a "corrective" to Alan Bold's "awful performance" in *Thom Gunn & Ted Hughes* (1976).[35] A tonic, of sorts, arrived in 1990 with A. E. Dyson's casebook, *Three Contemporary Poets: Thom Gunn, Ted Hughes and R. S. Thomas*. It collected the best writing about Thom to date, including Wilmer's essay "Definition and Flow" and Dyson's own article about *The Passages of Joy*. Thom welcomed the book and was especially pleased with Dyson's article. *Passages*, Thom told him, "is the one book of mine that the critics (with a few exceptions) were unfair about—partly because they didn't get the versification, partly because they felt it was ungentlemanly to admit to being queer in the year AD 1982."[36]

Submitting the manuscript of *The Man with Night Sweats* seemed to free Thom. He began writing again and, over the summer, finished "An Operation," redrafted his old poem about the Folsom Street Barracks into "Saturday Night," and made extensive notes for what became "Sequel" and "A Home." It had become Thom's habit in the 1980s to write more reflectively in his notebooks, analyzing what he was drafting and why as he went along. "I am attracted by what is different to me, study it, and am altered," he wrote of that summer's preoccupations. "The balanced magnificence of Pope's malice, the bravado of Hotspur and Robert Duncan, the sulky boy with the Mohawk, Bunting's sturdy line, my cat's selfish beauty, and indifference of the foxglove. I am altered until I don't remember quite what I was in the first place."[37]

The new "Saturday Night" explored these alterations. Bathhouses such as the Barracks, Thom wrote, were "places of joy & excitement, not of despair, or rather they are places to which we bring what we want them to be. (That unspeakable excitement of the cock.)"[38] The 1975 version concludes with the speaker being cruised: Thom chose not to publish it because "its author seemed limited and complacent. 'Look, I scored!' he says with the defiance of an insecure stockbroker." If a certain self-regard and boastfulness was behind the 1975 version of "Saturday Night," its revision in 1990 was, instead, "a historical poem" about "a great imaginative experience—the excitements and intensities of a bathhouse, with the druggy fantasy always bordering on the dangerous."[39] A different kind of danger closed the bathhouses: AIDS is the unspoken background to the 1990 version. "The embraces slip," Thom reflected, "and nothing seems to stay / In our community of the carnal heart."[40]

A new affair also helped Thom's writing. Since Charlie Hinkle's death, Thom told Tony Tanner, "I haven't found myself close to falling for anybody. Exhaustion perhaps."[41] That changed during the spring semester.

On Folsom Street, Thom cruised "very hot young Hispanic Robert. We have drinks together & come home & have a fine time, with plans to repeat it next week."[42] Robert Gallegos was thirty-six, "fun, & nice, & imaginative, & bright & funny & sexy," Thom wrote. "What more cd I want?"[43] Thom saw him regularly for the rest of the year. "He is careful, I have noticed, to space out our times together," Thom told Douglas in September: "if I try to get him to come over more often, I don't succeed. That's OK: he has established, and I have agreed, that we are 'boy-friends and not lovers'. He is coolly adult, unlike yours truly." Thom was happy with that and felt "the whole thing will last much longer this way!"[44]

Thom's relationships with younger men were key to his perception of his own mortality. That winter, writing about Gallegos in "American Boy," Thom took the careful spacing of dates as the poem's subject:

> I do not seek you out
>   For if I do
> You say I might get tired of you.
>   To think I was afraid
> You'd be the one to tire while we both still
>   Warm to the naked thrill
> Precisely of that strangeness that has made
>   For such self-doubt.[45]

The poem reimagines "Modes of Pleasure"—"The Fallen Rake, being fallen from / The heights of twenty to middle age"—and finds Thom, in late middle age, not content to sit "rigid" as "[t]he will awaits its gradual end."[46] Thom "hated those old men / With turkey-necks / And undiminished love of sex," he writes in "American Boy": "Now I myself am old / We calculate / Our games for such and such a date." Thom grew less spontaneous as he aged and came to depend more on the thrill of anticipation than on impulsive cruising. He sent postcards to boyfriends to remind them about plans. "Sending this to remind you of HOT DATES," he wrote Gallegos in 1991, listing four dates, three in the same week.[47] "He rides me around glamorously on his motorcycle," Thom told John Holmstrom the same year, "and I am trying to get accustomed to the role of daddy."[48]

Although the fifteen-year gestation of "Saturday Night" was an anomaly, Thom's return to an old idea demonstrates the importance of revision to his writing process. "I can't conceive of doing without revision," he told an interviewer. "Occasionally a poem has come out almost on first draft, but there are always a few alterations I have to make."[49] That had been the case at Cambridge, where a poem often took him "four or five days—if I work at it everyday" and sometimes "[came] out fairly easily and fairly complete at the first draft."[50] Extensively revising those early Cambridge poems—which composed *Fighting Terms* (1954)—proved to be an instructive experience. Thom called its American edition, published in 1958, "over-revised" and later "took away a good deal of the revisions" for the subsequent Faber edition (1962).[51] "I kept trying to tidy up something better left alone," he reflected. "All I seemed to do was remove what was maybe the book's only charm, a certain rhetorical awkwardness."[52]

As a result, revision became an integral part of his writing process, not, as it had been for *Fighting Terms*, a way of trying to correct the record. Patience was sometimes the key. Rather than rush to finish a poem, only to want to amend it years later, Thom began to take his time. "Sometimes you find out how to carry on if you just let it rest for a while," he reflected.[53] Once he had embraced revision, his writing process remained remarkably consistent throughout his life. An idea would emerge in a notebook—sometimes a single line, image, or rhyme. "I will jot down my notes . . . kind of higgledy-piggledy all over the page," he remarked, "so that when I look at what I've got maybe the form will be suggested by what I have there."[54] This was the case unless he had a particular form in mind—an Elizabethan street song, as in "Midday Mick"; the terza rima of "Saturday Night"—or was working in a consistent mode: the rhyming couplets of *Moly*, for example, or the rhyme and meter of the AIDS elegies.[55] As a poem began to take shape over several drafts, lines would emerge from Thom's rough prose summary. In his notebooks, Thom drafted on the recto: the verso was typically used for notes, rhyme lists, line variants; or, in a long poem, for composition. Only when Thom had wrestled the poem into something coherent would he type it: then the process began again, revisions in black and red ink across multiple typed drafts until he was finally satisfied.

After Thom absorbed the idea of writing *as* process from Robert Duncan, he began to apply the language of adventure and exploration to his composition practice. "Sometimes all that will survive from the original version [of a poem] will just be a few phrases in the general scheme of the thing," he reflected in 1985. "One of the exciting things about writing for me is the process of exploration. And often for me the exploration takes place in successive drafts, with surprises along the way. Often the poem you end with is going to be different from, and better than, the first draft or your first notion of the poem. Sometimes I'll write a poem and realize that a quarter of it near the end is the real poem; the rest of it was just preliminaries."[56] This was the core of Thom's writing process. "He said that you start writing a poem [on the ground] and you're aiming at a point up here, vertically above it," Clive Wilmer recalled. "You can see a sequence of thought that is going to lead you to that point, and you set out on the journey. As you write, you move to the side. You don't actually reach the objective: you go slightly off course. It's the going off course that makes a good poem. It's the deviations from the course that make the poem worth reading. That's a very characteristic piece of Thommery. He was very good at talking about that process."[57] For Thom, "a poem is a record of activity": part of that activity is the act of writing the poem. "I do think of [poetry] as a making, of that I am sure, because my entire pleasure derives from that," he reflected: "the poem as a made thing, both an artefact like a statue but one containing activity like a performed ballet."[58] Fittingly, such ideas about making, movement, revision, and process inform "Duncan," Thom's elegy to his friend and mentor. It took him some eight or nine drafts to perfect its key line: "You add to, you don't cancel what you do."[59] Revision was not erasure; it was instead fusion and synthesis, a process onto which everything in one's writing and experience could be brought to bear. The finished poem on the page was only the last stage of writing. Its earlier stages—adventure, exploration, accumulation, revision—Thom realized, were just as important, if not more so, to his happiness and pleasure.

In the autumn of 1990, Thom made his first visit to New York since 1984. He knew it would be "strange," now that Allan and Norm were both dead. "Last time I was in NY I had a bad time because of all that," he told Douglas. "I'll see if I cope better with it now."[60] He stayed with Don Doody for a few days in his new, "filthy" apartment "with a great view of Central Park trees across the street," before moving to a place in SoHo, paid for by the DIA Art Foundation, for whom he gave an "overpaid reading."[61] He kept himself busy visiting old friends like Ted Tayler—"now on his third wife ('like Milton,' he says)"[62]—and was not as haunted by the losses of Allan and Norm as he had expected. He had dinner with Allan's old friends John Kelly and Suzanne Greene, "& thr 2 fine twin daughters Annie & Jane I loved. Of AN3's ten friends they knew, the gay ones that is," Thom reflected, "Suzanne said only Bob Curry & I had survived."[63] Back in San Francisco, Thom decided he had "got a little old for New York, too chic for me in some parts and too rundown for me in others," he told Clive. "I need a smaller place (like here) to feel comfortable."[64] Pleased to return, Thom drafted "American Boy" and "Nights with the Speed Bros." and made notes for "In the Post Office" after he had seen "a young short guy in the Post Office yesterday with lazy blond hair—in his sturdy air like Charlie, the shock it gave me."[65] The sight, he wrote, "roused . . . that old man's greed for youth."[66]

Thom had written "<u>evenly</u>" through 1990 and was surprised to receive so many prizes and awards.[67] In spring 1990 he received the Shelley Memorial Award. "The establishment giving to the establishment," he mused. "Not that I'm ungrateful. Just cynical."[68] The following January he was awarded a "huge" grant from the Lila Wallace–Reader's Digest Fund, "around $35,000" a year for three years, for which he was required to "be tied in with the community."[69] He helped Wendy Lesser, the editor of *The Threepenny Review*, organize an annual poetry reading at Berkeley High School, but felt guilty about receiving so much money. To "assuage" his guilt, Thom gave some of it to Mike and Bill.[70] He also gave August Kleinzahler and Jim Powell two thousand dollars each, "because they are the poorest poets I know, nominally for reading to my class."[71] In the same week as the Lila Wallace–Reader's Digest announcement, Thom received a letter from the Ingram Merrill Foundation "wanting to give me another 25 thousand. (I am King Midas.)"[72] Thom replied "saying I couldn't accept it, since I'd just been given so much money, and they shd find someone else. I am not a pig, I hope!"[73] Thom knew that he would be eligible for retirement when he turned sixty-five, in 1994, but his newly acquired wealth did not tempt him to leave Berkeley. "It's so nice to be subjected to a schedule that is not of my own choosing," he told his aunts, "though I quickly get tired of it, and am delighted to return to my own plans by the middle of the year." Being around young people prevented him from "getting stale." "They're good for me," he continued, "asking me difficult questions and challenging my assumptions and figuratively speaking giving the elderly Englishman a kick in the balls."[74]

When the spring semester concluded, Thom's own plans did not seem to involve writing. "My entire writing career has been a series of feasts and famines," he told Ted Hughes, "and I rather suspect I am in a famine too right now."[75] Hughes had written to seek advice about publishing what became *Birthday Letters*: a book of poems about Sylvia Plath. It was "the inside story I should probably have dumped into the public realm as soon after her death as I could," he told Thom. "Maybe I should publish these & confuse a few more issues. Maybe my long silence has done me no good. What do you think?"[76] Thom wondered how Hughes had coped with "all the posthumous nonsense" in the three decades since Plath's suicide. Publishing the poems, he thought, would help Hughes's "mental health" by standing up for himself. "As she got made more and more a symbol of whatever the reader needed, you got made into one too, but of the opposite to what the reader thought he (or more likely she) needed," he replied. "I certainly would encourage you to print whatever you have written about S.P. and that you should add to these pieces anything needed to make the story complete." Thom had no doubt that it would be "a fine book . . . as well as a piece of history and a necessary document."[77] When *Birthday Letters* was published in 1998, shortly before Hughes's death, Thom was unimpressed. "Laboring thro" it, Thom thought it "bombastic" and wondered whether Hughes had "forgotten all subtlety of approach? It is not exciting reading."[78] Shortly afterward, referring to the film *Sylvia* (2003), Thom told Clive Wilmer: "I may not be a modest person, but I do believe in modesty in poetry. [. . .] I will never see the movie about Sylvia and Ted, the very thought of it turns my stomach."[79]

Although he was not writing, Thom tried to commit to regular reading schedules. Early in the year he read "Wyatt in the mornings and Rimbaud in the afternoons."[80] Come summer, he was reading Hardy in the mornings, then Darwin, Browning, and Louise Glück in the afternoons.[81] Sir Thomas Wyatt served a double purpose: he was one of the first poets in Thom's English Lyric course and a major figure in his review of Emrys Jones's *New Oxford Book of Sixteenth-Century Verse*.[82] Thom saw the course as a conversation with both his students and many of the poets he most admired. "When I read, let's say, George Herbert, I really do think of him as being a kind of contemporary of mine," he remarked. "I don't think of him as being separated from me by an impossible four hundred years of history. [. . .] And I feel that way of all the poets I like."[83] Part of Wyatt's appeal was his uncanny ability to "examin[e] the assumptions governing conduct" in games of love, diplomacy, and power in Henry VIII's court.[84] Conduct in the game of love would become Thom's major theme in his late work.

In May, Thom began a new notebook "to reacquire that essential brain fever" he needed to write.[85] Quickly, he began "Ghost Neighbors," a minor poem about Bill's incipient addiction to crack cocaine.[86] Thom warned Bill that "if he ever smoked crack on the premises again he'd have to leave," but a week later he found Bill had "resumed [his] crack habit. I am more angry than I can well express."[87] Thom was naturally worried, but his anxiety could easily manifest itself in a kind of mothering that did little to get his point across to Bill. On one occasion, Thom

showed Bill "A System," about Bill's PCP addiction, which he had annotated: "We seem to be back there again. I never thought I'd need to show
it to you."[88] On another, when Thom thought Bill's alcohol consumption
was threatening his T-cell count and reducing his immunity from opportunistic infections, he tried to persuade Bill to drink less "without nagging him about it."[89] Thom knew that "no one accomplished anything
through nagging," but he could not always resist the temptation.[90] He
sometimes described himself as like a mother and Bill as a son. "He is
really, an <u>ideal</u> son in a way: his addictions, his charm, his anger, his love,
all being son-like," Thom reflected. "I'm like an old mother: <u>That Billy</u> is
so wild, but he's good to his parents!"[91]

Mothers and mothering were on Thom's mind that summer. He felt
Mike's love was, like a mother's love, unconditional. Throughout 1990,
Thom had made extensive notes about Mike, beginning with their first
meetings in Cambridge when Thom found Mike "a man already dreamt
of / or seen in comic books or / cowboy movies."[92] He tried to work
on his "long delayed poem to Mickey" that summer but, "predictably,"
found it "even harder to write."[93] Now, a year later, he felt ready and
drafted "Rapallo" about their European "honeymoon" in 1953:

> That summer I was twenty-three,
> You about twenty-one,
> We hoped to live together, as we
> (Not to be smug) have done.

He acknowledged that "separate beds" was "not exactly / What we then
had in mind," but found "something of that first impetus" had remained.
Moreover, Thom had come to see their love as synonymous with the Cole
Street house. "The structure creaks we hold together," he wrote: "Water
blurs all detail. / This wood will speak beneath worse weather / Yet than
the Yukon's hail."[94] Thom "refuse[d] to sentimentalize" a love that had
lasted four decades and would one day end.[95]

Thom was close to finishing "Rapallo" in June but wondered whether
the "new subject brought up" in the concluding stanzas—"the image of

the blurred detail seen in the present—blurred from bad vision & fatigue of age"[96]—required another poem. Shortly afterward he wrote "In Trust," which draws on several of his favorite poems, including Hardy's "I'll Say I Seek Her" and, in its opening lines—"You go from me / In June for months on end"—Wyatt's "They Flee from Me." In draft, Thom called the poem "an education in love":

> We'll hug each other while we can,
> Work or stray while we must.
> Nothing is, or will ever be,
> Mine, I suppose. No one can hold a heart,
> But what we hold in trust
> We do hold, even apart.[97]

Thom certainly had Wyatt in mind: he wanted to give the lyric poem "my own turn by writing a love poem of mere truth, without fudging, in which I avoided both the idealizations and the contempt found so often in Wyatt and Donne."[98] Although they had brought other men into their relationship and now spent lots of time apart—Thom stayed in San Francisco, for example, while Mike spent the summer months at the cabin—there remained a loving companionship that was essential to both their lives. "Here's hoping I don't last more than another 10 years," Thom told Douglas in 1994. "I certainly don't want to outlast Mike. I may not mention him often in my letters, but I would find it very difficult surviving his death."[99]

It was no coincidence, while writing poems about Mike, that Thom also wrote about the other great love of his life. "I drafted a poem today about Mother's death," he wrote in mid-June.[100] His first draft was called "Finding Mother," and in the margin he wrote: "Or cd be in 3rd person, i.e. she barricades it to keep the children out."[101] His recent, extensive reading of Hardy had put the idea in his mind, and Thom spent the rest of the month revising "Finding Mother" into "The Gas-poker." "Then it came easy, because it was no longer about myself," he remarked later. "I don't like dramatizing myself."[102]

The connection Thom drew between his mother and Mike is one of three reasons why, in the summer of 1991, he felt emboldened to tackle a subject that had hitherto "defeated" him.[103] The second came from a poem he had written the previous year. "My Mother's Pride" is a catalog of his mother's sayings and behaviors, some of which had appeared in his notebooks as early as 1975.[104] It begins with a warning—"She dramatized herself / Without thought of the dangers"—and concludes with a plaint: "I am made by her, and undone."[105] The present tense—"am made," not *was made*—suggests perpetual making. If the making is perpetual, so is the undoing. Glossing the line, Thom wrote: "Incarnation is an undoing as well as a doing."[106] The most obvious reading of "undone" is thwarted, defeated; but Thom does not discourage other readings, like unfinished or even unfastened, by which he suggests that his mother was there at the beginning of his life, remained in his thoughts, and would be there at its end.[107] Thom foresaw his own death as not unlike his mother's: not exactly a premeditated suicide, but not a slow unfastening either. "All this speed at my age will probably kill me soon," he later told John Holmstrom.[108]

The third reason is more literary. Earlier in the year, Thom attended his Berkeley colleague Janet Adelman's "excellent" lecture "Suffocating Mothers in *King Lear*," in which she argued that much of the play's power "comes from its confrontation with the landscape of maternal deprivation or worse, from the vulnerability and rage that is the consequence of this confrontation and the intensity and fragility of the hope for a saving maternal presence that can undo pain."[109] Thom appreciated the Freudian aspect of seeing Mike as a mother substitute and had said as much three decades earlier. "In Freudian and very relevant terms," he told Mike during their quarrels, "I am tormented by not being what my father ought to have been."[110] His torment lessened once he and Mike resolved their relationship problems, but Thom could not have left Adelman's lecture about maternal deprivation—and its concomitant feelings of anger and vulnerability—unaffected.

It also made him think about other Shakespearean mothers. When

Thom read Adelman's book, also called *Suffocating Mothers*, the following year, he would not have been surprised to see her extended analysis of *Coriolanus*.[111] "Neither Coriolanus nor *Coriolanus* can sustain the fantasy that he is motherless, the author of himself," Adelman argued.[112] To Thom, Coriolanus was the hero he had "most admire[d]."[113] Clive Wilmer found it "a very odd choice of hero," the "most fiercely and insensitively macho of Shakespeare's tragic protagonists."[114] For a time, with toughs and leather jackets, Thom overcompensated on the machismo, just as Coriolanus had sought to escape natural birth and become, as Cominius puts it, "a thing / Made by some other deity than nature, / That shapes man better."[115] In Adelman's words, this is the "fantasy of self-authorship" that the play "enacts, exposes, and then punishes."[116] As Coriolanus nears his capitulation, he cannot bring himself to say "mother" and addresses her instead as "the honoured mould / Wherein this trunk was framed."[117]

In "The Gas-poker," Thom cannot bring himself to say "mother," either. His rhyme of "other" with "brother" leaves "mother" unsaid; she remains "she," and "the children" are "her treasures." During adolescence and early adulthood, Thom may have wanted, like Coriolanus, to be "author of himself / And kn[o]w no other kin": his use of the third person in "The Gas-poker" acknowledges that wish.[118] But Thom also learned to articulate what Coriolanus could not. Although he wanted "to objectify the situation" in the poem, Thom had taken his mother's surname, Thomson, for his first while she was still alive: *his* name, then, served as an enduring testament to *her* life and death.[119]

34

ENGLAND

Thom was delighted with his new glut of poems, as were his friends. August Kleinzahler recorded "a sort of neuro-muscular episode of considerable pleasure bumping up against the beams and struts of your meters."[1] Clive Wilmer was also impressed; he gave Thom "<u>useful</u> and specific comments the way no one else does." Clive was especially helpful with the scansion of "A Home," which Thom had revised over the summer. "I need to have that pointed out to me," Thom told him; "my ear is imperceptive at times."[2] Many of Thom's poems dwell on abandonment, and it was no coincidence that he revised "A Home" shortly after finishing "The Gas-poker." Sending the latter to Ander, Thom was typically understated. "Enclosed is a poem I wrote this summer which might be of interest to you," he wrote. The "trouble," he thought, was whether "people younger than we are know what a gas poker is."[3]

In August, Thom gave a reading in Carroll's bookstore at Church and Twenty-fourth. He read many of his new poems for the first time, including "The Gas-poker," "A Home," "In the Post Office," and "American Boy." Thom was "too conscious of audience" and "misunderstood their reactions," he reflected. "I thought they were resistant & they weren't."[4] When he finished "In Trust" the same month, his last poem of the year, he felt like "an old man who has gone to the whorehouse. I'm getting too old for these bursts of Creativity, they are wonderful, and surprising, and <u>welcome</u>, but they certainly are demanding on the brink of 62."[5]

Thom had now written "one third to a half of a [new] book of poems," he told Donald Hall. "From this I get a feeling of security, which is indefensible and absurd [. . .] but at least I don't have to worry all the time about going dry—a worry that at times, I am convinced, has actually made me dry up for years on end, especially after publishing a book."[6] Thom later collected his 1991 poems as a limited edition fine-press book called *Unsought Intimacies*, with three etchings by Theophilus Brown.[7] "They are right out of the borderlands of my life, where nothing is regular, scheduled, or often as it seems to be," Thom reflected. "They are records of what really did happen, i.e. not the official record. I am saying, for example, that Mike is the love of my life, even though we may have boyfriends, even though we don't share a bed—that is not the way it is supposed to be, it is the way it in fact is. If that makes the reader uncomfortable, so much the worse." Thom saw these poems as "distinct from confessional poetry, which is a form of indirect boasting about pain, not so indirect maybe. Where there is pain in these poems, it is a cause for deep regret." He felt "In Trust" was the most "characteristic" poem in the book "because it exemplifies most fully the poem where truthfulness breaks the pattern of behavior considered appropriate."[8]

Thom turned sixty-two in August. "I had such a funny dream, more like a nightmare," he told Tony Tanner. "The dream was that I was really a young man but that I suddenly found myself in my sixties. Then I woke, thinking 'Whew, that was a nasty one', and then suddenly realized that it was true." But for all his dislike of aging, Thom had "more or less . . . exactly the life I want," he continued. "Living with Mike gets better and better: Bill is a bit of an anxiety, it's true, like a wild son— but he's a terrifically bright and nice man to have around, however troubled."[9] As he aged, Thom traveled less often for readings. In 1991, his only overnight stay outside San Francisco came in October, when he flew to Washington, DC, to read at the Library of Congress.[10] It was his first visit to DC, and among the "immense frigid public buildings" he felt "like a flea inside the works of a watch."[11] Charlie Hinkle's old friend William McPherson took him for crab cakes. "He told me how Charlie had anal gonorrhoea while a student at Wesleyan," Thom told Douglas. "At the infirmary, while getting examined by a (good-looking) doctor, Charlie remarked: 'One more inch, Doctor, and we're engaged!' At the moment I heard this, I caught the eye of the male half of a very sturdy young couple at the next table: he had heard the story as distinctly as I had. It was wonderful, a joke within a joke, the horror on his face."[12] On his final day in DC, Thom visited the National Gallery and the Phillips Collection, where he saw Bonnards, Rothkos, Titians, and Turners. "I felt a bit like those poor girls after they've eaten the fruit in Goblin Market," he told Clive, "oil paint dribbling down over my lascivious chin."[13]

Back in San Francisco, Don Doody visited Cole Street for the holidays. After their initial friction in the 1960s, he and Mike now got on "exceptionally well," much to Thom's delight.[14] "Don said of Mike that he loves him because he always tries so hard to live a good life," Thom told Tanner in the mid-1980s. "Not the good life, you notice, but a good life. I think that's well put."[15] For Christmas Day, Thom and Mike cooked for thirteen. "We had 4 Jews, 3 ½ Catholics, 1 woman, 1 black, 3 heterosexuals," Thom told Douglas. "I thought it was a nicely mixed group." August Kleinzahler joined them for Christmas but was subdued because his girlfriend, Deborah Treisman, had "left for New York two days before to 'make her own way' or something—well, she is only 21."[16] Thom had taught Treisman—"the best student in the class"[17]—and found her "quiet, beautiful, forceful, and I'd say rather sexy, insofar as I can judge of women."[18] They had gotten to know each other socially during "long evenings over Thai curry" with August. "My sense was that Thom was very protective of August, had seen him get hurt, and wanted to be sure that my motives—as a student, twenty years younger than August—were pure," Treisman reflected. "Thom's private life wasn't much aired around me, but he did seem sometimes a little lonely or distanced, and I think August felt as protective of him as he did of August; it was an enviable friendship."[19]

Thom was not looking forward to 1992. *The Man with Night Sweats* was scheduled for publication in February (UK) and April (US): Thom had agreed to spend July in England—his first visit since 1979—to promote it. He wondered how the book would be received. "I am past caring in a sense," he told A. E. Dyson. "I hope a lot of people like it, but it won't matter too much if they don't, and I shall be a bit worried if the critics who have disliked me so much in the past (Ian Hamilton, Peter Porter) should admire this one, because surely that would mean I had been inconsistent in some way?"[20] Thom had come to care little for reviews— "Mother said 'Never bother about the opinions of strangers,'" he told Ander, "and I have certainly found that a good rule to TRY to follow for the last forty years"[21]—but he could not help but be pleased with good press. Alan Sinfield's "sensational review"[22] in the *London Review of Books* made Thom "very happy [because] it did seem as though someone was beginning to understand what I was getting at."[23] However, he also felt Sinfield had "mistaken" him "for a responsible and talented fighter for gay rights," he told Jack Hagstrom. "I'd love to be such a hero."[24]

The fourth section of *The Man with Night Sweats* is "a form of book within a book" that collects Thom's seventeen AIDS poems, most of them elegies. At first, he thought that "putting all the AIDS poems together would be too much" and planned to intersperse them throughout the book.[25] Writing to Robert Pinsky, he realized that "an idea of a largely chronological order . . . simply doesn't work."[26] He had resisted grouping them together because he had "never thought about it being a single continuing work": he was just "writing about things that matter to me—about the people disappearing all around me."[27] But there was another connection: "the almost heroic way in which people die. On the whole, the people I've known have accepted their deaths with tremendous strength, even politeness."[28] Such artifice, or labor, is a crucial image in some of the later elegies, notably "The Missing," written in late 1987, in which Michelangelo's unfinished statues develop an idea of incompletion. "Their deaths have left me less defined," Thom wrote. "It was their pulsing presence made me clear."[29] Just as friends like Charlie Hinkle died too young—"unachieved," as he puts it in "The J Car"[30]—Thom is left "froze[n] / Between potential and a finished work."[31] That idea of artifice had been there from the beginning. The couplets of "Lament,"

Thom's first AIDS poem, written in 1984, had set their tone and form. "I was trying to do justice to my subject, to be as artificial as I could, to bring as much artifice as I could, to do them justice," he reflected. "I was trying to build little monuments."[32] Thom was using "artifice" less in its modern sense of trickery or cunning and more in its original sense of craftsmanship: the making of something by technical skill and/or artistic ingenuity.[33] That is a sixteenth-century definition; many of Thom's elegies have roots in, and take their form and tone from, sixteenth- and seventeenth-century poetry. "What we must remember," Thom wrote in his essay about Ben Jonson, "is that artifice is not necessarily the antithesis of sincerity."[34] The fourth section of *The Man with Night Sweats* is a monument hewn from language, not from stone. The elegies are not *about* Thom, but Thom felt the obligation, as a poet, to write the elegies and to make a record of what was happening in San Francisco.[35] "This dying," wrote Alan Sinfield, "is part of a huge, continuing, subcultural event—civil and yet intimate." Thom's elegies "are part of that," he continued. "And this, I think, is what enables Gunn to write them, and what makes them so important."[36]

Sinfield set the tone: critics on both sides of the Atlantic were almost universal in their praise for *The Man with Night Sweats*. In Britain, Stephen Spender wrote admiringly of the book in *The Manchester Guardian Weekly*.[37] For Andrew Motion, writing in *The Observer*, Thom's elegies contained "a whole universe of anguish" and were "some of the best poems anyone has written in English in recent years."[38] Ian Hamilton did not review it; Peter Porter did, indifferently, in *The Sunday Telegraph*, comparing its "dark side of the ledger" to the more "hedonistic" *Passages of Joy*.[39] Thom thanked Clive for his "perceptiveness" in *PN Review*, and Belle for hers in *Common Knowledge*.[40] American reviews, which rolled in for the rest of the year, were just as laudatory. "To read this book," remarked David Biespiel in *The Washington Post*, "is to understand that great poetry so fuses emotion with language that you can't tell them apart."[41] In *The Boston Globe*, Matthew Gilbert called "restraint" the book's "great and undeniable potency," and argued that Thom had "furthered the language of sorrow, the language of recuperation."[42] Writing at length in *The Nation*, Henri Cole praised Thom for "continually attempting to grasp or understand . . . the condition of those around him, strangers and lovers alike, and we treasure his tone of brotherly forbearance as he makes his way." Cole called "A Blank," and its hopeful ending, "a human story unwritten in American poetry to date."[43]

Thom was especially pleased with Hugh Haughton's review in *The Times Literary Supplement*, which focused on the recurrence of embraces throughout the book. "It is quite something to find my book appreciated not only for the things I knew I was putting into it but for a consistency I hadn't been aware of, a consistency that is not of intentions but of the mind," Thom told Haughton, writing to thank him. "I really hadn't known that the book was held together by all those appeals to the embrace. [. . .] Anyway, thank you for a wonderful review. Everybody should have that kind of thing written about him once in his life!"[44] Haughton's articulate and insightful review was a bonus: after the mauling of *Passages*, Thom was "delighted by anything that is not malicious."[45] He met the avalanche of praise with a mixture of pride and cynicism. "It seems to be going down better than [*Passages*]," he told Douglas. "Death is so [much] more acceptable a partner to Queer Love than defiance, but I do have some defiance there too."[46] More immediately, having written almost nothing since "In Trust" the previous August, Thom felt the reviews "serve as a nagging, a pull on the essential energies, as if I had to justify myself continually."[47] His one new poem, "Herculaneum," "just falls to pieces—into dullness, really."[48]

Years earlier, Thom had joked that Ted Hughes had started to believe his "newspaper reputation."[49] Now, Thom was finding out what it was like to have one in America, where—compared to the leather-wearing, LSD-taking bon vivant image that had stubbornly persisted in England—he had remained, to his glee, resolutely unfamous. One contributing factor had been an almost complete absence of self-promotion. "[Thom] once fell into friendly conversation for half an hour with a woman in a bar, telling one another their occupations and so forth," recalled Robert Pinsky.

"When she left, her parting wish to him was 'I hope you get published some day.'"[50] To mark the publication of *The Man with Night Sweats*, Steven Saylor interviewed Thom in the *San Francisco Review of Books*.[51] Thom found the result "charming," but felt Saylor "makes me out to be something of a sex machine, which is more flattering than real at the age of 62."[52] Flattering, perhaps, but not inaccurate: Thom still saw Robert Gallegos regularly and brought home lots of other men from My Place, a druggy dive bar on Folsom popular with the leather crowd. On one occasion, Thom "behaved very badly indeed, going back w/ a certain Jim" instead of Gallegos. Thom felt "v guilty" the next day and phoned Gallegos: "he was nice," Thom wrote, "but I feel guiltier than ever."[53] Their relationship recovered and in June, at the Haight Street Fair, Robert "[told] me he loves me."[54]

As July, and England, approached, Thom felt confused and "deeply depressed." "I lack energy, I lack strength in the gym, I fart continuously, I have twisted my foot, it seems my blood pressure is up, & I am so distraught I drink too much wine in the evenings," he reflected. "Today I eat a great deal between meals, being ravenously hungry, I am a puzzle to myself. What is this: the dread of England, the self-consciousness of publication, AIDS, or the folly of age?"[55] His "dread" mingled with "excitement": Thom had not visited England for thirteen years. "Everybody, for example, tells me I will be appalled by the state of London, kids begging on the streets," he told his aunts. "But that's what we have here too, also the half crazy, since Reagan when governor decided to release all the mentally disturbed (not positively violent) from the looney bins 'back into the community', which effectively meant sending them back to sleep in doorways and in the parks."[56] Thom also dreaded spending an entire month away from his family. Bill's crack cocaine addiction had resurfaced. He described it as "a need in the head" rather than "a physical addiction": this struck a chord with Thom, who often described his own obsession as "sex in the head."[57] Thom had managed to control it, since becoming Gallegos's boyfriend, but it was no coincidence that his working title for "American Boy" had been "The Last Boyfriend." He likely had one of his and Mike's catchphrases in mind: "Nobody fucks old gays."[58]

Thom arrived in England two days late: it was "a horror journey," he told Mike, "out of Dante."[59] London became his base: he stayed in Thérèse's basement, which he still called "my room," in "gentrified Hampstead." What he most liked about the new London was that "English boys now wear engineer boots."[60]

To try to prevent the suffocating introspection that often over-whelmed him while in England, Thom had arranged a busy itinerary of visits and readings. First, he stayed with Tony Tanner for a week in Cambridge. Tanner was "on 2 sticks, fat, inactive, drinking a lot." Thom found Cambridge "all set up for tourists. Millers Wine Bar is now The Cambridge Teddy Bear." Tanner hosted dinner and champagne for ten at King's, among them Frank Kermode ("unexpectedly charming") and Clive, "who is as good as ever, sharp & fun."[61] Over three days, he and Clive recorded a long interview for *The Paris Review*. "Clive was tremendously reassuring," Thom told Robert Wells, who had accompa-nied Thom and Clive to Kettle's Yard, Jim Ede's eclectic collection of twentieth-century art, while in Cambridge: "that somebody can simply carry that much talent in conjunction with that much good sense so modestly and unfailingly IS reassuring, isn't it? It is amazing in a way that I can feel Clive is one of my best friends when we have lived on sepa-rate continents for most of our adult lives." Tanner, though, was less than reassuring. "I hadn't seen him since his balance became impaired, but it wasn't just that," Thom told Wells. "He kept on telling me how happy he was, and he was clearly unhappy and lonely and terribly hampered by his condition."[62]

Thom's mood did not improve in Snodland. "Mary is really batty now," he wrote. "'You're weak, you're weak,' she says up to my face, like a crazed Bette Davis."[63] Her indignation was the result of Thom's long-standing refusal to take sides in what he called the "Ander disputes," namely, the best way to help his nephew Will, who had developed schizophrenia, and the ongoing tensions caused by Ander's ex-wife, Margaret, living close to Ander and Bett in Cornwall.[64] Catherine, though, was "sane & nice."[65] Glad that his visit lasted only for a weekend—"I cd go nuts this way"[66]— Thom returned to London and gave a reading at the Purcell Room in the Southbank Centre, "where I am Mr Success."[67] The next day he read at Gay's the Word, a Bloomsbury bookshop, after which "a goodlooking man with an even betterlooking lover (chunky redhead) came over for me to sign his book, and said: 'I want you to know that yours was the first poetry I read, when I was 14.' (Now I can die happy.) That made me feel like Sid Vicious bathing in the audience's spit," he told Douglas, "or Lord Foppington having his balls tied up by the new footman."[68]

London was "almost too much" for Thom after his "quiet life in San Francisco."[69] He recalled his childhood excitement traveling on the Underground, only now the excitement was "watching all the young men sitting with their legs apart facing you."[70] After Thom's reading at St. Mary Woolnoth, the Hawksmoor-designed church in the City of London, Ander and Bett drove him southwest for a short visit to Cornwall. "A & B make a wonderful balance," Thom reflected, "A managing to deal with much of his belligerence these days." Their home in St. Just was "small & clean & cute."[71] The visit was "the best time with my brother in 20 years" and Thom was amazed he and Ander "failed altogether to have our routine quarrel."[72] While in the southwest, Thom visited Donald and Doreen Davie in Devon. Doreen "looks younger than ever," he told Robert Pinsky, "but Donald is fat and scant of breath, and I wonder how long he has left. He was very cheerful, very hospitable, and didn't mind at all when I kidded him about religion and such." It was "a cheerful little stay," but Thom felt Davie had "the last laugh . . . since the last thing before going to bed was a discussion of 'heresies.'"[73]

Thom returned to Kent to celebrate Mary's eighty-fifth birthday. Aunt and nephew were tentatively reconciled, although Thom still thought Mary "the last Stalinist" and was relieved he "need never spend another night in Snodland."[74] Back in London, Thom gave a benefit reading at the London Lighthouse, a hospice for people with HIV and AIDS. The reading was a mix of established poets—Thom, John Heath-Stubbs, Maureen Duffy—and younger ones: Clive Wilmer and "Jeremy Reid who thinks he is Mick Jagger."[75] The next day, Thom met Michael Schmidt for the first time, and Schmidt took him to a party in Highgate to celebrate the twenty-first anniversary of Carcanet Press. The party "couldn't have been more fun," he told Schmidt, and he enjoyed meeting Brian Cox, the coeditor—with A. E. Dyson—of the influential *Critical Quarterly*, who "was as jovial as I always knew he would be."[76] Thom left the party when Adam Johnson—a promising young poet who would die of AIDS a year later—whisked him across London to the Coleherne, Thom's old haunt, which was "full of sexy men. But I am 62 & not in leather, so all I do is pine."[77] His final days in London were full of other literary activities. He returned to University College School, "strangely the same," and was interviewed for its magazine, *The Gower*.[78] Later, the writer Blake Morrison showed him the graves of Bunyan, Defoe, and Blake in Bunhill Fields. At Adam Johnson's own party, Thom saw Charles Monteith, "far more likeable than in his latter days at F&F," he told Ted Hughes, "where he had begun to be rather imperious."[79] Monteith gossiped about Philip Larkin's Nazi father: Anthony Thwaite had recently edited Larkin's *Selected Letters*, and Andrew Motion's *A Writer's Life*, Larkin's official biography, would follow in 1993. "I'm still reeling under the impact of this information," Thom wrote Christopher Reid. "I'm not quite sure about what it does to L's poetry: it's almost too crudely specific as a cause for the insularity and sourness and loneliness. On the other hand, maybe it makes no difference to the poetry at all."[80]

In England, the success of *The Man with Night Sweats* had made Thom "Little Mr Celebrity." To his "guilty surprise," he found it "fun."[81] Back in San Francisco, he was "trying to dilute my overconcentrated life," but it "didn't help" that his favorite street fair, Dore Alley, occurred two days after his return.[82] "July has destabilized me!" he wrote in mid-August. "As if I was that stable. I avoid the gym, drink too much wine, cannot imagine composing poetry."[83] Thom rarely wrote while traveling, and it often took him a few months to get going again once he had returned to San Francisco. Having not finished a poem since "In Trust" the previous summer, Thom was "saved" in September when he was invited to contribute to *After Ovid: New Metamorphoses*, an anthology of poems based on Ovid's magnum opus. Thom chose two stories—Arethusa and Arachne—and began "composing again, though with a terrible straining and creaking of joints."[84] His relief to be writing again was tempered by the realization that he had been "permanently influenced" by "a phrase of Keats, a theory of Eliot's, a practice of Auden's—all long before I came to the U.S." Auden taught him that "all forms (e.g. stanzaic, metrical, rhyming) could be useful and all should be tried," and Eliot's "ideas about tradition" had convinced Thom, as an undergraduate, that "if I was good enough I was to be the fellow in one sense of Donne or Baudelaire, even of Shakespeare." But it was Keats who had set Thom's course. "His phrase about wishing he could have entered (as he did) <u>the company of English poets</u>," he reflected. "I really did make that my ambition—it was like being admitted to an elite academy, printed in Everyman's Library, of which the French (& later American) poets were members too. It gave me an aristocratic assurance that I as a poet could do what I wanted."[85]

This realization was a cause for pessimism: it seemed to confirm Thom's earlier suspicion that he was "a rather derivative poet."[86] Auden, Eliot, and Keats had made him "look less to the future" and he felt his "experiment has not been true experiment, it has merely been learned from such poets as WCW and RD as I learned earlier from Shakespeare and Donne. I don't think I am a very original poet."[87] There were two distinct reasons for Thom's self-deprecating pessimism. "Just sending off my Collected Poems to London and New York," he told Douglas, having compiled the book in August. "Complicated feelings about all that. Complicated feelings about my birthday coming up, which I resolve by taking lots of drugs, having lots of sex with perverted young men, drinking lots of wine, and—this list gets milder and milder—going to lots of movies."[88] When the proofs arrived in 1993, Thom felt "a good deal of it reads like something written by a stranger."[89] All he could see "in forty years of poetry is pretentiousness, datedness, and boredom, boredom, boredom."[90]

Thom's "complicated feelings" about turning sixty-three were due, in part, to the slow fade of his relationship with Robert Gallegos. When Thom returned from England, Robert canceled a series of dates. "I think Robert is losing interest in me sexually, perhaps has lost," Thom told Douglas. "I don't blame him, I wouldn't even touch an old educator of 63. We still go out and have fun together, though, like going to dinner and orgies and movies together."[91] When Robert flaked on Christmas Day, Thom knew he was "on the way out, if not actually out."[92] With Robert, he had felt less inclined to cruise Folsom Street three or four times a week or partake in twelve- or fifteen-hour methamphetamine marathons, as he had with the Speed Brothers. Without Robert, Thom needed to hit the bars more often to find sex. He connected physical and poetic virility. Physically, he felt "in such good shape": "I am HIV negative, I find, and the local gym has installed all-new apparatus . . . so I look forward to being the only poet besides Sophocles, Hardy, and Janet Lewis to continue writing poetry at the age of 90!"[93] On Folsom Street, "I hardly attract much attention at my age," Thom felt, but he developed other ways of finding sex: namely, by offering guys drugs to get them to go home with him. From the Castro Street Fair, he brought home a Utahan steelworker, "gave him some acid, and introduced him to some other things too, all of which he responded to with huge enthusiasm. That seems to be my new role: sexual educator to wonderful gerontophiles from out of town."[94]

Just as Thom was beginning to write again, he learned that he was not free of England quite yet. He was informed that he had won the inaugural Forward Prize (Best Collection) for *The Man with Night Sweats* and would be obliged to travel to London to receive the award in December. Thom had not wanted to return to England so soon, if ever, "but they are paying me so much money and putting me up in a hotel . . . I couldn't really see any way to refuse."[95] He thought the ten-thousand-pound (fifteen-thousand-dollar) prize would be "useful" for his retirement fund. "Maybe [the trip] will kill me," he told Ander, "then I shan't have to worry about pensions and retirement."[96]

Thom spent four nights in London. Faber put him up at the Hazlitt Hotel in Soho. On the day of the ceremony, Thom woke "feeling terrible" from jet lag and sped through the National Gallery, "only looking at Bacchus & Ariadne."[97] In the afternoon, "bright alert" Kate Kellaway interviewed him—"I doubt if I'll ever have anybody else treat me so well in print"[98]—before he received the Forward Prize at the Groucho Club. Simon Armitage and Jackie Kay placed second and third, respectively, for best collection. Thom found Armitage "absolutely charming, a darling, flattered me by saying how did I ever think up a line like 'the sniff of the real.'" At the ceremony, Thom "conducted myself well, gave a tiny speech, read 'Lament' [and] was noblesse obliging all over the place." The following day, lunch was held in his honor at the Ivy. Christopher Reid, Stephen Spender, "doddery & bright by turns," Hugo Williams, Andrew Motion, and Michael Hofmann were all invited, as was Christopher Logue, "drunk (I suppose) & v belligerent."[99] Thom and Logue did not get along. "I am not sure I have ever had anyone come on so strong with a lot of aggressive categorical opinions," he told Clive, "so that after ten minutes of this (the others at the lunch table stunned) I said 'you're bullying me' and turned away."[100] Thom tapped Motion's leg "& said (as I have not in 40 years) save me."[101]

Of all his old friends at the ceremony, Thom was most delighted to see Karl Miller. "You and I were a little vain, as undergraduates, that we had already read Proust," Thom wrote him afterward, "and we always knew that around this age our lives would be like the last volume of the Novel: all the familiar faces topped by white hair as if it had snowed overnight. It was wonderful seeing you the other day at that confused function: you really do look the same, but with white hair."[102] On Boxing Day, Thom received "a nice note from Karl, almost as if he is finally putting an end to the falling out we never actually had."[103] The following year, at Thom's request, Karl sent him a copy of his memoir, *Rebecca's Vest*. "It is of especial interest to me," Thom told him, having read the book in a single day: "you have said more about my life, by speaking of yours, than I could have said myself."[104] Miller had written that, at Cambridge, Thom "came to know there what he was, and to know that he wished to be what he was."[105] Thom thought that was "true, but I hadn't realised that anybody knew how fully true it was besides myself."[106]

Back on Cole Street, Thom tried once again to dilute his life. "Fun to be famous," he wrote, leaving London, "but I can't take any more of it, so I'm glad to leave."[107] He looked forward to a quieter year without the strange dread of England that had colored 1992 and made it seem overconcentrated. "Now to get ready for teaching," he told Ander. "Mike must go East (New Jersey) to move his mother down to a nice cousin in Florida . . . Then we must work on getting Bill off his crack addiction. Life is certainly full of good sport."[108]

35

DEƧIRE

"I am unbelievably depressed—quite the worst New Years depression in years," Thom wrote in mid-January. "I am living alone, M in the East, Bill sleeping every day & drugging every night." Nor was he writing any poetry. "I'm old & horny & unhappy & sorry for myself," he continued. "I look forward to school, to take me out of it."[1] Reflecting on his depression, Thom realized it was "rooted in the end of 1944."[2] "I am always depressed in January," he told Tanner a year later. "My mother killed herself on Dec 29, 1944, and I think I set my moods an annual pattern from that."[3] Mike did not return until February, "in good spirits, after having walked eye-deep in hell," clearing out the old family home in Kearny and helping his widowed mother relocate to Florida.[4] Thom feared that "we will lose Bill in the next 12 months" because of his addiction. "This thought is so dreadful I don't know how to handle it."[5] Mike thought Thom was too patient with Bill—"Bill is very spoiled," he reflected, "and Thom is one reason for that"[6]—but Thom's patience had its limits. Come summer, Thom was "pissed off at Bill, having let him sweet talk me into paying his utility bills (a lot) <u>again</u>, thus indirectly leading me to finance his habit, something I swore I'd never do. I am ashamed."[7]

When Robert Gallegos "more or less tactfully dropped"[8] him, Thom asked himself: "Why <u>should</u> I expect anyone to take notice of me at this age?"[9] In the spring he began—and quickly abandoned—"A Goodbye," another poem about Robert, in which he wrote, "my impulse all my life has always been to keep things nice/easy, / while knowing very well / I have things in me by which they won't stay nice: / I let people down / I disappoint / I lust after every man I see."[10] Against this depressing backdrop, Thom was even more pleased to be teaching. "I need to have a rigorous outside body (i.e. the university) give me a schedule that has nothing to do with my own choice," he told Clive, "mainly to get me out of a solipsistic existence at my own interior desk." Thoughts of retirement—he would turn sixty-five in August 1994—were far from his mind. His "really unusual and inconsistent career at Berkeley" meant he would "only have a minute pension to live on." The Forward Prize had been welcome: Thom put "everything like that into savings to live off whenever I do retire."[11] His two classes—verse composition and The English Lyric—went well, but Thom felt he was "a bit behind with everything but the classes."[12] In May, he gave the commencement address for the graduating English students in front of five thousand people in the Greek Theatre. He was "nervous for 6 months" about addressing so large an audience, but he need not have worried. "Everybody was in a marvellous mood, and thought my pieties were right in place," he told Clive. "The new graduates in their gowns and all were swigging champagne from bottles in the front row."[13] Thom's own gown was "so overpowering that it covered everything, like the 6 wings of the angels in Isaiah. It was an M.A. gown," he told Clive, "since I once went to the trouble of buying my Cambridge M.A. degree, in absentia."[14]

During the semester, Thom struggled to write—"I've lost the key to the door," he wrote in February, "I don't know how I could have let it go"—but in May an unexpected letter kick-started his imagination.[15] The composer John Adams wrote suggesting they work together on "'a new theater piece,'" Thom told Clive. "I waited and thought about it, and then got (madly) taken by the idea of Jeffrey Dahmer for an opera."[16] The timing was fortuitous. Thom had recently read Patricia Highsmith's article about Dahmer, "From Fridge to Cooler," in *The Times Literary Supplement*.[17] "In the course of it [Highsmith] describes the circumstances of the first murder," Thom later wrote:

The eighteen-year-old Dahmer picked up a hitchhiker notable for his bare chest . . . and asked him home for a beer. After the beer and some conversation, the hitchhiker turned to leave, on the way to see his girlfriend. "Dahmer began to feel the pangs of loss; in minutes Steve would leave the house, and he would never see him again." This is the sentence that lit up the whole account.[18]

Thom did not hear from Adams again—he subsequently learned that "Adams [had] contacted about every other poet in the US"[19]—but felt "bombarded by language, suddenly"[20] and began to write. What interested him was "the idea of an obsessive desire that probably finds itself as pure and single-minded as Romeo's or Tristan's."[21] The idea was a twist on the heroic, operatic ideals Thom had explored in earlier poems like "Das Liebesleben" and "The Kiss at Bayreuth."[22] Thom imagined that Dahmer "felt the same obsessive emotions as all of us, but just carried them a little farther and in a different direction."[23] Thom's own obsessive desires, and the connection he drew between desire and loss, are the emotional subtext of the poems. "[They] are about Dahmer," he wrote, "but they're also about me."[24] He chose to write in Dahmer's voice and felt enthusiastic about "dealing with another character, not having to speak for myself!"[25] "Hitch-hiker," the first poem of the sequence, begins:

> Oh do not leave me now.
> All that I ever wanted is compressed
> In your sole body. As you turn to go
> I know that I must keep you, and know how,
> For I must hold the ribbed arch of your chest
> And taste your boyish glow.[26]

"I do think it might work as a song-cycle," he told Clive. "I have already written two songs. [. . .] I call the cycle 'Troubadour' because a necrophiliac is dealing in a sense with an ideal."[27] The new project made Thom feel like "everything's a possibility again."[28] Between May 27 and

June 10 he finished four Dahmer poems—"Hitch-hiker," "Iron Man," "The Visible Man," and "A Borrowed Man"[29]—and wrote a fifth, "Final Song," later in the year. Reviews of *The Man with Night Sweats* had stifled Thom, but now—as they continued to trickle in[30]—they seemed to liberate him. "I think I have got tired of my saintly reputation of writing virtuous poems about AIDS," he told Ander, "[and] want to revert to my previous reputation for dubious morality."[31] Two years later, at the Art Institute of Chicago, "about ten old ladies rose and left after I read the Dahmer poems," Thom told John Holmstrom. "'You wouldn't be leaving if I'd written some poems about Napoleon or Julius Caesar, Ladies,' I said to their retreating backs, 'and they both killed many more people.' Understand, I said this in a friendly voice, not derisively, but none of them turned or answered. But I suppose it was the masturbatory bits that really got to them!"[32]

In early June, Thom received a surprise telephone call from the MacArthur Foundation. "I have received a MacArthur grant for 5 years . . . I find it a touch difficult to handle the whole idea," Thom wrote, "& drink a lot on Castro at night."[33] In 1993, MacArthur Fellowships—also known as "Genius Grants"—were worth around $369,000 and did much to allay Thom's fears about having "something to retire on."[34] Thom was delighted to learn that among his two dozen fellow awardees was his friend and fellow poet Jim Powell, whom he found "always sane and wonderful on the subject of poetry." Although their friendship was at times fractious, Thom had "the best chats about poetry with [Jim] that I've ever had with anyone except perhaps Yvor Winters."[35] When the MacArthurs were announced in mid-June, "the phone [was] off the hook, people (inc strangers) on street congratulating me," and the news was carried in all the Bay Area newspapers.[36] "Getting the award has made me momentarily famous in SF," he told Clive, "where I have never been much known as a poet or anything."[37] With his first installment of MacArthur money, Thom did two "grand" things: first, he bought "a first edition of [Yeats's] The Tower, which I have always considered the most physically beautiful book of the 20th century (cover in gold leaf by T. Sturge Moore)." Second, he organized a European holiday for him and Mike: a week in Prague followed by a week in Venice. Prague "because everyone tells me how beautiful it is," and Venice because "I <u>know</u> it is beautiful," Thom told Ander. "Somehow I don't want to travel abroad anymore without Mike, a sign of age I guess."[38]

The summer saw Bob return; he rejoined the Cole Street family after a three-year absence. "He is [a] sweet-natured man and very good at helping round the house (and a superlative cook)," Thom enthused.[39] Bob settled into the front bedroom and Thom was "happy to be cooking for 4 again."[40] Thom took his cooking responsibilities seriously. The family had a predetermined schedule—"Each cooks one night, and each cooks well"[41]—and there were often large dinner parties thrown for birthdays and visits. "Thom's company dish was always the same," Mike recalled. "A beef stew. It was good, but we got a little tired of it."[42] Another signature dish was "The Meatloaf," in which Thom baked a mixture of packet soup, sour cream, two eggs, and lightly sautéed beef until it looked "as crisp as shit."[43] "He wasn't a greatly gifted cook (he was, after all, an Englishman, and an Englishman of a particular generation)," recalled August Kleinzahler, "but he was more than passable: his pasta dishes were quite good, and he had a turkey recipe that involved cheesecloth, resulting in an uncommonly moist bird." Thom's approach was "fastidious, methodical and quietly determined, and a bit fussy: sober, spectacles resting on the tip of his nose, recipe book open at the appropriate page, stirring grimly away, eyes on the clock."[44] The family often hosted friends for Thanksgiving and Christmas: Thom and Bob rotated responsibility for the turkey. Mike typically made side dishes—sprouts, carrots, cranberry sauce—while Bill's specialty was a dessert called "bourbon on a cloud": "a huge blancmange made in a circular mould," Thom explained to his aunts, made with "bourbon (whiskey) and lots of heavy cream and some gelatine and I think eggs, or perhaps just whites of eggs."[45] Thom liked to drink while cooking the turkey. "He drank cheap wine," Mike recalled. "He would take out the bird roast then basically pass out. That was a pattern because he would be drinking the whole time."[46]

Before his European adventure, Thom traveled alone to Saratoga Springs to give classes and a reading for the summer school at Skidmore College. He "astonish[ed]" himself by writing while away: he made notes for the fifth Dahmer poem and wrote "Coffee Shop," based on two Weegee photographs, for *The Threepenny Review*.[47] Thom premiered his first four Dahmer songs at his public reading—"Pretty good, I think!"—and was "much taken" with Drew Limsky, a twenty-seven-year-old bodybuilder with "colossal arms & Gold's Gym Tshirt & wt lifting belt" who spoke to him after the reading.[48] A few days later, Thom took Drew for dinner. "Nothing happened," he wrote, "but nothing was <u>meant</u> to happen."[49] They corresponded a little: Thom wrote Drew some letters of recommendation and took him for dinner when he passed through San Francisco. "I remember I was going through my broken-hearted love affairs," Limsky recalled. "I wrote to him and said I couldn't believe after all my experiences I hadn't developed any armor. And Thom said, I don't know why you'd want to."[50]

On his last day in the East, Thom attended the Balanchine Celebration at the New York State Theater. "One of my best times ever in a theater," he reflected, "all Balanchine (a) Bourrée Fantasque (b) HAIEFF Divertimento (c) Valse Fantaisie & (best) (d) Symphony in C. All that athletic grace so beautiful I was in tears."[51] The ballets brought to mind the conclusion of Dante's *Paradiso* and lent Thom the concluding image for "A Wood near Athens," which he drafted on his return to San Francisco and originally called "A History of Love."[52] Together, the angels "sang and played / The intellect as powerhouse of love."[53] "It was incredibly moving," he told Clive of the Balanchine Celebration. "Dante's angels are dancing as well as <u>that</u>!"[54] The poem mentions Dahmer by name—Thom worked on "A Wood" concurrently with "Final Song," the last "Troubadour" poem—and confirmed to Thom that he wanted his next book to conclude with a series of love poems, in which the unusually tight and complex interplay of images, figures, and metaphors between the poems was his attempt to consolidate his ideas about love, desire, friendship, and sex. "This is either Dahmer-stuff or me-stuff (doesn't make much difference as the only part that interests me is the parts of us that overlap)," he reflected. "The wonder at the sheer <u>biology</u> of sex: that we have thought about & given values to & <u>believe in</u> so much that is simply cock and cunt and asshole & nipples, that what is sheerly flesh's contrivance for continuing the race shd have <u>meanings</u> that have floated free—into a great deal of other 'areas', perhaps into everything." Thom found it strange that this "matter of friction and juices" was "the source of almost all I care about—I mean Mike, and poetry, and my friends, etc. It's amazing, and it only stops being amazing for long periods because it is so large we're in it & can't get outside of it (like Alice's wood)."[55]

Realizing that his recent poems were all the results of commissions—"Troubadour" for John Adams, "Coffee Shop" for *Threepenny*—Thom hoped that "A Wood,"[56] which he considered "self-occasioned," might help him continue to write for the rest of the year. "If I am so prompt in coming up to an occasion," he reflected, "can't I try to create occasions as precise in their demands as these were—or as I took them to be?"[57] He would be disappointed. Through summer, with Mike and Bob at the cabin and Bill away visiting family, Thom felt "profoundly lonely in this big house."[58] He later drafted a poem about how difficult he found these extended separations. "Whenever you leave for a weekend or a week/ I feel you will never come back, but you do," he wrote, addressing Mike:

> This never coming back, this fear
> where does it come from
> Being left by my mother at the boarding school during the Blitz
> standing forlorn in the familiar dormitory
> of the Progressive school
> thrust from the womb again.[59]

Thom sought company at the bars and began "to pick up speed freaks."[60] He was no stranger to methamphetamine—one playmate thought "Thom was addicted to speed even in the 1970s"[61]—but that summer he witnessed firsthand the enormous demand for "poor man's cocaine" in the Bay Area. Its street value was "about $80 to $120 a gram" and "about $10 worth" could provide a high of "a good 12 hours."[62] What began as a summer habit continued for the rest of the year. He started taking speed on his own and used "tweaking"—a slang term for taking speed—in his diary to describe tricks. One, who "roamed from room to room" on speed, stole Thom's "(considerable) money-stash."[63] Another did not realize that Thom was sixty-four. "Doing it at that age actually surprises me," he reflected later, "realizing how old Thom was and that he was doing as much [speed] as he was, because the recovery is just brutal."[64] Thom knew what he was doing. "I have to admit, we snorted a great deal of speed (which seems to be the drug of the year—again)," he told Douglas after one threesome, "and I had a horrifying hangover until at least the next Thursday. I'll probably kill myself doing this kind of thing one of these days. Still, it's worth it: such a fulness of pleasure could convert anybody into a panting young Romantic in a moment."[65]

In September 1993, Faber published Thom's *Collected Poems*; Farrar, Straus and Giroux published its American edition the following summer. Since the late 1970s, Thom had helped Jack Hagstrom, his lead bibliographer, collect reviews of his books. "Most of them I could do without having read even once," he told Hagstrom. "I think in future, starting with Collected, I'll be leaving it all to you and no longer sharing the work of collecting them." He felt that "being systematic" about collecting, and thereby reading, all the reviews put him "in a false position with myself."[66]

Many reviews of Thom's work dwelled on an aspect of his life in which he took little interest: nationality. When he described himself as "Mid-Atlantic" or "Anglo-American" it was not from a shared affinity—a foot in both camps, as it were—but from the sheer necessity of having to live somewhere. "I feel now that I'm almost American, even though I'm still British by nationality," he told James Campbell in 1999. "I don't think nationality matters that much. It's a symbol of something, but not of anything I'm interested in."[67] Thom saw his Mid-Atlanticism as productive. Others did not. "His departure from England almost 40 years ago stranded him between two cultures, and within his insulating privacy he has written of America without being of America," complained William Logan. "His poems are wry, self-consumed, a little eaten up with their advantages, charmingly stiff in an Old World way."[68] But some critics were able to grasp Thom's point that nationality was immaterial. "The truly mysterious poise that runs through [Gunn's work] could be described as the power to be at home with the alien or unlikely," Robert Pinsky remarked: "with various metrical extremes and modes; with the manners of various kinds of people, like Odysseus; with many countries and cities and cultures . . . *Moly* is a book about being at home even in transformation, in distortion." For Pinsky, Thom "live[s] inside the rhythms and meanings and structures of our English language with a fresh, venturesome eagerness, and a mastery that make being merely an American poet or an English one seem beside the point."[69]

When American reviewers came to pay sustained attention to Thom—around the time of *The Man with Night Sweats* and *Collected Poems*—they were as reluctant to make a strong case for him as British critics had been since the late 1950s. His work received warm praise, in most cases, but opinions were caveated and judgments postponed. "Mr. Gunn, in the 40 years during which he has been publishing poetry, has always been elusive, hard to place both as to nationality and as to poetic affiliation," remarked Richard Tillinghast in *The New York Times*. "His 'Collected Poems' are sane, accessible, impressive in their versification and command of language—testaments to intelligence, warmth and integrity."[70] Thom was such an enigma to *The New York Review of Books* that they chose British or Irish reviewers for all his books, beginning in 1973 with Stephen Spender on *Moly and My Sad Captains*, then Richard Murphy on *Selected Poems 1950–1975* (1980), Michael Wood on *The Man with Night Sweats* (1993), and James Fenton on *Boss Cupid* (2000).[71] Not that this always displeased him. Wood's review "astonished" him, perhaps for its somewhat unlikely pairing of Thom with John Ashbery.[72] "Both have sought, in different ways, to bring poetry to bear on difficult and elusive contemporary conditions," Wood reflected: "loss, displacement, affection, loyalty, bewilderment, abrupt and brutal death."[73]

When a consensus emerged among American critics, it was largely informed by their British counterparts. Thom was a curiosity: Anglo-American, gay, pro-Winters but also pro-Duncan, he seemed to exist outside any kind of established critical apparatus. Thom called it "the Gunn-theory": A. Alvarez perpetuated it in England in the 1950s and 1960s and "recycle[d]" it in his review of the *Collected Poems* in *The New Yorker*.[74] In essence, Thom "started out brilliantly and full of purpose," Alvarez wrote, "and then seemed to lose his way." Thom's achievement in those middle years is questioned: "Maybe . . . Gunn was happy in San Francisco—and happiness, for the past two centuries, has not been a great inspirer of poetry." And praise is qualified: "All of [Gunn's poems] have virtues that a serious teacher, like Winters, or Gunn himself, could recognize and teach: technical skill, lucidity, discipline," Alvarez continued. "A large proportion of them are also rather dull. That, too, is par for the course. Coleridge was a great poet, but his reputation rests on five poems."[75] When Alvarez's review was published, friends telephoned and wrote to Thom to complain about it.[76]

By the time of Alvarez's review, this attitude was established on the East Coast. "He has rarely recovered the deftness or speed that drove him through the metrical register of 'Fighting Terms' or 'The Sense of Movement,'" Logan concluded.[77] What Colin Falck called "the vacant counter-cultural slovenliness of [Gunn's] Californian ethic"[78] in 1976 was, for Logan, the "overheated poems on surfers and LSD [which] are simply embarrassing."[79] Although Thom was more widely praised on the West Coast—reviews in the *San Francisco Chronicle* and *The Threepenny Review* were routinely positive—it was the eastern press that drove his American reception. In essence, Thom was never caught in the prevailing winds of American poetry. "The *I* of the poetry carries almost no tangible personality," reflected August Kleinzahler in *Threepenny*. "This can be upsetting to American readers acclimated to the dramatic personalities of recent poetry, Lowell, Berryman, Sexton, Ginsberg et al. [. . .] The 'I' in Lowell or Ginsberg, say, is no less willed, and in no regard is it the 'I' you'd encounter in conversation with the man. But the American reader is accustomed to the illusion of familiarity, intimacy, and Gunn doesn't fork over." This was "the popular line" on Thom, which culminated in

The Man with Night Sweats. "Gunn was rehabilitated by the AIDS crisis and became an important poet once again," Kleinzahler concluded, "because he became a *feeling* poet at last."[80]

Despite his ambivalent critical reception, Thom was nevertheless held in high esteem in the United States. Between 1988 and 1998, he won the Sara Teasdale Prize; the Robert Kirsch Award (for lifetime achievement, at the Los Angeles Times Book Awards); the Shelley Memorial Award from the Poetry Society of America; a Lila Wallace–Reader's Digest Writers' Award; the PEN Center USA West Literary Award for poetry; the Lenore Marshall Prize for *The Man with Night Sweats*; a MacArthur Fellowship; the Bay Area Book Reviewers' Award for poetry; and the Award of Merit for Poetry from the American Academy of Arts and Letters. Presenting Thom with the Robert Kirsch Award in November 1988, Charles Champlin, arts editor of the *Los Angeles Times*, quoted an admiring critic: "[Gunn's poetry] will serve as a reference point to this era in California and American history long after other forms of testimony have receded into oblivion. Great poetry saves experience by making it permanent."[81]

If Thom saw England as a representation of his vulnerable, gauche, teenage self, America was his new one: more masculine, more confident, more open. Thom was always looking forward, but his English reception—much to his irritation—seemed to matter most to him. He partook in American literary culture, contributing poems and essays to American publications, judging American poetry prizes, giving readings across the country, and supporting young American poets whose work he held in high regard. But as far as his own work was concerned, he could not help but keep one eye on England. When he mentioned reviews in letters and diaries, they are most often English ones. Ian Hamilton—his English bête noire, about whom he wrote "Hatchet, the Reviewer"[82]—never had an American equivalent.[83] The coolness of Thom's English reception bothered him more than he let on, but, feeling accepted in American life more generally, the opinions of American critics did not greatly stir him. "Neither country has offered him approval at its most resounding," reflected Alfred Corn, "almost as though neither trusts him to be entirely loyal."[84] Thom's loyalty was more to the West

Coast, to San Francisco. "Absurd to think of Thom Gunn as an expatriate," reflected Robert Pinsky. "San Francisco is his home city as few people find homes."[85] Donald Hall, in a perceptive essay about Thom in the *Los Angeles Times*, went one step further. "If he belongs to a nation it is San Francisco; or perhaps homosexuality is his country," Hall remarked, "but I do not find him pledging allegiance to anything except his own alert, unforgiving, skeptical independence."[86]

In October, Thom and Mike flew to Prague. It was Thom's first visit to mainland Europe since his jaunt to Paris with Tony White in 1974. It was also the first time he visited Europe from the United States without stopping in England. He looked forward to it. "I imagine the young men of Prague will set the tone of my sexual fantasies from now until my death," he told Tanner.[87] Mike was more apprehensive. "I was nervous about it because of the distance between us, and that we were sharing the room and the bed," he reflected. "But what was good about it was that we were so together. We'd get up and go sightseeing, then we ate together and slept in the same bed. It was so much togetherness where there had been almost none, except for meals. I didn't know how it would turn out, but it was a huge success."[88]

They took an apartment in the Old Town, on Dlouhá, and spent each day wandering at random, climbing hills, dawdling along cobbled streets. They "stumbled across fresh beauty at every street corner."[89] They browsed as many antiques shops as they could find, looking to add to Mike's already considerable collection, and drank pilsner together in the Old Town Square. "Thom would say let's have another one . . . And I would say, as long as we can go home and I can take a nap before we eat!" Mike recalled. "He was a good sport about that because [he] was such a drinker and I'm not."[90] Prague lived up to Thom's "high but vague" expectations. "It is breathtaking," he told Douglas, "and somehow especially delightful in that nothing there was predictable."[91]

In Venice, Thom and Mike stayed at the Hotel Flora, a boutique hotel behind St. Mark's Square, and spent most of the week visiting galleries and churches. At the Gallerie dell'Accademia they saw Tintoretto's *Cain and Abel* (1550–1553) and "OD'd on Tintoretto—all that melodrama" at the Scuola di San Rocco.[92] They delighted in a visit to the island of Torcello, with its array of palaces. Thom was especially taken with the "oceans of gold mosaic" in the Cathedral of Santa Maria Assunta. Eating outdoors, they were "hustled by wild cats like sparrows at Berkeley Union."[93] "Mike and I had a terrific time, as you can tell," Thom told Ander. "It was the first time we had gone anywhere together in I don't know how long— probably 1960 or so, when we started not getting on very well for about 5 years." He found it "very exhausting, all those cobbled streets, all that walking and climbing, all that eating and drinking, all that traveling," but "all very good for my body and mind."[94] The grand tour concluded with a short stop in Chicago, where Thom attended the MacArthur Fellowship ceremony. "It has been all I planned it to be," he reflected, "in company w/ M night & day for 2 weeks."[95]

Back in San Francisco, Thom received a letter from Ted Hughes asking him to accept the Queen's Gold Medal for Poetry. "We were unanimous (and instantaneous) in wanting to see it go to you," Hughes wrote on behalf of the committee he chaired as Poet Laureate. "We all thought The Collected Poems was stunning—a monument. Moreover, it actually grows in strength towards the end. There's a great feeling for you over here. I hope you'll accept."[96] Thom "politely refuse[d], on the grounds of absenteeism—surely it is a national award?"[97] Hughes "wondered" whether Thom was "the first to have declined" the medal. He asked Thom to reconsider but realized that his attempts at persuasion were futile. "Thom if you still feel you must refuse," Hughes wrote, "I shall go into a tiny round graveyard on a cliff over the River Thurso in the NE of Scotland, where about thirty Gunns, under variously elaborate, marvellously lichen-patched gravestones and crumbling monuments, defend your ancestral bit of body-garden, behind a 6 foot high whistling stone-wall, out on the blasted heath there, not a visible roof in any direction—and I shall shout: 'He says No!'"[98] Unmoved, Thom still would not accept. "The ceremony would have had Ted (as Poet Laureate) showing me in for a ¼ of an hour's chat with the Queen before she actually presented it to me,"

Thom told Ander. "I rather regret not doing that, I would be interested in talking with her, we might have exchanged a few tips about how to get through the 1990s." He knew it was "more fun telling" Ander he would "turn down the Queen's Medal than accepting it!"[99]

That November, Thom published *Shelf Life*, his second prose collection. It was part of the University of Michigan Press's Poets on Poetry series, for which Donald Hall acted as general editor. *Shelf Life* collected Thom's finest essays from the eighties and early nineties, including his memoirs of Christopher Isherwood and Yvor Winters and his important critical assessment of Robert Duncan.[100] As with *The Occasions of Poetry*—Thom's 1982 prose book, edited by Clive Wilmer—the essays in *Shelf Life* were the direct result of the project Thom had started in the sixties when he gave up regular poetry reviewing. "I kept feeling that the criticism should go deeper in some way," he reflected at the time: "it began to get rather distasteful."[101] At its core, this was a moral position: weary of maliciously destructive critiques of his own work, Thom felt it was unprincipled to perpetuate them against others. Of that, he was more than capable: Ian Hamilton, his own critical bogeyman, called Thom's early reviews the work of "a sprightly hatchet-man."[102] When Wilmer came to edit *Occasions*, Thom asked him not to include any of his early criticism.[103] He called those essays—typically long group reviews for *Poetry* and *The Yale Review*—"the product of a period 'sensibility'" and "derivative in tone and in judgement. The influences were those of FRL and YW—strange bedfellows, strange except in so far as they were both prescriptive and scornful," he added. "So I find a lot of my writing around this time rather unpleasant to read."[104]

Although Thom dropped the dismissive tone and judgmental statements from his subsequent critical writing, Leavis and Winters remained important to his approach. In a sense, Thom remained the Cambridge student: while his poetry was continuously searching, formally restless, and at its finest when exploring the tensions between open and closed, his prose did not lose any of the critical rigor drilled into him while studying for the English Tripos. This was his approach to every poet, from Fulke

Greville, Thomas Hardy, and Ben Jonson to Elizabeth Bishop, Mina Loy, and Walt Whitman. But despite the New Critical foundations, and his focus on textual analysis, Thom's criticism is not overly formal or stiff. "I view poetry criticism as something very practical," he reflected. "I see it as an extension of my role as teacher. I'm trying to show people how to read some poets they don't know about. I'm pointing to things, showing them a way into a new poet."[105] Thom's later prose writing combines the close textual scholarship he admired in his Cambridge models with the tone and purpose he found in the criticism of a friend: Tony Tanner. Vowing only to review poets he liked, Thom reached for the Tanneresque approach of joyousness and conviviality.[106] His reviews, in that sense, are a record of his reading. "It is possible to see the act of reading as a kind of bestowing of life, a contributive rather than passive act," Tanner reflected in 1974, in terms of his own engagement with contemporary American fiction. "I want to be a good reader; and I want to try to find the most appropriate words, drawn from whatever disciplines and discourses, to recreate my readings into texts. I regard myself as an explorer."[107] Tanner wrote about almost everything and everyone, from Shakespeare and Jane Austen to James Purdy and Thomas Pynchon. Commenting on Tanner's book about Austen, Thom told Wilmer: "I thought I knew Jane Austen backwards—well I do, but he showed me things I hadn't noticed in her."[108] For Thom, this was high praise and a reflection of his own aims.

If his critical approach seems quintessentially English, Thom wrote mainly about American poets. His essays about English poets rarely venture beyond the Renaissance.[109] *Occasions* contains essays about Greville, Hardy, Jonson, and Dick Davis; the other essays focus on twentieth-century American poets. In *Shelf Life*, except for a sixteenth-century anthology and Basil Bunting, Thom's range is again American, from Whitman and Pound through Marianne Moore and H.D. to Allen Ginsberg and August Kleinzahler. "I find most English poetry terribly timid," he remarked in 1991. "American poetry is much more interesting."[110] Thom admired Ted Hughes's work, for the most part, and wrote him appreciative notes, but did not review any of his collections after *Lupercal* (1960). He praised contemporary poets such as Clive Wilmer,

Robert Wells, Dick Davis, and Glyn Maxwell—and developed passions for certain books, such as Stephen Romer's *Idols* (1986) and Michael Longley's *Gorse Fires* (1991)—but he took little interest in the currents of poetry in the United Kingdom or Ireland. "I'm really not sure Heaney is that good," he once reflected. "I think he was invented by a committee of teachers with a sense of high fashion."[111] The more time Thom spent in the United States, and the more his own poetry loosened up, the more he came around to American poets whom he had previously dismissed: by the time he published *Shelf Life*, his views on Williams, Pound, Whitman, and Ginsberg had all changed from negative to positive. Thom's assessment of Larkin is indicative of what he came to disdain in English poetry and value in American poetry. "His distrust of rhetoric was also a distrust of feeling, a distrust of daring," Thom told Jim Powell. "Certainly he was right to be distrustful of rhetoric, but on the other hand I would sooner read poets who are able to take those risks."[112]

Once teaching began in January 1994, Thom "hardly" went to Folsom Street. The new semester kept him "fully occupied" and he did not have "much energy left over."[113] Some of his tiredness came from his decision to teach a freshman seminar on Shakespeare's sonnets: "one hour a week, no extra pay."[114] This proved to be a "handful" and, rereading the sonnets, it became "completely clear" to Thom "that WS was a fag like us," he told Douglas, "an extremely renaissance fag indeed, the kind that led a highly idealised but I am sure sexually consummated love-life with men, and considered women good for nothing but sex alone." Shakespeare "went <u>into</u> the psychology of it, he broached the subject."[115] Thom approached the one-off course with relish. Instructing his students to write a short essay about one of the sonnets, Thom reminded them that "succinctness is a virtue in writing. Shakespeare thought so, I think so, and I hope you think so too."[116] He told his students that the course was "a grounding not only for dealing with poetry, but also for what I take to be the chief aim of all studies in the humanities/English: the attempt to understand how words interpret experience, and also become part of experience."[117]

Thom began preparing his sonnets course in November, around the same time he had "ambitious thoughts of some poems about David, the O.T. King. Wonder if I'm up to them? Not sure how to go about the whole thing yet, probably have to let the stories stew for a few months."[118] Throughout the semester he made notes for "3 poems about King David, a kind of balance to my Dahmer poems, perhaps," and wrote them in late May.[119] He based "God" on 2 Samuel 6; King David dances before the Ark, "Uncovered in the sight / Of slaves and slave girls," to the disdain of his wife, Michal, whose womb becomes "closed and empty like a light nutshell."[120] In "Bathsheba," based on 2 Samuel 12, David lusts over Bathsheba and arranges the killing of her husband, Uriah: "A common sequence, I observed: / Love leading to duplicity."[121] "Abishag" is based on 1 Kings 1. In it, the titular young girl, brought to warm the aging David, "lay on my bosom" and was "source of merely temporary mild heat / So innocent she might have been a dog."[122] Thom called the sequence "Dancing David."

Although Thom wrote "Dancing David" to balance "Troubadour," he was uncertain about their precise relationship. He wanted to capture "the sense, however weird, of a career lived in terms specified in the first poem."[123] Thom sent the sequences to Robert Pinsky, who saw the phrase "Taste, taste, good taste," as key to the relationship: taste meaning decorum in "Dancing David" and the more literal tastes of "Troubadour." "Surely, to begin with, Michal stands in for the disapproving reader of the other sequence," Pinsky reflected. "The idea I get is something like, if [Dahmer] is incapable of thinking whether or how to deny himself what he enjoys, 'taste' makes the opposite person do the thinking and denying before experiencing any idea of what might be enjoyed. Also, here is one of our favorite poets and well-thought-of leaders, father of the etc., sneakily and with elaborate premeditation <u>killing</u> for a fuck: and killing in a way so elaborate [. . .] that especially given David's power there is something a little . . . perverse about it."[124] The sequences—"Troubadour" especially—are an extension of what Pinsky called Thom's "nearly clinical sympathy" for people. Thom accepted the phrase, "with all its various limitations," noting that "I do not like, or even believe in empathy: how can I claim to feel <u>inside</u> somebody else, even as a stretch of the imagination? To feel <u>with</u>, however, I see as an achievement, giving from the self without obliterating it."[125] Writing the sequences in the voices of Dahmer and David, Thom allowed himself to explore his own ideas and interests (sexual greed, obsessive desire) through characters and avoid self-dramatization. "Dahmer does not think of himself as abnormal," Thom reflected. "He is obsessed in his desire—but then most people are at some time or other."[126] The poems were an exercise "to get inside [Dahmer's] head in the same way Shakespeare was trying to get inside Macbeth's head."[127] Moreover, "Troubadour" and "Dancing David" were part of Thom's project to "work on other people's stories" as a way of understanding himself. He wanted to "work out my own mythology—I guess Jeffrey & David make a start in one direction."[128]

The final lines of "Abishag"—"The ultimate moment of improvisation, / A brief bow following on the final leap"—would become the final lines of *Boss Cupid*, Thom's final book. His mind brimming with Shakespeare, Thom had Prospero's farewell salutation—"Let your indulgence set me free"[129]—in mind for his own concluding gesture, but he was also thinking about Robert Duncan. "Abishag" is all about heat; or, rather, the lack of it. "I gat no heat," David says; Abishag's purpose is "to take the chill off my old age" but she provides instead "merely temporary mild heat"; Bathsheba took "less notice" of her "than if / I had a closed pan of warm embers on me."[130] In "Adventurous Song," his essay about Duncan, Thom discussed "Food for Fire, Food for Thought," the last poem in Duncan's 1960 book, *The Opening of the Field*. It, too, has echoes of Prospero's farewell speech, but to Thom the poem was "a magnificent paradox, for how can there be a last poem when you believe in a form so open that there are no closures and so no last things possible in it."[131] Duncan's "great dread / Was closure," Thom had written, and all the images in "Food for Fire" refuse it. Duncan's poem gave Thom his heat imagery— from "a fire on the hearth / Leapd up where you bankd it" to "palaces of heat in the fire's mouth"—and its concluding image combines heat and open-endedness: "flickers of unlikely heat / at the edge of our belief bud forth."[132] While there is closure in "Abishag"—the "final leap"—Thom's poem is also open-ended: Bathsheba wants David's "assurance / Of the succession of her Solomon."[133] Duncan's "whole poem looks both backward and forward," Thom thought, and he had something similar in mind for "Dancing David."[134]

With the David poems finished, Thom's thoughts turned to his new collection. It did not yet have the name *Boss Cupid*, but it had grown steadily, if unevenly, since the summer of 1988, and Thom now had around half a book. He sent "the balance of unpublished poems" to Clive that summer, which he called "for lack of a better title, Preliminaries 2." He thought the collection "does not look like a book yet" and that "only the love poems seem to stick together."[135] They included "Troubadour," "A Wood near Athens," and "Dancing David," which Thom called "a kind of anatomy of desire."[136] But they were also summations, as Thom would have known, just as "Duncan" was a summation. Thom would end *Boss Cupid* with "Dancing David"—a sequence of open-endedness and closure—and begin it with "Duncan," an ars poetica that disguised his own fear that, like Duncan, he would soon become "a posthumous poet." Thom did not fear death; rather, he feared that his next writing block would be his last, and that, like the aging King David, he would have "no heat."

36

CUPID

Thom hoped that "Dancing David" would set him up for a summer of writing, but this proved premature. He made progress with "A Young Novelist"—about his friend Brian Bouldrey, whose debut novel was published the same week his lover died—but dried up in mid-June. "I have somehow put myself in [a] position completely opposed to composition," he reflected. "There is a secret place, of the imagination?, I go sometimes when I read, always when I write. About 1 July, it was closed to me again. That's why I've done so much speed, I think, tho of course that closes it up even more."[1] He still hoped "to get sumpn out of this summer" but felt hindered by "this hysteria about finality. This last strange 2 months. Call it 'Confessional.'"[2]

Thom would turn sixty-five in August 1994. "It does seem like a time of closing off wherever I look," he told Donald Hall.[3] In the spring, Thom had read Brad Gooch's biography of Frank O'Hara, *City Poet*. Hall had known O'Hara at Harvard, and Thom was "struck" by Hall's "kindness and fairness" when Gooch quoted him in the book. Thom thought about all the help Hall had given him over the years—encouraging him to apply to Stanford, recommending his work to Oscar Mellor, attempting to secure Thom his first American publisher, and overseeing the publication of *Shelf Life* for the University of Michigan Press. "You have done as much for heaps of other people," Thom told him, "and you have done it for poets, for poetry, not for yourself, with true generosity and selflessness.

[. . .] I expect we shall all go on for ever, but I thought I might express a bit of this kind of gratitude in case it is too late tomorrow."⁴

Thom's valedictory tone was a sign of his difficult spring and summer. Something about seeing Hall historicized in *City Poet* jolted Thom into realizing that his "difficult year" of hysteria, discontent, and lethargy was "a reaction to the symbolic importance of completing my 65th year." "I have really no good reason to feel uneasy," he told Douglas. "I get more applause than one man needs, I do not run completely dry of ideas for poems, I couldn't be more contented with my household, I make out sexually pretty well for my age, and startlingly gorgeous men keeping turning up at my gym. But I feel tired and discontented much of the time."⁵ He had begun to lead "a dissipated life, and a rather foolish one" that involved "excessive amounts of speed every weekend, which just about deals with the following week, devoted to sleep. [. . .] Better stop this kind of thing or I'll get a heart attack."⁶ The more speed Thom took, the less likely he was to write: he called himself "weak" and vowed in early August "not to do speed for several weeks," having taken it "7 times in 9 weeks."⁷ He spent a quiet birthday and began to feel better. "I was hysterical all this year, unsettled, unhappy for no good reason, never at my best," he told Ander and Bett, "and then suddenly I think my actual 65th birthday broke the jynx."⁸ To celebrate, Thom brought home a tweaker from Folsom and, after they had taken "all the rest of the speed I had (double the usual)," Thom "unfortunately [did] the most self-destructive thing in about 10 years."⁹ To his relief, he "still test[ed] Negative" for HIV at his annual physical, "in spite of Sep 9 folly."¹⁰

After an "all night" speed marathon with a Vietnam veteran in mid-November, Thom abstained for a fortnight to prepare himself for public readings in New York. He and Mike flew east together: while Thom gave a talk about Mina Loy at Poets' House, Mike saw the original Broadway production of Tony Kushner's *Perestroika*; the next night they saw Stephen Daldry's "remarkable" production of *An Inspector Calls*.¹¹ Thom gave a "solid reading, a retrospective" at the Educational Alliance on East Broadway and, two nights later, read at the New School with Simone Di Piero, his friend, fellow poet, and neighbor on Cole Street. Thom read his "Love Group"—"Troubadour," "A Wood near Athens," and "Dancing David"—"as well as I ever read (M said)."[12]

Within days of his return to San Francisco, Thom received a letter from a young photographer named Billy Lux, who had approached him after his reading at the New School. Lux liked "the way you walked across the stage and threw your bag against the podium," he told Thom. "Then I was stunned by your introduction because I wasn't expecting Jeffrey Dahmer at all. I don't go to readings very often because I'm a terrible listener and an incessant daydreamer."[13] Lux had first read Thom a decade earlier when his then boyfriend, an Italian, showed him the Caravaggio in Santa Maria del Popolo and gave him a copy of Thom's *Poems 1950–1966*.[14] At the New School, Thom's poem "A Home" had struck Lux for its similarities to a series of his own photographs of a young hustler named Don. "The Don Saga: it is so terrific because it contains so many opposites—toughness and pathos, unsentimentality and desire, unfinishedness and completion," Thom remarked after Lux sent him copies of the photographs.[15] Through correspondence, at first, Thom and Lux became close friends. "You are such a thorough romantic and yet so cool (in the regular sense) about it. Obsessed but observing yourself with detachment," Thom told him, "like a character in Stendhal."[16]

With Lux's photographs in mind, Thom thought "about the difficulties / & obstacles of love, not just love, / but of desire itself, which seems (so) easy"[17] and began to "scratch a few words in my notebook."[18] His notes anticipated "To Cupid," of which Thom made an early draft on December 29, 1994—the fiftieth anniversary of his mother's suicide—but did not finish for another twelve months.[19] "Haven't written a poem (hardly any prose, either) since May," he told Ander on Christmas Eve. "Probably the old unconscious is reprocessing a lot of experience, humming and buzzing away, even as I write this letter. At least I hope that's what's happening."[20] His dry period persisted into the new year. "When I'm not writing the imagination does have the look of a world after a nuclear bombing," he told Michael Schmidt in February. "I don't see quite how anything is going to start growing there again."[21]

In mid-January, Thom took his "last speed before term" and walked to his new favorite South of Market bar: the Hole in the Wall Saloon.[22] The Hole opened on Eighth Street in 1994 and became known as a "carnal meat-packing house."[23] The crowd was grungy, the music loud rock, the drug of choice speed; a motorcycle hung suspended from the ceiling and a thick leather curtain covered the door. Such was the allure of the Hole, Thom's "last speed before term" resolution lasted only two weeks: he brought home "a sexy & resourceful man" named Alan with whom he took speed "all night & ha[d] ecstatic sensations."[24] Moreover, Thom felt he was teaching well—"the self-doubts of half a year laid to rest, at least for a while"[25]—which made him think that weekend speed marathons did not affect his alertness and concentration in the classroom. Anticipation was behind his desire to teach half-time: when it worked, ideas for poems gestated over several months and Thom eagerly awaited the end of semester so that he could write them. Folsom Street worked on the same principle: Thom went easy during the semester, feeling that, for the rest of the year, he could cruise and drug as much as he wanted. But in 1995 that relationship broke down and Thom spent many more term-time weekends on Folsom than usual. "A strange night," Thom wrote in February, "I end up smoking crack with someone called Allen on the street."[26] That was Thom's first and last experience with crack, the effects of which he had seen firsthand with Bill, but it was a sign that the delicate balance between teaching, writing, bar-going, drugging, and family—on which he had built his life—could easily be upset.

During the semester, Thom had "no poem even in sight."[27] "I tell myself I can't write because I am disorganized," he told Jack Hagstrom, "but I am really disorganized because I can't write."[28] "It's a curious thing about writing," he told Ander, "it isn't _that_ agreeable to do, but it is only when I'm doing it—when I have one or two poems in progress on my desk—that I feel my life is centered. I have felt uncentered for several months now—not badly, certainly not unhappy (how could I be unhappy, since I've got all I want?), but somewhat loose and irresponsible."[29] Impatient for the term to end, Thom bought more speed from his dealer. "Another year of tweaking," he vowed, "then try to start writing again next May, is my plan."[30] For Thom, sex and speed were complementary:

he liked "infinite cockplay without coming" and found it "wonderful to both be on the edge of orgasm for 12 hours or more."[31] The downsides were sleeplessness and terrible hangovers, which did nothing to help the strict writing routine that Thom had developed over several decades. Uneasy with his decision not to write for a year, he continued to make notes for possible poems. "Had an idea for a sequence about speed," he wrote. "I mean if I'm doing so much, why not write about it?"[32]

A summer that Thom hoped would be a speed-driven celebration was in fact overshadowed by unfamiliar and unsettling feelings of anxiety and depression. He had not finished a poem since "Dancing David" and had begun to realize that he could not compartmentalize speed like he could other aspects of his life. "My life is in disorder," he wrote in June. "I have all I want, & it should be ordered, but I am unable to will it to order. I cannot write—I don't know why—I couldn't even make a short list of subjects to write about; writing, which makes sense of my life, would bring it to order, interpreting as I go." Feeling like "an unsettled country" waiting for "a dictator to replace its feeble democracy," Thom wondered what "event" was coming. "I think it must be death. I do not desire death," he reflected, "but it would put an end to this mess I live in. I had never realised, until I stopped so abruptly last May, how dependent I am on my writing for an understanding, & thus an ordering, of experience."[33] Thom kept his despair from family and friends—"I seem to specialize in wonderful young hunks in big boots who are being unfaithful to their lovers," he boasted to Douglas[34]—but continued to reflect on his perceived "mediocrity" in his notebook. "I am a mediocre person, but neither I nor most people realize this most of the time," he wrote, "& do not realize it because of my poetry." Wondering about "who leads the best lives," Thom settled on Mike, Tony White, Clint Cline, and Aunt Barbara. "These are people of generosity (magnanimity): they help others, cheerfully & efficiently, not always understanding how much they give."[35]

The only tranquility Thom found during the summer came from books. Alone in the sunny garden, reading a biography of F. R. Leavis, Thom thought about a phrase from Wallace Stevens's poem "The

House Was Quiet and the World Was Calm": "The reader became the book." The poem was important to him—he mentioned it in his Berkeley commencement address and a short piece about "disinterestedness" for *Threepenny*[36]—and, absorbed in the Leavis book, Thom felt "a great tranquillity containing my deep satisfaction that I am, with these people, in this house & in this city. It is out of this sanity/tranquillity I could write again."[37] Thom had not tweaked for a fortnight, but the day after reading the Leavis book was "Krystaltag." A week later, another speed marathon prompted a realization. "That settles it," Thom wrote. "I must not get it in: I can't keep it: I must use it. So I'd better stop buying it."[38] This proved easier said than done: Thom continued to tweak and cruise for the rest of the summer and was particularly taken with a French-Canadian former commando named Wolf, "now deaf with his body half metal as a result of Vietnam injuries," with whom he shared five quarters of a gram of speed across two nights.[39] "He was the hottest man of the year," Thom gushed. "Wonder if I <u>will</u> see him again."[40]

Shortly after his sixty-sixth birthday—"which I hope can qualify as two-thirds the number of the Beast"[41]—Thom took Mike to Spain for a fortnight's holiday. He had refused to visit while Franco was in power and wanted to go "now or it will be too late."[42] He hoped it would be "like Almódovar's movies (which are about as realistic as A Midsummer Night's Dream)," and looked forward to traveling with Mike again.[43] "We live the same life as when we were first lovers," he reflected of their European holidays. "Married folks, as we are most of the time, do not live the same life, they have separate jobs, errands, schedules, and meet together only at dinner."[44] Part of their happiness, Mike suspected, was because "Thom couldn't go to bars" while they were traveling.[45]

Their first stop was Madrid, "a slightly boring city," where they stayed for a week at the Hotel Carlos V.[46] Thom thought it "full of banks & bank architecture" and most enjoyed seeing the Goyas at the Prado, "a kind of education you seldom are able to get with a painter."[47] From Madrid they made the seven-hour train ride through "craggy but often fertile country" to Barcelona.[48] They stayed on Las Ramblas, which Thom loved, and each day began and ended at the "queerish dearish" Café de L'Òpera.[49] "The old city is really a medieval city still . . . narrow winding smelly streets," he told Ander. "People are very pretty—we walk along the Ramblas all the time—a walking street for tourists & natives alike, with seats on it, & acrobats, & bird & hamster shops. There are 20 geese in the cathedral—really—in honor of a virgin saint who liked geese."[50] One day, Mike remembered, "Thom saw some guy in a leather jacket and that was it. I said to him, many times, nothing's more important to you than a trick. And truer words were never spoken!"[51] Thom did not trick with Mario, a "handsome NY born Puerto Rican guy," but his immediate change in manner irritated Mike.[52] Reflecting on Thom's promiscuity, Mike thought it was "almost a kind of insecurity. I don't mean that literally, but I mean when Thom said I was the first person who loved him, it wasn't love with all his sexual carrying on . . . He didn't have crushes like I do, but it was his nature. When Thom saw this guy in Barcelona, his sexy way of carrying on used to drive me crazy. He was a whole different person."[53] After his summer adventures, Thom was perhaps restless to return to San Francisco. By the time they did return, Thom had not taken speed for three weeks. At his annual physical, his blood pressure, usually high, was "marvellously normal."[54]

Flying home, Thom read the obituary of his "old friend and ally" Donald Davie.[55] "He was a man who was very dear to me personally—there! I don't say that often, do I?—and whose critical judgment meant more to me than anybody else of my generation," he told Jack Hagstrom. "He was a royalist, a conservative, a homophobe, and a Christian (all the things I loathe), and yet he knew what literature was really about, and his mind was ultimately one of the most open I have come across for the discovery of unexpected talent."[56] Davie's was "the only body of criticism by a contemporary that meant anything to me in terms of my own practice."[57] Although Thom refused an invitation to Davie's memorial service—"the ceremonies of death, marriage, etc., have never been of much importance to me"[58]—he drew on Davie's openness of mind for his elegy "To Donald Davie in Heaven":

I was reading Auden—But I thought
you didn't like Auden, I said.
Well, I've been reading him again,
and I like him better now, you said.
That was what I admired about you
your ability to regroup
without cynicism, your love of poetry
greater
than your love of consistency.[59]

"Davie actually made that remark about Auden (with me, characteristically, interrupting) when I last saw him," Thom told Clive, "but it's even better if imagined as a remark attributed Dantesquely post mortem."[60] He imagined Davie joining the warriors of faith in the fifth sphere of Dante's *Paradiso*, "But maybe less druggy, / a bit plainer, / more Protestant."[61] Thom hoped "the teasing may be taken as a sign of the personal affection that goes arm in arm with my admiration for the dear man."[62]

A short reading tour of New York, Washington, DC, and Chicago followed Thom's return from Spain. Back in San Francisco, he read at Intersection with August Kleinzahler and husband-and-wife poets Forrest Gander and C. D. Wright. Gander, "a poet in cowboy boots," immediately attracted Thom, and after the reading they had "a sweet little interlude alone at the bar near the Roxie before the others joined us."[63] Mike was well informed about how "hot" Thom was for Gander. "He was straight," Mike recalled, "and Thom was hoping to change that around. Thom would give us progress reports with how he was doing with this guy."[64] This was part of what the family called "Thom Talk." "It was dirty talk," Bob explained. "He could bring sex into any conversation, through any thread. It would be so much that you would get tired of it after a while because you couldn't have a regular conversation with him because he'd want to joke about it. He didn't like talking about serious things between us all. He liked to keep it light."[65] Bill thought Thom had "a potty mouth."[66] One playmate called Thom "a lot sleazier than a lot of [other] guys. Our whole conversation was always just sex and sleaziness and drugs."⁶⁷ "Thom was a good flirt," recalled another. "He knew how to talk, he knew how to butter you up."⁶⁸ Through autumn and winter, Thom established a routine: on Saturdays he would snort two or three lines and hit Folsom Street, and when Mike and Bob spent weekends at the cabin, he hosted speed marathons.

Given his traveling and speed use, Thom surprised himself by starting to write again. He resumed work on "First Song," another poem about King David, which he had started in May 1994. Although the poem "had been mostly written before," Thom was still pleased to finish it. "If I resume writing, as I hope to," he told Jack Hagstrom, "I will do so in my own time."⁶⁹ Finishing "First Song" was the spark he needed: by Christmas he had drafted "A Los Angeles Childhood," "Nasty Jokes," "Cat Island," "Front Bar of the *Lone Star*," and "To Cupid," his first poems in eighteen months. "I don't usually feel fully alive unless I am in the middle of writing. That sounds pretentious, I am sure," he told Belle Randall, "but you must know what I mean: it's not a question of happiness, or of achievement, but of the satisfaction that comes from being able to speak about something as well as experiencing it."⁷⁰

Like "First Song," "To Cupid" developed in fits and starts. Thom made notes for a poem about Cupid and desire in late 1993, wrote a very rough draft in December 1994, and spent most of 1995 thinking about the idea without success. "First it was in rhyming quatrains, but they were too smart-ass, for some reason," he told Clive. "Then I tried it in short free verse lines, then in long free verse lines—or was it the other way round? Finally got it to work in blank verse—which is at this stage perhaps a bit too silkily smooth for its I hope troubled subject, but I won't be able to judge that for some time."⁷¹ By the time Thom finished "To Cupid" in December 1995, his reading had deepened and expanded its conceit. Teaching Shakespeare's sonnets had returned Thom to the plays and thus to blank verse—"outstandingly Shakespeare's form and used by Gunn in the spirit of the master," as Clive Wilmer put it⁷²—in poems like "Abishag" and "A Wood near Athens." Moreover, Thom drew his image of Cupid as a bullying tough guy from his extensive reading of Mina Loy, who depicts "Pig Cupid his rosy snout / Rooting erotic garbage."[73] Thom was "delighted" that Clive thought "To Cupid" was "based on a real man. He wasn't, but I wanted to make him seem so."[74]

The poem was Thom's final addition to the "love group" that makes up the final part of *Boss Cupid*. Cupid, "the devious master of our bodies," presided over Thom's final years and poems. "Love is usually with us an obsession," he remarked in 2000:

> It's still what we want, still what we have in mind, but we often screw it up because of our obsessions, [which are] curiously mixed with what Freud would call perversions. I don't mean perversions in the ordinary sense, but obstructions to itself. And at the end [of "To Cupid"] I'm saying how wonderful that the wedding feast should be not only a prelude to the wedding bed, but a postponement of it. D. H. Lawrence always [criticized] "sex in the head," or sex in the brain, but that's part of its beauty! That's part of what makes sex so exciting for human beings, that we think about it, and look forward to it, and maybe in some ways even deliberately postpone it. That's what I'm talking about.[75]

Like "A Wood near Athens" and "Dancing David," "To Cupid" is a summation. In it, Thom refers to Fabrice, the hero of Stendhal's *La chartreuse de Parme*, one of his "big books."[76] He adored its blend of "spontaneities and calculation" and saw himself, like Fabrice, as one of Cupid's servants, all of whom "compose their amorous scripts—scripts of confinement, / Scripts of displacement, scripts of delay, and scripts / Of more delay."[77] Fabrice "hankered / After the distance of his prison cell," from which he had fallen in love with "the jailer's daughter." Unlike in his earlier poems—from "La Prisonnière" to the "little ease" of "Jack Straw's Castle"—a cell could now be a place of love and consolation. "To Cupid" is set in Thom's own room on Cole Street. Lying in bed, "dog-tired," he could hear

The pleasant sounds of voices from next door
Through windows open to the clement darkness.
A dinner for the couple one floor up,
Married today. [. . .]
                                    Chatting, the sounds
Of friendliness and feeding often broken
By laughter. It's consoling, Mr Love,
That such conviviality is also
One more obedience to your behest,
The wedding bed held off by the wedding feast.[78]

It was a small room, the smallest of the three Cole Street bedrooms. Bob thought it was "like a monk's room, or a cell."[79] Clive called it "extremely spartan": Thom had little furniture other than his bed.[80] His bedspread was leather and denim patchwork; there were grease marks on the walls. Listening to the "wedding feast" upstairs, Thom likely thought about the "amorous scripts" that had played out within his own four walls.

Friendship, conviviality, and companionship were all aspects of love, and all subject to Cupid's calculations and manipulations. "There are so many people I first met through sleeping with them who later became life-long friends," he reflected. "I love the mixture of categories."[81] Thom experienced conviviality in many forms, from the druggy, mind-expanding 1960s through "the sexual New Jerusalem"[82] of the 1970s and into the more urgent togetherness of the AIDS epidemic in the 1980s and '90s. "The idea of sexual energy as an anarchic force that nonetheless pulls people together, connects them, gives their lives meaning, creates new life, and governs how we live the life we have," writes Joshua Weiner, persuasively and insightfully, is "a fundamental value running through Gunn's poetry."[83]

Desire and writing were so intricately entwined in Thom's life that one often became the other. He felt "uncentred" when he was not writing, just as "sex in the head" could destabilize him, toppling from anticipatory thrill into debilitating obsession. "Motives in sex & writing are for me the same," he had established: "joyful possession of, mastery over, a piece of life."[84] But in "To Cupid," Thom is alone, and happily alone—noteworthy, given his fear of loneliness and abandonment—because he feels part of the overheard "conviviality." He could rest easy, having found an occasion for a poem in which he could address the idea that underpinned his entire system of thought and action. "Learning," he told the Berkeley graduates in his 1993 commencement address, is like "love in the simultaneous passion and openness of its commitment":

> when we open a book or read the first line of a poem we have
> to be ready for anything, that we can learn how to read it only
> from itself, that the exercise each time extends the sympathy
> along with the imagination (however imperceptibly)—all this
> feeds into the way we deal with our future experience, giving
> and taking from it too.[85]

To be "ready for anything" is to be Stendhalian. In a poem about desire that crystalizes almost five decades of Thom's ideas, preoccupations, and philosophies, it is unsurprising that he drew on *La chartreuse de Parme*, the book that had given him "a great feeling of release, as if anything were possible," when he read it for the first time in 1950.[86] "In later life," Fabrice and Clelia, the jailer's daughter, "touched, they did touch, but in darkness only." Devoting himself to Cupid, Thom knew the devotion would last a lifetime. In the absence of God, Cupid was his driving force, his daily energy. His "better rest," he seems to be saying, after his despairing summer of 1995, would be death.[87] "There was a death-drive in Thom," remarked Joshua Weiner, "or at the very least a square facing of the abyss."[88]

In the week before he finished "To Cupid," Thom had taken "most of 5 quarters" of a gram of speed and had ended up "clearly drunk, shamefully so" at the Lone Star Saloon, a leather bar on Harrison.[89] Later that month, after another speed marathon, he experienced his first aural hallucinations, "endless imaginary dialogs between made-up characters—

aloud. But I was alone, so that was OK."[90] Speed had become an ever-greater part of his own "amorous scripts"; rest had become more difficult to obtain; risk, so long balanced with discipline and order, had begun to take over. Thom knew that his writing life was coming to an end. He must also have known, on some level, that his pursuit of desire, already obsessive, would come to push family and poetry to the fringes of his life.

37

GO*SS*IP

Writing to Ander on December 28, 1995, Thom stopped himself short. "Typing that date, I realise it is 51 years since the event that altered our lives," he wrote. "Well, it did, but I can't say my subsequent life has been the worse for it. What I mean is, disasters try you, but usually if they don't wipe you out you find ways of coping which may make you stronger. Well, that IS a cliché, isn't it, and of course it can only be partly true. But I can hardly imagine a life more to my taste than mine."[1]

Thom's recent flurry of poems had lifted his spirits, as had a night of speed with a Tony he had met in the Hole in the Wall. "We adventure thru the night," Thom wrote. "The sp[eed] is 'very stray.' We have a great time, I like him a lot."[2] On the twenty-ninth, after he had written to Ander, Thom returned to Tony's Chinatown apartment and they "went flying thru the night, thru next morning too, not very sexual, w/ many visitors, most of them small-time dealers & pretty sleazy." With Mike and Bob at the cabin, Thom and Tony relocated to Cole Street the following day. "It doesn't sound good, but it was, I was speeding at least 2 days," he reflected. "I think the attraction of [Tony] is that he takes charge, looks after people, makes decisions—& as I have found I have always been attracted by strength, or the appearance of it—tho who knows, maybe such people are NOT stronger than I (is Don [Doody], for example, really stronger than me?)"[3] Alone on New Year's Eve, Thom was "happy & wobbly all day": this was when he experienced his first speed hallucinations. Hungover and exhausted, he felt "the big drowsies" for an entire week.[4]

Returning to his idea for a sequence of poems about speed, Thom drafted "The Last Weekend of 1995." It describes, in a "flat conversational voice," the comings and goings in Tony's apartment while he shot speed:

> A knock on the door
> just as my friend inserts the point
> which, surprised, he
> pushes <u>through</u> his vein
> causing a small lump beside it,
> envelope of unusable speed.
> Oh well, another time.
> (He's flying already.)[5]

"I guess I can't publish it, but I'm interested in trying to get it right," he told Douglas. "It is not nearly as reprehensible as it looks: the guy was a trained nurse, used clean needles, etc. [. . .] I don't want to shock, for once . . . But maybe it's another disaster." That "disaster" was "What Humans Do," also written in early 1996, about which August Kleinzahler told Thom "two things: a) it is an awful poem (awful was his exact word) b) birds do it also, bees do it, even educated fleas, etc. He was right on both counts."[6]

When the new semester began, Thom spent his weekends at the Hole. One Saturday, he introduced himself to Robert Prager, a sandy-haired guy in his mid-thirties whom he knew by sight as a former bartender at My Place. "He caught my attention right away," Prager recalled, "because he looked like he had stepped into the bar not from off the street but from a time machine directly out of 1981 or 82. [. . .] He was dressed in what people once would have called 'heavy leather' or full leather." Thom "squeezed through the crowd, reached out his hand to shake mine, and said, 'Hi, I'm Thom.' 'I know,'" Prager replied. "'People warned me about you.'"[7] Prager gave Thom his number. "I phoned him next day & he sounded ridiculously enthusiastic (must be a geriatric specialist, I suppose)," Thom told Billy Lux, "& we made a date, talking for a long time."[8] Thom planned their speed date "while my parents are at the cabin."[9] Prager arrived on his bicycle. "We carry on, wonderfully, till 6am, when he bicycles off," Thom wrote. "Two quarters [of a gram of speed]. He is a very interesting slightly odd guy, v. unexpectedly attractive, his eyes different colors."[10] Prager was "a whole night of fun," Thom thought, "but he's not interested in me. I love complicated people & he doesn't know how he fits a certain pattern."[11] Like Clint Cline, among others, Thom began giving Prager money—fifty dollars or so a month toward rent and expenses—and Prager became a regular visitor to Cole Street. Mike thought he was "downright rude. He came to see Thom, and we were out of the way. Prager was into celebrities."[12]

Prager had always wanted to be a writer. He was rarely seen without a reporter's notebook and pencil. "It was almost a security blanket," remarked his long-term partner Gordon Schneemann, "or part of wanting to be seen as a writer."[13] In his twenties, Prager started corresponding with gay novelists and developed friendships with Andrew Holleran, Dirk Vanden, and Edmund White. While a student at Wayne State, Prager drove to Key West and engineered an encounter with the aging Tennessee Williams.[14] When he moved to San Francisco in the early 1990s, Prager became obsessed with Chuck Arnett and began to gather material to write his biography. Thom encouraged Prager and gave him two of his Arnett paintings to look after because "I think he'd take better care of them than I would."[15] That summer, Prager interviewed Thom for his Arnett project. "David Barnard had told me that Chuck's life was a tragedy because he could never make enough money from his art to support himself," Prager told Thom, "but you said: 'his life was not a tragedy. He was always having sex and doing drugs and having the time of his life.' I appreciated that."[16]

Between teaching and tweaking, Thom also started writing again. Although "Last Weekend" and "What Humans Do" were false starts, Thom was intrigued by his casual tone in poems like "A Los Angeles Childhood" and "Front Bar of the *Lone Star*" and quickly drafted two more: "Famous Friends" and "To Donald Davie in Heaven." These short, funny, free verse poems were a reaction to the "predictable and lifeless" meter of "To Cupid." Thom found them "flexible," but feared they were "probably very derivative—from Augie and O'Hara." In style and tone, "Famous Friends" was a "deliberate echoing" of Frank O'Hara's *Lunch Poems*.[17] Short, funny poems had appealed to Thom ever since he read Brad Gooch's biography of O'Hara, *City Poet*, two years earlier. He found it "absolutely brilliant. Partly because it is full of great gossip, and that's appropriate because you can hardly separate O'H's poetry from gossip."[18] He admired O'Hara's "caught spontaneity" and wondered if he could achieve a similar effect.[19] He decided to call his new poems "Gossip" and planned "to go up to twenty or so, and to make it the middle section of my next book."[20] When the term ended, Thom had "an astonishing few weeks . . . writing more Gossip poems."[21] Thom himself was an enormous gossip. When the *Bay Area Reporter* called gossip "the Esperanto of queer culture," they cited "ex-Brit and SF personality poet Thom Gunn" to back them up. "'I'm the soul of indiscretion,' admits Gunn, and a million heads nod in synchronicity throughout the Bay Area."[22] Once, Thom heard that the handle of a toilet had been broken in a friend's apartment when it was being used by a mutual acquaintance. He then, according to the friend, "went into this whole fantasy routine about the sex that [the acquaintance and their lover] had had on the toilet that resulted in the breaking of the handle. And forever after, for years after, he would allude to it."[23]

"Gossip" sustained him through summer. He wrote "The Artist as an Old Man," based on "a remarkable nude self-portrait" by Lucian Freud, *Painter Working, Reflection* (1993), a postcard of which he stuck above his desk at Berkeley.[24] Looking at Freud, "nude and embattled, and old"—he painted himself as unforgivingly as he painted others—made Thom reflect on his own mortality.[25] "I feel both young and old in a curious way. No doubt about it, I feel 17 years old every morning. But also I am a bit listless in the afternoons," he told Ander. "I couldn't have had more terrific things happen in [my life], all that I have wanted, and far more. I should now go on to say I would die contented tomorrow, but I doubt it. We are so greedy for <u>everything</u>!"[26] Freud was seventy when he painted the self-portrait; Thom was almost sixty-seven when he wrote the poem. The Freud Thom sketched was vulnerable but vigorous: "Vulnerable because / naked because / his own model." Holding the palette "like a shield," the painter "faces off / the only appearance / reality has and makes it / doubly his," an act of defiance and possession that appealed to Thom.[27] Aspiring to Freud's vigor, Thom changed the poem's working title from "The Painter as an Old Man" to "The Artist as an Old Man": in the "assessing glare," the poem is a self-portrait, a kind of self-exposure, but one mediated through Thom's identification with Freud's painting, just as he had used Dahmer's and David's voices in "Troubadour" and "Dancing David" to explore his own thoughts and feelings. Thom "knew more about the visual arts than he let on," recalled Simone Di Piero, and Freud's portrait "reminded him of himself."[28]

Despite their relatively slight stature, many of Thom's "Gossip" poems deal with complex ideas like identity and self-reflection. The sequence also allowed him to experiment with voice, tone, and character, which he had relished while writing "Troubadour" and "Dancing David." Some of his Folsom Street tricks were, in themselves, occasions for poems. One, Mike B, was so frenetic that Thom recorded his stories and sayings. "(1) MB says 'I love you' to me, (2) tells me he has 6 months to live on lung cancer, (3) had half his body shot away in Vietnam, (4) was in jail 24 years (5) having shot a cop. Item 3 I believe & perhaps 2 & 4," Thom mused. "But he is so sexy I give him $200 to 'set him up' viz as a dealer."[29] Thom did not hear from him again. "My first thoughts of him were as a friend, then—as the days passed & he never contacted me—as a con man," he reflected. "Suddenly, today, I pitied his desperation, his need to take charge (power = identity; 'now the dealers will be buying from ME'), his frenetic plan-changing on the hour. I was conceited to think myself special. Why didn't I realize all this before?"[30] Thom drafted a poem about Mike B—called, variously, "An Identity," "Self-Fashioning in the 1990s," "The Con Man," and "The Pathos of the Confidence Man." The first part mimics Mike B's storytelling—"I was on Death Row, I shot a cop, I was crazy"—whereas, in the second, Thom speaks at a remove: "a terrific desperation informed him, how <u>could</u> he think of anyone else when he was searching for a self?" There was pathos: Mike B's "prime need is to con himself into believing he has an identity."[31] Thom abandoned the poem but developed its ideas in other poems, such as "Stories of bar-fights" and "Hi." In the latter, a waiter named Hugo—"deeply charming you, / as if charm could be deep"—constructs a new identity to suit each diner.[32]

That autumn, Thom gave an interview to *San Francisco Frontiers Newsmagazine* in which he called the Hole in the Wall his "favorite bar in the city" because "it's friendly and everybody's sexy. [. . .] Half the people in there are homeless," he continued. "I find that out when I've brought them home for the night and the next morning when I ask them what part of town they're going to—they tell me, 'no particular place.' I hear, 'I sleep in the back of somebody's truck,' or something like that."[33] After reading the interview, a friend phoned Thom "and said, it's more like a twentieth than a half: what you meant, he said, is that half the people you are attracted by turn out to be homeless. How right he was."[34] Thom felt "so guilty about the homeless": cruising homeless guys in the Hole was an extension of that guilt.[35] "I don't think I'd ever been with him when someone, a panhandler, was touching us or him for money and he didn't give them money. He did, scores and scores of times," recalled August Kleinzahler. "He was magnanimous, but his magnanimity leached into his sexuality. I think he found a certain kind of needy young male sexually attractive on account of that neediness, that vulnerability. [. . .] Whitman's Civil War service and writings about it would not have been lost on him in the slightest. A beautiful young wounded boy would have probably been one of his sexual ideals. Later in life, when he was inviting homeless people into the house, I don't know if there was so much guilt, but I think he was very attracted—sexually attracted and maybe aesthetically attracted—to their desperation. He did have that powerful mommy, nurse impulse."[36]

Thom continued writing "Gossip" poems through the autumn. After a fortnight in New York, where he saw lots of Billy Lux, Thom reread all the letters he had received from Lux in the past two years. "I admire the way you put things and you have been a lot in my mind," Thom told him. "I was trying to turn it and selected passages from others of your letters into a kind of collage-poem for my series (does that make you feel used?), but I don't think I can do it, your prose rhythms are so good."[37] He kept trying: he reread Pound's conversational "Canto XIII," "modelled" his approach on "WCW's use of letters," and within a fortnight had finished "Letters from Manhattan." Mike thought it was "too prosy and random."[38] Robert Pinsky, to whom Thom sent the poem for *Slate*, "thought it was all about <u>my</u> experiences in Manhattan, and didn't like it because it seemed like 'the gay poet' kind of dipping his wick into Manhattan then boasting about it, aged 67."[39] To solve the problem, Thom added "Hello T.G." at the beginning and was "very fond of it, because it is you," he told Lux, "that lovely understated wit of yours, making jokes against yourself."[40] Moreover, Thom was pleased to include another voice in the "Gossip" sequence. He worried his own would "predominate, because I don't have the imagination or reportorial power to bring in as many as I'd like."[41]

In late September, Thom was eighty-sixed from the Hole in the Wall. "I had this guy's cock out and he had mine out and we were doing enjoyable things to them," he explained to Lux.[42] His expulsion, he thought, "will help me cut down on my consumption of speed, it really can't be good for a 67 year old with high blood pressure."[43] Thom stayed clean for two months. More focused, he finished poems like "Letters from Manhattan," "Hi," and "7 a.m. in the bar," and began work on a prose project to which he had committed the previous summer in "a moment of madness." He had promised William Cookson, the editor of *Agenda*, "a short introductory book about Bunting" to be published by Cookson's Agenda Editions imprint.[44] Thom had stalled for a year, "dismayed" at how Peter Makin's book, *Bunting: The Shaping of His Verse*, left him "with little to do" and was "already better than what I can do."[45] The project kept him "virtuously busy" for the rest of the year.[46] "One page a day, I say to myself, like a recovering alcoholic," he told Clive, "but I doubt if I can finish it by the end of next summer as I promised."[47]

With Robert Prager's help, Thom was welcomed back to the Hole in late November. "It was like coming home," he reflected.[48] He invited Prager to Cole Street for Thanksgiving. "I could fall for RP, as I let him know," Thom wrote, "& he clearly let me know that's no good, tho nothing was said. Maybe that's for the best."[49] They made a speed date for New Year's Eve, but Prager caught pneumonia: Thom looked after him instead, running errands and bringing him groceries. Their aborted plan informed Thom's "Gossip" poem "Blues for the New Year, 1997":

> He has different-
> colored eyes and nothing
> about him quite matches.
> A challenge.
>
> [. . .]
>
>   Anyway
> I'm sixty-seven,
> and have high blood pressure,
> and probably shouldn't
> be doing speed at all.
>
> Let's reschedule![50]

Thom often felt compelled to look after his friends. He lent Prager money and fed him when he sometimes showed up "starving" on the Cole Street doorstep.[51] In the spring, Prager left his "Tenderloin shit-room" and stored his belongings at Cole Street while he searched for new accommodation. He eventually found a "birdcage" apartment on Perry, next to the freeway overpass: Thom lent him eighteen hundred dollars for his rent deposit.[52]

Thom had vowed to quit speed in 1997 and had anticipated his New Year's marathon with Prager as a final blowout. When Prager fell ill, Thom revised his plans. "No more speed after the age of 70, no more alcohol after 75, no more sex after 80 (probably not much more available at that age anyway), and die at 85," he wrote, "the last years being full of really good meals and lots of jokes." Thom was "still horny all the time" and found sex easy to come by in the Hole in the Wall. "I meet people who, because of the drugs I offer them and because of the poor lighting," he told Lux, "come back with me for an extraordinary night or so."[53] He began a new notebook early in the new year and spent "a slightly sad day—very characteristic of early spring term, <u>avoiding</u> bars & drugs & sex & keep fresh for teaching, also wondering & hoping about GOSSIP poems. I like what I'm doing, but they sure come few & far between."[54] He finished "Blues for the New Year, 1997" and "Aubade," both about Prager, and "Convergence" in the spring but felt "diffident," calling them "pieces of trivia."[55] Prager informed a third "Gossip" poem, "The Search," about gay classified ads: "Movie stars / OK, insensitivity a big +."[56] Thom often called classified-ad numbers in the *Bay Area Reporter* and used the prefix "HL"—hotline—in his diary to label successful hookups. Prager claimed to have told Thom that "all the poetry in gay life can be found in gay personal ads . . . the same way that people in Elizabethan [times] cultivated writing sonnets to express themselves."[57] By mid-April Thom had twenty-one "Gossip" poems: he aimed "to do 35 or more until I stop in mid-1999" and select the best ones for *Boss Cupid*. "If it turns out they are all trivia," he told Clive, "well, there are some firmish things in the rest of the book to keep a certain variety."[58] He warned his aunts that, after the "virtuous compassionate" poems of *The Man with Night Sweats*, he would be "reverting to the sneering bad boy again (bad <u>old man</u>) with poems about mass murderers and drugs."[59]

Summer brought troubling news of an old friend. Don Doody's emphysema was much advanced: Thom phoned but found Don "cheerful & stoical & admitted no pain."[60] Don's seemingly imminent demise made Thom think about Tony Tanner; Thom wrote and encouraged him to reconcile with Don. "I have no idea how you feel about him nowadays," Thom reflected. "Of course it would be hypocritical to write if you still feel about him as you did in the early 1970s." Thom saw parallels between their limited lives: Don lived off cigarettes and hamburgers in his New York apartment; Tanner, on two sticks, rarely ventured beyond King's College. "My own tendency is to be cheerful, to be evasive about ugly things and about my own troubles, to avoid talking about unhappinesses as if to disregard them would be to banish them," he told Tanner, "and I think you share something of the same tendency, though heaven knows you have had a Packard's van load more of misfortunes than I have had." Thom had learned from Don that "the abrasiveness and difficultness he exemplifies so often is also a good and truthful way of dealing with one's life." Don, he thought, "tells the truth a lot more than I do . . . and I know he has far more courage." Moreover, Thom respected Don for having "always refused to take easy ways. Anyway, I feel for him in his pain, admire his stoicism, and already miss him."[61] Tony wrote Don "a warm and long letter" and Don was "delighted," Thom told Clive. "Tony has acted with exemplary charity."[62] He took pleasure in having engineered Tony and Don's reconciliation but took little pleasure in the limited lives of two of his oldest and closest friends. When Thom visited Don in New York the following spring, he found him "blown up in face as well as body." Don suggested they go for a walk. "About 6 blocks each way, the longest he has taken in 2 years," Thom wrote. "The walk is to a store where he buys 6 cartons of Salems. I say, I suppose you are doing this so I can tell everybody? He knows I will not judge, but I <u>report</u>."[63] Thom led a much fuller and more active life than Don or Tony, but was beginning to look forward to his retirement from teaching in 1999. "I was thinking of dying about five years after that," he told Ander, "but haven't completely made up my mind up yet."[64]

When the semester concluded, Thom tweaked with Prager and tricked with guys he met at the Hole or through personal ads. One trick, an artist named Leslie, recalled the quality of Thom's drugs. "I saw the rocks Thom had, they were crystal clear," he reflected. "They were good quality, and that's more addictive."[65] Speed hangovers meant Thom slept a lot and struggled to concentrate on finishing his Bunting book. He had "trouble" starting his *Briggflatts* chapter and thought "too much speed" had "unnerved" him.[66] Sleeping eleven hours a night and "passing happy 'somatime' days," Thom resolved "to rest another week," thinking it was "all just prolonged speed hangover."[67] He hoped his "Puritan ethic" would guilt him into working on the Bunting book, poems, and an essay about Lord Rochester he had "madly" agreed to write.[68] "I have all the ideas inside my head but they won't come out right," he told Belle. "I haven't had writer's block like this since the late fifties."[69] Struggling on all fronts, Thom made peace with his "extraordinarily idle and wasteful summer" and wrote nothing, enjoying instead "the sunshine and the alcohol."[70] It concluded with a visit from Billy Lux, who had such a good time he moved to San Francisco the following year. Lux "charm[ed] Mike as he has charmed everyone else," Thom reflected.[71] "I can't thank you enough for your kindness, muesli-hospitality, and wicked bad-boy good cheer," Lux told Thom. "I had a blast at your place."[72]

Having entered his final year of "MacArthur loot," Thom booked another European adventure with Mike.[73] They flew to Venice in mid-October, stayed at the Pensione Accademia, and, as before, mostly wandered around and visited galleries. "From Rialto I got us lost & M got us found around Campo di S Polo," Thom wrote on their first day, "he quite surprised I find it hard to keep up with him nowadays."[74] Once a ferocious walker, Thom now relied on public transportation to get around San Francisco: the long walk to and from Folsom, up and over the hill at Seventeenth, was a thing of the past. "I'm much slower than I was," he told Clive. "'Walking with you is like walking with my mother,' [Mike] said, his mother being 93. Yes, TG, the young gazelle, now walks <u>old</u>. Not Mike though, only 2 years younger than I."[75] Chancing on the Santa Maria dei Miracoli, "<u>all</u> marble outside and inside," Thom thought it was "like lining a leather jacket with leather."[76] They returned to Torcello, expecting to be hustled, but "a Holocaust has taken the wild cats." Thom was most enthralled by a group of "the handsomest young firemen ever," glimpsed through an open door, and assumed "they must have been discussing beauty treatments." Thom felt he and Mike "saw everything"—from Giudecca and

Torcello to the Carpaccios and Giorgiones—and wondered whether he had seen Venice for the last time. "Such a long journey makes me feel my age," he told Clive, "and I wonder if I'll ever feel up to doing it again!"[77]

Back in San Francisco, Thom and Mike found that Bill's new boyfriend, Ralph, had moved in upstairs. "He was a heavy muffin," Mike reflected. "I can get along with everybody, pretty much: it's the actor in me. So it wasn't so bad for me, but . . . he was thrust upon us."[78] Thom saw little of them but was relieved that they "do seem happy together."[79] Instead, he began to prepare for his penultimate semester of teaching and tried hard to finish three "Gossip" poems he had started in Venice: "For the Sexes," "Familiar," and "New Manager." He abandoned all three and wondered whether it was "time to halt the Gossip poems?—or at least interrupt them?"[80] He expected to have *Boss Cupid* finished in late 1998. "Probably my last book?" he told Clive. "But I have always thought each book was my last."[81]

In December, Thom stayed overnight in Salt Lake City to read at the University of Utah. When he returned, Mike told him that Clint Cline had died, "his heart stopping in hospital."[82] For Thom it was the saddest of several deaths that year: Fred Kuh, his Old Spaghetti Factory friend, died "of an unexpected heart attack"; Thom O'Malley, whom he knew through Don Doody, died "under anaesthesia for a third throat operation" to treat cancer. Writing to Ander, Thom also recalled two Berkeley colleagues—Jim Breslin and Bill Nestrick[83]—who died in 1996, both "fairly young, from heart attacks." He had expected Clint's death—he had had five bouts of pneumonia through the year and had been in and out of the hospital since April—but the accumulated weight of so many unexpected heart attacks made him reflect on his own mortality. "I rather like the thought that I could pop off at any moment," he told Ander. "It's kind of comfortable, I've had such a wonderful life but I've almost had enough of it—better than going on into my nineties and becoming a helpless old bore everyone wants out of the way."[84]

38

JOHN

In mid-January, Thom "astonished" himself by writing two new "Gossip" poems on the same day: "Stories of bar fights" and "First saw him." "I'm terrifically pleased by them," he told Billy Lux, "the first real stuff since last May, after all."[1] The poem beginning "First saw him" is about Pat, "an obvious loser," whom Thom had seen rifling through trash cans outside the Hole and swigging the dregs from beer bottles. "Why was I so attracted?" he asked himself. "Something about his looks & attitude, I guess, I can't understand it really."[2] Like many "Gossip" poems, "First saw him" pays attention to appearance: in this case, the absence of self-reflection. "He had little idea of his looks," Thom wrote, "caught on a brief sill / between youthful lean times / and blowziness to come."[3] Thom fought his own "blowziness" but sometimes his looks caught him by surprise. Seeing himself on a CCTV screen in a bank, he wrote in his diary: "I look like a pig now."[4]

During the semester, Thom surprised himself again by writing another poem. The conversational free verse of "Gossip" influenced "The Dump," a poem about "a poet who concentrates on a body of work that is compressed into brilliance, all the mistaken poetry, the failures, the boring stuff omitted. (Bunting? for example Marvell? you can think of others)," he remarked at a reading in San Francisco. "And then the archivists who are intent on something completely other—scholarship or history, which is splendid—but also the kind of fetishism which would actually collect a poet's sneakers as the library of a university not 30 miles from here did with Allen Ginsberg."[5] A "compressed" body of work—"the crisp vehemence / of a lifetime reduced to / half a foot of shelf space"[6]— was Thom's own aim. He was disciplined about what he collected: many poems published in journals, magazines, and newspapers were omitted from major collections. He disliked *Touch* so much that he refused to have it reissued and included only its best pieces in his *Collected Poems*. Thom may have had Ginsberg's sneakers in mind for "The Dump," but he wrote the poem a week after attending a leather art show at the then Gay and Lesbian Historical Society of Northern California.[7] The experience may have made Thom think about his own posthumous "avalanche of letters, paid bills, / sexual polaroids" and "a cliff of notebooks / with every draft and erasure / of every poem he / published or rejected."[8]

Writing three poems during the semester was especially astonishing because Thom was already busier than usual. When his colleague Robert Hass "announced suddenly that he wouldn't be teaching this semester," Thom "rashly and indignantly offered to take on his writing course with no extra pay (I felt sorry for [the students], and also I think I was showing off to myself), so now I am teaching three courses, just at a time of my life when I feel a mixture of tiredness and laziness every afternoon."[9] Thom had little time for Hass or his poetry. When asked for remarks about Hass's tenure as United States Poet Laureate, Thom was "smooth, dishonest, manipulative, praising Hass for organizational abilities and avoiding saying anything at all about the quality of his poetry. I told no lies. But I told no major truths either."[10] Hass's abandonment of his students was "really the moment," according to a friend, that Thom turned against him. "Thom didn't like Bob Hass," they recalled. "On a certain level he's a sleaze, very charming, and would get away with murder. Thom wasn't going to leave those students high and dry when Hass had been willing to."[11] Hass's class, scheduled for 4:00 to 7:00 p.m. every Friday, made Thom feel "as overworked and depressed as at Trinity University, San Antonio in the mid fifties."[12] The highlight of the term came when August Kleinzahler, newly returned from teaching stints at Brown and Iowa, read to Thom's own poetry-writing class. "A really triumphant hour," Thom reflected, "he was a justification in person of the whole value of poetry."[13] But Thom, feeling old and tired, found teaching a struggle. "I was running to catch up with myself all term," he told his aunts. "It all went off well, I get on well with my students, and I must say the older I get the more I feed off their youth and energy, like a wicked old vampire."[14]

In May, Ander arrived for a short stay on Cole Street. Bett did not accompany him because complications from a broken back made it "difficult" for her to travel. "But they spoke every day on the phone," Thom told his aunts, "which I thought was sweet, like young lovers. I am glad he found someone to love him at last."[15] Ander's visit began "spikily": the brothers snapped at each other most mornings and Ander got on Thom's nerves. Thom criticized him for leaving only a 10 percent tip for a waiter, writing afterward that, on Ander's next visit, he would provide him with "a remedial course on tipping in the USA."[16] As usual, Mike came to the rescue. "Suddenly, everything is fine with Ander," Thom wrote. "He & M talked a long time after dinner last night, & somehow that got <u>my</u> mind right & it's my mind that is the problem here."[17] Reconciled, the brothers enjoyed Ander's last few days in the city. One thing in particular "shook" Thom during Ander's stay. "He told me that Father, seeing some poor person on the street, would say 'there but for the grace of god go I,'" Thom told his aunts. "That is something I constantly think about the beggars everywhere. I know he didn't originate the phrase (!), but it certainly makes me like the old bastard a little better that he should think on it and act on it."[18]

Through summer, Thom labored to finish his Rochester essay. That struggle, combined with Peter Makin's unassailable monograph, made Thom tell William Cookson that he "cannot write the Bunting book."[19] Nor had he written any poems since finishing "The Dump" in March. "That's another thing about old age," he told Ander: "the imagination dries up."[20] When he struggled to write poems, Thom also found it difficult to write letters. "Our friendship is a friendship of all sorts I hope by now," he told Clive, "and yet it was originally just a literary friendship (from which everything else sprang) and I still feel that when I have nothing to show you by way of composition I am not worth your consideration." He wondered whether his dry spell was "a prelude to the last barrenness which most writers enter a good time before dying."[21] Clive felt "very slightly hurt" as their correspondence tailed off. "I was a bit baffled by it, really, because we'd written a lot," he reflected. "He didn't often hurt me. He was a very considerate person. But it seemed like the only reason he'd written to me was because he wanted me to comment on his poems."[22] When Clive asked Thom to review Donald Davie's posthumous essay collection, *With the Grain*, which Clive had edited for Carcanet, Thom refused. "I am sorry, and in another year I would delight in making such a review a place for setting down my thoughts about Donald and his importance," Thom replied, "but the whole thought of writing a review— any review—is somehow repellent to me." Frustrated at having written so little poetry, combined with the exhaustion of a difficult semester and a summer of speed, Thom was unusually curt in his letter to Clive. "I'm a bitter old asshole," he wrote, "sitting under my umbrella in the yard and jealous of all the people who publish a new book every two years."[23]

The highlight of Thom's summer was "an exquisite holiday," a four-day trip to Los Angeles with Robert Gallegos, now a good friend. They stayed at Coral Sands, a famously cruisy motel where "everyone was on crystal." Thom cruised a guy named Randy, "the most sexually depraved man I ever met . . . like Clark Kent in street clothes, Superman without." They pooled their speed and went to Long Beach to buy more. By the third night, Thom was "hallucinating magnolia bushes as Bosnian refugees with their luggage." Gallegos, who had spent the day in Ventura celebrating his parents' wedding anniversary, returned to find Thom sprawled in the bathroom: he had fainted, "having forgotten about eating altogether." Gallegos bought him a hamburger.[24] It was all "drugs and brittle fun," Thom told Ander, "swimming pools and frivolity."[25]

Back in San Francisco, Thom's increasing speed use led him to have riskier sex. It was another cycle: the speed gave him energy and he came to rely on it to engage in weekend-long sex marathons. "The experiences we shared were a little on the dark side," recalled one trick. "Thom was not vanilla by any means."[26] Mike thought it "became more S&M with Thom as the years went on." Thom always wore engineer boots, "never anything else on his feet," and would typically wear a leather jacket and jeans to the Folsom bars. From the mid-nineties, however, he started wearing full leather. "When Thom would go out for the night," Mike reflected, "I was surprised he wasn't wearing leather underwear."[27] Bob also felt that "the leather became too much a part of [Thom's] life. When I first met him, it wasn't that way. It was separate. Then at the end he would wear the leather stuff around the house and it smelled bad."[28]

Around his sixty-ninth birthday, Thom became involved with a "very hot, slightly crazy" twenty-nine-year-old named Andy.[29] Within days of their first meeting, at the Hole, Andy ruptured a testicle and spent several days in San Francisco General. When he was discharged, Andy stayed with Thom for a week. Delighted to be looking after a handsome, vulnerable street boy, Thom was also quizzical. "He said last time he wants me as a boyfriend," he wrote, "but it turns out the term means nothing to him—Mark is also his boyfriend, & Stuart I have not met."[30] Andy's behavior became increasingly difficult. "Andy is great for drugs and sex," Thom wrote, "terrible for conversation (he has <u>attention deficit disorder</u>.)"[31] When Andy left, he took with him Thom's door key and Fast Pass for the Muni, "but I'm sure not thro malice."[32] A fortnight later, the day before Thom was due to fly east for a reading tour of Connecticut, New York, and Washington, DC, Andy showed up "after untold days on speed" and spent the day asleep on Thom's bed.[33]

At Yale, Thom read to "a very large and knowledgeable" audience. "I was so stimulated by all that attention that I started writing again," he told Ander, "my first two poems since February, I had thought I had dried up for ever."[34] Visiting the National Gallery, Thom "fell in love" with Vuillard's *Two Women Drinking Coffee* (c. 1893) and, on the steps of the gallery, in the hot sun, drafted "Painting by Vuillard" the same afternoon.[35] The women in the painting "had grown so old / That everything had got less complicated," Thom wrote, before an abrupt pivot: "But it's not like that for me: age is not simpler / Or less enjoyable, not dark, not whitewashed."[36] His second poem was testament to that. "Front Door

Man" began life as "Andrew, Pigboy" and, as he told Douglas, "every word of the poem is literally true."[37] Its first half, "prelude," describes Andy's appearance at the door and Thom's confusion between "love or duty"; its second, a "plaint" addressed to Cupid, "is based on Sappho's Hymn to Aphrodite. But I figured—she's a lesbo, so addresses Aphrodite—I'm a homo, so address Cupid."[38] "I most want to protect— / To care for you like a mother," Thom wrote, but, confronted by Andy's "full daunting beauty," he "barely can reject / The impulse of quite other." Having left Andy to "recover / The strength" to "resume the cycle" of his tweaking, Thom reflected on his own patterns of behavior:

> What on earth can I hope?
> This, Cupid, is my plaint.
> I seem to be more and more
> Attracted by the unstable
> Bright and accident-prone
> Homeless, who look a lot
> Like hustlers but are not.
> And in this I am shown
> A cycle of my own.[39]

The "cycle" is Thom's routine of picking up homeless guys at the Hole and caring for them "like a mother." Mike described Thom as "mothering" the men he brought home.[40] August Kleinzahler recalled Thom's "powerful mommy, nurse impulse." Thom had played that role at length in the 1980s, caring for Allan Noseworthy and making endless hospital visits to Charlie Hinkle, Lonnie Leard, and others. "That would have fascinated him beyond almost anything else," Kleinzahler reflected, "the mixture of sexual attraction and someone wasting away, the object of his love wasting away and him being able to feed him and nurse him."[41]

Recurrent dreams about his mother informed Thom's own "cycle." Once he had "the recurrent dream of Mother Returns, but for the first time [I] was not plaintively reproachful but <u>angry</u> with her."[42] Another time, Thom "woke from a mother-suicide dream, distraught, the worst ever. She was conflated, this time, with MK, & Jesus. (An empty shroud in M's clothes closet.)"[43] Thom wrote about these dreams in a never-published poem called "At Last," which dates to the "strange 2 months" he called "confessional" in early 1994:

> I stared down, as I had done year by year,
> At her pathetic body, always near,
> And suddenly said, "Oh not this time my dear,
> I'm not going through it now, I'm leaving here."
>
> I walked away from her in the belief
> The nurturing anguish could at least be brief,
> And made myself wake up from all that grief
> Into a difficult delayed relief.[44]

Thom saw his own abandonment in vulnerable, challenging street boys like Andy. He had lived with "reproach, guilt, desolation, rounds of pain" for five decades, "linked in an exquisite embracing chain."[45] In "Front Door Man," Thom was torn between "love or duty," whereas he framed his mother's suicide as a dereliction of both, thus his plaintive reproach gives way, eventually, to anger. He had come to realize that Mike—"my anchor, my love"—was a mother substitute as well as lover and life partner: Mike fulfilled Thom's need for a mother's unconditional love.[46] It was little wonder Thom had told Douglas that he would find it "difficult" to outlive Mike: it would be like losing his mother all over again. "Front Door Man" is not ultimately about a street boy named Andy; rather, it is Thom's closest examination, in print, of his complicated, unresolved feelings about his mother and how the traumatic effects of her suicide informed his own patterns of behavior. Marking fifty-four years since his mother's death, Thom found himself with "the New Year blues." "It's like this every year," he wrote. "I must be ruled by dates / Being haunted by a death."[47] Back in San Francisco, Thom was surprised when Andy "turned up several times in [a] day with his wife I'd heard about, Jane, likeable girl!" while they were "trying to sell home made acid on the Haight."[48] After several more encounters—during which they had sex, or Thom lent Andy money, or both—Thom saw Andy for the last time when Andy asked him to cash a couple of checks. To Thom's "disappointment," both checks "(in his wife's non-existent account) bounced, total $300. Boy, am I a simpleton."[49]

More distressing, however, was a letter from Clive Wilmer that arrived in October 1998. Tony Tanner had cancer of the prostate and kidneys, and was about to undergo a liver biopsy. He had only weeks to live: Thom wrote to him immediately. He found Tony's continued vitality and "strength" in the face of "the depression and the incapacitation and the subsequently limited life you have been forced to lead" remarkable. Although their friendship had faded from its heights of the sixties and early seventies, Thom still had great affection and respect for Tony. "I must say that you have been without question one of the friends who has meant most to me in my life," he told him.

> I know it is difficult to keep up the full vitality of a friendship when separated by 6000 miles, but you have always been and will go on being a reference point and a reminder to me not only of affection but of the way to lead a life. [. . .] I think of things you have said, jokes you have made, quotations, judgments, conclusions, funny stories, and they constantly recur to me as reference points as they do from Mike, my mother, Tony White and I am not sure anybody else in such profusion.[50]

Tanner died on December 5. His wife, Nadia Fusini, wrote Thom days later giving a "blow by blow account."[51] "He went on eating pate and drinking white wine on his deathbed," Thom told Ander. "I admire people who die as they have lived."[52] Clive mailed him the British obituaries, of which Thom most admired Colin MacCabe's "frank account of Tony's troubles" in *The Independent*.[53] "We corresponded pretty regularly for years, I seem to remember, but after his worst breakdown at Johns Hopkins, where I did visit him for a day and a night, he didn't seem able to write to me much," Thom told Clive. "I think I was part of America, and America was associated with all the worst things that had happened to him." He recalled that Tanner had been happiest in London during Thom's year there in the mid-sixties. "I remember his giving a party at Kings . . . and putting on a record," he told Clive, "then new, of Tom Jones' 'It's not unusual / to be in love with anyone,' and as the first line was sung saying to himself, but audibly, 'it <u>is</u>, actually.' He was rejoicing in Marcia being there and I suppose of their marriage being assured. He was very happy that year."[54]

The same month Thom heard about Tanner's prognosis, Ted Hughes died of cancer. "Everybody (TLS, BBC, Sunday Times) has been on at me to write memories of Ted, but I had nothing to say, not at this stage anyway," Thom told Clive. "I wrote a note to his widow instead."[55] A mutual friend of Thom and Hughes, A. E. Dyson, wrote Thom a remarkably candid account of Hughes and Plath's relationship. "Soon after Sylvia's death, Ted confided in me that he knew she was 'attempting' suicide, & but for her psychiatrist's arrival (two hours late) would have lived on, as Lady Lazarus," Dyson wrote. "Ted added that they would have got together again, & he felt wretched. Maybe they would; but Ted was not naturally monogamous & Sylvia's illness—which I never saw—would not have improved."[56] Elaine Feinstein, Hughes's first biographer, contacted Thom shortly after Hughes's death. Mentioning their joint *Selected Poems*, their *Five American Poets* anthology, and their abandoned *Faber Book of English Verse* project—"we never got it done because we decided we had to read everything, <u>everything</u> ever written in English poetry"—Thom suggested that they had never been especially close. "I never knew him pre-Sylvia," he wrote. "He and I always had good, but hardly close relations, and came to realize soon that our lives were widely different projects, though we wrote appreciative letters to one another every few years."[57]

After the deaths of Clint Cline, Hughes, and Tanner within twelve months, Thom was confronted by "a new kind of death—my contemporaries, not my juniors and not from AIDS." He feared Don Doody would soon follow; "the effects of emphysema were [even] more apparent" when Thom saw him in New York that October. Such deaths and declines made Thom feel guilty that he continued to "bounce along . . . in dreadfully good health, as full of sexual greed as ever and it seems usually getting what I want."[58]

Preparing for his final semester at Berkeley, Thom felt he had made the correct decision to retire. It was "a good idea to retire while you're still on top of things," he had once told Tony Tanner, "having had enough doddering teachers in my past to choose not to be among them."[59] In fact, Thom felt he taught "badly, these days" and was "careless & lazy."[60] He had more than 140 students in his Modern Poetry course, and his decision to revise his notes and teach D. H. Lawrence's poetry "for the first time in years" only increased his workload.[61] Exhausted, and in generally poor spirits, Thom was not at his social best during the semester. His childhood friend Ruth [Pearce] Townsend passed through San Francisco and Thom took her to lunch. "It was nice to see Ruth," he told Ander, "but she's becoming a rather self-righteous old woman (left-wing type of self-righteous, of course). But then I may be turning into a self-righteous old man myself."[62] Hardened attitudes toward important women from his youth—Ruth was "moralistic & frivolous,"[63] Aunt Mary "batty and drips poison,"[64] Thérèse a "lion-hunter"[65]—symbolized his hardening of attitudes toward England and the "self-pitying, vulnerable" adolescent he had fought to outgrow.[66] "I realised that half a century of hard work, fame, good & tragic times," Ruth wrote to him two years after their meeting, "left you so remarkably unchanged in every respect."[67] Her words likely horrified him.

During the spring term, Thom met the man who would become the central erotic and romantic figure of his retirement. John Ambrioso was thirty-six, of Cuban parentage, but born and raised in Kentucky. Moving to San Francisco in the mid-nineties, he met Robert Prager in My Place and they became casual boyfriends. Prager introduced Thom to John at the Hole in late December, but it was not until February that John "encouraged" Thom, having "always seemed distant." They partied on Cole Street one weekend while Mike and Bob were at the cabin. Thom was enthralled. "Handsome, articulate, melancholy hero," he gushed, "we got on wonderfully & fantastic sex."[68] It had been a "36 hour sexual epiphany,"

Thom told August Kleinzahler. "[John] has great verve and energy and good looks coupled with a puzzling low esteem for himself. I will make it my ambition to increase said esteem, since I can think of several reasons why anyone would want to be John Ambrioso."[69]

According to Prager, John "did the most skilled fancy needle work" he had ever seen. Thom typically snorted speed; after meeting John, he began shooting up. "Thom was unable to 'hit' himself," Prager reflected. "He always had to have somebody else perform 'nursing duties' when he shot up. This was always part of the tacit arrangement Thom had with guys he had sex with." Prager was Thom's on-off dealer for several years. "Whenever I took him several hundred dollars' worth I'd give him a couple of complimentary 'points' for free," he told a friend. "I also know how John operates. He'd prepare the points and give himself 3/4 or 4/5s of it. John told me this was his way of looking after Thom and taking care of him. I saw it as John's way of taking care of himself."[70] The first weekend of spring break, Thom and John shared the "best crystal ever." Thom had a "generous amount of hallucinations" and felt "crazy" about John.[71] He slept for the rest of the week, "without word from the wonderful man himself."[72] Thom could easily come across as too keen and wrote to John within days of their weekend marathon. "I'm writing just to say hello, and to say that our 2 times together were out of this world, and thank you!" he wrote. "I have never been so high in my life as this last time, & it was all great—you are the best, my friend. Sleeping in your wooden bed that 2nd night was in a way as good as anything. You are as generous and as hospitable as you are hot."[73] Telling Prager about his adventures, Thom was irritated that he "wants me to be Henry Higgins to JA's Eliza & 'Take him to the theater!' !!! I never go to SF theater anyway & am fully happy with JA's world of bikes & grease & drugs. I learn from him."[74]

Back on campus, Thom mailed the manuscript of *Boss Cupid* to Faber and Farrar, Straus and Giroux. He had not written anything since "Front Door Man" and "Painting by Vuillard" in the autumn; nor had he written a new "Gossip" poem for more than a year. "Maybe it's the end of my writing life," he mused. "I suppose it had to stop some time."[75] With the book scheduled for spring 2000, Thom thought "nobody will notice for a few years" that he was no longer writing.[76] After he submitted the manuscript, Thom struggled to distinguish between his typical post-submission slump and a writing life that had become steadily drier since the early nineties. His thoughts turned to retirement, and to John. As the semester concluded, Thom heard from his aunt Catherine. "Can't imagine your being retired," she wrote. "What will you do except study your body à la Buddha? & get drunk rather early?"[77] It was a good question. Thom found "all the grading murderous": the thought of his next date with John—"the immediate pleasure, waiting, waiting"—kept him going.[78]

At the end of Thom's final lecture, the students "applauded for a long time & that made me feel conceited at being so popular, they had probably heard I was retiring."[79] After final exams, grading, and administrative chores, he was finished. "Now I will do nothing for a long while," he reflected. "I don't seem to write any poetry, so I will take drugs & drink & stay in bed late."[80] He felt he had done "reasonably well (no more) in an honorable profession" and would miss "being surrounded by bright young people" and giving the "occasional lecture . . . which made me feel I'd done so well that it was like being a rock star."[81] Many former students wrote to congratulate him on a fine teaching career. "You were a damn good teacher-poet, and I often return to poems you first showed me—esp. material from your surveys of Elizabs & Romantics," wrote the poet Peter Spagnuolo. "I credit you with making me hear Donne & Marvell as real voices, in my language."[82] For Thom, this kind of praise ranked as high as offbeat compliments about his own poetry. When Robert Potts interviewed him for *The Guardian* in 2003, "he told me that he had admired my poetry for so long that he had stolen a copy of one of my books from the school library (what a terrific compliment)."[83]

For Memorial Day weekend, Thom partied with John while Mike and Bob were at the cabin. They invited Prager "to share the dope & sex" and Prager "was impressed by the easy relationship he observed betw J &

me."[84] Subsequent adventures included motorcycle rides to Bodega Bay. "I was riding behind him on his motorcycle and thought we were going rather fast, so I peered over his shoulder and noticed that there was no speedometer," Thom told Douglas. "He later told me he has no license for the bike nor a driver's license. That's what I mean by daredevil." Thom knew that John was "very independent" and that "trying anything except a sexual relationship would probably be impossible." That was part of John's attraction. Alluding to Wyatt's "Whoso List to Hunt," Thom thought it was "impossible to imagine [John] in a 'Stable relationship,' which to achieve would be like trying to trap the wind in a net."[85]

But that did not stop him from trying to keep hold of John. What began as a "huge crush" quickly became, for Thom at least, something more serious. John's independence likely reminded him of Charlie Hinkle, a similarly vivacious free spirit with whom he had also become obsessed. "Thom was not a spontaneous kind of guy," John reflected. "He had to plan things out. I'd get a note, like a week or two weeks before . . . Very regimented. Something that's totally foreign to me."[86] Thom went for days, sometimes weeks, without hearing from or seeing John. When John did drop by, often on his motorbike, he "lights up my life."[87] Without teaching and writing, Thom's leather and bar life became more consuming. He wanted John and wanted him often: the patience that had prolonged his relationship with Robert Gallegos had evaporated. He wanted "scripts of delay" *and* the certainty of anticipation. On their next weekend together, six weeks after their Memorial Day marathon, they shared two grams of speed. "It seemed to me he took less trouble with me," Thom reflected, "but maybe he was more tired than usual."[88] In the same way Thom wanted to possess a poem, he wanted to possess John, or what John represented. He had long realized that writing poetry was his attempt to deal with and understand his experience. Now that he was no longer writing, speed—and John—had become his attempt to seek escape from that experience. But John, as Thom knew, could not be possessed. "I leave off therefore," wrote Wyatt, "Sithens in a net I seek to hold the wind." Thom had no such plans to give up, but knew that to chase John, "wild for to hold," meant he "may spend his time in vain."[89]

39

ʃPEED

Initially, retirement seemed no different from ordinary life: because Thom taught only the spring semester, he was free from June through December anyway. The first few weeks were "a hoot," he told Ander. "The cat sits on my lap . . . and I drink a glass of wine and think of nothing. Sometimes, for variety, I think of something, but not for too long."[1] Summer 1999 was full of friends: August was back from a teaching stint in Texas; he saw plenty of Billy Lux and Robert Gallegos; Belle Randall passed through town; he took Robert Glück for lunches. Thom even began a new project: his new editor at Faber, Paul Keegan, suggested he edit the selected poems of Ezra Pound, whom Thom considered "the most important critic and poetic influence" of the twentieth century.[2] "No previous editors would have dreamt of asking me," he told Clive, "but Paul Keegan has evidently read my prose."[3] Thom spent the next year compiling the book and writing an introduction "designed to help the reader new to EP in explicit ways." Pound's "politics were abhorrent, but if we forgive Hazlitt for his admiration of Napoleon then we should be prepared to do likewise to Pound for his delusions about Mussolini," Thom reflected. "And at least he apologized for his anti-Semitism at the last minute, which is more than his genteeler contemporaries did."[4]

But Thom was increasingly obsessed with John. Thom told him he could bring over "a huge sack of laundry" whenever he wanted and promised to take him for slap-up meals at Zuni's. They would meet for "a marathon, all the trimmings" around once a month, and Thom's speed use became heavy and consistent.[5] After one party, Thom hallucinated "8 shrunken 14 yr olds—fairies from MN's Dream" in his room and could not sleep. Bob thought Thom was "acting like a schizophrenic."[6] Another time, Thom hallucinated "so hard" he saw "hieroglyphics everywhere on ceiling & needles everywhere on floor." When Mike and Bob returned from the cabin, Mike was "deeply resentful because I am obviously high & haven't cleaned up."[7] Thom had never before failed to uphold his end of their tacit arrangement. "We wanted the place to be cleaned up, and it wasn't," Mike recalled. "That was the first time that I thought Thom was in trouble."[8] Bob agreed. "You could tell he didn't know what to do with himself," he reflected. "He would sit on the sofa and read. He would go out to the garden and count the hours until it was late enough to go to the bars. Then he started drinking before that. By the time I came home from work he'd be pretty soused. It was soon after his retirement that you could tell Thom was uncomfortable and didn't know what to do."[9] Thom knew his "crystal hangovers" were becoming "worse & worse" but felt "to give up crystal wd mean giving up John, & I can't do that."[10] Sometimes John brought friends with him, "sex animals," Thom called them, "crises tracked across floors etc," one of whom broke Bob's television.[11] "Thom started bringing people around who were questionable. People I didn't quite trust," Bob reflected. "He'd think, 'This person loves me,' and not realize that sometimes he was being used for drugs and a place to sleep. He would always supply the drugs."[12] Thom's other friends knew something was wrong. Robert Gallegos "berate[d] me for drug use, in a friendly kind of way," Thom wrote on one occasion, laughing it off.[13]

Attempting to moderate his drug use, Thom "felt the benefits of snorting for a change."[14] He made notes for a poem called "The Wake Up Call," in which he imagined John "entering thru the wall / like a hologram or ghost":

> Clothed & handsome with intent,
> you seat yourself carefully on the bed
> take out the needle already loaded

& tenderly, without waking me,
discharge it into my arm.
[. . .]
constantly exploring & taking me with you
You know that my not knowing wd add to the thrill.[15]

One of Thom's hallucinations—which he had termed "ghost part[ies]"—
that winter was "pure love centred around a hallucinated John & his
friends who are parts of him." His hallucinations lasted for almost a
week, by which time Mike and Bob were home to witness it. "Bob, irritated by my roaming around the house, & his horror at my seeing people
who aren't there, gets me to bed," Thom wrote. Bill was "sympathetic,
Bob forgiving, Mike cold."[16] Thom spent the rest of the week "catching
up" on sleep and attributed his hallucinations "more [to] the sleep deprivation caused by speed than the speed itself."[17] For all Thom's intellectual
interest in the experience—it made him think about Blake's thistle and
wonder if "ghosts, spirits, drug-induced hallucinations are . . . all the
same?"[18]—he knew he had a problem. The intensity and duration of his
hallucinations were indicative of methamphetamine psychosis, in which
he heard and saw things that were not there; experienced paranoia about
those hallucinations; and continued to experience symptoms days after
having last taken methamphetamine. What had begun as an accompa-
niment to sex likely became an addiction, although Thom's distinction
between sex and drugs was blurred. "I can't do speed any more, now
I know how to hallucinate," he wrote. "I am not yet scared, rather interested, even amused, but it will turn bad, but John is addicted, & no
speed, no John."[19]

In October, Thom attended a two-day celebration at UC Berkeley honoring his teaching career. "I would have stopped it if I could," he told Clive,
"but it was really rather agreeable, and hardly ever embarrassing." He
thought it "highly gratifying to be praised for the qualities I most doubt
I actually have" and most enjoyed a joint reading by Jim Powell and Belle

Randall.[20] Concurrently, Thom was "flattered" by a lengthy supplement in *Agenda* to mark his seventieth birthday. "Well, thank you—you are as usual too kind," he told Clive, who edited the supplement, "and isn't it rather soon after the last one? I am flattered, but you are going to get increasingly weary of this sort of thing at my 80th, 90th, and maybe 100th birthdays."[21]

When the new semester began without him, Thom had his first real taste of retirement. "I enjoyed teaching so much I was afraid I would miss it, but I don't," he told Douglas. "I get up, have breakfast, and go back to bed for a nap, in winter time anyway. Most afternoons I sit with the cat on my lap and a glass or two of wine, thinking about John Ambrioso, and take another nap. I write nothing, no poetry, anyway, and it will be a wrench when I am able to write again—if I ever do."[22] Come spring, he was contemplating a tattoo. "Not, you notice, Born to Lose, Born to Raise Hell, Born to Surf," he told Ander, "but Born to Retire."[23] Lunch was often the signature event of the day. Thom regularly took people to Zazie, a neighborhood bistro named after the Queneau novel and Malle film *Zazie dans le Métro*, and "love[d] to sit in its back yard eating Salade Nicoise."[24] John's favorite spot was Chow's, a food bar at Market and Church, "the kind of place where queers take their mothers to show them that queers are really quite nice people after all."[25] Thom liked to plan lunches with John as well as their weekend sessions. He preferred the anticipatory thrill of prearranged dates but often did not know until the last minute if Mike and Bob would spend the weekend at the Russian River. "Hope this isn't too complicated," he wrote John when cabin plans, a reading in Dallas, and the unavailability of good speed all conspired to disrupt a weekend date.[26] "I love the idea of being spontaneous, but I just can't manage to do it," he once told Wendy Lesser, "so I figure out ways around it, like writing in my pocket diary a week ahead of time, 'Remember to spontaneously ask Mike out to the movies tonight.'"[27] Sometimes John took the initiative and made an impromptu visit, with a gram or two, and they would spend the night "fucked up & fucking."[28]

. . .

Boss Cupid was published in the spring of 2000. Thom was especially pleased with the cover designs: Freud's self-portrait *Interior with Hand Mirror* (1967) for Faber, and an Attila Richard Lukacs painting of a tough skinhead—*True North: Highlander* (1989)—for Farrar, Straus and Giroux. "The British cover illustrates me," he told Douglas, "the American cover illustrates the title."[29] In England, the book received mixed reviews. While Anthony Thwaite found Thom as "alert and compelling as ever," Sean O'Brien thought that "for some readers *Boss Cupid* will seem full of unexploited potential."[30] In the *London Review of Books*, Jeremy Noel-Tod found Thom's poems "merely drab" ("Duncan"), "modern English poetic autopilot" ("Shit"), "the literary equivalent of Dad Rock" ("First saw him"), before concluding: "Pottering about in his poetry, Thom Gunn comes across as an eminently likeable person."[31] For once, Thom seemed to pay no attention to negative reviews, while commenting that his favorable notices were "what you get anyway when you have been around so long that they are all bored with you."[32] In the *PN Review*, Gregory Woods called *Boss Cupid* a "bizarre and rather lovely book" and noted how the book's Hardy epigraph—"Well, it's a cool queer tale!"— amounted to "a combination of chic, detachment, oddity and homosexuality" that had "fuelled Gunn's work since the beginning of his career." Woods also found "a new openness in the use of the word 'queer' to denote something more complex than the mere 'lifestyle' of being gay. It is an identification with marginality, but with margins (poverty, sexuality) which are—if anything is—universal."[33] Thom hoped Woods was right. "You say all the things and more that I would most wish said," he told him.[34] Thom was likely pleased that Woods had picked up on the central image of "Duncan"—margins—and had praised him for a continued openness in a book that was mostly about closure.

In America, *Boss Cupid* also garnered a mixed reception. Although it drew thoughtful critical examinations from Langdon Hammer (in *Raritan*) and Will Aitken (in *Threepenny*)—both reserved particular praise for "The Gas-poker"—the collection otherwise seemed to frustrate reviewers keen to give the final word on Thom.[35] Many focused on the overtly sexual poems. William Deresiewicz posited "Still Horny After

All These Years" as an alternative title, but postponed judgment on the work. "Is Gunn signaling his intention to bow out after a half-century of making poems?" he wondered. "Unlikely: his boss clearly wants him for a few more jobs."[36] "I don't want to remember Gunn as just a gay poet, though the more his recent poems have been praised the more he's written as one," remarked William Logan. "The formal poems [in *Boss Cupid*] suffer from their cautiousness (as if they'd set out to discover exactly what they'd discovered, and nothing more), while the free verse lacks authority, the lines failing to provide enough resistance to work against."[37] In *Poetry*, David Orr thought that *Boss Cupid* "doesn't quite equal" *The Man with Night Sweats* but "still contains poetry that any critic would admire and that any poet—British, American, formalist, or free verser—would embrace."[38] Writing later, Paul Dean, in *The New Criterion*, called *Boss Cupid* "a rather disappointing finale." Of Thom's collected works, he continued, "fifty or sixty" poems were "successful: not a bad proportion."[39] In its blend of polite praise, slight bewilderment, and outright hostility, the reception of *Boss Cupid* put the bow on what had been, throughout Thom's life, a distinctly mixed critical evaluation. "Everybody loves Thom Gunn," Orr wrote in *Poetry*: "the tweed jacket crowd, for his sculpted stanzas and his careful attention to poetic tradition; the tattoo brigade, for his continuing allegiance to I-Am-Poet types like the Beats and the Black Mountain refugees; and sophomores at Bard, because he wears a lot of black and writes poems about serial killers."[40] Poetry reviewers, he perhaps implies, were the exception.

Common to English and American reviews were comments about Thom's lifestyle. "No, given his blood pressure he shouldn't be doing speed," wrote Blake Morrison in *The Independent on Sunday*, referring to "Blues for the New Year, 1997," "and it would be more seemly not to be stirred by young flesh. But since he's here still, unlike many of his friends, he won't give up the thing that makes him feel most alive."[41] A review in *Time* also quoted "Blues," prompting Mike to say, "in view of Time Mag's quote re speed, I should be very cautious about drugs. He is right, of course."[42] Other friends echoed Mike's view. Robert Wells enjoyed

Boss Cupid but found it "a troubling book—as you surely mean it to be. Troubling, because troubled—by those enigmas of Cupid you worry at in 'A Wood Near Athens'," he told Thom. "Or is it because of the need of the poems, despite their plenty, for bareness and hardness? Or because of the insistence on appetite and restlessness? Are the poems forgiving or un-forgiving? [. . .] I think I may simply mean that you remain the moralist, and make the reader put such questions to himself."[43] Thom was simply being honest. "Someone was interviewing me for a local gay magazine," Thom told *Out* magazine when *Boss Cupid* was published, "and he said, 'What's old age like?' And I said, 'Well, I still fuck and I still take drugs and I still drink.'" After the interview was published, a young man approached Thom in a bar. "He said, 'I saw what you said in that magazine. I think you should be trying to set an example.' Now, I don't think of myself as a role model for anybody," Thom told *Out*, "but I thought I *was* setting an example—by telling the truth."[44]

In April, Thom had "the wildest & maybe best of all weekends with John. We did 2½ grams together & it was the last time I use a point except for special occasions." Thom hoped he would have "the judgement to recog-nize a special occasion."[45] He knew the family "thoroughly disapproved of John" but were "too nice to say anything against him."[46] Thom was unamused when Prager told him that John only encouraged him because "I cd keep him satisfactorily in drugs, which I more or less do. Is this true?" Thom asked himself. "If it is true, do I care? (yes) Might it not be a further instance of RP's cynicism, this time as jealousy? [. . .] I don't believe [John] sees himself as exploiting me. But then I have to believe he likes me for myself, don't I?"[47] His use of needles also created tension with Prager, who claimed that they had "a major falling out" when he told Thom "he should stop shooting speed."[48] When Prager threatened to tell Mike, Bill, and Bob about the needles, Thom said he would "never speak to me again." "If John hadn't been shorting him all those years," Prager thought—by which he meant John lessened Thom's dosage, possibly without his knowledge—Thom would likely have died during one of their speed sessions. "I told him he obviously preferred to die. He needed to find some new reasons for living." Given "the havoc crystal wrecked on him," Prager reflected, "you wouldn't doubt" Thom had a death wish. "It was the cause of his writers' block."[49]

Thom thought John would tire of him because of his age. Another reason may have been Thom's stringent moral code. "Given what an extraordinarily wild kind of life he led," Clive Wilmer reflected, "he did have extremely strict moral principles and he didn't mind laying down the law about them. You don't tell lies, you tell the truth. He was really, really strict about things like that."[50] According to Jim Powell, "Thom respected and honored courage, candor, generosity of spirit, kindness, resistance to meanness, pettiness and spite in face of accomplishment and merit, forthright honesty, plainspeaking."[51] Those principles applied to everyone, from family, friends, and colleagues to fellow poets, boyfriends, and tricks. Although Thom was "obsessed" with John, he found him "only marginally honest."[52] John rarely returned borrowed money: for Thom, it was the principle that mattered, not the money. He once took John "to task . . . for borrowing 100 from me, promising faithfully to repay me by Thursday, & then not keeping his word."[53] There seemed to be, almost from the beginning, a power imbalance. Thom tried to mold John into the kind of vulnerable street boy who needed him; John found such a role too constricting and overwhelming. In the young, often homeless, addicts whom Thom brought home from the Hole in the Wall, he saw his own abandonment. When they in turn abandoned him, like Andy in "Front Door Man" and countless others, Thom was essentially replaying his own abandonment. With John, however, the stakes were higher. "JA comes round & acts self-defeatingly flighty—in 3 minds at once," Thom wrote in September, "to try for one apt, then another, or get a truck & drive back to Kentucky."[54] The thought that he could lose John at any moment made him feel frightened and unsettled.

Although John spent lots of time on Cole Street, Thom tried to keep him separate from the family. Mike and Bob disliked John, but Bill "accept[ed]" him.[55] "He was a get out there and do it kinda guy," Bill reflected. "Thom ended up going out a lot, and frankly, at that time, we related better than we probably had most of the years I knew him. We found solace in each other in a druggy kind of way."[56] Once, John told Thom he had had "a brief chat with Mickey about me, which I greatly resent, his trying to ingratiate himself with Mike."[57] Another time, John brought Mike some "ornamental stones" as a gift: "M is glacial," Thom recorded.[58] Recalling the scene, Mike remained puzzled: "Why the fuck would I want ornamental stones?"[59] When Thom spent part of Christmas Day with John and Prager before joining the family for dinner, Mike was again "glacial. I wonder why," Thom wrote. "It must be jealousy of John."[60] For Mike, it was obvious that John was using Thom. "John took him out someplace on his motorcycle. Diverted him. Gave him some thrills. John liked having a good time and Thom liked people who liked having a good time. That was his thing." John "knew he was onto a good thing" and was "using" Thom for drugs.[61] Sending a newsy letter to Douglas that autumn, Thom called Mike "the sole source of common sense in our house."[62]

There was "no trace of literary activity" in Thom's life until October, when he spent three weeks as the visiting Hurst Lecturer at the University of Washington, St. Louis.[63] "When I was young," he told Clive, "I could simply pop out the door in a strange town, go to a queer bar & go to bed with a comely stranger or three, but that's not so easily done at the age of 71, when it's only a hardened gerontophile who will so much as look at me."[64] With minimal responsibilities—he met with some classes, gave one public reading, and held a colloquium on the craft of poetry, which he "dreaded"[65]—Thom used his time to make notes for poems. "Lunch and then a Nap" described his daily life back home; "Trust Me" and "John" were about his ongoing affair with Ambrioso.[66] He abandoned all three and could not wait to leave St. Louis. He had been so "disconsolately lonely" that he rejected other offers to teach elsewhere, including the position of Mohr Visiting Poet at Stanford, which paid eighty thousand dollars for ten classes over ten weeks.[67] "I discussed it with Mike—did we need such money? what would we do with it if we had it?" he told Ander, "and since we have no desire for a butler or for a yacht, we could see no reason for breaking my pattern of afternoon naps." In the end, "indolence won out over greed."[68]

Travel exhausted him and, back in San Francisco, Thom knew he was in poor shape. Walking a block uphill was a struggle. He tried walking to the Hole but made it only as far as Buena Vista Park, about half a mile, before giving up.[69] In January 2001, he felt pains in his left arm and neck: thinking it was a heart attack, he took two aspirins and had Mike drive him to UC's emergency room on nearby Parnassus. "This was 7 in the evening & I didn't get released from ER until 11a.m. next day," he told Ander.[70] Subsequent tests showed "no sign of [a] heart attack."[71] Thom connected his physical decline with his inability to write. "I get so easily tired walking these days," he told Clive. "I used to walk like a demon, & a lot of my poeticizing took place while walking: the physical energy was somehow connected with the imaginative energy: now I get tired just walking to Haight Street & back."[72] In "Abishag," Thom had written about aging in terms of warmth and chill; now, to his friends, it became a matter of drought. "I got no juice," he told Clive on several occasions.[73] "I have not written anything in 2½ years," he told Peter Spagnuolo in March, "all dried up."[74]

As the year went on, Thom became "increasingly convinced" that John had lost interest in him.[75] Dates were canceled, excuses made; other men entered John's orbit. In May, Thom had a "sad bad day" in which he "woke from a dream of writing two poems (I who haven't finished one since 1998)" and took John to lunch at the Oyster Bar on Castro. "He is not interested in getting together, ever, for one of our weekends," Thom wrote. "Well, I should be grateful for having had so many wonderful times with him in the last 2 years & more, & not surprised he has gotten bored with me. But I don't see much to look forward to now."[76] He began "stumblingly laboring through draft after draft of a new poem" addressed to John.[77] That it took a year to finish "A Gratitude" convinced

Thom that his powers had dimmed for good. "We'd carry on like animals / And stay high all the weekend," he wrote:

> A bit of a bully in truth
> —Though who had charm as you did?—
> Rewarding me with a second youth
> Otherwise precluded.[78]

"But it seems I misunderstood J," Thom wrote, two days after he had been dumped, "or he says I did."[79] This became another cycle. Later in the year, John dumped Thom again. "I guess I am not that good in response, but I do try to take it well," Thom reflected. He felt he had been "hit by a house" and spent "a very black hour feeling sorry for myself."[80] John returned four days later, but Thom felt anxious instead of elated. Their next date was marked by "successive childishness from him & pigheadedness from me," and Thom spent the autumn "deeply unhappy."[81] One "disastrous" get-together ended in "a full rejection."[82]

John spent Christmas in Kentucky. Thom bought him a farewell lunch at Chow's. "Really, I love him as much as ever," he reflected, "though I think he is being just polite with me." That night, Thom woke "feeling like Tolstoy's Ivan Ivanovich," a probable slip for the eponymous hero of *The Death of Ivan Ilyich*, who struggles to accept his own impending death from terminal illness.[83] Thom had other reasons for introspection. He heard from England that Aunt Mary, aged ninety-four, had died. Her final years were unhappy. She had fallen out with Catherine and refused to come downstairs; Catherine, who needed a walker, could not get upstairs. Both required at-home care and used "one of the maids" to pass notes between them.[84] "Those Thomson girls, who taught them, I wonder, that you can die just when you want to?" Thom asked Ander late in Mary's life. "Our mother actually carried it out, much to the inconvenience of about twenty other people, Barbara tried, briefly and unsuccessfully, to starve herself to death, and now Mary thinks that, just by taking to her bed, she can die by being tired of it all. Actually, I like going back to bed after breakfast, but I don't expect to die there."[85] Mary's death left Catherine, then ninety-two, Thom's lone surviving aunt. "Will we live that long?" Ander asked Thom.[86] Thom hoped not.

In 2002, Thom slowed down even more. He wrote fewer letters, read fewer new books—preferring to reread old ones—and his diary entries, already short, became fewer and farther between. He stopped going to the gym and rarely traveled farther than the Hole. Mike became responsible for the garden and, while Thom still shopped and cooked for the house, he became less reliable the more he had to look beyond John for sex. One regular trick was a homeless guy named JR. "Has been thrown thro a window a few days ago, & is very ornery, & just wants to do drugs and have sex with me," Thom wrote. "I get ornery too, & am probably equally to blame that we just go off in different directions (from the Hole). But I also feel he is not being honest with me."[87] When John moved to a new high-rise apartment at Turk and Fillmore, Thom hired the moving truck and helped load John's possessions. "He now wants to make a date," Thom reflected. "Well, that makes me happy, but he does bounce me around. Confused."[88] He did not know "what to do about John emotionally" and felt "on the verge of just becoming a sugar daddy, which I don't want to be from vanity."[89]

In April, Thom flew east for a reading tour of New York, Amherst, and Laramie, Wyoming. He saw Don Doody, whose apparent emphysema had turned out to be acute malnutrition. "He lives on hamburgers and brandy, after all, with the occasional bit of cold pizza as a variation," Thom told Ander. "His friends in NY are all angry with him, he is so obstinate, and it took his passing out to get him to see a doctor."[90] Thom had been invited to Amherst by Daniel Hall, now a professor, whom he had met in 1981 when he was Robert Frost Library Fellow in Poetry. One morning, Hall walked with Thom to campus. "He was dressed the same as always, somewhat forbiddingly in jeans, leather jacket, and black boots," Hall recalled, "but when we reached a (very low) rise on our way there, he asked if we could stop a moment: he was out of breath. Thom was someone I had expected to live forever, but that morning I thought: maybe not."[91] Arriving in Laramie, some two thousand meters above sea level, Thom felt "the altitude problem" immediately and experienced "dehydration, dizziness, pounding heart, fatigue, like some diabolical new drug." He was looked after by "tall, red-head, bearded beauty" Kent Drummond, a professor at the University of Wyoming, whom Thom had met years earlier in San Francisco.[92] It was obvious that Thom was not well; he looked drawn, and Drummond thought he might have AIDS.[93] Thom visited classes and gave a reading at the University Art Museum but was glad to go home. "I'm wondering if I will ever feel like travelling again," Thom told Ander when he was safely back in San Francisco.[94]

With Bill in France, and Mike and Bob back and forth to the cabin, Thom spent much of the summer alone. When Mike returned for a few days around Thom's seventy-third birthday—"a joy"—they talked openly about their shared life. "M says he thinks I sleep so much since my retirement because I am depressed," Thom reflected. "(I don't teach, I don't write, the 2 things I used to enjoy doing. Also, I would add, John doesn't give me much joy.) Maybe he is right."[95] According to Bill, Thom was "the biggest Pollyanna I've ever met. He wouldn't let anyone catch him being down. But after a while, I couldn't believe it."[96] Bob thought Thom "was probably depressed, but he would never say that to anyone. He would never act depressed. He would always be cheerful, dancing around the house in his big clompy boots."[97] "He needed people to think he was happy," Mike wrote later. "And mostly he appeared happy, even manic. But sometimes, when no one else was around, he'd lean against the kitchen sink and bow his head and moan, 'I'm old! I'm old!' I never thought I'd hear him complain like that or admit to being depressed, but in his last year or so, I did."[98] For his birthday, Thom spent several "spaced & anxious" days taking "a lot of speed" with John.[99] A week later, on his cooking night, he was still hungover and tried to make "pasta without water."[100] Mike and Bob "both shout at me," he wrote in his diary. "I will not discuss the household problem."[101]

Feeling as though his family was turning against him, Thom became laxer about cleaning up after speed weekends. "We'd be at the cabin," Mike recalled, "and we'd come home late Sunday, and they'd be flying high."[102] He thought Thom "changed" dramatically over a short period. "Thom was so selfish," he reflected. "In order for us to live together there has [to be] some respect for boundaries, and suddenly Thom didn't have it."[103] Mike, Bob, and Bill met several times outside the house to discuss the problem. "Are we going to have to split up? Are we going to have to find another place to live?" Bob reflected. "I thought about moving up-stairs because I couldn't live down here anymore because it was too much craziness."[104] In October, Mike and Bob returned from the cabin to find Thom high and hallucinating. "I faint, Bob cries (in eve). Back to the dog-house," Thom wrote, "our place of love & permissions is broken. Through my fault."[105] On one occasion, Mike said to Thom: "I don't know what you want from me." Thom replied, "with some fierceness," according to Mike: "I thought you'd be more understanding." Mike, understandably hurt, ascribed Thom's changes in attitude and behavior to speed. "He was a little bit lost," Mike reflected. "Thom was not lost at all, ever, until then. So I think you have to separate the decline and fall from the rest of him."[106]

As the year concluded, Thom was in a rut. "I grow lazy in retirement and am working on the development of the dirty old man into very dirty old man," he told Douglas. "I probably owe you two letters. I will write in the end, though apparently not poetry."[107] August saw him often for lunch at Zazie and for trips to the movies. "This didn't happen just once, this happened on about a dozen occasions," he recalled. "Thom spoke like he'd had a stroke. I only said it to him once and he didn't like it. 'Here, you're hitting it pretty hard, you're gonna hurt yourself.' And he didn't like it."[108] Thom felt like the walls were closing in: the pursuit of sex, through the pursuit of drugs, had become a closed loop. Like the person at the center of "A System," written some fifteen years earlier, Thom was trapped:

> He dreams at the center of a closed system,
> Like the prison system, or a system of love,

Where folktale, recipe, and household custom
Refer back to the maze that they are of.[109]

Thom's life, full of patterns and cycles, had entered its death spiral. "He wasn't writing, and what little he had written, the last couple years of his life, wasn't really very good. He knew it," reflected Kleinzahler. "He was an older man. His attractiveness, his vigor, were receding. He was really starting to have to buy the sexual company. He kept drugs and so forth . . . I'm quite convinced he was killing himself."[110]

Thom knew his best times with John were over; nor had he written a good poem for four years. Worst of all, relations with his family were at an all-time low. "We sort of lost touch with Thom because he was no longer like we were anymore," Bob recalled. "I'll never forget the day he got up from the table upstairs—someone was coming over and he was going to meet them downstairs—and as he was going out the door he said, 'Oh, well, roommates are all just interchangeable.' I was devastated when he said that."[111]

40

CLOSURE

Thom thought he had seen the last of England in 1992, but fate held one final surprise. In February 2003, he learned he was to receive the David Cohen Prize for Literature, a biennial award for lifetime achievement. "They expect me to go to London to receive it," he wrote. "I probably will, but don't want to."[1] He shared the prize with Beryl Bainbridge: *The Guardian* called them "two of the most enduring but passed-over figures in modern English writing."[2] "I stop writing poetry and am rewarded by a colossal prize from England," he told Douglas. "It pays, apparently, to run dry."[3]

Faber put Thom up in Hazlitt's hotel for ten nights. He spent most of his time in nearby Soho Square, "ogling the attractive young men . . . catching up on a bit of sleep."[4] There was not enough time to visit Ander in Cornwall, but Thom traveled to Snodland to see Catherine. She was "in the pink mentally," he thought, "but can only walk with a frame."[5] In Hampstead, Thérèse had begun to "show her 95 years, cracked voice, bad memory."[6] Thom also spent an "exhausting interview day" with Bainbridge, meeting journalists from *The Guardian*, *The Daily Telegraph*, and *The Times*.[7] Accompanying a long profile of Thom in *The Guardian* was his portrait, taken by Eamonn McCabe.[8] For those who had not seen Thom for several years, the photograph came as a shock. "For me it seemed to illustrate a vision of you I had never seen . . . nor would want to," wrote Ruth Townsend: "the lack of generosity—the meanness of the mouth, the lack of humour in the eyes—it was alien to me & I just disliked it."[9] Thom's niece, Charlotte, also saw it. "I remember being so shocked at his deterioration," she recalled. "He looked quite bloated. That was really upsetting."[10]

The night before the David Cohen ceremony, Thom gave a reading at Faber's offices on Queen's Square. "Thom walked into the room with Paul Keegan, who was then his editor," recalled Clive Wilmer. "I went over and said hi, and he didn't know who I was. He just didn't recognize me. I told him, and he lit up." Clive also thought that Thom looked different. "He'd become quite hunched. He had a spinal curve. In a way it was quite glamorous looking," Clive reflected. "But as a result he'd shrunk quite a lot in old age. He looked much less impressive a figure, more subdued, smaller."[11] At the ceremony, "Gunn stepped forward, unintroduced, to make his brief speech of thanks at the prizegiving [and] began: 'I'm Beryl Bainbridge.'"[12] He thanked Karl Miller, Tony White, Tony Tanner, and August Kleinzahler. "My guide has been above all a prose writer, the late Christopher Isherwood," he told the audience. "Obviously, I have my personal reasons for identifying with Isherwood, but what I enormously admire about him is the way—especially in works of his like Goodbye to Berlin and A Single Man—he uses what is virtually autobiography with a light fictionalization to get rid of all but the essentials. And this has been what I have attempted in my own practice." Thom saw his kind of poem as "comprising at the same time the subject—the experience of thing—and the attempt to understand it. If they are folded in together, so much the better."[13] Returning to Hazlitt's, Thom "had some more wine at the Café Rouge, which put me nicely out of it."[14]

Thom's acceptance speech alluded to another important mentor: Yvor Winters. The previous summer, Thom had been approached to edit a selection of Mina Loy's poetry for the Library of America's American Poets Project, a series of books that would be kept perpetually in print. Thom suggested he select Winters instead.[15] He labored through an introduction—"far harder work than I thought it would be"[16]—which proved to be his last major piece of prose. His failing powers were likely on his mind when he suggested an edition of Winters: it was almost fifty years since Thom had arrived in California to study with "the most exciting teacher" he ever had. Thom called Winters "the maverick's maverick," and his selection focused on Winters's early, Imagist work—which he admired enormously—in part to demonstrate the seriousness of Winters's subsequent shift from romance to reason.[17] Thom made a point of including Winters's short, "autobiographical" story "The Brink of Darkness," believing it to be "a connecting link between the two parts of his career as a poet."[18] In the story, darkness represents insanity, and Thom agreed with Donald Hall that Winters "feared madness all his life." Hall suspected Winters "wanted or needed to leave this clue behind, a clue to the function throughout his life of what he called reason."[19] At the conclusion of the story, the speaker "glance[s] up at the darkened corner of the window to be fixed with horror. There, standing on the air outside the window, translucent, a few lines merely, and scarcely visible, was a face, my face, the eyes fixed upon my own."[20] Thom, who had written about doubles and doppelgängers for some fifty years, was now in thrall to the aural and visual hallucinations brought on by methamphetamine psychosis.

Back from England, Thom did not "feel like going beyond the limits of California ever again," but was soon flying east with August Kleinzahler to give a joint reading in Maryland.[21] "Over time we got very much at ease with each other," August reflected. "As my poetry became more interesting, he became more interested in it."[22] Paul Keegan, their editor at Faber, approached them to compile an anthology, provisionally called *101 Modern American Poems*. Thom hated anthologies, but freedom from inclusivity and proscription, plus the opportunity to work with a close friend, made him agree.[23] They sent Keegan a list of ninety-nine poems, including Thom standards—Loy's "Der Blinde Junge," Pound's "Canto XLVII," Robinson's "Eros Turannos"—and more contemporary favorites like Jim Powell's "It Was Fever That Made the World," section three of Forrest Gander's "Librettos for Eros," and Daisy Fried's "The Bombing of Serbia: Part II." August included friends and lesser-known poets like Robert VanderMolen, A. F. Moritz, and William Corbett. "We sent [Keegan] a preliminary list," August reflected, "and he was appalled."[24] The anthology was dropped.

Alongside John, Thom had two regular tricks through 2003. He had met "auburn haired Russell" at the Hole the previous September: Russell was in his early thirties and flitted between San Francisco and his hometown, Modesto.[25] In May, Thom let Russell stay with him for a week, which led to much tweaking and a long and difficult hangover.[26] "M's concentrated fury at me," Thom wrote, after he had let Russell stay for another few days. "Bill also gives me a talking-to, but much kinder & more acceptable than Mike's."[27] Later in the year, Thom became involved with a "very nice, homeless" man named Dane.[28] He soon learned that Dane was not easy to be around. Dane "shouts at me up & down the street," Thom wrote after one confrontation. The following day, they had another "terrible shouting bout" in which "he called me Satan. (He thinks he is Jesus.)"[29]

One-off tricks stole from him. Jackson "goes off (in my vest & jacket) leaving me high & dry." Thom dialed the Hot Line to find somebody else. "When will this stop?" he asked.[30] Days later, Jackson returned, stole Thom's wallet, and spent more than a hundred dollars on his bank card.[31] Another time, "crazy Larry" stole his watch.[32] Thefts became more common because Thom often allowed homeless men to keep their possessions at Cole Street, which gave him a near-certain guarantee of seeing them again. One, Steve, did not pick up his things when he said he would: Thom learned he had been "thru detox" and gave him money.[33] Another guy, Joey, "accuses me of leading him astray (!) & we leave one another on poor terms."[34] Some tricks made "unwanted" visits expecting handouts; Thom gave them "ten bucks" to get them to go away.[35] Sometimes, however, he needed John's help to get rid of them: "the dread Jamie" was removed "nicely but sternly" after John came to Thom's rescue.[36]

.   .   .

In the summer, Thom and Mike became legal domestic partners. The following year, when newly elected San Francisco mayor Gavin Newsom "encourages gay marriages at City Hall, defying the law," Thom thought it was "wonderful."[37] He and Mike, however, did not feel the need to participate. "Mike and I are already registered as 'domestic partners' with the State of California," he explained to Ander, "which means that whoever dies first the house remains [the surviving partner's], and I have not observed much about marriage that makes me respect it that much."[38] Mike thought they were "the wrong generation" for gay marriage. "We thought it was silly or unnecessary. My stock response was, 'What's next? Gay alimony?'"[39]

Thom had not written a poem since finishing "A Gratitude" in summer 2002. He had not written a collectable poem since "Painting by Vuillard" in fall 1998.[40] The summer brought "vivid dreams about working on some wonderful new poem," but nothing materialized.[41] "He would bring it up and say that he was blocked," recalled Wendy Lesser. "And he would bring it up as a very painful thing."[42] Lunches with Robert Glück often began with Thom saying he had not written anything. "He was just putting it out there," Glück recalled. "It was very much on his mind that he wasn't writing."[43] Mike knew firsthand about Thom's struggle to write. "Do you try and it doesn't come, or don't you try?" he asked. "Well, of course I try!" Thom replied. "It was very unusual for Thom to snap at me," Mike reflected, "but he did."[44] They were at their lowest ebb since their relationship-defining quarrels in the early 1960s. Mike felt they had become distant from each other. "I've never said this before: I would say that went back to Thom's retirement," he reflected. "Maybe that's the beginning of the decline."[45]

When Thom was again offered the position of Mohr Visiting Poet at Stanford, Mike "prevailed upon him to take it, the only time that ever happened in fifty-two years together."[46] Thom claimed he was "greedy enough to accept" the position, but really he had listened to Mike: he needed something to do, something to occupy his mind.[47] Before his first class, he felt "mildly hysterical."[48] He feared that, having not taught for four years, "the slickness and confidence are all slipped down the drain."[49] He turned to the poet Peter Campion, then Jones Lecturer at Stanford, for help with the practicalities. "Thom hadn't titled his course in the proper way for the Stanford administrators," Campion recalled:

> So we were on the phone, and he was quite sweet because he was understandably pissed off over this course titling business, but he wanted to make it clear that he wasn't pissed off at me. He said, "why don't we title the course Pirates of the Fucking Caribbean?" Which led to laughter, and a long conversation about movies of the day. We started talking about *The Matrix* at some point, and he stopped abruptly and said, "I know what I'll do at Stanford. I'll fly through the air like Keanu Reeves, and shoot everyone. But I won't shoot you."[50]

Thom renamed the course "The Occasions of Poetry." Admission was selective: Thom chose twelve students based on writing samples. Auditing his first class, "in a dingy, nondescript classroom," was the literary critic Cynthia Haven. "With his trademark black leather jacket slung over his chair, he gives them Ezra Pound's 'Canto XLVII' as a reading assignment," Haven wrote. "'It's enough to make one consider whether one wants this course or not,' he mutters. 'What I'm asking you to do is give it a chance,' he exhorts the class. 'Read it four times. If possible, aloud. Read it the following day.'"[51] Thom also assigned a selection of Basil Bunting's poems and Daisy Fried's recent collection *She Didn't Mean to Do It* (2000). "I never met Thom Gunn," Fried later remarked. "I thought it was wonderful . . . picking a poet he never met and helping her like this. I never told Thom that when I get in a funk about my writing, his encouragement has been one of the things that helps me get out of it."[52]

In October, Thom gave a large public reading at Stanford. He read exclusively from *Boss Cupid*, including "The Gas-poker" and "To Cupid," and concluded with "Painting by Vuillard."[53] It proved the highlight of his semester. "He had either been drinking or taking drugs, and he did badly one Wednesday," Mike recalled, "and he was shaken up because he prided himself as a teacher. He came in to [my room] and said, 'Why do

I do such things? Why did I do this?' 'I think because you're bored.' And he said, 'Does it show?'"⁵⁴ Thom's "lousy class" may have prompted his subsequent "action packed weekend." An "ex jailbird" named Tim "first of all does speed with me, then smack." It was Thom's "first time with the latter, & last." He was "higher than I've ever been. I look at the sky & it is emptier of meaning than ever." The next day he spoke to Bill, "who is v sympathetic. Shaken, alone, John takes me in for afternoon . . . I spend a strange night alone, hallucinating & go in to M early, to talk."⁵⁵ Thom taught his last class of a "depressing" semester in early December.⁵⁶ "I have been boring in this course, even to myself," he wrote, and spent the following day in "laziness & reading & wine."⁵⁷

In February 2004, Thom gave what proved to be his final reading, with David Biespiel at Cody's bookstore in Berkeley. He began with three older poems—"The Idea of Trust," "The Cherry Tree," "Nasturtium"— and concluded with three recent ones: "A Gratitude," "Front Door Man," and "To Cupid."⁵⁸ "We drove back across the bay," recalled Biespiel. "I asked Thom if he was working on anything, and he said: 'Well, I'm retired. What happens to me is I sit down in the afternoon to read. The cat jumps up on my lap. The cat falls asleep. Then I fall asleep. And at that point I'm kinda ruined. I don't have it in me.' I was struck by the resignation."⁵⁹

The day after the reading, Thom learned that Thérèse Megaw had died. "I owed her a lot," he reflected.⁶⁰ "She was always wonderful to me, considerate and sweet, and treated me better than her own sons, I thought," he told Ander. "Her weakness, which irritated Mother, was in being a lion-hunter—she loved celebrities quite shamelessly. So I was rather pleased that I became a minor celebrity, and was in a sense able to pay her back through her glee at that."⁶¹ The same month, Thom began rereading E. Nesbit and George MacDonald, authors from his child-hood, as though returning mentally one final time to that period of his life. Wendy Lesser had asked him to contribute to a *Threepenny* sympo-sium about realism, "but he called me apologetically in early March . . .

to say that he just hadn't been able to do it." He "promised instead to write something on Flaubert's *Sentimental Education*, one of his favorite novels."[62] Thom had had Nesbit in mind for realism. What he liked about her books was the "idea of a big friendly family having adventures together," something he had experienced with his mother's extended family in Snodland and had sought to replicate, after a fashion, in San Francisco.[63] Now, Thom's family felt like it was coming apart at the seams.

Early in the year, with Mike and Bob at the cabin, Thom had Russell stay for a "3 hit" weekend.[64] Although Russell was gone by the time Mike and Bob returned, "there is civil war," Thom wrote. "I cannot cover up my tweaking, alas." The next day, he wrote: "unforgiving things are said. I long for more loving & trusting roommates."[65] Bob stopped eating with the family because he heard Thom "recorded on message machine saying, 'My family hates me, & I hate them,' an inexcusable piece of petulance."[66] The family were used to leading largely independent lives, with the proviso that mealtimes were shared and convivial. Now, Thom kept more to himself, ate separately from Mike and Bob, and slept a lot, usually because of crystal. He spent ever more time at the Hole and, though he still saw John, their sexual relationship was over. His two regular tricks, Russell and Dane, were homeless speed freaks.

Amid the "civil war," Thom had a cataract procedure that had been postponed for a year. "I hope [that] will be all the doctoring I get this year," he told Ander.[67] The "doctoring" kept him mostly clean; although, after his cataract pre-op, he snorted two lines of speed and went to the Hole. "Toward the end of his life he had a problem with his hip," Lesser recalled. "The hip wore down and was grinding against the bone. I said you can have this operation and it will fix it completely. He didn't believe in that, somehow. It was like his body was deteriorating and he wouldn't do what he needed to do to get it to function again, like he'd already decided to just ride it into the ground."[68] That spring, other friends and neighbors detected a similar fatalism in Thom's attitudes and behavior. "He was always with somebody who didn't have great energy about him," recalled the writer Steve Silberman, a friend and neighbor on Cole Street who had studied under Thom at Berkeley. "He looked like he was tweak-ing. They seemed to be on a frequency together that didn't admit of oth-ers. At some point I thought Thom isn't interested in living anymore."[69]

In early March, Thom had his pocket picked at the Hole. "Almost im-mediately" he met "the splendid Phil Monsky," a forty-eight-year-old drifter whom he brought to Cole Street and let stay for "several weeks." Thom's tricks sometimes stayed a few nights, maybe a week, but he had never moved anybody in. "He is a comforter to me, as well as being a hunk, in this difficult time," Thom wrote. "They hate him, M being the fair Miss Frigidaire, & Bob blustery angry."[70] Moving Phil in was seen as provocation. "Thom distanced himself from us because we weren't part of that whole drug-taking scene anymore," Bob recalled. "He had a guy, a homeless person, living back there. We were very unhappy about it because it was as if Thom was trying to get him to be part of the fam-ily. None of us wanted that. He was all camped out in Thom's room, and he would come and go. It wasn't working for anybody but Thom. I can't imagine why it was working for him, other than the fact that he had someone. It was a really, really difficult time."[71]

After meeting Phil, Thom did not make another diary entry for al-most three weeks. The last weekend of March, they booked into Beck's Motor Lodge, a cheap motel on Market Street, "to be alone and away from my family," Thom wrote. "It was better than ever, we got really inti-mate (& of course we were high most of the time)." He thought Phil was "a lovely & in some ways unlucky man."[72] Thom likely ascribed Phil's lack of luck to a difficult upbringing. His father, Aaron, ran a prosper-ous hardware business in San Francisco. His mother, Myrtle, was from Hawaii. Aaron was her third husband by the age of thirty. Phil was born before they were married and was not quite three when they divorced. Myrtle remarried soon after: perhaps Thom saw a parallel with his own adored mother and hated stepfather.

When he was twenty-two, Phil had posed shirtless as the "White Russian" in the *San Francisco Crusader*, a short-lived gay newspaper, and was drifting around the city.[73] "Aaron's son was a druggie and spent most of his life in and out of prison," recalled a family friend. "Aaron tried to help him, but the son got into trouble and never wanted to have anything to do with him. Then he would show up out of the blue and ask for money every few years."[74] Thom sometimes accompanied Phil to San Francisco General, where he "get[s] methadone . . . every day," and met his probation officer, who "came to look the place over. The pretence is that Phil will be living here," Thom wrote, "but I can't let him. He is a fine man, only one battle so far (yesterday), but I can't just go against Mike (& the others), and ultimately he is not of that kind of importance to me."[75]

When Thom returned from Beck's, he found Bob "reinforcing the barriers/walls & doors to his bedroom to shut out noise (all mine & my friends, he says.)" Thom interpreted this as an indication "he & M can accept Phil, I think."[76] Bob's bedroom, at the front of the house, overlooked the street and had doors into the hallway and open-plan kitchen and dining room. "I told Thom I was doing it to save our friendship," Bob recalled, "and that he doesn't seem to respect his roommates anymore. He didn't understand what was going on with him."[77] Thom and Phil were taking speed "almost on a daily basis."[78] This led to one "unfriendly night" and subsequent "reconciliation."[79] On April 5, Mike left to visit his mother in Florida for a fortnight: Thom "promised" that Phil "wouldn't be here when he returned." Their five weeks together were "happy," Thom wrote, "& we had only 2 slight spats, each time when he was on heroin. [. . .] I have never before taken so much speed in 5 weeks as I did with Phil. He now owes me a lot of money, but I know will pay me back."[80]

On April 19, Phil moved out and Mike returned from Florida. Thom barely saw Mike that day because he visited Robert Glück's class at San Francisco State University. "Every week a different writer came in," Glück recalled, "and Thom was, as always, very generous and very frank, very open. That's what the students felt afterward. [. . .] He was light with them. He was joking and very regular. Not pretentious. He didn't have a pretentious bone in his body and was very wary of pretension."[81] Thom was going to take the bus home, but Glück paid for a taxi. They talked about "this hustler being at his house, and then Mike, and the scene that seemed to be getting out of hand," Glück reflected. "I think he admired Mike for his forbearance."[82] The next night, Thom and Bill went to Martin Rosen's apartment for "a good evening" with their old friend Bryan Condon, who was visiting from New Zealand with his lover, David. Bryan was seventy-four, the same age as Thom, "and looks splendid."[83]

Two days later, Phil turned up. Thom left him at the house while he took August to lunch at Zazie. "Then Dane comes, I cut 3 lines each," Thom wrote. Phil left, and Thom "only just got rid of [Dane] before M's return."[84] Thom began to answer a letter from Christian Wiman, then the editor of *Poetry*, who wanted him to have "an exchange via mail with Donald Hall about . . . how you see poetry now at this time of your life."[85] Thom thought it "a splendid idea, if I am up to it," but abandoned his note and "answered by phone" instead.[86] The following day, Friday, April 23, Mike went to the hospital for electrical cardioversion to correct an irregular heartbeat. That evening, Thom joined Bryan, David, Martin, and Martin's lover Michael for dinner upstairs in Bill's apartment. "M & Bob not there, it was peaceful," he wrote. "Meanwhile Phil comes by, so I bought him hamburgers etc."[87]

Neither Mike nor Bob recalled seeing Thom on Saturday the twenty-fourth until the small hours of Sunday morning. "I'd gotten up to go to the bathroom," Bob recalled. "Thom was standing in the hallway. This was late, like maybe 2 in the morning or something, and he was all decked out in his leathers like he was going out. I said something to him—I don't remember what. Then I went back to bed, and maybe a little while later the doorbell rang. Someone came upstairs. They were here for a little while, and then they left. Then I fell asleep."[88]

On Sunday morning, Mike and Bob heard the television going in Thom's room. "Bob, being in the front room, heard the doorbell—I'm guessing it was 6 a.m.—and Thom going up and down the stairs," Bill recalled. "Thom must have known somebody was coming over. From there on we don't quite know what happened because there were times when none of us were home on that Sunday."[89] "I assumed, as Mike and Billy assumed, that the guy who was living in there was with him and they were in bed watching TV," Bob reflected. "It went on all day, the TV going, nobody coming out of the room. And we began to think that it seemed a little strange that we hadn't seen Thom or anybody come out."[90]

After dinner, Bill went back upstairs. "Finally, when Mike went to bed, I thought, damn it, I'm going to knock on Thom's door because something doesn't seem right," Bob recalled. "Even if he gets pissed at me, I don't care. So I knocked on the door and there was no answer. I knocked again and there was still no answer. I opened the door a little and looked in, and I was relieved because there was nobody on the bed. I thought, oh . . . And then I looked over to the side and I saw Thom's feet sticking out from the other side of the bed. I went over to him and I could see that he was dead and maybe had been dead for hours that day. I totally freaked. I remember first thinking, I don't want to tell Mike, I don't want to tell Mike."[91] Bob frantically rang the upstairs bell: Bill came down and, seeing Thom's body on the floor, "tried giving him mouth-to-mouth resuscitation, and I can to this day remember thinking that I'm giving the last breath to this poet, Thom Gunn. But it wasn't even his last. He was dead already."[92] They called an ambulance. Thom Gunn was pronounced dead at 8:58 p.m. on Sunday, April 25, 2004.

"It was very difficult for a long time after that," Bob reflected. "Mike and Bill were sitting on the sofa with their arms around each other. Mike was just out of it. He didn't know what to think or say. He was devastated, for a long time. For a year or so he was in a terrible way."[93] Mike announced Thom's death to the press. "I'm thinking it was probably a heart attack," he told the *San Francisco Chronicle*, "but the medical examiner won't know the cause of death for weeks."[94] The initial autopsy proved inconclusive. After further tests, an amended death certificate was issued five months later. Thom's death was ruled a drug-related accident: "acute polysubstance abuse" was the immediate cause of death.[95] After cremation, Mike, Bill, and Bob scattered his ashes in the garden at Cole Street. Obituaries on both sides of the Atlantic called him "one of the late 20th century's finest poets."[96]

"I remember being quite cross about Thom dying," recalled his niece, Charlotte, "because it just left my dad. I remember thinking, 'Oh, Thom! Why did you do that to yourself? You've left Ander now . . .' And that reflects on their relationship. Ander definitely depended on Thom. Thom was all Ander had, I think."[97] Ander was in Yorkshire, taking photographs of the Dales, when he heard the news. "I got a phone call from Bob saying Thom's dead, he's OD'd," he reflected. "It's awful, an awful thing. It's quite possible he self-destructed."[98] That was the consensus among Thom's immediate family and friends. "My own theory is that he died of boredom," observed Wendy Lesser. "I think he was taking a lot of drugs and having a lot of casual sex to ward off that boredom. But if it's that kind of deep, existential boredom, I don't think those things work."[99] "I just don't believe that he decided to kill himself," remarked Robert Glück. "If he did, I don't think it would have been in such disarray, with people fleeing the scene. It would have been done with more order, more systematically. On the other hand, I think in some part of his mind he probably thought: I'm ready to die."[100] Mike thought it "wasn't suicide, but Thom was no fool. He was seventy-four years old and he's taking drugs, and drinking, and carrying on like he's young. You must know you're in risky territory now. That's why I say it wasn't suicide, but you're taking chances that you shouldn't take if you want to hang around for a while."[101]

The amended death certificate does not elaborate on "acute polysubstance abuse," but it was later suggested that Thom had been using heroin. Phil was a user—Thom wrote as much in his diary, but he does not himself suggest that he had taken it again after his "first & last" time in November 2003. Robert Prager learned from a mutual friend that Phil "loved to do speedball"—in this case, a mix of heroin and methamphetamine—and thought he "must have injected [Thom] with it, assuming that Phil bothered to tell Thom about what drugs he was injecting."[102] John

Ambrioso—who "didn't get along v well" with Phil when Thom introduced them[103]—thought Phil "wasn't the best sort of fella. First of all, Thom was not into that sort of thing [i.e., speedballs]. I don't know if Thom would have known that was going on. I don't know if the guy told him that was what was going on. Thom may have been doing it willingly, and knowingly, but then again he may not have. Which is a problem."[104] Mike was "very surprised" about the suggestion that Thom had been using heroin. Shortly after Thom's death, he mentioned it to Louis Bryan. "I think I said, in so many words, I didn't know that he took heroin," Mike recalled. "And Louis said, almost with some superiority, 'Oh really? Everybody knew that.' What he meant by 'everybody' I don't know."[105]

A memorial for Thom was held in the Doe Library at UC Berkeley on August 29, 2005: what would have been his seventy-sixth birthday. Clive Wilmer flew to San Francisco to attend the memorial and stayed in Thom's old room on Cole Street. "Early on, Mike took me into his room at the back of the house and talked me through the truth of Thom's death and the period leading up to it," Clive wrote. "When I told Mike how amazed I was that someone who had taken recreational drugs so rationally for so much of his life should fall into addiction—which is what it amounted to—he completely agreed. [. . .] The simple explanation would be that, despite his health, fitness, strength and superhuman energy, he was aging—no surprise there—and had so much investment in his youthfulness that he couldn't cope with becoming an old man."[106]

Bill also took Thom's death hard. In the days before Thom's death, Bill had written him a letter he later called "the letter that didn't get to Thom in time." "I am grateful to you for much of my life's security and wellbeing," Bill told him. "The idea of dismissing you [from the house] cause you don't remember or care is unbelievable to me. [. . .] It's not your house: it's ours, as you always insisted. 'I am so bored of this' as you said about Ralph and my relationship problems. This is your problem with speed. This is your problem with alcohol."[107] Bill telephoned Douglas Chambers and gave him the news. "It is impossible to think all that gusto for life is gone," Douglas wrote to him later. "I am sad in a way that is far beyond the grief that I obviously feel for the loss of Thom. I never knew anyone who could so strongly look bullshit in the face and laugh at it . . . or feel so strongly for the people and things he loved. Cole St. was so full of that energy and love—and I hope it still is."[108]

Thom always insisted his childhood was a happy one. His youth, however, was brought to an end with his mother's suicide: on the morning of December 29, 1944, he became an adult. As a fifteen-year-old, Thom knew what it was like to survive the one he loved the most. From his retirement, perhaps earlier, he knew he could not let it happen again. The "better rest" of "To Cupid" is death.

"Life seemed all / loss," he once wrote of his seventeen-year-old self.[109] In "A Gratitude," Thom rather fussily corrects himself. John Ambrioso gave him "a second youth / Otherwise precluded. // Or 'second childhood', some / Might say, and with good reason."[110] In his second youth, he was not going to be the little boy left behind again. He had watched scores of friends waste away from AIDS while still young men. He had lost Tony White to a freak accident. He had seen contemporaries like Clint Cline and Tony Tanner predecease him. It was enough loss for one lifetime.

In "Merlin in the Cave," an early poem, Thom wrote that "possession means the risk of loss": for a man who later remarked that "the streets that I move through are part of my life that I enjoy and wanted to possess," his intense desire to possess was tied inexorably to the fear of loss.[111] Thom often said he would find it very difficult to survive Mike. When his friend the poet Edgar Bowers died in early 2000, Thom learned that "Edgar's companion . . . had died just the night before, I think during an operation," he told Clive. "Neither knew of the other's death. This I take to be a wonderful stroke of good fortune—isn't it what we would all choose if we could, to die at the same time as the one we most love?"[112]

Mike, "the root/cause of all my happiness," was the one thing Thom could not lose.[113]

NOTES

These notes use abbreviations for the names of frequently cited sources. Abbreviations and the corresponding full sources can be found in the bibliography, on page 651.

PROLOGUE

1. William Probert, "Metropolitan Police Statement of Witness," 31 December 1944, LMA MSS.
2. Charles Hawkridge, "Metropolitan Police Statement of Witness," 31 December 1944, LMA MSS.
3. Scrapbook (1967–1977), Bancroft MSS.
4. Scrapbook (1967–1977), Bancroft MSS.
5. Hawkridge, "Statement," LMA MSS.
6. "Copy of notes of evidence of witnesses taken by [William Purchase] at St. Pancras Coroner's Court on 1st January, 1945, at an inquest upon the body of Ann Charlotte HYDE," LMA MSS.
7. "Wife Found Dead After Trial Separation," *Evening Despatch* (London) (1 January 1945), 4.
8. "Suicide Follows Separation," *Holborn and Finsbury Guardian* (5 January 1945), 1.
9. "Copy of notes," LMA MSS.
10. "Suicide Follows Separation," 1.
11. Thomas Day, "General Report," LMA MSS.
12. Hawkridge, "Statement," LMA MSS.

1. BEGINNINGS

1. "Tom" legally became "Thom" in September 1949, although TG may have called himself "Thom" as early as 1942; see chapter 6, pp. 71–72, for a full discussion. To prevent confusion, "Thom" is used throughout.
2. James Logan, *The Clans of the Scottish Highlands* (London: Ackermann, 1843), np.
3. Prose Notebook (1973), Bancroft MSS.
4. Prose Notebook (1972), Bancroft MSS.
5. Prose Notebook (1973), Bancroft MSS.
6. Dr. George Rose, sometime Chief Medical Officer of Schools for Aberdeen, quoted in Bessie D. Jones, *Charles Thomson (1852–1928): A Memoir by His Daugh-*

ter (1930), 7. Jones's short memoir informed several unpublished autobiographical essays TG wrote in the 1970s. See "The Flirt" (1978), Bancroft MSS.

7. W. I. Scobie, "Gunn in America: A Conversation in San Francisco with Thom Gunn," *The London Magazine* N.S. 17, no. 6 (December 1977), 7.

8. Jones, *Charles Thomson*, 10.

9. The name is perhaps a historic transcription error of "coney," a heraldic name for rabbit.

10. Prose Notebook (1972), Bancroft MSS.

11. In 2000, TG was surprised to learn from a cousin that the Gunns had "made a fortune" as bakers. See Diary (1986–2000), 9 August 2000, Bancroft MSS.

12. See Verax [pseud.], "Town and Country Notes," *South Eastern Gazette* (10 September 1889), 2.

13. "The Flirt" (1978), Bancroft MSS.

14. Nan Thomson [Ann Charlotte Gunn], "A Song of the Flapper," *Kent Messenger & Maidstone Telegraph* (9 October 1920), 5.

15. "'Spurious Independence.' Women and Housing," *The Manchester Guardian* (19 July 1919), 11.

16. Nan Thomson [Ann Charlotte Gunn], "Concerning Farm," *Kent Messenger & Maidstone Telegraph* (23 October 1920), 2. Compare Tennyson's "Morte d'Arthur": "God fulfils Himself in many ways, / Lest one good custom should corrupt the world."

17. "The Flirt" (1978), Bancroft MSS.

18. Ann Charlotte Thomson, Photograph album #1. Private collection.

19. Jean Nicol, *Meet Me at the Savoy* (London: Museum Press, 1952), 151.

20. "The Flirt" (1978), Bancroft MSS.

21. C. M. Turnbull, *Dateline Singapore: 150 Years of The Straits Times* (Singapore: Singapore Press Holdings, 1995), 69.

22. John Calhoun Merrill and Harold Fisher, *The World's Great Dailies: Profiles of Fifty Newspapers* (New York: Hastings House, 1980), 305.

23. "Overseas Journalism," *London and China Express* (3 July 1924), 9.

24. George Peet, *Rickshaw Reporter* (Singapore: Eastern Universities Press, 1985), 22.

25. Peet, *Rickshaw Reporter*, 41–42. Peet was actually a year older than Bert.

26. Helen M. Staunton, "War Killed Keyhole Stories, Britisher Says," *Editor & Publisher* (20 October 1945), 62.

27. Peet himself had realized that "marriage would be out of the question" until his "fifth or sixth year" in Singapore. Peet, *Rickshaw Reporter*, 41, 23.

28. This would not have been an unusual arrangement. Peet, for example, spent three decades at *The Straits Times* and served as editor from 1945 until 1951.

29. Peet, *Rickshaw Reporter*, 42.

30. Prose Notebook (1973), Bancroft MSS.

31. "My mother told me she read the whole of Gibbon [*The Decline and Fall of the Roman Empire*] when she was pregnant with me," TG told an interviewer. "I hate to think what that might mean." Tony Sarver, "Thom Gunn," *Gay News* 134 (12–25 January 1978), 16.

32. "The Flirt" (1978), Bancroft MSS.

33. Arthur Christiansen, *Headlines All My Life* (London: Heinemann, 1961), 41.

34. Barbara married William Francis Godfrey in 1924. She called him by his surname and TG knew him as Godfrey. Ander called him Frank.

35. Prose Notebook (1972), Bancroft MSS.

36. Ann Charlotte Thomson, Photograph album #2. Private collection. Seeing the album in later life, TG would have laughed at the Oedipal displacement of Bert.

37. Ander Gunn, interview with the author, 2 May 2018.

38. Ann Charlotte Thomson, Photograph album #1. Private collection.

39. "The Flirt" (1978), Bancroft MSS.

40. Prose Notebook (1972), Bancroft MSS. The Thomsons were Baptists, but of Charlotte's sisters only Barbara was baptized. After Daisy's death in 1920, Alexander "let the business of baptism slide." See "The Flirt" (1978), Bancroft MSS.

41. TG to Mary and Catherine Thomson, 26 October 1998. Private collection.

42. "The Flirt" (1978), Bancroft MSS.

43. See TG to Ander Gunn, 9 December 1981. Private collection.

44. "The Flirt" (1978), Bancroft MSS.

45. Margot Corbett, *A Family of Thomsons* (Maidstone, UK: Modern Press, 1989), 92.

46. See Corbett, *Thomsons*, 96.

47. Prose Notebook (1973), Bancroft MSS.

48. TG to Mary and Catherine Thomson, 20 June 1990. Private collection.

49. TG to Ander and Bett Gunn, 2 September 1994, in *Letters*, 555–56.

50. Prose Notebook (1973), Bancroft MSS.

51. Corbett, *Thomsons*, 96.

52. "The Flirt" (1978), Bancroft MSS.

53. "The Flirt" (1978), Bancroft MSS.

54. Clive Wilmer, "Gunn, Shakespeare, and the Elizabethans," in Joshua Weiner, ed., *At the Barriers: On the Poetry of Thom Gunn* (Chicago: University of Chicago Press, 2009), 45–46.

55. Maurice Wiggin, *Faces at the Window* (London: Thomas Nelson, 1972), 138.

56. For a vivid account of life at the *Evening Standard*, see Geoffrey Goodman, interview with Louise Brodie, part of the British Library's "Oral History of the British Press" series, C638/16, recorded in 2008.

2. ITINERANCY

1. "The Flirt" (1978), Bancroft MSS.

2. Margot Corbett, email to the author, 20 September 2018.

3. "The Flirt" (1978), Bancroft MSS.

4. *A Child's Garden of Verses* was first published in 1885. TG's edition was a 1928 reprint, with an introduction by Lawrence Alma-Tadema and illustrations by Kate Elizabeth Olver.

5. TG to Tony Tanner, 9 November 1994, in *Letters*, 562.

6. "The Flirt" (1978), Bancroft MSS.

7. "A Letter to Mark Rudman," in Michael Dorris and Emilie Buchwald, eds., *The Most Wonderful Books: Writers on Discovering the Pleasures of Reading* (Minneapolis: Milkweed Editions, 1997), 83.

8. Scobie, "Gunn in America," 7.

9. Tim Teeman, "When Beryl Met Thom," *The Times* (29 March 2003), WE1.

10. "A Letter to Mark Rudman," 83.

11. Beatrix Potter, *The Tale of Samuel Whiskers or The Roly-Poly Pudding* (London: Frederick Warne, 1908), 49. Clive Wilmer notes that this scene influenced the

third part of "Jack Straw's Castle" (*NSP*, 244). There is also an echo of E. A. Robinson's "Eros Turannos," one of TG's favorite poems, and its line "And waits and looks around him," which TG later borrowed in "7 a.m. in the bar" (*BC*, 65).

12. The *Daily Express*, also a Beaverbrook paper, had offices on Fleet Street abutting the Shoe Lane offices of the *Evening Standard*. The art deco, black glass *Express* building, opened in 1933, was nicknamed the Black Lubyanka after the KGB headquarters on Lubyanka Square, Moscow.

13. "An Apprenticeship," *The Threepenny Review* 168 (Winter 2022), 14. TG gave "An Apprenticeship" as a lecture at Lake Forest College, Illinois, in May 1977.

14. "The Flirt" (1978), Bancroft MSS.

15. "The Flirt" (1978), Bancroft MSS.

16. "Book Withdrawn from Publication," *The Times* (28 November 1935), 9.

17. "Should Men Be Faithful?," *Daily Mirror* (24 October 1935), 21.

18. "The Flirt" (1978), Bancroft MSS.

19. "The Flirt" (1978), Bancroft MSS.

20. Ander Gunn, interview with the author, 2 May 2018.

21. "The Flirt" (1978), Bancroft MSS.

22. Poetry Notebook 3 (May 1980), Bancroft MSS. TG worked intermittently on a poem about Pit Cottage called "First Light." See Poetry Notebook 12 (May 1991), Bancroft MSS. For the connection TG drew between witches and homosexuality in the late 1950s, see chapter 11, p. 136.

23. TG to Ander Gunn, 8 January 1991. Private collection.

24. Ann Charlotte Thomson, Photograph album #3. Private collection.

25. Wiggin, *Faces at the Window*, 140.

26. Prose Notebook (1972), Bancroft MSS.

27. Ander Gunn, interview with the author, 2 May 2018. TG also wrote "Lousy Land" in one of his mother's photograph albums.

28. "The Ryleys School," *Alderley & Wilmslow Advertiser* (16 July 1920), 3.

29. Hank Nuwer, "Thom Gunn: Britain's Expatriate Poet," *Rendezvous* 21, no. 1 (Fall 1985), 75.

30. Prose Notebook (1972), Bancroft MSS.

31. In *Little Men*, TG's favorite character was Dan, "the rebellious boy who is out of place among the pieties of Dr Baer's model school." See "My Life Up to Now," *OP*, 170–71.

32. Prose Notebook (1972), Bancroft MSS.

33. "The Flirt" (1978), Bancroft MSS.

34. Vernon Noble, "Autobiography" (unpublished manuscript, c. 1987), PDF file.

35. By 1941, Sir Harry was a local county councillor, chairman of the Conservative Men's Association, president of the Conservative Association, a governor of Ashton Secondary and Grammar School, and a member of numerous other local boards and committees. He rose to prominence through H. Hyde & Co., wholesale merchants and importers, which he established in 1897.

36. Standing for the then Unionist Party, now the Conservatives, Beaverbrook won the seat by 196 votes. He remained the MP for Ashton-under-Lyne until his resignation in December 1916.

37. Derek Tangye, *The Way to Minack* (1968; London: Sphere, 1975), 75.

38. Ander Gunn, interview with the author, 2 May 2018.

39. Nicol, *Meet Me at the Savoy*, 67.

40. Prose Notebook (1972), Bancroft MSS.

41. Diana Dean, interview with the author, 15 November 2021.

42. Stuart Kuttner, interview with the author, 28 October 2021.

43. "Ronald Hyde," *The Daily Telegraph* (13 July 1995), 19.

44. Wiggin, *Faces at the Window*, 141.

45. Noble, "Autobiography."

46. "I sometimes wonder where Ronnie's loyalties lay and whether there was a file on him," reflected his stepson, John Eddowes. "Left wing at Cambridge in the 30s—he [was there] at the time of Philby, Burgess and Maclean—he would have preferred to live in Moscow." John Eddowes, email to the author, 23 May 2022.

47. See "The Flirt" (1978), Bancroft MSS.

48. "These Names Make News: Spring Snubs Mars," *Daily Express* (21 March 1938), 6.

49. "The Flirt" (1978), Bancroft MSS.

50. Prose Notebook (1972), Bancroft MSS.

51. Charlotte Gunn to TG, c. 10 July 1937, Scrapbook (1930), Bancroft MSS. The postcard is postmarked Hornbæk, a fashionable resort town just north of Elsinore: both places are a short distance by train from Copenhagen. The party arrived weeks after the Old Vic staged four performances of *Hamlet* outside Kronberg Castle in Elsinore, the setting Shakespeare envisioned for the play. See Ivor Brown, "The World of the Theatre," *Illustrated London Evening News* (19 June 1937), 21. Laurence Olivier played Hamlet, Vivien Leigh Ophelia.

52. "The Flirt" (1978), Bancroft MSS.

53. Charlotte Gunn, Ronald Hyde, and Christina Beldam in Elsinore, Denmark, c. July 1937. Private collection.

54. "The Flirt" (1978), Bancroft MSS.

55. "The Flirt" (1978), Bancroft MSS.

56. The Infant Life (Preservation) Act (19 and 20 George 5, c. 34), Section 1, Subsection 1. See also Stephen Brooke, "'A New World for Women'? Abortion Law Reform in Britain During the 1930s," *The American Historical Review* 106, no. 2 (April 2001), 431–59.

57. Charlotte's postmortem examination provides no evidence of a backstreet abortion, in which one might expect to see perforation of the uterine wall. Otherwise, a suprapubic scar suggests that she may, at one stage, have had a cesarean section. See Bernard Spilsbury, "Notes of the Post-Mortem Examination of Anne [*sic*] Charlotte Hyde," LMA MSS.

58. "The Flirt" (1978), Bancroft MSS.

59. Ander Gunn, interview with the author, 2 May 2018.

60. "The Flirt" (1978), Bancroft MSS.

61. Ander Gunn, interview with the author, 2 May 2018.

62. TG to Barbara Godfrey, c. January 1938. Private collection.

3. HAMPSTEAD

1. TG to Jack Hagstrom, 15 September 1993, Hagstrom MSS.

2. "My Life Up to Now," *OP*, 171.

3. Joined for a time to 108, the two houses had formed a pub called, at various times, the Three Pigeons, Ye Pilgrim, the Windmill, and the Duke of Cumberland.

4. Ander Gunn, interview with the author, 2 May 2018.

5. Scrapbook (1930), Bancroft MSS.

6. John Sutherland, *Stephen Spender: The Authorized Biography* (Oxford: Oxford University Press, 2004), 54.

7. Terry Walker, "World War II Day," *The Gower* 56, no. 7 (December 2013), 115.

8. "Miss Polimeni," *The Gower* 32, no. 1 (December 1946), 35.

9. Jago Lee, "Thom Gunn (1942–47): The Laundromat Cowboy," *The Gower* 52, no. 3 (December 1992), 16.

10. T. W. Gunn, "A Thousand Cheers for Authors," *The Gower* 28, no. 6 (July 1940), 402, reprinted in *Biblio (I)*, 163. Bumpus, on the south side of Oxford Street near Marble Arch, was one of London's oldest and most prestigious bookshops.

11. TG to Clive Wilmer, c. November 2003, in *Letters*, 675. See André Maurois, *Ariel: A Shelley Romance*, trans. Ella D'Arcy (London: John Lane, 1924).

12. "My Life Up to Now," *OP*, 171. Clive Wilmer suspects, quite reasonably, that TG associated Nesbit with his mother, "who shared Nesbit's utopian politics and her sense of the practical value of literature" (*NSP*, xxiii).

13. "Miscellaneous Notes undated," Bancroft MSS. In 1884, Nesbit and her first husband, Hubert Bland, were founding members of the Fabian Society.

14. "Miscellaneous Notes undated," Bancroft MSS.

15. TG to A. E. Dyson, 15 July 1994, in *Letters*, 551.

16. TG Autograph book. Private collection.

17. Noble, "Autobiography."

18. The phrase "Je me bats devant Paris; je me bats à Paris; je me bats derrière Paris" is attributed to Georges Clemenceau. See John Buchan, *A History of the Great War*, vol. 4 (London: Thomas Nelson, 1922), 257.

19. TG Autograph book. Private collection.

20. Ruth [Pearce] Townsend to TG, 3 September 2003, Bancroft MSS.

21. "An Apprenticeship," 14.

22. Prose Notebook (1972), Bancroft MSS.

23. See Ruth [Pearce] Townsend to TG, c. December 2002, Bancroft MSS; TG to Ruth [Pearce] Townsend, c. December 2002. Private collection.

24. TG to Robert Glück, 16 May 1992. Private collection.

25. Ruth [Pearce] Townsend, telephone interview with Edward Guthmann, 15 April 2005.

26. Ander Gunn, interview with the author, 2 May 2018.

27. Ruth [Pearce] Townsend, telephone interview with Edward Guthmann, 15 April 2005; see also Edward Guthmann, "A Poet's Life: Part One," *San Francisco Chronicle* (25 April 2005), C3.

28. TG to Ander Gunn, 12 May 2002, in *Letters*, 670.

29. "The Flirt" (1978), Bancroft MSS.

30. Ralph Ingersoll, *Report on England: November 1940* (New York: Simon & Schuster, 1940), 44.

31. Quoted in Anne Sebba, *Battling for News: The Rise of the Woman Reporter* (London: Hodder & Stoughton, 1994), 161.

32. See "Round and About," *World's Press News and Advertisers' Review* (10 April 1941), 6.

33. TG Autograph book. Private collection.

34. "The Flirt" (1978), Bancroft MSS.

35. Ander Gunn, interview with the author, 3 May 2018.

36. Ruth [Pearce] Townsend to TG, c. December 2002, Bancroft MSS.

37. See "Memorial Service," *Chatham, Rochester and Gillingham News* (23 June 1939), 5. TG is listed among the mourners as "Tom Gunn," likely his first appearance in print.

38. "The Flirt" (1978), Bancroft MSS.

39. Lawrence Stone, *Road to Divorce: England 1530–1987* (Oxford: Oxford University Press, 1990), 399.

40. Guthmann, "A Poet's Life: Part One," C3.

41. See "Probate, Divorce, and Admiralty Division," *The Times* (30 April 1940), 2.

42. Noble, "Autobiography."

43. In August 1942, when Charlotte submitted a planning application to rebuild a bombed-out potting shed and lavatory in the rear garden of 110 Frognal, she told the Council that "Mr H. S. Gunn, my former husband, is the householder." See Ann Hyde to J. H. Forshaw, 14 August 1942, and planning application TPBR29279/2775, Camden Council.

44. See "Hyde Replaces Bliss as 'Standard' News Editor," *World's Press News and Advertisers' Review* (28 March 1940), 3.

45. Charles A. Smith, "Looking for News in London," *The Quill* 29, no. 10 (October 1941), 5.

46. "The Flirt" (1978), Bancroft MSS.

47. Nuwer, "Britain's Expatriate Poet," 75.

48. The lines "a big boy slips you a comic book / Because his heart is big, no other reason" in TG's late poem "A Home" (*BC*, 7–8) recall Porritt's benign influence.

49. "A Thousand Cheers for Authors" draws on the solace of reading Dumas at Ryleys.

50. Prose Notebook No. 3 (undated), Bancroft MSS.

51. "The Flirt" (1978), Bancroft MSS.

52. Ander Gunn, interview with the author, 3 May 2018.

53. "The Flirt" (1978), Bancroft MSS.

54. Herbert Gunn to Lord Beaverbrook, 22 July 1950, Beaverbrook MSS.

55. "The Flirt" (1978), Bancroft MSS.

56. Prose Notebook (1972), Bancroft MSS.

57. Ander Gunn, interview with the author, 2 May 2018.

58. Prose Notebook (1972), Bancroft MSS.

59. TG likely had in mind his aunt Christina's marriage to the much older George Beldam.

60. "The Flirt" (1941), Bancroft MSS. TG kept the original manuscript. In the 1970s, during his interest in autobiography, he typed "The Flirt" along with a lengthy introduction: see "The Flirt" (1978), Bancroft MSS.

61. Tommy Gunn, "Rain," *Bedales Chronicle* 28, no. 4 (March 1942), 6, reprinted in *Biblio (I)*, 164–65.

62. Prose Notebook (1972), Bancroft MSS.

63. Billy Lux, "It's the Instances That Hit You," *The Gay and Lesbian Review* 7, no. 3 (Summer 2000), 42.

64. Prose Notebook (1972), Bancroft MSS.

65. Michael Wishart, *High Diver* (London: Blond and Briggs, 1977), 30.

66. Lux, "It's the Instances," 42.
67. Wishart, *High Diver*, 31.
68. "Ahead of her years, and wild," wrote Cressida Connolly, biographer of the Garman sisters, "[Lorna, aged fourteen] 'seduced the much older Wishart in a hayrick.'" Cressida Connolly, *The Rare and the Beautiful: The Lives of the Garmans* (London: Fourth Estate, 2004), 49.
69. Wishart, *High Diver*, 6.
70. TG to Mary and Catherine Thomson, 1 September 2000. Private collection.
71. TG to Jack Hagstrom, 2 November 1996, Hagstrom MSS. "Lorna was a dream for any creative artist because she got them going," Michael Wishart's daughter, Yasmin, told Laurie Lee's biographer, Valerie Grove. "She was a natural Muse, a catalyst and an inspiration, and she had the same effect on both [Freud and Lee]. She was a symbol of their imagination, of their unconscious, she was nature herself; savage, wild, romantic, and completely without guilt." Quoted in Valerie Grove, *Laurie Lee: The Well-Loved Stranger* (London: Viking, 1999), 181.
72. TG to Mary and Catherine Thomson, 1 September 2000. Private collection. TG did not know for certain until he read Lorna Garman's obituary: see John Cunningham, "Muse and Mistress," *The Guardian* (21 January 2000), A5. For the Freud, Lee, and Lorna entanglement, see William Feaver, *The Lives of Lucian Freud: Youth* (London: Bloomsbury, 2019), 171–75.
73. Philip Hoare, "Obituary: Michael Wishart," *The Independent* (2 July 1996), 14.
74. TG to Jack Hagstrom, 17 March 1993, Hagstrom MSS.
75. TG to Jack Hagstrom, 27 February 1977, Hagstrom MSS.
76. TG to Jack Hagstrom, 9 January 1977, Hagstrom MSS.
77. Prose Notebook (1972), Bancroft MSS.
78. TG to Douglas Chambers, 15 November 1996, in *Letters*, 611. See "Julian the Apostate" (*CP*, 62–63).
79. "My Suburban Muse," *OP*, 153.
80. Hillary Morrish, "Thom Gunn: Violence and Energy: An Interview," *Poetry Review* 57, no. 1 (Spring 1966), 32.
81. "My Suburban Muse," *OP*, 153.
82. David Gewanter, "An Interview with Thom Gunn," *Agni* 36 (1992), 293.
83. See W. H. Auden and John Garrett, eds., *The Poet's Tongue: An Anthology* (London: George Bell, 1935), 97.
84. Auden and Garrett, introduction to *The Poet's Tongue*, v.
85. "My Suburban Muse," *OP*, 153.

4. MOTHER

1. Prose Notebook (1972), Bancroft MSS.
2. Ander Gunn, interview with the author, 3 May 2018.
3. Prose Notebook (1972), Bancroft MSS.
4. "The Flirt" (1978), Bancroft MSS. The incomplete prose project "Letters of the Dead" also prompted a draft poem, part of which is quoted in Clive Wilmer, "Poor Lovely Statue!," *The Times Literary Supplement* 5960 (23 June 2017), 17. Ander found Hyde "very neutral . . . not a person you could hate," and was surprised that TG hated him. Ander Gunn, interview with the author, 2 May 2018.
5. "The Flirt" (1978), Bancroft MSS.

6. Ander Gunn, interview with the author, 2 May 2018.

7. Prose Notebook (1950), Bancroft MSS.

8. Prose Notebook (1972), Bancroft MSS.

9. Lux, "It's the Instances," 42. They may also have reminded TG of American comics, which he found "rather sexy" and "used to masturbate thinking about."

10. "A GI in 1943," *BC*, 53–54.

11. Interviewing TG for *The Guardian*, Elgy Gillespie claimed TG "kn[e]w he was gay by early childhood, five or so." See Gillespie, "Poems of the Plague," *The Guardian* (24 February 1992), 33.

12. Ann Charlotte Thomson, Photograph album #3. Private collection.

13. Poetry Notebook K (8 January 1963), Hornbake MSS. The friend is Don Doody.

14. "Thom Gunn: October 23, 2002," Prager MSS.

15. *Thom Gunn in Conversation with James Campbell* (London: Between the Lines, 2000), 19.

16. Prose Notebook (1972), Bancroft MSS.

17. TG to Billy Lux, 7 May 1995, in *Letters*, 572.

18. *Thom Gunn in Conversation*, 19.

19. See Peter Wildeblood's memoir *Against the Law* (London: Weidenfeld & Nicolson, 1955).

20. John Gallagher, "Top Gunn," *The Advocate* 635 (10 August 1993), 58.

21. *Thom Gunn in Conversation*, 19. Compare the man whose story—"The first man he had sex with, at thirteen"—informed "A Wood near Athens" (*BC*, 102–104). "He remembered the experience with pleasure and gratitude," TG told a friend. "As indeed I would have remembered it if I had been lucky enough to have a mother with bisexual tattooed boyfriends." TG to John Holmstrom, 15 August 1990, Bancroft MSS.

22. TG to Robert Glück, 16 May 1992. Private collection.

23. "My Life Up to Now," *OP*, 172.

24. Richard Pike, *The Far Side of Years* (Leek, UK: Three Counties Publishing, 2002), 41, 49.

25. Nigel Watson, *A Tradition for Freedom: The Story of University College School* (London: James & James, 2007), 93.

26. Paul Thompson, "Interview with Peter Townsend," in *Pioneers of Social Research, 1996–2018*, 4th ed., UK Data Service, SN: 6226, para. 45, doi.org/10.5255 /UKDA-SN-6226-6. Peter Brereton Townsend (1928–2009) was a pioneering sociologist best known for his work on poverty and social justice.

27. "My Life Up to Now," *OP*, 172.

28. Prose Notebook (1972), Bancroft MSS.

29. "My Suburban Muse," *OP*, 153.

30. The lines "Power / as beauty, beauty / power" in "A GI in 1943" allude not only to "Ode on a Grecian Urn" but also to the experience of reading Keats around the same time he first saw American GIs.

31. Prose Notebook (1972), Bancroft MSS.

32. "My Suburban Muse," *OP*, 154.

33. Prose Notebook (1972), Bancroft MSS.

34. "Table Talk" [on *Low Life*, by Lucy Sante], *The Threepenny Review* 48 (Winter 1992), 3.

35. See, for example, "Berlin Halts Prisoner Exchange," *Daily Mail* (4 October 1941), 1.
36. Ander Gunn, interview with the author, 2 May 2018.
37. Prose Notebook (1972), Bancroft MSS.
38. Ander Gunn, interview with the author, 2 May 2018.
39. TG to Barbara Godfrey, 15 December 1976. Private collection.
40. Ander Gunn, interview with the author, 3 May 2018.
41. T. W. Gunn, "The Heights," *The Gower* 31, no. 1 (December 1944), 8, reprinted in *Biblio (I)*, 165.
42. "Notes of Evidence," LMA MSS.
43. "Notes of Evidence," LMA MSS.
44. Ander Gunn, interview with the author, 3 May 2018.
45. See "Appointment with Fear," *Radio Times* 86, no. 1108 (22 December 1944), 14. Valentine Dyall voiced "The Man in Black."
46. Diary (1944–1945), Bancroft MSS. TG kept Charlotte's two notes: see Scrapbook (1967–1977), Bancroft MSS. Bert obtained them from the coroner and presumably gave them to TG. See Herbert Gunn to the St. Pancras Coroner, 1 January 1946, LMA MSS.
47. Ander Gunn, interview with the author, 2 May 2018. "I think he was quite generous with her," Ander continued, "but she always wanted more."
48. Diary (1944–1945), Bancroft MSS.
49. *Thom Gunn in Conversation*, 19.
50. Ander Gunn, interview with the author, 2 May 2018.
51. Diary (1944–1945), Bancroft MSS.
52. Diary (1944–1945), Bancroft MSS.
53. Thérèse Megaw, interview with J. V. S. Megaw, c. spring 1999.
54. Diary (1944–1945), Bancroft MSS.
55. Prose Notebook (1950), Bancroft MSS.
56. Diary (1944–1945), Bancroft MSS.
57. Diary (1944–1945), Bancroft MSS. Hyde left on the twenty-eighth, not the twenty-seventh.
58. Nicol, *Meet Me at the Savoy*, 102.
59. Nicol subsequently married the journalist and intelligence agent Derek Tangye after Hyde introduced them.
60. Eddowes is remembered for his interest in the Rillington Place murders, his minor role in the Profumo affair, and his part in the exhumation of Lee Harvey Oswald's body in 1981.
61. John Eddowes, email to the author, 8 September 2021.
62. "Mr. R. Hyde and Mrs. Eddowes," *The Times* (4 June 1945), 6. They remained married until Daphne's death in April 1975. John Eddowes recalled that Hyde was not a bad stepfather, noting in particular their shared interest in cricket. John Eddowes, interview with the author, 31 May 2022.
63. Diary (1944–1945), Bancroft MSS. TG's diary entry is reprinted in part in *NSP*, 271–72.
64. "The Gas-poker," *The Threepenny Review* 49 (Spring 1992), 10; collected in *BC*, 10–11.
65. Wilmer, "Poor Lovely Statue!," 18.

66. Chris Jones, "A Transit of Thom," *Poetry Review* 86, no. 3 (Autumn 1996), 56.
67. *Thom Gunn in Conversation*, 19. It is unclear whether TG read newspaper reports of his mother's suicide in which Charlotte's body was discovered by "some children." See "Suicide Follows Separation," 1.
68. "The Gas-poker," *BC*, 10.
69. Wilmer, "Poor Lovely Statue!," 18.
70. "The Gas-poker," *BC*, 11.
71. "My Mother's Pride," *BC*, 9.
72. TG to Ander Gunn, 22 October 1978. Private collection.
73. W. S. Di Piero, in Wendy Lesser et al., "A Symposium on Thom Gunn," *The Threepenny Review* 102 (Summer 2005), 8.
74. Clive Wilmer, telephone interview with the author, 29 July 2020.
75. "My Mother's Pride," *BC*, 9.
76. Diary (1944–1945), Bancroft MSS.

5. RECUPERATION

1. Prose Notebook (1972), Bancroft MSS.
2. Margot Corbett, email to the author, 20 September 2018.
3. Margot Corbett, email to the author, 1 October 2018.
4. Margot Corbett, email to the author, 20 September 2018.
5. TG to Mary Thomson, 10 February 1945, in *Letters*, 4.
6. Poetry Notebook 6 (August 1984), Bancroft MSS. TG also remarked that "depression" was his "main feeling" for "several more years" after his mother's death.
7. Guthmann, "A Poet's Life: Part One," C3.
8. TG to Mary and Catherine Thomson, 11 May 1945, in *Letters*, 8.
9. "Celebrating Victory in North-West London," *Hampstead and Highgate Express* (11 May 1945), 1.
10. TG to Mary and Catherine Thomson, 11 May 1945, in *Letters*, 8.
11. "School Certificate," July 1945, Stanford MSS.
12. TG to Mary Thomson, 10 February 1945, in *Letters*, 4.
13. See Penelope Fitzgerald, *The Knox Brothers* (London: Macmillan, 1977), 266.
14. Bacon was away, probably in Paris. See Michael Peppiatt, *Francis Bacon: Anatomy of an Enigma*, rev. ed. (London: Constable, 2008), 421.
15. "Dr. E. C. S. Megaw," *The Times* (8 February 1956), 11.
16. J. V. S. Megaw, telephone interview with the author, 4 November 2021.
17. TG to Ander Gunn, 20 February 2004, in *Letters*, 677.
18. Poetry Notebook 6 (August 1984), Bancroft MSS.
19. "My Suburban Muse," *OP*, 155.
20. Prose Notebook (1972), Bancroft MSS.
21. TG to Ander Gunn, 29 August 1993. Private collection.
22. Prose Notebook (1972), Bancroft MSS.
23. See Nuwer, "Britain's Expatriate Poet," 73.
24. See A. J. P. Taylor, *Beaverbrook* (London: Hamish Hamilton, 1972), 550.
25. Ander Gunn, interview with the author, 2 May 2018.
26. Nuwer, "Britain's Expatriate Poet," 73.
27. Poetry Notebook 6 (August 1984), Bancroft MSS.

28. Poetry Notebook (Summer 1966–February 1967), Hornbake MSS. Compare "The Birthplace Revisited," in which a man balks when he returns to his child-hood room: "Such disparate past and present would not bear / A compromise." See "The Birthplace Revisited," *Trio* 2 (January 1953), 20, reprinted in *Biblio (I)*, 172.

29. The image is repeated in "Talbot Road," where TG imagined bumping into his nineteen-year-old self, full of "the prickly heat of adolescent emotion." There, however, the scene is celebratory: "I forgave myself for having had a youth." See "Talbot Road," *CP*, 383. Encounters with past selves recur in TG's work.

30. "'Twelfth Night,'" *The Gower* 31, no. 5 (March 1946), 143.

31. For example, see Alan Sinfield, "Thom Gunn in San Francisco: An Interview," *Critical Survey* 2 (1990), 224.

32. Sarver, "Thom Gunn," 16.

33. Sinfield, "Thom Gunn," 224.

34. Gallagher, "Top Gunn," 58.

35. Ruth [Pearce] Townsend, telephone interview with Edward Guthmann, 15 April 2005. The only friend TG described as "campy" was Peter Holgate.

36. C. Q. Forester, "Re-experiencing Thom Gunn," *The Gay and Lesbian Review* 12, no. 5 (September–October 2005), 16.

37. Poetry Notebook 6 (August 1984), Bancroft MSS.

38. Prose Notebook (1972), Bancroft MSS.

39. Poetry Notebook 6 (August 1984), Bancroft MSS. TG was wary of both words, calling the first "from Rimbaud" and the second "too Christian."

40. Poetry Notebook 6 (August 1984), Bancroft MSS.

41. Poetry Notebook 6 (August 1984), Bancroft MSS.

42. TG was called up under the 1939 National Service (Armed Forces) Act, which remained in place until the 1948 Act superseded it on 1 January 1949. All able-bodied men between eighteen and thirty were legally required to serve between twelve and twenty-four months in the armed forces.

43. Herbert Gunn to Robert Rattenbury, 7 February 1947, Trinity MSS. Soft power was at work: Bert used an *Evening Standard* letterhead and signed himself "Her-bert Gunn, Editor."

44. Robert Rattenbury to Herbert Gunn, 12 February 1947, Trinity MSS.

45. Herbert Gunn to Robert Rattenbury, 17 February 1947, Trinity MSS.

46. C. S. Walton to Robert Rattenbury, 18 February 1947, Trinity MSS. Walton's perception of TG is more accurate than his grasp of the details of Bert and Char-lotte's marriage.

47. Robert Rattenbury to C. S. Walton, 20 February 1947, Trinity MSS.

48. TG achieved advanced standards in English and French and a subsidiary standard in German. "Higher School Certificate," July 1947, Stanford MSS.

49. This written examination in Greek, Latin, or Paley's *Evidences of Christianity* was compulsory for all students until 1960. It was originally taken in second year, but TG, had he not achieved credit in School Certificate Latin, would have taken it as a de facto entrance examination. Before TG had achieved his Latin mark, Rat-tenbury's secretary, B. M. Gorse, wrote to Bert in November 1947 asking whether TG wished to be entered for the Latin papers of the Previous Examination that December.

50. Prose Notebook (1972), Bancroft MSS.
51. Immediately before his national service, TG read Tolstoy's pacifist writings, namely *The Kingdom of God Is Within You* and letters including "Non-Activity," "A Letter to the Liberals," and "Thou Shalt Not Kill."
52. TG to Ruth [Pearce] Townsend, 18 May 1948. Private collection.
53. TG to Mary and Catherine Thomson, 23 June 1948, in *Letters*, 10. "N.C.O.": noncommissioned officer.
54. "Some Autobiographical Notes: Thom Gunn," in Richard Burns, ed., *Rivers of Life: A Gravesham Anthology* (Gravesend: Victoria Press, 1980), 105.
55. "My Life Up to Now," *OP*, 172.
56. Prose Notebook (1972), Bancroft MSS.
57. TG to Ruth [Pearce] Townsend, 9 August 1948. Private collection.
58. "Buchanan Castle, 1948," *The London Magazine* N.S. 19, no. 9–10 (December 1979–January 1980), 45, uncollected.
59. Ingrey became a television screenwriter and wrote two moderately successful novels: *Me and Victor and Mrs Blanchard* (1962) and *Pig Boy* (1963).
60. "I *began* novels," he later quipped. See Steve Abbott, "Writing One's Own Mythology: An Interview with Thom Gunn," *Contact II* (Summer 1982), 20.
61. See TG to Ander Gunn, 13 April 1960. Private collection.
62. Ander Gunn, interview with the author, 2 May 2018.
63. Poetry Notebook "Libertad" (September 1963), Hornbake MSS. They last saw each other in 1970, when Ingrey acted "unspeakabl[y]" in a pub with Ander and Tony White. See Diary (1966–1970), 14 August 1970, Bancroft MSS. "He pretended to believe that Tony White and I were lovers," TG later reminded Ander. See TG to Ander Gunn, 4 September 1996. Private collection.
64. See the Freya Stark Collection, MS-03975, box 24, Harry Ransom Center, University of Texas at Austin.
65. David Walker, *Lean, Wind, Lean: A Few Times Remembered* (London: Collins, 1984), 94.
66. Henry Channon, *The Diaries: 1938–43*, ed. Simon Heffer (London: Hutchinson, 2021), 640. A batman is a soldier assigned as a personal servant to a commissioned officer.
67. TG to Mary and Catherine Thomson, 5 December 1948. Private collection.
68. Poetry Notebook 6 (August 1984), Bancroft MSS.
69. "A Letter to Mark Rudman," 84–85.
70. TG to Robert Glück, 16 May 1992. Private collection.
71. Prose Notebook (1972), Bancroft MSS. TG recalled "almost drowning" but did not elaborate.
72. Poetry Notebook 6 (August 1984), Bancroft MSS. The novel was called "An Anatomy of Youth" and featured "a romance against a winter landscape" between a boy and girl who meet while ice skating.
73. TG to Robert Glück, 16 May 1992. Private collection.
74. Prose Notebook (1972), Bancroft MSS.
75. TG to Robert Rattenbury, 28 November 1949, Trinity MSS.
76. "Cambridge in the Fifties," *OP*, 157.

6. CAMBRIDGE

1. TG to Alice Collings, Barbara and Frank Godfrey, 9 March 1950. Private collection.
2. Poetry Notebook H (February 1958), Hornbake MSS.
3. Lee, "Laundromat Cowboy," 17.
4. Poetry Notebook H (February 1958), Hornbake MSS.
5. Prose Notebook (1950), Bancroft MSS.
6. There was perhaps another affinity: Stendhal also lost his mother during childhood.
7. TG to Clive Wilmer, 19 October 1981, in *Letters*, 363.
8. TG to Clive Wilmer, 10 October 1994, in *Letters*, 560.
9. Poetry Notebook No. 3 (undated), Bancroft MSS.
10. Prose Notebook (1972), Bancroft MSS.
11. Prose Notebook (1950), Bancroft MSS.
12. Joan Smith, "Cold Comfort," *San Francisco Examiner Magazine* (11 January 1998), 7.
13. "Some Autobiographical Notes," 105.
14. Lee, "Laundromat Cowboy," 17.
15. *Thom Gunn in Conversation*, 17.
16. Prose Notebook (1972), Bancroft MSS. TG maintained this belief throughout his life. See the lines "mimicking each friend / I answer expectations" in "Transients and Residents: Interruption," *CP*, 379.
17. Prose Notebook (1950), Bancroft MSS.
18. Marcel Proust, *Within a Budding Grove*, trans C. K. Scott Moncrieff (London: Chatto & Windus, 1923), 129. TG would have read Moncrieff's original translation.
19. Prose Notebook (1950), Bancroft MSS.
20. TG knew by 1958. Referring to his 1952 poem "Light Sleeping," he "tried to avoid the Albertine Strategy as dishonest," but called the poem "not a real example of it, anyway." See TG to Donald Hall, 12 May 1958, New Hampshire MSS. See also "Light Sleeping," *New World Writing* 7 (April 1955), 115–16, reprinted in *The Missed Beat* (Newark, VT: Janus Press; Sidcot, UK: Gruffyground Press, 1976).
21. Clive Wilmer, "Thom Gunn: The Art of Poetry LXXII," *The Paris Review* 135 (Summer 1995), 150.
22. "My Life Up to Now," *OP*, 173.
23. The collection, which does not survive, perhaps contained poems TG showed to Archie John Wavell.
24. See Prose Notebook (1972), Bancroft MSS.
25. Prose Notebook (1950), Bancroft MSS.
26. "Table Talk," 3.
27. Prose Notebook (1950), Bancroft MSS.
28. Brendan Bernhard, "Boss Cupid's Poet: The Good Life and Hard Times of Thom Gunn," *LA Weekly* 22, no. 52 (17–23 November 2000), 34.
29. TG knew Pradelles from Robert Louis Stevenson's *Travels with a Donkey in the Cévennes* (1879), although TG's journey ended around where Stevenson's began.
30. Prose Notebook (1972), Bancroft MSS.

31. See TG to Clive Wilmer, 23–25 August 1994, in *Letters*, 553–54.
32. TG to Clive Wilmer, 10 October 1994, in *Letters*, 560.
33. TG to Clive Wilmer, 23–25 August 1994, in *Letters*, 554.
34. *Thom Gunn in Conversation*, 20–21.
35. TG to A. G. Lee, 9 September 1953, John's MSS.
36. Bert's solicitor, Arnold Maplesden, handled the paperwork, which can be found in Stanford MSS.
37. TG to A. G. Lee, 9 September 1953, John's MSS.
38. Two postcards to Aunt Barbara demonstrate the change. Arriving in Paris in March 1950, he signed "Tom"; back in England in September, preparing for Cambridge, he was "Thom."
39. *Thom Gunn in Conversation*, 52.
40. "Cambridge in the Fifties," *OP*, 157–58.
41. Prose Notebook (1972), Bancroft MSS.
42. "Cambridge in the Fifties," *OP*, 158.
43. This vantage point is the scene of "The Secret Sharer," *CP*, 13.
44. TG to Tony Tanner, 26 March 1992, in *Letters*, 515.
45. Prose Notebook (1950), Bancroft MSS.
46. TG to Tony Tanner, 26 March 1992, in *Letters*, 516.
47. *Thom Gunn in Conversation*, 21.
48. "Cambridge in the Fifties," *OP*, 158–59.
49. "My Life Up to Now," *OP*, 173.
50. TG to Karl Miller, c. summer 1953, Emory MSS.
51. "Cambridge in the Fifties," *OP*, 158.
52. Helena Shire, Michaelmas term report, 1950 ("Mrs Shire, Mich. '50"), Trinity MSS.
53. *Thom Gunn in Conversation*, 22.
54. August Kleinzahler and John Tranter, "An Interview with Thom Gunn," *Scripsi* 5, no. 3 (1989), 185. TG spoke often about what Leavis called "realisation," the process of turning reality into art. See F. R. Leavis, *The Common Pursuit* (London: Chatto & Windus, 1952), 213. See also chapter 6, p. 71.
55. Prose Notebook (1972), Bancroft MSS.
56. Wilmer, "Art of Poetry," 154.
57. "Cambridge in the Fifties," *OP*, 160.
58. *Thom Gunn in Conversation*, 23.
59. Michael Kitay, Julian Jebb, and Ronald Hayman, "Interview: Thom Gunn," *Chequer* 6 (Summer 1954), 17.
60. "Cambridge in the Fifties," *OP*, 158.
61. See "'Oasis': An Experiment in Selling Poetry," *The Bookseller* (15 March 1952), 782.
62. TG to Herbert Gunn, 21 February 1951. Private collection.
63. Driberg spoke about "Korea—the present situation." See "Cambridge Notebook," *Varsity* (3 February 1951), 12; and "Socialist Dilemma," *Varsity* (10 February 1951), 5. See also TG to Herbert Gunn, 10 February 1951, in *Letters*, 12.
64. Tom Driberg, "Tories Bay for War," *Reynold's News* (London) (2 July 1950), 4.
65. See "Refresher Training for Many Reservists," *The Times* (30 January 1951), 6.
66. TG to Herbert Gunn, 21 February 1951. Private collection.

67. TG to Herbert Gunn, 10 February 1951, in *Letters*, 12.
68. *You* ran for eight issues between November 1950 and August 1951 and almost bankrupted the Gunns. Many of its contributors, including Enid Blyton, Ronald Duncan, and Rebecca West, wrote for free as a favor to Bert.
69. "Son or Father—Who Is Right?," *You* 73, no. 782 (April 1951), 18–21.
70. See "Poem," *Cambridge Today* 4, no. 16 (June 1951), 15, republished as "The Soldier" in *The Missed Beat* (1976).
71. Prose Notebook (1972), Bancroft MSS.
72. "Cambridge in the Fifties," *OP*, 159.
73. "Poem," 15.
74. Peter Green, "Our Contemporaries," *The Cambridge Review* LXXII, no. 1768 (9 June 1951), 603.
75. "Cambridge in the Fifties," *OP*, 159.

7. TONY

1. "Cambridge in the Fifties," *OP*, 159.
2. "South," *The Times Literary Supplement* 4393 (12 June 1987), 637, uncollected.
3. "Cambridge in the Fifties," *OP*, 159. TG was preparing to sit for exams for the Charles Oldham Shakespeare Scholarship.
4. TG to Tony Tanner, 25 August 1995, King's MSS.
5. "Cambridge in the Fifties," *OP*, 159.
6. Wilmer, "Art of Poetry," 152.
7. "Cambridge in the Fifties," *OP*, 159.
8. "Cambridge in the Fifties," *OP*, 160.
9. TG to John Coleman, 9 March 1952, in *Letters*, 16.
10. Christopher Bayliss, "Oasis 5," *Granta* 55, no. 1131 (23 February 1952), 18; "Two Ghosts," *Oasis* 5 (February 1952), 8, reprinted in *Biblio (I)*, 168–69.
11. TG to John Coleman, 9 March 1952, in *Letters*, 15.
12. Don May, "Cambridge Poetry," *Varsity* (14 February 1953), 5.
13. "Cambridge in the Fifties," *OP*, 161. Coleman is the subject of "Birthday Poem," which begins: "You understand both Adolphe and Fabrice / The speculative man or passionate" (*CP*, 48).
14. Caught after dark without their mandatory black gowns, Coleman and Baron answered the university proctors "with assumed voices and farcical accents." The incident occurred in February and they were suspended for the remainder of the academic year. See "Cambridge in the Fifties," *OP*, 161.
15. TG to John Coleman, 9 March 1952, in *Letters*, 15. The most infamous rustication during TG's time at Cambridge occurred the following year when *Granta* editor Mark Boxer was rusticated for publishing Antony de Hoghton's supposedly blasphemous poem "God is in his garage." The case made the national press and Boxer's supporters held a mock funeral on his rustication day. See "'Funeral' for Editor of 'Granta,'" *The Times* (25 May 1953), 2.
16. "Cambridge in the Fifties," *OP*, 161.
17. Nick Tomalin, "Northern Light," *Varsity* (1 March 1952), 7.
18. Miller chaired the program from December 1951 through March 1952.
19. "An orphan self took hold," Miller later reflected, "vulnerable and fierce, bereaved and aggrieved. It came and went; in time, it was to be tempered and concealed,

rather than outgrown." Karl Miller, *Rebecca's Vest: A Memoir* (London: Hamish Hamilton, 1993), 15.

20. Karl Miller, "Thom Gunn: Cambridge Poet," *Varsity* (18 October 1952), 4.

21. "Cambridge in the Fifties," *OP*, 161.

22. Wilmer, "Art of Poetry," 152.

23. "Cambridge in the Fifties," *OP*, 159.

24. Prose Notebook (1972), Bancroft MSS.

25. When James Campbell suggested the "temperature" of TG's work was "point-Zero," TG replied, "Yes, I'm a *cold* poet, aren't I?" See *Thom Gunn in Conversation*, 26.

26. Helena Shire, Lent term 1952 report ("Shire, Lent '52"), Trinity MSS.

27. Ian Hamilton, "Four Conversations: Thom Gunn," *The London Magazine* N.S. 4, no. 8 (November 1964), 69.

28. Kitay, Jebb, and Hayman, "Interview," 18.

29. Hamilton, "Four Conversations," 70.

30. Kitay, Jebb, and Hayman, "Interview," 18.

31. Wilmer, "Art of Poetry," 149–50. Auden's example also encouraged TG to "try out every form," which in part accounts for the formal range of *FT*. See Kleinzahler and Tranter, "An Interview," 192.

32. Hamilton, "Four Conversations," 69. "Empsonian" was a pejorative term. Reviewing Empson, TG found his "five separate difficulties [were] muddled imagery, difficulty of reference, an excessive telescoping of statement, unclearness of tone, and some very odd ways with scansion." TG felt that "the object of a poem is to say something and, though this something may be very complicated, it is not said well by the means of irrelevant figures or a style as complicated as the subject matter." Untitled review of William Empson, *Collected Poems* (1955), *The London Magazine* 3, no. 2 (February 1956), 71, 75.

33. Sinfield, "Thom Gunn," 229.

34. "An Anglo-American Poet," *SL*, 223.

35. Scobie, "Gunn in America," 9.

36. TG to A. E. Dyson, 8 September 1991, in *Letters*, 507.

37. Tony White was "lithe, tough, and sexy as Petruchio." See George Wilcox, "The Taming of the Shrew," *The Cambridge Review* LXXIII, no. 1792 (7 June 1952), 572.

38. "Cambridge in the Fifties," *OP*, 164.

39. "Cambridge in the Fifties," *OP*, 161–62.

40. "Cambridge in the Fifties," *OP*, 162.

41. Wilmer, "Art of Poetry," 151.

42. TG Autograph book. Private collection.

43. "Cambridge in the Fifties," *OP*, 162–63.

44. Prose Notebook (1972), Bancroft MSS.

45. "Cambridge in the Fifties," *OP*, 163.

46. "Tony White," *Varsity* (8 November 1952), 4. TG later acknowledged his own fascistic streak. Calling himself "a Shakespearean, Sartrean fascist," he noted that his early goal, "the heroic in the modern world," was "a slightly fascistic quest because the heroic is so often a martial kind of virtue." See Wilmer, "Art of Poetry," 165.

47. "Tony White," 4. White informed TG's own attraction to Coriolanus. In "A

Plan of Self-Subjection" (*CP*, 46) TG wrote: "As Alexander or Mark Antony / Or Coriolanus, whom I most admire, / I mask self-flattery." TG also refers to the adventure novelist Rafael Sabatini (1875–1950), whose most famous works include *Scaramouche* (1921) and *Captain Blood* (1922).

48. "Tony White," 4.

49. "Cambridge in the Fifties," *OP*, 163. White wrote about his unease as an actor in "Rant," *Granta* 56, no. 1136 (1 November 1952), 17–19.

50. "Cambridge in the Fifties," *OP*, 164.

51. Quoted in "Cambridge in the Fifties," *OP*, 163. They picked up "espagnolisme" (youthful folly) from Stendhal.

52. TG to Karl Miller, 14 July 1952, in *Letters*, 17. It would not have been lost on TG that Ann shared a name with his mother.

53. Miller, *Rebecca's Vest*, 134. TG was another such "avatar." In his dismissal of Cambridge undergraduate poetry, Philip Hobsbaum felt "the strength of [TG's] initial external virtuosity and (what he called) panache" meant he could "get away with" a minor piece like "Elizabeth Barrett Barrett," which "combines flaccid rhythm, platitude, and irrelevant vulgarity into a much admired poem." See Hobsbaum, "Why Read Cambridge Poetry?," *Varsity* (8 May 1954), 4; Hobsbaum is referring specifically to the poem's third stanza. See "Elizabeth Barrett Barrett," *Gadfly* 4, no. 4 (November 1953), 11, uncollected.

54. Jane [Collet] Miller, interview with the author, 8 August 2018.

55. TG to Karl Miller, 14 July 1952, in *Letters*, 17.

56. "Carnal Knowledge," *CP*, 15–16.

57. "To His Cynical Mistress" (*CP*, 5) and "The Secret Sharer" (*CP*, 13).

58. John Fuller noted a "strong riddle element in *Fighting Terms*," especially in poems like "The Wound" and "Without a Counterpart," but felt the term was only applicable "where the demand for solution asserts itself above the symbolic structure." See Fuller, "Thom Gunn," in Ian Hamilton, ed., *The Modern Poet: Essays from the Review* (London: Macdonald, 1967), 20.

59. Poems Annotated for Readings 1961–1999, Bancroft MSS.

60. The refrain came from the Rodgers and Hammerstein musical *South Pacific* (1949): TG liked Mary Martin's rendition of "I'm in Love with a Wonderful Guy." Elgy Gillespie, "Smokin' Gunn," *San Francisco Bay Guardian* (28 September 1994), 7.

61. Gillespie, "Smokin' Gunn," 7.

62. Poems Annotated for Readings 1961–1999, Bancroft MSS.

63. "My Life Up to Now: Postscript," *OP*, 188.

64. TG to John Holmstrom, 15 December 1952, in *Letters*, 21.

65. TG to Karl Miller, 26 August 1952, Emory MSS.

66. TG to John Holmstrom, 15 December 1952, in *Letters*, 20.

67. "Lerici," *CP*, 23. Compare "the large gesture of solitary man" in "In Santa Maria del Popolo," *CP*, 94.

68. TG to Karl Miller, 19 September 1952, Emory MSS.

69. Lux, "It's the Instances," 42.

70. TG to Karl Miller, 19 September 1952, Emory MSS. The scholarship was worth one hundred pounds per annum.

71. Helena Shire, Easter term 1952 report ("Shire, Easter '52"), Trinity MSS.

72. R. R. Bolgar to Robert Rattenbury, 9 June 1952, Trinity MSS.

73. *New Soundings* ran for twelve episodes between January 1952 and March 1953 on the BBC Third Programme. "The Secret Sharer" was broadcast on episode seven (24 September 1952).

74. Donald Hall, "In Memoriam: Thom Gunn," *Poetry* 184, no. 4 (August 2004), 329.

75. "Cambridge in the Fifties," *OP*, 164–65.

76. "Cambridge in the Fifties," *OP*, 165.

77. Prose Notebook (1972), Bancroft MSS.

8. MIKE

1. Mike Kitay, email to the author, 23 August 2021.

2. Mike Kitay, email to the author, 9 February 2020.

3. Mike Kitay, email to the author, 5 June 2020.

4. Mike Kitay, email to the author, 9 February 2020.

5. "Kearny Lad Wins National Sermon Test," *New Jersey Jewish News* (28 March 1947), 3.

6. "I was a hit . . ." Mike Kitay, email to the author, 10 August 2021.

7. Rutgers University, *The 1952 Scarlet Letter* (Newark, NJ: Rutgers, 1952), 148–49. Philip Dunning and George Abbott's *Broadway* was a smash hit at the Broadhurst Theatre, New York, from 1926 to 1928. It was less of a hit at Rutgers. Bob Comstock, later a prominent journalist and editor, called it "a horrible little hodgepodge." See "First-Nighters Ask Why?," *The Targum* (30 November 1951), 1.

8. "Queens Players Present First Performance of *Winslow Boy*," *The Daily Home News* (New Brunswick, NJ) (1 March 1951), 8.

9. New Jersey College for Women, *The 1951 Quair* (New Brunswick: New Jersey College for Women, 1951), 135. That "realistic world" perhaps alludes to Polly's difficult childhood: her mother was committed to a psychiatric hospital in the early 1930s; her father, no longer able to support his daughters, sent Polly and her sister Elizabeth to a home for girls in Helmetta, New Jersey. Mike knew nothing about her background.

10. Mike Kitay, interview with the author, 25 June 2019.

11. Mike Kitay, interview with the author, 25 June 2019.

12. Mike Kitay, email to the author, 5 June 2020.

13. Mike Kitay, interview with the author, 25 June 2019.

14. Mike Kitay, interview with the author, 20 October 2018.

15. Mike Kitay, interview with the author, 10 October 2018.

16. Mike's research project focused on "expressionism in modern literature." See J. Milton French to R. N. Walters, 14 June 1952, Fitzwilliam MSS.

17. John Berryman addressed the society while Mike was a member. See "Philosopheans Plan Banquet for Thursday," *The Targum* (1 May 1951), 1.

18. "Melvin Kitay," A–Z (1945–1971), Series 1, Disk 8, Wilson MSS.

19. J. Milton French to Whitney J. Oates, 3 March 1952, Wilson MSS.

20. Donald J. McGinn to Whitney J. Oates, 3 March 1952, Wilson MSS.

21. Donald J. McGinn to Whitney J. Oates, 3 March 1952; Mason W. Gross to Whitney J. Oates, 4 March 1952, Wilson MSS.

22. Mike Kitay, email to the author, 10 August 2021.

23. According to Mason W. Gross, Mike was "the first student [at Rutgers] who has

ever won such a fellowship." See Mason W. Gross to R. N. Walters, 13 June 1952, Fitzwilliam MSS.

24. Quoted in "Rutgers Grad Gets Fellowship," *The Daily Home News* (New Brunswick, NJ) (10 June 1952), 22.

25. Mike Kitay, interview with the author, 9 October 2018.

26. Mason W. Gross to R. N. Walters, 13 June 1952, Fitzwilliam MSS.

27. Robert M. Rattenbury to Whitney J. Oates, 10 June 1952, Wilson MSS.

28. R. N. Walters to Whitney J. Oates, 10 June 1952, Wilson MSS. Established in 1869 to allow men who could not afford to belong to a college to belong to the university, Fitzwilliam would not become a full college until 1966. See John Cleaver, ed., *Fitzwilliam: The First 150 Years of a Cambridge College* (London: Third Millennium Publishing, 2013), 68–79.

29. "Censor" is a specific term for the master—the head of a Cambridge college—of the noncollegiate students and their residence, Fitzwilliam House.

30. Melvin [Mike] Kitay to W. S. Thatcher, 27 May 1952, Fitzwilliam MSS.

31. J. Milton French to R. N. Walters, 14 June 1952, Fitzwilliam MSS.

32. Mike Kitay, interview with the author, 10 October 2018.

33. Mike Kitay, interview with the author, 23 October 2018.

34. R. N. Walters, Terminal Report, Michaelmas 1952, Fitzwilliam MSS.

35. "The Beach Head," *CP*, 27.

36. TG likely had in mind Aufidius's speech at IV.5.102–36. See *Coriolanus* in Stanley Wells and Gary Taylor, eds., *The Oxford Shakespeare: The Complete Works* (Oxford: Clarendon Press, 1998), 1091.

37. See "Tony White," 4; see also chapter 7, p. 85.

38. Mike Kitay, in Lesser et al., "A Symposium on Thom Gunn," 12–13. "The Beach Head" was published in full in *Granta* in February 1953.

39. An American accent did not prevent another American student, Mike's friend Gordon Gould, from becoming president of the ADC (1953–54). "[Gould] has to look on each part where he is not playing an American as a character portrayal because of the accent," commented a *Varsity* journalist, "but he overcomes this drawback very successfully." See "Name in Lights," *Varsity* (20 February 1954), 5.

40. Mike Kitay, interview with August Kleinzahler, undated.

41. Edmond Rostand, *Cyrano de Bergerac*, trans. Brian Hooker (New York: Henry Holt, 1923), 36.

42. Stephen Culverwell, "Theatre: 'Cyrano de Bergerac,'" *The Cambridge Review* LXXIV, no. 1801 (17 January 1953), 232.

43. Jane [Collet] Miller, interview with the author, 8 August 2018.

44. Margaret [Baron] Owen, interview with the author, 24 July 2018. Margaret later acted alongside Mike in Bernard Shaw's *The Shewing-Up of Blanco Posnet* at the ADC Theatre.

45. Poetry Notebook 11 (January 1990), Bancroft MSS. The poem became "Rapallo," *BC*, 94–95.

46. "My Life Up to Now," *OP*, 175.

47. Prose Notebook (1972), Bancroft MSS.

48. Mike Kitay, interview with the author, 9 October 2018.

49. Kitay, in Lesser et al., "A Symposium on Thom Gunn," 13. Wilson read from his novel *Hemlock and After* (1952), an account of homosexuality in postwar Britain.

50. Tony Tanner, "A Talk with Thom Gunn," King's MSS.
51. "Collected Poet," review of Dylan Thomas, *Collected Poems 1934–1952* (1953), *The Cambridge Review* LXXIV, no. 1799 (22 November 1952), 160.
52. See Jonathan Bate, *Ted Hughes: The Unauthorised Life* (London: HarperCollins, 2015), 74.
53. "Cambridge in the Fifties," *OP*, 167.
54. John Mander, TG, F. S. Grubb, and E. J. Hughes, letter to the editor, *Varsity* (9 May 1953), 8.
55. See "Comments About Books at Sotheby's," March 1992, box 7, folder 1, Hughes BL MSS. Bate has claimed that Hughes wrote "The Thought Fox" "in 1955, sitting in bed at one o'clock in the morning after an evening in the flat of fellow-poet Thom Gunn." See Bate, *Ted Hughes*, 94. However, TG left for the United States in 1954 and did not return to England at all during 1955. Bate's source is a page from a notebook in which Hughes listed the dates and places of composition of many of his early poems. Bate has misread "Thom" for "Than"—a reference to Hughes's Cambridge friend Nathaniel Minton. See Add MS 88918/7/2, Hughes BL MSS. For Minton, see *Letters of Ted Hughes*, ed. Christopher Reid (London: Faber, 2007), 81–82.
56. TG to Elaine Feinstein, 3 August 1999, in *Letters*, 644.
57. "Cambridge in the Fifties," *OP*, 160.
58. TG to Douglas Chambers, 4 October 1976, in *Letters*, 334.
59. Richard Butler, "Thom Gunn's Poems," *Varsity* (6 June 1953), 5.
60. Apemantus, "Springtime," *Gadfly* 2, no. 2 (30 May 1953), 27.
61. TG to Donald Hall, 30 April 1953, New Hampshire MSS.
62. Prose Notebook (1972), Bancroft MSS. TG saw a parallel between two Americans on cultural and educational visits to Europe: Mike's fellowship year at Cambridge and Hudson's attempt to become a sculptor in Rome. Later, TG probably saw another parallel between their overprotective mothers.
63. TG to Karl Miller, 10 December 1952, Emory MSS.
64. Mike Kitay, interview with the author, 19 September 2016.
65. TG to Karl Miller, 18 December 1952, in *Letters*, 22. At school, Tony had "romantic attachments to his fellow schoolboys" and wrote letters about his "crushes" to John Holmstrom, a close friend at Haileybury. Through school and into his early twenties, Tony "had a series of relationships with young men, which were undoubtedly sexual in intent, if not always in practice." See Sam Miller, *Fathers* (London: Jonathan Cape, 2017), 89. Holmstrom recalled that, at school, Tony had been "in love [with] a shy, graceful little boy." See John Holmstrom, "Whisper It Easily" (unpublished manuscript, c. 2013), PDF file.
66. "Cambridge in the Fifties," *OP*, 166.
67. TG to Karl Miller, 10 December 1952, Emory MSS.
68. TG to Mike Kitay, 2 March 1953, Stanford MSS. Always one to choose an apt postcard, TG presumably meant *The Ironers* to signify the removal of wrinkles or creases following their misunderstanding about the Paris trip.
69. Mike Kitay, quoted in "Thom Gunn: Appropriate Measures," *Sunday Feature*, BBC Radio 3, first broadcast 4 January 2015.
70. Prose Notebook (1972), Bancroft MSS.
71. Poetry Notebook 11 (January 1990), Bancroft MSS.

72. Marc Breindel, "Top Gunn," *San Francisco Sentinel* 16, no. 32 (5 August 1988), 19.

73. Christopher Hennessy, *Outside the Lines: Talking with Contemporary Gay Poets* (Ann Arbor: University of Michigan Press, 2005), 20.

74. Prose Notebook (1972), Bancroft MSS.

75. Theodore Redpath, Easter term 1953 report ("Redpath, Easter '53"), Trinity MSS. Redpath now saw TG more "as a creative writer and sensitive critic than as an academic scholar."

76. Prose Notebook (1972), Bancroft MSS.

77. Mike Kitay, interview with the author, 19 September 2016.

78. Margaret [Baron] Owen, interview with the author, 24 July 2018.

79. Miller, *Fathers*, 47–48.

80. "Cambridge in the Fifties," *OP*, 167.

81. TG to Tony White, c. June 1953, in *Letters*, 26.

82. Mike Kitay, interview with the author, 25 June 2019.

83. TG to Mike Kitay, 4 March 1961, Stanford MSS.

84. "Tamer and Hawk," *CP*, 29.

85. TG to Mike Kitay, c. February 1961, Stanford MSS.

86. Mike Kitay, interview with the author, 9 October 2018.

87. Prose Notebook (1972), Bancroft MSS.

88. TG to Karl Miller, c. spring 1953, Emory MSS.

89. "Legal Reform," *CP*, 77–78.

90. TG to Karl Miller, c. spring 1953, Emory MSS.

91. "Without a Counterpart," *CP*, 31.

92. TG to Donald Hall, 13 May 1953, New Hampshire MSS.

93. TG to Mike Kitay, 21 May 1953, in *Letters*, 25–26.

94. W. S. Thatcher to Commanding General, First Air Force, 19 June 1953, Fitzwilliam MSS.

95. Mike Kitay, interview with the author, 10 October 2018. "My fellowship money paid for the trip," Mike recalled: another sign that a deferment was not at all certain.

96. TG to Helena Mennie Shire, 9 September 1953, in *Letters*, 27.

97. Mike Kitay to W. S. Thatcher, 20 August 1953, Fitzwilliam MSS. Mike could not renew his Woodrow Wilson Fellowship: instead, he relied on "app[rox.] $1500" in financial aid "from my parents" to support his second year at Cambridge. See "Questionnaire," Wilson MSS.

98. Poetry Notebook L (23 February 1963), Hornbake MSS.

99. Mike Kitay, interview with the author, 19 September 2016.

100. Poetry Notebook 2 (May 1979), Bancroft MSS.

101. See Poetry Notebook 11 (January 1990), Bancroft MSS; see also chapter 33, p. 427.

9. POET

1. Fantasy published fifteen single-author pamphlets alone in 1952: poets included Hall, Adrienne Rich, Elizabeth Jennings, Geoffrey Hill, and A. Alvarez. See *Thom Gunn: Fantasy Poets 16* (Oxford: Fantasy Press, 1953). "Incident on a Journey" was broadcast on episode eleven of *New Soundings* (4 February 1953).

2. "The Shield of Irony," *The Times Literary Supplement* 2722 (2 April 1954), 218.

3. See James Gibson, ed., *Let the Poet Choose* (London: Harrap, 1973), 69.

4. "The Wound," *CP*, 3.

5. The title presumably came from Patroclus's warning to Achilles that "wounds heal ill that men do give themselves." See *Troilus and Cressida*, III.3.220–22, *Oxford Shakespeare*, 734.

6. Poetry Notebook X (December 1971), Bancroft MSS.

7. *Troilus and Cressida*, III.3.210–12, *Oxford Shakespeare*, 734.

8. Compare the ending of "Without a Counterpart," a companion poem to "The Wound," where the help of another—"I only spoke your name"—provides comfort in a similar landscape to that of "The Wound": i.e., "The bad hole in the ground no longer gaped" ("Without a Counterpart") and "I had to let those storm-lit valleys heal" ("The Wound"). TG wrote "The Wound" before he knew Mike, and "Without a Counterpart" months later, after they had become lovers.

9. TG to Donald Hall, 22 May 1953, New Hampshire MSS.

10. Theodore Redpath, Easter term 1953 report ("Redpath, Easter '53"), Trinity MSS.

11. Hall, "In Memoriam," 329.

12. See D. A. Routh to TG, 10 September 1953, Trinity MSS.

13. TG to Karl Miller, 25 September 1953, Emory MSS.

14. TG to Donald Hall, 13 May 1953, in *Letters*, 24. TG had in mind Philip Toynbee's assessment of "Carnal Knowledge" as "slick and empty facility": see Toynbee, "The Budding Grove," *The Observer* (3 May 1953), 9.

15. TG to Donald Hall, 28 September 1953, New Hampshire MSS.

16. TG to Donald Hall, 3 November 1953, New Hampshire MSS.

17. TG to Helena Mennie Shire, 9 September 1953, in *Letters*, 28.

18. See "Thomson William Gunn" student card, John's MSS.

19. TG to John Lehmann, 8 October 1953, Texas MSS. Eight stanzas of "The Furies" were published in *Chequer* 2 (May 1953), 14–15, reprinted in *Biblio (I)*, 174–76.

20. For *New Writing*, see John Lehmann, *In My Own Time: Memoirs of a Literary Life* (Boston: Little, Brown, 1969), 155–72. Lehmann wrote an account of his time at the Hogarth Press called *Thrown to the Woolfs* (London: Weidenfeld and Nicolson, 1978).

21. "A First Meeting," in A. T. Tolley, ed., *John Lehmann: A Tribute* (Ottawa: Carleton University Press, 1987), 25.

22. TG to Tony White, 10 March 1954, Tulsa MSS. TG had in mind "Hungry" and "Palinode": see *The London Magazine* 1, no. 4 (May 1954), 25–26.

23. TG to Tony White, 10 March 1954, Tulsa MSS.

24. "A First Meeting," 25.

25. Adrian Wright, *John Lehmann: A Pagan Adventure* (London: Duckworth, 1998), 189.

26. TG to Donald Hall, 14 August 1954, New Hampshire MSS. Two years later he called himself, uneasily, Lehmann's "blue-eyed boy." See TG to Donald Hall, 21 January 1956, New Hampshire MSS. He later mellowed, calling Lehmann "the editor of all editors to whom I owe the most." See "A First Meeting," 25.

27. Breindel, "Top Gunn," 19.

28. TG to Donald Hall, 28 September 1955, New Hampshire MSS.

29. "The circles they moved in may well have been those of rough trade," Wright

summarized, "and they certainly brought with them problems that Lehmann could well have done without." See Wright, *John Lehmann*, 222. Dadie Rylands, Lehmann's friend from undergraduate days—and whom Thom knew from the Cambridge theater scene—called him "a romantic old ninny." Quoted in Wright, *John Lehmann*, 39.

30. TG to Tony White, 10 March 1954, Tulsa MSS.
31. TG to Oscar Mellor, c. September 1953, Morgan MSS.
32. Prose Notebook (1972), Bancroft MSS.
33. Stephen Haskell, "A.D.C.—*The Heiress*," *The Cambridge Review* LXXV, no. 1818 (17 October 1953), 50.
34. Frederic Raphael, *Going Up: To Cambridge and Beyond—A Writer's Memoir* (London: Robson Press, 2015), 169.
35. Stanley Price, "Lady at the Wheel," *Varsity* (14 November 1953), 4.
36. "He has a personality on stage which is surprisingly attractive," TG wrote. "I thought he made the best Hamlet I've seen." TG to Karl Miller, c. December 1953, Emory MSS.
37. TG to Donald Hall, 11 December 1953, New Hampshire MSS. Hall was poetry editor of *The Paris Review*.
38. TG to Donald Hall, 11 December 1953, New Hampshire MSS.
39. TG to Karl Miller, c. December 1953, Emory MSS.
40. TG to Karl Miller, 9 January 1954, in *Letters*, 29.
41. Poetry Notebook 12 (May 1991), Bancroft MSS.
42. TG to Karl Miller, 9 January 1954, in *Letters*, 29.
43. TG to Tony White, 10 March 1954, Tulsa MSS.
44. "A District in Rome," *The London Magazine* 2, no. 7 (July 1955), 14, uncollected.
45. TG to Donald Hall, 23 February 1954, in *Letters*, 33.
46. The lines are a slight misquotation from Yeats's "Ego Dominus Tuus," which reads: "A style is built with sedentary toil / And constant imitation of great masters." See Poetry Notebook (undated) [1954], Bancroft MSS.
47. "An Apprenticeship," 17.
48. TG to Donald Hall, 3 November 1953, New Hampshire MSS.
49. The first chapter of MacDonald's *At the Back of the North Wind* (1871) is called "The Hayloft."
50. Note that "After a Dream" bears no resemblance to "The Book of the Dead" (*CP*, 104–105), TG's subsequent poem about Book XI of *The Odyssey*.
51. Homer, *The Odyssey*, trans. Samuel Butler (London: Jonathan Cape, 1925), 168. Butler notes that "tradition says that she had hanged herself."
52. "After a Dream," Hornbake MSS. The "sweating post" alludes to Shakespeare's "reeking post": see *King Lear*, II.2.206, in *Oxford Shakespeare*, 956.
53. In alternative lines sent to Donald Hall, TG had "A rain of meteors only tide and fuel / Where welled the ceaseless fire in her head." He alludes to Butler's "consuming fire" as well as Yeats's "Song of Wandering Aengus," in which "a fire was in my head."
54. Poetry Notebook (undated) [1954], Bancroft MSS.
55. Prose Notebook (1972), Bancroft MSS. TG joked to Karl that he "might dedicate" his Fantasy pamphlet "to you instead of to my wife." See TG to Karl Miller, c. summer 1953, Emory MSS.

56. TG published "Apocryphal" and "Excursion" in *Botteghe Oscure* 14 ([Autumn] 1954), 173–75. As with *The London Magazine*, TG used it as a venue for minor poems.

57. Prose Notebook (1972), Bancroft MSS.

58. TG to Karl Miller, 9 January 1954, in *Letters*, 31.

59. TG to Karl Miller, 9 January 1954, in *Letters*, 31.

60. TG kept a photograph of the portrait in his scrapbook. See Scrapbook (1954–1960), Bancroft MSS. Timner's inscription is legible—"To Thom from Jim 10.3.54 ROME"—in another photograph of the painting. See Timner. The artist sometimes signed his early paintings "Jim."

61. TG to Tony White, 10 March 1954, in *Letters*, 35.

62. Prose Notebook (1972), Bancroft MSS.

63. Mike Kitay, interview with the author, 10 October 2018. Their correspondence from this period is lost.

64. Money was also a factor. TG returned from Rome "a bit broke" and requested the remainder of his Harper-Wood grant earlier than planned. See TG to A. G. Lee, 12 April 1954, John's MSS.

65. TG to Karl Miller, 9 January 1954, in *Letters*, 29.

66. TG to Tony White, 10 March 1954, in *Letters*, 34–35.

67. TG to Tony White, 14 May 1954, in *Letters*, 37.

68. TG to Tony White, 10 March 1954, in *Letters*, 34–35.

69. Prose Notebook (1972), Bancroft MSS.

70. TG to Tony White, 10 March 1954, in *Letters*, 34–35.

71. Arthur Guy Lee (1918–2005) was a fellow of St. John's from 1945 until his death. A classicist and poet, he published translations of (among others) Catullus, Cicero, Horace, Ovid, and Virgil.

72. A. G. Lee to TG, 25 November 1953, John's MSS.

73. TG to Donald Hall, 3 November 1953, New Hampshire MSS.

74. "Brief statement of writing interests. (continued)," Hornbake MSS.

75. TG to Donald Hall, 23 February 1954, in *Letters*, 32.

76. TG to Donald Hall, 3 April 1954, New Hampshire MSS.

77. Yvor Winters to TG, 17 March 1954, Bancroft MSS.

78. See *Stanford University Bulletin* 9, no. 27 (12 May 1954), 168–69.

79. Yvor Winters to TG, 17 March 1954, Bancroft MSS.

80. TG to Donald Hall, 14 August 1954, New Hampshire MSS.

81. In subsequent editions, TG reordered the poems so that "The Wound" came first.

82. TG to Karl Miller, 25 September 1953, Emory MSS. The title comes from a nineteenth-century music hall song called "She Was One of the Early Birds." See Sam Leith, "A Writer's Life," *The Daily Telegraph* (12 April 2003), B12.

83. TG to Oscar Mellor, 23 September 1953, Morgan MSS.

84. David Jones, "Cambridge Poetry," *Varsity* (5 June 1954), 8.

85. Anne Ridler, "Two Poets," *The Guardian* (30 July 1954), 4; G. S. Fraser, "Texture and Structure," *The New Statesman and Nation* 48, no. 1221 (31 July 1954), 138.

86. Gordon Wharton, "Plain Speech and Pedantry," *The Times Literary Supplement* 2755 (19 November 1954), 741.

87. Sinfield, "Thom Gunn," 224. TG had thought of "Lofty" as a series and drafted "Lofty in the Showers," a poem about the "daily sensual experience" of communal showers in an army barracks. See "Lofty in the Showers," Hornbake MSS.

88. "My Life Up to Now," *OP*, 173–74.

89. "Lofty in the Palais de Danse," *CP*, 9. Clive Wilmer finds "the speaker's mask" in the poem "hopelessly transparent. Who is the woman no other can compete with if not the speaker's mother?" See Wilmer, "The Self You Choose," *The Times Literary Supplement* 5482 (25 April 2008), 14.

90. "I don't feel very proud about that," TG continued. See Gallagher, "Top Gunn," 59.

91. Jones, "A Transit of Thom," 53.

92. Karl Miller, "Thom Gunn's *Fighting Terms*," *Granta* 57, no. 1147 (8 June 1954), 27–28.

93. In his first year, Mike had achieved a third in the English Prelim. "I cannot help feeling," Walters told him, "that with a real effort next year you should be able to raise your Class." R. N. Walters to Mike Kitay, 16 July 1953, Fitzwilliam MSS.

94. "Reading List," Stanford MSS.

95. Helena Shire, Terminal Report, Easter [1954], Fitzwilliam MSS.

96. W. S. Thatcher, "To Whomsoever It May Concern," 25 June 1954, Fitzwilliam MSS.

97. TG to Helena Mennie Shire, 19 August 1954, Aberdeen MSS.

98. TG to Donald Hall, 14 August 1954, New Hampshire MSS.

99. TG to Mike Kitay, 19 August 1954, in *Letters*, 38–39. "I read it right away," Mike recalled. Mike Kitay, interview with the author, 10 October 2018.

10. STANFORD

1. F. O. Matthiessen, ed., *The Oxford Book of American Verse* (New York: Oxford University Press, 1950), 971. Like Auden, Crane's "you" is genderless, and TG may not have realized at first that Crane was queer.

2. TG did not read *The Letters of Hart Crane: 1916–1932*, ed. Brom Weber (Berkeley: University of California Press, 1952), until 1957.

3. Hart Crane to Grace Hart Crane, 16 November 1924, in *Letters of Hart Crane*, 193.

4. "Storm Lashes City," *The New York Times* (1 September 1954), 20.

5. Poetry Notebook E [1954–57], Hornbake MSS. TG's notes about meeting Dora informed his subsequent poem "First Meeting with a Possible Mother-in-Law" (*CP*, 49).

6. Mike Kitay, interview with the author, 10 October 2018. "This was 1954," he reflected. "Gays were in the closet with the door closed and locked. Being 'out' meant you weren't home." Mike Kitay, "The Way We Were," *The Threepenny Review* 174 (Summer 2023), 25.

7. Prose Notebook (1972), Bancroft MSS.

8. TG to John Lehmann, 21 September 1954, Princeton MSS.

9. *Thom Gunn in Conversation*, 28.

10. TG to Eugene Walter, 18 October 1954, Walter MSS.

11. TG to Donald Hall, 28 September 1954, New Hampshire MSS.

12. TG to Helena Mennie Shire, 11–12 October 1954, in *Letters*, 40.

13. "On a Drying Hill," *SL*, 198. Winters could also fret like a grandmother. "When he gave Thom Gunn the Fellowship," Hall remarked, "Winters called me and said, 'He won't be able to drive, can't afford a car. Will he ride a bicycle? I have a

bicycle.'" See *Donald Hall in Conversation with Ian Hamilton* (London: Between the Lines, 2000), 41.

14. "On a Drying Hill," *SL*, 199–200.
15. Malcolm Bradbury and Angus Wilson founded the first MA program in creative writing at the University of East Anglia in 1970.
16. TG to Mary and Catherine Thomson, 25 February 1955. Private collection.
17. "On a Drying Hill," *SL*, 205.
18. Donald Hall, *Their Ancient Glittering Eyes: Remembering Poets and More Poets* (New York: Ticknor & Fields, 1992), 126.
19. "On a Drying Hill," *SL*, 205.
20. "On a Drying Hill," *SL*, 202.
21. TG to Donald Hall, 20 November 1954, in *Letters*, 42.
22. TG to Karl Miller, 26 November 1954, Emory MSS. This extract is not collected in *Letters* but is quoted in Wilmer, introduction to *NSP*, xxviii.
23. TG to Donald Hall, 28 September 1954, New Hampshire MSS.
24. "On a Drying Hill," *SL*, 207.
25. "An Apprenticeship," 18.
26. TG to Helena Mennie Shire, 11–12 October 1954, in *Letters*, 40–41.
27. Scobie, "Gunn in America," 9.
28. TG to Helena Mennie Shire, 11–12 October 1954, in *Letters*, 41.
29. "You write so well when you simply tell stories and describe," White told him. "I wish you would trust this power rather more." Tony White to TG, 22 September 1955, Bancroft MSS.
30. "St Martin and the Beggar," *CP*, 66.
31. "My Life Up to Now," *OP*, 177.
32. Yvor Winters, *Edwin Arlington Robinson* (Norfolk, CT: New Directions, 1946), 63.
33. For a more detailed account of "Merlin in the Cave" as an exposition of the limits of existentialism, see David Richards, "'Each challenge to the skin': The Significance of the Body in the Poetry of Thom Gunn," PhD dissertation (King's College London, 2004), 51–53.
34. "Merlin in the Cave: He Speculates Without a Book," *CP*, 84.
35. TG to Tony White, 25 November 1955, Tulsa MSS.
36. TG to Tony White, 24 January 1955, in *Letters*, 48. Winters likened its "method" to that of his own poem "John Sutter" and to Baudelaire's "Le Jeu." See Yvor Winters to TG, 21 July 1956, in *The Selected Letters of Yvor Winters*, ed. R. L. Barth (Athens, OH: Swallow Press, 2000), 352.
37. TG had not read the Sartre; rather, he found the image in Iris Murdoch's critical book, *Sartre: Romantic Rationalist* (Cambridge: Bowes & Bowes, 1953), 56. See TG to Tony White, 24 January 1955, in *Letters*, 48.
38. TG to Tony White, 25 November 1955, in *Letters*, 62.
39. "The Corridor," *CP*, 85–86.
40. TG to Robert Conquest, 28 May 1956. Private collection.
41. *Thom Gunn in Conversation*, 30.
42. TG to Donald Hall, 20 November 1954, New Hampshire MSS.
43. TG to John Lehmann, 17 October 1954, Princeton MSS.
44. "On a Drying Hill," *SL*, 200.
45. TG to Helena Mennie Shire, 11–12 October 1954, in *Letters*, 42.

46. TG to Donald Hall, 20 November 1954, in *Letters*, 43.

47. "A Visit from Mr Auden," Hornbake MSS.

48. Untitled prose statement about Yvor Winters, *Per/Se* 3, no. 3 (Fall 1968), 40.

49. TG to Eugene Walter, 1 May 1955, Walter MSS.

50. TG to Karl Miller, 26 November 1954, in *Letters*, 45.

51. Allen Ginsberg called it "maybe the best gay bar in America. It was totally open, bohemian, San Francisco, Viennese; and everybody went there, heterosexual and homosexual." Allen Ginsberg and Allen Young, *Gay Sunshine Interview* (Bolinas, CA: Grey Fox Press, 1974), 33.

52. "Thom Gunn: October 23, 2002," Prager MSS.

53. TG to Tony White, 24 January 1955, in *Letters*, 51.

54. TG to Billy Lux, 23 January 1996, in *Letters*, 596.

55. Wilmer, "Art of Poetry," 171–72.

56. Gayle S. Rubin, "Thinking Sex: Notes for a Radical Theory of the Politics of Sexuality," in Carole S. Vance, ed., *Pleasure and Danger: Exploring Female Sexuality* (Boston: Routledge & Kegan Paul, 1984), 270.

57. For an account of this time, see Nan Almilla Boyd, *Wide-Open Town: A History of Queer San Francisco to 1965* (Berkeley: University of California Press, 2003), 114–47.

58. Wilmer, "Art of Poetry," 159. "[Winters] hated rhetoric and sprawling, generalised feelings—which rather ruled out Whitman," TG reflected. See Scobie, "Gunn in America," 9.

59. TG to Yvor Winters, 16 January 1956, in *Letters*, 67.

60. TG to Donald Hall, 20 November 1954, in *Letters*, 44.

61. TG to Mary and Catherine Thomson, 25 February 1955. Private collection.

62. Ander Gunn to TG, 7 March 1956, Bancroft MSS.

63. Mike Kitay, interview with the author, 10 October 2018.

64. See Gerald Ashford, "On the Aisle," *San Antonio Express* (2 December 1954), 6D.

65. Mike Kitay, interview with August Kleinzahler, undated.

66. TG to Tony White, 24 January 1955, in *Letters*, 50.

67. TG to Karl Miller, 26 November 1954, Emory MSS.

68. See Roger Wood and Mary Clarke, *Shakespeare at the Old Vic* (London: Adam and Charles Black, 1956).

69. TG to Tony White, 24 January 1955, in *Letters*, 50.

70. TG to Tony White, 24 January 1955, in *Letters*, 50–51.

71. *Thom Gunn in Conversation*, 29. Motorcycles as a metaphor for disaffected American youth first came to mainstream attention in 1947 when a racing event in Hollister, California, descended into a thirty-six-hour riot. See "Motorcyclists Put Town in an Uproar," *The New York Times* (7 July 1947), 19.

72. "Man, you gotta Go" was the epigraph for "On the Move" in its first appearance in print: see "On the Move," *Encounter* 5, no. 6 (December 1955), 50. Retained in *SM*, the epigraph was dropped thereafter and is absent from *CP* and *NSP*.

73. "On the Move" was a break from the classical mythology that TG had used for the content and structure of many poems in *FT*. TG seemed to realize the importance of keeping the poem strictly contemporary while writing it: early drafts refer to Perceval and the Knights of the Grail legend. TG also abandoned an idea of

writing "10 poems stealing saints etc from religion for Existentialism." See TG to Tony White, 25 November 1955, in *Letters*, 61.

74. "On the Move," *CP*, 39–40. Later, TG questioned whether "the last line means anything" and found the use of "One" "very stilted." See *Thom Gunn in Conversation*, 29.

75. Wilmer, "Art of Poetry," 154. "I didn't find out till years later that when Shakespeare uses the word *will* it means the penis," TG reflected.

76. "Four Young Poets—IV: Thom Gunn," *Times Educational Supplement* 2150 (3 August 1956), 995.

77. TG to Donald Hall, 18 April 1955, New Hampshire MSS.

78. TG to Mary and Catherine Thomson, 25 February 1955. Private collection.

79. TG to Tony White, 25 November 1955, in *Letters*, 61.

80. TG to Donald Hall, 6 June 1955, New Hampshire MSS.

81. "On a Drying Hill," *SL*, 208.

82. TG to Donald Hall, 6 June 1955, New Hampshire MSS.

83. Wilmer, "Art of Poetry," 159–60. Compare TG's definition of poetry as "memorable speech," which he drew from *The Poet's Tongue*. See "My Suburban Muse," *OP*, 153.

84. Scobie, "Gunn in America," 9.

85. Helen Deutsch and Ted Braun, "Voice of the Poet," *In Other Words* 2, no. 7 (8 May 1981), 8.

86. Wilmer, "Art of Poetry," 172.

87. "To Yvor Winters, 1955," *CP*, 70.

88. Prose Notebook (1972), Bancroft MSS.

11. SAN ANTONIO

1. At Stanford, TG had reviewed Isherwood's novel *The World in the Evening* (1954), a study in repressed homosexuality, finding it "far more serious, far more complex," than his earlier work: "if its local failures are more frequent, its successes are more impressive, because this time we are not just interested, we are involved." See *The London Magazine* 1, no. 9 (October 1954), 85.

2. "Getting Things Right," *SL*, 173. John Lehmann had given TG a letter of introduction to Isherwood; the difference in TG's attitude to Lehmann (compare chapter 9, p. 110) and his immediate attraction to Isherwood's lifestyle is instructive. As to Isherwood's own feelings about Lehmann, a friend of some four decades, he reflected in 1973: "I think, as everybody in London thinks, that he's an ass and that he has almost no talent. But I am fond of him, which is more than most people are." See Christopher Isherwood, *Diaries: Volume Three: Liberation: 1970–1983*, ed. Katherine Bucknell (London: Chatto & Windus, 2012), 393.

3. "Getting Things Right," *SL*, 173. This is somewhat revisionist. At the time, TG found Isherwood "very very charming, but at the same time [a] terribly passive person" and "wondered how much I'd have liked him if I hadn't so loathed the other lit. celebrities I've met, like Auden." See TG to Tony White, mid-August 1955, Tulsa MSS.

4. Christopher Isherwood, *Diaries: Volume One: 1939–1960*, ed. Katherine Bucknell (London: Methuen, 1996), 506.

5. "Getting Things Right," *SL*, 175–76.

6. "Getting Things Right," *SL*, 181.

7. "An Apprenticeship," 18.

8. "Getting Things Right," *SL*, 181, 184.

9. TG to Helena Mennie Shire, 27 December 1955, Aberdeen MSS.

10. "Thom Gunn: October 23, 2002," Prager MSS.

11. Poetry Notebook XIV (December 1973), Bancroft MSS.

12. TG to Ander Gunn, 9 June 1955, in *Letters*, 55. Mike helped him pay the first installments. Faculty salaries at Trinity University in 1955–56 did not exceed thirty-eight hundred dollars. As an instructor, TG would have earned significantly less.

13. TG to Tony White, mid-August 1955, in *Letters*, 59.

14. TG to Tony White, 25 November 1955, in *Letters*, 63.

15. TG to Helena Mennie Shire, 27 December 1955, in *Letters*, 65.

16. Nuwer, "Britain's Expatriate Poet," 74.

17. "New Poet Joins Staff," *San Antonio Light* (2 October 1955), 9A.

18. TG to Donald Hall, 20 September 1955, New Hampshire MSS.

19. Doris Polunsky, "Ode to Mr. Gunn," *The Trinitonian* 54, no. 27 (20 April 1956), 3, Special Collections and Archives, Coates Library, Trinity University, San Antonio, Texas.

20. *Thom Gunn in Conversation*, 28.

21. TG to Tony White, mid-August 1955, in *Letters*, 58.

22. Mike Kitay, interview with the author, 10 October 2018.

23. TG to Tony White, mid-August 1955, in *Letters*, 58–59.

24. TG to Tony White, 25 November 1955, in *Letters*, 60.

25. TG to Tony White, 20 July 1956, in *Letters*, 75. White had worked with Richard Burton at the Old Vic.

26. Mike Kitay, interview with the author, 12 October 2018.

27. "Elvis Presley," *CP*, 57.

28. A. L. Stone, "Crowning King Anchovy: Cold War Gay Visibility in San Antonio's Urban Festival," *Journal of the History of Sexuality* 25, no. 2 (May 2016), 300.

29. Kitay, "The Way We Were," 25.

30. Mike Kitay, interview with the author, 10 October 2018.

31. Prose Notebook (1972), Bancroft MSS.

32. Teeman, "When Beryl Met Thom," WE2.

33. "Anyone aware that I am homosexual is likely to misread the whole poem," TG remarked of "Carnal Knowledge." See "My Life Up to Now: Postscript," *OP*, 188.

34. See Wilmer, "Art of Poetry," 181.

35. TG to Tony White, 21 April 1956, in *Letters*, 69.

36. Poetry Notebook I (c. 1958–1961), Hornbake MSS.

37. TG to Donald Hall, 18 April 1955, New Hampshire MSS. Conversely, in 2000 TG told Alexandra Chang—an artist who wanted to work with TG on a video project in which visual imagery would accompany his poems—that "I am not a poet whose strength is in his imagery" and that his "dependence on image is more superficial" than that of other poets such as Gary Snyder. See Poetry Notebook 15 (February 1997), Bancroft MSS.

38. TG to Donald Hall, 20 November 1954, in *Letters*, 43. TG had Anthony Hartley's article "Poets of the Fifties" in mind, in which Hartley considered TG and

Donald Davie adept in "the handling of words and metre which metaphysical verse requires." See Hartley, "Poets of the Fifties," *The Spectator* 6583 (27 August 1954), 261.

39. Zachary Leader, introduction to Zachary Leader, ed., *The Movement Reconsidered* (Oxford: Oxford University Press, 2009), 2.

40. See J. D. Scott, "In the Movement," *The Spectator* 6588 (1 October 1954), 399–400, in which he summarizes "this new Movement of the Fifties—its metaphysical wit, its glittering intellectuality, its rich Empsonian ambiguities." See also Blake Morrison, *The Movement: English Poetry and Fiction of the 1950s* (London: Methuen, 1980), and Leader, ed., *The Movement Reconsidered.*

41. TG to Karl Miller, 26 November 1954, in *Letters*, 45.

42. TG to Robert Conquest, 11 March 1955, in *Letters*, 53.

43. TG to John Lehmann, 2 March 1955, Texas MSS.

44. Robert Conquest, introduction to Robert Conquest, ed., *New Lines: An Anthology* (London: Macmillan, 1956), xv.

45. TG to Robert Conquest, 24 July 1956. Private collection.

46. Conquest called Hall's work "absolutely first class," but told TG that selection criteria for *New Lines* was "English poets only." See Robert Conquest to TG, 16 February 1956, Bancroft MSS.

47. TG to Donald Hall, 6 June 1955, New Hampshire MSS.

48. Donald Hall to TG, 12 August 1955, Bancroft MSS.

49. TG to Donald Hall, 1 April 1958, New Hampshire MSS.

50. Yvor Winters to TG, 30 January 1956, Bancroft MSS.

51. See TG to Henry Rago, 7 April 1955, Chicago MSS.

52. TG to Tony White, 25 November 1955, in *Letters*, 60.

53. "Lines for a Book," *CP*, 56. The poem alludes to Spender's "My Parents" and "The Truly Great," which begin, respectively, "My parents kept me from children who were rough" and "I think continually of those who were truly great."

54. See Henry Rago to TG, 27 April 1955, Bancroft MSS.

55. TG to Henry Rago, 29 April 1955, Chicago MSS. This likely benefited "On the Move," which TG sent to *Encounter*—where Spender was literary editor—hoping for quick publication around the time "Lines for a Book" appeared in *Poetry.*

56. Kenneth Allott, ed., *The Penguin Book of Contemporary Verse: 1918–60* (London: Penguin, 1962), 373.

57. Scobie, "Gunn in America," 10.

58. TG to John Lehmann, 28 December 1955, Texas MSS.

59. Untitled review of Wallace Stevens, *Collected Poems* (1955), *The London Magazine* 3, no. 4 (April 1956), 81, 83–84.

60. "I'm not that much influenced by Stevens," TG later claimed, but agreed that "Winters was right—WS was the greatest poet of the century." See TG to Douglas Chambers, 21 January 2000, in *Letters*, 648.

61. See TG to Yvor Winters, 16 January 1956, in *Letters*, 67.

62. TG to Tony White, 21 April 1956, in *Letters*, 68.

63. TG to Donald Hall, 20 September 1955, New Hampshire MSS.

64. See Donald Hall to TG, 17 November 1955, Bancroft MSS.

65. TG to Karl Miller, 25 February 1955, Emory MSS. A copy of the *FT* contract can be found in Morgan MSS.

66. TG to Oscar Mellor, 6 March 1956, Morgan MSS.

67. TG to Oscar Mellor, 2 April 1956, Morgan MSS.

68. Fantasy did not collapse at that point but shuttered for good in 1962. See John Cotton, *Oscar Mellor: The Fantasy Press* (Hitchin, UK: Dodman Press, 1977).

69. See Robert Conquest to TG, 16 May 1956, Bancroft MSS.

70. TG to Oscar Mellor, 30 May 1956, Morgan MSS.

71. Charles Monteith to TG, 6 July 1956, Bancroft MSS.

72. TG to Tony White, 20 July 1956, in *Letters*, 74.

73. TG to John Lehmann, 27 April 1956, Texas MSS.

74. Mike Kitay, interview with the author, 10 October 2018. For Mike's full account of the investigation, see "The Way We Were," 25.

75. Jon Randall and Wesley Joost, "Smokin' Gunn," *Goblin Magazine* 8 (1996), 6–7.

76. Mike Kitay, interview with the author, 10 October 2018.

77. TG to Tony White, 27 May 1956, Tulsa MSS.

78. TG to Tony White, c. May 1956, in *Letters*, 71.

79. TG to Sasha Moorsom, 23 June 1956, Churchill MSS.

80. Mike Kitay, interview with the author, 10 October 2018.

81. TG to Tony White, 20 July 1956, in *Letters*, 73.

12. LEATHER

1. TG to Tony White, 12 October 1956, in *Letters*, 77–78.

2. Yvor Winters to TG, 21 July 1956, Bancroft MSS.

3. TG to Robert Conquest, 14–18 October 1956, in *Letters*, 80.

4. TG to Tony White, 12 October 1956, in *Letters*, 78.

5. "Thom Gunn: October 23, 2002," Prager MSS.

6. "The Beaters," *SM*, 36–37. Published as "Canzone: The Flagellants" in Cecil Day Lewis, Kathleen Nott, and Thomas Blackburn, eds., *New Poems 1957* (London: Michael Joseph, 1957), 59–60. Its epigraph—"None but my foe to be my guide"—is from the Scottish ballad "Helen of Kirkconnel," to which TG was likely introduced by Helena Shire.

7. TG to Gregory Woods, 2 October 1982, in *Letters*, 377. TG published "The Beaters" in *SM* but cut it from *CP*. Once, when Oliver Sacks mentioned the poem, TG "seemed embarrassed, and reprimanded me delicately: 'You mustn't confuse the poem with the poet.'" See Oliver Sacks, in Lesser et al., "A Symposium," 7.

8. TG to Robert Conquest, 6 January 1957. Private collection.

9. Prose Notebook (1972), Bancroft MSS. TG made this comment in 1972 in notes for an autobiography, specifically for a chapter about his trip to New York in 1956.

10. TG to Tony White, 12 October 1956, in *Letters*, 78.

11. Mike Kitay, interview with August Kleinzahler, undated.

12. Yvor Winters, "Report on English 201A for Autumn 1956." Private collection.

13. TG to Alice Collings, 7 November 1956. Private collection.

14. TG to Tony White, 12 December 1956, in *Letters*, 82.

15. TG to Robert Conquest, 14–18 October 1956, in *Letters*, 80.

16. See TG to Charles Monteith, 26 December 1956, Faber Archive.

17. "Market at Turk," *CP*, 58; "In Praise of Cities," *CP*, 59–60; "The Allegory of the Wolf Boy," *CP*, 61; "The Beaters," *SM*, 36–37.

18. See "At the street corner, hunched up, / he gestates action" and "bootstraps and

Marine belt, / reminders of the will" in "Market at Turk" (*CP*, 58); "desires hoarded against his will" in "The Allegory of the Wolf Boy" (*CP*, 61); and "I see them careful, choosing limitation" in "The Beaters" (*SM*, 36).

19. Hennessy, *Outside the Lines*, 16.
20. TG to John Lehmann, 30 December 1956, Texas MSS.
21. Kitay, in Lesser et al., "A Symposium," 13.
22. TG to Tony White, 12 December 1956, in *Letters*, 83.
23. See *Stanford University Bulletin* 9, no. 58 (13 May 1956), 293–94.
24. They were "thrilled to meet Aldous," remarked Isherwood. See Isherwood, *Diaries: Volume One*, 688–89.
25. Ander Gunn to TG, 30 December 1957, Bancroft MSS.
26. TG to Donald Hall, 8 August 1957, New Hampshire MSS.
27. TG to Donald Hall, 29 July 1957, in *Letters*, 85.
28. Poetry Notebook H (February 1958), Hornbake MSS.
29. TG to Donald Hall, 29 July 1957, in *Letters*, 85.
30. TG to Tony White, 16 October 1957, Tulsa MSS.
31. "Thom Gunn Writes," *Poetry Book Society Bulletin* 14 (May 1957), 2.
32. TG to Donald Hall, 9 November 1956, New Hampshire MSS.
33. Pierre Corneille, *Cinna: ou, La clémence d'Auguste*, ed. John E. Matzke (Boston: D. C. Heath, 1905), V.3.1697.
34. "Thom Gunn Writes" (1957), 2.
35. "My Life Up to Now," *OP*, 176–77.
36. Robert Conquest, "A Major New Poet?," *The Spectator* 6729 (14 June 1957), 787.
37. Frank Kermode, "The Problem of Pleasure," *Listen* 2, no. 4 (Spring 1958), 17. Kermode's italics.
38. Dannie Abse, "New Poetry," *Time & Tide* 38, no. 32 (10 August 1957), 1000.
39. John Press, "Tough and Tender," *The Sunday Times* (16 June 1957), 8.
40. Anne Ridler, "Verses of the Season," *The Guardian* (5 July 1957), 7.
41. Graham Hough, "Landmarks and Turbulences," *Encounter* 9, no. 5 (November 1957), 86.
42. Writing in 1994, A. Alvarez remarked of "Carnal Knowledge": "This, I thought (and still think), was what the new poetry should sound like." See A. Alvarez, "Marvell and Motorcycles," *The New Yorker* 70, no. 23 (1 August 1994), 77.
43. TG to Donald Hall, 29 July 1957, in *Letters*, 84. Samuel French Morse praised *SM* but felt TG would hereon "struggle to avoid repetition and parody." See Morse, "A Transatlantic View," *Poetry* 92, no. 5 (August 1958), 329.
44. Jerome W. Clinton, "'Separate Tables' Stimulating, Fine," *The Stanford Daily* (25 November 1958), 2.
45. TG to John Lehmann, 27 March 1958, Texas MSS.
46. Mike Kitay, interview with the author, 13 October 2018.
47. Mike Kitay, interview with the author, 10 October 2018.
48. Mike Kitay, interview with the author, 13 October 2018.
49. "Thom Gunn: October 23, 2002," Prager MSS.
50. Email to the author, 14 December 2020. The correspondent asked to remain anonymous.
51. "Cycle Riots Ended at Angels Camp," *San Francisco Chronicle* (3 June 1957), 5.
52. "Black Jackets," *CP*, 109.

53. TG to John Lehmann, 4 December 1957, in *Letters*, 89.
54. Poetry Notebook G (1957–1958), Hornbake MSS.
55. TG to Tony White, 15 December 1957, in *Letters*, 92.
56. Hart Crane to Alfred Stieglitz, 4 July 1923, in *Letters of Hart Crane*, 138. See also Poetry Notebook G (1957–1958), Hornbake MSS.
57. "A Map of the City," *CP*, 103.
58. TG to Tony White, 25–27 February 1959, in *Letters*, 113.
59. Poetry Notebook G (1957–1958), Hornbake MSS.
60. Poetry Notebook H (February 1958), Hornbake MSS. "Malady" recalls TG's use of "malaise" to describe the general feeling of *SM*.
61. "Whenever I thought seriously about it," TG told C. Q. Forester in 2003, "some nasty little war would come up and I wouldn't want to be identified with it." See Forester, "Re-experiencing Thom Gunn," 15.
62. TG to Donald Hall, 29 July 1957, in *Letters*, 85.
63. "My Life Up to Now," *OP*, 185.
64. TG to Donald Hall, 12 May 1958, New Hampshire MSS.
65. TG to Donald Hall, 24 March 1958, New Hampshire MSS. Based in Paris, Obelisk Press published pornography and avant-garde literature, including Henry Miller's *Tropic of Cancer* (1934) and Lawrence Durrell's *The Black Book* (1938).
66. TG to John Lehmann, 27 March 1958, Texas MSS.
67. TG to Tony White, 15 December 1957, in *Letters*, 91.
68. Josephine Miles to TG, 12 November 1957, Bancroft MSS.
69. Josephine Miles to TG, 27 November 1957, Bancroft MSS.
70. TG to Tony White, 15 December 1957, in *Letters*, 91.
71. TG to John Lehmann, 4 December 1957, in *Letters*, 90.
72. TG to Donald Hall, 26 December 1957, New Hampshire MSS.
73. TG to Tony White, 17 July 1958, in *Letters*, 102–103.
74. TG to John Lehmann, 15 July 1958, Texas MSS.
75. TG to Tony White, 20 July 1956, in *Letters*, 75.
76. TG to John Lehmann, 27 March 1958, Texas MSS.
77. TG to Tony White, 26 November 1958, in *Letters*, 106.
78. Prose Notebook (1972), Bancroft MSS.
79. Mike Kitay, interview with August Kleinzahler, undated.

13. BERKELEY

1. TG to Ander Gunn, 20 September 1958. Private collection.
2. TG to Tony White, 26 November 1958, in *Letters*, 106.
3. TG to Ander Gunn, 20 September 1958. Private collection.
4. TG to Donald Hall, 25 September 1958, New Hampshire MSS.
5. TG to August Kleinzahler, 31 October 1996, in *Letters*, 608.
6. Spender gave the prestigious Beckman Lectures; his themes included "Nostalgia for the Past and Hatred for the Present" and "The Myth of Poetry in a World Without Values."
7. TG to Tony White, 25–27 February 1959, in *Letters*, 112–13.
8. TG to John Lehmann, 22 October 1958, Texas MSS.
9. TG to Tony White, 26 November 1958, in *Letters*, 109–10.

10. See Graham Cleverley, "Footlights to Street Lamps," *Picture Post* 74, no. 10 (11 March 1957), 34–35.

11. Miller, *Fathers*, 99.

12. Tony White to TG, 28 October 1956, Bancroft MSS.

13. Tony White to TG, 30 January 1959, Bancroft MSS.

14. "A quarter of a century earlier he might have gone off to fight in the Spanish Civil War," reflected his son, Sam Miller, "but Tony White never found his cause." Miller, *Fathers*, 128. For Sam Miller and Tony White, see chapter 33, p. 417.

15. Tony White to TG, 30 January 1959, Bancroft MSS.

16. John Holmstrom's unpublished autobiography "Whisper It Easily" includes Tony's list of forty trades and professions.

17. "Cambridge in the Fifties," *OP*, 168.

18. "In Santa Maria del Popolo," *CP*, 93–94.

19. Not to be confused with the published "Loot" (*CP*, 127–28), which addresses the same ideas but is not directly about Tony White. For more on the unpublished "Loot," see TG to Tony White, 26 November 1958, in *Letters*, 110–11.

20. "Writing a Poem," *OP*, 152. The "loot" theory corresponds with TG's desire, in a poem, to "convey an experience [and] try to understand it."

21. Poetry Notebook G (1957–1958), Hornbake MSS.

22. "Loot (to Tony White)," King's MSS.

23. Poetry Notebook G (1957–1958), Hornbake MSS.

24. A. Alvarez, "Signs of Poetic Life," *The Observer* (16 June 1957), 19.

25. TG to Tony White, 15 December 1957, in *Letters*, 91.

26. TG to Tony White, 15 December 1957, in *Letters*, 91.

27. TG to Donald Hall, 29 January 1958, New Hampshire MSS.

28. TG to Tony White, c. January 1958, in *Letters*, 94.

29. TG to Tony White, 17 July 1958, in *Letters*, 101.

30. TG to Tony White, 25–27 February 1959, in *Letters*, 114.

31. "Claus von Stauffenberg," *CP*, 111.

32. Claudia Collins et al., "An Interview with Thom Gunn," *Cauldron* (Winter 1969), 14.

33. TG to Robert Conquest, 20 February 1956. Private collection.

34. Alfred Alvarez, "Poetry Chronicle," *Partisan Review* 25, no. 4 (Fall 1958), 604.

35. John Thompson, "A Poetry Chronicle," *Poetry* 95, no. 2 (November 1959), 110.

36. James Dickey, "The Suspect in Poetry or Everyman as Detective," *The Sewanee Review* 68, no. 4 (October–December 1960), 663.

37. TG to A. Alvarez, 19 October 1959, Alvarez MSS.

38. TG to Tony White, 25–27 February 1959, in *Letters*, 113.

39. TG to Donald Hall, 13 January 1960, New Hampshire MSS.

40. TG to Donald Hall, 12 May 1958, New Hampshire MSS.

41. TG to Robert Conquest, 26 May 1958, in *Letters*, 100. TG later revised this opinion: he found Ginsberg's *Collected Poems* (1984) "more exemplary with each succeeding year" ("A Record," *SL*, 115) and asked of Whitman's "defiant admiration of impulse . . . What poet is more generous?" ("Forays Against the Republic: Whitman," *SL*, 20.)

42. TG to Robert Conquest, 27 March 1958. Private collection.

43. Charles Monteith to TG, 18 March 1959, Bancroft MSS.

44. "The Marginal Muse," *The Sunday Times* (22 March 1959), 5.

45. TG to Karl Miller, 31 March 1959, Emory MSS. The *Mail* called him a "husky six-footer." See Paul Tanfield [pseud.], "The £500 Poet," *Daily Mail* (20 March 1959), 20. There is no comparable characterization in the *Express* article, but TG may have been surprised by its reference to his mother, "[who] died 15 years ago." This may have been the first occasion that TG's mother's death was mentioned in an article about his work. See William Hickey [pseud.], "Now Freedom of Movement," *Daily Express* (24 March 1959), 3.

46. TG to Tony White, 25–27 February 1959, in *Letters*, 112.

47. TG to Tony White, 26 November 1958, in *Letters*, 106. See chapter 14, p. 175.

48. TG to Tony White, 25–27 February 1959, in *Letters*, 113.

49. TG to A. Alvarez, 4 April 1960, Add MS 88485, Alvarez MSS.

50. TG to Donald Hall, 22 May 1959, New Hampshire MSS.

51. TG to Tony White, 25–27 February 1959, in *Letters*, 113.

52. "An Inhabitant," *The London Magazine* 7, no. 5 (May 1960), 14–15, uncollected.

53. TG to Mike Kitay, c. 14 April 1961, Stanford MSS. The first "MoP" ("I jump with terror") is *CP*, 101; the second "MoP" ("New face, strange face") is *CP*, 102.

54. Writing "Market at Turk" in 1955, TG "wondered how much I could get away with." See Sinfield, "Thom Gunn," 223.

55. TG to Donald Hall, 25 September 1958, New Hampshire MSS.

56. See TG to Tony White, 20 July 1956, in *Letters*, 74.

57. TG to Tony White, 26 November 1958, in *Letters*, 106.

58. TG to Tony White, 25–27 February 1959, in *Letters*, 112.

59. See Barbara Bladen, "'Six Appeal' a Real Gas at the Troupe," *San Mateo Times* (17 September 1959), 20; and Stanley Eichelbaum, "'Six Appeal' Also Has Laugh Appeal," *San Francisco Examiner* (29 September 1959), 4.

60. Mike Kitay, interview with the author, 12 October 2018.

61. TG to Tony White, 4 February 1959, Tulsa MSS.

62. TG to Donald Hall, 13 January 1960, New Hampshire MSS.

63. TG to John Lehmann, 22 September 1959, Princeton MSS.

64. TG to Donald Hall, 29 July 1957, in *Letters*, 85–86.

65. TG to John Lehmann, 29 April 1959, Texas MSS.

66. TG to Tony White, 6 June 1963, Tulsa MSS.

67. "My Life Up to Now," *OP*, 179. TG did not value his omnibus reviews and did not allow Clive Wilmer to reprint them in *OP*: see chapter 35, p. 457.

68. TG to John Lehmann, 22 September 1959, Princeton MSS.

69. Collins et al., "An Interview," 12.

70. Albert Camus, *The Plague*, trans. Stuart Gilbert (London: Penguin, 1960), 209.

71. TG to Tony White, 4 February 1960, in *Letters*, 118.

72. Jean Bloch-Michel, "Camus: The Lie and the Quarter-Truth," *The Observer* (17 November 1957), 16. TG kept a copy of the interview in his scrapbook. See Scrapbook (1954–1960), Bancroft MSS.

73. TG to Tony White, 15 December 1957, in *Letters*, 90–91.

74. Bloch-Michel, "Camus," 16. TG grapples with these ideas most obviously in "Misanthropos," *CP*, 133–51.

75. "Camus' death breaks me up," TG told White, following Camus's fatal car accident on 4 January 1960. "As you say, he was not to be spared." TG to Tony White, 4 February 1960, in *Letters*, 118.

76. TG to John Lehmann, 9 February 1960, Princeton MSS.
77. TG to Tony White, 4 February 1960, in *Letters*, 116.
78. TG to Irene Worth, c. 9 or 16 January 1960, Boston MSS.
79. TG to Donald Hall, 13 January 1960, New Hampshire MSS.
80. TG to John Lehmann, 9 February 1960, Princeton MSS.

14. INNOCENCE

1. Thomas R. Arp (1932–2015), a Shakespeare specialist, taught at colleges including the University of California, Berkeley, and Southern Methodist University. Edward W. Tayler (1931–2018), known as Ted, was a Shakespeare and Milton scholar who taught at Columbia University from 1960 until his retirement in 1999.
2. Isherwood, *Diaries: Volume One*, 844. When Isherwood's *Diaries* were first published in 1996, TG looked up all the references to himself. "Things wr never as they seemed," he wrote: "the trouble it appeared was always my neglecting Don B, who flew into rages becos he had a crush on me . . . I'd been blaming myself all this time." See Diary (1986–2000), 28 January 1997, Bancroft MSS.
3. TG to Donald Hall, 13 January 1960, New Hampshire MSS. TG included Simpson in his "Young American Poets" supplement: see "Young American Poets 1956," *The London Magazine* 3, no. 8 (August 1956), 21–35. TG also included Edgar Bowers, Donald Hall, Anthony Hecht, Joseph Langland, James Merrill, Robert Pack, and Adrienne Cecile Rich.
4. Randall already knew Mike: she had seen his production of *Separate Tables* in Palo Alto and introduced herself to him afterward.
5. Belle Randall, "Thom and Belle: A Closet Drama" (unpublished manuscript, last modified 2 August 2022), Microsoft Word file.
6. TG to Donald Hall, 13 January 1960, New Hampshire MSS.
7. TG to Tony White, 4 February 1960, in *Letters*, 116.
8. See Tony Tanner, *The Reign of Wonder: Naivety and Reality in American Literature* (Cambridge: Cambridge University Press, 1965). "He's a fucking genius, that one," TG remarked. See TG to Donald Doody, 8 June 1965. Private collection.
9. TG to Clive Wilmer, 9 January 1999, in *Letters*, 641.
10. William Plowden, "Tony Tanner: A Memoir," *King's Parade* (Spring 2006), 7.
11. TG to Tony White, 4 February 1960, in *Letters*, 118.
12. TG to John Haffenden, 28 February 1975, in *Letters*, 314.
13. For Berryman's time at Berkeley, see John Haffenden, *The Life of John Berryman* (London: ARK, 1983), 286–94.
14. TG to John Haffenden, 28 February 1975, in *Letters*, 315.
15. John Berryman, *The Selected Letters of John Berryman*, ed. Philip Coleman and Calista McRae (Cambridge, MA: Belknap Press, 2020), 463, 397.
16. TG to Tony Tanner, 15 August 1960, in *Letters*, 123–24.
17. Diary (1974–1986), 5 November 1974, Bancroft MSS. TG made this remark about Allan Noseworthy. See chapter 23, p. 286.
18. Wilmer, "Art of Poetry," 184–85.
19. Mike Kitay, interview with the author, 13 October 2018.
20. TG to Donald Hall, 13 October 1960, New Hampshire MSS.
21. TG to Tony Tanner, 20 July 1960, in *Letters*, 120.
22. TG to Tony Tanner, 15 August 1960, in *Letters*, 122–23.

23. Poetry Notebook I (c. 1958–1961), Hornbake MSS. TG later called Tony White "heroic & maybe without a center," and asked of John Ambrioso, "What if J is the man without a center?" See Prose Notebook (1972) and Diary (1986–2000), 16–17 October 1999, both Bancroft MSS. For Ambrioso, see chapter 38, p. 497.

24. Poetry Notebook I (c. 1958–1961), Hornbake MSS.

25. "Das Liebesleben," *Encounter* 16, no. 3 (March 1961), 5, uncollected. TG alludes to "Liebestod," literally "love death," from Wagner's *Tristan und Isolde*. See also "The Kiss at Bayreuth," *CP*, 156. Wagner typified the kind of heroism TG had started to leave behind.

26. TG to Tony White, 27 August 1960, Tulsa MSS.

27. TG to Robert Conquest, 10 August 1960. Private collection.

28. TG to Donald Hall, 10 July 1956, New Hampshire MSS.

29. "Vox Humana," *CP*, 87. Tanner thought "Vox Humana" was central to TG's "task of endlessly grasping and naming the purposeless drifting matter which we see— and which we are." See Tony Tanner, "An Armour of Concepts," *Time & Tide* 42, no. 35 (31 August 1961), 1440, and TG to Tony Tanner, 7 October 1961, in *Letters*, 146.

30. Wilmer, "Art of Poetry," 151.

31. See Stefania Michelucci, "Cole Street, San Francisco: A Conversation with Thom Gunn," in *The Poetry of Thom Gunn*, trans. Jill Franks (Jefferson, NC: McFarland, 2009), 170. The interview was conducted in March 1990.

32. Gewanter, "Interview with Thom Gunn," 290. TG found that his rhythms in eight- or nine-syllable lines became "too prosy." See "Syllabics," in Jon Silkin, ed., *The Life of Metrical and Free Verse in Twentieth-Century Poetry* (London: Macmillan, 1997), 375.

33. Hamilton, "Four Conversations," 65.

34. Before battle, Antony demands "one other gaudy night. Call to me / All my sad captains. Fill our bowls once more. / Let's mock the midnight bell." See *Antony and Cleopatra*, III.13.185–87, in *Oxford Shakespeare*, 1024.

35. "My Sad Captains," *CP*, 129.

36. Collins et al., "An Interview," 14.

37. "'Blackie, the Electric Rembrandt,'" *CP*, 118.

38. Collins et al., "An Interview," 14.

39. TG to John Lehmann, 22 August 1960, Princeton MSS.

40. Poems Annotated for Readings 1961–1999, Bancroft MSS.

41. Poetry Notebook I (c. 1958–1961), Hornbake MSS.

42. Poetry Notebook (October 1960), Hornbake MSS. "A House Without Doors" is a possible allusion to Emily Dickinson's "Doom Is the House Without the Door."

43. According to TG, this was the first time he met Hughes. See TG to Elaine Feinstein, 3 August 1999, in *Letters*, 644. See also chapter 8, n55.

44. TG had recently praised Hughes's new book, *Lupercal* (1960), for *Poetry*. "I would very much like to review [it]," TG told its editor, Henry Rago. "He strikes me as the best poet out of England since the war (apart from Larkin, I guess) . . . I think he is still not enough admired, in spite of the prizes he has had." TG to Henry Rago, 21 March 1960, Chicago MSS. In private, TG was more cautious. "I'm awfully afraid that he is on the brink of adopting some half-wit system of personal mythology like Blake or Yeats," he told John Lehmann. "But as he is, he is fine—

there's a beautiful strength about his poetry." TG to John Lehmann, 22 August 1960, Princeton MSS. For TG's review of Hughes, see "Certain Traditions," *Poetry* 97, no. 4 (January 1961), 260–70.

45. TG to Josephine Miles, c. October 1960, Miles MSS.
46. TG to Donald Hall, c. October 1960, New Hampshire MSS.
47. The Berlin Wall was not constructed until August 1961.
48. TG to Tony Tanner, 11 November 1960, in *Letters*, 127.
49. TG to John Lehmann, c. November 1960, in *Letters*, 124.
50. TG to Tony Tanner, 11 November 1960, in *Letters*, 127.
51. TG listed Pension Ansbach, on Ansbacher Strasse, Hotel-Pension Baku, on Fuggerstrasse, and Pension D'Este, on Kurfürstendamm, in his address book. He gave the American Express in Berlin-Dahlem as his correspondence address. See Address Book (1960), Bancroft MSS.
52. See Christopher Isherwood, *Goodbye to Berlin* (1939; reprint, London: Vintage, 1992), 243; see also Isherwood, *Christopher and His Kind* (New York: Avon Books, 1977), 56.
53. For an account of the Kleist Casino in the 1920s, see Robert Beachy, *Gay Berlin: Birthplace of a Modern Identity* (New York: Knopf, 2014), 203–205.
54. TG to John Lehmann, c. November 1960, in *Letters*, 125.
55. Poetry Notebook (2 May 1963), Hornbake MSS. For the photograph of Stötzner, see Scrapbook (1960–1967), Bancroft MSS.
56. TG to Tony Tanner, 11 November 1960, in *Letters*, 127.
57. TG, "Meeting the Merrills in Berlin," enc. to Langdon Hammer, c. November 2002, quoted in Hammer, *James Merrill: Life and Art* (New York: Knopf, 2015), 286–87.
58. James Merrill to John and Anne Hollander, 14 November 1961, in Langdon Hammer and Stephen Yenser, eds., *A Whole World: Letters from James Merrill* (New York: Knopf, 2021), 176.
59. TG to Tony Tanner, 11 November 1960, in *Letters*, 126–27.
60. TG to Tony Tanner, 29 November 1960, in *Letters*, 130.
61. TG to Tony White, 18 November 1960, in *Letters*, 129.
62. Poetry Notebook I (c. 1958–1961), Hornbake MSS. The entry is dated 18 October 1960.
63. TG to Tony Tanner, 29 November 1960, in King's MSS.
64. TG to Tony Tanner, 11 November 1960, in *Letters*, 128.
65. TG to Tony White, 18 November 1960, Tulsa MSS. Richard Murphy, a mutual friend, connected "Innocence" with *La Peste* and thought TG dedicated the poem to White "because many of [White's] friends caught in the abstract pestilence found that he acted like Doctor Rieux." See Richard Murphy, "Fierce Games," *The New York Review of Books* 27, no. 4 (20 March 1980), 30.
66. TG to Tony Tanner, 29 November 1960, in *Letters*, 131.
67. TG titled his notes for the poem "The training of an SS man" and referred to him as such in letters to Tanner and White. See Poetry Notebook (October 1960), Hornbake MSS.
68. "Innocence," *CP*, 100.
69. TG to Tony Tanner, 28 November 1960, in *Letters*, 131.
70. TG to Tony White, 8 April 1958, in *Letters*, 97–98. TG discussed Nazism with

almost no one other than White. See chapter 7, p. 84, for what TG called White's "positively Fascist streak."

71. Murphy, "Fierce Games," 30.
72. TG to Tony White, 4 February 1960, in *Letters*, 118. Given TG's own interest in "the will," the title perhaps gave him pause.
73. TG to Tony White, 8 April 1958, in *Letters*, 97–98.
74. "Where did you get yours and mine in England?" See TG to Tony White, 18 November 1960, in *Letters*, 129. Richard Murphy recalled that the "buckle of [White's] leather belt bore the eagle and swastika emblem of the German army whose defeat at Cassino in 1944 had cost Tony's older brother, a poet, his life." Richard Murphy, *The Kick: A Memoir* (London: Granta, 2002), 186.
75. TG kept a photograph of Tiemersma and Kennedy, sharing a motorcycle, in his scrapbook. See Scrapbook (1960–1967), Bancroft MSS.
76. Address Book (1960), Bancroft MSS.
77. TG to Donald Hall, 15 January 1961, New Hampshire MSS. Plath thought TG "very sweet" and "a rare, unaffected & kind young chap." See Sylvia Plath, *The Letters of Sylvia Plath, Volume II: 1956–1963*, ed. Peter K. Steinberg and Karen V. Kukil (London: Faber, 2018), 569.
78. R. P. McDouall to Charles Monteith, 3 January 1961, Faber Archive.
79. Charles Monteith to R. P. McDouall, 4 January 1961, Faber Archive. Monteith also blamed Hughes, who "arrived so late that the opportunity for quick action was lost."
80. Poetry Notebook (December 1960), Hornbake MSS.
81. TG to Donald Hall, c. October 1960, New Hampshire MSS.
82. TG to Christopher Isherwood, 11 December 1961, in *Letters*, 147.
83. TG to Tony White, 1 March 1961, Tulsa MSS.

15. SAN FRANCISCO

1. TG to John Lehmann, 23 June 1961, Princeton MSS.
2. TG to Mike Kitay, c. March/April 1961, Stanford MSS.
3. TG to Tony White, 1 March 1961, Tulsa MSS.
4. TG to Mike Kitay, c. February 1961, Stanford MSS.
5. TG to Mike Kitay, c. January/February 1961, Stanford MSS.
6. TG to Tony White, 1 March 1961, Tulsa MSS.
7. Mike Kitay, interview with the author, 15 October 2018.
8. TG to Mike Kitay, 20 March 1961, in *Letters*, 138–39.
9. TG to Mike Kitay, c. spring 1961, Stanford MSS. TG's poem "Driving from Florida" was "not about Don Magner," he claimed, "but becomes me as the masculine principle being smothered by the feminine principle, in my imagination." See TG to Mike Kitay, c. 27 February 1963, in *Letters*, 158; and "Driving to Florida," *The Observer* (31 March 1963), 27, uncollected.
10. TG to Mike Kitay, c. February 1961, Stanford MSS.
11. Mike Kitay, interview with the author, 13 October 2018.
12. TG to Mike Kitay, "Sunday," c. early 1961, Stanford MSS.
13. TG to Mike Kitay, c. February 1961, in *Letters*, 136.
14. TG to Mike Kitay, c. February 1961, in *Letters*, 136–37.
15. TG to Mike Kitay, c. spring 1961, Stanford MSS.
16. TG to Mike Kitay, c. February 1961, Stanford MSS.

17. TG to Mike Kitay, "Sunday," c. early 1961, Stanford MSS.

18. TG to Mike Kitay, c. early 1961, fragment on blue paper, Stanford MSS.

19. Mike Kitay, interview with the author, 19 June 2019.

20. TG to Mike Kitay, c. February 1961, Stanford MSS.

21. TG to Mike Kitay, c. 10 April 1961, Stanford MSS. "All I knew was that I was unhappy," Mike reflected. "Was I ever suicidal? No. Did I say I was because I wanted Thom to know how unhappy? Obviously. Did I want us to break up? No. What did I want? For things to be different . . ." Mike Kitay, email to the author, 29 October 2023.

22. TG to Mike Kitay, c. 10 April 1961, Stanford MSS.

23. TG to Mike Kitay, c. April 1961, Stanford MSS.

24. Prudence Martin, "From Cotillion to Cabaret," *San Francisco Examiner* (22 April 1962), PL-11.

25. TG to Mike Kitay, c. May 1961, Stanford MSS.

26. TG to Mike Kitay, c. February 1961, Stanford MSS.

27. TG to Mike Kitay, c. March/April 1961, Stanford MSS.

28. TG to Mike Kitay, c. February 1961, in *Letters*, 135.

29. Oliver Sacks, *On the Move: A Life* (London: Picador, 2015), 76. Sacks named this book, his second autobiography, after TG's poem.

30. TG to Mike Kitay, 20 March 1961, in *Letters*, 138.

31. Sacks, *On the Move*, 77.

32. TG liked the idea of a motorcycle journal and had sketched out a poem called "Nineteen Entries from a Journal" four years earlier, parts of which included "sadists and masochists," "orgies," and "initiation into the gang." See Poetry Notebook G (1957–1958), Hornbake MSS.

33. TG had in mind "a scathingly satirical piece" Sacks had written about an acquaintance. "It was very unsympathetic toward someone whom Oliver basically liked personally," TG told Lawrence Weschler. "And then he went and showed the guy." See Lawrence Weschler, *And How Are You, Dr. Sacks?* (New York: Farrar, Straus and Giroux, 2019), 43. Weschler interviewed TG in 1982.

34. Weschler, *And How Are You*, 43–44.

35. Chuck Arnett and Bill Tellman, interview with Gayle Rubin, 5 July 1984, Prager MSS.

36. See Jack Fritscher, "Artist Chuck Arnett: His Life/Our Times," in Mark Thompson, ed., *Leatherfolk: Radical Sex, People, Politics, and Practice* (Boston: Alyson Books, 1991), 106–18.

37. "Thom Gunn: July 25, 1996," Prager MSS.

38. Boyd, *Wide-Open Town*, 102.

39. Donald Doody, telephone interview with Edward Guthmann, 19 March 2005.

40. Donald Doody, telephone interview with Edward Guthmann, 19 March 2005.

41. Chuck Arnett and Bill Tellman, interview with Gayle Rubin, 5 July 1984, Prager MSS.

42. Gayle S. Rubin, "Elegy for the Valley of Kings: AIDS and the Leather Community in San Francisco, 1981–1996," in Martin P. Levine, Peter M. Nardi, and John H. Gagnon, eds., *In Changing Times: Gay Men and Lesbians Encounter HIV/AIDS* (Chicago: University of Chicago Press, 1997), 106–107.

43. Paul Welch, "Homosexuality in America," *Life* (26 June 1964), 66–74. When the

Tool Box building was demolished in 1975, the mural on the southern wall stood eerily over the rubble for several years.

44. TG to John Lehmann, 23 June 1961, Princeton MSS.
45. TG to Tony White, 4 August 1961, Tulsa MSS.
46. TG to Tony Tanner, 7 October 1961, in *Letters*, 146.
47. TG to Christopher Isherwood and Don Bachardy, 12 February 1962, Huntington MSS.
48. Stanley Eichelbaum, "Sparkling Peninsula Revue," *San Francisco Examiner* (30 January 1962), 22.
49. "There's a very real Spenderish temptation I feel to remain in the Public Eye," he mused. TG to Donald Hall, 19 February 1961, New Hampshire MSS.
50. TG to Tony White, 4 August 1961, Tulsa MSS.
51. John Simon, "More Brass Than Enduring," *The Hudson Review* 15, no. 3 (Autumn 1962), 463.
52. M. L. Rosenthal, "What Makes a Poet Interesting?," *The New York Times* (24 December 1961), 14.
53. Anthony Thwaite, "Good, Bad and Chaos," *The Spectator* 6949 (1 September 1961), 298.
54. Bernard Bergonzi, "A Mythologising Tendency," *The Guardian* (1 September 1961), 5.
55. Frank Kermode, "Towards Transparency," *New Statesman* 62, no. 1595 (6 October 1961), 479.
56. A. Alvarez, "The Poet of the Black Jackets," *The Observer* (10 September 1961), 24.
57. A. Alvarez, "Four New Poems," *The Observer* (24 September 1961), 28.
58. TG to Robert Conquest, 11 December 1961. Private collection.
59. Donald Davie to TG, 9 December 1964, Bancroft MSS.
60. TG to Charles Gullans, 29 May 1975, UCLA MSS.
61. "From an Asian Tent," *CP*, 172.
62. "My Life Up to Now: Postscript," *OP*, 187–88.
63. TG to Mike Kitay, 20 March 1961, Stanford MSS.
64. TG to Mike Kitay, 15 March 1963, Stanford MSS.
65. TG to Donald Hall, 13 October 1960, New Hampshire MSS.
66. TG to Mary and Catherine Thomson, 14 January 1961, in *Letters*, 134.
67. Tudor Jenkins, "Herbert Gunn—Three Times an Editor," *Evening Standard* (3 March 1962), 3.
68. Ander Gunn to TG, 10 July 1961, Bancroft MSS.
69. TG to Tony Tanner, 7 October 1961, in *Letters*, 147.
70. Ander Gunn to TG, 21 January 1962, Bancroft MSS.
71. Olive Gunn to George Malcolm Thomson, 25 January 1962. Private collection.
72. TG to Mike Kitay, 5 March 1962, Stanford MSS. "Fais molt" is code for "I love you a lot."
73. See TG to Olive Gunn, 12 March 1962, in *Letters*, 149. Bert left TG "the gold cigarette case bearing my initials" and the sum of five hundred pounds. See "The last will and testament of Herbert Smith Gunn," Leeds.
74. See "Herbert Gunn, 57, British Newsman," *The New York Times* (3 March 1962), 21.
75. Mike Kitay, interview with the author, 13 October 2018.
76. TG to Robert Conquest, c. March 1962, in *Letters*, 150.

16. HEPATITIS

1. Prose Notebook (1972), Bancroft MSS.
2. During their quarrels, TG once wrote Mike an eight-page defense of promiscuity, called "Promiscuity, a White Paper." See TG to Mike Kitay, "Friday," c. early 1961, Stanford MSS.
3. Mike Kitay, interview with the author, 13 October 2018.
4. TG to Mike Kitay, c. March 1963, in *Letters*, 159.
5. Poetry Notebook J (5 May 1961), Hornbake MSS. This imagery recurs throughout TG's work: for "firm embrace," see "The Hug" (*CP*, 407) and "At the Barriers" (*CP*, 399–402).
6. Poetry Notebook J (5 May 1961), Hornbake MSS.
7. Prose Notebook (1972), Bancroft MSS.
8. TG to Mike Kitay, c. spring 1963, Stanford MSS.
9. TG to Mike Kitay, 6 May 1963, in *Letters*, 162.
10. TG to Mike Kitay, c. February 1961, Stanford MSS.
11. Donald Doody, telephone interview with Edward Guthmann, 19 March 2005. "I don't let people go, as you know." See TG to Tony Tanner, 3 June 1986, in *Letters*, 423; and chapter 30, p. 385.
12. TG to Donald Hall, 3 October 1962, New Hampshire MSS.
13. TG to Tony White, 27 November 1962, Tulsa MSS.
14. TG to Herbert Gunn, 30 September 1961, in *Letters*, 145.
15. TG to Oliver Sacks, 26 December 1962, in *Letters*, 152.
16. TG to Donald Hall, 8 December 1962, New Hampshire MSS.
17. TG to Mike Kitay, 6 May 1963, in *Letters*, 162–63.
18. Mike was in Boston, preparing to stage a musical revue called *Five Faces Out* at the Statler Hilton, on Park Square.
19. TG to Mike Kitay, c. 27 February 1963, in *Letters*, 158.
20. TG to Mike Kitay, 28 May 1963, in *Letters*, 164. Once TG left Fell Street, he concluded "any <u>sexual</u> relationship" with Don was "totally out of the question." See "On 1963," in Diary (1962–1966), Bancroft MSS.
21. TG to Mike Kitay, c. March 1963, in *Letters*, 159.
22. TG to Tony White, 7 February 1963, in *Letters*, 153.
23. TG to Mike Kitay, c. 27 February 1963, in *Letters*, 157.
24. TG to Mike Kitay, 28 May 1963, in *Letters*, 163.
25. TG to Mike Kitay, c. early 1963, Stanford MSS.
26. TG to Mike Kitay, c. March 1963, in *Letters*, 159.
27. TG to Mike Kitay, c. early 1963, Stanford MSS.
28. TG to Mike Kitay, c. March 1963, in *Letters*, 159.
29. TG to Mike Kitay, 11 April 1963, in *Letters*, 161.
30. TG to John Lehmann, 6 March 1963, Princeton MSS.
31. TG to Mike Kitay, 6 May 1963, in *Letters*, 162.
32. TG to Mike Kitay, c. 27 February 1963, in *Letters*, 158; and "Tending Bar," *Critical Quarterly* 6, no. 1 (Spring 1964), 33–34, uncollected.
33. Poetry Notebook M (8 March 1963), Hornbake MSS.
34. See Poetry Notebook M (8 March 1963), Hornbake MSS. See also chapter 17, p. 203.
35. "The Doctor's Own Body," *The Observer* (15 December 1963), 25, uncollected.

36. Poetry Notebook J (5 May 1961), Hornbake MSS.
37. Poetry Notebook K (8 January 1963), Hornbake MSS.
38. Poetry Notebook J (5 May 1961), Hornbake MSS. This builds on the idea TG had begun to explore in "In Santa Maria del Popolo" in 1958.
39. TG to Mary and Catherine Thomson, 5 June 1963. Private collection.
40. Diary (1962–1966), 8 June 1963, Bancroft MSS.
41. TG to Mike Kitay, 26 June 1963, Stanford MSS.
42. Diary (1962–1966), 30 June 1963, Bancroft MSS.
43. Diary (1962–1966), 27–28 June 1963, Bancroft MSS.
44. Diary (1962–1966), 3–4 July 1963, Bancroft MSS.
45. TG to Mike Kitay, 19 July 1963, Stanford MSS.
46. TG to Charlotte Gunn, 13 December 1982. Private collection.
47. When Doody met him in 1957, Shaw was writing a play about Antonio de Ulloa, the first Spanish governor of Louisiana.
48. Vincent Bugliosi, *Reclaiming History* (New York: W. W. Norton, 1998), 1347–48.
49. TG to Mike Kitay, 4 August 1963, Stanford MSS.
50. Diary (1962–1966), 4 August 1963, Bancroft MSS.
51. Diary (1962–1966), 22 August 1963, Bancroft MSS.
52. TG to Tony Tanner, 31 August 1963, in *Letters*, 166.
53. TG to John Lehmann, 25 September 1963, Texas MSS.
54. TG to Tony Tanner, 31 July 1961, in *Letters*, 142.
55. Yvor Winters to TG, 26 June 1961, Bancroft MSS.
56. "I haven't had time to work on the article about W. C. Williams," he told Stephen Spender. See TG to Stephen Spender, 27 April 1961, Oxford MSS. For TG's Williams essay, see chapter 17, p. 210.
57. TG to Tony White, 15 September 1963, Tulsa MSS.
58. Diary (1962–1966), 7 September 1963, Bancroft MSS.
59. Diary (1962–1966), 5 November 1963, Bancroft MSS.
60. "On 1963," in Diary (1962–1966), Bancroft MSS.
61. Diary (1962–1966), 10 January 1964, Bancroft MSS.
62. Diary (1962–1966), 30 December 1963, Bancroft MSS.
63. "On 1963," in Diary (1962–1966), Bancroft MSS.
64. Diary (1962–1966), 28 January 1964, Bancroft MSS.
65. "The Vigil of Corpus Christi," *CP*, 170–71.
66. Poetry Notebook VII (May–December 1970), Bancroft MSS.
67. Tony Tanner to TG, 28 October 1963, Bancroft MSS.
68. Poetry Notebook "Libertad" (September 1963), Hornbake MSS.
69. "The Girl of Live Marble," *T*, 51.
70. Poetry Notebook "Libertad" (September 1963), Hornbake MSS.
71. Diary (1962–1966), 5 October 1963, Bancroft MSS.
72. TG to Tony Tanner, 22 October 1963, King's MSS.
73. Tony Tanner to TG, 28 October 1963, Bancroft MSS.
74. TG to Tony Tanner, 23 December 1963, in *Letters*, 167.
75. TG to Tony Tanner, 23 February 1964, King's MSS.
76. TG to Tony Tanner, 23 December 1963, in *Letters*, 167.
77. Diary (1962–1966), 4 March 1964, Bancroft MSS.
78. Diary (1962–1966), 12 March 1964, Bancroft MSS.

79. Diary (1962–1966), 3 April 1964, Bancroft MSS.

80. Diary (1962–1966), 30 May 1964, Bancroft MSS.

81. The Old Spaghetti Factory "looked a little like a used furniture store," recalled Bill Morgan, "with an odd collection of junk and painted chairs of every sort suspended from the ceiling." Bill Morgan, *The Beat Generation in San Francisco: A Literary Tour* (San Francisco: City Lights Books, 2003), 52.

82. Justice, on a yearlong leave of absence from his teaching position at the University of Iowa, attended the Actor's Workshop in San Francisco as a Ford Foundation Fellow in Theater.

83. See John Francis Hunter, *The Gay Insider* (New York: Olympia, 1971), 290.

84. Diary (1962–1966), 25 June 1964, Bancroft MSS.

85. See Wendell C. Stone, *Caffe Cino: The Birthplace of Off-Off-Broadway* (Carbondale: Southern Illinois University Press, 2005), 52.

86. Diary (1962–1966), 29 June 1964, Bancroft MSS.

87. Diary (1962–1966), 4 July 1964, Bancroft MSS.

88. Diary (1962–1966), 5 July 1964, Bancroft MSS.

17. RETURN

1. Diary (1962–1966), 8 July 1964, Bancroft MSS.

2. "My Life Up to Now," *OP*, 180.

3. Diary (1962–1966), 10 July 1964, Bancroft MSS.

4. Diary (1962–1966), 11 July 1964, Bancroft MSS.

5. Diary (1962–1966), 20 July 1964, Bancroft MSS.

6. Diary (1962–1966), 18 September 1964, Bancroft MSS.

7. Diary (1962–1966), 28 September 1964, Bancroft MSS.

8. Diary (1962–1966), 23 July 1964, Bancroft MSS.

9. Mike Kitay, interview with the author, 13 October 2018.

10. TG to Mike Kitay, 19 October 1964, Stanford MSS.

11. Diary (1962–1966), 22 October 1964, Bancroft MSS.

12. Diary (1962–1966), 28 October 1964, Bancroft MSS.

13. White spent a month in Yugoslavia, digging roads as a shock worker, before touring Romania with John Holmstrom. See Roger Gellert [John Holmstrom], "To Ovid with Love," *The Guardian* (27 January 1965), 9.

14. "Talbot Road," *CP*, 380.

15. "My Life Up to Now," *OP*, 180–81.

16. White's translation credits include Claude Faux's *The Young Dogs*, Jacques Lanzmann's *Qui Vive*, and Georges Simenon's *Maigret and the Hundred Gibbets* and *Maigret and the Saturday Caller*.

17. "My Life Up to Now," *OP*, 180.

18. For a full account of the influences behind and the writing of "Misanthropos," see Joshua Weiner, "From Ladd's Hill to Land's End (and Back Again): Narrative, Rhythm, and the Transatlantic Occasions of 'Misanthropos,'" in Weiner, ed., *At the Barriers*, 105–26.

19. "My Life Up to Now," *OP*, 180.

20. TG to Mike Kitay, c. March 1963, Stanford MSS.

21. "Misanthropos," *CP*, 133.

22. "What Hope for Poetry?," *Granta* 68, no. 1229 (19 October 1963), 8.

23. TG to Tony White, 30 December 1963, Tulsa MSS. TG likely had in mind the novels of Philip K. Dick; through the 1960s, he also read many collections of science fiction short stories.
24. Poetry Notebook M (8 March 1963), Hornbake MSS. See Thomas Mann, *The Magic Mountain*, trans. H. T. Lowe-Porter (1927; reprint, New York: Modern Library, 1992), 295.
25. "Misanthropos," *CP*, 141–43.
26. Mann, *Magic Mountain*, 295–96.
27. Poetry Notebook M (8 March 1963), Hornbake MSS.
28. Poetry Notebook "Libertad" (September 1963), Hornbake MSS.
29. "On 1963," in Diary (1962–1966), Bancroft MSS.
30. Poetry Notebook K (8 January 1963), Hornbake MSS.
31. "Misanthropos," *CP*, 138–39.
32. "Misanthropos," *CP*, 151.
33. "Ben Jonson," *OP*, 110. "It was Gunn's misfortune," Wilmer reflects, "that this highly moralistic view of poetry and its purposes was not what most people wanted to hear in the later twentieth century." Wilmer, introduction to *NSP*, xxi.
34. "My Life Up to Now," *OP*, 180.
35. Morrish, "Violence and Energy," 34.
36. "Misanthropos," *Encounter* 25, no. 2 (August 1965), 19–25; collected in *CP*, 133–51.
37. Poetry Notebook R (March–April 1967), Hornbake MSS.
38. Kenneth Martin, "Love Me, Love My Poem," *The Observer* (7 March 1965), 23.
39. TG to Mike Kitay, 11 December 1964, in *Letters*, 175.
40. See Diary (1962–1966), 20 August 1964, Bancroft MSS.
41. See Diary (1962–1966), 2 September 1964, Bancroft MSS.
42. T. S. Eliot to Leon M. Little, 7 August 1964, quoted in Robert Crawford, *Eliot After "The Waste Land"* (New York: Farrar, Straus and Giroux, 2022), 481.
43. TG to Belle Randall, 18–20 March 1965, in *Letters*, 182.
44. See TG to Charles Monteith, 14 January 1965, Faber Archive.
45. Marcia Tanner, interview with the author, 9 October 2018.
46. Marcia Tanner, interview with the author, 9 October 2018.
47. TG to Tony White, 4 May 1964, Tulsa MSS.
48. TG to Mike Kitay, 11 November 1964, Stanford MSS.
49. TG to Mike Kitay, 22 March 1965, Stanford MSS.
50. TG to Mike Kitay, 3 April 1965, Stanford MSS.
51. Marcia Tanner, interview with the author, 9 October 2018.
52. Marcia Tanner, interview with the author, 9 October 2018.
53. TG to Mike Kitay, 30 November 1964, Stanford MSS.
54. Clive Wilmer, interview with the author, 13 December 2018.
55. TG to Donald Hall, 13 January 1965, New Hampshire MSS.
56. TG to Mike Kitay, 8 December 1964, Stanford MSS.
57. TG to Donald Hall, 13 January 1965, New Hampshire MSS. TG perhaps alludes to two related reasons for his "need to be an exile" having "vanished." First, the death of his father; second, the recommendation of the Wolfenden Report (1957) that "homosexual behaviour between consenting adults in private should no longer be a criminal offence." There was widespread support for decriminalization by

1965: a private member's bill was introduced into the House of Commons that year, although the reform was not ultimately made until the enactment of the Sexual Offences Act in 1967.

58. TG to Donald Hall, 13 January 1965, New Hampshire MSS.

59. Martin Green and Tony White, *Guide to London Pubs* (London: Heinemann, 1965), 42. The *Guide* was published after TG returned to America. "I look forward very much to reading it," TG told White. See TG to Tony White, 3 August 1965, Tulsa MSS.

60. Gil Sutherland, email to the author, 14 April 2020. TG's other regular cruising spots included the Biograph Cinema (nicknamed the Biogrope) in Victoria; the underground toilets by Marble Arch and on Westbourne Park Road; and Bolton's, a leather bar close to the Coleherne on Old Brompton Road.

61. Poetry Notebook N (11 January 1965), Hornbake MSS.

62. Diary (1962–1966), 17, 24 October 1964, Bancroft MSS.

63. Diary (1962–1966), 9 January 1965, Bancroft MSS.

64. TG to Mike Kitay, 22 March 1965, Stanford MSS.

65. Poetry Notebook N (11 January 1965), Hornbake MSS.

66. TG to Clive Wilmer, 25 February 1965, in *Letters*, 180. For an extended comparison between TG and Plath, see Paul Giles, "Crossing the Water: Gunn, Plath, and the Poetry of Passage," in *Virtual Americas: Transnational Fictions and the Transatlantic Imaginary* (Durham, NC: Duke University Press, 2002), 182–224. As William Wootten observed, "the connection between one mother who dramatised herself without thought of the dangers, who gassed herself leaving two children behind, and another is not a difficult one to make." See Wootten, *The Alvarez Generation* (Liverpool: Liverpool University Press, 2015), 182. "Ted Hughes left his wife Sylvia and she committed suicide," TG told Mike at the time. "I feel very sorry for him, poor bastard." TG to Mike Kitay, 18–20 February 1963, in *Letters*, 155.

67. TG to Belle Randall, 18–20 March 1965, in *Letters*, 182.

68. TG to Donald Hall, c. spring 1959, New Hampshire MSS.

69. "Excellence and Variety," *The Yale Review* 49, no. 2 (December 1959), 304–305.

70. TG to Donald Hall, c. 18 February 1966, in *Letters*, 190.

71. TG to Tony Tanner, 31 March 1966, in *Letters*, 197.

72. Poetry Notebook N (11 January 1965), Hornbake MSS. TG did not start writing autobiographical essays until the 1970s. See chapter 22, p. 271.

73. Poetry Notebook N (11 January 1965), Hornbake MSS.

74. Diary (1962–1966), 23, 26 February 1965, Bancroft MSS.

75. TG to Mike Kitay, 22 February 1965, Stanford MSS. Lehmann's letter itself is lost.

76. TG to John Lehmann, 25 February 1965, in *Letters*, 179.

77. Poetry Notebook N (11 January 1965), Hornbake MSS.

78. *Collected Later Poems* (London: MacGibbon and Kee, 1965); *Paterson*, vols. 1–5 (London: MacGibbon and Kee, 1964); and *Pictures from Brueghel and Other Poems* (London: MacGibbon and Kee, 1964).

79. "A New World: The Poetry of William Carlos Williams," *OP*, 22.

80. "A New World," *OP*, 35.

81. TG to Mike Kitay, 21 May 1965, Stanford MSS.

82. TG to Tony White, 11 September 1965, Tulsa MSS. Williams had died in March 1963.

83. TG called it the "Anderbook" in his notes; White came up with the name *Positives*.
84. "My Life Up to Now," *OP*, 181.
85. Poetry Notebook N (11 January 1965), Hornbake MSS.
86. Poetry Notebook "Libertad" (September 1963), Hornbake MSS.
87. Poetry Notebook O (September 1965), Hornbake MSS. TG called his contributions "poems or captions." See "My Life Up to Now," *OP*, 181. He also described this verse form as "unrhymed syllabics i.e. virtually free verse." TG to Mike Kitay, 22 February 1965, Stanford MSS. Before *P*, almost all of TG's syllabic poems were rhymed. For an exception, see "The Kiss at Bayreuth," *CP*, 156. In other poems, the rhymes are often faint: see "Berlin in Ruins," *CP*, 157–58.
88. Morrish, "Violence and Energy," 33.
89. Poetry Notebook "Misanthropos" (January 1965), Hornbake MSS.
90. Poetry Notebook "Positives" (c. March 1965), Hornbake MSS.
91. Diary (1962–1966), 1 April 1965, Bancroft MSS.
92. TG to Charles Monteith, 26 August 1965, in *Letters*, 183.
93. TG to Charles Monteith, 5 April 1965, Faber Archive.
94. Diary (1962–1966), 14 May 1965, Bancroft MSS. TG alludes to *Othello* but was slow to admit his own jealousy over Mike's other partners.
95. Poetry Notebook N (11 January 1965), Hornbake MSS.
96. Tony and Marcia married in August 1965, shortly after TG left London. Via Tony White, TG sent them a case of wine as a wedding present after Tanner had told him about a dream in which he was "living temporarily in a house made up of extremely amiable men whom I later realised were queer . . . One of the men was very nice indeed—he gave me 20 bottles of vintage wine!" Quoted in TG to Tony White, 11 September 1965, Tulsa MSS. "I would like it to look flashily magnificent," TG told White, "so choose a good (old) year." TG to Tony White, 15 August 1965.
97. Diary (1962–1966), 12 June 1965, Bancroft MSS.
98. "Talbot Road," *CP*, 384.
99. "My Life Up to Now," *OP*, 180.
100. "Talbot Road," *CP*, 382–83.
101. TG to Mike Kitay, 21 May 1965, Stanford MSS.

18. TOGETHER

1. See Stanley Eichelbaum, "Witty, Stylish 'Funny Side Up,'" *San Francisco Examiner* (20 July 1965), 21.
2. TG to Tony White, 3 August 1965, Tulsa MSS.
3. Diary (1962–1966), 20–21 July 1965, Bancroft MSS.
4. TG to Tony Tanner, 28 August 1965, in *Letters*, 185.
5. Diary (1962–1966), 27 August 1965, Bancroft MSS.
6. TG to Peter Tangen, 11 August 1965, Stanford MSS.
7. TG to Peter Tangen, 11 August 1965, Stanford MSS.
8. TG to Tony White, 3 August 1965, Tulsa MSS.
9. Poetry Notebook O (September 1965), Hornbake MSS.
10. Mike Kitay, interview with the author, 16 October 2018.
11. TG to Tony Tanner, 27 December 1965, in *Letters*, 188.
12. TG to Tony Tanner, 4 October 1965, King's MSS.

13. Quoted in Wendy Lesser, "Thom Gunn's Sense of Movement," *Los Angeles Times Magazine* (14 August 1994), 36.

14. TG to Tony Tanner, 24 December 1965, in *Letters*, 187.

15. Cynthia L. Haven, "'No Giants': An Interview with Thom Gunn," *The Georgia Review* 59, no. 1 (Spring 2005), 121.

16. "Got a tattoo of a panther as a kind of substitute for writing." TG to Robert Conquest, 1 March 1962. Private collection.

17. TG to Tony Tanner, 4 October 1965, King's MSS.

18. TG to Tony Tanner, 24 December 1965, in *Letters*, 187.

19. TG to Tony Tanner, 31 March 1966, in *Letters*, 197.

20. TG to Tony Tanner, 5 March 1966, in *Letters*, 192. See D. H. Lawrence, "The Poetry of the Present" (1919), in Vivian de Sola Pinto and F. Warren Roberts, eds., *D. H. Lawrence: The Complete Poems* (London: Penguin, 1993), 181–86. TG mentions this essay in Wilmer, "Art of Poetry," 165.

21. TG to Tony White, 26 March 1966, in *Letters*, 195.

22. For example, "Snowfall" uses a seven-line stanza: line one has two feet; lines two, three, five, and six have five feet, and lines four and seven have three feet. The rhyme scheme is *abcabcb*. TG also called this "the Lycidas form": see John Haffenden, *Viewpoints: Poets in Conversation* (London: Faber, 1981), 46.

23. TG thought this "scarcely a departure," having borrowed the form from Cavalcanti via Pound. See TG to Tony Tanner, 10 June 1966, in *Letters*, 199.

24. TG recycled "The Colour Machine" (*CP*, 205–206) as a prose poem; another section became "Bravery" (*T*, 16–17), about Arnett's portrait of TG wearing a red leather jacket.

25. "Pierce Street," *CP*, 177–78. Robert Prager claimed that the mural was the work of Arnett's partner, Bill Tellman. See Prager to Martin Meeker, 2 September 2006, ONE MSS. The photograph shows TG with his friend Tom Medcalf, a photographer and model at Andy Warhol's Factory.

26. Compare "fulness" in "The Vigil of Corpus Christi" (*CP*, 171); and "Talbot Road" (*CP*, 384): "The mind / is an impermanent place, isn't it, / but it looks to permanence."

27. TG to Tony Tanner, 31 March 1966, in *Letters*, 197.

28. Tony Tanner to TG, 18 July 1966, Bancroft MSS.

29. TG to Tony Tanner, 31 March 1966, in *Letters*, 197.

30. TG to Tony Tanner, 19 December 1966, King's MSS.

31. TG to Donald Hall, 9 July 1969, in *Letters*, 248.

32. TG to Tony Tanner, 31 March 1966, in *Letters*, 197.

33. TG to Donald Hall, c. 18 February 1966, in *Letters*, 191.

34. TG to Tony Tanner, 5 March 1966, in *Letters*, 192–93.

35. TG to Robert Conquest, 6 September 1963. Private collection. Reviewing *Thrones: Cantos 96–109* (1960), TG questioned whether Pound was "partially and indirectly to blame for the modern emphasis on what [I. A.] Richards calls tone . . . In fact, we have reached a stage where the highest (and often the only) recommendation we find on the jacket of a new book of poetry is that 'this poet has a voice of his own.' (The Elizabethans would not even have considered this to be praise.) . . . Whether the voice is a good one, whether it is firm and coherent, whether it ever succeeds in saying anything, does not apparently matter: it merely has to be 'your own.'" See "Voices of Their Own," *The Yale Review* 49, no. 4 (June 1960), 591.

36. TG to Tony Tanner, 10 June 1966, in *Letters*, 200.
37. See Wilmer, introduction to *NSP*, xviii.
38. Kleinzahler and Tranter, "An Interview," 176.
39. TG to Charles Monteith, 28 May 1964, in *Letters*, 172. TG tried to persuade Monteith (unsuccessfully) that Faber should publish Snyder in Britain.
40. "The Early Snyder," *OP*, 37. "The Early Snyder" collects two separate TG essays about Snyder: "Interpenetrating Things," *Agenda* 4, no. 3–4 (Summer 1966), 39–44; and "Waking with Wonder," *The Listener* 79, no. 2036 (April 4, 1968), 432.
41. "Early Snyder," *OP*, 38.
42. "Early Snyder," *OP*, 44.
43. "Early Snyder," *OP*, 42.
44. "Early Snyder," *OP*, 46. Later, TG found Snyder's work overly repetitive: "he's written little else but the Gary Snyder poem since about 1970." See TG to Clive Wilmer, 6 November 1993, in *Letters*, 541.
45. TG to Tony White, 26 March 1966, in *Letters*, 195.
46. TG to Donald Hall, c. 18 February 1966, in *Letters*, 190.
47. TG to Tony Tanner, 12 August 1966, quoted in Wilmer, *NSP*, 224. See also Winters, "The Scansion of Free Verse," in *In Defense of Reason* (London: Routledge & Kegan Paul, 1947), 112–29.
48. "Touch," *CP*, 168.
49. "Small Persistent Difficulties," *SL*, 95. "The World" begins with the lines "I wanted so ably / to reassure you," which TG later echoed in "The Reassurance" (*CP*, 471). For "The World," see *The Collected Poems of Robert Creeley, 1945–1975* (Berkeley: University of California Press, 1982), 328–29.
50. "Touch," *CP*, 169.
51. "Small Persistent Difficulties," *SL*, 94.
52. TG to Tony White, 26 March 1966, in *Letters*, 195.
53. Yvor Winters to TG, 20 October 1966, Bancroft MSS. The criticism recalls Winters's description of TG's early syllabic poems as "melodramatic and journalistic." See Yvor Winters to TG, 26 June 1961, Bancroft MSS.
54. TG to Yvor Winters, 16 December 1966, Winters MSS.
55. Diary (1966–1970), 1–2 June 1966, Bancroft MSS.
56. Diary (1966–1970), 7 June 1966, Bancroft MSS.
57. TG to Donald Hall, c. 18 February 1966, in *Letters*, 189. Probably a reference to Helena Shire's remark that reading the entirety of Shakespeare "adds a cubit to anybody's stature." See chapter 7, p. 79.
58. TG to Ander Gunn, 18 March 1966. Private collection.
59. TG to Donald Hall, c. 18 February 1966, in *Letters*, 189.
60. TG's Rockefeller grant was worth seventy-five hundred dollars and funded his yearlong sabbatical from UC Berkeley. He proposed three projects: to finish his edition of Greville; to work on a critical book about American poetry, provisionally titled "A New World," which would include his essay about William Carlos Williams; and to continue his experiment in combining meter and free verse, to find "a poetry in which both the organized and the improvised rhythm may have a place without conflicting, and of which the province would be both the past and the present." TG saw this "search" as "the crucial one for poets at the moment." See Rockefeller MSS.

61. TG to Tony White, 28 July 1966, Tulsa MSS.
62. Diary (1966–1970), 7 May 1966, Bancroft MSS.
63. TG to Tony White, 26 November 1958, in *Letters*, 110.
64. TG to Tony Tanner, 4 October 1965, King's MSS.
65. Mike Caffee, email to the author, 27 August 2020. For Fransway's burnoose, see "Transients and Residents: Falstaff," *CP*, 374–75. "Jere was a leader of people," recalled Bill Schuessler. "He influenced people to be more druggy, more into [a] free lifestyle and everything. He was a huge man and commanded the scene just when he walked into a room." Bill Schuessler, interview with the author, 29 June 2019.
66. Diary (1966–1970), 12 June 1966, Bancroft MSS.
67. See Diary (1966–1970), 19 June 1966, Bancroft MSS. The Capri was TG's favorite North Beach bar. "It is the only really bisexual bar I have ever known," he told Tanner, "and is very wild and delightful." See TG to Tony Tanner, 13 September 1966, in *Letters*, 206.
68. TG to Tony Tanner, 10 June 1966, in *Letters*, 199.
69. TG to Tony Tanner, c. August 1966, King's MSS.
70. TG to Tony Tanner, 13 September 1966, in *Letters*, 206.
71. Diary (1966–1970), 20 August 1966, Bancroft MSS.
72. TG to Tony Tanner, 27 October 1966, in *Letters*, 209.
73. TG to Tony White, 22 November 1966, Tulsa MSS. TG recorded the dates of his LSD trips. After tripping with Don Doody on 15 September 1966, he did not take acid again until 26 October 1968, at the Renaissance Pleasure Fair in San Rafael.
74. TG to Tony Tanner, 9 November 1966, King's MSS.
75. Diary (1966–1970), 16 November 1966, Bancroft MSS. Bryan Condon, Don's roommate at Fell Street, did not commit suicide. He later moved to New Zealand with his lover, David Fitchew.
76. TG to Ander Gunn, 18 October 1966. Private collection.
77. James Deraspe (1931–1988), known as James Dimitrius, was a writer, model, and photographer. Originally from Maine, he settled in New York, where he coproduced the gay leather periodical *DAM* with his longtime partner, the artist Greg Maskwa. In 1988, Dimitrius was murdered by a man he had invited to live with him and Maskwa in New York. See Jennifer Sullivan, "Murderer of Former Mexico Man Gets 10–20 Years," *Lewiston (ME) Daily Sun* (26 January 1989), 10.
78. Diary (1966–1970), 14 October 1966, Bancroft MSS. Peter Tangen (1928–2008) was a visual artist and a friend of TG and Mike Kitay. He worked at the Museum of Modern Art in the 1960s and later moved to San Francisco, where he lived for many years in North Beach.
79. See Jerome Taylor, ed., *The N.Y.C. Gay Scene Guide 1969* (New York: Apollo, 1968), 14.
80. Don Bachardy to Christopher Isherwood, 12 October 1966, in *The Animals: Love Letters Between Christopher Isherwood and Don Bachardy*, ed. Katherine Bucknell (London: Chatto & Windus, 2013), 224.
81. Diary (1966–1970), 17 October 1966, Bancroft MSS.
82. TG to Tony Tanner, 27 October 1966, in *Letters*, 208.
83. TG to Ander Gunn, 18 October 1966. Private collection. See p. 583, n46.
84. TG to Tony White, 22 November 1966, Tulsa MSS. Ivan Goncharov's *Oblomov* (1859) was one of TG's mother's favorite novels.

85. TG to Tony Tanner, 19 December 1966, King's MSS.
86. TG to Tony White, 22 November 1966, Tulsa MSS.
87. Poetry Notebook (Summer 1966–February 1967), Hornbake MSS.
88. Diary (1966–1970), 10 January 1967, Bancroft MSS.
89. TG to Ander Gunn, 24 May 1988. Private collection.
90. TG to Thomas Parkinson, 11 February 1967, in *Letters*, 213.

19. ACID

1. Tony Tanner to TG, 11 January 1967, Bancroft MSS.
2. Quoted in TG to Tony White, 28 July 1966, Tulsa MSS. For an account of White's life in Cleggan, see Murphy, *The Kick*, 186–87.
3. Green and White, *Guide to London Pubs*, 74, 105. White knew some villains. Uncredited, he ghostwrote Alfred Hinds's autobiography *Contempt of Court* (1966); Hinds achieved notoriety in the 1950s for his escapes from three different high-security prisons.
4. Diary (1966–1970), 18 March 1967, Bancroft MSS.
5. TG to Tony White, 29 June 1968, Tulsa MSS.
6. "Flooded Meadows," *CP*, 215.
7. TG to Tony Tanner, 3 April 1967, King's MSS.
8. "One of Gunn's most frequent subjects in his poetry is the shape and contingency of excess," wrote W. S. Di Piero, "of the need to find a form to contain personal anarchy." See Di Piero, "Poetry Defined and Self-Defined," *The Sewanee Review* 93, no. 1 (Winter 1985), 146.
9. Haffenden, *Viewpoints*, 48.
10. Diary (1966–1970), 22–27 March 1967, Bancroft MSS. The dreamlike, kaleidoscopic images of "Penny Lane" perhaps made TG think about his LSD hallucinations.
11. TG to Michael Vince, 25 January 2000. Private collection.
12. Haffenden, *Viewpoints*, 47.
13. "From the Wave," *CP*, 198–99.
14. TG to Mike Kitay, 27 April–3 May 1967, in *Letters*, 216.
15. TG to Tony Tanner, 3 April 1967, King's MSS.
16. Diary (1966–1970), 1 April 1967, Bancroft MSS.
17. Diary (1966–1970), 9 April 1967, Bancroft MSS.
18. TG to Mike Kitay, 24 April 1967, Stanford MSS.
19. Diary (1966–1970), 16 April 1967, Bancroft MSS.
20. "My Life Up to Now," *OP*, 181.
21. "FBI Suspect Is Called," *San Francisco Chronicle* (24 March 1967), 9. The article misspelled his name Donald "Dooty." His subpoena made front-page news in New Orleans: see "New Subpenas Issued in JFK Death Inquiry," *The Times-Picayune* (24 March 1967), 1.
22. See Jim Garrison, *On the Trail of the Assassins* (1988; reprint, London: Penguin, 1992), 154–55.
23. TG to Tony Tanner, 3 April 1967, King's MSS.
24. Donald Doody, interview with Jim Garrison and James Alcock, 23 March 1967, Box 5, Folder 2, "Miscellaneous material re assassination. Includes newspaper clippings, photographs, reports, and memoranda," Garrison MSS.

25. "Interview with Donald Doody, 5 April 1967," Box 2, Dymond MSS.
26. Mike Kitay to TG, 21 March 1967, Bancroft MSS.
27. Mike Kitay to TG, 7 April 1967, Bancroft MSS. Many people interviewed as part of the investigation—including Don, David Ferrie, and Clay Shaw—were homosexual.
28. TG to Tony Tanner, 3 August 1972, in *Letters*, 287.
29. Diary (1966–1970), 5 April 1967, Bancroft MSS. "Flooded Meadows," "From the Wave," and "Sunlight" are collected in *CP*. See "North Kent," *The Listener* 79, no. 2030 (22 February 1968), 231, uncollected. "The Moon's Dark" and "Walks Round Silvertown" were abandoned.
30. TG to Mike Kitay, 27 April–3 May 1967, in *Letters*, 214–15.
31. *The Living Poet*, BBC Radio 3, London, 19 December 1968; quoted in Wilmer, *NSP*, 239.
32. "Thom Gunn Writes," *Poetry Book Society Bulletin* 54 (September 1967), 1.
33. TG to Mike Kitay, 27 April–3 May 1967, in *Letters*, 215.
34. "Thom Gunn Writes" (1967), 1.
35. Wilmer, "Art of Poetry," 152. TG did not allow *T* to be reissued, nor did he include it in *CP*. Instead, he included its best poems, alongside others previously uncollected, in a section called "Poems from the 1960s" (*CP*, 153–80).
36. Clive Wilmer, "Clive Wilmer on Thom Gunn," *Granta* 73, no. 1247 (22 April 1967), 20–21. Wilmer thought TG's reputation had "suffered rather unjustly . . . through a failure on the part of his critics to come to terms with the status of the conceptual in his verse."
37. Christopher Isherwood to TG, 9 April [1968], Bancroft MSS.
38. Ian Hamilton, "Dead Ends and Soft Centres," *The Observer* (12 November 1967), 28.
39. TG to Tony Tanner, 3 December 1967, in *Letters*, 224.
40. "Thom Gunn Writes" (1967), 1.
41. TG to Tony Tanner, 14 October 1967, King's MSS.
42. Diary (1966–1970), 9 July 1967, Bancroft MSS.
43. TG to Tony White, 15 August 1967, in *Letters*, 219.
44. Diary (1966–1970), 9–11 June 1967, Bancroft MSS.
45. TG to Tony White, 5 January 1968, Tulsa MSS.
46. Diary (1966–1970), 31 July 1967, Bancroft MSS; *Selected Poems of Fulke Greville* (London: Faber, 1968).
47. "Three," *CP*, 196.
48. "Writing a Poem," *OP*, 151–52. TG wrote this short essay for Dannie Abse, ed., *Corgi Modern Poets in Focus* 5 (London: Corgi, 1973), 37–39. Five years later, when Donald Hall asked TG for a "poetics," TG sent him this essay. "It isn't a poetics in the strict sense," TG told Hall, "but it implies one, and is probably the closest I'll ever get to one." See TG to Donald Hall, 3 March 1978, New Hampshire MSS.
49. Poetry Notebook (Summer 1966–February 1967), Hornbake MSS.
50. Diary (1966–1970), 1 August 1967, Bancroft MSS.
51. TG to Tony White, 15 August 1967, in *Letters*, 218.
52. TG to Tony Tanner, 14 October 1967, King's MSS.
53. TG to Tony Tanner, 3 January 1968, King's MSS. TG was fifteen when his mother killed herself.
54. TG to Tony Tanner, 28 October 1967, in *Letters*, 221.

55. Yvor Winters, *Forms of Discovery* (Chicago: Alan Swallow, 1967), 345. TG found Winters's discussion of his poems "very perceptive" and had "no complaints." See TG to Tony Tanner, 28 October 1967, in *Letters*, 221.

56. TG to Yvor Winters, c. October–November 1967, Winters MSS.

57. TG to Janet Lewis, 30 January 1968, in *Letters*, 228.

58. TG to Tony White, 27 January 1968, in *Letters*, 226.

59. "Wes Trimpi wept," TG remarked. "I felt like Charles Dickens." TG to Tony and Marcia Tanner, 15 February 1968, in *Letters*, 229. Trimpi, a poet and professor at Stanford, had studied under Winters.

60. Diary (1966–1970), 25 August 1967, Bancroft MSS.

61. TG to Tony and Marcia Tanner, 15 February 1968, in *Letters*, 229.

62. "My Life Up to Now," *OP*, 183.

63. TG to Tony Tanner, 21 May 1968, in *Letters*, 230.

64. TG to Tony White, 29 June 1968, Tulsa MSS.

65. TG to Tony Tanner, 21 May 1968, in *Letters*, 231.

66. Mike Caffee, email to the author, 27 August 2020.

67. TG to Tony White, 26 January 1968, in *Letters*, 227.

68. See "Reported 'Mr. LSD,' and Four Others Seized," *Los Angeles Times* (22 December 1967), A2.

69. Diary (1966–1970), 15 January 1968, Bancroft MSS.

70. Mike Caffee, email to the author, 27 August 2020.

71. Gary Owsley to James Scannell, 18 April 1986. Private collection. In a subsequent court case, Gary White's ex-boyfriend, Laurence Bartholomew, testified that "the fashion in which he made this money [i.e., to purchase 400 Clayton] strongly suggested the winding up of a drug processing operation." Brief for Appellant at 3, *Bartholomew v. Doody and Talley* (A040877) in the Court of Appeals for the State of California, 1987.

72. Mike Kitay, interview with the author, 16 October 2018. Later, Mike received "a new pair of blue leather pants" for his fortieth birthday. "And very nice they look, too," he told Tony White, "provided I don't eat." Mike Kitay to Tony White, 23 May 1971, Tulsa MSS.

73. Diary (1966–1970), 29 September 1968, Bancroft MSS.

74. TG to Tony Tanner, 30 September 1968, in *Letters*, 233.

75. Mike Kitay, interview with the author, 16 October 2018.

76. Diary (1966–1970), 10 September 1968, Bancroft MSS.

77. Poetry Notebook I (September–November 1968), Bancroft MSS.

78. TG to Tony White, 5 January 1968, Tulsa MSS. The title comes from *The Epic of Gilgamesh*, which TG read in October 1967. Drafts of the poem use a quotation from *Gilgamesh* as an epigraph: "There was the garden of the gods; all round him stood bushes bearing gems." See N. K. Sandars, ed., *The Epic of Gilgamesh* (Harmondsworth, UK: Penguin, 1972), 100. Compare TG's suggestion that some people "think green, blue, and crimson gems / Hang from the vines and briars here" in "The Garden of the Gods," *CP*, 213.

79. "The Garden of the Gods," *CP*, 214.

80. Diary (1966–1970), 28 February 1968, Bancroft MSS. "There was a long poem of his, all of his poems are long," TG told Henri Coulette, "and there was something about horns growing out of his head, and I thought it was a lovely image and I

connected that in my mind with the Doors album which was still quite new at that time." See Henri Coulette, *The Unstrung Lyre: Interviews with Fourteen Poets* (Washington, DC: National Endowment for the Arts, [1971]), C-22. TG had in mind the Doors' song "The End," which alludes to Oedipal desire: see *NSP*, 233. The long Ferlinghetti poem was perhaps "Dog," in which "the great gramaphone / of puzzling existence / with its wondrous hollow horn / [. . .] always seems / just about to spout forth / some Victorious answer / to everything." See Lawrence Ferlinghetti, *A Coney Island of the Mind* (New York: New Directions, 1958), 68.

81. TG's Los Angeles notes are lost. A draft of "Rites of Passage" does not appear in TG's notebooks until c. September 1968, when it is almost finished. See Poetry Notebook I (September–November 1968), Bancroft MSS.

82. Compare the similar transformation in "The Allegory of the Wolf Boy," *CP*, 61.

83. "Rites of Passage," *CP*, 185.

84. Coulette, *Unstrung Lyre*, C-12. Compare "clean exception to the natural laws, / Only to instinct and the moon being bound," in "The Allegory of the Wolf Boy," *CP*, 61.

85. Coulette, *Unstrung Lyre*, C-12.

86. Coulette, *Unstrung Lyre*, C-16.

87. Coulette, *Unstrung Lyre*, C-18–C-19. Compare TG on the muse as a mother, chapter 23, p. 290.

88. Coulette, *Unstrung Lyre*, C-15.

89. Coulette, *Unstrung Lyre*, C-11.

90. Breindel, "Top Gunn," 22. TG made the remark in connection with gay liberation, but the principle can also be applied to how acid altered TG's perceptions more generally, including his attempt to live without alibis.

91. Paul Mariah sounded TG out about taking over the workshop when Duncan stepped down, but TG thought the "difference" in their approaches "would be such that it would cause resentments." See TG to Paul Mariah, 25 October 1968, Mariah MSS.

92. Diary (1966–1970), 14 September 1968, Bancroft MSS.

93. TG to Tony Tanner, 30 September 1968, in *Letters*, 234.

94. Wilmer, "Art of Poetry," 171.

95. Wilmer, "Art of Poetry," 171.

96. Wilmer, "Art of Poetry," 173–74.

97. Wilmer, "Art of Poetry," 175.

98. "My Life Up to Now," *OP*, 183.

99. Diary (1966–1970), 26 October 1968, Bancroft MSS. Literally, "the sound of the horn, in the evening, deep in the woods": see Alfred de Vigny's poem "Le Cor" ["The Horn"] (1826).

100. TG to Tony White, 12 November 1968, Tulsa MSS. "The Fair in the Woods" (*CP*, 209–210) is dedicated to Jere Fransway.

101. TG to Tony Tanner, 9 December 1968, King's MSS. "By 1968 taking the drug was no longer an unusual experience," he later reflected; "probably hundreds of thousands had had at least one experience with it." See "My Life Up to Now," *OP*, 182.

102. The only free verse acid poem TG liked was Allen Ginsberg's "Wales Visitation," which he thought "much better" than "The Fair in the Woods." See TG to Tony Tanner, 9 December 1968, King's MSS.

103. "My Life Up to Now," *OP*, 182.

20. THE STUD

1. "Thom Gunn: July 25, 1996," Prager MSS.
2. "Interview of Donald Doody by Robert Prager on 4 October 1996," Prager MSS.
3. "Thom Gunn: July 25, 1996," Prager MSS.
4. "Interview of Donald Doody," Prager MSS.
5. TG to Tony Tanner, 30 September 1968, in *Letters*, 233.
6. "Thom Gunn: July 25, 1996," Prager MSS.
7. "Thom Gunn: July 25, 1996," Prager MSS.
8. Mike Caffee, email to the author, 9 July 2022.
9. Mike Kitay, interview with the author, 19 October 2018.
10. TG to Tony Tanner, 30 September 1968, in *Letters*, 233.
11. "What none of us knew at the time," TG recalled, "was that this was Doody's birthday. It was his way of giving a birthday party for himself." See "Thom Gunn: July 25, 1996," Prager MSS.
12. Tom Wolfe's account of Kesey's adventures, *The Electric Kool-Aid Acid Test*, was first published in August 1968, shortly after Don had taken over the Stud. TG thought it "the best thing written about drugs in California" and identified with Sandy Lehmann-Haupt because he was "a little unstable." See TG to Tony Tanner, 13 January 1969, King's MSS. TG put this identification to Doody. "He said, of me, 'well that speaks volumes' (as it does), and then 'of course I identify with Kesey.' (Which also speaks volumes.)" See TG to Tony Tanner, 11 April 1969, in *Letters*, 246. Doody planned to move to Australia in 1969, "intend[ing] to be the Ken Kesey of Australia," TG wrote, "which I find heroic & beautiful." See Diary (1966–1970), 6 March 1969, Bancroft MSS. Doody's plan failed when he was arrested at the Renaissance Pleasure Fair in September 1969 and pled guilty to amphetamine possession. See "Guilty Plea to Dope Burglary," *Daily Independent Journal* (San Rafael, CA) (27 January 1970), 5.
13. TG to Tony Tanner, 25 December 1968, in *Letters*, 237.
14. "Thom Gunn: July 25, 1996," Prager MSS.
15. Diary (1966–1970), 17 December 1968, Bancroft MSS.
16. Mike Kitay, interview with the author, 19 October 2018.
17. TG to Tony Tanner, 13 January 1969, King's MSS. TG thought *The Brothers Karamazov* "the best novel of all." See TG to Douglas Chambers, 5 October 1992, in *Letters*, 520. Alyosha, its saintly nineteen-year-old hero, is called "an early lover of mankind" and signified for TG a combination of innocence, courtesy, and sympathy. TG also mentions Alyosha in "A Wood near Athens," *BC*, 102–104.
18. "Alyosha is a dealer (AA)," TG wrote in notes for the poem. "The dealer/saint—at his center, the intact untouchable core—he spreads though, giving generously without wasting himself . . . true to his impulses, impulses ruled by standards he made & learnt in 6 months of solitary." See Poetry Notebook II (December 1968–February 1969), Bancroft MSS. Compare the "smiling sexual saint" in "Front Door Man," *BC*, 100–101.
19. Diary (1966–1970), 23 December 1968, Bancroft MSS.
20. Diary (1966–1970), 29 December 1968, Bancroft MSS. Elizabeth Bishop lived in an apartment at 1559 Pacific Avenue, about a fifteen-minute walk from TG and Mike at 975 Filbert. "This note is to say how much I enjoyed having you live over the hill and how sorry I am that you are not coming back," TG wrote when

Bishop moved east to teach at Harvard. See TG to Elizabeth Bishop, 12 September 1970, Vassar MSS.

21. Diary (1966–1970), 30 December 1968, Bancroft MSS.
22. Diary (1966–1970), 31 December 1968, Bancroft MSS.
23. TG to Tony Tanner, 13 January 1969, King's MSS.
24. Diary (1966–1970), 19 January 1969, Bancroft MSS.
25. Diary (1966–1970), 28 January 1969, Bancroft MSS.
26. Diary (1966–1970), 5 January 1969, Bancroft MSS.
27. Diary (1966–1970), 25–26 January 1969, Bancroft MSS.
28. TG to Tony Tanner, 10 February 1969, in *Letters*, 239.
29. Diary (1966–1970), 10 February 1969, Bancroft MSS.
30. Hayward achieved university status in 1972 and was renamed California State University, East Bay, in 2005.
31. TG to Tony White, 9 March 1969, Tulsa MSS.
32. TG to Tony Tanner, 13 January 1969, King's MSS.
33. TG to Tony Tanner, 30 September 1968, in *Letters*, 234. The 1968 Democratic National Convention was marked by a practically unprecedented level of public resistance against the war in Vietnam. City authorities violently quashed protests, with 668 people arrested and hundreds injured.
34. TG to Tony White, 9 March 1969, Tulsa MSS.
35. TG to Tony Tanner, 28 March 1969, King's MSS. TG called Frank Reynolds "the literary Hell's Angel" because of his book: *Freewheelin Frank, Secretary of the Angels, As Told to Michael McClure* (New York: Grove Press, 1967).
36. TG to Tony Tanner, 3 December 1967, in *Letters*, 224. See "Vote Yes on P," *Vector* 3, no. 12 (November 1967), 11.
37. A barrel-shaped blue tablet that contained LSD. See Eugene Landy, *The Underground Dictionary* (New York: Simon & Schuster, 1971), 36; and Hunter S. Thompson, *Fear and Loathing in Las Vegas* (New York: Random House, 1971), 114.
38. TG to Tony Tanner, 13 January 1969, King's MSS. Compare TG's definition of writing as "a stage in the process of my dealing with what happened to me" (see chapter 28, p. 352) and his definition of experience as "carry[ing] the burden of everything you know" (see chapter 22, p. 272).
39. TG to Tony Tanner, 10 February 1969, in *Letters*, 239–40.
40. Diary (1966–1970), 8–9 February 1969, Bancroft MSS.
41. TG to Tony Tanner, 13 January 1969, King's MSS.
42. The loss of a stable identity recalls "Street Song" (*CP*, 207): "Pure acid—it will scrape your brain, / And make it something else again."
43. TG to Tony Tanner, 10 February 1969, in *Letters*, 239.
44. Poetry Notebook III (February–April 1969), Bancroft MSS. See also "Duncan" (*BC*, 3–4), where TG calls poetic inspiration "an unstopping flood."
45. Poetry Notebook III (February–April 1969), Bancroft MSS.
46. Lee Bartlett, *Talking Poetry: Conversations in the Workshop with Contemporary Poets* (Albuquerque: University of New Mexico Press, 1987), 100.
47. Diary (1966–1970), 15 April 1969, Bancroft MSS.
48. TG to Tony Tanner, 19 April 1969, in *Letters*, 246.
49. TG to Tony Tanner, 19 April 1969, in *Letters*, 244.
50. "Being Born," *CP*, 218.

51. "For Signs," *CP*, 188; "The Garden of the Gods," *CP*, 214; "Rites of Passage," *CP*, 185; "Tom-Dobbin," *CP*, 201.

52. Diary (1966–1970), 28 September 1968, Bancroft MSS.

53. "For Signs," *CP*, 188; TG to Tony Tanner, 25 December 1968, in *Letters*, 238.

54. See TG to Tony White, 9 March 1969, Tulsa MSS.

55. "For Signs," *CP*, 188.

56. TG to Tony Tanner, 15 February 1968, in *Letters*, 229. In 1970, TG made a list of dreams he had had or had heard about from others. It includes his recurrent dream about finding his mother's body: "I was tired of finding her body. I had done so in too many other dreams." In that version, TG let someone else find it "and went away. I didn't dream that dream again." See Poetry Notebook VI (February–May 1970), Bancroft MSS.

57. Poetry Notebook II (December 1968–February 1969), Bancroft MSS.

58. TG to Tony Tanner, 13 January 1969, King's MSS.

59. "For Signs," *CP*, 189. TG also reflects on "a cycle of my own"—his sexual attraction to "the unstable / Bright and accident-prone / Homeless"—in "Front Door Man," *BC*, 100–101. See chapter 38, p. 493.

60. TG to Donald Davie, 18 January 1969, Davie MSS.

61. Diary (1966–1970), 16 March 1969, Bancroft MSS.

62. Bill Schuessler, interview with the author, 29 June 2019.

63. Diary (1966–1970), 2 July 1967, Bancroft MSS.

64. Bill Schuessler, interview with the author, 29 June 2019.

65. Diary (1966–1970), 22 March 1969, Bancroft MSS.

66. Mike Kitay, interview with the author, 19 October 2018.

67. Bill Schuessler, interview with the author, 29 June 2019.

68. Mike Kitay, interview with the author, 20 October 2018.

69. TG to Tony White, 28 September 1969, Tulsa MSS.

70. TG to Tony White, 28 September 1969, Tulsa MSS.

71. TG to Donald Hall, 26 March 1969, in *Letters*, 242–43.

72. Jean W. Ross, "CA Interview," in James G. Lesniak, ed., *Contemporary Authors: New Revision Series*, vol. 33 (Detroit: Gale, 1991), 198.

73. TG to Tony Tanner, 25 November 1969, in *Letters*, 253.

74. Diary (1966–1970), 1 November 1969, Bancroft MSS.

75. Diary (1966–1970), 28 October 1969, Bancroft MSS.

76. Diary (1966–1970), 2 November 1969, Bancroft MSS.

77. TG to Donald Hall, 26 November 1969, New Hampshire MSS. Hall later married one of his students, Jane Kenyon, whom he had met at Michigan in spring 1969. See John H. Timmerman, *Jane Kenyon: A Literary Life* (Grand Rapids, MI: William B. Eerdmans, 2002), 19.

78. TG to Tony Tanner, 25 November 1969, in *Letters*, 253.

79. TG to Tony Tanner, 21 May 1968, in *Letters*, 232.

80. Poetry Notebook V (September 1969–February 1970), Bancroft MSS.

81. TG to Tony Tanner, 25 November 1969, in *Letters*, 255.

82. TG to Tony Tanner, 19 January 1970, in *Letters*, 259.

83. Diary (1966–1970), 17 December 1969, Bancroft MSS.

84. TG to Tony Tanner, 25 November 1969, in *Letters*, 255.

85. Poetry Notebook V (September 1969–February 1970), Bancroft MSS.

86. Poetry Notebook VII (May–December 1970), Bancroft MSS.
87. Breindel, "Top Gunn," 23.
88. Pico Iyer, "Thom Gunn and the Pacific Drift," *Isis* 1671 (2 June 1977), 21.
89. TG to Tony and Marcia Tanner, 22 April 1970, in *Letters*, 269.

21. MOLY

1. Diary (1966–1970), 16–17 October 1969, Bancroft MSS.
2. TG to Tony Tanner, 19 January 1970, in *Letters*, 258.
3. Diary (1966–1970), 19, 27 January 1970, Bancroft MSS.
4. TG to Donald Hall, 12 February 1970, New Hampshire MSS. Lippard was away in Spain.
5. Diary (1966–1970), 17 January 1970, Bancroft MSS.
6. TG to Tony Tanner, 10 March 1970, King's MSS.
7. Poetry Notebook V (September 1969–February 1970), Bancroft MSS.
8. TG to Tony and Marcia Tanner, 13 February 1970, in *Letters*, 261–62.
9. Poetry Notebook V (September 1969–February 1970), Bancroft MSS.
10. TG to Tony Tanner, 10 March 1970, King's MSS.
11. Tony Tanner to TG, 4 March 1970, Bancroft MSS. Tanner echoed Wilmer's comment that some of TG's early *M* poems, like "Apartment Cats" and "Sunlight," showed a "loss of energy" and that TG had adopted a "watcher-stance," which seemed to work against his "commitment to the subject." See Clive Wilmer to TG, 4 February 1968, Bancroft MSS.
12. TG to Donald Hall, 12 February 1970, New Hampshire MSS.
13. TG to Tony Tanner, 19 August 1969, King's MSS.
14. Writing in a woman's voice was extremely rare for TG. Another example is "Rita," a minor poem written about a San Francisco sex worker. See "Rita," *Sebastian Quill* 2 (Spring 1971), 12, reprinted in *Songbook* (New York: Albondocani Press, 1973). Compare another minor poem, "The Stylist," which begins: "I am the woman with red-rimmed eyes / drinking and weeping and talking to myself, / thinking I am Jean Rhys in Paris, / mourning a loss, as always." See "The Stylist," *A Just God* 1, no. 1 (November 1982), 91, uncollected.
15. "Phaedra in the Farm House," *CP*, 191.
16. "Dobbin" is a common child's name for a horse. TG likely would not have known that Isherwood adopted the pet name "Dobbin" in love letters to Don Bachardy. See Bucknell, introduction to *The Animals*, ix.
17. Wilmer, "Art of Poetry," 168.
18. "Tom-Dobbin," *CP*, 200–201.
19. Poetry Notebook V (September 1969–February 1970), Bancroft MSS.
20. Poetry Notebook VI (February–May 1970), Bancroft MSS.
21. Poetry Notebook V (September 1969–February 1970), Bancroft MSS.
22. "Tom-Dobbin," *CP*, 201.
23. See "The Flirt" (1978), Bancroft MSS. "Perhaps neither statement is true," TG qualified.
24. "Tom-Dobbin," *CP*, 202.
25. Genesis 2:24, King James Bible (1611).
26. TG to Donald Davie, 18 April 1970, Davie MSS.
27. See TG to Tony and Marcia Tanner, 2 April 1970, in *Letters*, 264.

28. TG to Donald Hall, 12 February 1970, New Hampshire MSS.
29. TG to Tony and Marcia Tanner, 13 February 1970, in *Letters*, 261.
30. John Peck, email to the author, 2 October 2018.
31. TG to Donald Davie, 18 April 1970, Davie MSS.
32. TG revised his Hardy lecture into the essay "Hardy and the Ballads" (*OP*, 77–105).
33. TG to Tony and Marcia Tanner, 2 April 1970, in *Letters*, 263–64.
34. "My Life Up to Now," *OP*, 184.
35. For contemporaneous accounts of these bars, see Hunter, *Gay Insider*, 48–49 (Den), 102–104 (Zoo).
36. TG to Tony and Marcia Tanner, 22 April–3 May 1970, in *Letters*, 268.
37. TG to Tony White, 18 April 1970, Tulsa MSS.
38. "My Life Up to Now," *OP*, 184.
39. Diary (1966–1970), 5 May 1970, Bancroft MSS.
40. "My Life Up to Now," *OP*, 184.
41. Special thanks to Richard Kaye for bringing this to my attention. See Douglas Robinson, "Townhouse Razed by Blast and Fire; Man's Body Found," *The New York Times* (7 March 1970), 1.
42. "My Life Up to Now," *OP*, 184.
43. TG to Donald Davie, 18 April 1970, Davie MSS.
44. An echo of "Street Song," in which the drug dealer Midday Mick is "too young to grow a beard" (*CP*, 207).
45. "Moly," *CP*, 186.
46. TG to Tony and Marcia Tanner, 22 April–3 May 1970, in *Letters*, 268.
47. Sarver, "Thom Gunn," 16.
48. TG to Tony and Marcia Tanner, 22 April–3 May 1970, in *Letters*, 268.
49. Poetry Notebook V (September 1969–February 1970), Bancroft MSS.
50. Diary (1966–1970), 25 May 1970, Bancroft MSS.
51. TG to Belle Randall, 15 June 1970, Randall MSS.
52. TG to Donald Davie, 1 May 1970, in *Letters*, 270.
53. Diary (1966–1970), 24–25 June 1970, Bancroft MSS.
54. Diary (1966–1970), 26 June 1970, Bancroft MSS. The Queen Elizabeth Hall had opened in March 1967 as part of London's Southbank Centre.
55. TG to Tony Tanner, 31 December 1971, in *Letters*, 284.
56. Robert Tait, "Evening of Poetry Drew 900," *The Scotsman* (29 June 1970), 4. TG pasted this review into his scrapbook. See Scrapbook (1967–1977), Bancroft MSS.
57. Charles Osborne, *W. H. Auden: The Life of a Poet* (London: Macmillan, 1982), 322. For Osborne's diary of the 1970 Poetry International Festival, see "A Rhyme of Poets," *The Sunday Times* (5 July 1970), 27.
58. Angus McGill, "Nobody Heckled Lord Tennyson," *Evening Standard* (25 June 1970), 23. McGill and TG's stepfather, Ronald Hyde, were colleagues at the *Standard* from 1957 onward.
59. Diary (1966–1970), 29 June 1970, Bancroft MSS.
60. Green and White, *Guide to London Pubs*, 34.
61. Diary (1966–1970), 3 July 1970, Bancroft MSS. For example: "End of eve— John . . . young, handsome, great body, long blond hair, long cock—we do acid

(twice), nameless wildness, get to sleep at 5." Diary (1986–2000), 6 November 1993, Bancroft MSS.

62. Diary (1966–1970), 14 August 1970, Bancroft MSS.
63. Charlotte Gunn, interview with the author, 29 November 2018.
64. TG to Tony White, 8 October 1970, Tulsa MSS.
65. TG to Tony Tanner, 4 November 1970, King's MSS.
66. "My Life Up to Now," *OP*, 184.
67. TG to Tony Tanner, 19 January 1970, in *Letters*, 259.
68. See "Let It Bleed," *Rolling Stone* 50 (30 January 1970), 16.
69. Diary (1966–1970), 24 August, 8 September 1970, Bancroft MSS.
70. TG to Tony White, 8 October 1970, Tulsa MSS. TG never finished the novel: a draft of some early chapters can be found in Bancroft MSS.
71. Poetry Notebook VII (May–December 1970), Bancroft MSS.
72. TG to Tony Tanner, 15 December 1970, King's MSS.
73. TG to Tony Tanner, 10 January 1971, King's MSS.
74. TG to Tony Tanner, 15 December 1970, King's MSS.
75. TG to Tony Tanner, 10 January 1971, in *Letters*, 272–73.
76. Poetry Notebook VIII (December 1970–March 1971), Bancroft MSS.
77. "My Life Up to Now," *OP*, 184.
78. Poetry Notebook VIII (December 1970–March 1971), Bancroft MSS.
79. TG to Tony Tanner, 10 January 1971, in *Letters*, 273. MDA is not the same drug as MDMA: while both are hallucinogens, stimulants, and amphetamines, MDA tends to enhance empathy and affection (hence "love drug") whereas MDMA (ecstasy/molly) causes increased euphoria and energy.
80. Poetry Notebook VIII (December 1970–March 1971), Bancroft MSS.
81. See also "Tom-Dobbin," where Tom "plunges into orgy" (*CP*, 201); and "The Feel of Hands," in which the hands "plunge together in a full / formed single fury" (*CP*, 120).
82. "The Plunge," *CP*, 253.
83. Poetry Notebook XI (August 1972), Bancroft MSS. In *Mandrakes* (London: Rainbow Press, 1974), "The Plunge" begins with the lines "A pure / bold plunge into," which TG cut from the version included in *JSC*.
84. Poetry Notebook XI (August 1972), Bancroft MSS.
85. Poetry Notebook VIII (December 1970–March 1971), Bancroft MSS.
86. TG to Tony Tanner, 15 December 1970, King's MSS.
87. Alan Brownjohn, "Gunn & Sun," *New Statesman* 81, no. 2087 (19 March 1971), 393.
88. Michael Fried, "Approximations," *The Review* 25 (Spring 1971), 60.
89. Ian Hamilton, "Soul Expanding Potions," *The Observer* (4 April 1971), 36.
90. Donald Davie, "The Rhetoric of Emotion," *The Times Literary Supplement* 3682 (29 September 1972), 1142.
91. Clive Wilmer, "Clive Wilmer on New Poetry," *The Spectator* 7457 (29 May 1971), 743–44.
92. TG to Clive Wilmer, c. August 1971, Wilmer MSS.
93. Reviewing Taylor's debut collection, *Florida East Coast Champion* (1972), TG called him "the best poet to turn up in the last fifteen years." See "New Lineaments," *OP*, 137. Taylor subsequently disappeared, resurfacing years later as a rock

singer and screenwriter. TG addressed "Night Taxi" (*CP*, 386–88) to "Rod Taylor, wherever he is."

94. Diary (1970–1974), 22 March 1971, Bancroft MSS.
95. Tony Tanner to TG, 11 May 1970, Bancroft MSS.
96. Diary (1970–1974), 25 March 1971, Bancroft MSS.
97. TG to Tony White, 23 May 1971, Tulsa MSS.
98. Mike Kitay, interview with the author, 20 October 2018.
99. Marcia Tanner, interview with the author, 9 October 2018.
100. TG to Tony White, 23 May 1971, Tulsa MSS. TG wrote Tanner some four or five letters a year between 1971 and 1977, but it is difficult to say for certain whether Tanner answered them. Tanner seems to have kept most if not all of TG's letters, whereas TG did not typically keep all his correspondence from anyone. After Tanner's letter dated 5 August 1971—in which he thanked TG "for writing to me again so quickly and so warmly and encouragingly," a reference to TG's letter dated 24 June 1971—there is a break in Tanner's letters to TG (with the exception of a postcard postmarked 23 June 1972) until 24 February 1977 (see chapter 24, p. 303). See also TG to Tony Tanner, 24 June 1971, King's MSS; and Tony Tanner to TG, 5 August 1971, Bancroft MSS.
101. TG to Tony Tanner, 3 June 1971, in *Letters*, 277.
102. Poetry Notebook VII (May–December 1970), Bancroft MSS.

22. AUTOBIOGRAPHY

1. "John Guggenheim Fund Gives $3.7-Million in Grants to 354," *The New York Times* (12 April 1971), 40.
2. TG to Ander Gunn, 11 January 1971. Private collection.
3. David Talbot, *Season of the Witch: Enchantment, Terror and Deliverance in the City of Love* (New York: Free Press, 2012), 124, 126.
4. Mike Kitay, interview with the author, 19 October 2018.
5. TG to Tony Tanner, 3 June 1971, in *Letters*, 277.
6. Mike Kitay, interview with the author, 19 October 2018.
7. TG to Tony Tanner, 3 June 1971, in *Letters*, 277.
8. TG's tastes were more spartan. "I always felt a little guilty about the stuff in the kitchen and the front room, where I have all the bottles, because it wasn't to Thom's taste," Mike reflected. "But he let me do it, which was very sweet of him." Mike Kitay, interview with the author, 24 June 2019. "It's endless," TG warned during an interview on Cole Street in 2003. See Haven, "No Giants," 104.
9. TG to Tony Tanner, 19 March 1972, King's MSS.
10. Diary (1970–1974), 10 August 1971, Bancroft MSS.
11. TG to Tony Tanner, 16 August 1971, in *Letters*, 278–79.
12. TG to Tony White, 2 August 1971, Tulsa MSS.
13. TG to Tony White, 14 September 1971, Tulsa MSS.
14. TG to Tony Tanner, 27 September 1971, in *Letters*, 282.
15. Diary (1966–1970), 6 October 1967, Bancroft MSS.
16. Marcus Hernandez maintained the column—originally called "Southern Scandals"—until his death in 2009.
17. Diary (1970–1974), 23 October 1971, Bancroft MSS.

18. "Faustus Triumphant," *CP*, 267.
19. Poetry Notebook XIV (December 1973), Bancroft MSS. See "The Idea of Trust," *CP*, 290–91.
20. See *The Organ* IX (July 1971), 21. TG included poems by Belle Randall, Gary Snyder, Rod Taylor, David Ignatow, and Donald Moyer. By the time *The Organ* folded, TG had compiled an August poetry page, which included poems by Robert Duncan and Donald Davie.
21. Diary (1970–1974), 3 December 1971, Bancroft MSS. See also Hunter, *Gay Insider*, 49–63.
22. Diary (1970–1974), 7 December 1971, Bancroft MSS.
23. Poetry Notebook IX (March 1971), Bancroft MSS. Compare TG's poem about leather bars, "The Menace" (*CP*, 337–43), and his attempt to subvert the "dreary mythology" of sadomasochism: see chapter 27, p. 338.
24. Diary (1970–1974), 16 December 1971, Bancroft MSS.
25. "'Drug Supermarket' Is Raided in S.F.—5 Held," *San Francisco Chronicle* (30 October 1971), 3.
26. Baron Muller, "Rope Saves 2 in Big Polk Fire," *San Francisco Examiner* (6 December 1971), 1, 4.
27. TG to Tony Tanner, 31 December 1971, in *Letters*, 285.
28. Diary (1970–1974), 5 November 1971, Bancroft MSS.
29. Diary (1970–1974), 20 December 1971, Bancroft MSS.
30. TG to Tony Tanner, 31 December 1971, in *Letters*, 285.
31. TG to Tony Tanner, 31 December 1971, in *Letters*, 285. Dondson and Doody were mutual friends of Clay Shaw. For Dondson's connection with Shaw, and for his small role in Jim Garrison's investigation into the Kennedy assassination, see Donald H. Carpenter, *Man of a Million Fragments: The True Story of Clay Shaw* (Lexington, KY: Carpenter LLC, 2014), 249–50.
32. TG to Tony Tanner, 19 March 1972, King's MSS.
33. Diary (1970–1974), 30 January 1972, Bancroft MSS. TG quotes Robert Hunter, a lyricist for the Grateful Dead.
34. TG to Tony Tanner, 3 August 1972, in *Letters*, 287.
35. TG to Tony White, 5 December 1972, in *Letters*, 292.
36. "American Guilty in LSD Case in Denmark," *Arizona Daily Star* (14 August 1971), A13. Dale subsequently escaped from the Danish prison and returned to California. Two years earlier, when Dale fled San Francisco for London following an arrest for possession, he used Tony White's apartment as a safe house at TG's suggestion. "He is nice, completely trustworthy—a real charmer," TG told White. "Anyway I wouldn't write this letter unless I thought you'd like him!" TG to Tony White, 21 November 1969, Tulsa MSS.
37. TG to Tony White, 29 June 1972, Tulsa MSS. See also Diary (1970–1974), 8 May 1972, Bancroft MSS.
38. TG to Tony Tanner, 3 August 1972, in *Letters*, 289.
39. Poetry Notebook XII (December 1972), Bancroft MSS.
40. TG did not write "As Expected" (*CP*, 335–36) until 1978.
41. TG to Tony Tanner, 16 August 1971, in *Letters*, 279–80. In his review of *M*, Wilmer concluded that its only "significant flaw" was "a kind of hippie sentimen-

talism that creeps into a couple of the poems." See Wilmer, "Clive Wilmer on New Poetry," 744.

42. Jack Fritscher, email to the author, 22 October 2018. See also Fritscher, *Profiles in Gay Courage* (Sebastopol, CA: Palm Drive Publishing, 2022), 157–60.

43. The poem took eighteen months to write. Its first publication, in TG's pamphlet *To the Air* (Boston: David R. Godine, 1974), contains a fifth part called "Discourse from the Deck."

44. "I always felt that doing something for Penguin would mean I was a real author." See TG to Tony White, 29 June 1972, Tulsa MSS.

45. "Ben Jonson," *OP*, 106–107. TG's essay was first published as the introduction to *Ben Jonson: Poems* (Harmondsworth, UK: Penguin, 1974).

46. TG to Tony Tanner, 3 August 1972, in *Letters*, 289. The line recalls Henryson's "Orpheus and Eurydice"—"And on thay went talkand of play and sport"—given TG's allusion to Orpheus's fate in the final poem of "The Geysers."

47. "The Geysers," *CP*, 246.

48. "The Geysers," *CP*, 244.

49. Poetry Notebook X (December 1971), Bancroft MSS.

50. Prose Notebook (1972), Bancroft MSS.

51. "Autobiography," *CP*, 285.

52. Poetry Notebook XI (August 1972), Bancroft MSS.

53. Barbara lived for another seventeen years: she died in December 1989. See chapter 32, p. 412.

54. "Breaking Ground," *CP*, 303–305. Barbara was a keen gardener. On visits to Kent, TG would help her with digging and planting. He appears in the poem as "some nephew."

55. Haffenden, *Viewpoints*, 53.

56. Poetry Notebook XII (December 1972), Bancroft MSS. Compare "branching streams" in "The Geysers," *CP*, 244.

57. Poetry Notebook XIV (December 1973), Bancroft MSS.

58. "Bringing to Light," *CP*, 256.

59. TG to Ander Gunn, 10 February 1973. Private collection.

60. TG to Mary and Catherine Thomson, 14 February 1973. Private collection.

61. "Bringing to Light," *CP*, 257.

62. Poetry Notebook IX (March 1971), Bancroft MSS.

63. TG to Tony White, 5 December 1972, in *Letters*, 292.

64. TG to Tony Tanner, 3 August 1972, in *Letters*, 288.

65. TG to Barbara Godfrey, 21 July 1973. Private collection.

66. Mike Kitay, interview with the author, 21 October 2018.

67. Diary (1970–1974), 2 January 1973, Bancroft MSS.

68. Clyde Wildes, email to the author, 14 July 2022.

69. Quoted in Peter du Sautoy to Morris Philipson, 12 July 1971, Faber Archive.

70. Eric P. Swenson, an editor at W. W. Norton, told Matthew Evans—then Peter du Sautoy's assistant at Faber—that Norton's "poetry experts . . . seem to think that [TG] is on his way down while our other poets, Adrienne Rich and A. R. Ammons, are on their way up." Eric P. Swenson to Matthew Evans, 3 December 1970, Faber Archive.

71. TG to Peter du Sautoy, 18 December 1971, Faber Archive.

72. TG to Matthew Evans, 25 September 1972, Faber Archive.
73. TG to Tony Tanner, 25 September 1973, King's MSS. "Too often, in these new experiments with the Roethkean mode, Gunn's form seems to be at odds with his theme," wrote Marjorie Perloff. "The ecstatic Lawrentian sun-worship, the Roethkean ability to enter the life of the other, are absent." See Perloff, "Roots and Blossoms," *The Washington Post* (16 September 1973), BW6.
74. Duncan received a copy of the British edition from a friend and wrote his poems in the margins of TG's book. They were reprinted in *Manroot* 9 (Fall 1973), 32–38.
75. TG to Michael Davidson, 29 December 1990, in *Letters*, 492.
76. TG to Tony White, 13 September 1973, in *Letters*, 298.
77. Poetry Notebook XIII (June 1973), Bancroft MSS.
78. TG to Oliver Sacks, 2 October 1973, in *Letters*, 300.
79. Poetry Notebook XIV (December 1973), Bancroft MSS.
80. "The Release," *CP*, 301.
81. Poetry Notebook XIV (December 1973), Bancroft MSS.
82. Poetry Notebook XIII (June 1973), Bancroft MSS.
83. In "From the Wave," as Adam Scheffler remarks, "it is easy to imagine the surfers walking up the beach and back to the lives they have outside the poem." See Scheffler, "Thom Gunn's Humane Prisons," *Essays in Criticism* 68, no. 1 (2018), 114.
84. "The Release," *Gay News* 74 (2 July 1975), 12.

23. RELATIONSHIPS

1. Diary (1974–1986), 15 February 1974, Bancroft MSS.
2. Poetry Notebook XIV (December 1973), Bancroft MSS.
3. Diary (1974–1986), 5 March 1974, Bancroft MSS; TG to Ander Gunn, 12 July 1974. Private collection.
4. TG to Mike Kitay, 7 May 1974, Stanford MSS.
5. Diary (1974–1986), 18 April 1974, Bancroft MSS.
6. Diary (1974–1986), 19 April 1974, Bancroft MSS. In 1949, Ruth married Peter Townsend. TG had known him at UCS and they had also overlapped at Cambridge: Townsend studied anthropology at St. John's. For an account of Peter and Ruth's marriage—its importance to Peter's life as a social scientist, and Ruth's often underappreciated contributions to his work—see Chris Renwick, "The Family Life of Peter and Ruth Townsend: Social Science and Methods in 1950s and Early 1960s Britain," *Twentieth Century British History* (31 May 2023), 1–23, doi.org/10.1093/tcbh/hwad040.
7. Diary (1974–1986), 20 April 1974, Bancroft MSS.
8. August Kleinzahler, email to the author, 4 September 2022.
9. "Talbot Road," *CP*, 382.
10. Diary (1974–1986), 22 April 1974, Bancroft MSS.
11. TG read at the Mermaid on 9 June 1974. "The thought of all those people paying to see me made me nervous," he told John Lehmann, "and somehow being nervous made me do my best." See TG to John Lehmann, 18 October 1975, Princeton MSS.
12. TG to Tony and Marcia Tanner, 30 July 1974, in *Letters*, 306.
13. TG to Tony White, 17 July 1974, in *Letters*, 304.
14. Diary (1974–1986), 23 April 1974, Bancroft MSS.

596 NOTES TO PAGES 278-281

15. Diary (1974–1986), 6 May 1974, Bancroft MSS.
16. Diary (1974–1986), 7 May 1974, Bancroft MSS.
17. Diary (1974–1986), 6 June 1974, Bancroft MSS.
18. "Hampstead: the Horse Chestnut Trees," *CP*, 287–88.
19. Diary (1974–1986), 6 June 1974, Bancroft MSS.
20. TG to Mike Kitay, 7 May 1974, Stanford MSS.
21. TG to Mike Kitay, 1 May 1974, Stanford MSS.
22. Diary (1974–1986), 29 May 1974, Bancroft MSS. TG alludes to Plath's poem "Totem."
23. Diary (1974–1986), 31 May 1974, Bancroft MSS.
24. Poetry Notebook IX (March 1971), Bancroft MSS.
25. Poetry Notebook 2 (May 1979), Bancroft MSS. TG first had his hair permed in London in summer 1974. "I got a perm," he told the Tanners, "so I now look like someone who has put his finger in a light-socket." TG to Tony and Marcia Tanner, 30 July 1974, in *Letters*, 306. He maintained it, and by December had "a mass of <u>tight</u> curls. None of that beginner's loose stuff for me," he told Tony White. "I'm doing a real Shirley Temple trip." TG to Tony White, 12 December 1974, in *Letters*, 311. TG kept the style for five years. "I put safflower oil on my hair (brylcreem is too expensive)," he told a friend, "and nobody recognizes me." TG to Joseph Mockus, 18 June 1979. Private collection.
26. TG to Mike Kitay, 7 May 1974, Stanford MSS.
27. See Diary (1974–1986), 9 April 1974, Bancroft MSS.
28. Allan Noseworthy to TG, 26 August 1977, Bancroft MSS.
29. TG to Tony White, 12 December 1974, in *Letters*, 313.
30. Diary (1974–1986), 29–30 June 1974, Bancroft MSS.
31. TG to Tony White, 17 July 1974, Tulsa MSS.
32. TG to Tony and Marcia Tanner, 30 July 1974, in *Letters*, 306. The New York City Council did not pass a homosexual rights bill until 1986. See Joyce Purnick, "Homosexual Rights Bill Is Passed by City Council in 21-to-14 Vote," *The New York Times* (21 March 1986), 1.
33. Poetry Notebook XV (July 1974), Bancroft MSS. Note the repetition of the final line from TG's abandoned poem "A photograph of my brother." See chapter 23, pp. 278–79.
34. "My Life Up to Now," *OP*, 184.
35. Wilmer, "Art of Poetry," 177–78.
36. See "On the Move" (*CP*, 39–40), "Market at Turk" (*CP*, 58), and "The Beaters" (*SM*, 36–37). The same argument applies to several poems from *MSC*, including the two poems called "Modes of Pleasure" (*CP*, 101–102), "The Feel of Hands" (*CP*, 120), and "Rastignac at 45" (*CP*, 122–23). For a discussion of "An Inhabitant"—an overtly queer poem TG chose not to collect in *MSC*—see chapter 13, p. 161.
37. TG to Tony Tanner, 3 August 1972, in *Letters*, 288.
38. Scobie, "Gunn in America," 14–15.
39. "The Goddess," *CP*, 155.
40. Poetry Notebook XV (July 1974), Bancroft MSS. See Gertrude Stein, *The Autobiography of Alice B. Toklas* (1933; reprint, London: Penguin, 1966), 91–92.
41. Poetry Notebook XIV (December 1973), Bancroft MSS.

42. Diary (1974–1986), 21 July 1974, Bancroft MSS.
43. See chapter 2, p. 24: TG describes his father as "cowardly."
44. Poetry Notebook XIV (December 1973), Bancroft MSS.
45. See Poetry Notebook XIV (December 1973), Bancroft MSS. "HSG" and "The Journalist" feature in TG's lists of ideas from this period.
46. "Hampstead: the Horse Chestnut Trees," *CP*, 288.
47. Haffenden, *Viewpoints*, 52.
48. Poetry Notebook XIV (December 1973), Bancroft MSS. Compare "I like the things / That help me if not lose then leave behind, / What else, the self," in "Transients and Residents: Interruption," *CP*, 379.
49. "Behind the Mirror," *CP*, 293.
50. TG likely saw Caravaggio's *Narcissus* (1597–1599) at the National Gallery of Ancient Art in Palazzo Barberini during his visit to Rome in 1954.
51. With "identical twins," TG may have had in mind "another story about Narcissus" in which he had an identical twin sister. "Narcissus loved his sister, and when the girl died he used to haunt the spring," wrote Pausanias, "knowing that what he saw was his own reflection, but finding solace in imagining that he was looking not at his own reflection, but at his sister's likeness." See J. G. Frazer, ed. and trans., *Pausanias's Description of Greece*, vol. 1 (1898; Cambridge: Cambridge University Press, 2012), 483.
52. Poetry Notebook XV (July 1974), Bancroft MSS.
53. Diary (1974–1986), 30 August 1974, Bancroft MSS.
54. Poetry Notebook XIII (June 1973), Bancroft MSS.
55. "So: grotesques, or irrational images rising from trips and dreams. Night-work (isn't that Freud's phrase?)" Poetry Notebook XIII (June 1973), Bancroft MSS. "Jack Straw" is the title of one of TG's favorite Grateful Dead songs. See Wilmer, "Art of Poetry," 176.
56. Scobie, "Gunn in America," 11.
57. Poetry Notebook XV (July 1974), Bancroft MSS. In one outline, TG assigned each poem a particular room.
58. Wilmer, "Art of Poetry," 176.
59. "Jack Straw's Castle," *Manroot* 10 (Late Fall 1974–Winter 1975), 52–54, uncollected.
60. TG to Tony and Marcia Tanner, 30 July 1974, in *Letters*, 307.
61. Poetry Notebook XV (July 1974), Bancroft MSS.
62. Poetry Notebook XIV (December 1973), Bancroft MSS.
63. "Jack Straw's Castle," *CP*, 279. "When do people say that?" TG later remarked: "when they're not very sure of themselves. Richard III says 'Richard's not himself again.'" See Haffenden, *Viewpoints*, 51.
64. Wilmer, "Art of Poetry," 178.
65. Poetry Notebook XV (July 1974), Bancroft MSS.
66. Charles Hovland, telephone interview with the author, 5 April 2022.
67. Compare TG's sale of his old notebooks to the University of Maryland in 1974. "I am homosexual, and the homosexuality is extremely overt in these notebooks," he told the rare book dealer George Bixby, who arranged the sale. "I am certainly not ashamed of being homosexual, but I am an alien & could conceivably be deported

for it if anybody wanted to get me. [. . .] I would like to have them unavailable to the public for 10 years." See "Stuff for Bixby, Descriptive List," c. 1974. Private collection.

68. TG to Pat Strachan, 22 March 1976, FSG MSS.
69. TG to Tony White, 12 December 1974, in *Letters*, 310. TG likely had in mind the global recession, famines in Bangladesh and Ethiopia, various IRA bombings across England and Ireland, and the Cypriot coup d'état.
70. Diary (1974–1986), 22 November 1974, Bancroft MSS.
71. TG to Tony White, 12 December 1974, in *Letters*, 311–12.
72. Diary (1974–1986), 5 November 1974, Bancroft MSS.
73. TG to Barbara Godfrey, 13 August 1975. Private collection.
74. "My Life Up to Now," *OP*, 186.
75. See chapter 33, p. 414.
76. Bartlett, *Talking Poetry*, 98–99.
77. TG to Ander Gunn, 5 January 1975. Private collection.
78. TG to Tony White, 13 February 1975, Tulsa MSS.
79. Diary (1974–1986), 13/14 March 1975, Bancroft MSS.
80. TG and Mike stayed at Tanner's place overnight. "[It was] nice hugging M all night," TG wrote: "He is 44 today." Diary (1974–1986), 21 May 1975, Bancroft MSS. TG had this night in mind when he started writing "The Hug" (*CP*, 407) five years later.
81. Diary (1974–1986), 20 May 1975, Bancroft MSS.
82. Mike Kitay, interview with the author, 19 June 2019.
83. Jack Collins, interview with the author, 20 June 2019.
84. TG to Tony White, 28 June 1975, in *Letters*, 319.
85. Mike Kitay, interview with the author, 19 June 2019.
86. Bill Schuessler, interview with the author, 29 June 2019.
87. Mike Kitay, interview with the author, 21 October 2018.
88. Diary (1974–1986), 1 June 1975, Bancroft MSS.
89. An eight-page draft introduction and a list of poems for "A Choice of Donne" can be found in Bancroft MSS.
90. TG to Charles Monteith, 6 June 1975, Faber Archive.
91. TG to Jack Hagstrom, 24 July 1975, Hagstrom MSS.
92. TG to Ander Gunn, 9 December 1975. Private collection.
93. TG to Tony White, 28 June 1975, in *Letters*, 318–19.
94. "Haven't written a thing in six months," he told Tanner in October. TG to Tony Tanner, 21 October 1975, King's MSS.
95. TG to Douglas Chambers, 12 December 1975, Toronto MSS. See "Homosexuality in Robert Duncan's Poetry," in Robert Bertholf and Ian Reid, eds., *Scales of the Marvellous* (New York: New Directions, 1979), 143–60, reprinted in *OP*, 118–34.
96. Robert Duncan, "The Homosexual in Society" (1944), in Duncan, *Collected Essays and Other Prose*, ed. James Maynard (Berkeley: University of California Press, 2014), 5–18.
97. Robert Duncan, *Caesar's Gate: Poems 1949–50* (San Francisco: Sand Dollar, 1972), xv.
98. "Homosexuality," *OP*, 123.
99. "Homosexuality," *OP*, 122. The lines are from "The Venice Poem": see Robert

Duncan, *Collected Early Poems and Plays*, ed. Peter Quartermain (Berkeley: University of California Press, 2012), 221. TG's introductory sentence is insightful in terms of his own poetic interest in doubles and doppelgängers.

100. "Homosexuality," *OP*, 134.
101. TG to Barbara Godfrey, 22 December 1975. Private collection.
102. TG to Ander Gunn, 9 December 1975. Private collection.
103. "Homosexuality," *OP*, 131.
104. See Robert Duncan, "My Mother Would Be a Falconress," in *Bending the Bow* (New York: New Directions, 1968), 52–54.
105. "Homosexuality," *OP*, 131.
106. "The Flirt" (1978), Bancroft MSS.
107. The falcon even dreams in the poem: "I dream in my little hood with many bells / jangling when I'd turn my head."
108. "Homosexuality," *OP*, 131.
109. Duncan, "My Mother," 54.
110. TG to Douglas Chambers, 8 January 1976, Toronto MSS.

24. LOSS

1. Tony White to TG, 10 October 1975, Bancroft MSS.
2. TG to Tony Tanner, 21 October 1975, King's MSS.
3. TG to Barbara Godfrey, 22 December 1975. Private collection.
4. TG to Ander Gunn, 9 December 1975. Private collection.
5. Diary (1974–1986), 13 January 1976, Bancroft MSS.
6. TG to Tony White, 14 January 1976, in *Letters*, 321.
7. Tony White to TG, 3 March 1975, Bancroft MSS.
8. Quoted in Miller, *Fathers*, 176.
9. Quoted in Miller, *Fathers*, 177. For a more detailed account of White's final weeks, see Miller, *Fathers*, 176–85.
10. John Holmstrom to TG, 10 January 1976, Bancroft MSS.
11. TG to Ander and Margaret Gunn, 19 January 1976, in *Letters*, 322.
12. TG to Tony Tanner, 27 January 1976, in *Letters*, 323.
13. TG to Tony Tanner, 27 January 1976, in *Letters*, 322–23.
14. "When the life that began in 1959 with our meeting on the Inishbofin quay ended with Tony's death in 1976," Murphy reflected, "I felt it was time to leave the west of Ireland." Murphy, *The Kick*, 335.
15. John Holmstrom to TG, 15 March 1976, Bancroft MSS.
16. Sasha Moorsom to TG, 19 March 1976, Bancroft MSS.
17. Bill Schuessler to TG and Mike Kitay, c. January 1976, Bancroft MSS.
18. TG to Tony Tanner, 27 February 1976, King's MSS.
19. Margaret Gunn to TG, 23 January 1976, Bancroft MSS.
20. TG to Tony Tanner, 27 February 1976, King's MSS.
21. TG to Tony White, 28 June 1975, in *Letters*, 319.
22. TG to Tony Tanner, 27 January 1976, in *Letters*, 323.
23. Mike Kitay, interview with the author, 18 June 2019.
24. "Mike's father is dying," TG wrote. See Diary (1974–1986), 27 February 1976, Bancroft MSS. See also "Abraham Kitay," *New Jersey Jewish News* (4 March 1976), 50.

25. Mike Kitay, interview with the author, 22 October 2018.

26. TG to Tony Tanner, 20 April 1976, in *Letters*, 326.

27. TG to John Holmstrom, 17 June 1976, in *Letters*, 331–32.

28. TG's Cambridge contemporary, the biographer Ronald Hayman, solicited the piece in December 1975. See Ronald Hayman, ed., *My Cambridge* (Cambridge: Robson Books, 1977), 135–48, reprinted in *OP*, 157–68.

29. "Cambridge in the Fifties," *OP*, 168.

30. TG to John Holmstrom, 17 June 1976, in *Letters*, 332.

31. TG published three pamphlets with Bixby's Albondocani Press: *Sunlight* (1969), *Poem After Chaucer* (1971), and *Songbook* (1973), the latter with drawings by Bill Schuessler. The poem "Poem After Chaucer" was subsequently retitled "All Night, Legs Pointed East" (*CP*, 238).

32. TG to Jack Hagstrom, 23 December 1976, Hagstrom MSS.

33. TG to Charles Monteith, 18 May 1977, Faber Archive.

34. "My Life Up to Now," *OP*, 186.

35. Donald Davie, *Collected Poems* (Manchester: Carcanet, 2002), 346.

36. TG to Donald Davie, 6 January 1976, Davie MSS.

37. TG to Tony Tanner, 20 April 1976, in *Letters*, 326.

38. "An Anglo-American Poet," *SL*, 230.

39. Glenn Jordan, email to the author, 25 May 2020.

40. Glenn Jordan, email to the author, 27 April 2020.

41. TG to Tony Tanner, 22 July 1976, King's MSS.

42. John Holmstrom to TG, 15 March 1976, Bancroft MSS.

43. Diary (1974–1986), 30 July, 29 August 1976, Bancroft MSS.

44. Diary (1974–1986), 9 September 1976, Bancroft MSS.

45. TG to Ander Gunn, 14 December 1976. Private collection.

46. "Two Saturday Nights," *SL*, 213.

47. Poetry Notebook XVII (May 1977), Bancroft MSS. See "Saturday Night" (*BC*, 43–44) and "Two Saturday Nights" (*SL*, 213–17): TG started a poem about the Barracks in 1975 but rewrote it in 1990.

48. Jim Stewart, "The Slot," *Bay Area Reporter* (29 September 2013), www.ebar.com /bartab/nightlife/148795, accessed 23 July 2022. The Slot refers to the streetcar line that runs along Market Street: anything south of Market is known colloquially as South of the Slot.

49. Dennis Charles, "South of Market," *Kalendar* 4, no. 19 (3 October 1975), 2.

50. Robert E. Roberts, *Mad Dogs and Queer Tattoos: Tattooing the San Francisco Queer Revolution* (Springfield, PA: Fair Page, 2018), 25.

51. Mark I. Chester, "The Ambush," *Bay Area Reporter* 16, no. 51 (18 December 1986), 45.

52. Roberts, *Mad Dogs*, 29.

53. Chester, "Ambush," 45–46.

54. Diary (1974–1986), 18 May 1977, Bancroft MSS.

55. TG to Bill Schuessler, "Where to Go in New York," undated. Private collection. See also Diary (1974–1986), 20 November 1976, Bancroft MSS.

56. Edmund White, *City Boy: My Life in New York During the 1960s and 1970s* (London: Bloomsbury, 2009), 235.

57. Diary (1974–1986), 30 May 1977, Bancroft MSS.

58. TG's poem "Song of a Camera" (*CP*, 347–48) is about Mapplethorpe taking his picture.

59. Mike Kitay, interview with the author, 22 October 2018.

60. TG to Clive Wilmer, 26 October 1976, Wilmer MSS. The reviewer, John Bayley, felt TG was "counterfeiting poetry with a highly accomplished and covertly malignant skill." John Bayley, "Castles and Communes," *The Times Literary Supplement* 3889 (24 September 1976), 1194.

61. "I do not court impersonality so much as try to avoid personality, which I'd prefer to leave to the newspapers," TG remarked. "It is not an anonymous voice, but I hope that when you hear it you will be inclined to listen to what it is saying before you start noticing its mannerisms." See "Thom Gunn Writes," *Poetry Book Society Bulletin* 90 (Autumn 1976), 1.

62. Peter Porter, "Gunn Metal," *The Observer* (17 October 1976), 33.

63. Martin Booth, "Established Poets, New Approaches," *Tribune* (22 October 1976), 8.

64. TG to Ander Gunn, 14 December 1976. Private collection.

65. TG to Charles Monteith, 10 March 1977, Faber Archive.

66. TG stuck a copy of the poster above his desk.

67. See Roger Austin, "Books," *San Francisco Sentinel* 3, no. 21 (7 October 1976), 8, 11; and Tony Sarver, "Thom Gunn," *The Advocate* 220 (27 July 1977), 39–40.

68. TG to Jack Hagstrom, 20 September 1976, Hagstrom MSS.

69. W. I. Scobie, "Jack Straw's Castle," *The Advocate* 220 (27 July 1977), 40.

70. Douglas Chambers, "Jack Straw's Castle," *Body Politic* 34 (July 1977), 16.

71. TG to Douglas Chambers, 31 May 1977, in *Letters*, 339.

72. On Tanner's visit to San Francisco in 1975, TG ensured that he and Doody were "completely reconciled." See Diary (1974–1986), 9 August 1975, Bancroft MSS.

73. See TG to Tony Tanner, 22 July 1976, King's MSS.

74. Charles Newman (1938–2006) edited *TriQuarterly* at Northwestern and moved to Johns Hopkins in 1975.

75. Marcia Tanner, email to the author, 5 August 2021.

76. TG to Tony Tanner, 22 July 1976, King's MSS.

77. Diary (1974–1986), 13 July 1976, Bancroft MSS. From TG, "sensible" was a real mark of admiration. Compare chapter 3, p. 32.

78. TG to Tony White, 28 June 1975, in *Letters*, 318.

79. Diary (1974–1986), 14 October 1976, Bancroft MSS.

80. Diary (1974–1986), 3 November 1976, Bancroft MSS.

81. Diary (1974–1986), 8 November 1976, Bancroft MSS.

82. Diary (1974–1986), 10 November 1976, Bancroft MSS.

83. Diary (1974–1986), 11 November 1976, Bancroft MSS.

84. Jack Collins, interview with the author, 20 June 2019.

85. TG to Ander Gunn, 14 December 1976. Private collection.

86. Diary (1974–1986), 13 December 1976, Bancroft MSS.

87. Diary (1974–1986), 16 December 1976, Bancroft MSS.

88. Mike Kitay, interview with the author, 20 October 2018.

89. Mike Kitay, interview with the author, 18 June 2019.

90. Diary (1974–1986), 23 December 1976, Bancroft MSS.

91. Diary (1974–1986), 12 January 1977, Bancroft MSS.

92. Marcia Tanner, email to the author, 5 August 2021. Because they were still married, albeit separated, Marcia felt obligated to come to Baltimore and clear out Tony's apartment. "The Baltimore cleanup was one of the worst experiences of my life," she reflected.

93. Tony Tanner to TG, 24 February 1977, Bancroft MSS.

94. Jack Collins, interview with the author, 20 June 2019.

95. TG to Barbara Godfrey, 6 December 1977. Private collection. No letters from TG to Tanner survive between 22 July 1976 and 5 December 1977.

96. TG to Barbara Godfrey, 15 December 1976. Private collection.

25. BLOCK

1. TG to Mary and Catherine Thomson, 9 December 1976. Private collection.

2. Diary (1974–1986), 4 March 1977, Bancroft MSS. THC is the main psychoactive ingredient in cannabis; TG typically took it in pill form.

3. TG to Barbara Godfrey, 17 April 1977. Private collection.

4. Diary (1974–1986), 19 February 1977, Bancroft MSS.

5. TG to Douglas Chambers, 8 March 1976, in *Letters*, 324.

6. Diary (1974–1986), 26 February 1977, Bancroft MSS.

7. Allan Noseworthy to TG, 26 March 1977, Bancroft MSS.

8. Allan Noseworthy to TG, 3 April 1977, Bancroft MSS.

9. TG to Belle Randall, 18 April 1977, Randall MSS.

10. TG to Douglas Chambers, 31 May 1977, in *Letters*, 340. Lady Britomart is the "very typical managing matron of the upper class" in Shaw's play *Major Barbara* (1905).

11. TG to Mike Kitay, 26 April 1977, Stanford MSS.

12. "An Apprenticeship," 18.

13. Poetry Notebook XIV (December 1973), Bancroft MSS. See also "Getting Things Right," *SL*, 173–96.

14. "Expression," *CP*, 321.

15. TG to Douglas Chambers, 31 May 1977, in *Letters*, 340.

16. "Expression," *CP*, 321.

17. See chapter 23, p. 290.

18. Poetry Notebook XVII (May 1977), Bancroft MSS.

19. TG to Charles Monteith, 8 June 1977, Faber Archive.

20. TG to Barbara Godfrey, 17 April 1977. Private collection.

21. Diary (1974–1986), 19 May 1977, Bancroft MSS.

22. Diary (1974–1986), 4 May 1977, Bancroft MSS; Poetry Notebook XVII (May 1977), Bancroft MSS.

23. TG's four published autobiographical essays are collected in *OP*, 151–88.

24. TG to Ander Gunn, 7 November 1977. Private collection.

25. Diary (1974–1986), 24 August 1977, Bancroft MSS.

26. Poetry Notebook J (5 May 1961), Hornbake MSS.

27. Diary (1974–1986), 28 July 1977, Bancroft MSS. TG often used "euphoric" and "euphoria" in his diaries to describe good moods and feelings of well-being associated with drug-taking, community, and conviviality. For example: "Euphoric day. Hot sun. To Haight St. Gus' [Pub] lovely." Diary (1974–1986), 19 April 1976, Bancroft MSS. Compare "In Time of Plague" (*CP*, 463): "Brad and John thirst

heroically together / for euphoria—for a state of ardent life / in which we could all stretch ourselves / and lose our differences."

28. "Modes of Pleasure," *CP*, 101.
29. TG to John Holmstrom, 16 December 1977, Bancroft MSS.
30. TG to Ander Gunn, 7 November 1977. Private collection.
31. TG to Tony White, 5 December 1972, in *Letters*, 293. TG made the remark after reading Hughes's *Selected Poems* (1972).
32. TG to John Holmstrom, 16 December 1977, Bancroft MSS.
33. TG to Charles Monteith, 24 May 1970, in *Letters*, 271.
34. Edward Lucie-Smith, ed., *British Poetry Since 1945* (Harmondsworth, UK: Penguin, 1970), 143.
35. TG to Douglas Chambers, 23 March 1977, in *Letters*, 337.
36. "An Anglo-American Poet," *SL*, 225. TG and Larkin never met. Their only surviving correspondence relates to Larkin's accidental omission of the last two stanzas of TG's poem "The Byrnies" from *The Oxford Book of Twentieth Century English Verse* (1973). "To my anguish!" TG wrote. "Any chance of getting an erratum slip put into the copies?" TG to Philip Larkin, 5 March 1973, Hull MSS. The missing stanzas were printed in *The Times Literary Supplement* with an explanatory note and Larkin's profuse apologies. See Philip Larkin, "Twentieth Century English Verse," *The Times Literary Supplement* 3708 (30 March 1973), 353.
37. TG to Charles Monteith, 8 June 1977, Faber Archive.
38. Diary (1974–1986), 28 May 1977, Bancroft MSS.
39. Mike Kitay, interview with the author, 19 June 2019.
40. Diary (1974–1986), 25 February 1977, Bancroft MSS.
41. Bob Bair, interview with the author, 21 June 2019.
42. Bob Bair, interview with the author, 28 June 2019.
43. Bob Bair, interview with the author, 21 June 2019.
44. Diary (1974–1986), 19 July 1977, Bancroft MSS.
45. Diary (1974–1986), 28 July 1977, Bancroft MSS.
46. Diary (1974–1986), 20 August 1977, Bancroft MSS. Upstairs the following summer, Jere was "seriously perturbed" to hear that TG had marched in the gay pride parade. "'Activist!' he hissed at me, with a touch of real anger." See TG to Donald Doody, 18 July 1978. Private collection.
47. Day later moved to San Francisco. TG introduced him to another friend, Louis Bryan, who became his life partner. TG had met Louis, and introduced him to MDA, at the Polk Street Fair in July 1974. "I enquired whether Thom might be able to provide some of this stuff for me," Louis recalled. "He said sure." Louis became a friend of the Cole Street family and was often a guest at large birthday and holiday dinners. Louis Bryan, interview with the author, 20 October 2018.
48. Diary (1974–1986), 7 September 1977, Bancroft MSS.
49. TG to Barbara Godfrey, 6 December 1977. Private collection.
50. TG to Tony Tanner, 5 December 1977, King's MSS.
51. TG to Donald Doody, 18 July 1978. Private collection.
52. White, *City Boy*, 229–30.
53. Diary (1974–1986), 3 January 1978, Bancroft MSS.
54. Diary (1974–1986), 31 December 1977, Bancroft MSS.
55. Diary (1974–1986), 7 March 1978, Bancroft MSS.

56. Diary (1974–1986), 30 January 1978, Bancroft MSS. Course number 141 was Modes of Writing; 143B, Verse (composition).
57. TG to Belle Randall, 13 May 1978, Randall MSS.
58. Having managed to negotiate a better offer from the department chair, Brom Weber, TG remarked, "I shall be able to afford coke!" See Diary (1974–1986), 20 August 1977, Bancroft MSS.
59. Diary (1974–1986), 3 April 1978, Bancroft MSS.
60. TG to Belle Randall, 13 May 1978, Randall MSS.
61. Diary (1974–1986), 24 April 1978, Bancroft MSS.
62. TG to Joshua Odell, 20 May 1978. Private collection.
63. Diary (1974–1986), 5 April 1978, Bancroft MSS.
64. TG to Clive Wilmer, 19 June 1978, Wilmer MSS.
65. Diary (1974–1986), 7 May 1978, Bancroft MSS.
66. TG to Charles Monteith, 26 May 1978, Faber Archive.
67. "Selves," *CP*, 322–23. See Haffenden, *Viewpoints*, 53, and above, chapter 22, p. 272.
68. "Selves," *CP*, 322. TG once copied out "Selves" by hand with the dedication "for Jim, who appears in the poem briefly as a lolling nude." Private collection.
69. Diary (1974–1986), 13 April 1978, Bancroft MSS.
70. Robby (Gunner) Robinson, email to the author, 20 November 2020.
71. "Bally *Power Play*," *CP*, 315–16.
72. "Sweet Things," *CP*, 328. Delay is a recurrent theme in TG's work. Compare "scripts of delay, and scripts / Of more delay" in "To Cupid" (*BC*, 98).
73. Poetry Notebook 1 (April 1978), Bancroft MSS.
74. Belle Randall to TG, 30 April 1979, Bancroft MSS.
75. TG to Belle Randall, 15 May 1979, in *Letters*, 345. TG regularly made lists of his tricks—sometimes by year, sometimes by month—and often ranked them, dividing the page into three columns. Names vie with descriptions—"Dimitrius' friend Greg," "guy with crazy stepfather who killed mother," "big nose & ganz in Brig recently." See Diary (2000–2004), list beginning "Mohawk–Baldy Haight Street," Bancroft MSS.
76. Poetry Notebook 1 (April 1978), Bancroft MSS.
77. "Sweet Things," *CP*, 327. For the prolific leather and fetish artist Rex, see his website rexwerk.com.
78. Sinfield, "Thom Gunn," 225.
79. Diary (1974–1986), 14 September 1978, Bancroft MSS.
80. TG to Charles Monteith, 2 March 1978, Faber Archive.
81. TG to Mike Kitay, 19 September 1978, Stanford MSS.
82. Diary (1974–1986), 24 September 1978, Bancroft MSS.
83. Diary (1974–1986), 24 September 1978, Bancroft MSS. Prendergast is the subject of TG's poem "His Rooms in College," *CP*, 351.
84. Christopher Prendergast, email to the author, 26 May 2020.
85. TG to Barbara Godfrey, 21 October 1978. Private collection.
86. TG to John Holmstrom, 24 October 1978, Bancroft MSS.
87. "Slow Waker," *CP*, 364.
88. Diary (1974–1986), 30 September 1978, Bancroft MSS.
89. Diary (1974–1986), 4 October 1978, Bancroft MSS.

90. Diary (1974–1986), 7 October 1978, Bancroft MSS.
91. TG to John Holmstrom, 24 October 1978, in *Letters*, 344.
92. Poetry Notebook 1 (April 1978), Bancroft MSS. Compare "My Mother's Pride," *BC*, 9.
93. Poetry Notebook 3 (May 1980), Bancroft MSS.
94. Poetry Notebook 1 (April 1978), Bancroft MSS.
95. Poetry Notebook 3 (May 1980), Bancroft MSS.
96. Poetry Notebook XVII (May 1977), Bancroft MSS.

26. MARRIAGES

1. Mike Kitay, interview with the author, 22 October 2018.
2. Bob Bair, interview with the author, 28 June 2019.
3. Diary (1974–1986), 8 November 1978, Bancroft MSS.
4. Poetry Notebook 1 (April 1978), Bancroft MSS.
5. The essay was originally published in *San Francisco Review of Books* 5, no. 3 (August 1979), 3–4, and reprinted in *OP*, 142–47.
6. TG to Clive Wilmer, 26 April 1979, Wilmer MSS.
7. "A Heroic Enterprise," *OP*, 146–47. Compare this ordinary, casual heroism with TG's earlier ideas: see chapter 7, p. 83, and chapter 13, p. 156.
8. Wendy Lesser, interview with the author, 4 April 2019.
9. Diary (1974–1986), 5 April 1979, Bancroft MSS.
10. TG to Belle Randall, 15 May 1979, in *Letters*, 346.
11. Diary (1974–1986), 12 April 1979, Bancroft MSS.
12. Diary (1974–1986), 25 January 1979, Bancroft MSS.
13. Poetry Notebook XVII (May 1977), Bancroft MSS.
14. Diary (1974–1986), 11 December 1978, Bancroft MSS.
15. Diary (1974–1986), 22 October 1979, Bancroft MSS.
16. "A Heroic Enterprise," *OP*, 144.
17. Poetry Notebook 1 (April 1978), Bancroft MSS. Compare "I realize that love is an arranging" in "Thoughts on Unpacking," *CP*, 80.
18. Poetry Notebook 2 (May 1979), Bancroft MSS. Compare "In Trust," *BC*, 96–97.
19. Poetry Notebook 1 (April 1978), Bancroft MSS.
20. Poetry Notebook 3 (May 1980), Bancroft MSS.
21. "June," *CP*, 352.
22. "The Married Men," *PN Review* 24, vol. 8, no. 4 (March–April 1982), 21, uncollected.
23. Diary (1974–1986), 21 July 1974, Bancroft MSS.
24. Diary (1974–1986), 7 June 1979, Bancroft MSS.
25. Diary (1974–1986), 25 May 1979, Bancroft MSS.
26. TG to Barbara Godfrey, 12 June 1979. Private collection.
27. TG to Joseph Mockus, 18 June 1979. Private collection.
28. TG to Jack Hagstrom, 2 June 1979, Hagstrom MSS. The "solid book" is *Selected Poems 1950–1975* (London: Faber; New York: Farrar, Straus and Giroux, 1979). The "next book" is *PJ*.
29. Poetry Notebook 2 (May 1979), Bancroft MSS.
30. Diary (1974–1986), 27 November 1978, Bancroft MSS. For the circumstances

and aftermath of the assassination, see Randy Shilts, *The Mayor of Castro Street: The Life and Times of Harvey Milk* (New York: St. Martin's Press, 1982), 263–95.

31. Diary (1974–1986), 27 November 1978, Bancroft MSS.

32. Poetry Notebook 1 (April 1978), Bancroft MSS.

33. TG to Ander Gunn, 23 January 1979. Private collection. When Dan White was convicted of voluntary manslaughter, not first-degree murder, pleading diminished capacity, and received a seven-year sentence, San Francisco rioted. TG thought the verdict "astonishing" but was not present at the White Night riots: it was Mike's birthday party. See Diary (1974–1986), 21 May 1979, Bancroft MSS.

34. Poetry Notebook 1 (April 1978), Bancroft MSS.

35. "Thom Gunn: July 25, 1996," Prager MSS.

36. Lesser, "Sense of Movement," 38. "What I remember, and will remember, most vividly about our friendship was traveling around town with Thom on public transport," recalled August Kleinzahler. "The prospect and the adventure of getting to the cinema seemed to put Thom in high spirits. To travel with Thom was to participate in an erotic mapping of San Francisco out the bus window." August Kleinzahler, *Cutty, One Rock: Low Characters and Strange Places, Gently Explained*, rev. ed (New York: Farrar, Straus and Giroux, 2005), 139.

37. Poetry Notebook 1 (April 1978), Bancroft MSS. Visiting Don in New York in autumn 1978, TG wrote this down on a scrap of paper and later copied it into his notebook.

38. Poetry Notebook 1 (April 1978), Bancroft MSS.

39. "Drug Raid at Eel Home Nabs Six," *Ukiah (CA) Daily Journal* (3 January 1972), 2.

40. Mike Caffee, email to the author, 27 August 2020. Jere cultivated an entourage of younger men. One of them, Robert Lee Nugent, with whom Jere was arrested in 1972, took his own life when sought in connection with the rape of a woman in 1976. See "Rape Suspect on Parole Apparently Kills Himself," *The Press Democrat* (Santa Rosa, CA) (16 December 1976), 2.

41. Poetry Notebook 2 (May 1979), Bancroft MSS.

42. Poetry Notebook 3 (May 1980), Bancroft MSS.

43. See chapter 14, p. 168.

44. "Transients and Residents: Interruption," *CP*, 378. Compare "he is the same, he is other" in "Behind the Mirror," *CP*, 293.

45. Poetry Notebook 2 (May 1979), Bancroft MSS.

46. Poetry Notebook 3 (May 1980), Bancroft MSS.

47. "Transients and Residents: Crystal," *CP*, 375–76.

48. "Transients and Residents: Falstaff," *CP*, 375.

49. "Transients and Residents: Crystal," *CP*, 376.

50. Diary (1974–1986), 21 July 1974, Bancroft MSS.

51. TG to Douglas Chambers, 20 July 1979, Toronto MSS.

52. Diary (1974–1986), 8 August 1979, Bancroft MSS.

53. "Transients and Residents: Crosswords," *CP*, 376–77. Doody visited in August 1979 and TG wrote the poem in April 1980. The title comes from Doody's life-long habit of reading a daily newspaper and doing the crossword.

54. "Transients and Residents: Crosswords," *CP*, 378.

55. Compare TG's first impression of Karl Miller, chapter 7, pp. 80–81. For Don and alibis, see chapter 17, p. 204.

56. Diary (1974–1986), 10 August 1979, Bancroft MSS.
57. TG to Ander Gunn, 22 July 1969. Private collection.
58. "Transients and Residents: Crosswords," *CP*, 378.
59. Diary (1974–1986), 21 November 1982, Bancroft MSS. TG was "flattered."
60. Diary (1974–1986), 23 July 1979, Bancroft MSS.
61. TG to Douglas Chambers, 20 July 1979, Toronto MSS.
62. TG to Jack Hagstrom, 20 August 1979, Hagstrom MSS.
63. Diary (1974–1986), 8 September 1979, Bancroft MSS.
64. Diary (1974–1986), 10–11 October 1979, Bancroft MSS.
65. Diary (1974–1986), 22 October 1979, Bancroft MSS.
66. Diary (1974–1986), 24 October 1979, Bancroft MSS.
67. Diary (1974–1986), 23 October 1979, Bancroft MSS.
68. TG to John Holmstrom, 16 September 1979, Bancroft MSS. The "Poetry Secretariat" was Pamela Clunies-Ross; Ted Hughes's brother-in-law, Richard Orchard, organized the school readings.
69. TG to Tony Tanner, 23 October 1979, King's MSS.
70. TG to Barbara Godfrey, 6 December 1979. Private collection.
71. TG to Ander Gunn, 15 December 1979. Private collection.
72. TG to Douglas Chambers, 23 December 1979, in *Letters*, 347.
73. Diary (1974–1986), 9 December 1979, Bancroft MSS.
74. Diary (1974–1986), 13 December 1979, Bancroft MSS.
75. TG to Douglas Chambers, 23 December 1979, in *Letters*, 348.
76. Diary (1974–1986), 22 December 1979, Bancroft MSS.
77. TG to Douglas Chambers, 23 December 1979, in *Letters*, 348.
78. Diary (1974–1986), 19 January 1980, Bancroft MSS.
79. TG to John Lehmann, 6 March 1980, Princeton MSS.
80. TG to Ander Gunn, 3 February 1980. Private collection.
81. Diary (1974–1986), 28 November 1979, Bancroft MSS.
82. Diary (1974–1986), 27 January 1980, Bancroft MSS.
83. Bob Bair, interview with the author, 21 June 2019.
84. Diary (1974–1986), 12–13 March 1980, Bancroft MSS.
85. "Angel-Dust Raid Nets 9 Near Haight-Ashbury," *San Francisco Examiner* (13 March 1980), 4.
86. Mike Kitay, interview with the author, 21 June 2019.
87. Diary (1974–1986), 13, 15 March 1980, Bancroft MSS.
88. See Lise Gaston, "Collaging with Thom Gunn," *Brick* 101 (2018), 61–65.
89. Mike Kitay, interview with the author, 20 October 2018. TG also published a pornographic short story under the pseudonym Sam Browne, "Star Clone," *Son of Drummer* (September 1978), 6–7, 58–59. Robert Prager asked TG to sign a copy after TG's reading at the San Francisco Public Library in June 2001. "From the look on Thom's face, I could tell I had finally done something unforgivable, putting our friendship at risk," Prager recalled. "Thom quizzed me who else I told about 'Star Clone.' [. . .] 'I thought you didn't care about your literary reputation,' I reminded him. 'I don't,' Thom said, 'but that would be misleading people with false information.'" Undated note, Prager MSS. Jack Fritscher, editor of *Drummer* when "Star Clone" was published, examines TG's attributed authorship in *Profiles in Gay Courage*, 151–54. A Sam Browne is a belt

with a shoulder strap, fashionable in leather subculture. For Robert Prager, see chapter 37, p. 477.

90. "Not exactly an <u>English</u> garden, but nice none the less," Don Doody wrote to him from the Henry Francis du Pont Winterthur Museum in Delaware. "Your other postcard categories are even harder to find." See Donald Doody to TG, 17 February 1981, Stanford MSS.

91. TG to Barbara Godfrey, 9 May 1980. Private collection.

92. TG to Jack Hagstrom, 21 May 1980, Hagstrom MSS.

27. AGING

1. Charles Monteith to TG, 21 December 1979, Faber Archive.

2. Donald Davie, untitled review, *The New Republic* 181, no. 15 (13 October 1979), 38. See also Colin Falck, "Uncertain Violence," *The New Review* 3, no. 32 (November 1976), 37.

3. TG to Charles Monteith, 3 February 1980, Faber Archive.

4. See TG to Douglas Chambers, 28 December 1980, Toronto MSS.

5. TG to Ted Hughes, 24 April 1980, in *Letters*, 353.

6. Diary (1974–1986), 24 March 1980, Bancroft MSS.

7. Diary (1974–1986), 1, 3 April 1980, Bancroft MSS.

8. Diary (1974–1986), 17 May, 3 June 1980, and Poetry Notebook 3 (May 1980), both Bancroft MSS.

9. TG to Jack Hagstrom, 21 May 1980, Hagstrom MSS.

10. TG to Douglas Chambers, 22 July 1980, in *Letters*, 355.

11. TG to Ted Hughes, 24 April 1980, in *Letters*, 353.

12. TG to Douglas Chambers, 22 July 1980, in *Letters*, 354.

13. Diary (1974–1986), 16–17 July 1980, Bancroft MSS.

14. TG to Charles Monteith, 22 July 1980, Faber Archive.

15. TG to Douglas Chambers, 22 July 1980, in *Letters*, 354.

16. Diary (1974–1986), 17 July 1980, Bancroft MSS.

17. TG to Ander Gunn, 29 July 1980. Private collection.

18. TG to Douglas Chambers, 22 July 1980, in *Letters*, 354.

19. Mike Kitay, interview with the author, 21 October 2018.

20. Bob Bair, interview with the author, 21 June 2019.

21. Diary (1974–1986), 22 August 1980, Bancroft MSS.

22. Diary (1974–1986), 3 September 1980, Bancroft MSS.

23. TG to Douglas Chambers, 22 July 1980, in *Letters*, 355.

24. TG to Douglas Chambers, 24 November 1981, Toronto MSS.

25. Poetry Notebook 1 (April 1978), Bancroft MSS. See Gregory Bateson, *Steps to an Ecology of Mind* (1972; reprint, Chicago: University of Chicago Press, 2000), 180.

26. TG to Gregory Woods, 2 October 1982, in *Letters*, 377.

27. Poetry Notebook 3 (May 1980), Bancroft MSS.

28. Poetry Notebook 3 (May 1980), Bancroft MSS.

29. TG to Douglas Chambers, 22 July 1980, in *Letters*, 355.

30. TG to Douglas Chambers, 13 October 1980, Toronto MSS.

31. "Talbot Road," *CP*, 381–83.

32. "Transients and Residents: Interruption," *CP*, 379.

33. "Talbot Road," *CP*, 384.

34. See TG to Douglas Chambers, 28 December 1980, in *Letters*, 358.
35. Diary (1974–1986), 6 November 1980, Bancroft MSS. TG recommended the Bar to everyone for the next fifteen years.
36. Ned Rorem, *The Nantucket Diary of Ned Rorem, 1973–1985* (San Francisco: North Point Press, 1987), 305.
37. Diary (1974–1986), 18 November 1980, Bancroft MSS. See Josh Barbanel, "Gunman Kills One and Wounds 7 in Village," *The New York Times* (20 November 1980), B1.
38. Robert Wells to TG, 26 September 1977, Bancroft MSS.
39. TG to Clive Wilmer, 18 April 1977, Wilmer MSS.
40. C. H. Sisson, "Editorial," *PN Review* 12, vol. 6, no. 4 (March–April 1980), 2.
41. TG to Michael Schmidt, 5 February 1981, in *Letters*, 360.
42. TG to Douglas Chambers, 28 December 1980, in *Letters*, 358.
43. TG to Michael Schmidt, 5 February 1981, in *Letters*, 360.
44. See *PN Review* 8, vol. 5, no. 4 (July–September 1979), 2. "Elegy" and "Hide and Seek" were first published two years earlier in *The Southern Review* 13, no. 3 (July 1977), 582–84; and "Adultery" in *Canto* 1, no. 1 (Spring 1977), 14–15.
45. TG to Douglas Chambers, 28 December 1980, in *Letters*, 357–58.
46. TG to A. E. Dyson, 5 February 1981, Dyson MSS.
47. TG to Michael Schmidt, 5 February 1981, in *Letters*, 360.
48. Michael Schmidt to TG, 14 February 1981, Carcanet MSS.
49. TG to Michael Schmidt, 2 May 1981, in *Letters*, 362.
50. Michael Schmidt to TG, 1 June 1981, Carcanet MSS.
51. Diary (1974–1986), 14 January 1981, Bancroft MSS.
52. Diary (1974–1986), 28 January 1980, Bancroft MSS.
53. TG to Douglas Chambers, 8 March 1981, Toronto MSS.
54. TG to Donald Davie, 29 July 1982, in *Letters*, 374.
55. TG to Robert Pinsky, 17 June 1981, Pinsky MSS.
56. TG to Douglas Chambers, 22 July 1980, in *Letters*, 355.
57. TG to Charles Monteith, 6 April 1981, Faber Archive.
58. TG to Douglas Chambers, 23 June 1981, Toronto MSS.
59. Diary (1974–1986), 25 March 1981, Bancroft MSS.
60. Jerry Reneau, email to the author, 3 February 2022. Reneau taught at Exeter.
61. Diary (1974–1986), 22 April 1981, Bancroft MSS.
62. TG based his lecture on the essay he had recently written about Winters. See "On a Drying Hill," *The Southern Review* 17, no. 4 (Autumn 1981), 681–93, reprinted in *SL*, 197–212.
63. Daniel Hall, email to the author, 5 June 2020. Hall was not a student at the time. He later won Yale's Series of Younger Poets competition—*Hermit with Landscape* (1989)—and taught at Amherst.
64. Diary (1974–1986), 3 May 1981, Bancroft MSS.
65. TG to Barbara Godfrey, 16 June 1981. Private collection.
66. Diary (1974–1986), 22, 28 April 1981, Bancroft MSS.
67. TG to Mike Kitay, Bob Bair, and Bill Schuessler, 28 April 1981, Stanford MSS.
68. Diary (1974–1986), 8 July 1981, Bancroft MSS.
69. TG to Douglas Chambers, 29 September 1981, Toronto MSS.
70. Diary (1974–1986), 2 September 1981, Bancroft MSS.
71. Diary (1974–1986), 29 August 1981, Bancroft MSS.

72. Diary (1974–1986), 5 September 1981, Bancroft MSS. Compare "Perhaps I should open a home for wayward boys. / At least I might get help from the State," in "The Stylist," 91.

73. Diary (1974–1986), 15 September 1981, Bancroft MSS.

74. TG to Douglas Chambers, 29 September 1981, Toronto MSS.

75. Diary (1974–1986), 26–27 September 1981, Bancroft MSS.

76. TG to Douglas Chambers, 29 September 1981, Toronto MSS.

77. Diary (1974–1986), 3 October 1981, Bancroft MSS.

78. See chapter 6, p. 68.

79. Diary (1974–1986), 27 November 1981, Bancroft MSS.

80. TG to Douglas Chambers, 29 September 1981, Toronto MSS.

81. Diary (1974–1986), 3–4 October 1981, Bancroft MSS.

82. TG to Jack Collins, 8 November 1981, Collins MSS.

83. TG to Mike Kitay, Bob Bair, and Bill Schuessler, 11 November 1981, in *Letters*, 366.

84. TG to Mike Kitay, 25 October 1981, Stanford MSS.

85. TG to Donald Davie, 19 November 1981, Davie MSS.

86. TG to Douglas Chambers, 29 September 1981, Toronto MSS.

87. TG to Jack Collins, 26 October 1981, Collins MSS.

88. TG to Clive Wilmer, 19 October 1981, in *Letters*, 363–64.

89. "Wings Deep with Inner Gloss," *The Threepenny Review* 10 (Summer 1982), 6.

90. See the famous axiom, "Dichten = condensare," in Ezra Pound, *ABC of Reading* (New York: New Directions, 1934), 36.

91. "A Record," *SL*, 110. Compare "JVC," *CP*, 448.

92. Basil Bunting, *Collected Poems* (London: Fulcrum Press, 1970), 156.

93. "Wings Deep," 6.

94. "Adventurous Song: Robert Duncan as Romantic Modernist," *SL*, 168.

95. "Transients and Residents: Interruption," *CP*, 379.

96. Mike Kitay, interview with the author, 21 June 2019.

97. Diary (1974–1986), 6, 11 December 1981, Bancroft MSS.

98. Diary (1974–1986), 9 December 1981, Bancroft MSS.

28. FOREBODING

1. Allen White, "The Fallout from a Blaze," *Bay Area Reporter* 11, no. 15 (16 July 1981), 1, 4.

2. Mr. Marcus [Marcus Hernandez], "Southern Scandals," *Bay Area Reporter* 11, no. 16 (30 July 1981), 34.

3. "Health Shorts," *Bay Area Reporter* 11, no. 14 (2 July 1981), 34.

4. Lawrence K. Altman, "Rare Cancer Seen in 41 Homosexuals," *The New York Times* (3 July 1981), 20.

5. CDC, "Update on Acquired Immune Deficiency Syndrome (AIDS)—United States," *Morbidity and Mortality Weekly Report* 31, no. 37 (24 September 1982), 507. The number of cases per million population reported in that period "in New York City and San Francisco was roughly 10 times greater than that of the entire country." The report went on to note that "the eventual case-mortality rate of AIDS, a few years after diagnosis, may be far greater than the 41% overall case-mortality rate noted above." See "Update," 507, 513–14.

6. TG to Douglas Chambers, 13 February 1982, Toronto MSS.
7. Diary (1974–1986), 18 February 1982, Bancroft MSS.
8. Diary (1974–1986), 6, 9 April 1982, Bancroft MSS.
9. Diary (1974–1986), 14 April 1982, Bancroft MSS.
10. Diary (1974–1986), 17–18 April 1982, Bancroft MSS.
11. TG to Mike Kitay, 17 April 1982, Stanford MSS.
12. Diary (1974–1986), 27 April 1982, Bancroft MSS.
13. Diary (1974–1986), 15 May 1982, Bancroft MSS.
14. Poetry Notebook 4 (September 1981), Bancroft MSS.
15. TG to Don Bogen, 11 May 1982. Private collection.
16. "What the Slowworm Said," *SL*, 53–65; "Wings Deep," 6–7.
17. For the importance of 544 Natoma to South of Market culture, see Karl Stewart, "My Knights in Leather: Little Daddy and the Royal Ring," *Bay Area Reporter* 13, no. 40 (6 October 1983), 32–33.
18. See William Corbett, "August Kleinzahler: The Art of Poetry XCIII," *The Paris Review* 182 (Fall 2007), 32–34.
19. August Kleinzahler, interview with the author, 12 October 2018.
20. Kleinzahler, *Cutty, One Rock*, 132.
21. August Kleinzahler, interview with the author, 12 October 2018.
22. TG to Douglas Chambers, 29 September 1983, in *Letters*, 389.
23. Allan Noseworthy to TG, 30 March–9 April 1982, Bancroft MSS.
24. See Joel Laski, "Castro Service for Michael Maletta," *Bay Area Reporter* 12, no. 32 (12 August 1982), 5.
25. Arthur Evans, "Lethal Lifestyle," *Bay Area Reporter* 12, no. 35 (2 September 1982), 7.
26. CDC, "A Cluster of Kaposi's Sarcoma and Pneumocystis carinii Pneumonia Among Homosexual Male Residents of Los Angeles and Orange Counties, California," *Morbidity and Mortality Weekly Report* 31, no. 23 (18 June 1982), 305–307.
27. CDC, "Update," 507.
28. "Skateboard," *CP*, 433.
29. Diary (1974–1986), 18 August 1982, Bancroft MSS. See "Bow Down," *The Threepenny Review* 14 (Summer 1983), 3, uncollected.
30. TG to Belle Randall, 23 May 1983, Randall MSS.
31. Poetry Notebook 4 (September 1981), Bancroft MSS.
32. "To a Friend in Time of Trouble," *CP*, 409.
33. Mike Kitay, interview with the author, 18 June 2019.
34. "Thom Gunn Writes," *Poetry Book Society Bulletin* 113 (Summer 1982), 1.
35. Diary (1974–1986), 11 August 1982, Bancroft MSS.
36. Ian Hamilton, "The Call of the Cool," *The Times Literary Supplement* 4138 (23 July 1982), 782.
37. Gavin Ewart, "Moving Verse," *The Guardian* (1 July 1982), 8.
38. Mark Caldwell, untitled review of *PJ* and *OP*, *The Village Voice* 27, no. 43 (26 October 1982), 55.
39. Andy Brumer, "Exploring an Exceptional Literary Mind," *San Francisco Chronicle* (2 January 1983), R4.
40. Mary Kinzie, "No Connection," *The American Poetry Review* 12, no. 1 (January–February 1983), 32.

41. Don Bogen, "Energy and Control," *The Threepenny Review* 15 (Autumn 1983), 16.
42. Steve Abbott, untitled review of *PJ*, *The Advocate* 356 (25 November 1982), 30.
43. TG to Donald Davie, 29 July 1982, in *Letters*, 373.
44. Donald Davie, "Looking Up," *London Review of Books* 4, no. 13 (15 July–4 August 1982), 19.
45. Donald Davie to TG, 9 July 1982, Bancroft MSS.
46. Donald Davie to TG, 13 January 1982, Bancroft MSS.
47. TG to Donald Davie, 17 May 1982, in *Letters*, 372.
48. Wilmer, "Art of Poetry," 180.
49. TG to Douglas Chambers, 5 August 1982, Toronto MSS.
50. Wilmer, "Art of Poetry," 180.
51. TG to Douglas Chambers, 5 August 1982, Toronto MSS.
52. TG to Ander Gunn, 13 October 1982. Private collection.
53. Mike Kitay, interview with the author, 21 October 2018.
54. Charlotte Gunn, interview with the author, 29 November 2018.
55. Bob Bair, interview with the author, 21 June 2019.
56. Mike Kitay, interview with the author, 21 October 2018.
57. Charlotte Gunn, interview with the author, 29 November 2018.
58. Charlotte Gunn, interview with the author, 29 November 2018.
59. TG to Charlotte Gunn, 13 December 1982. Private collection.
60. TG to Barbara Godfrey, 17 December 1982. Private collection.
61. Mike Kitay, interview with the author, 21 October 2018.
62. TG could be hostile to expressions of femininity in masculine spaces. One Bay Area poet, an acquaintance, once ran into TG at a South of Market leather bar. "I was completely in drag and I looked fabulous," he recalled. "I came up to Thom, tapped him on the shoulder, he turned around and, without recognizing me, was none too pleased. And he was none too pleased *after* recognizing me. I think it was like blowing his cover in some way. He was uncomfortable. He really didn't want to talk to me like that. It was guilt by association or something." Aaron Shurin, interview with the author, 10 October 2018.
63. Mike Kitay, interview with the author, 12 October 2018.
64. TG to August Kleinzahler, c. 25 November 1995, in *Letters*, 588.
65. "Three Hard Women," *SL*, 55. The essay is about H.D., Mina Loy, and Marianne Moore.
66. Wendy Lesser, "Notes to Readers," *The Threepenny Review* 14 (Summer 1983), 26.
67. Robert Glück, interview with the author, 23 October 2018.
68. Wendy Lesser, interview with the author, 2 April 2019.
69. See chapter 34, p. 432.
70. Margaret [Baron] Owen, interview with the author, 24 July 2018.
71. TG to Jack Hagstrom, 17 December 1982, Hagstrom MSS.
72. Diary (1974–1986), 16 January 1983, Bancroft MSS.
73. Poetry Notebook 4 (September 1981), 12 January 1983, Bancroft MSS.
74. Poetry Notebook 4 (September 1981), 10 January 1983, Bancroft MSS. This made TG think of "that poem of Hardy's about the ghost surviving only as long as there is someone to remember the dead person"—a reference to "The To-be-forgotten," in which the dead fear their "future second death . . . / When, with the living, memory of us numbs, / And blank oblivion comes!"

75. Poetry Notebook 4 (September 1981), 14 January 1983, Bancroft MSS.
76. Allan Noseworthy to TG, 18–23 February 1983, Bancroft MSS.
77. Diary (1974–1986), 2 May 1983, Bancroft MSS.
78. Mike Kitay, interview with the author, 24 June 2019.
79. TG also emphasized "the importance of friendship, which may well have emerged from tricking in the first place." See Poetry Notebook 4 (September 1981), 9 January 1983, Bancroft MSS.
80. TG to Douglas Chambers, 16 May 1983, in *Letters*, 380.
81. TG to Douglas Chambers, 23 April 1982, in *Letters*, 371.
82. TG to Douglas Chambers, 8 June 1983, in *Letters*, 382.
83. Poetry Notebook 4 (September 1981), Bancroft MSS.
84. TG to Clive Wilmer, 17 April 1983, Wilmer MSS.
85. TG to Douglas Chambers, 16 May 1983, in *Letters*, 380.
86. TG to Ander Gunn, 14 August 1983. Private collection.
87. Poetry Notebook 4 (September 1981), Bancroft MSS.
88. TG to Clive Wilmer, 5 January 1984, in *Letters*, 390.
89. TG to Ander Gunn, 12 May 1983. Private collection.
90. TG to Douglas Chambers, 4 August 1983, in *Letters*, 386.
91. Diary (1974–1986), 17 January 1976, Bancroft MSS.
92. Diary (1974–1986), 7 June 1979, Bancroft MSS.
93. Mike Kitay, interview with the author, 24 June 2019.
94. Diary (1974–1986), 20 May 1983, Bancroft MSS.
95. Diary (1974–1986), 1, 3, 6 June 1983, Bancroft MSS.
96. TG to Barbara Godfrey, 16 June 1983. Private collection.
97. TG to Mary and Catherine Thomson, 28 July 1983, in *Letters*, 384.
98. Konstantin Berlandt and Wayne April, "Ad-Hoc Group Urges Bathhouses to Post AIDS Warnings," *Bay Area Reporter* 13, no. 21 (26 May 1983), 1.
99. See "Supervisors Pass AIDS Funding 11–0," *Bay Area Reporter* 13, no. 21 (26 May 1983), 1.
100. Diary (1974–1986), 7 June 1983, Bancroft MSS.
101. John Donne, "Of the Progress of the Soul: The Second Anniversary," in *The Complete English Poems of John Donne*, ed. C. A. Patrides (London: J. M. Dent, 1990), 355.

29. ALLAN

1. Diary (1974–1986), 9 July 1983, Bancroft MSS.
2. TG to Douglas Chambers, 4 August 1983, in *Letters*, 386.
3. Diary (1974–1986), 21–22 August 1983, Bancroft MSS.
4. Poetry Notebook 4 (September 1981), Bancroft MSS; *Ben Jonson*, 128.
5. Poetry Notebook 4 (September 1981), Bancroft MSS.
6. TG to Douglas Chambers, 30 August 1983, Toronto MSS.
7. Diary (1974–1986), 24 August 1983, Bancroft MSS.
8. Diary (1974–1986), 3 September 1983, Bancroft MSS.
9. TG to Douglas Chambers, 29 September 1983, in *Letters*, 388.
10. TG to Ander Gunn, 30 September 1983. Private collection.
11. TG to Clive Wilmer, 5 January 1984, in *Letters*, 391.
12. TG to Douglas Chambers, 29 September 1983, in *Letters*, 389.

13. Diary (1974–1986), 20 September 1983, Bancroft MSS.
14. TG to Douglas Chambers, 31 May 1977, in *Letters*, 339.
15. Diary (1974–1986), 26 August 1983, Bancroft MSS.
16. Diary (1983–1989), 25–26 October 1983, Bancroft MSS.
17. TG to Douglas Chambers, 5 December 1983, Toronto MSS.
18. Diary (1974–1986), 1 December 1983, Bancroft MSS.
19. TG to Douglas Chambers, 30 May 1984, in *Letters*, 393. See "Bone," *CP*, 410.
20. TG to Charlotte Gunn, 30 December 1983. Private collection.
21. TG to Douglas Chambers, 5 December 1983, Toronto MSS.
22. TG to Douglas Chambers, 5 December 1983, Toronto MSS.
23. Thomas Nashe, *The Unfortunate Traveller and Other Works*, ed. J. B. Steane (London: Penguin, 1985), 204.
24. Poetry Notebook 5 (December 1983), Bancroft MSS. Their names are Tony Tavarossi, Michael Maletta, Gemini Mike [Shiell], Joe Salek, Paul Joseph, John Ponyman, Rick Jacobi, AN3 [Allan Noseworthy], and Tom Tyler. TG likely suspected Allan had AIDS because he had been in poor health for much of 1983.
25. TG notes that Greville and Camus also used this image. Camus used it "for the state of a man constrained by a sense of guilt in a world where there is no god and thus where there can be no redemption for that guilt." See "Fulke Greville," *OP*, 67.
26. TG to Douglas Chambers, 29 December 1983, Toronto MSS.
27. Diary (1974–1986), 26 December 1983, Bancroft MSS.
28. Diary (1974–1986), 27 December 1983, Bancroft MSS.
29. Diary (1974–1986), 29 December 1983, Bancroft MSS.
30. Diary (1974–1986), 30 December 1983, Bancroft MSS.
31. White had served five years of his seven-year sentence for the assassinations of Harvey Milk and George Moscone. "The question of the day," asked Brian Jones in the *Bay Area Reporter*: "Were people still Mad As Hell at the Dan White verdict? The answer of the day: You Better Believe It!" Brian Jones, "White Protests Bigger Than Expected," *Bay Area Reporter* 14, no. 2 (12 January 1984), 4. White took his own life in October 1985.
32. Diary (1974–1986), 13 January 1984, Bancroft MSS.
33. TG to Mary and Catherine Thomson, 15 January 1984. Private collection.
34. Diary (1974–1986), 6 January 1984, Bancroft MSS.
35. Diary (1974–1986), 20 January 1984, Bancroft MSS.
36. Poetry Notebook 5 (December 1983), 22 January 1984, Bancroft MSS.
37. Diary (1974–1986), 10 February 1984, Bancroft MSS.
38. Diary (1974–1986), 19 February 1984, Bancroft MSS.
39. Diary (1974–1986), 25 March 1984, Bancroft MSS.
40. Poetry Notebook 5 (December 1983), Bancroft MSS.
41. "The Differences," *CP*, 414. TG developed this metaphor in "Philemon and Baucis" (*CP*, 416), which he wrote around six months later.
42. Diary (1974–1986), 17 April 1984, Bancroft MSS.
43. TG to Jack Hagstrom, 15 May 1984, Hagstrom MSS.
44. TG to Douglas Chambers, 30 May 1984, in *Letters*, 392.
45. Diary (1974–1986), 4 May 1984, Bancroft MSS.
46. TG to Douglas Chambers, 30 May 1984, in *Letters*, 392.

47. Diary (1974–1986), 3 March 1984, Bancroft MSS. Siniard took his own life in November 1990, at the age of fifty-two. See "Roy Will Siniard," *Bay Area Reporter* 21, no. 2 (10 January 1991), 22.
48. Diary (1974–1986), 8 February 1984, Bancroft MSS.
49. Diary (1974–1986), 30 March 1984, Bancroft MSS.
50. See Rubin, "Elegy," 108.
51. Poetry Notebook 6 (August 1984), Bancroft MSS.
52. Allan Noseworthy to TG, 18 March 1984, Bancroft MSS.
53. Diary (1974–1986), 7 April 1984, Bancroft MSS.
54. Diary (1974–1986), 5 May 1984, Bancroft MSS.
55. Diary (1974–1986), 8 May 1984, Bancroft MSS.
56. Diary (1974–1986), 11 May 1984, Bancroft MSS.
57. TG to Ander Gunn, 23 May 1984. Private collection.
58. TG to Douglas Chambers, 30 May 1984, in *Letters*, 392.
59. Poetry Notebook 5 (December 1983), Bancroft MSS. TG called this note "Theory of Consolation."
60. Diary (1974–1986), 4 June 1984, Bancroft MSS.
61. TG to Barbara Godfrey, 14 June 1984, in *Letters*, 396.
62. Mike Kitay, interview with the author, 24 June 2019.
63. Diary (1974–1986), 8 June 1984, Bancroft MSS.
64. TG to Barbara Godfrey, 14 June 1984, in *Letters*, 397.
65. TG to Douglas Chambers, 2 July 1984, in *Letters*, 398.
66. Diary (1974–1986), 15 June 1984, Bancroft MSS.
67. Diary (1974–1986), 14 June 1984, Bancroft MSS.
68. Diary (1974–1986), 13 June 1984, Bancroft MSS.
69. TG to Barbara Godfrey, 14 June 1984, in *Letters*, 396–97.
70. Diary (1974–1986), 18 June 1984, Bancroft MSS.
71. TG to Ander Gunn, 13 July 1984. Private collection.
72. Diary (1974–1986), 19 June 1984, Bancroft MSS.
73. Diary (1974–1986), 21 June 1984, Bancroft MSS.
74. TG to Mary and Catherine Thomson, 24 August 1984. Private collection.
75. Diary (1974–1986), 22 June 1984, Bancroft MSS.
76. Diary (1974–1986), 25 June 1984, Bancroft MSS.
77. TG to Tony Tanner, 30 July 1984, in *Letters*, 402.
78. Diary (1974–1986), 22 June 1984, Bancroft MSS.
79. Diary (1974–1986), 11 June 1984, Bancroft MSS.
80. Diary (1974–1986), 12 July 1984, Bancroft MSS.
81. Diary (1974–1986), 19 May 1984, Bancroft MSS.
82. Diary (1974–1986), 18 July 1984, Bancroft MSS.
83. Diary (1974–1986), 25 July 1984, Bancroft MSS.
84. Poetry Notebook 5 (December 1983), Bancroft MSS.
85. TG to Clive Wilmer, 28 August 1984, Wilmer MSS.
86. Poetry Notebook 5 (December 1983), Bancroft MSS.
87. "Lament," *CP*, 468.
88. "The Reassurance," *CP*, 471.
89. Poetry Notebook 6 (August 1984), Bancroft MSS.
90. *Thom Gunn in Conversation*, 19.

91. Like "Lament," "An Invitation" (*CP*, 411–12) is in TG's Jonsonian mode. "Inevitably it calls to mind Ben Jonson's great poem 'On Inviting a Friend to Supper,'" remarked Wilmer, "which, analogously, sets the candour and liberality of good fellowship against the paranoia of a repressive state." Wilmer, "The Dangerous Edge of Things," *PN Review* 85, vol. 18, no. 5 (May–June 1992), 62. See chapter 34, p. 436.

92. Poetry Notebook 6 (August 1984), Bancroft MSS.

93. TG to Douglas Chambers, 9 October 1984, in *Letters*, 404.

94. Diary (1974–1986), 29 September 1984, Bancroft MSS.

95. Diary (1974–1986), 10 September 1984, Bancroft MSS.

96. Diary (1974–1986), 29 September 1984, Bancroft MSS.

97. Diary (1983–1989), 9 November 1984, Bancroft MSS.

98. Poetry Notebook 5 (December 1983), Bancroft MSS.

99. TG to Ander Gunn, 24 November 1984. Private collection.

100. TG to Mary and Catherine Thomson, 14 December 1984, in *Letters*, 408–409.

101. Diary (1974–1986), 20 November 1984, Bancroft MSS.

102. Diary (1983–1989), 19 November 1984, Bancroft MSS.

103. TG to Mary and Catherine Thomson, 14 December 1984, in *Letters*, 409.

104. Diary (1974–1986), 11 December 1984, Bancroft MSS.

105. Poetry Notebook 5 (December 1983), Bancroft MSS.

106. Poetry Notebook 6 (August 1984), Bancroft MSS. See chapter 23, p. 289.

107. Poetry Notebook 6 (August 1984), Bancroft MSS.

108. Diary (1974–1986), 22 November 1984, Bancroft MSS.

109. Diary (1974–1986), 31 December 1984, Bancroft MSS.

110. Diary (1974–1986), 1–2 January 1985, Bancroft MSS.

111. Diary (1986–2000), 18 August 1988, Bancroft MSS. See "Dennis Leon Hrlic," *Bay Area Reporter* 18, no. 33 (18 August 1988), 19.

30. ILLUMINATIONS

1. Diary (1974–1986), 22 September 1984, Bancroft MSS.

2. TG to Robert Duncan, 25 September 1984, Duncan MSS.

3. Egbert Faas, "An Interview with Robert Duncan," *boundary 2*, vol. 8, no. 2 (Winter 1980), 18.

4. TG to Tony Tanner, 30 July 1984, in *Letters*, 402.

5. Poetry Notebook 5 (December 1983), Bancroft MSS.

6. Diary (1974–1986), 11 October 1984, Bancroft MSS.

7. Diary (1974–1986), 5 November 1984, Bancroft MSS.

8. Poetry Notebook 6 (August 1984), Bancroft MSS.

9. "Odysseus on Hermes," *CP*, 418.

10. Poetry Notebook 6 (August 1984), 3 February 1985, Bancroft MSS; see also chapter 5, p. 61. TG does not mention the summer 1951 "revelation" in these initial notes but it belonged to the same set of experiences. See "Cambridge in the Fifties," *OP*, 159; "South," 637; and chapter 7, p. 79.

11. TG to Ander Gunn, 24 February 1985. Private collection.

12. Diary (1974–1986), 6, 8 January 1985, Bancroft MSS.

13. Poetry Notebook 6 (August 1984), Bancroft MSS. There are remarkably few revisions between the "extempore" and final versions of "In Time of Plague." Com-

pare the opening lines of the final version: "My thoughts are crowded with death / and it draws so oddly on the sexual" (*CP*, 463).

14. "In Time of Plague," *CP*, 463–64.
15. By summer 1984, TG had not heard from Tanner "for many a twelvemonth." See TG to Tony Tanner, 30 July 1984, in *Letters*, 401. TG is likely exaggerating for comic effect: he had not heard from Tanner for about two years. See Tony Tanner to TG, 12 June 1982, Bancroft MSS.
16. TG to Tony Tanner, 8 January 1985, King's MSS.
17. Clive Wilmer, interview with the author, 13 December 2018.
18. TG to Tony Tanner, 8 January 1985, King's MSS.
19. Diary (1974–1986), 11 January 1985, Bancroft MSS.
20. TG to Mary and Catherine Thomson, 30 January 1985, in *Letters*, 411–12.
21. Diary (1974–1986), 13 January 1985, Bancroft MSS.
22. TG to Mary and Catherine Thomson, 30 January 1985, in *Letters*, 411–12.
23. TG to Robert Conquest, 6 March 1985, in *Letters*, 412.
24. TG to Barbara Godfrey, 27 May 1985. Private collection.
25. Poetry Notebook 6 (August 1984), 8 January 1985, Bancroft MSS.
26. TG to Tony Tanner, 17 May 1985, in *Letters*, 414.
27. TG to Tony Tanner, 8 January 1985, King's MSS.
28. Diary (1974–1986), 5, 12, 24 June 1985, Bancroft MSS.
29. Diary (1974–1986), 26 April 1985, Bancroft MSS.
30. TG to Ander Gunn, 10 May 1985. Private collection.
31. TG to Douglas Chambers, 16 May 1985, Toronto MSS.
32. Poetry Notebook 7 (November 1985), Bancroft MSS.
33. TG to Douglas Chambers, 16 May 1985, Toronto MSS.
34. See "Josephine Miles," *California Monthly* 95, no. 6 (June–July 1985), 29.
35. Poetry Notebook 6 (August 1984), Bancroft MSS. "The sloth which is the reverse of life" alludes to what moly counteracts, "putting pig within." See "Moly," *CP*, 187.
36. Diary (1974–1986), 15 May 1985, Bancroft MSS.
37. Diary (1974–1986), 13, 19 November 1985, Bancroft MSS.
38. TG to Douglas Chambers, 16 July 1985, Toronto MSS.
39. TG to John Lehmann, 7 August 1985, Princeton MSS.
40. TG to Clive Wilmer, 19 August 1985, Wilmer MSS.
41. Poetry Notebook 6 (August 1984), Bancroft MSS.
42. TG to Douglas Chambers, 26 September 1985, in *Letters*, 417.
43. Poetry Notebook 6 (August 1984), Bancroft MSS.
44. Diary (1974–1986), 22 September 1985, Bancroft MSS.
45. TG to Douglas Chambers, 26 September 1985, in *Letters*, 417.
46. Poetry Notebook 6 (August 1984), Bancroft MSS.
47. Poetry Notebook 7 (November 1985), Bancroft MSS.
48. "Nights with the Speed Bros.," *BC*, 34. At first, TG mistakenly thought Eric and Rick were half brothers.
49. Diary (1974–1986), 29 September 1984, Bancroft MSS.
50. Poetry Notebook 6 (August 1984), Bancroft MSS.
51. Diary (1974–1986), 12–13 October 1985, Bancroft MSS.
52. TG to John Holmstrom, 22 February 1986, Bancroft MSS.
53. Clive Wilmer, email to the author, 23 November 2022.

54. TG to John Holmstrom, 22 February 1986, Bancroft MSS.

55. Poetry Notebook 7 (November 1985), Bancroft MSS.

56. TG to Ander Gunn, 28 November 1985, in *Letters*, 419–20.

57. TG to Clive Wilmer, 27 December 1985, Wilmer MSS.

58. Poetry Notebook 6 (August 1984), Bancroft MSS.

59. Poetry Notebook 7 (November 1985), Bancroft MSS.

60. "The Man with Night Sweats," *CP*, 461–62.

61. Poetry Notebook 6 (August 1984), Bancroft MSS.

62. Poetry Notebook 7 (November 1985), Bancroft MSS.

63. "South," 637.

64. Poetry Notebook 7 (November 1985), Bancroft MSS.

65. TG to Jack Hagstrom, 31 December 1985, Hagstrom MSS.

66. Diary (1974–1986), 12 November 1985, Bancroft MSS.

67. "Gary died, without a will and without relatives . . . and a huge house full of treasures," TG continued. "Don decided that it was a waste for the State to get all this & is selling off all the treasures as fast as he can, so as to distribute the money among [Gary]'s best friends. And Don is such that you can be sure none of this is for himself, though he is risking jail by doing it. (But something about Don loves the drama of risk.)" TG to Ander Gunn, 28 November 1985, in *Letters*, 419. TG himself received "the compact OED w/ magnifier." Diary (1974–1986), 19 November 1985, Bancroft MSS. Gary's art and antiques collection included Biedermeier-style furniture, eighteenth-century French porcelain, numerous sixteenth- and seventeenth-century Dutch and Flemish paintings, as well as an extensive pewter and silver collection. Not all of Gary's friends agreed with TG's assessment of Don's motives. "The prevailing opinion among Gary's friends was that Don looted Gary's estate," recalled one. "Gary would be pissed at how things turned out." Another was "enraged" to find that a subsequent appraisal of Gary's estate did not include "a large number of art objects" that were known to be in his collection. See Clyde Wildes, email to the author, 21 September 2023; see also Gary Owsley to James Scannell, 18 April 1986. Private collection. Moreover, because Gary died intestate, a dispute arose between his ex-boyfriend, Laurence Bartholomew, and Don—who occupied 400 Clayton with another of Gary's friends, Al Talley—as to whether Gary had revoked the trust that named Don his sole trustee. Litigation ensued. Don won the case: he sold 400 Clayton for $560,000 in late 1988 and subsequently moved to New York. See *Bartholomew v. Doody and Talley* (A040877) in the Court of Appeals for the State of California, 1987.

68. Diary (1974–1986), 15 March 1986, Bancroft MSS.

69. TG to Ander Gunn, 8 March 1986. Private collection.

70. Diary (1974–1986), 11 January 1986, Bancroft MSS.

71. TG copied the paragraph from *Great Expectations* beginning "My first most vivid and broad impression of the identity of things" in his notebook while writing the poem. The "little churchyard clogged with nettles" is an almost exact lift. See Poetry Notebook 7 (November 1985), Bancroft MSS.

72. *Thom Gunn in Conversation*, 52.

73. "A Sketch of the Great Dejection," *CP*, 424.

74. Poetry Notebook 7 (November 1985), Bancroft MSS.

75. "A Sketch of the Great Dejection," *CP*, 424.

76. TG to Wendy Lesser, 15 April 1986. Private collection.
77. TG to Wendy Lesser, 30 June 1986. Private collection. See "The Liberty Granted," *In Folio* 29 (8 August 1986), 2–3, uncollected.
78. TG to Clive Wilmer, 1 June 1987, Wilmer MSS.
79. Poetry Notebook 7 (November 1985), Bancroft MSS.
80. Diary (1974–1986), 18 March 1986, Bancroft MSS.
81. TG to Ander Gunn, 8 March 1996. Private collection.
82. Diary (1974–1986), 26 March 1986, Bancroft MSS.
83. TG to Tony Tanner, 3 June 1986, in *Letters*, 423.
84. TG to Jack Hagstrom, 9 March 1986, Hagstrom MSS.
85. TG to Tony Tanner, 3 June 1986, in *Letters*, 423.
86. TG to John Holmstrom, 4 June 1986, Bancroft MSS.
87. Diary (1974–1986), 15 August 1986, Bancroft MSS.
88. TG to Mary and Catherine Thomson, 15 March 1987. Private collection.
89. TG to Mary and Catherine Thomson, 9 August 1986. Private collection.
90. TG to Timothy Steele, 11 June 1986. Private collection.
91. Clive Wilmer, email to the author, 28 November 2022.
92. August Kleinzahler, email to the author, 31 December 2022.
93. TG to Douglas Chambers, 16 July 1986, in *Letters*, 427.
94. Diary (1974–1986), 24 June 1986, Bancroft MSS.
95. Diary (1974–1986), 13 July 1986, Bancroft MSS.
96. Diary (1974–1986), 15 May 1986, Bancroft MSS.
97. Diary (1974–1986), 13 September 1986, Bancroft MSS.

31. THE MISSING

1. TG to Ander Gunn, 27 September 1986. Private collection. Jim worked at the University of California San Francisco Medical Center at Parnassus Heights.
2. TG to Clive Wilmer, 22 September 1986, Wilmer MSS.
3. See Poetry Notebook 8 (September 1986), Bancroft MSS.
4. Poetry Notebook 8 (September 1986), Bancroft MSS.
5. TG to Douglas Chambers, 24 October 1986, in *Letters*, 428.
6. TG to Ander Gunn, 27 September 1986. Private collection.
7. Diary (1986–2000), 20 September 1986, Bancroft MSS.
8. TG to Ander Gunn, 7 November 1986. Private collection.
9. "Terminal," *CP*, 469.
10. Diary (1986–2000), 15, 19 September 1986, Bancroft MSS.
11. Diary (1986–2000), 18 September 1986, Bancroft MSS.
12. TG to Ander Gunn, 27 September 1986. Private collection.
13. Diary (1986–2000), 8 November 1986, Bancroft MSS.
14. Diary (1986–2000), 29 November 1986, Bancroft MSS.
15. Charlie Hinkle to TG, 14 October 1986, Bancroft MSS. TG used three lines from "Rain" as the epigraph to the elegies section of *MNS* (*CP*, 459). For Hinkle's pamphlet *Poems*, see chapter 32, pp. 404–405.
16. Poetry Notebook 9 (August 1987), Bancroft MSS. The phrases are from an early draft of "To a Dead Graduate Student," *CP*, 482.
17. Diary (1986–2000), 4 December 1986, Bancroft MSS.
18. Diary (1986–2000), 5 December 1986, Bancroft MSS.

19. Diary (1986–2000), 6 December 1986, Bancroft MSS.
20. "Still Life," *CP*, 470. Compare the "backwards flute" in "The Gas-poker," *BC*, 11.
21. TG to Douglas Chambers, 16 December 1986, in *Letters*, 429.
22. Diary (1986–2000), 5 December 1986, Bancroft MSS.
23. TG to Ralph Pomeroy, 14 December 1986, Bancroft MSS.
24. Diary (1986–2000), 13 December 1986, Bancroft MSS.
25. Diary (1986–2000), 17 December 1986, Bancroft MSS.
26. TG to Clive Wilmer, 24 November 1986, Wilmer MSS.
27. Diary (1986–2000), 20 December 1986, Bancroft MSS.
28. Diary (1986–2000), 24 December 1986, Bancroft MSS.
29. TG to Ander and Bett Gunn, 30 December 1986, in *Letters*, 431.
30. Diary (1986–2000), 25 December 1986, Bancroft MSS.
31. TG to Belle Randall, 9 October 1987, in *Letters*, 441.
32. TG to Ander and Bett Gunn, 30 December 1986, in *Letters*, 431.
33. Diary (1986–2000), 26 December 1986, Bancroft MSS.
34. TG to Douglas Chambers, 3 January 1987, Toronto MSS.
35. Diary (1986–2000), 31 December 1986, Bancroft MSS. This incident informed "Sequel" (*BC*, 35–36).
36. Diary (1986–2000), 29 December 1986, Bancroft MSS.
37. "Words for Some Ash," *CP*, 472.
38. TG to Douglas Chambers, 3 January 1987, Toronto MSS; Diary (1986–2000), 21 January 1987, Bancroft MSS.
39. Diary (1986–2000), 29 January 1987, Bancroft MSS.
40. TG to Ander Gunn, 26 February 1987. Private collection.
41. Poetry Notebook 8 (September 1986), Bancroft MSS.
42. Diary (1986–2000), 29 January 1987, Bancroft MSS.
43. TG to Mary and Catherine Thomson, 24 February 1987. Private collection.
44. TG to Douglas Chambers, 1 March 1987, Toronto MSS.
45. TG to Ander Gunn, 19 April 1987. Private collection.
46. Charlie Hinkle to TG, 19 April 1987, Bancroft MSS.
47. TG to Ander Gunn, 19 April 1987. Private collection.
48. Diary (1986–2000), 31 March 1987, Bancroft MSS.
49. Diary (1986–2000), 4 April 1987, Bancroft MSS.
50. Louis Bryan, interview with the author, 20 October 2018.
51. TG to Ander Gunn, 19 April 1987. Private collection.
52. Diary (1986–2000), 14 April 1987, Bancroft MSS.
53. TG to Ander Gunn, 19 April 1987. Private collection.
54. Diary (1986–2000), 30 April 1987, Bancroft MSS.
55. Poetry Notebook 8 (September 1986); Diary (1986–2000), 1 May 1987, Bancroft MSS.
56. Diary (1986–2000), 3 May 1987, Bancroft MSS. TG quotes from Pound's "The River-Merchant's Wife."
57. Diary (1986–2000), 17 June 1987, Bancroft MSS.
58. Poetry Notebook 8 (September 1986), Bancroft MSS.
59. Charlie Hinkle to TG, 19 April 1987, Bancroft MSS.
60. Diary (1986–2000), 30 May 1987, Bancroft MSS.
61. Diary (1986–2000), 4 June 1987, Bancroft MSS. An alternate reading would be

"young man"—TG's handwriting here is ambiguous—although after 1:00 p.m. on this date, a first quarter moon was visible from San Francisco.

62. Diary (1986–2000), 23 June 1987, Bancroft MSS.

63. Diary (1986–2000), 9 July 1987, Bancroft MSS.

64. "The J Car," *CP*, 480–81. "Unready, disappointed, unachieved" echoes "unhoused, disappointed, unannealed": see *Hamlet*, I.5.77, in *Oxford Shakespeare*, 661.

65. Mike Kitay, interview with the author, 16 October 2018.

66. Diary (1986–2000), 8 August 1987, Bancroft MSS. Norm was from Dayton, Ohio.

67. Diary (1986–2000), 12 August 1987, Bancroft MSS.

68. Diary (1986–2000), 17 August 1987, Bancroft MSS.

69. Diary (1986–2000), 18 August 1987, Bancroft MSS.

70. TG to Ander Gunn, 31 August 1987, in *Letters*, 439.

71. Diary (1986–2000), 24 August 1987, Bancroft MSS.

72. Diary (1986–2000), 25 August 1987, Bancroft MSS.

73. The opening line echoes Camus's *La Peste*, "Le graphique des progrès de la peste," which reads, in Gilbert's translation, "the progress of the plague." See Camus, *The Plague*, trans. Gilbert, 96. TG had first admired *La Peste* in the 1960s for its account of everyday heroism; in the late 1980s, it took on much greater significance for him in light of the AIDS epidemic.

74. "The Missing," *CP*, 483.

75. Diary (1986–2000), 27 August 1987, Bancroft MSS.

76. Balbiani's tomb can be found in the Musée du Louvre, Paris. TG saw its photograph in Michael Levey's *High Renaissance* (Harmondsworth, UK: Penguin, 1975), 129.

77. "Her Pet," *CP*, 475.

78. Diary (1986–2000), 8 September 1987, Bancroft MSS.

79. Diary (1986–2000), 9 September 1987, Bancroft MSS.

80. Diary (1986–2000), 15 September 1987, Bancroft MSS.

81. TG to Belle Randall, 9 October 1987, in *Letters*, 441.

82. "Memory Unsettled," *CP*, 479.

83. Diary (1986–2000), 10–11 September 1987, Bancroft MSS.

84. Diary (1986–2000), 18 September 1987, Bancroft MSS.

85. Mike Kitay, interview with the author, 24 June 2019.

86. Diary (1986–2000), 18 September 1987, Bancroft MSS.

87. Mike Kitay to TG, c. August 1987, Bancroft MSS. Mike's father had suffered from early-onset Alzheimer's; for Mike, the thought he might suffer the same fate was a constant source of anxiety.

88. Diary (1986–2000), 24 August 1987, Bancroft MSS.

89. TG to Clive Wilmer, 5 January 1988, Wilmer MSS.

90. Diary (1986–2000), 21 September 1987, Bancroft MSS.

91. Diary (1986–2000), 27 September 1987, Bancroft MSS.

92. See Diary (1986–2000), 30 September 1987, Bancroft MSS. "Memory Unsettled" (*CP*, 479) was originally called "The Arboretum."

93. Poetry Notebook 9 (August 1987), Bancroft MSS. TG refers to three famous elegies: Milton's "Lycidas"; Yeats's "In Memory of Major Robert Gregory"; and Jonson's "To Sir Robert Wroth."

94. Diary (1986–2000), 6 October 1987, Bancroft MSS.
95. TG to Ander Gunn, 10 November 1987. Private collection.
96. Diary (1986–2000), 9 November 1987, Bancroft MSS.
97. TG to Ander Gunn, 10 November 1987. Private collection.
98. Poems Annotated for Readings 1961–1999, Bancroft MSS.
99. "In the Post Office," *BC*, 15.
100. "Postscript: the Panel," *BC*, 16.
101. Poetry Notebook 9 (August 1987), Bancroft MSS.
102. "Postscript: the Panel," *BC*, 16–17.
103. "Death's Door," *CP*, 485.
104. Poetry Notebook 9 (August 1987), Bancroft MSS.
105. Diary (1986–2000), 15 December 1987, Bancroft MSS.
106. TG to Mary and Catherine Thomson, 23 December 1987. Private collection.
107. Diary (1986–2000), 27 December 1987, Bancroft MSS.
108. See "Postscript and Notes," *CP*, 492.
109. Not to be confused with the poet Paul Mariah (1937–1996), who lived for many years in the Bay Area and knew TG socially. For Mariah and Robert Duncan's poetry workshop, see p. 585, n91.

32. CONSOLATION

1. Diary (1986–2000), 17 December 1987, Bancroft MSS.
2. "Chuck Arnett," *Bay Area Reporter* 18, no. 10 (10 March 1988), 18.
3. "Thom Gunn: July 25, 1996," Prager MSS.
4. TG to Jack Hagstrom, 3 November 1987, Hagstrom MSS.
5. Diary (1986–2000), 3 February 1988, Bancroft MSS.
6. TG to Gregory Woods, 27 February 1988, in *Letters*, 445; see "Robert Duncan's Romantic Modernism," *European Gay Review* 4 (1989), 54–55.
7. TG to Gregory Woods, 27 February 1988, in *Letters*, 444.
8. See Diary (1986–2000), 18 November 1986, Bancroft MSS; TG to Clive Wilmer, 5 January 1988, Wilmer MSS.
9. Diary (1986–2000), 15 April 1988, Bancroft MSS.
10. August Kleinzahler to TG, 23 March 1988, Bancroft MSS.
11. Diary (1974–1986), 30 July 1985, Bancroft MSS.
12. Steven Fritsch Rudser, interview with the author, 16 October 2018.
13. TG to Jack Hagstrom, 13 November 1989, Hagstrom MSS.
14. "A Blank," *CP*, 487–88.
15. See TG to Steven Fritsch Rudser, 9 April 1988, in *Letters*, 446.
16. Diary (1986–2000), 13 April 1988, Bancroft MSS.
17. TG borrowed his title from a favorite Elizabethan song, Thomas Campion's "Now Winter Nights Enlarge." See chapter 18, p. 217.
18. Poetry Notebook 9 (August 1987), Bancroft MSS. For "math," see "The Problem," *BC*, 22–23.
19. Poetry Notebook 9 (August 1987), Bancroft MSS.
20. Diary (1986–2000), 15 September 1987, Bancroft MSS.
21. Diary (1986–2000), 15 June 1988, Bancroft MSS. See Charlie Hinkle, *Poems*, ed. TG and William McPherson (San Francisco: Eon Press, 1988).
22. See advertisement in *Bay Area Reporter* 18, no. 31 (4 August 1988), 45.

23. Diary (1986–2000), 20 June 1988, Bancroft MSS.
24. TG to Jack Hagstrom, 17 July 1988, in *Letters*, 452.
25. Poetry Notebook 10 (June 1988), Bancroft MSS. See Robert Duncan, "Sonnet 2," *Roots and Branches: Poems* (New York: Charles Scribner's Sons, 1964), 123.
26. "The High Road," *SL*, 130.
27. TG to Clive Wilmer, 28 July 1988, in *Letters*, 455.
28. TG to Jack Hagstrom, 12 September 1988, Hagstrom MSS.
29. Poetry Notebook 10 (June 1988), 26 July 1988, Bancroft MSS.
30. "A Symposium on the Strange, the Weird, and the Uncanny," *The Threepenny Review* 85 (Spring 2001), 21.
31. Poetry Notebook 3 (May 1980), Bancroft MSS.
32. TG to Jack Hagstrom, 1 August 1995, Hagstrom MSS.
33. Diary (1986–2000), 7 August 1988, Bancroft MSS.
34. Diary (1986–2000), 8, 13 August 1988, Bancroft MSS.
35. TG to Douglas Chambers, 7 September 1988, in *Letters*, 460–61.
36. TG to Douglas Chambers, 7 September 1988, in *Letters*, 460–61.
37. "At the Barriers," *CP*, 399.
38. "At the Barriers," *San Francisco Sentinel* 16, no. 41 (7 October 1988), 22, collected in *CP*, 399–402. For TG, two months was an uncommonly short time between starting and publishing a poem.
39. "At the Barriers," *CP*, 402. The phrase "returning to roots of first feeling" is the title of a Duncan poem. See Duncan, *The Collected Later Poems and Plays*, ed. Peter Quartermain (Berkeley: University of California Press, 2014), 79–80.
40. Gewanter, "Interview with Thom Gunn," 296.
41. Clive Wilmer, *Poets Talking: Poet of the Month Interviews from BBC Radio 3* (Manchester: Carcanet, 1994), 5. Compare TG's approach to writing about LSD in rhyme and meter, "to render the infinite through the finite." See "My Life Up to Now," *OP*, 182.
42. "Duncan," *BC*, 4. TG called the use of this image a "pun." See Wilmer, *Poets Talking*, 5. The image is from the Venerable Bede. In the poem's first printing in *The Threepenny Review*, TG had "swallow," not "sparrow." Denise Levertov wrote to correct him. See TG to Levertov, 1 April 1991, Levertov MSS.
43. "Duncan," *BC*, 3–4.
44. TG to Clive Wilmer, 13 November 1990, Wilmer MSS.
45. "Adventurous Song," *SL*, 154, 153.
46. TG to Douglas Chambers, 19 September 1990, in *Letters*, 490. TG discusses this definition in "Adventurous Song," *SL*, 150–51, 168.
47. TG to Ander Gunn, 24 May 1988. Private collection. Here, TG perhaps demonstrates a lack of self-reflection.
48. Poetry Notebook 9 (August 1987), Bancroft MSS. TG kept a typed copy of the letter in his notebook.
49. Diary (1986–2000), 11 June 1988, Bancroft MSS.
50. "A System," *BC*, 34.
51. Diary (1986–2000), 8 January 1989, Bancroft MSS.
52. TG to Ander Gunn, 5 February 1989. Private collection.
53. Diary (1986–2000), 10 January 1989, Bancroft MSS.
54. Diary (1986–2000), 12 January 1989, Bancroft MSS.

55. Diary (1986–2000), 13 January 1989, Bancroft MSS.
56. Diary (1986–2000), 18 January 1989, Bancroft MSS.
57. TG to Ander Gunn, 23 March 1989. Private collection.
58. TG to Douglas Chambers, 26 January 1989, Toronto MSS.
59. Diary (1986–2000), 13 February 1989, Bancroft MSS.
60. TG to Douglas Chambers, 26 January 1989, Toronto MSS; TG to Jack Hagstrom, 11 February 1989, Hagstrom MSS.
61. TG to Ander Gunn, 29 June 1989. Private collection.
62. Poetry Notebook 10 (June 1988), 26 July 1988, Bancroft MSS.
63. Diary (1986–2000), 6 May 1989, Bancroft MSS.
64. Diary (1986–2000), 27 April 1989, Bancroft MSS.
65. Diary (1986–2000), 24 May 1989, Bancroft MSS.
66. Diary (1986–2000), 10 May 1989, Bancroft MSS.
67. Diary (1986–2000), 16 July 1989, Bancroft MSS.
68. Poetry Notebook 10 (June 1988), 26 July 1988, Bancroft MSS.
69. Bob Bair, interview with the author, 21 June 2019.
70. Diary (1986–2000), 12 November 1989, Bancroft MSS.
71. TG to Douglas Chambers, 8 February 1990, Toronto MSS.
72. TG to Douglas Chambers, 21 August 1988, Toronto MSS.
73. Poetry Notebook 10 (June 1988), 26 July 1988, Bancroft MSS.
74. "As If Startled Awake: The Poetry of Janet Lewis," *SL*, 66–73; "Fever in the Morning: Jim Powell," *SL*, 121–25; and "Living the Present: Donald Hall," *SL*, 96–101.
75. "Forays Against the Republic: Whitman," *SL*, 15–21; and "Christopher Isherwood: Getting Things Right," *SL*, 173–96.
76. TG to A. E. Dyson, 21 November 1989, in *Letters*, 473.
77. Diary (1986–2000), 26 July 1989, Bancroft MSS.
78. See Clive Wilmer, ed., "Thom Gunn at Sixty," *PN Review* 70, vol. 16, no. 2 (November–December 1989), 25–56; Douglas Chambers, ed., *A Few Friends* (Walkerton, ON: Stonyground Press, 1989).
79. TG to Clive Wilmer, 25 September 1989, in *Letters*, 468.
80. Poetry Notebook 10 (June 1988), 26 July 1989, Bancroft MSS.
81. Diary (1986–2000), 12 December 1989, Bancroft MSS.
82. TG to Ander Gunn, 2 January 1990, in *Letters*, 476.
83. Diary (1986–2000), 30, 31 December 1989, Bancroft MSS.
84. TG to Tony Tanner, 7 January 1990, in *Letters*, 478–79.

33. NEEDS

1. TG to Ander Gunn, 22 March 1990. Private collection.
2. Regardless of which courses he taught, TG valued the connection between reading and writing and insisted his students compose short informal reports about "the ways in which [your reading] may have helped you as a writer." See "Reading for the rest of the winter quarter," February 1981, Bancroft MSS.
3. Diary (1986–2000), 20 February 1987, Bancroft MSS.
4. TG to Douglas Chambers, 1 March 1987, Toronto MSS.
5. TG to Douglas Chambers, 30 May 1984, in *Letters*, 392.
6. TG to Mary and Catherine Thomson, 15 April 1986. Private collection.
7. TG to August Kleinzahler, 31 October 1996, in *Letters*, 608.

8. TG to Douglas Chambers, 12 June 1989, Toronto MSS.
9. TG to Belle Randall, 19 October 1992, Randall MSS.
10. TG to August Kleinzahler, 31 October 1996, in *Letters*, 608.
11. Michael Colleary, email to the author, 21 January 2021.
12. Anne Winters, email to the author, 27 June 2021.
13. TG to John Holmstrom, 21 April 1990, Bancroft MSS.
14. David Gewanter, "Domains of Ecstasy," in Weiner, ed., *At the Barriers*, 318, n. 45. TG's reticence in the classroom extended to the bars. In 1993, the year he won the MacArthur Fellowship, TG began tricking with a leatherman named Doug whom he had met in My Place. "I did not know who he was," Doug reflected. "Pretty much the whole time I knew him. Once I said to a friend I had gone somewhere with Thom Gunn, and my friend said: 'Thom Gunn, the poet?' My friend, who was a lot more literarily aware than me, was impressed. 'He's a big deal,' he said. 'He's a great writer.' I was totally taken aback because I had no idea. Thom never brought that up." Doug H., telephone interview with the author, 30 March 2022.
15. Diary (1986–2000), 29 January 1992, Bancroft MSS.
16. TG to Jack Hagstrom, 25 February 1991, Hagstrom MSS.
17. "A week or so later, he told me the results wr negative." Diary (1986–2000), 25 February 1991, Bancroft MSS.
18. Weiner dedicated his dissertation to TG, "who encouraged me to write on [Loy], kept me honest while I tried to do so, pulled no punches, and speedily conveyed the curiosity and interest in the research and writing of this dissertation to keep me going." Joshua Weiner, "Mina Loy Among the Moderns" (PhD dissertation, University of California, Berkeley, 1998), v.
19. Joshua Weiner, letter to the author, 5 March 2018.
20. Diary (1986–2000), 20 March 1990, Bancroft MSS.
21. TG to Ander Gunn, 22 March 1990. Private collection.
22. Diary (1986–2000), 20 March 1990, Bancroft MSS.
23. Diary (1986–2000), 23 March 1990, Bancroft MSS.
24. TG to Mary and Catherine Thomson, 29 March 1990. Private collection.
25. See Miller, *Fathers*.
26. Craig Raine to TG, 23 May 1990, Faber Archive.
27. Craig Raine, "Bad Trip," *The London Magazine* N.S. 17, no. 1 (April–May 1977), 97.
28. Diary (1986–2000), 8 August 1989, Bancroft MSS.
29. Craig Raine to Clive Wilmer, 23 March 1988, Faber Archive. TG thought "the reason my reputation wasn't higher is because I'm not homosexual enough to please a homosexual audience and I'm not heterosexual enough to please a heterosexual audience. Because I want to write about everything! I never set out to be a homosexual poet. I never dreamt that anybody could be one or the other." See Randall and Joost, "Smokin' Gunn," 6–7.
30. Diary (1986–2000), 22 September 1989, Bancroft MSS.
31. TG to Craig Raine, 21 September 1989, Faber Archive. Raine succeeded Monteith as Faber poetry editor in 1981. Reid occasionally filled in when Raine was on sabbatical and took over from Raine permanently in 1991.
32. Craig Raine to TG, c. September 1989, Faber Archive.
33. TG to Craig Raine, 20 October 1989, Faber Archive.
34. Diary (1986–2000), 8 August 1989, Bancroft MSS.

35. TG to Neil Powell, 8 October 1989. Private collection.
36. TG to A. E. Dyson, 7 July 1989, Dyson MSS.
37. Poetry Notebook 11 (January 1990), Bancroft MSS.
38. Poetry Notebook XVII (May 1977), Bancroft MSS.
39. "Two Saturday Nights," *SL*, 213–17.
40. "Saturday Night," *BC*, 46. Compare "The stay of your secure firm dry embrace," in "The Hug," *CP*, 407.
41. TG to Tony Tanner, 7 January 1990, in *Letters*, 478.
42. Diary (1986–2000), 17 February 1990, Bancroft MSS.
43. Diary (1986–2000), 6 July 1990, Bancroft MSS.
44. TG to Douglas Chambers, 19 September 1990, in *Letters*, 490.
45. "American Boy," *BC*, 47. When *MNS* was published in 1992, TG handwrote "American Boy" in the copy he gave to Gallegos. "I wrote this poem too recently to be included," he told him in the inscription, "but you know it's about you. XX Thom."
46. "Modes of Pleasure," *CP*, 101.
47. TG to Robert Gallegos, 19 August 1991. Private collection.
48. TG to John Holmstrom, 13 July 1991, Bancroft MSS.
49. *Thom Gunn in Conversation*, 43.
50. Kitay, Jebb, and Hayman, "Interview," 17.
51. Hamilton, "Four Conversations," 68.
52. Scobie, "Gunn in America," 8.
53. *Thom Gunn in Conversation*, 42.
54. Wilmer, "Art of Poetry," 147.
55. One exception was "Meat" (*CP*, 451), which TG "completely finished as a free-verse poem" but found that it "didn't seem as strong as I wanted it to be; I wanted it more defined. It's the only time I've ever turned a free verse poem into meter." See Gewanter, "Interview with Thom Gunn," 298. See also Joshua Weiner, "Gunn's 'Meat': Notations on Craft," in Weiner, ed., *At the Barriers*, 129–32.
56. Nuwer, "Britain's Expatriate Poet," 76–77.
57. Clive Wilmer, interview with the author, 13 December 2018.
58. Poetry Notebook 10 (June 1988), Bancroft MSS. Compare the dance imagery that concludes "A Wood near Athens," *BC*, 104.
59. "Duncan," *BC*, 3–4. TG glossed an early version of the first stanza: "An improvising gift before self-revising." See Poetry Notebook 10 (June 1988), Bancroft MSS.
60. TG to Douglas Chambers, 19 September 1990, in *Letters*, 491.
61. Diary (1986–2000), 24, 30 October 1990, Bancroft MSS. For Doody's move to New York, see p. 618, n67.
62. TG to Clive Wilmer, 14 November 1990, Wilmer MSS.
63. Diary (1986–2000), 26 October 1990, Bancroft MSS.
64. TG to Clive Wilmer, 14 November 1990, Wilmer MSS.
65. Poetry Notebook 11 (January 1990), Bancroft MSS.
66. "In the Post Office," *BC*, 13.
67. TG to Timothy Steele, 16 January 1991. Private collection.
68. TG to Timothy Steele, 30 March 1990. Private collection.
69. Diary (1986–2000), 5 October 1990, Bancroft MSS.
70. TG to Douglas Chambers, 14 January 1991, Toronto MSS.
71. Diary (1986–2000), 9 March 1991, Bancroft MSS.

72. Diary (1986–2000), 12 January 1991, Bancroft MSS.
73. TG to Jack Hagstrom, 25 February 1991, Hagstrom MSS.
74. TG to Mary and Catherine Thomson, 6 January 1991, in *Letters*, 496.
75. TG to Ted Hughes, 14 April 1991, in *Letters*, 499–500.
76. Ted Hughes to TG, 25 January 1991, Bancroft MSS.
77. TG to Ted Hughes, 14 April 1991, in *Letters*, 500.
78. TG to Clive Wilmer, 19 February 1998, Wilmer MSS.
79. TG to Clive Wilmer, c. November 2003, in *Letters*, 675.
80. TG to Robert Pinsky, 21 January 1991, Pinsky MSS.
81. Diary (1986–2000), 31 May 1991, Bancroft MSS.
82. "Enmeshed with Time: The Sixteenth Century," *SL*, 3–14. "I feel like saying it is the best anthology ever put together," TG remarked, "(me, who hates anthologies)." TG to Douglas Chambers, 12 July 1991, Toronto MSS.
83. Wilmer, "Art of Poetry," 148–49. Compare "it is a poet / we flirt with / together" in "Office Hours," *BC*, 78.
84. "Enmeshed with Time," *SL*, 7.
85. Poetry Notebook 12 (May 1991), Bancroft MSS.
86. "Ghost Neighbors," *Common Knowledge* 1, no. 3 (Winter 1992), 157, uncollected.
87. Diary (1986–2000), 17, 24 June 1991, Bancroft MSS.
88. Annotated copy of "A System." Private collection.
89. Diary (1986–2000), 25 August 1989, Bancroft MSS.
90. TG to Ander Gunn, 8 September 1989. Private collection.
91. Poetry Notebook 12 (May 1991), Bancroft MSS.
92. See chapter 8, p. 98.
93. Diary (1986–2000), 13 July 1990, Bancroft MSS.
94. "Rapallo," *BC*, 95.
95. TG to John Holmstrom, 19 September 2000, Bancroft MSS.
96. Poetry Notebook 12 (May 1991), Bancroft MSS.
97. "In Trust," *BC*, 97.
98. "Note," *PN Review* 100, vol. 21, no. 2 (November–December 1994), 57.
99. TG to Douglas Chambers, 26 September 1994, in *Letters*, 558.
100. Diary (1986–2000), 11 June 1991, Bancroft MSS.
101. Poetry Notebook 12 (May 1991), Bancroft MSS.
102. See chapter 4, p. 53.
103. See chapter 23, p. 290. In his notebook, TG's first notes for "The Gas-poker" occur on the same page as an idea for a poem about seeing Mike for the first time in Cambridge: during an editorial meeting, *Granta* editor Mark Boxer had "point[ed] out MK . . . passing below the window." Poetry Notebook 12 (May 1991), Bancroft MSS.
104. See Poetry Notebook XV (July 1974), Bancroft MSS.
105. "My Mother's Pride," *BC*, 9. TG likely had Thérèse Megaw's take on his mother's suicide in mind when he wrote the poem. See chapter 4, p. 54; chapter 25, pp. 317–18.
106. Poetry Notebook 11 (January 1990), Bancroft MSS.
107. Compare "the needs of ghosts embarrass the living" in "Postscript: the Panel," *BC*, 16–17. "They present me with new problems, surprise me, contradict me, my dear, my everpresent dead." "Undone" also recalls TG's use of "unready" and "unachieved" in "The J Car" (*CP*, 480–81), written two years earlier. He would also

have been aware of Hardy's use of the "un-" prefix, and Donne's famous epigram: "John Donne, Ann Donne, Undone."

108. TG to John Holmstrom, 21 May 2000, in *Letters*, 655.
109. Janet Adelman, *Suffocating Mothers* (New York: Routledge, 1992), 104. See also Diary (1986–2000), 19 February 1991, Bancroft MSS.
110. See chapter 15, p. 187.
111. Diary (1986–2000), reading list, June 1992, Bancroft MSS.
112. Adelman, *Suffocating Mothers*, 162.
113. "A Plan of Self-Subjection," *CP*, 46.
114. See Wilmer, "The Self You Choose," 15, to which this discussion is indebted.
115. *Coriolanus*, IV.6.94–96, in *Oxford Shakespeare*, 1093.
116. Adelman, *Suffocating Mothers*, 161.
117. *Coriolanus*, V.2.22–23, in *Oxford Shakespeare*, 1096.
118. *Coriolanus*, V.2.35–36, in *Oxford Shakespeare*, 1096.
119. *Thom Gunn in Conversation*, 19.

34. ENGLAND

1. August Kleinzahler to TG, 24 June 1991, Bancroft MSS.
2. TG to Clive Wilmer, 15 August 1991, Wilmer MSS.
3. TG to Ander Gunn, 9 September 1991, in *Letters*, 508.
4. Diary (1986–2000), 13 August 1991, Bancroft MSS.
5. TG to Clive Wilmer, 15 August 1991, Wilmer MSS.
6. TG to Donald Hall, 29 October 1991, in *Letters*, 511.
7. See *Unsought Intimacies: Poems from 1991* (Berkeley: Peter Koch, 1993).
8. Poetry Notebook 12 (May 1991), Bancroft MSS.
9. TG to Tony Tanner, 21 October 1991, King's MSS.
10. Joseph Brodsky—"the worst poet writing in the language (if you call it the language)"—introduced him. TG to Robert Pinsky, 18 January 1992, Pinsky MSS.
11. Diary (1986–2000), 13 November 1991, Bancroft MSS.
12. TG to Douglas Chambers, 8 December 1991, in *Letters*, 513.
13. TG to Clive Wilmer, 4 December 1991, in *Letters*, 512.
14. Diary (1986–2000), 18 December 1991, Bancroft MSS.
15. TG to Tony Tanner, 30 July 1984, in *Letters*, 401.
16. TG to Douglas Chambers, 1 January 1992, Toronto MSS. In 2003, aged thirty-two, Treisman became fiction editor of *The New Yorker*.
17. TG to Clive Wilmer, 28 May 1991, in *Letters*, 504.
18. TG to Peter Spagnuolo, 31 July 1991, in *Letters*, 505.
19. Deborah Treisman, email to the author, 26 June 2019.
20. TG to A. E. Dyson, 8 September 1991, in *Letters*, 506–507.
21. TG to Ander Gunn, 9 January 1992. Private collection.
22. Diary (1986–2000), 11 January 1992, Bancroft MSS. See Alan Sinfield, "Thom Gunn and the Largest Gathering of the Decade," *London Review of Books* 14, no. 3 (13 February 1992), 16–17.
23. TG to Ander Gunn, 23 February 1992. Private collection.
24. TG to Jack Hagstrom, 21 March 1992, Hagstrom MSS.
25. Jones, "A Transit of Thom," 56.

26. TG to Robert Pinsky, 1 June 1989, in *Letters*, 466.

27. Hennessy, *Outside the Lines*, 14.

28. Gallagher, "Top Gunn," 59.

29. "The Missing," *CP*, 483.

30. "The J Car," *CP*, 481.

31. "The Missing," *CP*, 483. TG perhaps had a remark made by his friend Ralph Pomeroy in mind. Pomeroy had told TG, "with an honesty that sickened me, 'every death strengthens my life.' He is a dreadful little ogre," TG continued. "Doesn't he see how every death, viz. of a friend, weakens his context and so all that he is really nourished by. Consanguinity as opposed to vampiricism." Poetry Notebook 5 (December 1983), Bancroft MSS. See also "The Honesty," *Sulfur* 13 (1985), 46, uncollected.

32. Gewanter, "Interview with Thom Gunn," 291.

33. Compare TG's suggestion that the "underlying and implicit resentment" in English reviews of *PJ* was "that I was a Californian now, so I was altogether a creature of artifice." See "An Anglo-American Poet," *SL*, 224. The interview was conducted in 1989.

34. "Ben Jonson," *OP*, 111.

35. Interviewing TG about *MNS*, Alan Jenkins remarked: "He greets with unfeigned pleasure my suggestion that his could be read as, in a sense, a poetry of record: 'I'm not a journalist's son for nothing.'" Alan Jenkins, "In Time of Plague," *The Independent on Sunday* (2 February 1992), 25.

36. Sinfield, "Largest Gathering," 16.

37. Stephen Spender, "Ode to the Body Beautiful," *The Manchester Guardian Weekly* (8 March 1992), 27.

38. Andrew Motion, "Posing Over, Pain Begins," *The Observer* (9 February 1992), 63.

39. Peter Porter, "Doing What Comes Naturally," *The Sunday Telegraph* (23 February 1992), XII.

40. TG to Clive Wilmer, 2 May 1992, Wilmer MSS; TG to Belle Randall, 15 May 1992, Randall MSS.

41. David Biespiel, "Poetry," *The Washington Post* (22 November 1992), BW8.

42. Matthew Gilbert, "Furthering the Language of Sorrow," *The Boston Globe* (1 June 1992), 33.

43. Henri Cole, "Sketches of the Great Epidemic," *The Nation* 255, no. 6 (31 August–7 September 1992), 222–23.

44. TG to Hugh Haughton, 7 August 1992, in *Letters*, 518–19. See Haughton, "An Unlimited Embrace," *The Times Literary Supplement* 4648 (1 May 1992), 12–13.

45. TG to Jack Hagstrom, 21 March 1992, Hagstrom MSS.

46. TG to Douglas Chambers, 17 February 1992, Toronto MSS.

47. Diary (1986–2000), 4 March 1992, Bancroft MSS.

48. Poetry Notebook 12 (May 1991), Bancroft MSS. See "Herculaneum," *Conjunctions* 19 (1992), 139–41, uncollected.

49. TG to John Holmstrom, 16 December 1977, Bancroft MSS; see chapter 25, p. 309.

50. Robert Pinsky, "Thom Gunn," *PN Review* 70, vol. 16, no. 2 (November–December 1989), 42.

51. See Steven Saylor, "Thom Gunn on Love in the Time of AIDS," *San Francisco Review of Books* 16, no. 4 (March 1992), 14–16.

52. TG to Jack Hagstrom, 21 March 1992, Hagstrom MSS.
53. Diary (1986–2000), 4 April 1992, Bancroft MSS.
54. Diary (1986–2000), 7 June 1992, Bancroft MSS.
55. Diary (1986–2000), 12 June 1992, Bancroft MSS.
56. TG to Mary and Catherine Thomson, 24 May 1992. Private collection. Compare "An Invitation," *CP*, 411–12. In 1967, Reagan signed the Lanterman-Petris-Short Act, which all but ended the practice of institutionalizing mental health patients against their will. In 1981, as president, Reagan repealed most of the Mental Health Systems Act (1980), which had provided grants to community mental health centers. This left many who suffered from mental illness without support or income.
57. Diary (1986–2000), 11 May 1992, Bancroft MSS.
58. Mike Kitay, interview with the author, 28 June 2019.
59. TG to Mike Kitay, 7 July 1992, Stanford MSS.
60. Diary (1986–2000), 1–3 July 1992, Bancroft MSS. A staple of postwar biker culture, engineer boots are a type of mid- or high-shafted work boot, characterized by their buckled straps.
61. Diary (1986–2000), 6 July 1992, Bancroft MSS.
62. TG to Robert Wells, 7 October 1992, in *Letters*, 523.
63. Diary (1986–2000), 10 July 1992, Bancroft MSS.
64. TG had sought Oliver Sacks's "wisdom and knowledge" in an attempt to understand Will's condition and how it might best be treated. See TG to Oliver Sacks, 22 December 1981, Sacks Foundation.
65. Diary (1986–2000), 10 July 1992, Bancroft MSS.
66. Diary (1986–2000), 12 July 1992, Bancroft MSS.
67. Diary (1986–2000), 13 July 1992, Bancroft MSS.
68. TG to Douglas Chambers, 5 August 1992, Toronto MSS.
69. TG to Christopher Reid, 8 August 1992, Faber Archive.
70. TG to Jack Hagstrom, 12 August 1992, Hagstrom MSS.
71. Diary (1986–2000), 16–17 July 1992, Bancroft MSS.
72. TG to Douglas Chambers, 5 August 1992, Toronto MSS; TG to Robert Pinsky, 23 October 1992, in *Letters*, 524.
73. TG to Robert Pinsky, 23 October 1992, in *Letters*, 525.
74. Diary (1986–2000), 23, 26 July 1992, Bancroft MSS.
75. Diary (1986–2000), 27 July 1992, Bancroft MSS.
76. TG to Michael Schmidt, 18 August 1992, Carcanet MSS.
77. Diary (1986–2000), 28 July 1992, Bancroft MSS.
78. Diary (1986–2000), 29 July 1992, Bancroft MSS. The interviewer was a seventeen-year-old student named Jago Lee. TG thought the interview "well-researched, lively, interesting, and honest." See TG to Howard Moore, 11 February 1993, in *Letters*, 528.
79. TG to Ted Hughes, 7 August 1992, Hughes MSS.
80. TG to Christopher Reid, 8 August 1992, Faber Archive.
81. TG to Robert Pinsky, 23 October 1992, in *Letters*, 525.
82. TG to Douglas Chambers, 5 August 1992, Toronto MSS.
83. Diary (1986–2000), 10 August 1992, Bancroft MSS.
84. TG to Douglas Chambers, 5 October 1992, in *Letters*, 521.

85. Poetry Notebook 13 (October 1992), Bancroft MSS.
86. "My Life Up to Now," *OP*, 186.
87. Poetry Notebook 13 (October 1992), Bancroft MSS.
88. TG to Douglas Chambers, 26 August 1992, Toronto MSS.
89. TG to Douglas Chambers, 31 March 1993, Toronto MSS.
90. TG to Clive Wilmer, 15–17 April 1993, in *Letters*, 531.
91. TG to Douglas Chambers, 5 October 1992, in *Letters*, 522.
92. Diary (1986–2000), 25 December 1992, Bancroft MSS.
93. TG to Jack Hagstrom, 30 September 1992, Hagstrom MSS.
94. TG to Douglas Chambers, 5 October 1992, in *Letters*, 521.
95. TG to Margaret [Baron] Owen, 10 November 1992. Private collection.
96. TG to Ander Gunn, 4 November 1992. Private collection.
97. Diary (1986–2000), 7 December 1992, Bancroft MSS.
98. TG to Ander Gunn, 30 December 1992. Private collection.
99. Diary (1986–2000), 7–8 December 1992, Bancroft MSS.
100. TG to Clive Wilmer, 5 January 1993, in *Letters*, 526.
101. Diary (1986–2000), 8 December 1992, Bancroft MSS.
102. TG to Karl Miller, 12 December 1992, Emory MSS.
103. Diary (1986–2000), 26 December 1992, Bancroft MSS. See Karl Miller to TG, 17 December 1992, Bancroft MSS.
104. TG to Karl Miller, 21 September 1993, Emory MSS.
105. Miller, *Rebecca's Vest*, 134.
106. TG to Karl Miller, 21 September 1993, Emory MSS.
107. Diary (1986–2000), 9 December 1992, Bancroft MSS.
108. TG to Ander Gunn, 30 December 1992. Private collection.

35. DESIRE

1. Diary (1986–2000), 16 January 1993, Bancroft MSS.
2. Diary (1986–2000), 17 January 1993, Bancroft MSS.
3. TG to Tony Tanner, 1 January 1994, in *Letters*, 545.
4. TG to Douglas Chambers, 15 February 1993, Toronto MSS.
5. Diary (1986–2000), 12 July 1993, Bancroft MSS.
6. Mike Kitay, interview with the author, 28 June 2019.
7. Diary (1986–2000), 20 July 1993, Bancroft MSS.
8. TG to Mike Kitay, 10 January 1993, Stanford MSS.
9. Diary (1986–2000), 13 March 1993, Bancroft MSS.
10. Poetry Notebook 13 (October 1992), Bancroft MSS.
11. TG to Clive Wilmer, 15–17 April 1993, in *Letters*, 530–31.
12. TG to Greg Miller, 1 June 1993. Private collection.
13. TG to Clive Wilmer, 31 May 1993, Wilmer MSS.
14. TG to Clive Wilmer, 26 July 1993, Wilmer MSS. A Cambridge MA is a rank of seniority, not a postgraduate qualification. Holders of a Cambridge BA can apply for it no fewer than six years after the end of their first term in residence. There is no examination. TG received his Cambridge MA in 1958.
15. Poetry Notebook 13 (October 1992), 6 February 1993, Bancroft MSS.
16. TG to Clive Wilmer, 31 May 1993, Wilmer MSS.
17. Patricia Highsmith, "From Fridge to Cooler," *The Times Literary Supplement* 4698

(16 April 1993), 5–6; Highsmith reviewed Brian Masters's book *The Shrine of Jeffrey Dahmer* (London: Hodder & Stoughton, 1993).

18. "Note on Troubadour," in *In the Twilight Slot* (London: Enitharmon Press, 1995).

19. TG to Clive Wilmer, 26 July 1993, Wilmer MSS.

20. Diary (1986–2000), 17 May 1993, Bancroft MSS.

21. Poetry Notebook 13 (October 1992), 6 February 1993, Bancroft MSS.

22. TG had mixed feelings about opera. Many of his early poems explore operatic ideals of love and heroism, an interest perhaps sparked by his and Mike's opera-going on their European tour in summer 1953. By the 1990s, however, his interest had cooled. "Sometimes I hate opera, or rather I hate the connection with being queer—is it just an adjunct of homosexuality like teddy bears?" he wrote to Billy Lux. "Why do so many of my friends make such a <u>thing</u> about it? [. . .] An epigram: teddy bears are the poor faggot's opera." TG to Billy Lux, 26 February 1995, in *Letters*, 568. He sometimes accompanied Wendy Lesser to the opera in San Francisco, most notably in 2002 when they saw Handel's *Alcina* at the War Memorial Opera House. TG liked *Alcina* for its focus on mistaken sexual identities. He had never seen it live before but "listened to the Joan Sutherland recording all the time." "Thom came with me," Lesser recalled, "and he was dressed in black jeans with his keys hanging from his belt, the leather jacket . . ." Wendy Lesser, interview with the author, 2 April 2019.

23. TG to John Holmstrom, 21 July 1993, Bancroft MSS.

24. Poetry Notebook 13 (October 1992), Bancroft MSS.

25. TG to Clive Wilmer, 31 May 1993, Wilmer MSS.

26. "Troubadour: Hitch-hiker," *BC*, 85.

27. TG to Clive Wilmer, 31 May 1993, Wilmer MSS.

28. Poetry Notebook 13 (October 1992), 19 May 1993, Bancroft MSS.

29. Some of TG's plans suggest he had a sequence of up to eighteen songs in mind.

30. Michael Wood wrote glowingly of *MNS* in *The New York Review of Books*; John Updike wrote a short piece for *The New Yorker*; in *The Irish Times*, Colm Tóibín called TG's AIDS elegies "among the best short poems written in English this century." See Michael Wood, "Outside the Shady Octopus Saloon," *The New York Review of Books* 41, no. 10 (27 May 1993), 32–35; John Updike, untitled review of *MNS, The New Yorker* 68, no. 30 (14 September 1992), 108; Colm Tóibín, "Books of the Year 1992," *The Irish Times* (5 December 1992), WE3.

31. TG to Ander Gunn, 8 July 1993. Private collection. TG called it "the AIDS entertainment industry!" See TG to Jack Hagstrom, 13 February 1993, Hagstrom MSS.

32. TG to John Holmstrom, 2 November 1995, in *Letters*, 583–84.

33. Diary (1986–2000), 11 June 1993, Bancroft MSS.

34. TG to Clive Wilmer, 26 July 1993, Wilmer MSS. The funds were paid in quarterly installments over five years.

35. TG to Jack Hagstrom, 29 May 1991, Hagstrom MSS.

36. Diary (1986–2000), 15 June 1993, Bancroft MSS.

37. TG to Clive Wilmer, 17 September 1993, Wilmer MSS.

38. TG to Ander Gunn, 8 July 1993. Private collection.

39. TG to Ander Gunn, 27 May 1993. Private collection.

40. Diary (1986–2000), 22 June 1993, Bancroft MSS.

41. "An Invitation," *CP*, 412.
42. Mike Kitay, interview with the author, 22 June 2019.
43. "The Meatloaf." Private collection.
44. Kleinzahler, *Cutty, One Rock*, 131–32.
45. TG to Mary and Catherine Thomson, 6 January 1991, in *Letters*, 495.
46. Mike Kitay, interview with the author, 22 June 2019.
47. "Weegee V: Coffee Shop," *The Threepenny Review* 56 (Winter 1994), 18–19: the two photographs are printed next to the poem. Its working title was "Love and Friendship," although TG later revised and retitled the poem "Coffee Shop," *BC*, 93.
48. Diary (1986–2000), 6 July 1993, Bancroft MSS.
49. Diary (1986–2000), 9 July 1993, Bancroft MSS.
50. Drew Limsky, interview with the author, 29 May 2019.
51. Diary (1986–2000), 10 July 1993, Bancroft MSS.
52. Diary (1986–2000), 17 July 1993, Bancroft MSS.
53. "A Wood near Athens," *BC*, 104.
54. TG to Clive Wilmer, 26 July 1993, Wilmer MSS.
55. Poetry Notebook 13 (October 1992), Bancroft MSS.
56. See "Troubadour" (*BC*, 85–92), TG's five "songs for Jeffrey Dahmer"; "Coffee Shop" (*BC*, 93); and "A Wood near Athens" (*BC*, 102–104).
57. Poetry Notebook 13 (October 1992), Bancroft MSS. Other recent "commissions" included "The Antagonism" (*BC*, 5–6)—for the Helena Shire festschrift—and "Arachne" (*BC*, 28) and "Arethusa: Saved" (*BC*, 24–25) for Michael Hofmann and James Lasdun, eds., *After Ovid: New Metamorphoses* (London: Faber, 1994).
58. Diary (1986–2000), 8 August 1993, Bancroft MSS.
59. Poetry Notebook 14 (May 1994), Bancroft MSS.
60. Diary (1986–2000), 25 July 1993, Bancroft MSS.
61. Clyde Wildes, email to the author, 13 July 2022.
62. Erin Hallissy, "Use of 'Speed' Drug Rising in State," *San Francisco Chronicle* (24 March 1993), A8.
63. Diary (1986–2000), 18–19 July 1993, Bancroft MSS.
64. Doug H., telephone interview with the author, 30 March 2022.
65. TG to Douglas Chambers, 24 December 1993, in *Letters*, 542–43.
66. TG to Jack Hagstrom, 2 June 1993, Hagstrom MSS.
67. *Thom Gunn in Conversation*, 53.
68. William Logan, "Angels, Voyeurs, and Cooks," *The New York Times Book Review* (15 November 1992), 16.
69. Pinsky, "Thom Gunn," 42–43.
70. Richard Tillinghast, "Poetry, Plain and Tattooed," *The New York Times Book Review* (29 May 1994), 11.
71. See Stephen Spender, "Can Poetry Be Reviewed?" *The New York Review of Books* 20, no. 14 (20 September 1973), 8, 10–14; Murphy, "Fierce Games," 28–30; Wood, "Outside the Shady Octopus Saloon," 32–35; and James Fenton, "Separate Beds," *The New York Review of Books* 47, no. 10 (15 June 2000), 45–46. Their reviewing trend continued after TG's death: Colm Tóibín reviewed the 2009 *Selected Poems* (New York: Farrar, Straus and Giroux) and Mark Ford the *Letters* (2022). See Colm Tóibín, "The Genius of Thom Gunn," *The New York Review of Books* 57, no. 1 (14 January 2010), 43; and Mark Ford, "A Style of Revolt," *The*

New York Review of Books 69, no. 10 (9 June 2022), 30–32. *The New York Review of Books* did not review *PJ* or *CP*.

72. TG to Jack Hagstrom, 2 June 1993, Hagstrom MSS. TG found Ashbery's work "rather lively and fun, in small doses." See TG to Clive Wilmer, 22 May 1990, Wilmer MSS.

73. Wood, "Outside the Shady Octopus Saloon," 32.

74. TG to Belle Randall, 9 August 1994, Randall MSS. "He is a jerk," TG concluded.

75. Alvarez, "Marvell and Motorcycles," 79–80.

76. Diary (1986–2000), 29 July 1994, Bancroft MSS. See Philip Levine to TG, 2 August 1994, and Janet Lewis to TG, 13 August 1994, both Bancroft MSS.

77. Logan, "Angels," 16

78. Falck, "Uncertain Violence," 41.

79. William Logan, "You Betcha!," *The New Criterion* 27, no. 10 (June 2009), 65.

80. August Kleinzahler, "The Plain Style and the City," *The Threepenny Review* 60 (Winter 1995), 16.

81. Quoted in "Thom Gunn Intro—Los Angeles Times Book Awards 11/4/88," Bancroft MSS.

82. See TG's chapbook *Night Sweats* (Florence, KY: Robert L. Barth, 1987). Writing about an unfinished poem by TG called "Lit Critics 1994," Brian Teare makes the perceptive comment that TG's "deeply felt moral stance toward criticism [is] that it should be accurate to the intention of the poet him or herself, and not consist of 'proprietary' gestures of intellectual and/or aesthetic ownership that merely promulgate the critic's own views." See Brian Teare, "Our Dionysian Experiment," in Weiner, ed., *At the Barriers*, 185–86.

83. Calvin Bedient auditioned for the role with a rare negative review of *MNS*. Bedient found in TG's "D-side"—poems "pro-Dionysian and in free verse"—"a precious, mincing measure and diction," and thought TG's "A-side" was defined by "self-consciously superior diction, prosody, and irony [which] come off as a cold self-distancing from the ugliness and horror of [AIDS]." See Calvin Bedient, "These AIDS Days," *Parnassus: Poetry in Review* 20, nos. 1–2 (August 1995), 206.

84. Alfred Corn, untitled review, *Poetry* 161, no. 5 (February 1993), 291.

85. Pinsky, "Thom Gunn," 42.

86. Donald Hall, "A Minute Holds Them Who Have Come to Go," *Los Angeles Times* (6 November 1988), J1.

87. TG to Tony Tanner, 10 September 1993, in *Letters*, 536.

88. Mike Kitay, interview with the author, 30 June 2019.

89. TG to Douglas Chambers, 23 October 1993, Toronto MSS.

90. Mike Kitay, interview with the author, 30 June 2019.

91. TG to Douglas Chambers, 23 October 1993, Toronto MSS.

92. Diary (1986–2000), 10–11 October 1993, Bancroft MSS.

93. Diary (1986–2000), 9 October 1993, Bancroft MSS. See also "Cat Island," *BC*, 30–31.

94. TG to Ander Gunn, 27 October 1993, in *Letters*, 539.

95. Diary (1986–2000), 16 October 1993, Bancroft MSS.

96. Ted Hughes to TG, 2 December 1993, Bancroft MSS.

97. Diary (1986–2000), 9 December 1993, Bancroft MSS. TG's letter to Hughes does not survive.

98. Ted Hughes to TG, 16 December 1993, in *Letters of Ted Hughes*, 652–54.

99. TG to Ander Gunn, 15 December 1993. Private collection. In 2000, TG received his "2nd offer of Queen's Medal for Poetry, this time on phone from Andrew Motion." Again, he refused. See Diary (1986–2000), 26 February 2000, Bancroft MSS.

100. It also reprinted TG's interview with Jim Powell from the *PN Review* supplement celebrating TG's sixtieth birthday. See "An Anglo-American Poet," *SL*, 218–30.

101. Hamilton, "Four Conversations," 70

102. Hamilton, "The Call of the Cool," 782. One example was TG's assessment of Lee Anderson's *The Floating World and Other Poems* (1954) in his article "Eight Poets," *Poetry* 89, no. 4 (January 1957), 244–52. Calling Anderson's style a derivative blend of Hart Crane and T. S. Eliot, TG concluded: "I find it impossible to judge Mr. Anderson's talent until he at least makes an attempt to write like himself." This was a milder assessment than TG had intended. In a draft of the review sent to the editor, Henry Rago, TG's original sentence had read: "I find it impossible to judge whether Mr Anderson has any talent or not until he can at least <u>attempt</u> to write like himself, instead of mimicking every effect, every gesture, that Eliot has ever made." Rago suggested the amendment, feeling that TG had been "just a little rough" on Anderson and that the amended line "seems to me more humane." See Henry Rago to TG, 4 November 1956, Chicago MSS.

103. The earliest piece in *OP* is TG's generous assessment of William Carlos Williams, written in 1965.

104. TG to Clive Wilmer, 22 March 1979, Wilmer MSS.

105. Ross, "CA Interview," 198.

106. For an even-handed account of Tanner's style, see Denis Donoghue, "Tony Tanner's Convivial Criticism," *The New Criterion* 28, no. 8 (April 2010), 8–12. See also Stephen Heath, "The Reign of Reading," *Critical Quarterly* 41, no. 2 (July 1999), 20–29.

107. Tony Tanner, "My Life in American Literature," *TriQuarterly* 30 (Spring 1974), 108. As Englishmen in America, TG and Tanner shared some common ground. "Here [in America], I am still considered slightly odd or suspect for having decided to spend a lot of time writing about recent American fiction," Tanner mused. See Tanner, "My Life," 83.

108. TG to Clive Wilmer, 1 June 1987, Wilmer MSS.

109. One exception is a review of Clive Wilmer's poetry collection *Devotions* (1982). See "In the Brazen Age," *PN Review* 30, vol. 9, no. 4 (March–April 1983), 69–70.

110. Ross, "CA Interview," 199.

111. TG to Douglas Chambers, 30 May 1984, in *Letters*, 394.

112. "An Anglo-American Poet," *SL*, 225.

113. Diary (1986–2000), 13 February 1994, Bancroft MSS.

114. TG to Douglas Chambers, 15 February 1993, Toronto MSS.

115. TG to Douglas Chambers, 24 December 1993, in *Letters*, 543–44. In preparation, TG read Bruce R. Smith's *Homosexual Desire in Shakespeare's England* (Chicago: University of Chicago Press, 1991). "Talk about the scales falling from my eyes," TG told Douglas. "Why was I earlier taken in by the grave scholarly assertions that Elizabethan men spoke of passion and merely meant what <u>we</u> would call friendship?"

116. "English 24, Section 2, Spring 1994," Bancroft MSS.

117. "Teaching Materials—Shakespeare," Bancroft MSS.
118. TG to Clive Wilmer, 6 November 1993, in *Letters*, 542. Writing to Clive in September 1991, TG mentioned he had "been reading again the story of David in Samuel 1 & 2. Hot stuff. Interesting. The Saul business is as wonderful as ever. Poor Uriah. Nasty Michal, to look down on her husband because he did the hip-hop in front of the ark." See TG to Clive Wilmer, 7 September 1991, Wilmer MSS.
119. Diary (1986–2000), 7 January 1994, Bancroft MSS.
120. "Dancing David: God," *BC*, 107–108.
121. "Dancing David: Bathsheba," *BC*, 109–10.
122. "Dancing David: Abishag," *BC*, 111.
123. Poems Annotated for Readings 1961–1999, Bancroft MSS.
124. Robert Pinsky to TG, 1 July 1994, Bancroft MSS. TG thought it a "brilliant" explanation. "He has a pretty marvellous mind, doesn't he?" he told Wendy Lesser. "Certainly this is all the kind of stuff that was hovering around in my consciousness while I was writing DD." TG to Wendy Lesser, 17 September 1994. Private collection.
125. Poetry Notebook 10 (June 1988), 7 February 1989, Bancroft MSS. See also "Save the word," *BC*, 71. For Pinsky, TG's "nearly clinical sympathy" was one facet of his broader character. "Thom was slow to judge, in the sense he was slow to disapprove," Pinsky reflected. "He didn't go in for disapproval. That enabled him to write the Dahmer poems, among other things. He was more interested in behavior than in moral judgment and attempted to withhold judgment in favor of understanding." Robert Pinsky, telephone interview with the author, 20 May 2023. For example, see TG's reaction to the phone call hoaxes in Robert Pinsky, in Lesser et al., "A Symposium on Thom Gunn," 11–12.
126. Prose Notebook [1993], Bancroft MSS.
127. TG to Billy Lux, 13 January 1995. Private collection.
128. Poetry Notebook 14 (May 1994), Bancroft MSS.
129. See *The Tempest*, epilogue 1–20, *Oxford Shakespeare*, 1189.
130. "Dancing David: Abishag," *BC*, 111.
131. "Adventurous Song," *SL*, 156.
132. Robert Duncan, "Food for Fire, Food for Thought," in *The Opening of the Field* (New York: Grove Press, 1960), 95–96.
133. In 1 Kings 1, David makes Solomon king; Bathsheba says, "May my lord King David live forever." In TG's poem, however, David does not answer Bathsheba's demand for assurance.
134. "Adventurous Song," *SL*, 156.
135. TG to Clive Wilmer, 23–25 August 1994, in *Letters*, 553.
136. TG to John Holmstrom, 11 October 1994, Bancroft MSS.

36. CUPID

1. Diary (1986–2000), 17, 20 July 1994, Bancroft MSS.
2. Poetry Notebook 14 (May 1994), Bancroft MSS.
3. TG to Donald Hall, 30 May 1994, New Hampshire MSS.
4. TG to Donald Hall, 30 May 1994, in *Letters*, 547–48.
5. TG to Douglas Chambers, 8 June 1994, in *Letters*, 549.

6. TG to Douglas Chambers, 3 August 1994, Toronto MSS.
7. Diary (1986–2000), 7 August 1994, Bancroft MSS.
8. TG to Ander and Bett Gunn, 2 September 1994, in *Letters*, 555.
9. Diary (1986–2000), 9 September 1994, Bancroft MSS.
10. Diary (1986–2000), 15 November 1994, Bancroft MSS. TG did not take an HIV test until 1992. See Diary (1986–2000), 30 September 1992, Bancroft MSS. "Not wishing to know whether he was HIV-positive, for years [TG] avoided taking a test," wrote Kate Kellaway. "Then, a friend of his, an AIDS counsellor, took him to task, reminding him that there was a certain amount that could be done for HIV-positive people. 'So I had the test. It was negative. I was beyond fear, just clinically interested.'" Kate Kellaway, "A Poet Who's Still Firing on All Cylinders," *The Observer* (13 December 1992), R43.
11. TG to Douglas Chambers, c. Christmas 1994, Toronto MSS.
12. Diary (1986–2000), 4, 6 December 1994, Bancroft MSS.
13. Billy Lux to TG, 29 March 1995, Bancroft MSS.
14. See Billy Lux to TG, 7 December 1994, Bancroft MSS.
15. TG to Billy Lux, 30 December 1994. Private collection. Some of the photographs appeared in two German magazines: "Don NYC," *Männer aktuell* 10 (October 1993), and "Don Called," *Euros* 18 (1993).
16. TG to Billy Lux, 26 February 1995, in *Letters*, 569.
17. Poetry Notebook 14 (May 1994), Bancroft MSS.
18. Diary (1986–2000), 21 December 1994, Bancroft MSS.
19. TG did not start revising this early draft until fall 1995.
20. TG to Ander Gunn, 24 December 1994. Private collection.
21. TG to Michael Schmidt, 7 February 1995, Carcanet MSS.
22. Diary (1986–2000), 14 January 1995, Bancroft MSS.
23. Mark Mardon, "In a Castro Bar," *Bay Area Reporter* 31, no. 2 (11 January 2001), 35.
24. Diary (1986–2000), 27 January 1995, Bancroft MSS.
25. Diary (1986–2000), 25 January 1995, Bancroft MSS.
26. Diary (1986–2000), 11 February 1995, Bancroft MSS.
27. TG to Billy Lux, 26 February 1995, in *Letters*, 569.
28. TG to Jack Hagstrom, 29 March 1995, Hagstrom MSS.
29. TG to Ander Gunn, 2 March 1995. Private collection.
30. Diary (1986–2000), 12 May 1995, Bancroft MSS.
31. TG to Billy Lux, 26 June 1995, in *Letters*, 576.
32. Diary (1986–2000), 4 June 1995, Bancroft MSS.
33. Poetry Notebook 14 (May 1994), Bancroft MSS.
34. TG to Douglas Chambers, 28 July 1995, Toronto MSS.
35. Poetry Notebook 14 (May 1994), Bancroft MSS.
36. "Symposium on Disinterestedness," *The Threepenny Review* 53 (Spring 1993), 12.
37. Diary (1986–2000), 30 June 1995, Bancroft MSS.
38. Diary (1986–2000), 6 July 1995, Bancroft MSS.
39. In 1995, the street price of a quarter gram was between twenty and thirty dollars.
40. Diary (1986–2000), 18, 23 August 1995, Bancroft MSS.
41. TG to Clive Wilmer, 29 September 1995, in *Letters*, 579.
42. TG to Ander Gunn, 13 May 1995. Private collection. "The Spanish Civil War was part of the mythology of my youth," TG explained Jack Hagstrom, "and my

mother was intensely left wing." TG to Jack Hagstrom, 7 November 1995, Hagstrom MSS.

43. TG to Douglas Chambers, 22 May 1995, in *Letters*, 574.
44. Poetry Notebook 14 (May 1994), Bancroft MSS.
45. Mike Kitay, interview with the author, 30 June 2019.
46. Mike Kitay, interview with the author, 30 June 2019.
47. TG to Clive Wilmer, 29 September 1995, in *Letters*, 580.
48. Diary (1986–2000), 14 September 1995, Bancroft MSS.
49. Diary (1986–2000), 16 September 1995, Bancroft MSS.
50. TG to Ander Gunn, 17 September 1995. Private collection.
51. Mike Kitay, interview with the author, 18 June 2019.
52. Diary (1986–2000), 20 September 1995, Bancroft MSS.
53. Mike Kitay, interview with the author, 18 June 2019.
54. Diary (1986–2000), 3 October 1995, Bancroft MSS.
55. TG to Mary and Catherine Thomson, 2 October 1995. Private collection.
56. TG to Jack Hagstrom, 7 November 1995, Hagstrom MSS.
57. TG to Clive Wilmer, 29 September 1995, in *Letters*, 579–80.
58. TG to Michael Schmidt, 2 January 1996, Carcanet MSS.
59. "To Donald Davie in Heaven," *BC*, 57.
60. TG to Clive Wilmer, 28 June 1996, Wilmer MSS.
61. "To Donald Davie in Heaven," *BC*, 58.
62. TG to Clive Wilmer, 1 May 1996, Wilmer MSS.
63. Diary (1986–2000), 17 October 1995, Bancroft MSS.
64. Mike Kitay, interview with the author, 22 October 2018.
65. Bob Bair, interview with the author, 28 June 2019.
66. Bill Schuessler, interview with the author, 29 June 2019.
67. Doug H., telephone interview with the author, 30 March 2022.
68. Leslie Aguilar, telephone interview with the author, 22 April 2021.
69. TG to Jack Hagstrom, 7 November 1995, Hagstrom MSS.
70. TG to Belle Randall, 15 November 1995, in *Letters*, 586.
71. TG to Clive Wilmer, 18 January 1996, in *Letters*, 594.
72. Wilmer, "Gunn, Shakespeare, and the Elizabethans," 67.
73. Mina Loy, *The Lost Lunar Baedeker*, ed. Roger L. Conover (New York: Farrar, Straus and Giroux, 1996), 225.
74. TG to Clive Wilmer, 18 January 1996, in *Letters*, 594.
75. Bernhard, "Boss Cupid's Poet," 34. "Cupid is the Christ of the religion of love," TG remarked in "Fulke Greville," *OP*, 57. Compare also TG's earlier use of "perversion" to denote leather, sadomasochism, and promiscuity: see chapter 12, p. 151.
76. TG to August Kleinzahler, 24 December 1995, Kleinzahler MSS.
77. See John Hollander, ed., *The Best American Poetry 1998* (New York: Scribner, 1998), 299. Compare "We know delay makes pleasure great" in "Sweet Things," *CP*, 328.
78. "To Cupid," *BC*, 100–101.
79. Bob Bair, interview with the author, 28 June 2019.
80. Clive Wilmer, interview with the author, 13 December 2018.
81. Julian Machin, "Thom Gunn," *Gay Times* 193 (October 1994), 64.

82. "The 1970s," *BC*, 44.
83. Joshua Weiner, "Loy Gunn Cupid," *American Book Review* 38, no. 6 (September–October 2017), 27.
84. Poetry Notebook J (5 May 1961), Hornbake MSS.
85. "Commencement Speech for graduating English class, 1993," Bancroft MSS.
86. TG to Clive Wilmer, 10 October 1994, in *Letters*, 560.
87. "To Cupid," *BC*, 99.
88. Joshua Weiner, email to the author, 25 March 2022.
89. Diary (1986–2000), 2, 7 December 1995, Bancroft MSS.
90. Diary (1986–2000), 31 December 1995, Bancroft MSS.

37. GOSSIP

1. TG to Ander Gunn, 28 December 1995, in *Letters*, 591. Ander's reply does not survive.
2. Diary (1986–2000), 20 December 1995, Bancroft MSS.
3. Diary (1986–2000), 29 December 1995, Bancroft MSS.
4. Diary (1986–2000), 6 January 1996, Bancroft MSS.
5. Poetry Notebook 14 (May 1994), Bancroft MSS.
6. TG to Douglas Chambers, 20 April 1996, Toronto MSS.
7. "Thom Gunn's True Home," ONE MSS.
8. TG to Billy Lux, 23 January 1996, in *Letters*, 596.
9. TG to Douglas Chambers, 4 February 1996, Toronto MSS.
10. Diary (1986–2000), 10 February 1996, Bancroft MSS.
11. TG to Douglas Chambers, 26 February 1996, Toronto MSS.
12. Mike Kitay, interview with the author, 30 June 2019.
13. Gordon Schneemann, email to the author, 1 July 2020.
14. Robert Prager Journal, 1 November 1977, ONE MSS.
15. Diary (1986–2000), 6 June 1996, Bancroft MSS.
16. "Thom Gunn: July 25, 1996," Prager MSS.
17. TG to Clive Wilmer, 1 May 1996, Wilmer MSS. "Famous Friends" (*BC*, 51–52) recalls the time TG ran into "Frank O'Hara's last lover" in a New York City gay bar.
18. TG to Douglas Chambers, 8 June 1994, in *Letters*, 550.
19. TG to Robert Pinsky, 6 June 1994, Pinsky MSS.
20. TG to Douglas Chambers, 7 October 1996, in *Letters*, 605.
21. TG to Clive Wilmer, 7 May 1996, Wilmer MSS.
22. Aiva Nidnacs [Mark Finch], "Out There," *Bay Area Reporter* 24, no. 34 (25 August 1994), 34.
23. Interview with the author, 2 February 2020. The interviewee asked to remain anonymous.
24. Poems Annotated for Readings 1961–1999, Bancroft MSS.
25. TG to Clive Wilmer, 29 October 1996, Wilmer MSS.
26. TG to Ander Gunn, 23 April 1996. Private collection.
27. "The Artist as an Old Man," *BC*, 61.
28. Di Piero, in Lesser et al., "A Symposium on Thom Gunn," 8.
29. Diary (1986–2000), 25–27 May 1996, Bancroft MSS.
30. Diary (1986–2000), 3 June 1996, Bancroft MSS.

31. Poetry Notebook 14 (May 1994), Bancroft MSS.
32. "Hi," *BC*, 66.
33. Austin Lewis, "Poet Thom Gunn Shoots Off His Mouth," *San Francisco Frontiers Newsmagazine* 15, no. 14 (7 November, 1996), 20.
34. TG to Douglas Chambers, 15 November 1996, in *Letters*, 611.
35. Diary (1986–2000), 4 September 1994, Bancroft MSS.
36. August Kleinzahler, interview with the author, 29 June 2019.
37. TG to Billy Lux, 30 October 1996, in *Letters*, 606.
38. TG to Douglas Chambers, 15 November 1996, in *Letters*, 610.
39. TG to Billy Lux, 17 February 1997, in *Letters*, 619.
40. TG to Billy Lux, 9 November 1996. Private collection.
41. TG to Wendy Lesser, 10 December 1996. Private collection.
42. TG to Billy Lux, 30 October 1996. Private collection.
43. TG to Douglas Chambers, 7 October 1996, in *Letters*, 605.
44. TG to Douglas Chambers, 28 July 1995, Toronto MSS.
45. TG to Clive Wilmer, 18 January 1996, in *Letters*, 594.
46. TG to Billy Lux, 9 November 1996. Private collection.
47. TG to Clive Wilmer, c. November 1996, in *Letters*, 612.
48. Diary (1986–2000), 23 November 1996, Bancroft MSS.
49. Diary (1986–2000), 28 November 1996, Bancroft MSS.
50. "Blues for the New Year, 1997," *BC*, 74.
51. Diary (1986–2000), 27 February 1997, Bancroft MSS.
52. Diary (1986–2000), 29 March 1997, Bancroft MSS.
53. TG to Billy Lux, 17 February 1997, in *Letters*, 619.
54. Diary (1986–2000), 1 February 1997, Bancroft MSS.
55. TG to August Kleinzahler, 4 February 1997, in *Letters*, 616.
56. "The Search," *BC*, 76.
57. Robert Prager, email to "Vern," 6 December 2008, ONE MSS. A fist-fucking aficionado, Prager titled his own personal ad "Elbow Room Available."
58. TG to Clive Wilmer, 13 April 1997, Wilmer MSS.
59. TG to Mary and Catherine Thomson, 25 February 1997. Private collection.
60. Diary (1986–2000), 30 June 1997, Bancroft MSS.
61. TG to Tony Tanner, 2 July 1997, in *Letters*, 625.
62. TG to Clive Wilmer, 17 September 1997, Wilmer MSS.
63. Diary (1986–2000), 21 May 1998, Bancroft MSS.
64. TG to Ander Gunn, 22 March 1997. Private collection.
65. Leslie Aguilar, telephone interview with the author, 22 April 2021.
66. Diary (1986–2000), 2 July 1997, Bancroft MSS.
67. Diary (1986–2000), 7, 11 July 1997, Bancroft MSS.
68. TG to Clive Wilmer, 15 June 1997, Wilmer MSS. See "Saint John the Rake: Rochester's Poetry," in Jonathan F. S. Post, ed., *Green Thoughts, Green Shades: Essays by Contemporary Poets on the Early Modern Lyric* (Berkeley: University of California Press, 2002), 242–56.
69. TG to Belle Randall, 25 July 1997, Randall MSS.
70. TG to Ander Gunn, 4 September 1997. Private collection.
71. Diary (1986–2000), 14 September 1997, Bancroft MSS.
72. Billy Lux to TG, 9 December 1997, Bancroft MSS.

73. TG to August Kleinzahler, 11 October 1997, in *Letters*, 626.
74. Diary (1986–2000), 16 October 1997, Bancroft MSS.
75. TG to Clive Wilmer, 16 November 1997, in *Letters*, 628.
76. TG to Billy Lux, 11 January 1998. Private collection.
77. TG to Clive Wilmer, 16 November 1997, in *Letters*, 629.
78. Mike Kitay, interview with the author, 19 October 2018.
79. Diary (1986–2000), 10 November 1997, Bancroft MSS.
80. Poetry Notebook 15 (February 1997), Bancroft MSS.
81. TG to Clive Wilmer, 16 November 1997, in *Letters*, 629.
82. Diary (1986–2000), 12 December 1997, Bancroft MSS.
83. James E. B. Breslin (1935–1996) was a scholar of twentieth-century American poetry and art; William Virgil Nestrick (1940–1996) was a scholar of Renaissance and twentieth-century literature, drama, and the visual arts.
84. TG to Ander Gunn, 13 January 1998. Private collection.

38. JOHN

1. TG to Billy Lux, 26 January 1998. Private collection.
2. Diary (1986–2000), 10 January 1998, Bancroft MSS.
3. "First saw him," *BC*, 81.
4. Diary (2000–2004), 3 April 2001, Bancroft MSS.
5. Poems Annotated for Readings 1961–1999, Bancroft MSS. In 1994, Stanford purchased Allen Ginsberg's papers for one million dollars, including a pair of sneakers Ginsberg received as a gift in Czechoslovakia in 1965.
6. "The Dump," *BC*, 39.
7. It was renamed the Gay, Lesbian, Bisexual, Transgender (GLBT) Historical Society in 1999.
8. "The Dump," *BC*, 39–40. Mike sold TG's papers to the Bancroft Library at the University of California, Berkeley, in 2006. Dean Smith, the archivist who processed the collection, called it one of the most well-organized collections he had ever cataloged. "They were already in good order and all [I] had to do was simply folder and box them according to archival standards," he reflected. "What surfaced from the papers . . . was the emergence and conscious creation of a masculine sensibility/identity and culture in the mid-20th century." Dean Smith, email to the author, 12 May 2023.
9. TG to Joshua Weiner, 22 February 1998. Private collection.
10. TG to August Kleinzahler, 23 March 1997, Kleinzahler MSS.
11. Interview with the author, 7 March 2022. The interviewee asked to remain anonymous.
12. Diary (1986–2000), 23 January 1998, Bancroft MSS.
13. Diary (1986–2000), 27 April 1998, Bancroft MSS.
14. TG to Mary and Catherine Thomson, 22 June 1998, in *Letters*, 632.
15. TG to Mary and Catherine Thomson, 22 June 1998, in *Letters*, 633.
16. TG to Ander Gunn, 31 July 1998. Private collection.
17. Diary (1986–2000), 9 June 1998, Bancroft MSS.
18. TG to Mary and Catherine Thomson, 17 September 1998. Private collection.
19. TG to Clive Wilmer, 16 June 1998, Wilmer MSS.
20. TG to Ander Gunn, 31 July 1998. Private collection.

21. TG to Clive Wilmer, 14 September 1998, in *Letters*, 633–34.
22. Clive Wilmer, interview with the author, 13 December 2018.
23. TG to Clive Wilmer, 14 September 1998, in *Letters*, 634–35.
24. Diary (1986–2000), 9–13 July 1998, Bancroft MSS.
25. TG to Ander Gunn, 31 July 1998. Private collection.
26. Rick Carpenter, email to the author, 28 December 2018.
27. Mike Kitay, interview with the author, 28 June 2019.
28. Bob Bair, interview with the author, 28 June 2019.
29. Diary (1986–2000), 26 August 1998, Bancroft MSS.
30. Diary (1986–2000), 4 September 1998, Bancroft MSS.
31. Diary (1986–2000), 8 September 1998, Bancroft MSS.
32. Diary (1986–2000), 13–14 September 1998, Bancroft MSS.
33. Diary (1986–2000), 28 September 1998, Bancroft MSS.
34. TG to Ander Gunn, 25 October 1998. Private collection.
35. Diary (1986–2000), 14 October 1998, Bancroft MSS.
36. "Painting by Vuillard," *BC*, 47.
37. TG to Douglas Chambers, 20 October 1998, in *Letters*, 638.
38. TG to Billy Lux, 23 November 1998. Private collection.
39. "Front Door Man," *BC*, 100–101.
40. Quoted in Clive Wilmer Diary, 28 August 2005. Private collection.
41. August Kleinzahler, interview with the author, 29 June 2019.
42. Diary (1986–2000), 27 October 1999, Bancroft MSS.
43. Diary (1986–2000), 6 September 2000, Bancroft MSS.
44. Poetry Notebook 13 (October 1992), Bancroft MSS.
45. Poetry Notebook 13 (October 1992), Bancroft MSS. For "embracing chain," compare the images of embrace that structure *MNS*; see Haughton, "Unlimited Embrace," 12–13.
46. Diary (1986–2000), 5 July 1999, Bancroft MSS.
47. Diary (1986–2000), 29 December 1998, Bancroft MSS.
48. Diary (1986–2000), 27 November 1998, Bancroft MSS. "Well, it was lovely to see Andy, but he does not have a consciousness or memory like the rest of us," TG reflected; "he forgets us all in a while, as he has forgotten Stuart & will soon forget me & next year forget his wife."
49. Diary (1986–2000), 1 February 1999, Bancroft MSS.
50. TG to Tony Tanner, 18 October 1998, in *Letters*, 636.
51. Diary (1986–2000), 9 December 1998, Bancroft MSS.
52. TG to Ander Gunn, 7 February 1999. Private collection.
53. TG to Clive Wilmer, 9 January 1999, in *Letters*, 640. See Colin MacCabe, "Obituary: Professor Tony Tanner," *The Independent* (9 December 1998), 7.
54. TG to Clive Wilmer, 9 January 1999, in *Letters*, 640.
55. TG to Clive Wilmer, 19 November 1998, Wilmer MSS. TG's letter to Carol Hughes is in a private collection and was not shared with the author.
56. A. E. Dyson to TG, 8 November 1998, Bancroft MSS.
57. TG to Elaine Feinstein, 3 August 1999, in *Letters*, 644–45. Correspondence concerning *Selected Poems* (1962) and *Five American Poets* (1963) can be found in Bancroft MSS and Hughes BL MSS. Correspondence concerning the abandoned *Faber Book of English Verse* project can be found in Bancroft MSS and Hughes MSS.

58. TG to Douglas Chambers, 20 October 1998, in *Letters*, 638.
59. TG to Tony Tanner, 18 October 1998, in *Letters*, 637.
60. Diary (1986–2000), 22 February 1999, Bancroft MSS.
61. TG to Clive Wilmer, 14 September 1998, in *Letters*, 635.
62. TG to Ander Gunn, 27 May 1999. Private collection.
63. Diary (1986–2000), 25 February 1999, Bancroft MSS.
64. TG to Douglas Chambers, 5 August 1992, Toronto MSS.
65. TG to Ander Gunn, 20 February 2004, in *Letters*, 677.
66. Poetry Notebook 2 (Summer 1966–February 1967), Hornbake MSS.
67. Ruth [Pearce] Townsend to TG, c. June 2001, Bancroft MSS.
68. Diary (1986–2000), 13 February 1999, Bancroft MSS.
69. TG to August Kleinzahler, 28 February 1999, in *Letters*, 642.
70. Robert Prager, email to Charles Garber [Andrew Holleran], 27 July 2009, ONE MSS.
71. Diary (1986–2000), 20–22 March 1999, Bancroft MSS.
72. Diary (1986–2000), 25 March 1999, Bancroft MSS.
73. TG to John Ambrioso, 27 March 1999, in *Letters*, 643.
74. Diary (1986–2000), 30 March 1999, Bancroft MSS.
75. TG to William Cookson, 7 March 1999, Agenda MSS.
76. TG to Ander Gunn, 27 May 1999. Private collection.
77. Catherine Thomson to TG, 4 May 1999, Bancroft MSS.
78. Diary (1986–2000), 26 April 1999, Bancroft MSS. Compare "delay makes pleasure great" ("Sweet Things," *CP*, 328) and "scripts of delay" ("To Cupid," *BC*, 100).
79. Diary (1986–2000), 3 May 1999, Bancroft MSS.
80. Diary (1986–2000), 24 May 1999, Bancroft MSS.
81. TG to Douglas Chambers, 11 June 1999, Toronto MSS.
82. Peter Spagnuolo to TG, 4 November 1999, Bancroft MSS.
83. TG to Ander Gunn, 11 November 2003. Private collection.
84. Diary (1986–2000), 29 May 1999, Bancroft MSS.
85. TG to Douglas Chambers, 11 June 1999, Toronto MSS.
86. John Ambrioso, interview with the author, 15 October 2018.
87. Diary (1986–2000), 17, 24 June 1999, Bancroft MSS.
88. Diary (1986–2000), 10 July 1999, Bancroft MSS.
89. Thomas Wyatt, *The Complete Poems*, ed. R. A. Rebholz (London: Penguin, 1978), 77.

39. SPEED

1. TG to Ander Gunn, 19 June 1999. Private collection.
2. Lecture on Ezra Pound, 27 January 1997, Bancroft MSS.
3. TG to Clive Wilmer, 1 July 1999, Wilmer MSS.
4. Introduction to *Ezra Pound: Poems Selected by Thom Gunn* (London: Faber, 2001), xvi.
5. TG to John Ambrioso, 21 June 1999. Private collection.
6. Diary (1986–2000), 19 July 1999, Bancroft MSS.
7. Diary (1986–2000), 7 September 1999, Bancroft MSS.
8. Mike Kitay, interview with the author, 1 July 2019.

9. Bob Bair, interview with the author, 21 June 2019.
10. Diary (1986–2000), 30 August 1999, Bancroft MSS.
11. Diary (1986–2000), 18–19 September 1999, Bancroft MSS. TG uses "crisis" in the Lawrentian sense, as a term for orgasm. See D. H. Lawrence, *Lady Chatterley's Lover* (London: Vintage, 2011), 33.
12. Bob Bair, interview with the author, 21 June 2019.
13. Diary (1986–2000), 30 October 1999, Bancroft MSS. On another occasion, "[John] shouts at me for being so out of control." See Diary (1986–2000), 11 December 2000, Bancroft MSS.
14. Diary (1986–2000), 24 September 1999, Bancroft MSS.
15. Poetry Notebook 15 (February 1997), Bancroft MSS.
16. Diary (1986–2000), 27–30 November 1999, Bancroft MSS.
17. Diary (1986–2000), 3 December 1999, Bancroft MSS.
18. Diary (1986–2000), 30 November 1999, Bancroft MSS. See William Blake, "With happiness stretched across the hills" (1802), in Blake, *Selected Poetry*, ed. Michael Mason (Oxford: Oxford University Press, 1998), 141–42.
19. Diary (1986–2000), 30 November 1999, Bancroft MSS.
20. TG to Clive Wilmer, 10 October 1999, Wilmer MSS. There was also a one-day symposium held in London to coincide with the Berkeley event.
21. TG to Clive Wilmer, 14 September 1998, Wilmer MSS. See Clive Wilmer, ed., "Essays on Thom Gunn at Seventy," *Agenda* 37, no. 2–3 (Autumn–Winter 1999), 13–122.
22. TG to Douglas Chambers, 21 January 2000, in *Letters*, 648–49.
23. TG to Ander Gunn, 3 March 2000, in *Letters*, 653. TG had used the phrase "Born to Lose" in "Black Jackets," *CP*, 108–109. See also chapter 12, p. 149.
24. TG to Jack Hagstrom, 7 November 1995, Hagstrom MSS.
25. TG to Ander Gunn, 19 February 2002. Private collection.
26. TG to John Ambrioso, 26 January 2000. Private collection.
27. Wendy Lesser, in Lesser et al., "A Symposium on Thom Gunn," 6.
28. Diary (1986–2000), 9 January 2000, Bancroft MSS.
29. TG to Douglas Chambers, 26 October 1999, Toronto MSS.
30. Anthony Thwaite, "Time for Poetic Justice," *The Sunday Telegraph* (12 March 2000), R14; Sean O'Brien, "A Modest Bafflement," *The Times Literary Supplement* 5058 (10 March 2000), 23.
31. Jeremy Noel-Tod, "Out of the Eater," *London Review of Books* 22, no. 13 (6 July 2000), 31–32.
32. TG to John Holmstrom, 21 May 2000, in *Letters*, 655.
33. Gregory Woods, "Affectionate Gifts," *PN Review* 133, vol. 26, no. 5 (May–June 2000), 67.
34. TG to Gregory Woods, 9 May 2000. Private collection.
35. Langdon Hammer, "Thom Gunn and the Cool Queer Tales of Cupid," *Raritan* 20, no. 2 (Fall 2000), 114–25; Will Aitken, "Everyone Always Gets Lost," *The Threepenny Review* 86 (Summer 2001), 6–7.
36. William Deresiewicz, "Among the Bad Boys," *The New York Times Book Review* (6 August 2000), 25.
37. William Logan, "The Way of All Flesh," *The New Criterion* 18, no. 10 (June 2000), 65. Compare TG's discussion of his writing process: see chapter 33, p. 422.

38. David Orr, untitled review, *Poetry* 177, no. 5 (March 2001), 391.
39. Paul Dean, "Notebook: Thom Gunn, 1929–2004," *The New Criterion* 23, no. 3 (November 2004), 78.
40. Orr, untitled review, 394.
41. Blake Morrison, "Turkey-Necks and Sex," *The Independent on Sunday* (5 March 2000), R56.
42. Diary (1986–2000), 2 May 2000, Bancroft MSS. See Paul Gray, "Poems of Love and Death," *Time* (24 April 2000), 80.
43. Robert Wells to TG, 12 February 2001, Bancroft MSS.
44. Erik Jackson, "Profile: Thom Gunn," *Out* 77 (April 2000), 44.
45. Diary (1986–2000), 21–24 April 2000, Bancroft MSS.
46. TG to Douglas Chambers, 21 January 2000, in *Letters*, 649.
47. Diary (1986–2000), 29 April 2000, Bancroft MSS.
48. Robert Prager, email to Mike Kitay, 19 August 2009, ONE MSS.
49. Robert Prager, email to Charles Garber [Andrew Holleran], 16 August 2009, ONE MSS.
50. Clive Wilmer, interview with the author, 13 December 2018.
51. Jim Powell, email to Clive Wilmer, 28 November 2021.
52. Diary (1986–2000), 2 June 2000, Bancroft MSS; TG to Douglas Chambers, 5 October 2000, in *Letters*, 662.
53. Diary (1986–2000), 7 September 2000, Bancroft MSS.
54. Diary (1986–2000), 18 September 2000, Bancroft MSS. "I never had an unstable living situation," John reflected, "but there were certain legal issues." John Ambrioso, interview with the author, 15 October 2018.
55. Diary (2000–2004), 11 July 2001, Bancroft MSS.
56. Bill Schuessler, interview with the author, 29 June 2019.
57. Diary (2000–2004), 18 December 2000, Bancroft MSS.
58. Diary (1986–2000), 30 October 2000, Bancroft MSS.
59. Mike Kitay, interview with the author, 1 July 2019.
60. Diary (2000–2004), 26 December 2000, Bancroft MSS.
61. Mike Kitay, interview with the author, 26 June 2019.
62. TG to Douglas Chambers, 5 October 2000, in *Letters*, 661.
63. TG to Clive Wilmer, 20 July 2000, in *Letters*, 656.
64. TG to Clive Wilmer, 3 October 2000, in *Letters*, 660.
65. Diary (1986–2000), 12 October 2000, Bancroft MSS.
66. Poetry Notebook 15 (February 1997), Bancroft MSS.
67. Diary (1986–2000), 1 October 2000, Bancroft MSS.
68. TG to Ander Gunn, 25 November 2000. Private collection.
69. Diary (2000–2004), 5 January 2001, Bancroft MSS.
70. TG to Ander Gunn, 7 February 2001, in *Letters*, 663.
71. Diary (2000–2004), 27 January 2001, Bancroft MSS.
72. TG to Clive Wilmer, 20 November 2001, in *Letters*, 668–69.
73. Clive Wilmer, interview with the author, 13 December 2018.
74. TG to Peter Spagnuolo, 20 March 2001. Private collection.
75. Diary (2000–2004), 5 May 2001, Bancroft MSS.
76. Diary (2000–2004), 10 May 2001, Bancroft MSS.
77. TG to Douglas Chambers, c. 18 May 2001, in *Letters*, 664.

78. "Miscellaneous Poems, 1997–2001; undated," Bancroft MSS.
79. Diary (2000–2004), 12 May 2001, Bancroft MSS.
80. Diary (2000–2004), 8, 10 September 2001, Bancroft MSS.
81. Diary (2000–2004), 22, 26 September 2001, Bancroft MSS.
82. Diary (2000–2004), 10 November 2001, Bancroft MSS.
83. Diary (2000–2004), 12 December 2001, Bancroft MSS. "In the depths of his heart he knew he was dying but, so far from growing used to the idea," Tolstoy wrote, "he simply did not and could not grasp it." Leo Tolstoy, *The Death of Ivan Ilyich*, trans. Rosemary Edmonds (1960; reprint, Harmondsworth, UK: Penguin, 1995), 53–54.
84. TG to Mary and Catherine Thomson, 1 September 2000. Private collection.
85. TG to Ander Gunn, 5 September 2000, in *Letters*, 658.
86. Ander Gunn to TG, c. December 2001, Bancroft MSS.
87. Diary (2000–2004), 20 March 2002, Bancroft MSS.
88. Diary (2000–2004), 22 March 2002, Bancroft MSS.
89. TG to Billy Lux, 16 July 2002. Private collection.
90. TG to Ander Gunn, 12 August 1999. Private collection.
91. Daniel Hall, email to the author, 5 June 2020.
92. Diary (2000–2004), 16 April 2002, Bancroft MSS. They met through Ronald A. Rebholz, a professor of Renaissance literature at Stanford and author of *The Life of Fulke Greville* (Oxford: Clarendon Press, 1971).
93. Kent Drummond, interview with the author, 30 May 2022.
94. TG to Ander Gunn, 12 May 2002, in *Letters*, 671.
95. Diary (2000–2004), 24 August 2002, Bancroft MSS.
96. Bill Schuessler, interview with the author, 29 June 2019.
97. Bob Bair, interview with the author, 21 June 2019.
98. Kitay, in Lesser et al., "A Symposium on Thom Gunn," 13.
99. Diary (2000–2004), 28 August–1 September 2002, Bancroft MSS.
100. Mike Kitay, interview with the author, 18 June 2019.
101. Diary (2000–2004), 9 September 2002, Bancroft MSS.
102. Mike Kitay, interview with the author, 22 October 2018.
103. Mike Kitay, interview with the author, 25 June 2019.
104. Bob Bair, interview with the author, 28 June 2019.
105. Diary (2000–2004), 7–8 October 2002, Bancroft MSS.
106. Mike Kitay, interview with the author, 18 June 2019.
107. TG to Douglas Chambers, 6 December 2002, Toronto MSS.
108. August Kleinzahler, interview with the author, 12 October 2018.
109. "A System," *BC*, 33.
110. August Kleinzahler, interview with the author, 12 October 2018.
111. Bob Bair, interview with the author, 21 June 2019.

40. CLOSURE

1. Diary (2000–2004), 12 February 2003, Bancroft MSS. The David Cohen Prize is worth £40,000.
2. John Ezard, "Poetic Justice for Bainbridge and Gunn," *The Guardian* (28 March 2003), 17.
3. TG to Douglas Chambers, 14 April 2003, Toronto MSS.

4. TG to Douglas Chambers, 14 April 2003, Toronto MSS.

5. Diary (2000–2004), 23 March 2003, Bancroft MSS.

6. Diary (2000–2004), 20 March 2003, Bancroft MSS.

7. Diary (2000–2004), 24 March 2003, Bancroft MSS.

8. See Robert Potts, "Moving Voice," *The Guardian* (27 September 2003), R20–R23.

9. Ruth [Pearce] Townsend to TG, 3 September 2003, Bancroft MSS.

10. Charlotte Gunn, interview with the author, 29 November 2018.

11. Clive Wilmer, interview with the author, 13 December 2018.

12. "David Cohen Prize; Diary," *The Times* (2 April 2003), 21.

13. "List of Poems Read 1990–2004," Bancroft MSS.

14. Diary (2000–2004), 27 March 2003, Bancroft MSS.

15. See Geoffrey O'Brien to TG, 28 June 2002, Bancroft MSS.

16. TG to Clive Wilmer, c. December 2002. Private collection.

17. *Yvor Winters: Selected Poems* (New York: Library of America, 2003), xvii.

18. *Yvor Winters: Selected Poems*, xxiii.

19. Hall, *Ancient Glittering Eyes*, 136–38. See also TG to Donald Hall, 7 June 1991, New Hampshire MSS.

20. *Yvor Winters: Selected Poems*, 147–48.

21. TG to Ander Gunn, 15 April 2003. Private collection.

22. August Kleinzahler, interview with the author, 12 October 2018.

23. "What I have against them is that they are the mere hors d'oeuvres which many readers fill up on," he reflected, "thus losing their appetites for the main dish—the collection by a single poet, of which only the accumulation tells you the full story." See "The Postmodernism You Deserve," *The Threepenny Review* 57 (Spring 1994), 6. For an exception, see p. 627, n82.

24. August Kleinzahler, interview with the author, 24 October 2018.

25. Diary (2000–2004), 22 September 2002, Bancroft MSS.

26. Diary (2000–2004), 21 May 2003, Bancroft MSS.

27. Diary (2000–2004), 29–31 May 2003, Bancroft MSS.

28. Diary (2000–2004), 6–7 September 2003, Bancroft MSS.

29. Diary (2000–2004), 22–23 September 2003, Bancroft MSS.

30. Diary (2000–2004), 14 June 2003, Bancroft MSS.

31. Diary (2000–2004), 16–17 June 2003, Bancroft MSS.

32. Diary (2000–2004), 9 July 2003, Bancroft MSS.

33. Diary (2000–2004), 20 July 2003, Bancroft MSS.

34. Diary (2000–2004), 10–11 August 2003, Bancroft MSS.

35. Diary (1986–2000), 14 March 1998, Bancroft MSS.

36. Diary (2000–2004), 14 August 2003, Bancroft MSS.

37. Diary (2000–2004), 14 February 2004, Bancroft MSS.

38. TG to Ander Gunn, 20 February 2004, in *Letters*, 678.

39. Mike Kitay, interview with the author, 10 October 2018.

40. Two minor poems appeared in 2000 and 2001: "This Morning Light," in William Corbett, Michael Gizzi, and Joseph Torra, eds., *The Blind See Only This World: Poems for John Wieners* (New York: Granary Books, 2000), 53; and "To Edgar on His 70th," in a memorial publication for Edgar Bowers edited by William Conelly, *Profile, Full Face* (Hatfield, MA: Van Zora Press, 2001), 7.

41. TG to Belle Randall, 25 July 2003, Randall MSS.

42. Wendy Lesser, interview with the author, 2 April 2019.
43. Robert Glück, interview with the author, 23 October 2018.
44. Mike Kitay, interview with the author, 30 June 2019.
45. Mike Kitay, interview with the author, 2 July 2019.
46. Mike Kitay, interview with the author, 1 July 2019.
47. Diary (2000–2004), 8 November 2002, Bancroft MSS.
48. TG to Wendy Lesser, 23 September 2003. Private collection.
49. TG to Douglas Chambers, 10 February 2003, in *Letters*, 672.
50. Peter Campion, email to the author, 7 April 2022.
51. Cynthia L. Haven, "Thom Gunn Gets His," *Stanford Magazine* 32, no. 2 (March–April 2004), 68–69.
52. Daisy Fried, in Lesser et al., "A Symposium on Thom Gunn," 12.
53. "Lists of Poems Read 1990–2004," Bancroft MSS.
54. Mike Kitay, interview with the author, 16 October 2018.
55. Diary (2000–2004), 15–16 November 2003, Bancroft MSS.
56. TG to Belle Randall, 14 January 2004, Randall MSS.
57. Diary (2000–2004), 3–4 December 2003, Bancroft MSS.
58. "Lists of Poems Read 1990–2004," Bancroft MSS. It was the only time TG read "A Gratitude."
59. David Biespiel, telephone interview with the author, 13 April 2022.
60. Diary (2000–2004), 2 February 2004, Bancroft MSS.
61. TG to Ander Gunn, 20 February 2004, in *Letters*, 677.
62. Lesser, in Lesser et al., "A Symposium on Thom Gunn," 6.
63. "Miscellaneous Notes undated," Bancroft MSS.
64. Diary (2000–2004), 17 January 2004, Bancroft MSS.
65. Diary (2000–2004), 19, 20 January 2004, Bancroft MSS.
66. Diary (2000–2004), 23 January 2004, Bancroft MSS.
67. TG to Ander Gunn, 20 February 2004, in *Letters*, 678.
68. Wendy Lesser, interview with the author, 2 April 2019.
69. Steve Silberman, interview with the author, 9 October 2018.
70. Diary (2000–2004), 7 March 2004, Bancroft MSS.
71. Bob Bair, interview with the author, 21 June 2019.
72. Diary (2000–2004), 27 March 2004, Bancroft MSS.
73. "Muscles and More Muscles," *San Francisco Crusader* 65 (18 October–8 November 1978), 15.
74. Blaine Moss, text message to the author, 9 April 2022.
75. Diary (2000–2004), 2 April 2004, Bancroft MSS.
76. Diary (2000–2004), 27 March 2004, Bancroft MSS.
77. Bob Bair, interview with the author, 28 June 2019.
78. Diary (2000–2004), 27 March 2004, Bancroft MSS.
79. Diary (2000–2004), 4 April 2004, Bancroft MSS.
80. Diary (2000–2004), 19 April 2004, Bancroft MSS.
81. Robert Glück, interview with the author, 23 October 2018. See also Robert Glück, "Thom Gunn Memorial in the Morrison Reading Room," in *Communal Nude: Collected Essays* (Cambridge, MA: MIT Press, 2016), 260–62.
82. Robert Glück, interview with the author, 23 October 2018.
83. Diary (2000–2004), 20 April 2004, Bancroft MSS.

84. Diary (2000–2004), 22 April 2004, Bancroft MSS.
85. Christian Wiman to TG, 12 April 2004. Private collection.
86. TG to Christian Wiman, 22 April 2004. Private collection.
87. Diary (2000–2004), 23 April 2004, Bancroft MSS.
88. Bob Bair, interview with the author, 21 June 2019.
89. Edward Guthmann, "A Poet's Life: Part Two," *San Francisco Chronicle* (26 April 2005), E4.
90. Bob Bair, interview with the author, 21 June 2019.
91. Bob Bair, interview with the author, 21 June 2019.
92. Bill Schuessler, interview with the author, 29 June 2019.
93. Bob Bair, interview with the author, 21 June 2019.
94. Edward Guthmann, "Thom Gunn—Poet Defied Convention," *San Francisco Chronicle* (28 April 2004), B7.
95. "Thomson W. Gunn, Amendment of Medical and Health Data—Death," issued 28 September 2004.
96. Neil Powell, "Thom Gunn: Gifted Poet Who Explored the Balance of Life's Contradictions," *The Guardian* (28 April 2004), 25.
97. Charlotte Gunn, interview with the author, 29 November 2018.
98. Ander Gunn, interview with the author, 2 May 2018.
99. Wendy Lesser, interview with the author, 2 April 2019.
100. Robert Glück, interview with the author, 23 October 2018.
101. Mike Kitay, interview with the author, 22 October 2018.
102. Robert Prager, email to Eric Garber [Andrew Holleran], 12 November 2004, Prager MSS.
103. Diary (2000–2004), 27 March 2004, Bancroft MSS.
104. John Ambrioso, interview with the author, 15 October 2018.
105. Mike Kitay, interview with the author, 2 July 2019.
106. Clive Wilmer Diary, 28 August 2005. Private collection.
107. Bill Schuessler to TG, c. 2004. Private collection.
108. Douglas Chambers to Bill Schuessler, 3 May 2004. Private collection.
109. "Autobiography," *CP*, 285.
110. "Miscellaneous Poems, 1997–2001; undated," Bancroft MSS.
111. "Merlin in the Cave: He Speculates Without a Book," *CP*, 82; Wilmer, "Art of Poetry," 183.
112. TG to Clive Wilmer, 11 February 2000, in *Letters*, 651.
113. Poetry Notebook 3 (May 1980), Bancroft MSS.

BIBLIOGRAPHY

WORKS BY TG

Major collections

FT   *Fighting Terms*. Oxford: Fantasy Press, 1954.
SM   *The Sense of Movement*. London: Faber, 1957.
MSC   *My Sad Captains*. London: Faber, 1961.
P   *Positives*. Photographs by Ander Gunn. London: Faber, 1966.
T   *Touch*. London: Faber, 1967.
M   *Moly*. London: Faber, 1971.
JSC   *Jack Straw's Castle*. London: Faber, 1976.
PJ   *The Passages of Joy*. London: Faber, 1982.
MNS   *The Man with Night Sweats*. London: Faber, 1992.
BC   *Boss Cupid*. New York: Farrar, Straus and Giroux, 2000.

OP   *The Occasions of Poetry*. Edited by Clive Wilmer. London: Faber, 1982.
SL   *Shelf Life*. London: Faber, 1994.

CP   *Collected Poems*. London: Faber, 1993.
NSP   *New Selected Poems*. Edited by Clive Wilmer. New York: Farrar, Straus and Giroux, 2018.

Letters   *The Letters of Thom Gunn*. Edited by Michael Nott, August Kleinzahler, and Clive Wilmer. London: Faber, 2021.

For a complete bibliographical record of TG's publications, see:
Biblio (I)   *Thom Gunn: A Bibliography, 1940–78*. Edited by Jack Hagstrom and George Bixby. London: Bertram Rota, 1979.
Biblio (II)   *Thom Gunn: A Bibliography: Volume II, 1979–2012*. Edited by Jack Hagstrom and Joshua Odell. New Castle, DE: Oak Knoll Press, 2013.

Pamphlets (selected)

Thom Gunn: Fantasy Poets 16. Oxford: Fantasy Press, 1953.
Sunlight. New York: Albondocani Press, 1969.

Poem After Chaucer. New York: Albondocani Press, 1971.
Songbook. New York: Albondocani Press, 1973.
Mandrakes. London: Rainbow Press, 1974.
To the Air. Boston: David R. Godine, 1974.
The Missed Beat. Newark, VT: Janus Press; Sidcot, UK: Gruffyground Press, 1976.
Night Sweats. Florence, KY: Robert L. Barth, 1987.
Unsought Intimacies: Poems from 1991. Berkeley, CA: Peter Koch, 1993.
In the Twilight Slot. London: Enitharmon Press, 1995.

Editions

Poetry from Cambridge 1951–52. Edited by Thom Gunn. London: Fortune Press, 1952.
Selected Poems of Fulke Greville. Edited by Thom Gunn. London: Faber, 1968.
Ben Jonson: Poems. Edited by Thom Gunn. Harmondsworth, UK: Penguin, 1974.
Ezra Pound: Poems Selected by Thom Gunn. London: Faber, 2001.
Yvor Winters: Selected Poems. Edited by Thom Gunn. New York: Library of America, 2003.

Uncollected poems (selected)

"A Thousand Cheers for Authors." *The Gower* 28, no. 6 (July 1940): 402.
"The Heights." *The Gower* 31, no. 1 (December 1944): 8.
"Poem." *Cambridge Today* 4, no. 16 (June 1951): 15.
"Two Ghosts." *Oasis* 5 (February 1952): 8.
"The Furies." *Chequer* 2 (May 1953): 14–15.
"Elizabeth Barrett Barrett." *Gadfly* 4, no. 4 (November 1953): 11.
"Palinode." *The London Magazine* 1, no. 4 (May 1954): 25–26.
"Hungry." *The London Magazine* 1, no. 4 (May 1954): 26.
"Apocryphal." *Botteghe Oscure* 14 ([Autumn] 1954): 173–74.
"Excursion." *Botteghe Oscure* 14 ([Autumn] 1954): 174–75.
"Light Sleeping." *New World Writing* 7 (April 1955): 115–16.
"A District in Rome." *The London Magazine* 2, no. 7 (July 1955): 14.
"Canzone: The Flagellants." In Cecil Day Lewis, Kathleen Nott, and Thomas Black-
    burn, eds. *New Poems 1957*, 59–60. London: Michael Joseph, 1957.
"An Inhabitant." *The London Magazine* 7, no. 5 (May 1960): 14–15.
"Das Liebesleben." *Encounter* 16, no. 3 (March 1961): 5.
"Driving to Florida." *The Observer* (31 March 1963): 27.
"The Doctor's Own Body." *The Observer* (15 December 1963): 25.
"Tending Bar." *Critical Quarterly* 6, no. 1 (Spring 1964): 33–34.
"North Kent." *The Listener* 79, no. 2030 (22 February 1968): 231.
"Rita." *Sebastian Quill* 2 (Spring 1971): 12.
"Jack Straw's Castle." *Manroot* 10 (Late Fall 1974–Winter 1975): 52–54.
"Buchanan Castle, 1948." *The London Magazine* N.S. 19, no. 9–10 (December 1979–
    January 1980): 45.
"The Married Men." *PN Review* 24, vol. 8, no. 4 (March–April 1982): 21.
"The Stylist." *A Just God* 1, no. 1 (November 1982): 91.
"Bow Down." *The Threepenny Review* 14 (Summer 1983): 3.
"The Honesty." *Sulfur* 13 (1985): 46.
"The Liberty Granted." *In Folio* 29 (8 August 1986): 2–3.
"South." *The Times Literary Supplement* 4393 (12 June 1987): 637.

"Ghost Neighbors." *Common Knowledge* 1, no. 3 (Winter 1992): 157.

"Herculaneum." *Conjunctions* 19 (1992): 139–41.

"This Morning Light." In William Corbett, Michael Gizzi, and Joseph Torra, eds. *The Blind See Only This World: Poems for John Wieners*, 53. New York: Granary Books, 2000.

"To Edgar on His 70th." In William Conelly, ed. *Profile, Full Face*, 7. Hatfield, MA: Van Zora Press, 2001.

Uncollected essays, reviews, statements, stories, broadcasts (selected)

"Rain." *Bedales Chronicle* 28, no. 4 (March 1942): 6.

Anonymous [with Herbert Gunn]. "Son or Father—Who Is Right?" *You* 73, no. 782 (April 1951): 18–21.

"'Oasis': An Experiment in Selling Poetry." *The Bookseller* 2412 (15 March 1952): 782–85.

"Tony White." *Varsity* (8 November 1952): 4.

"Collected Poet." Review of Dylan Thomas, *Collected Poems 1934–1952* (1952). *The Cambridge Review* LXXIV, no. 1799 (22 November 1952): 158, 160.

Apemantus [pseud.]. "Springtime." *Gadfly* 2, no. 2 (30 May 1953): 27.

Untitled review of Christopher Isherwood, *The World in the Evening* (1954). *The London Magazine* 1, no. 9 (October 1954): 81–85.

Untitled review of William Empson, *Collected Poems* (1955). *The London Magazine* 3, no. 2 (February 1956): 70–75.

Untitled review of Wallace Stevens, *Collected Poems* (1955). *The London Magazine* 3, no. 4 (April 1956): 81–84.

"Young American Poets 1956." *The London Magazine* 3, no. 8 (August 1956): 21–22, 34–35.

"Eight Poets." *Poetry* 89, no. 4 (January 1957): 244–52.

"Thom Gunn Writes." *Poetry Book Society Bulletin* 14 (May 1957): 1–2.

"Excellence and Variety." *The Yale Review* 49, no. 2 (December 1959): 295–305.

"Voices of Their Own." *The Yale Review* 49, no. 4 (June 1960): 589–98.

"Certain Traditions." *Poetry* 97, no. 4 (January 1961): 260–70.

"What Hope for Poetry?" *Granta* 68, no. 1229 (19 October 1963): 8.

"Thom Gunn Writes." *Poetry Book Society Bulletin* 54 (September 1967): 1.

Untitled prose statement about Yvor Winters. *Per/Se* 3, no. 3 (Fall 1968): 40.

The Living Poet. BBC Radio 3, London, 19 December 1968.

Untitled prose statement about "The Wound" and "Three." In James Gibson, ed. *Let the Poet Choose*, 69. London: Harrap, 1973.

"Thom Gunn Writes." *Poetry Book Society Bulletin* 90 (Autumn 1976): 1.

"Some Autobiographical Notes: Thom Gunn." In Richard Burns, ed. *Rivers of Life: A Gravesham Anthology*, 105–107, 133. Gravesend: Victoria Press, 1980.

"Thom Gunn Writes." *Poetry Book Society Bulletin* 113 (Summer 1982): 1–2.

"Wings Deep with Inner Gloss." *The Threepenny Review* 10 (Summer 1982): 6–7.

"In the Brazen Age." *PN Review* 30, vol. 9, no. 4 (March–April 1983): 69–70.

"Josephine Miles." *California Monthly* 95, no. 6 (June–July 1985): 29.

"A First Meeting." In A. T. Tolley, ed. *John Lehmann: A Tribute*, 25. Ottawa: Carleton University Press, 1987.

Advertisement. *Bay Area Reporter* 18, no. 31 (4 August 1988): 45.

"Robert Duncan's Romantic Modernism." *European Gay Review* 4 (1989): 54–55.

"Table Talk." [On *Low Life*, by Lucy Sante.] *The Threepenny Review* 48 (Winter 1992): 3–4.

"Symposium on Disinterestedness." *The Threepenny Review* 53 (Spring 1993): 12–14.

"The Postmodernism You Deserve." *The Threepenny Review* 57 (Spring 1994): 6–8.

"Note." *PN Review* 100, vol. 21, no. 2 (November–December 1994): 57.

"A Letter to Mark Rudman." In Michael Dorris and Emilie Buchwald, eds. *The Most Wonderful Books: Writers on Discovering the Pleasures of Reading*, 83–85. Minneapolis: Milkweed Editions, 1997.

"Syllabics." In Jon Silkin, ed. *The Life of Metrical and Free Verse in Twentieth-Century Poetry*, 374–76. London: Macmillan, 1997.

Untitled prose statement about "To Cupid." In John Hollander, ed. *The Best American Poetry 1998*, 299. New York: Scribner, 1998.

"A Symposium on the Strange, the Weird, and the Uncanny." *The Threepenny Review* 85 (Spring 2001): 20–21.

"Saint John the Rake: Rochester's Poetry." In Jonathan F. S. Post, ed. *Green Thoughts, Green Shades: Essays by Contemporary Poets on the Early Modern Lyric*, 242–56. Berkeley: University of California Press, 2002.

"An Apprenticeship." *The Threepenny Review* 168 (Winter 2022): 14–19.

Other

Browne, Sam [pseud.]. "Star Clone." *Son of Drummer* (September 1978): 6–7, 58–59.

Hinkle, Charlie. *Poems*. Edited by Thom Gunn and William McPherson. San Francisco: Eon Press, 1988.

Untitled poetry page. Edited by Thom Gunn. *The Organ* IX (July 1971): 21.

PUBLISHED INTERVIEWS (SELECTED)

Kitay, Michael, Julian Jebb, and Ronald Hayman. "Interview: Thom Gunn." *Chequer* 6 (Summer 1954): 17–19.

Hamilton, Ian. "Four Conversations: Thom Gunn." *The London Magazine* N.S. 4, no. 8 (November 1964): 64–70.

Martin, Kenneth. "Love Me, Love My Poem." *The Observer* (7 March 1965): 23.

Morrish, Hillary. "Thom Gunn: Violence and Energy: An Interview." *Poetry Review* 57, no. 1 (Spring 1966): 32–35.

Collins, Claudia, Patrick Condon, Frank Schaller, Robert Vianello, and Bruce White. "An Interview with Thom Gunn." *Cauldron* (Winter 1969): 12–17.

Coulette, Henri. *The Unstrung Lyre: Interviews with Fourteen Poets*. Washington, DC: National Endowment for the Arts, [1971]: C-4–C-27.

Iyer, Pico. "Thom Gunn and the Pacific Drift." *Isis* 1671 (2 June 1977): 20–21.

Scobie, W. I. "Gunn in America: A Conversation in San Francisco with Thom Gunn." *The London Magazine* N.S. 17, no. 6 (December 1977): 5–15.

Sarver, Tony. "Thom Gunn." *Gay News* 134 (12–25 January 1978): 16, 26.

Deutsch, Helen, and Ted Braun. "Voice of the Poet." *In Other Words* 2, no. 7 (8 May 1981): 8–9, 11.

Haffenden, John. *Viewpoints: Poets in Conversation*. London: Faber, 1981: 35–56.

Abbott, Steve. "Writing One's Own Mythology: An Interview with Thom Gunn." *Contact II* (Summer 1982): 20–24.

Nuwer, Hank. "Thom Gunn: Britain's Expatriate Poet." *Rendezvous* 21, no. 1 (Fall 1985): 68–78.

Bartlett, Lee. *Talking Poetry: Conversations in the Workshop with Contemporary Poets.* Albuquerque: University of New Mexico Press, 1987: 88–101.

Breindel, Marc. "Top Gunn." *San Francisco Sentinel* 16, no. 32 (5 August 1988): 19, 22–23.

Kleinzahler, August, and John Tranter. "An Interview with Thom Gunn." *Scripsi* 5, no. 3 (1989): 173–94.

Sinfield, Alan. "Thom Gunn in San Francisco: An Interview." *Critical Survey* 2 (1990): 223–30.

Ross, Jean W. "CA Interview." In James G. Lesniak, ed. *Contemporary Authors: New Revision Series*, vol. 33, 197–99. Detroit: Gale, 1991.

Jenkins, Alan. "In Time of Plague." *The Independent on Sunday* (2 February 1992): 24–25.

Saylor, Steven. "Thom Gunn on Love in the Time of AIDS." *San Francisco Review of Books* 16, no. 4 (March 1992): 14–16.

Gillespie, Elgy. "Poems of the Plague." *The Guardian* (24 February 1992): 33.

Kellaway, Kate. "A Poet Who's Still Firing on All Cylinders." *The Observer* (13 December 1992): R43.

Lee, Jago. "Thom Gunn (1942–47): The Laundromat Cowboy." *The Gower* 52, no. 3 (December 1992): 16–18.

Gewanter, David. "An Interview with Thom Gunn." *Agni* 36 (1992): 289–99.

Gallagher, John. "Top Gunn." *The Advocate* 635 (10 August 1993): 56–59.

Lesser, Wendy. "Thom Gunn's Sense of Movement." *Los Angeles Times Magazine* (14 August 1994): 16–18, 36–38.

Gillespie, Elgy. "Smokin' Gunn." *San Francisco Bay Guardian* (28 September 1994): 7, 15.

Wilmer, Clive. *Poets Talking: Poet of the Month Interviews from BBC Radio 3*. Manchester: Carcanet, 1994: 1–7.

Wilmer, Clive. "Thom Gunn: The Art of Poetry LXXII." *The Paris Review* 135 (Summer 1995): 143–89.

Jones, Chris. "A Transit of Thom." *Poetry Review* 86, no. 3 (Autumn 1996): 52–57.

Lewis, Austin. "Poet Thom Gunn Shoots Off His Mouth." *San Francisco Frontiers Newsmagazine* 15, no. 14 (7 November, 1996): 19–20.

Randall, Jon, and Wesley Joost. "Smokin' Gunn." *Goblin Magazine* 8 (1996): 6–7. Last modified 5 April 2013. web.archive.org/web/20130405021602/http://www.sonic.net:80/-goblin/8gunn.html.

Lux, Billy. "It's the Instances That Hit You." *The Gay and Lesbian Review* 7, no. 3 (Summer 2000): 41–44.

Bernhard, Brendan. "Boss Cupid's Poet: The Good Life and Hard Times of Thom Gunn." *LA Weekly* 22, no. 52 (17–23 November 2000): 26–34.

Thom Gunn in Conversation with James Campbell. London: Between the Lines, 2000.

Teeman, Tim. "When Beryl Met Thom." *The Times* (29 March 2003): WE1–2.

Leith, Sam. "A Writer's Life." *The Daily Telegraph* (12 April 2003): B12.

Haven, Cynthia L. "'No Giants': An Interview with Thom Gunn." *The Georgia Review* 59, no. 1 (Spring 2005): 104–22.

Forester, C. Q. "Re-experiencing Thom Gunn." *The Gay and Lesbian Review* 12, no. 5 (September–October 2005): 14–19.

Hennessy, Christopher. *Outside the Lines: Talking with Contemporary Gay Poets*. Ann Arbor: University of Michigan Press, 2005: 7–20.

MONOGRAPHS AND ESSAY COLLECTIONS ABOUT TG (SELECTED)

Bold, Alan. *Thom Gunn & Ted Hughes*. Edinburgh: Oliver & Boyd, 1976.

Chambers, Douglas, ed. *A Few Friends*. Walkerton, ON: Stonyground Press, 1989.

Dyson, A. E., ed. *Three Contemporary Poets: Thom Gunn, Ted Hughes and R. S. Thomas: A Casebook*. Basingstoke, UK: Macmillan, 1990.

Michelucci, Stefania. *The Poetry of Thom Gunn*. Translated by Jill Franks. Jefferson, NC: McFarland, 2009.

Weiner, Joshua, ed. *At the Barriers: On the Poetry of Thom Gunn*. Chicago: University of Chicago Press, 2009.

Wilmer, Clive, ed. "Essays on Thom Gunn at Seventy." *Agenda* 37, no. 2–3 (Autumn–Winter 1999): 13–122.

———, ed. "Thom Gunn at Sixty." *PN Review* 70, vol. 16, no. 2 (November–December 1989): 25–56.

UNPUBLISHED INTERVIEWS, CORRESPONDENCE, EMAILS WITH THE AUTHOR

Aaron Shurin, interview with the author, 10 October 2018.

Ander Gunn, interview with the author, 2 May 2018.

Ander Gunn, interview with the author, 3 May 2018.

Anne Winters, email to the author, 27 June 2021.

August Kleinzahler, interview with the author, 12 October 2018.

August Kleinzahler, interview with the author, 24 October 2018.

August Kleinzahler, interview with the author, 29 June 2019.

August Kleinzahler, email to the author, 4 September 2022.

August Kleinzahler, email to the author, 31 December 2022.

Bill Schuessler, interview with the author, 29 June 2019.

Blaine Moss, text message to the author, 9 April 2022.

Bob Bair, interview with the author, 21 June 2019.

Bob Bair, interview with the author, 28 June 2019.

Charles Hovland, telephone interview with the author, 5 April 2022.

Charlotte Gunn, interview with the author, 29 November 2018.

Christopher Prendergast, email to the author, 26 May 2020.

Clive Wilmer, interview with the author, 13 December 2018.

Clive Wilmer, telephone interview with the author, 29 July 2020.

Clive Wilmer, email to the author, 23 November 2022.

Clive Wilmer, email to the author, 28 November 2022.

Clyde Wildes, emails to the author, 13 July 2022.

Clyde Wildes, email to the author, 14 July 2002.

Clyde Wildes, email to the author, 21 September 2023.

Daniel Hall, email to the author, 5 June 2020.

David Biespiel, telephone interview with the author, 13 April 2022.

Dean Smith, email to the author, 12 May 2023.

Deborah Treisman, email to the author, 26 June 2019.

Diana Dean, interview with the author, 15 November 2021.

Donald Doody, telephone interview with Edward Guthmann, 19 March 2005.

Doug H., telephone interview with the author, 30 March 2022.

Drew Limsky, interview with the author, 29 May 2019.

Gil Sutherland, email to the author, 14 April 2020.

Glenn Jordan, email to the author, 27 April 2020.

Glenn Jordan, email to the author, 25 May 2020.

Gordon Schneemann, email to the author, 1 July 2020.

J. V. S. Megaw, telephone interview with the author, 4 November 2021.

Jack Collins, interview with the author, 20 June 2019.

Jack Fritscher, email to the author, 22 October 2018.

Jane [Collet] Miller, interview with the author, 8 August 2018.

Jerry Reneau, email to the author, 3 February 2022.

Jim Powell, email to Clive Wilmer, 28 November 2021.

John Ambrioso, interview with the author, 15 October 2018.

John Eddowes, email to the author, 8 September 2021.

John Eddowes, email to the author, 23 May 2022.

John Eddowes, interview with the author, 31 May 2022.

John Peck, email to the author, 2 October 2018.

Joshua Weiner, letter to the author, 5 March 2018.

Joshua Weiner, email to the author, 25 March 2022.

Kent Drummond, interview with the author, 30 May 2022.

Leslie Aguilar, telephone interview with the author, 22 April 2021.

Louis Bryan, interview with the author, 20 October 2018.

Marcia Tanner, interview with the author, 9 October 2018.

Marcia Tanner, email to the author, 5 August 2021.

Margaret [Baron] Owen, interview with the author, 24 July 2018.

Margot Corbett, email to the author, 20 September 2018.

Margot Corbett, email to the author, 1 October 2018.

Michael Colleary, email to the author, 21 January 2021.

Mike Caffee, email to the author, 27 August 2020.

Mike Caffee, email to the author, 9 July 2022.

Mike Kitay, interview with the author, 19 September 2016.

Mike Kitay, interview with the author, 9 October 2018.

Mike Kitay, interview with the author, 10 October 2018.

Mike Kitay, interview with the author, 12 October 2018.

Mike Kitay, interview with the author, 13 October 2018.

Mike Kitay, interview with the author, 15 October 2018.

Mike Kitay, interview with the author, 16 October 2018.

Mike Kitay, interview with the author, 19 October 2018.

Mike Kitay, interview with the author, 20 October 2018.

Mike Kitay, interview with the author, 21 October 2018.

Mike Kitay, interview with the author, 22 October 2018.

Mike Kitay, interview with the author, 23 October 2018.

Mike Kitay, interview with the author, 18 June 2019.

Mike Kitay, interview with the author, 19 June 2019.

Mike Kitay, interview with the author, 21 June 2019.

Mike Kitay, interview with the author, 22 June 2019.

Mike Kitay, interview with the author, 24 June 2019.

Mike Kitay, interview with the author, 25 June 2019.

Mike Kitay, interview with the author, 26 June 2019.

Mike Kitay, interview with the author, 28 June 2019.

Mike Kitay, interview with the author, 30 June 2019.
Mike Kitay, interview with the author, 1 July 2019.
Mike Kitay, interview with the author, 2 July 2019.
Mike Kitay, email to the author, 9 February 2020.
Mike Kitay, email to the author, 5 June 2020.
Mike Kitay, email to the author, 10 August 2021.
Mike Kitay, email to the author, 23 August 2021.
Mike Kitay, email to the author, 29 October 2023.
Mike Kitay, interview with August Kleinzahler, undated.
Peter Campion, email to the author, 7 April 2022.
Rick Carpenter, email to the author, 28 December 2018.
Robby (Gunner) Robinson, email to the author, 20 November 2020.
Robert Glück, interview with the author, 23 October 2018.
Robert Pinsky, telephone interview with the author, 20 May 2023.
Ruth [Pearce] Townsend, telephone interview with Edward Guthmann, 15 April 2005.
Steve Silberman, interview with the author, 9 October 2018.
Steven Fritsch Rudser, interview with the author, 16 October 2018.
Stuart Kuttner, interview with the author, 28 October 2021.
Thérèse Megaw, interview with J. V. S. Megaw, c. spring 1999.
Wendy Lesser, interview with the author, 2 April 2019.
Wendy Lesser, interview with the author, 4 April 2019.

UNPUBLISHED SOURCES

Aberdeen MSS	Papers of Helena Mennie Shire, GB 231 MS 3407, Special Collections, University of Aberdeen.
Agenda MSS	Agenda Magazine Records Addition, GEN MSS 87, Beinecke Rare Book and Manuscript Library, Yale University.
Alvarez MSS	Alvarez Papers, Add MS 88482–88611, British Library, London.
Bancroft MSS	Thom Gunn Papers, BANC MSS 2006/235, Bancroft Library, University of California, Berkeley.
Beaverbrook MSS	The Beaverbrook Papers, BBK/H/252, Parliamentary Archives, Houses of Parliament, London.
Boston MSS	Irene Worth Collection #1649, Howard Gottlieb Archival Research Center, Boston University.
Carcanet MSS	Archive of Carcanet Press, GB 133 CPA2, John Rylands Library, University of Manchester.
Chicago MSS	Poetry: A Magazine of Verse. Records, Box 117, Folder 18, Hanna Holborn Gray Special Collections Research Center, University of Chicago.
Churchill MSS	Papers of Sasha Moorsom Young, GBR/0014/YONG, Churchill Archives Centre, University of Cambridge.
Collins MSS	Uncataloged Manuscript Holdings, Berg Collection, New York Public Library.
Davie MSS	Donald Davie Papers, GEN MSS 439, Beinecke Rare Book and Manuscript Library, Yale University.
Duncan MSS	Robert Duncan collection, PCMS-0110, Archival & Manuscript Collections, University at Buffalo.

Dymond MSS	F. Irvin Dymond Papers, 2000–102-L.1, Williams Research Center, Historic New Orleans Collection, Louisiana.
Dyson MSS	Papers of Tony Dyson and Cliff Tucker, GB 133 AED, John Rylands Library, University of Manchester.
Emory MSS	Karl Miller Papers, Stuart A. Rose Manuscript, Archives, and Rare Book Library, Emory University.
Faber Archive	The Faber Archive, Faber and Faber Ltd., London.
Fitzwilliam MSS	Mike Kitay Tutorial File, Fitzwilliam College Archive, University of Cambridge.
FSG MSS	Farrar, Straus and Giroux Records, MssCol 979, New York Public Library.
Garrison MSS	Jim Garrison Papers, National Archives and Records Administration, College Park, Maryland.
Hagstrom MSS	Jack W. C. Hagstrom (AC 1955) Collection of Thom Gunn Bibliography Papers, MA.00265, Archives and Special Collections, Amherst College Library.
Hornbake MSS	Thom Gunn Papers, 0007-LIT, Hornbake Library, University of Maryland.
Hughes MSS	Ted Hughes Papers, Stuart A. Rose Manuscript, Archives, and Rare Book Library, Emory University.
Hughes BL MSS	Edward James Hughes Papers, Add MSS 88918, British Library, London.
Hull MSS	Papers of Philip Arthur Larkin, U DPL2/3/61/63, Hull History Centre.
Huntington MSS	Christopher Isherwood Papers, Huntington Library, San Marino, California.
John's MSS	Thom Gunn Tutorial File, St. John's College Archives, University of Cambridge.
King's MSS	Tony Tanner Papers, King's College Archive, University of Cambridge.
Kleinzahler MSS	August Kleinzahler papers, YCAL MSS 1089, Beinecke Rare Book and Manuscript Library, Yale University.
Leeds	District Probate Registry, Leeds.
Levertov MSS	Denise Levertov Papers (M0601), Department of Special Collections and University Archives, Stanford University.
LMA MSS	COR/LN/1945/001, London Metropolitan Archives, City of London.
Mariah MSS	Manroot/Paul Mariah Collection, PCMS-0049, Archival & Manuscript Collections, University at Buffalo.
Miles MSS	Josephine Miles Papers, BANC MSS 86/107 c, Bancroft Library, University of California, Berkeley.
Morgan MSS	Carter Burden Collection of American Literature, MA 5518, Morgan Library and Museum, New York.
New Hampshire MSS	Donald Hall Papers, MC 53, Milne Special Collections and Archives, University of New Hampshire.
ONE MSS	Robert Prager Collection (unprocessed), ONE National Gay and Lesbian Archives, University of Southern California.

Oxford MSS | Papers of Stephen Spender, MS Spender 48, Bodleian Libraries, Oxford.

Pinsky MSS | Robert Pinsky Papers (M0697), Department of Special Collections and University Archives, Stanford University.

Prager MSS | Robert Prager Papers (1961–2003), 1998–20, Gay, Lesbian, Bisexual, Transgender Historical Society, San Francisco.

Princeton MSS | Lehmann Family Papers, Rare Books and Special Collections, Princeton University Library.

Randall MSS | Belle Randall Collection of Thom Gunn Letters, BANC MSS 2008/252, Bancroft Library, University of California, Berkeley.

Rockefeller MSS | Rockefeller Foundation records, Box 435, Folder 3743, Rockefeller Archive Center, New York.

Sacks Foundation | Oliver Sacks Foundation, New York.

Stanford MSS | Thom Gunn–Mike Kitay papers (M2559), Department of Special Collections and University Archives, Stanford University.

Texas MSS | John Lehmann Collection, MS-02436, Harry Ransom Center, University of Texas at Austin.

Timner | Carl Timner Archive, Holzheim, Germany.

Toronto MSS | Douglas Chambers Papers, Ms. Coll. 00386 and 00442, Thomas Fisher Rare Book Library, University of Toronto.

Trinity MSS | Thom Gunn Tutorial File, Wren Library, Trinity College, University of Cambridge.

Tulsa MSS | Richard Murphy Papers, 1988–014, McFarlin Library, University of Tulsa.

UCLA MSS | Charles B. Gullans Papers (Collection 2101), Department of Special Collections, Charles E. Young Research Library, University of California, Los Angeles.

Vassar MSS | Elizabeth Bishop Papers, Archives and Special Collections Library, Vassar College.

Walter MSS | Eugene Walter Collection, MS-04400, Harry Ransom Center, University of Texas at Austin.

Wilmer MSS | Papers of Clive Wilmer, GBR/0012/MS Ad.9958/2/19, Cambridge University Library.

Wilson MSS | Woodrow Wilson National Fellowship Foundation Files, Rockefeller Archive Center, New York.

Winters MSS | Yvor Winters and Janet Lewis Papers (M0352), Department of Special Collections and University Archives, Stanford University.

Letters to Alice Collings.
Letters to Ander Gunn.
Letters to Barbara Godfrey.
Letter to Bill Schuessler.
Letters to Billy Lux.
Letters to Charlotte Gunn (niece).
Letter to Don Bogen.

Letter to Greg Miller.
Letters to Gregory Woods.
Letters to Herbert Gunn.
Letters to Joseph Mockus.
Letters to John Ambrioso.
Letter to Joshua Odell.
Letter to Joshua Weiner.
Letter to Margaret [Baron] Owen.
Letters to Mary and Catherine Thomson.
Letter to Michael Vince.
Letter to Neil Powell.
Letters to Robert Glück.
Letters to Ruth [Pearce] Townsend.
Letters to Timothy Steele.
Letters to Wendy Lesser.

Ann Charlotte Thomson Photograph Albums (three).
TG Autograph Book.

Holmstrom, John. "Whisper It Easily." Unpublished manuscript, c. 2013. PDF file.
Noble, Vernon. "Autobiography." Unpublished manuscript, c. 1987. PDF file.
Randall, Belle. "Thom and Belle: A Closet Drama." Unpublished manuscript, last modified 2 August 2022. Microsoft Word file.

ARTICLES ABOUT AND REVIEWS OF TG (SELECTED)

Abbott, Steve. Untitled review of *PJ. The Advocate* 356 (25 November 1982): 30.
Abse, Dannie. "New Poetry." *Time & Tide* 38, no. 32 (10 August 1957): 1000.
Aitken, Will. "Everyone Always Gets Lost." *The Threepenny Review* 86 (Summer 2001): 6–7.
Alvarez, A. "Four New Poems." *The Observer* (24 September 1961): 28.
———. "Marvell and Motorcycles." *The New Yorker* 70, no. 23 (1 August 1994): 77–80.
———. "Poetry Chronicle." *Partisan Review* 25, no. 4 (Fall 1958): 603–609.
———. "Signs of Poetic Life." *The Observer* (16 June 1957): 19.
———. "The Poet of the Black Jackets." *The Observer* (10 September 1961): 24.
Austin, Roger. "Books." *San Francisco Sentinel* 3, no. 21 (7 October 1976): 8, 11.
Bayley, John. "Castles and Communes." *The Times Literary Supplement* 3889 (24 September 1976): 1194.
Bayliss, Christopher. "Oasis 5." *Granta* 55, no. 1131 (23 February 1952): 18.
Bedient, Calvin. "These AIDS Days." *Parnassus: Poetry in Review* 20, nos. 1–2 (August 1995): 197–231.
Bergonzi, Bernard. "A Mythologising Tendency." *The Guardian* (1 September 1961): 5.
Biespiel, David. "Poetry." *The Washington Post* (22 November 1992): BW8.
Bogen, Don. "Energy and Control." *The Threepenny Review* 15 (Autumn 1983): 14–16.
Booth, Martin. "Established Poets, New Approaches." *Tribune* (22 October 1976): 8.
Brownjohn, Alan. "Gunn & Sun." *New Statesman* 81, no. 2087 (19 March 1971): 393–94.
Brumer, Andy. "Exploring an Exceptional Literary Mind." *San Francisco Chronicle* (2 January 1983): R4.

Butler, Richard. "Thom Gunn's Poems." *Varsity* (6 June 1953): 5.

Caldwell, Mark. Untitled review of *PJ* and *OP*. *The Village Voice* 27, no. 43 (26 October 1982): 55.

Chambers, Douglas. "Jack Straw's Castle." *Body Politic* 34 (July 1977): 16.

Cole, Henri. "Sketches of the Great Epidemic." *The Nation* 255, no. 6 (31 August–7 September 1992): 221–23.

Conquest, Robert. "A Major New Poet?" *The Spectator* 6729 (14 June 1957): 786–87.

Corn, Alfred. Untitled review of *MNS*. *Poetry* 161, no. 5 (February 1993): 291–95.

"David Cohen Prize; Diary." *The Times* (2 April 2003): 21.

Davie, Donald. "Looking Up." *London Review of Books* 4, no. 13 (15 July–4 August 1982): 19.

———. "The Rhetoric of Emotion." *The Times Literary Supplement* 3682 (29 September 1972): 1141–43.

———. Untitled review of *Selected Poems 1950–1975* (1979). *The New Republic* 181, no. 15 (13 October 1979): 36–38.

Dean, Paul. "Notebook: Thom Gunn, 1929–2004." *The New Criterion* 23, no. 3 (November 2004): 78–80.

Deresiewicz, William. "Among the Bad Boys." *The New York Times Book Review* (6 August 2000): 25.

Dickey, James. "The Suspect in Poetry or Everyman as Detective." *The Sewanee Review* 68, no. 4 (October–December 1960): 660–74.

Di Piero, W. S. "Poetry Defined and Self-Defined." *The Sewanee Review* 93, no. 1 (Winter 1985): 140–49.

Duncan, Robert. *Poems from the Margins of Thom Gunn's "Moly"*. San Francisco: Author's Typescript Edition, 1972. Reprinted in *Manroot* 9 (Fall 1973): 32–38.

Ewart, Gavin. "Moving Verse." *The Guardian* (1 July 1982): 8.

Ezard, John. "Poetic Justice for Bainbridge and Gunn." *The Guardian* (28 March 2003): 17.

Falck, Colin. "Uncertain Violence." *The New Review* 3, no. 32 (November 1976): 37–41.

Fenton, James. "Separate Beds." *The New York Review of Books* 47, no. 10 (15 June 2000): 45–46.

Ford, Mark. "A Style of Revolt." *The New York Review of Books* 69, no. 10 (9 June 2022): 30–32.

"Four Young Poets—IV: Thom Gunn." *Times Educational Supplement* 2150 (3 August 1956): 995.

Fraser, G. S. "Texture and structure." *The New Statesman and Nation* 48, no. 1221 (31 July 1954): 138.

Fried, Michael. "Approximations." *The Review* 25 (Spring 1971): 59–60.

Fuller, John. "Thom Gunn." In Ian Hamilton, ed. *The Modern Poet: Essays from the Review*, 17–22. London: Macdonald, 1967.

Gaston, Lise. "Collaging with Thom Gunn." *Brick* 101 (2018): 61–65.

Gewanter, David. "Domains of Ecstasy." In Weiner, ed. *At the Barriers*, 257–68.

Gilbert, Matthew. "Furthering the Language of Sorrow." *The Boston Globe* (1 June 1992): 33.

Giles, Paul. "Crossing the Water: Gunn, Plath, and the Poetry of Passage." In *Virtual Americas: Transnational Fictions and the Transatlantic Imaginary*, 183–224. Durham, NC: Duke University Press, 2002.

Glück, Robert. "Thom Gunn Memorial in the Morrison Reading Room." In *Communal Nude: Collected Essays*, 260–62. Cambridge, MA: MIT Press, 2016.

Gray, Paul. "Poems of Love and Death," *Time* (24 April 2000): 80.

Guthmann, Edward. "A Poet's Life: Part One." *San Francisco Chronicle* (25 April 2005): C1, 3.

———. "A Poet's Life: Part Two." *San Francisco Chronicle* (26 April 2005): E1, 4–5.

———. "Thom Gunn—Poet Defied Convention." *San Francisco Chronicle* (28 April 2004): B7.

Hall, Donald. "A Minute Holds Them Who Have Come to Go." *Los Angeles Times* (6 November 1988): J1–2.

———. "In Memoriam: Thom Gunn." *Poetry* 184, no. 4 (August 2004): 329–31.

Hamilton, Ian. "Dead Ends and Soft Centres." *The Observer* (12 November 1967): 28.

———. "Soul Expanding Potions." *The Observer* (4 April 1971): 36.

———. "The Call of the Cool." *The Times Literary Supplement* 4138 (23 July 1982): 782.

Hammer, Langdon. "Thom Gunn and the Cool Queer Tales of Cupid." *Raritan* 20, no. 2 (Fall 2000): 114–25.

Hartley, Anthony. "Poets of the Fifties." *The Spectator* 6583 (27 August 1954): 260–61.

Haughton, Hugh. "An Unlimited Embrace." *The Times Literary Supplement* 4648 (1 May 1992): 12–13.

Haven, Cynthia L. "Thom Gunn Gets His." *Stanford Magazine* 32, no. 2 (March–April 2004): 68–69.

Hickey, William [pseud.]. "Now Freedom of Movement." *Daily Express* (24 March 1959): 3.

Hobsbaum, Philip. "Why Read Cambridge Poetry?" *Varsity* (8 May 1954): 4.

Hough, Graham. "Landmarks and Turbulences." *Encounter* 9, no. 5 (November 1957): 83–84, 86–87.

Jackson, Erik. "Profile: Thom Gunn." *Out* 77 (April 2000): 44.

Jones, David. "Cambridge Poetry." *Varsity* (5 June 1954): 8.

Kermode, Frank. "The Problem of Pleasure." *Listen* 2, no. 4 (Spring 1958): 14–19.

———. "Towards Transparency." *New Statesman* 62, no. 1595 (6 October 1961): 479–80.

Kinzie, Mary. "No Connection." *The American Poetry Review* 12, no. 1 (January–February 1983): 28–33.

Kitay, Mike. "The Way We Were." *The Threepenny Review* 174 (Summer 2023): 24–25.

Kleinzahler, August. "The Plain Style and the City." *The Threepenny Review* 60 (Winter 1995): 14–17. Reprinted in Weiner, ed. *At the Barriers*, 71–84.

Larkin, Philip. "Twentieth Century English Verse." *The Times Literary Supplement* 3708 (30 March 1973): 353

Lesser, Wendy, Philip Levine, Oliver Sacks, W. S. Di Piero, Jim Powell, Peter Spagnuolo, Joshua Weiner, Robert Pinsky, Daisy Fried, and Mike Kitay. "A Symposium on Thom Gunn." *The Threepenny Review* 102 (Summer 2005): 6–13.

Logan, William. "Angels, Voyeurs, and Cooks." *The New York Times Book Review* (15 November 1992): 15–16.

———. "The Way of All Flesh." *The New Criterion* 18, no. 10 (June 2000): 64–65.

———. "You Betcha!" *The New Criterion* 27, no. 10 (June 2009): 63–70.

Lucie-Smith, Edward, ed. *British Poetry Since 1945*. Harmondsworth, UK: Penguin, 1970.

McGill, Angus. "Nobody Heckled Lord Tennyson." *Evening Standard* (25 June 1970): 23.

Machin, Julian. "Thom Gunn." *Gay Times* 193 (October 1994): 64–65.

"The Marginal Muse." *The Sunday Times* (22 March 1959): 5.

May, Don. "Cambridge Poetry." *Varsity* (14 February 1953): 5.

Miller, Karl. "Thom Gunn: Cambridge Poet." *Varsity* (18 October 1952): 4.

———. "Thom Gunn's *Fighting Terms*." *Granta* 57, no. 1147 (8 June 1954): 27–29.

Morrison, Blake. *The Movement: English Poetry and Fiction of the 1950s*. London: Methuen, 1980.

———. "Turkey-Necks and Sex." *The Independent on Sunday* (5 March 2000): R56.

Morse, Samuel French. "A Transatlantic View." *Poetry* 92, no. 5 (August 1958): 318–29.

Motion, Andrew. "Posing Over, Pain Begins." *The Observer* (9 February 1992): 63.

Murphy, Richard. "Fierce Games." *The New York Review of Books* 27, no. 4 (20 March 1980): 28–30.

"New Poet Joins Staff." *San Antonio Light* (2 October 1955): 9A.

Noel-Tod, Jeremy. "Out of the Eater." *London Review of Books* 22, no. 13 (6 July 2000): 31–32.

O'Brien, Sean. "A Modest Bafflement." *The Times Literary Supplement* 5058 (10 March 2000): 23.

Orr, David. Untitled review of *BC*. *Poetry* 177, no. 5 (March 2001): 391–94.

Perloff, Marjorie. "Roots and Blossoms." *The Washington Post* (16 September 1973): BW6.

Pinsky, Robert. "Thom Gunn." *PN Review* 70, vol. 16, no. 2 (November–December 1989): 42.

Polunsky, Doris. "Ode to Mr. Gunn." *The Trinitonian* 54, no. 27 (20 April 1956): 3.

Porter, Peter. "Doing What Comes Naturally." *The Sunday Telegraph* (23 February 1992): XII.

———. "Gunn Metal." *The Observer* (17 October 1976): 33.

Potts, Robert. "Moving Voice." *The Guardian* (27 September 2003): R20–R23.

Powell, Neil. "Thom Gunn: Gifted Poet Who Explored the Balance of Life's Contradictions." *The Guardian* (28 April 2004): 25.

Press, John. "Tough and Tender." *The Sunday Times* (16 June 1957): 8.

Raine, Craig. "Bad Trip." *The London Magazine* N.S. 17, no. 1 (April–May 1977): 96–101.

Richards, David. "'Each Challenge to the Skin': The Significance of the Body in the Poetry of Thom Gunn." PhD dissertation, King's College London, 2004.

Ridler, Anne. "Two Poets." *The Guardian* (30 July 1954): 4.

———. "Verses of the Season." *The Guardian* (5 July 1957): 7.

Rosenthal, M. L. "What Makes a Poet Interesting?" *The New York Times* (24 December 1961): 4, 14.

Sarver, Tony. "Thom Gunn." *The Advocate* 220 (27 July 1977): 39–40.

Scheffler, Adam. "Thom Gunn's Humane Prisons." *Essays in Criticism* 68, no. 1 (2018): 108–25.

Scobie, W. I. "Jack Straw's Castle." *The Advocate* 220 (27 July 1977): 40.

Scott, J. D. "In the Movement." *The Spectator* 6588 (1 October 1954): 399–400.

"The Shield of Irony." *The Times Literary Supplement* 2722 (2 April 1954): 218.

Simon, John. "More Brass Than Enduring." *The Hudson Review* 15, no. 3 (Autumn 1962): 455–68.

Sinfield, Alan. "Thom Gunn and the Largest Gathering of the Decade." *London Review of Books* 14, no. 3 (13 February 1992): 16–17.

Smith, Joan. "Cold Comfort." *San Francisco Examiner Magazine* (11 January 1998): 4–7, 15–17.

Spender, Stephen. "Can Poetry Be Reviewed?" *The New York Review of Books* 20, no. 14 (20 September 1973): 8, 10–14.

———. "Ode to the Body Beautiful." *The Manchester Guardian Weekly* (8 March 1992): 27.

Tait, Robert. "Evening of Poetry Drew 900." *The Scotsman* (29 June 1970): 4.

Tanfield, Paul [pseud]. "The £500 Poet." *Daily Mail* (20 March 1959): 20.

Tanner, Tony. "An Armour of Concepts." *Time & Tide* 42, no. 35 (31 August 1961): 1440–41.

Teare, Brian. "Our Dionysian Experiment." In Weiner, ed. *At the Barriers*, 181–238.

Thompson, John. "A Poetry Chronicle." *Poetry* 95, no. 2 (November 1959): 107–16.

Thwaite, Anthony. "Good, Bad and Chaos." *The Spectator* 6949 (1 September 1961): 298–99.

———. "Time for Poetic Justice." *The Sunday Telegraph* (12 March 2000): R14.

Tillinghast, Richard. "Poetry, Plain and Tattooed." *The New York Times Book Review* (29 May 1994): 10–11.

Tóibín, Colm. "Books of the Year 1992." *The Irish Times* (5 December 1992): WE3.

———. "The Genius of Thom Gunn." *The New York Review of Books* 57, no. 1 (14 January 2010): 43.

———, ed. "Thom Gunn: Appropriate Measures." *Sunday Feature*. BBC Radio 3. First broadcast 4 January 2015.

Updike, John. Untitled review of *MNS*. *The New Yorker* 68, no. 30 (14 September 1992): 108.

Weiner, Joshua. "From Ladd's Hill to Land's End (and Back Again): Narrative, Rhythm, and the Transatlantic Occasions of 'Misanthropos.'" In Weiner, ed. *At the Barriers*, 105–26.

———. "Gunn's 'Meat': Notations on Craft." In Weiner, ed. *At the Barriers*, 129–32.

———. "Loy Gunn Cupid." *American Book Review* 38, no. 6 (September–October 2017): 14, 27.

Wharton, Gordon. "Plain Speech and Pedantry." *The Times Literary Supplement* 2755 (19 November 1954): 741.

Wilmer, Clive. "Clive Wilmer on New Poetry." *The Spectator* 7457 (29 May 1971): 742–44.

———. "Clive Wilmer on Thom Gunn." *Granta* 73, no. 1247 (22 April 1967): 20–21.

———. "Gunn, Shakespeare, and the Elizabethans." In Weiner, ed. *At the Barriers*, 45–67.

———. "Poor Lovely Statue!" *The Times Literary Supplement* 5960 (23 June 2017): 17–18.

———. "The Dangerous Edge of Things." *PN Review* 85, vol. 18, no. 5 (May–June 1992): 61–62.

———. "The Self You Choose." *The Times Literary Supplement* 5482 (25 April 2008): 13–15.

Wood, Michael. "Outside the Shady Octopus Saloon." *The New York Review of Books* 41, no. 10 (27 May 1993): 32–35.

Woods, Gregory. "Affectionate Gifts." *PN Review* 133, vol. 26, no. 5 (May–June 2000): 67–68.

RELATED BOOKS, ARTICLES, REVIEWS, AND OBITUARIES

"Abraham Kitay." *New Jersey Jewish News* (4 March 1976): 50.

Abse, Dannie, ed. *Corgi Modern Poets in Focus* 5. London: Corgi, 1973.

Adelman, Janet. *Suffocating Mothers.* New York: Routledge, 1992.

Allott, Kenneth, ed. *The Penguin Book of Contemporary Verse: 1918–60.* London: Penguin, 1962.

Altman, Lawrence K. "Rare Cancer Seen in 41 Homosexuals." *The New York Times* (3 July 1981): 20.

"American Guilty in LSD Case in Denmark." *Arizona Daily Star* (14 August 1971): A13.

"Angel-Dust Raid Nets 9 near Haight-Ashbury." *San Francisco Examiner* (13 March 1980): 4.

"Appointment with Fear." *Radio Times* 86, no. 1108 (22 December 1944): 14.

Ashford, Gerald. "On the Aisle." *San Antonio Express* (2 December 1954): 6D.

Auden, W. H., and John Garrett, eds. *The Poet's Tongue: An Anthology.* London: George Bell, 1935.

Barbanel, Josh. "Gunman Kills One and Wounds 7 in Village." *The New York Times* (20 November 1980): B1.

Bate, Jonathan. *Ted Hughes: The Unauthorised Life.* London: HarperCollins, 2015.

Bateson, Gregory. *Steps to an Ecology of Mind.* Chicago: University of Chicago Press, 2000. First published in 1972.

Beachy, Robert. *Gay Berlin: Birthplace of a Modern Identity.* New York: Knopf, 2014.

Berlandt, Konstantin, and Wayne April. "Ad-Hoc Group Urges Bathhouses to Post AIDS Warnings." *Bay Area Reporter* 13, no. 21 (26 May 1983): 1.

Berryman, John. *The Selected Letters of John Berryman.* Edited by Philip Coleman and Calista McRae. Cambridge, MA: Belknap Press, 2020.

Bladen, Barbara. "'Six Appeal' a Real Gas at the Troupe." *San Mateo Times* (17 September 1959): 20.

Blake, William. *Selected Poetry.* Edited by Michael Mason. Oxford: Oxford University Press, 1998.

Bloch-Michel, Jean. "Camus: The Lie and the Quarter-Truth." *The Observer* (17 November 1957): 16.

"Book Withdrawn from Publication." *The Times* (28 November 1935): 9.

Boyd, Nan Almilla. *Wide-Open Town: A History of Queer San Francisco to 1965.* Berkeley: University of California Press, 2003.

Brooke, Stephen. "'A New World for Women'? Abortion Law Reform in Britain During the 1930s." *The American Historical Review* 106, no. 2 (April 2001): 431–59.

Brown, Ivor. "The World of the Theatre." *Illustrated London Evening News* (19 June 1937): 21.

Brown, Olive Melville. "Berlin Halts Prisoner Exchange." *Daily Mail* (4 October 1941): 1.

Buchan, John. *A History of the Great War.* Vol. 4. London: Thomas Nelson, 1922.

Bugliosi, Vincent. *Reclaiming History.* New York: W. W. Norton, 1998.

Bunting, Basil. *Collected Poems.* London: Fulcrum Press, 1970.

"Cambridge Notebook." *Varsity* (3 February 1951): 12.

Camus, Albert. *The Plague.* Translated by Stuart Gilbert. London: Penguin, 1960.

Carpenter, Donald H. *Man of a Million Fragments: The True Story of Clay Shaw.* Lexington, KY: Carpenter LLC, 2014.

"Celebrating Victory in North-West London." *Hampstead and Highgate Express* (11 May 1945): 1.

Centers for Disease Control and Prevention (CDC). "A Cluster of Kaposi's Sarcoma and Pneumocystis carinii Pneumonia Among Homosexual Male Residents of Los Angeles and Orange Counties, California." *Morbidity and Mortality Weekly Report* 31, no. 23 (18 June 1982): 305–307.

———. "Update on Acquired Immune Deficiency Syndrome (AIDS)—United States." *Morbidity and Mortality Weekly Report* 31, no. 37 (24 September 1982): 507–508, 513–14.

Channon, Henry. *The Diaries: 1938–43*. Edited by Simon Heffer. London: Hutchinson, 2021.

Charles, Dennis. "South of Market." *Kalendar* 4, no. 19 (3 October 1975): 2.

Chester, Mark I. "The Ambush." *Bay Area Reporter* 16, no. 51 (18 December 1986): 45–46.

Christiansen, Arthur. *Headlines All My Life*. London: Heinemann, 1961.

"Chuck Arnett." *Bay Area Reporter* 18, no. 10 (10 March 1988): 18.

Cleaver, John, ed. *Fitzwilliam: The First 150 Years of a Cambridge College*. London: Third Millennium Publishing, 2013.

Cleverley, Graham. "Footlights to Street Lamps." *Picture Post* 74, no. 10 (11 March 1957): 34–35.

Clinton, Jerome W. "'Separate Tables' Stimulating, Fine." *The Stanford Daily* (25 November 1958): 2.

Comstock, Bob. "First-Nighters Ask Why?" *The Targum* (30 November 1951): 1.

Connolly, Cressida. *The Rare and the Beautiful: The Lives of the Garmans*. London: Fourth Estate, 2004.

Conquest, Robert, ed. *New Lines: An Anthology*. London: Macmillan, 1956.

Corbett, Margot. *A Family of Thomsons*. Maidstone, UK: Modern Press, 1989.

Corbett, William. "August Kleinzahler: The Art of Poetry XCIII." *The Paris Review* 182 (Fall 2007): 21–52.

Corneille, Pierre. *Cinna: ou, La clémence d'Auguste*. Edited by John E. Matzke. Boston: D. C. Heath, 1905.

Cotton, John. *Oscar Mellor: The Fantasy Press*. Hitchin, UK: Dodman Press, 1977.

Crane, Hart. *The Letters of Hart Crane: 1916–1932*. Edited by Brom Weber. Berkeley: University of California Press, 1952.

Crawford, Robert. *Eliot After "The Waste Land"*. New York: Farrar, Straus and Giroux, 2022.

Creeley, Robert. *The Collected Poems of Robert Creeley, 1945–1975*. Berkeley: University of California Press, 1982.

Culverwell, Stephen. "Theatre: 'Cyrano de Bergerac.'" *The Cambridge Review* LXXIV, no. 1801 (17 January 1953): 230, 232.

Cunningham, John. "Muse and Mistress." *The Guardian* (21 January 2000): A5.

"Cycle Riots Ended at Angels Camp." *San Francisco Chronicle* (3 June 1957): 5.

Davie, Donald. *Collected Poems*. Manchester: Carcanet, 2002.

"Dennis Leon Hrlic." *Bay Area Reporter* 18, no. 33 (18 August 1988): 19.

Donald Hall in Conversation with Ian Hamilton. London: Between the Lines, 2000.

Donne, John. *The Complete English Poems of John Donne*. Edited by C. A. Patrides. London: J. M. Dent, 1990.

Donoghue, Denis. "Tony Tanner's Convivial Criticism." *The New Criterion* 28, no. 8 (April 2010): 8–12.

"Dr. E. C. S. Megaw." *The Times* (8 February 1956): 11.

Driberg, Tom. "Tories Bay for War." *Reynold's News* (London) (2 July 1950): 4.

"Drug Raid at Eel Home Nabs Six." *Ukiah (CA) Daily Journal* (3 January 1972): 2.

"'Drug Supermarket' Is Raided in S.F.—5 Held." *San Francisco Chronicle* (30 October 1971): 3.

Duncan, Robert. *Bending the Bow*. New York: New Directions, 1968.

———. *Caesar's Gate: Poems 1949–50*. San Francisco: Sand Dollar, 1972.

———. *Collected Early Poems and Plays*. Edited by Peter Quartermain. Berkeley: University of California Press, 2012.

———. *Collected Essays and Other Prose*. Edited by James Maynard. Berkeley: University of California Press, 2014.

———. *The Collected Later Poems and Plays*. Edited by Peter Quartermain. Berkeley: University of California Press, 2014.

———. *The Opening of the Field*. New York: Grove Press, 1960.

———. *Roots and Branches: Poems*. New York: Charles Scribner's Sons, 1964.

Eichelbaum, Stanley. "'Six Appeal' Also Has Laugh Appeal." *San Francisco Examiner* (29 September 1959): 4

———. "Sparkling Peninsula Revue." *San Francisco Examiner* (30 January 1962): 22.

———. "Witty, Stylish 'Funny Side Up.'" *San Francisco Examiner* (20 July 1965): 21.

Evans, Arthur. "Lethal Lifestyle." *Bay Area Reporter* 12, no. 35 (2 September 1982): 7.

Faas, Egbert. "An Interview with Robert Duncan." *boundary 2*, vol. 8, no. 2 (Winter 1980): 1–19.

Faux, Claude. *The Young Dogs*. Translated by Tony White. London: Panther, 1964.

"FBI Suspect Is Called." *San Francisco Chronicle* (24 March 1967): 9.

Feaver, William. *The Lives of Lucian Freud: Youth*. London: Bloomsbury, 2019.

Ferlinghetti, Lawrence. *A Coney Island of the Mind*. New York: New Directions, 1958.

Fitzgerald, Penelope. *The Knox Brothers*. London: Macmillan, 1977.

Fried, Daisy. *She Didn't Mean to Do It*. Pittsburgh: University of Pittsburgh Press, 2000.

Fritscher, Jack. "Artist Chuck Arnett: His Life/Our Times." In Mark Thompson, ed. *Leatherfolk: Radical Sex, People, Politics, and Practice*, 106–18. Boston: Alyson Books, 1991.

———. *Profiles in Gay Courage*. Sebastopol, CA: Palm Drive Publishing, 2022.

"'Funeral' for Editor of 'Granta.'" *The Times* (25 May 1953): 2.

Garrison, Jim. *On the Trail of the Assassins*. 1988; London: Penguin, 1992.

Gellert, Roger [John Holmstrom]. "To Ovid with Love." *The Guardian* (27 January 1965): 9.

Ginsberg, Allen, and Allen Young. *Gay Sunshine Interview*. Bolinas, CA: Grey Fox Press, 1974.

Green, Martin, and Tony White. *Guide to London Pubs*. London: Heinemann, 1965.

Green, Peter. "Our Contemporaries." *The Cambridge Review* LXXII, no. 1768 (9 June 1951): 602–603.

Grove, Valerie. *Laurie Lee: The Well-Loved Stranger*. London: Viking, 1999.

"Guilty Plea to Dope Burglary." *Daily Independent Journal* (San Rafael, CA) (27 January 1970): 5.

Haffenden, John. *The Life of John Berryman*. London: ARK, 1983.

Hall, Donald. *Their Ancient Glittering Eyes: Remembering Poets and More Poets*. New York: Ticknor & Fields, 1992.

Hallissy, Erin. "Use of 'Speed' Drug Rising in State." *San Francisco Chronicle* (24 March 1993): A1, 8.

Hammer, Langdon. *James Merrill: Life and Art*. New York: Knopf, 2015.

Haskell, Stephen. "A.D.C.—*The Heiress*." *The Cambridge Review* LXXV, no. 1818 (17 October 1953): 50.

Hayman, Ronald, ed. *My Cambridge*. Cambridge: Robson Books, 1977.

"Health Shorts." *Bay Area Reporter* 11, no. 14 (2 July 1981): 34.

Heath, Stephen. "The Reign of Reading." *Critical Quarterly* 41, no. 2 (July 1999): 20–29.

"Herbert Gunn, 57, British Newsman." *The New York Times* (3 March 1962): 21.

Highsmith, Patricia. "From Fridge to Cooler." *The Times Literary Supplement* 4698 (16 April 1993): 5–6.

Hinds, Alfred. *Contempt of Court*. London: Bodley Head, 1966.

Hoare, Philip. "Obituary: Michael Wishart." *The Independent* (2 July 1996): 14.

Hofmann, Michael, and James Lasdun, eds. *After Ovid: New Metamorphoses*. London: Faber, 1994.

Homer. *The Odyssey*. Translated by Samuel Butler. London: Jonathan Cape, 1925.

Hughes, Ted. *Letters of Ted Hughes*. Edited by Christopher Reid. London: Faber, 2007.

Hunter, John Francis. *The Gay Insider*. New York: Olympia, 1971.

"Hyde Replaces Bliss as 'Standard' News Editor." *World's Press News and Advertisers' Review* (28 March 1940): 3.

Ingersoll, Ralph. *Report on England: November 1940*. New York: Simon & Schuster, 1940.

Isherwood, Christopher. *Christopher and His Kind*. New York: Avon Books, 1977.

———. *Diaries: Volume One: 1939–1960*. Edited by Katherine Bucknell. London: Methuen, 1996.

———. *Diaries: Volume Three: Liberation: 1970–1983*. Edited by Katherine Bucknell. London: Chatto & Windus, 2012.

———. *Goodbye to Berlin*. London: Vintage, 1992. First published in 1939.

Isherwood, Christopher, and Don Bachardy. *The Animals: Love Letters Between Christopher Isherwood and Don Bachardy*. Edited by Katherine Bucknell. London: Chatto & Windus, 2013.

Jenkins, Tudor. "Herbert Gunn—Three Times an Editor." *Evening Standard* (3 March 1962): 3.

"John Guggenheim Fund Gives $3.7-Million in Grants to 354." *The New York Times* (12 April 1971): 40.

Jones, Bessie D. *Charles Thomson (1852–1928): A Memoir by His Daughter*. 1930.

Jones, Brian. "White Protests Bigger Than Expected." *Bay Area Reporter* 14, no. 2 (12 January 1984): 1, 4.

"Kearny Lad Wins National Sermon Test." *New Jersey Jewish News* (28 March 1947): 3.

Kleinzahler, August. *Cutty, One Rock: Low Characters and Strange Places, Gently Explained*. Revised edition. New York: Farrar, Straus and Giroux, 2005.

Landy, Eugene. *The Underground Dictionary*. New York: Simon & Schuster, 1971.

Lanzmann, Jacques. *Qui Vive*. Translated by Tony White. London: Faber, 1967.

Larkin, Philip, ed. *The Oxford Book of Twentieth Century English Verse*. Oxford: Oxford University Press, 1973.

Laski, Joel. "Castro Service for Michael Maletta." *Bay Area Reporter* 12, no. 32 (12 August 1982): 5.

Lawrence, D. H. *The Complete Poems*. Edited by Vivian de Sola Pinto and F. Warren Roberts. London: Penguin, 1993.

———. *Lady Chatterley's Lover*. London: Vintage, 2011. First published in an unexpurgated English edition, 1960, by William Heinemann (London).

Leader, Zachary, ed. *The Movement Reconsidered*. Oxford: Oxford University Press, 2009.

Leavis, F. R. *The Common Pursuit*. London: Chatto & Windus, 1952.

Lesser, Wendy. "Notes to Readers." *The Threepenny Review* 14 (Summer 1983): 26.

"Let It Bleed." *Rolling Stone* 50 (30 January 1970): 14–30.

Logan, James. *The Clans of the Scottish Highlands*. London: Ackermann, 1843.

Loy, Mina. *The Lost Lunar Baedeker*. Edited by Roger L. Conover. New York: Farrar, Straus and Giroux, 1996.

MacCabe, Colin. "Obituary: Professor Tony Tanner." *The Independent* (9 December 1998): 7.

Makin, Peter. *Bunting: The Shaping of His Verse*. Oxford: Clarendon Press, 1992.

Mann, Thomas. *The Magic Mountain*. Translated by H. T. Lowe-Porter. New York: Modern Library, 1992. First published in 1927.

Marcus, Mr. [Marcus Hernandez]. "Southern Scandals." *Bay Area Reporter* 11, no. 16 (30 July 1981): 34.

Mardon, Mark. "In a Castro Bar." *Bay Area Reporter* 31, no. 2 (11 January 2001): 35.

Martin, Prudence. "From Cotillion to Cabaret." *San Francisco Examiner* (22 April 1962): PL-10–PL-13.

Masters, Brian. *The Shrine of Jeffrey Dahmer*. London: Hodder & Stoughton, 1993.

Matthiessen, F. O., ed. *The Oxford Book of American Verse*. New York: Oxford University Press, 1950.

Maurois, André. *Ariel: A Shelley Romance*. Translated by Ella D'Arcy. London: John Lane, 1924.

"Memorial Service." *Chatham, Rochester and Gillingham News* (23 June 1939): 5.

Merrill, James. *A Whole World: Letters from James Merrill*. Edited by Langdon Hammer and Stephen Yenser. New York: Knopf, 2021.

Merrill, John Calhoun, and Harold Fisher. *The World's Great Dailies: Profiles of Fifty Newspapers*. New York: Hastings House, 1980.

Miller, Karl. *Rebecca's Vest: A Memoir*. London: Hamish Hamilton, 1993.

Miller, Sam. *Fathers*. London: Jonathan Cape, 2017.

"Miss Polimeni." *The Gower* 32, no. 1 (December 1946): 35.

Morgan, Bill. *The Beat Generation in San Francisco: A Literary Tour*. San Francisco: City Lights Books, 2003.

"Motorcyclists Put Town in an Uproar." *The New York Times* (7 July 1947): 19.

"Mr. R. Hyde and Mrs. Eddowes." *The Times* (4 June 1945): 6.

Muller, Baron. "Rope Saves 2 in Big Polk Fire." *San Francisco Examiner* (6 December 1971): 1, 4.

Murdoch, Iris. *Sartre: Romantic Rationalist*. Cambridge: Bowes & Bowes, 1953.

Murphy, Richard. *The Kick: A Memoir*. London: Granta, 2002.

"Muscles and More Muscles." *San Francisco Crusader* 65 (18 October–8 November 1978): 15.

"Name in Lights." *Varsity* (20 February 1954): 5.

Nashe, Thomas. *The Unfortunate Traveller and Other Works*. Edited by J. B. Steane. London: Penguin, 1985.

New Jersey College for Women. *The 1951 Quair*. New Brunswick: New Jersey College for Women, 1951.

"New Subpenas Issued in JFK Death Inquiry." *The Times-Picayune* (24 March 1967): 1.

Nicol, Jean. *Meet Me at the Savoy*. London: Museum Press, 1952.

Nidnacs, Aiva [Mark Finch]. "Out There." *Bay Area Reporter* 24, no. 34 (25 August 1994): 34.

Osborne, Charles. "A Rhyme of Poets." *The Sunday Times* (5 July 1970): 27.

———. *W. H. Auden: The Life of a Poet*. London: Macmillan, 1982.

"Overseas Journalism." *London and China Express* (3 July 1924): 9.

Pausanias's Description of Greece. Vol. 1. Edited and translated by J. G. Frazer. Cambridge: Cambridge University Press, 2012. First published in 1898.

Peet, George. *Rickshaw Reporter*. Singapore: Eastern Universities Press, 1985.

Peppiatt, Michael. *Francis Bacon: Anatomy of an Enigma*. Revised edition. London: Constable, 2008.

"Philosopheans Plan Banquet for Thursday." *The Targum* (1 May 1951): 1.

Pike, Richard. *The Far Side of Years*. Leek, UK: Three Counties Publishing, 2002.

Plath, Sylvia. *The Letters of Sylvia Plath, Volume II: 1956–1963*. Edited by Peter K. Steinberg and Karen V. Kukil. London: Faber, 2018.

Plowden, William. "Tony Tanner: A Memoir." *King's Parade* (Spring 2006): 6–7.

Potter, Beatrix. *The Tale of Samuel Whiskers or The Roly-Poly Pudding*. London: Frederick Warne, 1908.

Pound, Ezra. *ABC of Reading*. New York: New Directions, 1934.

Price, Stanley. "Lady at the Wheel." *Varsity* (14 November 1953): 4.

"Probate, Divorce, and Admiralty Division." *The Times* (30 April 1940): 2.

Proust, Marcel. *Within a Budding Grove*. Translated by C. K. Scott Moncrieff. London: Chatto & Windus, 1923.

Purnick, Joyce. "Homosexual Rights Bill Is Passed by City Council in 21-to-14 Vote." *The New York Times* (21 March 1986): 1.

"Queens Players Present First Performance of *Winslow Boy*." *The Daily Home News* (New Brunswick, NJ) (1 March 1951): 8.

"Rape Suspect on Parole Apparently Kills Himself." *The Press Democrat* (Santa Rosa, CA) (16 December 1976): 2.

Raphael, Frederic. *Going Up: To Cambridge and Beyond—A Writer's Memoir*. London: Robson Press, 2015.

Rebholz, Ronald A. *The Life of Fulke Greville*. Oxford: Clarendon Press, 1971.

"Refresher Training for Many Reservists." *The Times* (30 January 1951): 6.

Renwick, Chris. "The Family Life of Peter and Ruth Townsend: Social Science and Methods in 1950s and Early 1960s Britain." *Twentieth Century British History* (31 May 2023): 1–23. doi.org/10.1093/tcbh/hwad040.

"Reported 'Mr. LSD,' and Four Others Seized." *Los Angeles Times* (22 December 1967): A2.

Reynolds, Frank. *Freewheelin Frank, Secretary of the Angels: As Told to Michael McClure*. New York: Grove Press, 1967.

Roberts, Robert E. *Mad Dogs and Queer Tattoos: Tattooing the San Francisco Queer Revolution*. Springfield, PA: Fair Page, 2018.

Robinson, Douglas. "Townhouse Razed by Blast and Fire; Man's Body Found." *The New York Times* (7 March 1970): 1.

"Ronald Hyde." *The Daily Telegraph* (13 July 1995): 19.

Rorem, Ned. *The Nantucket Diary of Ned Rorem, 1973–1985*. San Francisco: North Point Press, 1987.

Rostand, Edmond. *Cyrano de Bergerac*. Translated by Brian Hooker. New York: Henry Holt, 1923.

"Round and About." *World's Press News and Advertisers' Review* (10 April 1941): 6.

"Roy Will Siniard." *Bay Area Reporter* 21, no. 2 (10 January 1991): 22.

Rubin, Gayle S. "Elegy for the Valley of Kings: AIDS and the Leather Community in San Francisco, 1981–1996." In Martin P. Levine, Peter M. Nardi, and John H. Gagnon, eds. *In Changing Times: Gay Men and Lesbians Encounter HIV/AIDS*, 101–44. Chicago: University of Chicago Press, 1997.

———. "The Miracle Mile: South of Market and Gay Male Leather, 1962–1997." In James Brook, Chris Carlsson, and Nancy J. Peters, eds. *Reclaiming San Francisco: History, Politics, Culture*, 247–72. San Francisco: City Lights, 1998.

———. "Thinking Sex: Notes for a Radical Theory of the Politics of Sexuality." In Carole S. Vance, ed. *Pleasure and Danger: Exploring Female Sexuality*, 267–319. Boston: Routledge & Kegan Paul, 1984.

"Rutgers Grad Gets Fellowship." *The Daily Home News* (New Brunswick, NJ) (10 June 1952): 22.

Rutgers University. *The 1952 Scarlet Letter*. Newark, NJ: Rutgers, 1952.

"The Ryleys School." *Alderley & Wilmslow Advertiser* (16 July 1920): 3.

Sacks, Oliver. *On the Move: A Life*. London: Picador, 2015.

Sandars, N. K., ed. *The Epic of Gilgamesh*. Harmondsworth, UK: Penguin, 1972.

Sebba, Anne. *Battling for News: The Rise of the Woman Reporter*. London: Hodder & Stoughton, 1994.

Shakespeare, William. *The Oxford Shakespeare: The Complete Works*. Edited by Stanley Wells and Gary Taylor. Oxford: Clarendon Press, 1998.

Shilts, Randy. *The Mayor of Castro Street: The Life and Times of Harvey Milk*. New York: St. Martin's Press, 1982.

"Should Men Be Faithful?" *Daily Mirror* (24 October 1935): 21.

Simenon, Georges. *Maigret and the Hundred Gibbets*. Translated by Tony White. Harmondsworth, UK: Penguin, 1963.

———. *Maigret and the Saturday Caller*. Translated by Tony White. London: Hamish Hamilton, 1964.

Sisson, C. H. "Editorial." *PN Review* 12, vol. 6, no. 4 (March–April 1980): 2.

Smith, Bruce R. *Homosexual Desire in Shakespeare's England*. Chicago: University of Chicago Press, 1991.

Smith, Charles A. "Looking for News in London." *The Quill* 29, no. 10 (October 1941): 5.

"Socialist Dilemma." *Varsity* (10 February 1951): 5.

"'Spurious Independence.' Women and Housing." *The Manchester Guardian* (19 July 1919): 11.

Stanford University. *Stanford University Bulletin* 9, no. 27 (12 May 1954): 168–69.

———. *Stanford University Bulletin* 9, no. 58 (13 May 1956): 293–94.

Staunton, Helen M. "War Killed Keyhole Stories, Britisher Says." *Editor & Publisher* (20 October 1945): 62.

Stein, Gertrude. *The Autobiography of Alice B. Toklas*. London: Penguin, 1966. First published in 1933.

Stevenson, Robert Louis. *A Child's Garden of Verses*. London: Collins, 1928. First published in 1885.

Stewart, Jim. "The Slot." *Bay Area Reporter* (29 September 2013): www.ebar.com/bartab /nightlife/148795. Accessed 23 July 2022.

Stewart, Karl. "My Knights in Leather: Little Daddy and the Royal Ring." *Bay Area Reporter* 13, no. 40 (6 October 1983): 32–33.

Stone, A. L. "Crowning King Anchovy: Cold War Gay Visibility in San Antonio's Urban Festival." *Journal of the History of Sexuality* 25, no. 2 (May 2016): 297–322.

Stone, Lawrence. *Road to Divorce: England 1530–1987*. Oxford: Oxford University Press, 1990.

Stone, Wendell C. *Caffe Cino: The Birthplace of Off-Off-Broadway*. Carbondale: Southern Illinois University Press, 2005.

"Storm Lashes City." *The New York Times* (1 September 1954): 20.

"Suicide Follows Separation." *Holborn and Finsbury Guardian* (5 January 1945): 1.

Sullivan, Jennifer. "Murderer of Former Mexico Man Gets 10–20 Years." *Lewiston (ME) Daily Sun* (26 January 1989): 10.

"Supervisors Pass AIDS Funding 11–0." *Bay Area Reporter* 13, no. 21 (26 May 1983): 1.

Sutherland, John. *Stephen Spender: The Authorized Biography*. Oxford: Oxford University Press, 2004.

Talbot, David. *Season of the Witch: Enchantment, Terror, and Deliverance in the City of Love*. New York: Free Press, 2012.

Tangye, Derek. *The Way to Minack*. London: Sphere, 1975. First published in 1968.

Tanner, Tony. "My Life in American Literature." *TriQuarterly* 30 (Spring 1974): 83–108.

———. *The Reign of Wonder: Naivety and Reality in American Literature*. Cambridge: Cambridge University Press, 1965.

Taylor, A. J. P. *Beaverbrook*. London: Hamish Hamilton, 1972.

Taylor, Jerome, ed. *The N.Y.C. Gay Scene Guide 1969*. New York: Apollo, 1968.

"These Names Make News: Spring Snubs Mars." *Daily Express* (21 March 1938): 6.

Thompson, Hunter S. *Fear and Loathing in Las Vegas*. New York: Random House, 1971.

Thompson, Paul. "Interview with Peter Townsend." *Pioneers of Social Research, 1996–2018*. 4th Edition. UK Data Service. SN: 6226, Para. 45. doi.org/10.5255/UKDA -SN-6226-6.

Thomson, Nan. [Ann Charlotte Gunn] "A Song of the Flapper." *Kent Messenger & Maidstone Telegraph* (9 October 1920): 5.

———. "Concerning Farm." *Kent Messenger & Maidstone Telegraph* (23 October 1920): 2.

Timmerman, John H. *Jane Kenyon: A Literary Life*. Grand Rapids, MI: William B. Eerdmans, 2002.

Tolstoy, Leo. *The Death of Ivan Ilyich*. Translated by Rosemary Edmonds. Harmondsworth, UK: Penguin, 1995. First published in 1960.

Tomalin, Nick. "Northern Light." *Varsity* (1 March 1952): 6–7.

Toynbee, Philip. "The Budding Grove." *The Observer* (3 May 1953): 9.

Turnbull, C. M. *Dateline Singapore: 150 Years of the Straits Times*. Singapore: Singapore Press Holdings, 1995.

"'Twelfth Night.'" *The Gower* 31, no. 5 (March 1946): 141–45.

Verax. [pseud.]. "Town and Country Notes." *South Eastern Gazette* (10 September 1889): 2.

"Vote Yes on P." *Vector* 3, no. 12 (November 1967): 11.

Walker, David. *Lean, Wind, Lean: A Few Times Remembered*. London: Collins, 1984.

Walker, Terry. "World War II Day." *The Gower* 56, no. 7 (December 2013): 115.

Watson, Nigel. *A Tradition for Freedom: The Story of University College School*. London: James & James, 2007.

Weiner, Joshua. "Mina Loy Among the Moderns." PhD dissertation, University of California, Berkeley, 1998.

Welch, Paul. "Homosexuality in America." *Life* (26 June 1964): 66–74.

Weschler, Lawrence. *And How Are You, Dr. Sacks?* New York: Farrar, Straus and Giroux, 2019.

White, Allen. "The Fallout from a Blaze." *Bay Area Reporter* 11, no. 15 (16 July 1981): 1, 4.

White, Edmund. *City Boy: My Life in New York During the 1960s and 1970s*. London: Bloomsbury, 2009.

White, Tony. "Rant." *Granta* 56, no. 1136 (1 November 1952): 17–19.

"Wife Found Dead After Trial Separation." *Evening Despatch* (London) (1 January 1945): 4.

Wiggin, Maurice. *Faces at the Window*. London: Thomas Nelson, 1972.

Wilcox, George. "The Taming of the Shrew." *The Cambridge Review* LXXIII, no. 1792 (7 June 1952): 572.

Wildeblood, Peter. *Against the Law*. London: Weidenfeld & Nicolson, 1955.

Williams, William Carlos. *Collected Later Poems*. London: MacGibbon and Kee, 1965.

———. *Paterson*. Volumes 1–5. London: MacGibbon and Kee, 1964.

———. *Pictures from Brueghel and Other Poems*. London: MacGibbon and Kee, 1964.

Winters, Yvor. *Edwin Arlington Robinson*. Norfolk, CT: New Directions, 1946.

———. *Forms of Discovery*. Chicago: Alan Swallow, 1967.

———. *In Defense of Reason*. London: Routledge & Kegan Paul, 1947.

———. *The Selected Letters of Yvor Winters*. Edited by R. L. Barth. Athens, OH: Swallow Press, 2000.

Wishart, Michael. *High Diver*. London: Blond and Briggs, 1977.

Wolfe, Tom. *The Electric Kool-Aid Acid Test*. New York: Farrar, Straus and Giroux, 1968.

Wood, Roger, and Mary Clarke. *Shakespeare at the Old Vic*. London: Adam and Charles Black, 1956.

Wootten, William. *The Alvarez Generation*. Liverpool: Liverpool University Press, 2015.

Wright, Adrian. *John Lehmann: A Pagan Adventure*. London: Duckworth, 1998.

Wyatt, Thomas. *The Complete Poems*. Edited by R. A. Rebholz. London: Penguin, 1978.

ACKNOWLEDGMENTS

This book would have been impossible without the kindness and support of Thom Gunn's family. They are: Mike Kitay, Bill Schuessler, and Bob Bair in San Francisco; his brother, Ander Gunn, in Cornwall; his niece, Charlotte Gunn, in Devon; his cousin Jenny Fremlin, in London; his cousin Margot Corbett, in Wiltshire; and his half brother James Gunn, in West Sussex.

I am grateful to the following people for sharing their memories of Thom Gunn, Mike Kitay, and other people and events mentioned herein: Leslie Aguilar, Taylor Ahlgren, Jonathan Aitken, Daniel Amaral Jr., John Ambrioso, William Arp, Andrew Ashbee, Don Baird, Mel Baker, Paul Bertolli, David Biespiel, Jay Blakesberg, Brian Bouldrey, Don Bogen, Bob Boyers, Brandon Brown, the late Louis Bryan, Chris Burgess, Angela Burns, Mike Caffee, Peter Campion, Donald H. Carpenter, Rick Carpenter, the late Douglas Chambers, Alexandra Chang, Heather Clark, Janice Clark, Stephen Claypole, the late Michael Clayton, Ben Coleman, Michael Colleary, Jack Collins, Roger Conover, Elizabeth Neece Conquest, Pablo Conrad, Peter Conradi, Dave Cooper, Jean Corston, Jim Cyphers, Peter Daniels, Michael Davidson, Dick Davis, Jacqueline Davis, Diana and Philip Dean, Randolph Delehanty, W. S. Di Piero, Bob Doody, Kathy Doust, Kent Drummond, Ian Duncan, John Eddowes, Kate Edgar, Dorothy Fasthorse, Edward Field, Peter Fiske, David Fitchew, Sarah French, Daisy Fried, Jack Fritscher, Nadia Fusini, David Galbraith, Maria Del Mar Galindo, Forrest Gander, Alisoun Gardner-Medwin, Timothy Gerken, Robert Glück, David Godine, Matt Gonzalez, Adrian Goss, Gordon Gould, Helen Graham, Thomas Gross, Edward Guthmann, Doug H., the late Jack Hagstrom, Daniel Hall, the late Donald Hall, Langdon Hammer, Martin Harrison, Hugh Haughton, Cynthia Haven, Felix Hawlin, Billy Hayes, Stephen Heath, Wade Hinkle, Andrew Holleran, Michael Holmes, Thomas Horn, Charles Hovland, the late Richard Howard, Ben Ryder Howe, Annie Ingrey, Panayotis Ioannidis, Clive Irving, Valerie Jabir, Patrick Dale Jackson, David Johnson, Glenn Jordan, Alex Kanarek, Ann Karlstrom, Richard Kaye, Jim Kelly, John Kelly and Suzanne Greene, Devin King, Maude Kirk, Harriet Kuliopulos, Stuart Kuttner, Jago Lee, Emily Leider, Gerald Lewis, Drew Limsky, Cesar Love, Billy Lux, Sonia Lynch, Patricia McCarthy, Jane McPherson, Tony Marchant, Tom Martin, J. V. S. Megaw, Stefania Michelucci, Greg Miller, Jane Miller, Sam Miller, Joseph Mockus, A. F. Moritz, Ron Morrison, Michael Morton-Evans, Blaine Moss, the late Richard Murphy, Christopher Nealon, Louis Keith Nelson, Oliver Newman, Richard Niland, John Niles, Andrew Noble, Toke Nørby, Joshua Odell, Raymond Oliver, Stephen Orgel, Margaret Owen, Peter Parker, Craig Patterson, John Peck, Carl Phillips, Richard Pike, Robert Pinsky, Frances Pirie, Johnny Pomeroy, Jim Powell, Neil Powell, Christopher Prendergast, Vincent Quinn, Christina Rago, Craig Raine, Belle Randall, Christopher Reid, Jerry Reneau, Robert Roberts, Robby (Gunner) Robinson, Martin Rosen, Yohn Rosqui, Tod Rossi, Chuck Roth, Jerome Rothenberg, Lisa Rotondo-McCord, Gayle Rubin, Steven Fritsch Rudser, Nicholas Sansom, Lawrence Schimel, Michael Schmidt, Gordon Schneemann, René Schuppert, Tony Scotland, Tim Scully, Steve Silberman, Steven Simmons, Mona Simpson, J. F. Slattery, Lee Smith, Timothy d'Arch Smith, Bob Snow, Michael E. Snyder, Peter Spagnuolo, Lara Speyer, Peter Stansky, Timothy Steele, Ellen Stephen, Colin Still, Pat Strachan, Marek Stycos, Gil Sutherland, Peter Swaab, Hal and Peter Tangen, Marcia Tanner, Anthony Thwaite, Clara Moriconi Timner, Claire Tomalin, Ben and Chris Townsend, Paul Trachtenberg, Jess Turner, Mark Turpin, Chickie Vella, Michael Vince, Dan Vining, Jeff Wakefield, Joshua Weiner, Robert Wells, Edmund White, Clyde Wildes, Denise Wilkinson, Hugo Williams, Dean Williamson, Chris Wiman, Anne Winters, Melissa Winters, Tobias Wolff, Gregory Woods, Stephen Yenser, and Sophie and Toby Young.

As August Kleinzahler, Clive Wilmer, and I mentioned in our acknowledgments to *The Letters of Thom Gunn*, the tireless work of Gunn's three bibliographers—Jack W. C. Hagstrom, Joshua Odell, and George Bixby—has made all research into Gunn considerably easier. The two volumes of Gunn's bibliography have rarely left my desk in the last eight years. The Gunn community was deeply saddened by the passing of Jack, in November 2019, and Joshua, in May 2020. This book is a testament to their work and passion. I would also like to remember Jack's partner, Thomas Fleming, who passed away in February 2022; and to thank Joshua's widow, Cynthia, and their two sons, Gabriel and Alexander.

Many librarians and archivists have aided my research. I am particularly indebted to staff at the four main collections of Gunn material. They are James Eason, David Faulds, Lorna Kirwan, and Dean Smith at the Bancroft Library, University of California, Berkeley; Douglas McElrath at the Hornbake Library, University of Maryland; Christina E. Barber and Margaret Dakin at the Robert Frost Library, Amherst College; and Tim Edward Noakes at Special Collections and University Archives, Stanford University. The Bancroft Library holds the most extensive Gunn collection in the world: special thanks again to Dean Smith, who cataloged Gunn's papers back in 2007–2008, both for his diligence and for the personal interest he has taken in the collection.

I would also like to extend my thanks to Michelle Gait and Andrew MacGregor at the Special Collections Centre, the Sir Duncan Rice Library, University of Aberdeen; Judith Ayn Bernhard at the Andover Street Archives, San Francisco; Julie Swarstad Johnson at the University of Arizona Poetry Center; Colin McDowall at the Army Personnel Centre, Glasgow; Jane Kirby at Bedales School, Petersfield, Hampshire; Jane Parr at the Howard Gotlieb Archival Research Center, Boston University; Scot McKendrick at Western Heritage Collections, the British Library; Robin Wheelwright Ness at Special Collections, the John Hay Library, Brown University; Alison Fraser and James Maynard at the Poetry Collection, University at Buffalo, New York; Sara Gunasekara at Special Collections, the Peter J. Shields Library, University of California, Davis; Heather I. Briston at the Charles E. Young Library, University of California, Los Angeles; Heather Smedberg at Special Collections and Archives, the Geisel Library, University of California, San Diego; Yolanda Blue and Edward Fields at Special Research Collections, University of California, Santa Barbara; John Wells at the University of Cambridge; Daniel Croughton at the Camden Local Studies and Archives Centre, London; Jordan Wright and Christine Colburn at the Hanna Holborn Gray Special Collections Research Center, University of

Chicago; Julia Schmidt at the Churchill Archives Centre, Churchill College, University of Cambridge; Emma Sheinbaum and Hekang Yang in the History Department at Columbia University; Benjamin Panciera at the Linda Lear Center for Special Collections and Archives, Connecticut College; Laura Schieb at the Rauner Special Collections Library, Dartmouth College; Valerie Stenner at the Morris Library, University of Delaware; Kathleen Shoemaker at the Stuart A. Rose Manuscript, Archives, and Rare Book Library, Emory University; Robert Brown, formerly at Faber and Faber; John Cleaver at Fitzwilliam College, University of Cambridge; Caterina Fiorani at the archives of the Fondazione Camillo Caetani, Rome; Kelsi Evans, Isaac Fellman, and Ramon Silvestre at the Dr. John P. De Cecco Archives and Special Collections, the GLBT Historical Society, San Francisco; Ellen Shea at the Arthur and Elizabeth Schlesinger Library on the History of Women in America, Harvard University; Annie Pinder at the Parliamentary Archives, Houses of Parliament, London; Caoimhe West at the Hull History Centre, UK; Brian Moeller at the Huntington Library, San Marino, California; Ruthann Miller at the Lilly Library, Indiana University; Laura Michelson at Special Collections and University Archives, University of Iowa; Elspeth Healey and Kathy Lafferty at the Kenneth Spencer Research Library, University of Kansas, Lawrence; Denise Eaton at the *Kent Messenger*, Rochester, Kent, UK; Patricia McGuire and Peter Monteith at the Archive Centre, King's College, University of Cambridge; Mel Leverich at the Leather Archives and Museum, Chicago; Layla Hillsden at Special Collections and Galleries, Leeds University Library; the reading room staff at the London Metropolitan Archives; Nicholas Beyelia at the Los Angeles Public Library; Hayley Jackson at the Luther College Archives, Iowa; Fran Baker at the John Rylands Library, University of Manchester; Cecily Marcus and Kathryn Hujda at Archives and Special Collections, the Elmer L. Andersen Library, University of Minnesota; Christine Nelson at the Morgan Library & Museum, New York; Allison Chomet at the Fales Library and Special Collections, New York University; Kate Edgar at the Oliver Sacks Foundation, New York; Angie Goodgame, Victoria Joynes, and Samantha Sherbourne at Special Collections, Weston Library, Bodleian Libraries, University of Oxford; Sandra Bossert at the Department of Rare Books and Special Collections, Seeley G. Mudd Manuscript Library, Princeton University; Kathleen Leonard and Renee Pappous at the Rockefeller Archive Center, New

York; Jo Anne Bilodeau at the City College of San Francisco; Jamie McIntosh at the National Library of Scotland, Edinburgh; Michael Oliveira and Loni Shibuyama at the ONE Archives, University of Southern California; Lynsey Darby and Janet Chow at St. John's College Archives, University of Cambridge; Eric Colleary and Virginia Seymour at the Harry Ransom Center, University of Texas at Austin; Loryl MacDonald, Jennifer Toews, and Danielle Van Wagner at the Thomas Fisher Rare Book Library, University of Toronto; Nicolas Bell at the Wren Library, Trinity College, Cambridge; Abra Schnur at the Elizabeth Huth Coates Library, Trinity University, Texas; Ann Case at Tulane University Special Collections, New Orleans; Pamela S. M. Hopkins at the Tufts University Archives, Massachusetts; Amanda Vestal at the Department of Special Collections and University Archives, the McFarlin Library, University of Tulsa; Elana Dwek at University College School, Hampstead; Bernard Schwartz and Ricardo Maldonado at the Unterberg Poetry Center, 92nd Street Y, New York; Rebecca Bultman at the Albert and Shirley Small Special Collections Library, University of Virginia; Kate Goldkamp and Joel Minor at the Olin Library, Washington University in St. Louis; Jennifer Hadley at the Olin Memorial Library, Wesleyan University; and Rebecca Aldi at the Beinecke Rare Book and Manuscript Library, Yale University.

At Farrar, Straus and Giroux, I would like to thank my editor, Jonathan Galassi, for supporting this project from the very beginning. Katie Liptak *ran the show*, and there would not be a book without her. I would also like to thank Scott Auerbach, Greg Villepique, Songhee Kim, Na Kim, Tanya Heinrich, Rima Weinberg, and Laura Ogar for their brilliant and meticulous work at every stage. At Faber and Faber, thank you to Jane Feaver, Leigh Haddix, Matthew Hollis, Lavinia Singer, and Becky Taylor; and to Rali Chorbadzhiyska for all her assiduous work on *The Letters of Thom Gunn*. Thanks also to my agent, David Godwin, for his kindness and patience, and to the whole team at David Godwin Associates.

I would like to thank the Society of Authors and the Authors' Foundation, from whom I received a small grant in 2019. Some research for this book was undertaken in parallel to *The Letters of Thom Gunn*: in 2016 I was a visiting fellow at the University of California, Berkeley, with funding from the US–UK Fulbright Commission; from 2016 to 2018 I was a postdoctoral researcher at

University College Cork, Ireland, with funding from the Irish Research Council. I would also like to thank my friends and colleagues at Boston University London, as well as the remarkable students I meet every day.

I have been fortunate enough to encounter some extraordinary mentors over the last fifteen years. Kasia Boddy, Robert Crawford, Alex Davis, Kapka Kassabova, David Kinloch, and Tom Normand have all done much to shape my writing and thinking. (Special thanks to Robert for not laughing me out of his office when I suggested writing Gunn's biography back in 2014.) Wendy Lesser was there at the beginning of this project and supported me throughout, providing sage advice and stern words when stern words were required. August Kleinzahler and Clive Wilmer—Gunn's literary executors—deserve my enormous gratitude for rolling the dice on an unproven kid from the back hills. (Let's hope it all turns out fine.) August and Clive were redoubtable coeditors on the *Letters* and have become steadfast friends: our Sidneys and our perfect men, to adapt a Gunn favorite. It is to them I owe the opportunity to undertake this great adventure.

And lastly to Hannah; Tristan, Lee, and Sue; Caitlin; Liz; Anna; Sarah; Mamen; Hitesh; Randall; Andrew; Kevin and Chiara; Orla; Éadaoín; Alice and Rob; and Kerri, Peggy, and Kevin. And thanks to my parents, David and Debra, for all their support.

INDEX

PERMISSIONS ACKNOWLEDGMENTS

For permission to quote from the published and unpublished work of Thom Gunn I extend thanks to the Estate of Thom Gunn, Faber & Faber Ltd., and Farrar, Straus and Giroux.

"Ode to Mr. Gunn" by Doris Polunsky. Copyright © Trinity University, San Antonio, Texas, used by permission.

Excerpt from a postcard to Thom Gunn by Christopher Isherwood. Copyright © 2024 the Estate of Christopher Isherwood, used by permission of the Wylie Agency (UK) Limited.

Excerpts from letters to Thom Gunn by Tony Tanner. Copyright © the Literary Estate of Tony Tanner, used by permission.

Excerpts from letters by Charles Monteith and Craig Raine, taken from the Faber archive. Copyright © Faber & Faber Ltd., used by permission.

Excerpts from letters by Donald Davie and Michael Schmidt. Copyright © Carcanet Press Ltd., used by permission.

Letter from Ted Hughes to Thom Gunn, 16 December 1993, in *Letters of Ted Hughes*, ed. Christopher Reid (London: Faber, 2007). Reproduced by permission of Faber & Faber Ltd.

Letter from Ted Hughes to Thom Gunn, 2 December 1993, taken from the Bancroft Library, University of California, Berkeley. Copyright © Ted Hughes. Reproduced by permission of the Estate of Ted Hughes.

Letter from Ted Hughes to Thom Gunn, 25 January 1991, taken from the Bancroft Library, University of California, Berkeley. Copyright © Ted Hughes. Reproduced by permission of the Estate of Ted Hughes.

Excerpts from letters by Yvor Winters to Thom Gunn. Copyright © the Estate of Yvor Winters, used by permission.

Letter from A. E. Dyson to Thom Gunn, 8 November 1998. Copyright © the Estate of A. E. Dyson, used by permission of Centrepoint.

ILLUSTRATION CREDITS

1. Studio of D'Ath and Dunk, Maidstone. Courtesy of Ander Gunn.
2. Courtesy of Charlotte Gunn.
3. Courtesy of Charlotte Gunn.
4. Courtesy of Charlotte Gunn.
5. Scrapbook circa 1930–1952, Oversize Volume 2, Thom Gunn Papers, BANC MSS 2006/235, Bancroft Library, University of California, Berkeley.
6. *Grove Cottage in Frognal*, image copyright © London Metropolitan Archives, City of London.
7. Scrapbook circa 1930–1952, Oversize Volume 2, Thom Gunn Papers, BANC MSS 2006/235, Bancroft Library, University of California, Berkeley.
8. Carton 2, Folder 35, Thom Gunn Papers, BANC MSS 2006/235, Bancroft Library, University of California, Berkeley. Copyright © the Estate of Thom Gunn.
9. Scrapbook circa 1930–1952, Oversize Volume 2, Thom Gunn Papers, BANC MSS 2006/235, Bancroft Library, University of California, Berkeley.
10. Courtesy of Mike Kitay.
11. Collage from the office walls of Thom Gunn, Box 1, Folder Quadrant D-3, BANC PIC 2012.056, Bancroft Library, University of California, Berkeley.
12. Scrapbook circa 1954–1960, Oversize Volume 4, Thom Gunn Papers, BANC MSS 2006/235, Bancroft Library, University of California, Berkeley.

13. Scrapbook circa 1960–1967, Oversize Volume 5, Thom Gunn Papers, BANC MSS 2006/235, Bancroft Library, University of California, Berkeley.
14. Scrapbook circa 1954–1960, Oversize Volume 4, Thom Gunn Papers, BANC MSS 2006/235, Bancroft Library, University of California, Berkeley.
15. Copyright © Marcia Tanner.
16. Box 181, Folder 31, Contemporary Manuscripts Collection, Poetry Collection, University at Buffalo. Copyright © the Estate of Thom Gunn.
17. Collage from the office walls of Thom Gunn, Box 1, Folder Quadrant E-2, BANC PIC 2012.056, Bancroft Library, University of California, Berkeley.
18. Scrapbook circa 1960–1967, Oversize Volume 5, Thom Gunn Papers, BANC MSS 2006/235, Bancroft Library, University of California, Berkeley.
19. Copyright © Marcia Tanner.
20. Copyright © Marcia Tanner.
21. Copyright © Marcia Tanner.
22. Copyright © Faber & Faber, Ltd.
23. Henri Leleu Papers, 1997–13, Gay, Lesbian, Bisexual, Transgender Historical Society, San Francisco. Copyright © Henri Leleu.
24. Collage from the office walls of Thom Gunn, Box 1, Folder Quadrant D-2, BANC PIC 2012.056, Bancroft Library, University of California, Berkeley.
25. Collage from the office walls of Thom Gunn, Box 1, Folder Quadrant D-2, BANC PIC 2012.056, Bancroft Library, University of California, Berkeley. Copyright © the Estates of Chuck Arnett and Bill Tellman.
26. Box 162, Folder 5, Robert Duncan Collection, Poetry Collection, University at Buffalo.
27. Courtesy of the Leather Archive and Museum, Chicago.
28. Carton 2, Folder 39, Thom Gunn Papers, BANC MSS 2006/235, Bancroft Library, University of California, Berkeley. Copyright © the Estate of Thom Gunn.
29. Box 1, Folder 9, Thom Gunn–Mike Kitay papers (M2559), Department of Special Collections and University Archives, Stanford University.
30. Collage from the office walls of Thom Gunn, Box 1, Folder Quadrant D-3, BANC PIC 2012.056, Bancroft Library, University of California, Berkeley.
31. Scrapbook circa 1967–1977, Oversize Volume 6, Thom Gunn Papers, BANC MSS 2006/235, Bancroft Library, University of California, Berkeley.
32. Collage from the office walls of Thom Gunn, Box 1, Folder Quadrant C-2, BANC PIC 2012.056, Bancroft Library, University of California, Berkeley. Copyright © Ander Gunn.
33. Collage from the office walls of Thom Gunn, Box 1, Folder Quadrant E-3, BANC PIC 2012.056, Bancroft Library, University of California, Berkeley.
34. Collage from the office walls of Thom Gunn, Box 1, Folder Quadrant B-3, BANC PIC 2012.056, Bancroft Library, University of California, Berkeley.
35. Collage from the office walls of Thom Gunn, Box 1, Folder Quadrant A-3, BANC PIC 2012.056, Bancroft Library, University of California, Berkeley.
36. Copyright © Charles Hovland.
37. Poetry Notebook 5 (December 1983), Carton 4, Folder 5, Thom Gunn Papers, BANC MSS 2006/235, Bancroft Library, University of California, Berkeley. Copyright © the Estate of Thom Gunn.
38. Courtesy of Mike Kitay. Copyright © Billy Lux.
39. San Francisco LGBT Business Ephemera Collection, BUS-EPH, Gay, Lesbian, Bisexual, Transgender Historical Society, San Francisco.
40. Box 1, Folder 9, Thom Gunn–Mike Kitay papers (M2559), Department of Special Collections and University Archives, Stanford University.